Innovative Methods, User–Friendly Tools, Coding, and Design Approaches in People–Oriented Programming

Steve Goschnick
Swinburne University of Technology, Australia

A volume in the Advances
in Computer and Electrical
Engineering (ACEE) Book Series

Published in the United States of America by
    IGI Global
    Engineering Science Reference (an imprint of IGI Global)
    701 E. Chocolate Avenue
    Hershey PA, USA 17033
    Tel: 717-533-8845
    Fax: 717-533-8661
    E-mail: cust@igi-global.com
    Web site: http://www.igi-global.com

Library of Congress Cataloging-in-Publication Data

Names: Goschnick, Steve, 1956- editor.
Title: Innovative methods, user-friendly tools, coding, and design approaches
    in people-oriented programming / Steve Goschnick, editor.
Description: Hershey, PA : Engineering Science Reference, an imprint of IGI
    Global, [2018] | Includes bibliographical references and index.
Identifiers: LCCN 2017059192| ISBN 9781522559696 (hardcover) | ISBN
    9781522559702 (ebook)
Subjects: LCSH: Human-computer interaction. | User interfaces (Computer
    systems) | Electronic data processing.
Classification: LCC QA76.9.H85 .I5765 2018 | DDC 004.01/9--dc23 LC record available at https://
lccn.loc.gov/2017059192

This book is published in the IGI Global book series Advances in Computer and Electrical
Engineering (ACEE) (ISSN: 2327-039X; eISSN: 2327-0403)

British Cataloguing in Publication Data
A Cataloguing in Publication record for this book is available from the British Library.

All work contributed to this book is new, previously-unpublished material.
The views expressed in this book are those of the authors, but not necessarily of the publisher.

For electronic access to this publication, please contact: eresources@igi-global.com.

Advances in Computer and Electrical Engineering (ACEE) Book Series

ISSN:2327-039X
EISSN:2327-0403

Editor-in-Chief: Srikanta Patnaik, SOA University, India

MISSION

The fields of computer engineering and electrical engineering encompass a broad range of interdisciplinary topics allowing for expansive research developments across multiple fields. Research in these areas continues to develop and become increasingly important as computer and electrical systems have become an integral part of everyday life.

The **Advances in Computer and Electrical Engineering (ACEE) Book Series** aims to publish research on diverse topics pertaining to computer engineering and electrical engineering. **ACEE** encourages scholarly discourse on the latest applications, tools, and methodologies being implemented in the field for the design and development of computer and electrical systems.

COVERAGE

- Programming
- Computer Architecture
- Analog Electronics
- Microprocessor Design
- Sensor Technologies
- Electrical Power Conversion
- Digital Electronics
- Computer Hardware
- Optical Electronics
- Computer science

IGI Global is currently accepting manuscripts for publication within this series. To submit a proposal for a volume in this series, please contact our Acquisition Editors at Acquisitions@igi-global.com or visit: http://www.igi-global.com/publish/.

Titles in this Series

For a list of additional titles in this series, please visit:
https://www.igi-global.com/book-series/advances-computer-electrical-engineering/73675

EHT Transmission Performance Evaluation Emerging Research and Opportunities
K. Srinivas (Transmission Corporation of Andhra Pradesh Limited, India) and R.V.S. Satyanarayana (Sri Venkateswara University College of Engineerin, India)
Engineering Science Reference • ©2018 • 160pp • H/C (ISBN: 9781522549413) • US $145.00

Fuzzy Logic Dynamics and Machine Prediction for Failure Analysis
Tawanda Mushiri (University of Johannesburg, South Africa) and Charles Mbowhwa (University of Johannesburg, South Africa)
Engineering Science Reference • ©2018 • 301pp • H/C (ISBN: 9781522532446) • US $225.00

Creativity in Load-Balance Schemes for Multi/Many-Core Heterogeneous Graph Computing...
Alberto Garcia-Robledo (Center for Research and Advanced Studies of the National Polytechnic Institute (Cinvestav-Tamaulipas), Mexico) Arturo Diaz-Perez (Center for Research and Advanced Studies of the National Polytechnic Institute (Cinvestav-Tamaulipas), Mexico) and Guillermo Morales-Luna (Center for Research and Advanced Studies of the National Polytechnic Institute (Cinvestav-IPN), Mexico)
Engineering Science Reference • ©2018 • 217pp • H/C (ISBN: 9781522537991) • US $155.00

Free and Open Source Software in Modern Data Science and Business Intelligence ...
K.G. Srinivasa (CBP Government Engineering College, India) Ganesh Chandra Deka (M. S. Ramaiah Institute of Technology, India) and Krishnaraj P.M. (M. S. Ramaiah Institute of Technology, India)
Engineering Science Reference • ©2018 • 189pp • H/C (ISBN: 9781522537076) • US $190.00

Design Parameters of Electrical Network Grounding Systems
Osama El-Sayed Gouda (Cairo University, Egypt)
Engineering Science Reference • ©2018 • 316pp • H/C (ISBN: 9781522538530) • US $235.00

For an entire list of titles in this series, please visit:
https://www.igi-global.com/book-series/advances-computer-electrical-engineering/73675

701 East Chocolate Avenue, Hershey, PA 17033, USA
Tel: 717-533-8845 x100 • Fax: 717-533-8661
E-Mail: cust@igi-global.com • www.igi-global.com

Table of Contents

Section 1
Programming Environments for People-Oriented Programming

Section 4
Personalized Learning Environments and the People-Oriented Programming Paradigm

Detailed Table of Contents

Section 1
Programming Environments for People-Oriented Programming

Highly usable and well-engineered development tools are required for People-Oriented Programming so that the end-user can design, code, configure, make or mashup solutions to their own problems, either afresh or customised from solutions to similar problems or needs. This section is made up of four chapters that together present the state-of-the-art of the programming languages and coding environments of the People-Oriented Programming paradigm.

Chapter 1
Judith Good, University of Sussex, UK

In 2011, the author published an article that looked at the state of the art in novice programming environments. At the time, there had been an increase in the number of programming environments that were freely available for use by novice programmers, particularly children and young people. What was interesting was that they offered a relatively sophisticated set of development and support features within motivating and engaging environments, where programming could be seen as a means to a creative end, rather than an end in itself. Furthermore, these environments incorporated support for the social and collaborative aspects of learning. The article considered five environments—Scratch, Alice, Looking Glass, Greenfoot, and Flip—examining their characteristics and investigating the opportunities they might offer to educators and learners alike. It also considered the broader implications of such environments for both teaching and research. In this chapter, the author revisits the same five environments, looking at how they have changed in the intervening years.

She considers their evolution in relation to changes in the field more broadly (e.g., an increased focus on "programming for all") and reflects on the implications for teaching, as well as research and further development.

Chapter 2
Michael Kölling, King's College London, UK

Educational programming systems are booming. More systems of this kind have been published in the last few years than ever before, and interest in this area is growing. With the rise of programming as a school subject in ever-younger age groups, the importance of dedicated educational systems for programming education is increasing. In the past, professional environments were often used in programming teaching; with the shift to younger age groups, this is no longer tenable. New educational systems are currently being designed by a diverse group of developing teams, in industry, in academia, and by hobbyists. In this chapter, the authors describe their experiences with the design of three systems—Blue, BlueJ, and Greenfoot—and extract lessons that they hope may be useful for designers of future systems. The authors also discuss current developments, and suggest an area of interest where future work might be profitable for many users: the combination of aspects from block-based and text-based programming. They present their work in this area—frame-based editing—and suggest possible future development options.

Chapter 3
Antonio Rizzo, University of Siena, Italy
Francesco Montefoschi, University of Siena, Italy
Maurizio Caporali, University of Siena, Italy
Giovanni Burresi, University of Siena, Italy

This chapter describes the opportunities offered by an extension of MIT App Inventor 2 named UDOO App Inventor (UAPPI). UAPPI aims to facilitate learning in programming the behavior of objects in the physical world (e.g., internet of things). In addition, UAPPI offers the opportunity to experiment with the emerging field of interactive machine learning. Two case studies devoted to different user groups are described to illustrate these opportunities. In the first, dedicated to middle school students, a door is made interactive; in the second, aimed at interaction designers, a light source is controlled by the blink of the eyes and the smile intensity.

Chapter 4

Xiao Liu, Pennsylvania State University, USA
Dinghao Wu, Pennsylvania State University, USA

Programming remains a dark art for beginners or even professional programmers. Experience indicates that one of the first barriers for learning a new programming language is the rigid and unnatural syntax and semantics. After analysis of research on the language features used by non-programmers in describing problem solving, the authors propose a new program synthesis framework, dialog-based programming, which interprets natural language descriptions into computer programs without forcing the input formats. In this chapter, they describe three case studies that demonstrate the functionalities of this program synthesis framework and show how natural language alleviates challenges for novice programmers to conduct software development, scripting, and verification.

Section 2
New Methods for the People-Oriented Programming Paradigm

As with the programming languages and environments covered in Section 1, a similar rate of progress has been made to help along with the third element of People-Oriented Programming: employing self-ethnography, which may include the use of sensors (informational probes), to define and refine the individual's requirements and clarify the context. This is being enhanced with ongoing improvements and innovations in new methods for: requirements gathering, analysis, through to the design of applications - for individuals and around an individual's situatedness.

Chapter 5

Connor Graham, National University of Singapore, Singapore
Mark Rouncefield, Lancaster University, UK

This chapter reflects on some of the methodological aspects of the use of cultural probes (or probes) and the extent to which they constitute a people-oriented method. The authors review different kinds of probes, documenting and analyzing two separate deployments—technology probes and informational probes—in a care setting. They suggest that probes, when deployed in this fashion, reflect a "post-disciplinary" era of "messy" data and a shift of attention beyond "the social" to greater concern with individual variation, personal aggregated datasets in technology design, materiality, and the visual. The authors also suggest that in an era of big data, through considering everyday development in terms of personhood, everyday technology and practice, probes can play an important role in providing insights concerning the product of people-oriented programming and, potentially, its process.

Chapter 6

The miniature Raspberry Pi computer has become of interest to many researchers as a platform for building sociotechnical IoT systems for end-users; however, for the end-user to design and build such apps themselves requires new people-oriented tools and design methods. This chapter describes a people-oriented design method called TANDEM and demonstrates the use of it in detail, by way of a case study— the design of a mashup of services and local data stores—that solves the so-called movie-cinema problem. An implementation of the newly designed movie-cinema app is then built within the DigitalFriend, an end-user programmer IDE. Furthermore, a significant part of the TANDEM design method is then automated within the development tool itself. This automation removes the most skilled task required by TANDEM of the end-user: the automation of the process of data normalization. The automation applies data normalization to the initial model of components and data sources that feed into the mashup. The presentation here relies on some understanding of data normalization, so a simple example is presented. After this demonstrated example of the method and the implementation, the authors discuss the applicability of a model achievable by end-users using TANDEM coupled with the automated normalization process built into the IDE vs. using a top-down model by an experienced information analyst. In conclusion, the TANDEM method combined with the automation as demonstrated does empower an end-user to a significant degree in achieving a workable mashup of distributed services and local data stores and feeds. Such a powerful combination of methods and tools will help the Raspberry Pi to become a significant people-oriented platform, beyond just a platform for teaching novices to code. Furthermore, the TANDEM method does have broader applicability to designing a broad class of logic programs, complementing the use of collected patterns in logic programs.

Chapter 7

Translating ethnographic field data to engineering requirements and design models suitable for implementing socio-technical systems is problematic. Ethnographic field data is often "messy" and unstructured, while requirements models are organized and systematic. Cooperation and communication within an interdisciplinary design team makes the process even more complicated. A shared understanding between ethnographers, interaction designers, and software engineers is vital to ensure that complex and subtle social interactions present in the data are considered in the final system design. One solution for supporting team conversations uses the quality goal construct as a container for complex and ambiguous interaction attributes. Quality goals in system modelling promote shared understandings and collaborative design solutions by retaining a high level of abstraction for as long as possible during the design process. This chapter illustrates the effectiveness of abstract goals for conveying complex and ambiguous information in the design of a socio-technical system supporting social interaction between couples.

Chapter 8
Agent-Based Modelling of Emotional Goals in Digital Media Design
James Marshall, Swinburne University of Technology, Australia

The author promotes agent-oriented models to identify, represent, and evaluate high-level abstractions of digital media design projects. The models include emotional goals, in addition to functional goals and quality goals, to describe feelings such as having fun, being engaged, and feeling cared for. To establish emotional goals, digital media design methods and processes were employed including the development of emotional scripts, user profiles, mood boards and followed an iterative creative design process. Using agent-oriented models proved to be highly successful not only to represent emotional goals such as fun, tension, and empathy but also to facilitate the ideation, creation, and progressive evaluation of projects. The design process supported communication between designers, developers, and other stakeholders in large multidisciplinary development teams by providing a shared language and a common artefact. The process is demonstrated by describing the development of Aspergion, a multiplayer online role play game that promotes respect for people with Asperger's Syndrome.

Section 3
Theory in the People-Oriented Programming Paradigm

As previously highlighted, a new software design and development paradigm doesn't come into existence in a neat chronological order like: Theory, Tools, Methodology, Framework, Applications. And so it is with the theory part of People-Oriented Programming. However, there have been advances in the area of theory coming from disparate disciplines, that do sit well within the embryotic POP paradigm. The two chapters in this Section hold important aspects of how relevant theoretical considerations from diverse disciplines have already impacted the other areas of POP, namely, the theory behind some of the tools and the methods described in Section 2.

Chapter 9

Christine Yunn-Yu Sun, eBookDynasty.net, Australia
Steve Goschnick, Swinburne University of Technology, Australia

This chapter explores the construction of identity in online communities and websites for social purposes, and its consequences in terms of how one's online identity may be utilized to such an extent that one's real-world identity is either enforced or eroded. It does so by investigating the very nature of identity, coming predominantly from a cultural studies research and philosophical view, although it also cites some related findings and advances in computing and information systems (IS) research. The central argument across the chapter is two-fold: firstly, in promoting an initial shift in focus from the management of online identity to the nature and significance of identity itself whose construction may be conceptualized as a process of sense making and strengthening; and only then, armed with a better understanding of identity, one can focus back upon the management of it more effectively, with a view to the individual taking more control of their own identity within cyberspace, which is increasingly transitioning us all into a functioning global community, in both predictable and unforeseen ways.

Chapter 10

Leon Sterling, Swinburne University of Technology, Australia
Alex Lopez-Lorca, University of Melbourne, Australia
Maheswaree Kissoon-Curumsing, Deakin University, Australia

In modern software development, considering the viewpoints of stakeholders is an important step in building the right system. Over the past decade, several authors have proposed solutions to capture and model these viewpoints. While these solutions have been successful, emotions of stakeholders have been largely ignored. Considering the emotional needs of stakeholders is important because both the users' perceptions of a product and their use of a product are influenced by emotion as much as cognition. Building on recent work in modelling the emotional goals of stakeholders, the authors extend an existing viewpoint framework to capture emotions, and to use emotions in models from early-phase requirements to detailed software design. They demonstrate the models and framework with a case study of an emergency alarm system for older people, presenting a complete set of models for the case study. The authors introduce recent experience in using emotional models in requirements elicitation within an agile process.

Section 4
Personalized Learning Environments and the People-Oriented Programming Paradigm

We saw in Section 1 that a lot of the exciting developments in POP are in new programming environments for coding, and these coding environments are often much more than programming editors. Several of them including Scratch and Greenfoot, are prime examples of learning environments with large communities of likeminded people. In the recent book Lifelong Kindergarten: Cultivating Creativity through Projects, Passion, Peers, and Play the author and the prime-mover behind Scratch, Mitchel Resnick, outlines his reasons for being a strong advocate for teaching all young people to become fluent in coding: "Most people won't grow up to become professional programmers or computer scientists, but learning to code fluently is valuable for everyone. Becoming fluent, whether with writing or coding, helps you to develop your thinking, develop your voice, and develop your identity." While coding is only one aspect of learning in the modern school curriculum, there is considerable scope for coding activities and computational thinking in many other subjects that make up a comprehensive curriculum. For these reasons we include two chapters on Personalized Learning Environments (PLE) in this volume.

Chapter 11

Georg Weichhart, Johannes Kepler University, Austria
Chris Stary, Johannes Kepler University, Austria

Although a large number of e-learning systems for individual learning support exist today, many of them still deal with pedagogical issues in an isolated way. In contrast, intertwining interactive system features with educational concepts allows pedagogical designs that may be considered according to their educational rationale. However, pedagogical approaches also do not provide requirements for technologies; they rather consider tools and features as predefined design parameters. Taking an interoperability point of view allows focus on the interaction between the pedagogical and the technological systems. By interpreting technology and didactic approaches as systems and ensuring their interoperability, educators are able to adapt learning experiences and technological features in a way that the overall learning system becomes personalized. A key element of the described work is an architecture that captures the design elements from both progressive education focusing on individual learning support, and the enabling web-based e-learning technologies.

Chapter 12

Steve Goschnick, Swinburne University of Technology, Australia

The future of learning environments lies with the merging of the better aspects of learning management systems (LMS), with those popularized in social networking platforms, to personalize the individual learning experience in a PLE (personal learning environment). After examining the details of a particularly flexible LMS, followed by the investigation of several key data structures behind the Facebook social networking platform, this chapter demonstrates how such a merging can be done at the conceptual schema level, and presents a list of novel features that it then enables.

Foreword

I welcome the opportunity to introduce you to this volume, a representation of the varied contributions that have appeared in the *International Journal of People Oriented Programming* (IJPOP), a journal devoted to ideas concerning the generation of user-fashioned software products. Steve Goschnick, the editor of this eclectic collection of articles, co-taught with me the inaugural *Interactive System Design* subject offered in the late 1990s to 'hard core' computer scientists at the University of Melbourne. That subject and its various descendants benefited greatly from Steve's extensive ICT industry experience and his enthusiasm as an educator, and that same spirit is evident in the choice of the articles comprising this volume.

Steve has a longstanding passion for making coding and the associated activities more accessible and this volume includes many articles illustrating the remarkable progress that has been made internationally in bringing such ambitions to reality. As viewed by designers of programming environments such as described in Section 1, coding is a type of literacy. By this it is meant that practicing the discipline of coding is not just about writing programs, but can help in organising one's thinking more generally and so improve one's ability to express ideas. But the articles in Section 1 are not simply a contemporary view of novice programming languages and environments – they are written by leaders in the field who have generously shared their expert reflections and lessons learned.

Indeed, following the spirit of POP, the authors of this collection are not just spectators or commentators, but are themselves do-ers, drawn from varied disciplinary backgrounds. The four sections of the volume contain a broad sweep of styles and cover a range of topics relevant to the growing field of supporting People Oriented Programming: the art of programming language design for novice coders; the craft of requirements gathering in support of software engineering practice relevant to the design of individualisable socio-technical systems; an interesting excursion through a cultural studies perspective on identity; and material concerning the design of personalised learning environments.

A reader can use this book as a starting point from which to plunge into specific topics, or just to get a taste of diverse perspectives on what it will take to further progress the field of People Oriented Programming.

Liz Sonenberg
The University of Melbourne, Australia
January 2018

Liz Sonenberg *is a Pro Vice-Chancellor at The University of Melbourne, Australia, and also Professor of Information Systems in the Melbourne School of Engineering. In her Pro Vice-Chancellor role, Professor Sonenberg holds specific responsibilities for planning of university-wide research infrastructure, and for oversight of the University's digital and data strategies. Liz Sonenberg's research expertise is in computational science, with the integrating theme of her research being the conceptualisation and construction of adaptive, distributed, intelligent information systems.*

Preface

People from all walks of life use modern interactive systems in a multitude of ways across their lives, and the rate at which such devices and apps are created with evolved features and functionality, is placing new and urgent challenges upon the creators of these same devices, systems and apps. How do you anticipate what people need or want? How do you design them for ways of operation yet to be discovered or envisaged? How do you improve peoples' experience in each of their unique situations? These are among the most pressing design issues of our times. Furthermore, there are complexities in contemporary life that exacerbate these problems for designers and creators, including:

- A heightened need for flexibility.
- Constant consideration of the context of the user.
- Dynamic environments that include heightened degrees of uncertainty.
- Incomplete information about the tasks or activity at hand.
- A growing diversity in the users themselves and their needs as the uptake of technology continues into the far cultural reaches of the planet.
- A proliferation of sensors upon the user and within their environment, both near and far (e.g. satellite).
- Immersion of the user within multiple parallel social worlds including personal, family, recreational and work-related social groupings, not to mention civic engagements at the local, national and global levels.

The People-Oriented Programming paradigm is envisaged to address this multifaceted design and development problem. It has a particular strength over conventional paradigms within domestic and non-work settings, where people spend a significant amount of their time, often on non-work-related tasks or goals, and less results-orientated activities such as play and contemplation. However, it is an equally adept paradigm when supporting or enhancing goal-oriented activities. Under the descriptive umbrella of People-Oriented Programming, there are a diverse range of new and innovative methods, new requirements gathering and design tools, user-friendly coding environments and new programming languages aimed at introducing programming to everyone that wishes to write their own code, often with online social communities of people that help each other.

BACKGROUND TO THE POP PARADIGM

People-Oriented Programming (POP) is a relatively new design paradigm for developing individual-oriented, software-based applications and systems, with a rudimentary sketch of what the paradigm should encompass, outlined in (Goschnick, 2009). It has four *elements* of activity, the first three of which call upon the individual user themselves:

1. An individual user of the system or application is the central focus of the endeavour, with customisations directed specifically to fit their requirements, in what von Hippel and Katz (2002) described as a 'market of one' – emphasising that the user needs to be heavily involved in servicing the customisation. Conversely, this increasingly empowered individual, although a member of multiple communities both online and the more traditional, is progressively becoming a global citizen.
2. Highly usable and well-engineered development tools are employed by the end-user so that the individual in question can design and then code, configure, make or mashup solutions to their own problems and situations, either afresh or customised from solutions to similar problems or needs, usually drawing upon a community of like-minded people.
3. Self-ethnography (Arnold 2004; Goschnick & Graham, 2005) is employed to some degree including the use of sensors, to define and refine the individual's requirements and clarify the context. This is being enhanced with ongoing improvements and innovations in new methods for requirements gathering, analysis and design of applications for individuals and around an individual's situatedness.
4. Cognitive models are drawn from two disciplines: the Agent-Oriented (AO) paradigm, and Cognitive Task Modelling (from HCI) – both for the analysis and design of applications, and also in creating new end-user development tools and methods, that make the second and third elements immediately above increasingly viable to all who want to participate in POP.

Although the third element initially represented a big hurdle for POP to be viable, Goschnick (ibid) drew attention to the practice of modding by users of games in the likes of World of Warcraft, as a demonstration that tools of the required usability and effectiveness were possible, and indeed, were becoming more commonly available. That same year Minecraft - the popular 3D creative game - was released on the public with very fast uptake by 5-year-olds and up, accruing tens of millions of users in just a few years (currently it has in excess of 100 million paid downloads). Such a rapid uptake for a paid-for app is uncommon, attesting to the demand for user-friendly software that end-users of virtually all ages can use by themselves to create things that previously required (in that case) game developer level skills. The impact that Minecraft was having on young creativity was further underlined by the willingness of Microsoft Inc. to pay US$2.5 billion for the controlling company, Mojang AB, in 2014.

COMPARATIVE TIMELINES OF THE OBJECT-ORIENTED AND AGENT-ORIENTED PARADIGMS

To get something of a handle on what the future holds for the development and consolidation of POP, it is worth looking at parallels in other much older paradigms of software and system development. In the early years of the millennium the Agent-Oriented paradigm of software development came into focus. It happened after nearly a decade of research and development, coming from different players across the world, and it didn't come in an orderly or pre-defined manner. A new software design and development paradigm doesn't come into existence in a neat chronological sequence like: Theory, Tools, Methodology, Framework, Applications. Some AO researchers developed tools first (e.g. dMARS) which they eventually realized were AO paradigm tools, as others started with theory first and only then developed AO tools. While others began with a pressing application first (e.g. the intelligent software in a robot; the software for airport flight control systems). The results in one area of AO research were used as feedback to improve the other areas which were not a specific focus - e.g. Work on analysis and design, provided feedback to agent theory and tools, and fed-forward into improved implementation efforts in problem domain areas (applications), and both informal methods and more rigorous full-blown methodologies. So, there were early AO architectures that now have supporting methodologies, early tools that have now grown into sophisticated frameworks, and early AO applications that guided theory, tools and methodologies. Not so much chaotic as vigorous innovation by pockets of researchers spread around the world, each informed periodically by the developments of the others, each realizing at different times that they were indeed toiling away on one or a few aspects of what was a whole new paradigm of software design and development.

The same was true of the Object-Oriented Paradigm (OOP). For example, OOP languages were widely available in the 1980s, including C++, Objective C and

Smalltalk-80 (itself based on Simula-67, circa 1967); and yet the Unified Modelling Language (UML) used predominently in the analysis and design of OOP programs and systems, only culminated in a 1997 release of UML V1 of that agreed upon standard, bringing together the proponents of three earlier competing methodologies which themselves evolved separately in the early 1990s.

TIMELINE OF THE PEOPLE-ORIENTED PARADIGM

This same non-chronological manifestation of a paradigm, over a significant number of years, can be seen with the People-Oriented Programming paradigm. Researchers and developers are working on different aspects of POP, spread around the world, often without realizing they are putting in place, the pieces that will eventually reach some agreed upon paradigm, an enterprise much larger than the corner they are working on – which will eventually be called POP, or some other name with a very similar intent and coverage of human endeavour.

This book is a contribution to that realisation and the ongoing discussion. Each of the chapters makes a solid and unique contribution to this discussion. As what happened with the OOP paradigm the POP languages, such as Scratch and Greenfoot, are well ahead of the other aspects (methodologies, theories, analysis and design notations) of the paradigm. In this sense, the evolution of the POP paradigm is more like that of the OOP paradigm, than the AO paradigm. The AO paradigm had great trouble coming up with AO programming language – most of the AO frameworks and toolkits were based on Object-Oriented languages, e.g. dMars was based on C++, while other AO programming environments like JACK and JADE were heavily Java-oriented, as the underlying language. Whereas in the OOP paradigm, the languages came first.

Nonetheless, there are significant contributions to the methods, theories and analysis and design tools of POP, right here in this volume. And as with the AO paradigm which took decades for any firm consensus of what constitutes AO, the POP paradigm is in its earliest days and a widely agreed definition of it, is probably far off in the future. This book, drawing as it does from the most pertinent papers published in the International Journal of People-Oriented Programming (IJPOP), updated with new research and insights, taking into consideration the latest developments in their respective topics and areas of expertise, makes a significant contribution to the embryonic but impactful POP paradigm.

SECTION 1: PROGRAMMING ENVIRONMENTS FOR PEOPLE-ORIENTED PROGRAMMING

Highly usable and well-engineered development tools are required for People-Oriented Programming so that the end-user can design, code, configure, make or mashup solutions to their own problems, either afresh or customised from solutions to similar problems or needs. This section is made up of four chapters that together present the state-of-the-art of the languages of the People-Oriented Programming paradigm. There has been a push to bring computer programming languages to a much wider cohort of people, for several decades, with Basic and Logo signposting very early attempts. However, there has been something of a breakthrough with the block-based languages from about 2007, onward. New programming environments such as Scratch (Chapter 1) and Greenfoot (Chapter 2) on the web, Alice for 3D coding, and ScratchJr (Scratch Junior) on tablets, allow the effective teaching of coding concepts and the writing of code, to children as young as 5 or 6 Note: ScratchJr is realistically aimed at 5 to 7 year olds with an iPad or Android tablet.

These new language environments have coincided with the introduction of coding into the school curriculum in numerous countries, including the UK, Australia, and parts of the US. E.g. Judith Good (Chapter 1) notes that the English national curriculum introduced statutory computing programmes of study for all educational key stages, from age 5 to 16 in 2013. Estonia introduced coding into primary schools in 2012. How these young coders transition to the current traditional textural languages of the software engineering and computing world as undergraduates and beyond, is one subject of Michael Kölling's excellent work in Chapter 2. The new language environments have also coincided with the rise of the Maker movement, which most often brings hardware and software together in creating brand new artifacts though personal invention. New inexpensive single board computers (e.g. Raspberry Pi; many variants of Arduino) have arrived, that take the student and the hobbyist from coding to the hardware and sensor world, and back again. In Chapter 3 Antonio Rizzo and colleagues present their work on UAPPI, a platform that extends the App Inventor block-based language for Android, together with hardware that combines the processing functionality of Arduino and Raspberry Pi on a single board, into an IoT (Internet of Things) platform. They also use a Machine Learning toolkit from Google to do some surprisingly sophisticated things in their student-based case studies, for example *"a light source is controlled by the blink of the eyes and the (intensity of a) smile"*. Chapter 4 brings the focus away from the new block-based languages and back upon natural language for computational purposes, succinctly titled *From Natural Language to Programming Language*.

Chapter 1

Professor Judith Good re-examines five user-friendly coding environments for novice programmers – Scratch, Alice, Looking Glass, Greenfoot and Flip – a full 6 years after she first published a state-of-the-art investigation of the same five environments in the International Journal of People-Oriented Programming in 2011. All have evolved substantially in that time, in a number of different ways. She identifies a number of exciting trends, including the substantial advances in these programming environments for novices, with regard to the programming languages inherent in them, the sophistication of the user interfaces, the growth of the communities around them, and a recognition of the importance of the innovative collaborative options that coders themselves are pioneering, in this new type of creative social network (e.g. both Scratch and Greenfoot have online supportive communities of users, that are able to share code and much more). She highlights the significant expansion of resources around these coding environments, for both learners and educators.

Professor Good looks at the process one goes through in creating a program in each of the five environments, and discusses the special features that mark out each from the others. Each coding environment has gone on a specific journey in terms of: how the developers have seen their target user base, what they think are the most important features such an environment should have to support and encourage novice coders in their creative endeavours and progress, and so on. Growth has been exponent in the uptake of these environments, for example, Scratch now has in excess of 20 million projects online.

Alice now has a vast gallery of ready-to-use 3D objects from the SIM II game, made available to coders for their own purposes thanks to Electronic Arts. The Alice approach takes a *game-first* or *animation-first* approach to motivating the novice coder. Typical of many creative tools where the user is a prosumer of new virual artifacts, Alice 3 has two significant editors within the one environment: a Code Editor complete with drag and drop controls, and a Scene Editor, where the user 3D world is envisaged, created and populated with all manner of objects. There is significant support for students to transition to the Java language, for those wishing to move beyond/out-of block-language coding, into a regular IDE, in this case Netbeans.

Looking Glass was designed with the aim addressing the large gender disparity in undergraduate computer science. It is specifically aimed at helping middle school girls (aged 11-14 years) to create stories in a 3D world, based on the rationale they will be gain motivation in tackling the programming part of the exercise. The Looking Glass IDE (Integrated Development Environment) is itself based on Alice 3, and so it also has both a Scene Editor and a Code Editor.

Greenfoot is covered too, but much more so in Chapter 2, by its originator. Flip is a block-based language for constructing game dialogues in a dungeon-and-dragon style role-playing game (an RPG). There is much innovation here, and Flip is an outcome of Good's own applied research. Flip demonstrates much innovation, for example, there is a translation feature from the routines coded in blocks, into natural language, that has proven to be a signifcant communication aide in discussions amongst small teams of coders, such as debugging their logic via the English equivalent.

After a comparison of the 5 environments there is an extensive section of reflection, drawing upon both the chapter's coverage and a significant career down the path of bringing programming and computational thinking to everybody. For example, whether the current textual vs block-based coding discussion is the right level of investigation that researchers should be concentrating upon. Professor Good identifies these new POP tools as ideal environments for studying collaboration. However, she also emphasies that the collaborative e-nature of learning and advancement in environments like Scratch, shouldn't supplant the cognitive – that these tools need to continue to support and encourage external representations of individual cognitive activity and understanding.

Chapter 2

In this chapter titled 'Blue, BlueJ, Greenfoot: Designing Educational Programming Environments', Professor Michael Kölling begins with a brief history of the programming languages and development environments that were most focused on people learning to code, which began almost as early as programming itself. Professor Kölling is a pioneer in providing environments for learning to code. He is in the unique and valuable position of having been centrally involved in designing and developing three programming environments for teaching programming to novices, over a period of more than twenty years. The involvement includes cultivating and servicing input from communities of learners, and teachers, for ongoing improvements to both BlueJ and Greenfoot. BlueJ, introduced in the year 1999, was aimed at 1st year undergraduate students, teaching them 'objects first' in the Java language. Kölling soon realised that many 1st year undergraduate students were learning their first programming language well before beginning their tertiary studies. He then designed Greenfoot to address the needs of students and teachers at mid-level high school.

Kölling outlines that history, often in relation to other environments, notably Scratch and Alice. Significantly, he distils his hard-won advice gained in the design decisions he took with the three environments, and in supporting the large user communities of two of them. The advice is particularly well suited to current or would-be designers of new learning environments for coding. It is equally well suited to those wanting to choose between existing environments in teaching programming/coding to a particular target user base.

His sub-headings within the section The Lessons Learned, are good to repeat here as the briefest of a summary: Visualization, interaction, simplicity; Know your target group; Do one thing well; Say no (to features requests beyond the target group); Beware feature creep; Do not be afraid to make decisions; Availability; Support material matters (e.g. "*A software system—no matter how well designed—does not, by itself, make an impact in education. What actually drives adoption is an ecosystem of support material*"); The importance of motivation (e.g. "*We want to create motivation, show how a computer works, instill computational thinking, discuss problem solving, show the main aspects and limits of programming. In short, it is about concepts, not syntax*"); Taking control (and the learner taking ownership); Visualization of program execution; The power of community; Teacher communities.

His own endeavours over the extended period of time that has elapsed since the turn of the millennium, have seen the target user group for such environments go from first year university programming novices to high school student novices. Further, he has observed the block-based languages successfully targeting primary school kids as young as seven.

Greenfoot was written to address the high school cohort, whereas BlueJ had been envisaged for first year university students who had already chosen their career direction. In high school, everyone was being subjected to coding, and so *motivation* became the key design criteria.

In moving from a class diagram interface in BlueJ, Greenfoot went for interactive objects: "*we arrived at a well-known destination: micro-worlds. ... we had come full-circle... But most importantly, Greenfoot was not (just) a micro-world, but a micro-world meta framework.*" That is, any number of micro-worlds, and objects in a world, could be created by users, all within a fully developed coding environment (editor, debugger, runtime system, graphics library, and so on).

There is now a new cohort of students that go from block-based environments for their first foray into coding, then learn a text-based syntax language later on if they need to take programming more seriously. Some of the new tools do both styles of coding in the one environment, demonstrating a two-way approach to coding, sometimes in dual side-by-side windows.

Towards the latter part of the chapter Professor Kölling introduces his own new work on Greenfoot 3, with a technique he calls *frame-based editing* that combines aspects of both block and text code editing in a single merged approach. This frame-based editing approach is brought home with a new language called Stride, although Java can still be used instead. Indeed, the syntax of Stride is something of a subset of that of Java. The new version aims to enable novices who are first introduced to coding in the new environment, to be able to continue on in it, taking their coding as far as they want to go, without the necessity of a transition.

This is a valuable chapter from many perspectives, particularly with regard to those learning, teaching and researching in and around the high school cohort of people learning to code. However, its greatest value is perhaps the set of generic lessons and insights drawn from the experience of envisaging, developing and supporting two very significant and innovative coding environments in BlueJ and GreenFoot. There are tools available for the developers of new block-based languages, principally Blockly, a JavaScript code base from a joint Google and MIT project – the same people who brought App Inventor to Android, discussed in the next chapter. All sorts of block-based environments based on Blockly have appeared in the last year or two, including the Code.org site, which runs the well-subscribed to Hour-of-Code, a school-focused event held each December. If you are thinking of joining the few research teams that currently supply a block-based coding environment, and in so doing, adding to the toolsets available for the People-Oriented Programming paradigm, then this chapter is a must read.

Chapter 3

Titled 'UAPPI: A Platform for Extending App Inventor Towards the Worlds of IoT and Machine Learning', this chapter by Professor Antonio Rizzo and colleagues, is complementary to the previous two chapters, in that it is about another block-based language, namely App Inventor, but an extended version that gives new coders access to the new frontier of the Internet of Things (IoT) via an UDOO board. The UDOO board allows microcontroller-managed sensors and actuators to be accessed from code (note: It has two ARM processors integrated on the one board – one much like the Raspberry Pi single-board computer but which instead runs Android apps, while the other is capable of running Arduino like programs).

Apps have been a great motivator for novices wanting to learn to code, and App Inventor for Android has arguably been the most successful approach to date, in terms of novices programming apps for mobile devices. The authors present an extension to App Inventor called UAPPI (short for UDOO App Inventor), that adds some new functional blocks to the block-based language, to deal with the new hardware – beyond what an Android mobile phone normally has. This has been possible since the original source code of App Inventor is open source. The chapter shows how they use App Inventor and the UDOO hardware to connect it to all sorts of sensors, all from within the widely-used block-based language of the App Inventor environment (i.e. there were over 6 million registered users of App Inventor who had created over 21 million apps by Dec 2017). UDOO App Inventor empowers novices further, by giving them the means for direct experience in coding sensors and firing up actuators in the real world beyond the touchscreen of their everyday mobile devices.

Three case studies are presented using UAPPI. The researchers followed the Research through Design (RtD) approach. RtD in Human-Computer Interaction (HCI) is a practice focused on improving the current state-of-the-art by enabling new behaviours and interactions between technology and humans. Participants are pro-active makers of a world they desire to live in. In the more sophisticated case they used UdooVision components, that integrate the Google Vision framework, which is able to find objects in photos and video, in real-time by use of on-device vision technology. The Google mobile face API finds human faces in photos, tracks positions of *facial landmarks* (eyes, nose, mouth) providing information about the state of those facial features, e.g. Are the subject's eyes open? Are they smiling? This allowed them to control an LED light with a smile, or by simply blinking their eyes. The three application scenarios presenting in this chapter, are examples of interaction with everyday objects and related activities, that were transformed by merging physical objects with digital technology. All from a block-based coding language, highly accessible to novice programmers.

Chapter 4

The title of this chapter is 'From Natural Language to Programming Language' by Associate Professor Dinghao Wu and colleague Xiao Liu. Natural language programming is one of the current research directions being pursued, as an easier way for people with limited programming experience to compose solutions to practical problems, where a programming task is currently required. After analysis of research on the language features used by non-programmers in describing their problem-solving approaches, the authors proposed and built a general framework that synthesizes programming languages from natural language descriptions, with considerable success.

They present three case studies, the first of which aimed at lowering the bar for novice programmers or children, to draw graphs. They prototyped a domain-specific *program synthesis* system called Programming in Eliza (PiE), to draw graphs, taking as input, conversations in English with a computer. PiE is capable of synthesizing programs in the LOGO programming language to draw graphs, taking input from the English conversation between Eliza and the user.

Their second case study, called Natural Shell, is about turning natural language describing a task, into a shell script that does the deed. Shell scripting is widely used for automating tasks at the Operating System level - sometimes tasks involving multiple applications from different sources or vendors. Despite the popularity of shell scripting, it remains difficult to use for both beginners and experts alike, but for different reasons. Beginners are confronted by a barrage of cryptic commands and concepts, while experts struggle with the often incompatible syntaxes across different systems, made worse by seemingly similar syntax, that can be used for some completely different tasks. The authors solution is a system they call *Natural Shell* that transforms the natural language describing a task we want done on our computer, into the appropriate shell scripts that make it happen. It is a multi-step process. Firstly, it translates the natural language of the user into an intermediate, system-agnostic script called Uni-shell. In the remaining steps, Natural Shell transforms the Uni-shell script into the appropriate underlying native script, executes it, then reports details about the resulting action. In an affirming and reinforced-learning manner, the user then gets to see all the steps involved: the natural language they entered, the generated Uni-shell script, the converted native script, together with the system-reported results. Their system was applied to tasks that together require some 50 common shell commands.

The third case study aimed to lower the bar for network administration training and reduce the configuration complexity, so they proposed EasyACL, a tool that synthesizes ACL configuration commands for different platforms directly from natural language descriptions. EasyACL can port the synthesized commands to different platforms, namely, Cisco and Juniper.

Natural Shell and EasyACL both provide an intermediate phase, where the sytem provides a formal interpretation of what the end-user was requesting in natural conversation. The user can thereby quickly see if the system really interpreted what they really meant. In addition to ensuring that the user understands the meaning of tasks undertaken in a programming language, the use of a natural language translation into an intermediate language that is understood by both the user and the system, also reduces the time it takes for the user to learn and do appropriate tasks. Furthermore, the intermediate representation is platform-independent, so the commands can be ported to any platforms with same functionalities, e.g., Bash, Csh and Winbat for Natural Shell, and various Cisco and Juniper systems for EasyACL. The conversational dialogue allows the user to transition from English to programming syntax at his or her own pace – if they want to go beyond natural language dialogue.

In user testing of the resultant applications from the two latter case studies, reportage that it (the intermediate language) was very useful in successfully troubleshooting problems, was a common response. This is an interesting parallel with a finding by Professor Good back in Chapter 1, where the Flip language had a translation from block-based code to plain English feature, where it also greatly helped in team communication and debugging. This reinforces one of the author's conclusions here, that such systems can significantly help end-users learn technical programming languages, not just replace them with natural language.

There are great efficiencies in programming languages with regards to specifying and communicating issues around complex tasks, that should not be under-valued going into a future with more People-Oriented Programming.

As our user interfaces in general move further towards natural language and voice input, solutions such as this framework by Wu and Liu are becoming increasingly important to People-Oriented Programming. At the significant vendor level we already have intelligent agent products such as Apple's Siri, Google Assistant (and now Google Now), Amazon's Alexa, Microsoft's Cortana and Wolfram Alpha - that extensively draw upon data, services and knowledge *out on* the Internet. However, it is at the personal level, that we tend to organise our own data, and where we service those requests and tasks, asked of us by others. We ourselves are often a part of a complex human-agent system, increasingly supported by algorithms and AI, inputting our own individual specialised knowledge into the system. The authors of this chapter are addressing issues that are physically closer to our end of the deal, as the human in these human-agent collaborations of which we are all steadily becoming a part. Solutions on our desktops and our laptops and tablets, and in our phones, which are not always connected to a network. They are also applying their natural language framework to a number of divergent cases, where programming language and scripting presents a significant hurdle to people, to cases where formalised languages were previously a requirement.

SECTION 2: NEW METHODS FOR THE PEOPLE-ORIENTED PROGRAMMING PARADIGM

As with the programming languages and environments covered in the last section, a similar rate of progress has been made to help along with the third element of People-Oriented Programming: employing self-ethnography, which may include the use of sensors (informational probes), to define and refine the individual's requirements and clarify the context. This is being enhanced with ongoing improvements and innovations in new methods for: requirements gathering, analysis, through to the design of applications - for individuals and around an individual's situatedness.

Sophisticated sensors in smartphones (e.g. NASA has sent them into orbit as cheap satellites) and smart watches, and various sensors in other wearable technology and in the home, are leading to collections of vast amounts of data about an individual, and about the immediate environment of the individual. The Internet of Things (IoT) is just one strand of research addressing these new sensor technologies. POP research is interested in how real-time *data* can be turned into highly useful *information* about the individual for the individual, but also for greater society. I.e. the empowered individual is increasingly becoming a global citizen - one such example is the Citizen Science projects aimed at helping prevent further loss of endangered species (Preece, 2017). Self-ethnography - such as the keeping of diaries, photos and video, including those in social media - and quantifying information from arrays of sensors on and about the user in their environment, is quickly helping to bridge a long-recognised information gap between ethnographers capturing user requirements, and software engineers developing a system based on their interpretation of what a 'typical' end-user wants and needs. That the users themselves may become coders is helping to bridge the gap between the software that an individual needs, and those able to write/create it. The following chapters cover a range of people-oriented methods that can bridge that gap successfully.

The first chapter in this section by Graham and Rouncefield, covers the variants of *cultural probes* that are eminently suitable for self-ethnography as a *requirements method* for POP. They present significant insights and concluding recommendations about how such data can and should be used. In the second chapter, I showcase a *design method* suitable for a significant class of applications that end-users could develop themselves, given the tools. Chapter 7 outlines a significant body of work by an eminent group of collaborative professors, that also calls upon cultural probes for requirements gathering, but then develop an innovative *design method* incorporating models from the agent-oriented paradigm (goals and roles), and combines these with *quality goals* and *functional goals*. Chapter 8 builds on the initial work in Chapter 7, in a digital media design context, adding *emotional goals* to the quality goals and functional goals, evolving the initial design method into a full people-oriented *development methodology* that has been successfully used in teams of as many as 300 digital media students "right down to teams as small as one".

Chapter 5

In this chapter Connor Graham and Mark Rouncefield explore the use of Cultural Probes as a method in People-Oriented Programming. They investigate Cultural Probes that have previously been used by ethnographers and designers, to gain fresh perspectives in areas of technology usage, that are very sensitive and often domestic in nature. They begin with a literature review of the different branches of probes since the seminal paper on cultural probes by Gaver et al in 1999. They discuss the variety of 'x' probes available: empathy probes, digital cultural probes, mobile probes, urban probes, value probes, domestic probes and cognitive probes – which have common features, including: they capture some biographical account of individual people; they give visibility to the things in a person's life; they focus on people being experts in their own lives. Two other types of probes are detailed in the literature: technology probes, and informational probes. The first involved exploring the potential for new technologies to support communication for diverse, distributed and multi-generational families. While information probes were first deployed to help understand and assist people and their carers in residential care centres for: elderly people living at home; and hostels for former psychiatric patients.

The usefulness of ethnographic approaches was being questioned in the late 1990s, in terms of both general applicability and design relevance, regarding the observations and documentation coming from them. Cultural Probes were one response to such criticisms. These probes provide a way in which we can see everyday activities as social actions embedded within some larger socially organised domain. The various ways that the day-to-day activities of people are documented, provides access to the ways in which people understand and conduct their lives.

Furthermore, insights gained on individuals' lives are closely coupled with insights about design, particularly the design of new things and new solutions. Some see this as a sign that we have entered a 'post-methodology' era where diversity is key and fitness for purpose and flexibility are critical; and that a multitude of probes are available to help achieve this. Whereas Graham and Rouncefield see that culture probes actually *"constitute a 'people-oriented' method if not a methodology."*

Probes allow the movement away from laboratory confined studies with generalised outcomes, to context-aware and people-oriented observation, down at the individual level, and how we interact socially with those people closest to us in work, leisure and home-based situations. We can build up a unique picture of personhood, of self, with the help of such probes. Interestingly, the study that Graham and Rouncefield embarked on, can be seen as a middle-ground between laboratory and study of individuals – they chose to study a community residential care setting for former psychiatric patients, with both information probes and technology probes. One site was staffed with shift workers around the clock, while the second nearby site supported semi-independent living with support staff as needed. This gave them access to a site where domestic lives are already heavily observed, routinized and facilitated, removing the novelty of introducing technology and overseers, while still being able to observe the workflow and patterns of individual lives via their new probes. The second site, one kilometer away, allowed them a more normalized arrangement.

Many of the insights they gained are applicable to the wider population. Think of parents as a team of two, responsible for their children and themselves 24/7, as well as situations where neighbours and relatives look out for elderly citizens in their midst. Also, the most generic of insights were gained. For example, technology probes required a reactive and adaptive participation, while the informational probes encouraged investigative and reflective participation. Both forms of participation made available descriptive data that acted as a resource for design: one that was more temporal and thematic, while the other, more spatial and episodic.

Another observation they make is that the work required to maintain the technical order of domestic technologies, has now filtered down to the individual, to non-expert household members. This can range from what is described as system administration work, to more broadly, the *"digital plumbing"* or *"the actual work of installing digital technologies in a setting*" that ensures newly installed technologies "*fit with a whole constellation of pre-existing organisational arrangements, both physical and social*". Beyond administration, home users are also buying, upgrading, customising and even making new domestic software and hardware solutions that "*contribute to the socio-technical order of their households*" … "*the individual person is increasingly subject to and responsible for the work of maintaining their digital personhood*". This discussion of probes as a method has implications beyond my second element of POP above regarding coding. They note that: "*programming-like activities have entered, even sneaked, into many people's everyday lives. There is a raft of everyday, unnoticed work that people do to configure, administer, tailor and even create and publish through computing systems*". Which suggests that the revolution we are seeing in block-based coding amongst current school students, for example, may well flow into the domestic space in many of those areas of *digital plumbing*. Allowing "*home users (to) also upgrade, tailor, purchase and even develop new domestic software and hardware solutions that contribute to the socio-technical order of their households*". There is already something of this evident in the early adopters of block-based coding within the maker movement.

They explore other opportunities that probes present for People-Oriented Programming as a people-oriented method. For example, that 'probing' can include automatically collected datasets of different scales and specificity, which can happen in parallel with people's domestication of a technology. However, the pertinent questions that arise are what can one (ethically) do with such data and how we can make sense of it. The methods the authors discuss in this chapter, give appropriate perspective to these questions, so that they can be more easily answered in a given situation. For example, the demonstrated information flows, shine light on the pathways that people make around and through different technologies. And beyond the insights gained, some probes have the potential to highlight, record and even replay to the individual concerned, how they did it 'last time' in a perfect memory sense.

On the increasing amount of automation in the collection of data about an individual, the authors outline questions regarding responsibility, visibility, performance and expertise that are essential to ethically understand, and to further develop the potential of new forms of probing for People-Oriented Programming. That the kinds of efforts made by some researchers in the spirit of 'total capture' of a life, autonomously, at least for People-Oriented Programming, seems to miss the point entirely. "*What we choose to collect through Probes is informed and selective and helps drive how we 'make sense' through selection, extraction and presentation of the data we collect. In addition, what people effortfully collect and choose to put on display (e.g. with Informational Probes) is of some importance to us*", and if such 'work' is outsourced to autonomous probes, gone too is that effort that made it so.

Through the probes used, the researcher may acknowledge 'the user' not only as a content producer but also as a cultural commentator, a diarist, a photographer, and so on, in a place in the real world, as a unique person who exhibits their identity and self, in and through the physical and digital worlds. We return to these last most important subjects about Identity and Self, in depth in Chapter 9 titled 'Formation and Control of Identity in a Social Media World'.

Chapter 6

This chapter is titled 'A Design Method for People-Oriented Programming: Automating Design of Declarative Language Mashups on the Raspberry Pi'. In it, I detail a method that was conceived as a People-Oriented Programming method, from the ground up. From a coding point of view, it applies to declarative languages rather than procedural languages. While the logic languages such as Prolog are very much less used than mainstream procedural and object-oriented languages, the widely used and easily understood SQL language is declarative in nature. SQL has a *function point count* (a metric used to measure the expressiveness of programming languages, based on large databases of past projects) which is in the top 3 languages of most comparisons done (e.g. http://www.qsm.com/resources/function-point-languages-table; http://www.ifpug.org/Conference%20Proceedings/ISMA3-2008/ISMA2008-14-Jones-using-function-point-metrics-for-software-economic-studies.pdf). The SQL language is ideally suited to first-time coders for certain types of applications, an opportunity that has not been exploited well in the movement to bring coding to novices. One aspect responsible for that lack of adaption is that good information design skills greatly reduce the complexity of the SQL needed to solve a particular set of problems. The TANDEM method detailed in this chapter significantly eases the need for those information design skills. By applying a series of rudimentary steps, a novice is able to find an acceptably good way to structure domain level data. Having some measure (a starting data set) of the domain data assumes a previous requirements gathering exercise. For a People-Oriented Programming approach to requirements gathering, the range of cultural probes discussed in the previous chapter, offer an eminently suitable choice for gathering the data needed for a starting point with TANDEM. Other traditional requirements methods are also a possible precursor to using TANDEM.

The application developed in the case study within the chapter, does so on a Raspberry Pi miniature computer, fast becoming a useful POP platform, used heavily in the UK primary and secondary education sectors (Banks Gatenby, 2017), and gaining a significant footprint in those school sectors in other countries, and also in the maker movement market in general.

The case study describes the TANDEM design method and demonstrates the use of it in detail, calling upon it to design a mashup application of services and local data stores that solves the so-called *movie-cinema problem*. An implementation of the newly designed movie-cinema app is then built within the DigitalFriend, an end-user oriented IDE that fits into the second element of POP defined above. The DigitalFriend example uses an inbuilt declarative logic language called CoLoG, but it can equally use SQL scripts. The early part of TANDEM uses a simple task analysis technique, describing all the *doing* activities in the proposed system, always beginning with a verb, e.g. *Reserve* seats. *Read* a book. These verb-first activities from Task Analysis, are familiar to all Facebook users, which are discussed below in Chapter 9. Furthermore, a significant part of the TANDEM design method is then automated within the development tool itself. This automation removes the most skilled task required by TANDEM of the end-user: the automation of the process of data normalisation. The automation applies data normalisation to the initial model of components and data sources that feed into the mashup. The presentation here relies on some understanding of data normalization, so a simple example is presented. After this demonstrated example of the method and the implementation, a discussion ensues on the applicability of a model achievable by end-users using TANDEM coupled with the automated normalization process built into the IDE, versus using a top-down model by an experienced information analyst. In conclusion, the TANDEM method combined with the automation as demonstrated, does empower an end-user to a significant degree in achieving a workable mashup of distributed services and local data stores and feeds. Such a powerful combination of methods and tools will help the Raspberry Pi become a significant people-oriented programming platform, beyond just a platform for teaching novices to code. Furthermore, the TANDEM method does have broader applicability to designing a broad class of logic programs, complementing the use of collected patterns in logic programs.

With 15 million units of the Raspberry Pi having sold (by August 2017) it is not only a formidable common platform for makers and for teaching school kids something of coding and computer science, but is also a fully functional Linux machine with desktop level tools, together with low level interfaces to all sorts of sensors and physical world devices to be controlled. Therefore, it is not surprising that the Raspberry Pi has also raised the interest of many researchers as a platform for building sociotechnical IoT systems for end-users (see Chapter 3 for an IoT application upon a *similar* low-cost computer board). It is with this in mind that the DigitalFriend was ported to the Raspberry Pi. Using the DigitalFriend, end-users are able to build mashups of REST and SOAP web services, together with local resources and processes, and other information sources including data streams from sensors and devices, into newly envisaged and often personalised POP applications.

Chapter 7

Professors Paay, Sterling, Pedell, Vetere and Howard have assembled an important body of work over 8 or 9 years that bridges a previous gap in the understanding between ethnographers, interaction designers and software engineers, whenever they came together to design and create socio-technical systems. They were early adopters of cultural probes (discussed back in Chapter 5), and have also adapted models from the Agent-Oriented paradigm - in which several methodologies use goal models that are tied to role models - in the requirements, analysis and design phases of system development. They take their agent models from those detailed in (Sterling & Taveter, 2009). While ethnographic data is often 'messy', the models used by software engineers are conversely, systematic and well organised. This can lead to either, a regular clash between those different ways of working, or to a productive team with complementary strengths via a shared understanding across the whole process. The authors have developed a method which promotes such a shared understanding, very effectively, during the whole time the team are together. In this chapter they consolidate their findings and present them with some clarity.

To uncover the social requirements for a new system a design team must identify non-work-focussed and non-goal-oriented interactions that happen between people. Cultural probes are particularly good for collecting data about personal and intimate aspects of people's lives. Data generated from cultural probes by the user themselves, can include photographs, postcards, drawings, diary and scrapbook entries, and more, which can be supplemented with contextual interviews to enrich understanding. With such ethnographic field data, the problem is how to derive usable and useful system requirements while retaining the insights and inspirations collected from the alternative views. Mulling over this material, an interdisciplinary team will often uncover and generate ambiguity in the system requirements.

Traditionally, software engineers do away with ambiguity before the design stage, by forcing choices early on during the analysis phase. However, ambiguity can be seen as an opportunity rather than a problem, particularly when developing social systems, as it allows people to interpret situations for themselves, and thereby establish a deeper understanding of what is needed. The authors use high level *quality goals* to capture such ambiguity and carry it through the whole design process. Quality goals are non-functional goals used to encapsulate social aspects of the context of use, bringing them into the models. They include *emotional goals* within the quality goals, such as: *having fun*, and *feeling secure*. Quality goals become a vehicle to carry subtle nuances of social interactions from the field data through to the final system design. The authors turn quality goals into quality attributes that in turn both enrich and constrain the goal and role models from the agent methods.

They present their method in a case study, the *Secret Touch* system, with quality goals representing information about intimate interactions that occur between couples. The study is an extension of their earlier Mediating Intimacy project: a study focused on supporting intimates (i.e. life partners, parents and younger children, adult offspring with dependent parents, and so on) with both co-present or separated by distance. The *Secret Touch* scenario was chosen for the design and implementation of a prototype of a socio-technical device for mediating intimacy in couples.

They have since extended their experience with the methodology through modelling a range of more complex socio-technical situations: guiding the building of software systems to encourage grandparents and grandchildren to have fun over the internet; in the mental health area, the development and pilot study of a novel digital intervention to promote personal recovery in people with persisting psychotic disorders; and the design of an emergency alarm monitor systems to help older people wishing to continue living at home.

These quality goal and role models, together with an innovative notation have been incorporated into an agile development methodology, that is now routinely used in teaching interaction design and software engineering at tertiary education level - which is detailed in the next chapter.

Feedback from the members of the interdisciplinary design team confirm that the role and goal models, together with the innovative notation, are easily understand by all team members, which is a major contributing factor of the success of the method. For that reason, there is every chance that the study subjects and actual users of these systems could also easily understand the method. Combine that with the fact that the cultural probes used in requirement gathering, were self-administered by the study subjects in this project, and what you have here is a method that is very well placed to play a bigger role in People-Oriented Programming into the future.

Chapter 8

Where the previous chapter presents a case study with an interdisciplinary design team made up of software engineers, ethnographers and interaction designers, research in this chapter involves the same starting method, but within Digital Media Design courses where the projects are generally about the design and creation of video games, and the student team members are a younger and more diverse group. As such, for the method it is a good further proving ground as a People-Oriented Programming method, demonstrating that it should be well placed in the future of POP. Particularly as there is some evolution of the method through the work presented here, involving human emotions, that has been folded back into the usage of it in general.

A striking difference in the domain and the digital design discipline, as compared to the software engineering and interaction disciplines, comes up early in the chapter:

Realising emotional factors is fundamental to design disciplines, from industrial and communication design to architecture and fashion design ... The consideration of emotions is important in the development of many sociotechnical systems. If a computer game does not feel fun, we will not play it; if an ecommerce website does not feel trustworthy we will not purchase from it; and if a social networking application does not feel engaging we will not use it. We describe these as the emotional goals of the system, which we define as goals that aim to affect people's emotional state or wellbeing... Digital media design methodologies have a tradition in realising emotional goals by using tools and processes such as: emotional colour scripts, flowcharts, rich pictures and mood boards... Designers model emotion and communicate the feel to clients and to each other using this visual, and in some cases, audio and textural language.

However, Marshall recognised the need for an inter-disciplinary design approach to solve the increasingly complex digital technologies being used and the diverse collaborations taking place in creating new digital media applications. The agent-oriented models (Sterling & Taveter, 2009) that were being applied to sociotechnical systems by the Paay et al. the authors of Chapter 7, fitted the need that Marshall had personally identified. He incorporated emotional goals and gave them equal importance, to the quality and functional goals duo, that Paay et al. had used to hold ambiguity in the minds of all team members for as long as possible in the design process. By advocating this new category of goal – *the emotional goal* (and introducing a new icon to the visual notation, in the shape of a heart) – the method has been evolved considerably, improving the way that sociotechnical systems are designed and created by inter-disciplinary teams, large and small.

Indeed, in the case study in this chapter - Aspergion Galaxy, a video game (a learning resource) for secondary school students that promotes *respect* for people with Asperger's Syndrome - Marshall applied the method to a team of 160 student developers over two semesters, and got a significant result. Conversely, the method has been used successfully by individuals. Marshall concludes with some statistics and results around the success of the method, with regard to teaching new digital media design:

Between 2011 and (late) 2017 the process has been repeated in over 200 separate projects, ranging in scale from 1 to approximately 300 developers, and at academic levels including 3rd year, Honours, Masters, Doctoral, Post-doctoral students,

Industry-based and Research projects. Outcomes have included the development of computer games, websites, animations … software applications, systems and services, advertising campaigns, branding and physical products.

Student feedback consistently reported that the goal models were intuitive and easy to use, and they provided common, well-understood artefacts around which progress can be communicated to all, and also helped to focus students on the primary project objectives throughout the life of the project.

From a marketing perspective, what the author's research is reporting at the end of this chapter, is a strategic advantage no less, in the way his university is teaching Digital Design, based squarely upon this new method that incorporates emotional, quality and functional goals, in equal measure. A method that has all the hallmarks of a good *POP methodology*, both scalable to large and diverse groups of people, and that still works right down to teams as small as *one*.

SECTION 3: THEORY IN THE PEOPLE-ORIENTED PROGRAMMING PARADIGM

As previously highlighted, a new software design and development paradigm doesn't come into existence in a neat chronological order like: *Theory, Tools, Methodology, Framework, Applications*. And so it is with the *theory* part of People-Oriented Programming. However, there have been advances in the area of theory coming from disparate disciplines, that do sit well within the embryotic POP paradigm. The two chapters in this Section hold important aspects of how relevant theoretical considerations from diverse disciplines have already impacted the other areas of POP, namely, the theory behind some of the tools and the methods described in Section 2. The focus in Chapter 9 upon the nature, formation and control of *Identity*, is timely, as there is something of a groundswell lately, aimed at harnessing the multitude of smartphone-empowered individuals, into groupings that both think and shoulder some responsibility at a global level, but act locally within their immediate communities. Two such initiatives are mentioned in the chapter. The first is from the social media platform industry itself, with the founder of Facebook, Mark Zuckerberg, flagging the intentions of his significant development resource, to provide the infrastructure for building a global community (Zuckerberg, 2017). While the second, mentioned earlier, is the various existing citizen science projects, such as those cited by Jennifer Preece in (Preece, 2017). This groundswell is very relevant to POP as it is a paradigm about empowering the individual, and the subject of Identity is right at the core of 'individual'.

There is a case study in Chapter 10 that thoroughly documents the complete process in specifying and designing an emergence alarm system for elderly people, who wish to continue living independently at home for as long as possible. It is a safety critical system. There is people-oriented method here within an overall software engineering methodology. The chapter also brings into focus, both the original and the ongoing role of software engineering in the People-Oriented Programming paradigm.

Chapter 9

This chapter by Dr Christine Yunn-Yu Sun et al. is titled 'Formation and Control of Identity: In a Social Media World'. It largely comes from the Cultural Studies discipline, but then that investigation of identity is reinforced with parallel and complementary theory from the *Psychology of Sub-selves* which is presented by way of a case study. The chapter begins by exploring the construction of identity in online communities and websites for social purposes, and its consequences in terms of how one's online identity may be utilized to such an extent that one's real-world identity is either enforced or eroded. It does so by investigating the very nature of Identify, coming predominantly from a Cultural Studies and philosophical view, although it also cites some related findings and advances in Computing and Information Systems (IS) research. In section: *Identity as a Self-Produced Continuity and the Media* - the authors investigate the concept of identity in the real world. They then investigate it in the online world in the section: *Online Identity, Its Construction and Circulation*. The section titled: *Social Media, Identity and the Meaning of Self* - examines how an individual positions herself, including who she associates with and why she flags this positioning, to others. For context, it looks at several mainstream social media platforms used, when doing so. This includes an overview of Facebook's recently divulged plan to build a global community, and compares that to certain citizen science projects that also often have global-level goals.

Interestingly, the biodiversity data collected by individual in these communities, is typically "*collected using smartphones (which) can include photos, comments, numerical data, video, and sound, together with metadata (e.g., time, date, and geolocation logging)*" – i.e. crowd-sourcing people with their increasingly sophisticated smartphones and attached/nearby sensors, as *information probes*, discussed by Graham & Rouncefield at length back in Chapter 5 on cultural probes as a POP method. That chapter was focused on self-ethnography. The biodiversity citizen science usage of these same probes, often scales to *ethnography* at the global level.

The section: *A Case Study in Representation and Control of Identity and Privacy* - presents an innovative approach to dealing with those issues and actions that revolve around the control and disclosure of identity, as detailed in earlier sections. Initial emphasis is on *knowing oneself well* through the interests and roles in one's life. Conceptual models of example POP software and an instantiated digital-self built using the software, are shown, as a pro-active tool that helps a person manage identity as their life evolves and as they interact in the online world, both through social media platforms and the greater Internet.

The central argument that runs across this chapter is two-fold, firstly, it promotes and demonstrates an initial shift in focus from the management of online identity to the nature and significance of *Identity* itself, whose construction may be conceptualized as a process of sense making and strengthening. Then, armed with a better understanding of identity, one can focus back upon the management of it more effectively, with a view to the individual taking more control of their own identity, particularly with regard to privacy. They emphasise the importance of this with: *"At stake is mass trust in the service providers of these new social media and search platforms. Also at stake is the last interior privacy firewall of Self"*. They further emphasise the importance of this at the global level, as the technology space (most notably but not limited to, social media, search engines, and mobile apps) is increasingly transitioning us all into members of a global community, one that needs to be functional not dysfunctional.

In several chapters of this book including this one, there is a recognition that the increasingly empowered individual, while a member of multiple communities both online and in the physical world, is progressively becoming a global citizen, or in this case: forming or reinforcing something of a global identity. This chapter demonstrates that the People-Oriented Programming tools and methods have a significant part to play in this ongoing empowering process, and that *Identity* research from multiple disciplines, including - cultural and philosophical studies, psychology, computing and information systems - is an important theatre for the *theory* that will continue to play a part in the POP paradigm.

Chapter 10

In this chapter by Leon Sterling, Antonio Lopez-Lorca, and Maheswaree Kissoon-Curumsing, a case study is used to show how they incorporate *emotions* as a first-class entity in the requirements and modelling phase of a software engineered system. The case study is one of emergency alarms for elder people who continue to live independently in their own homes, with the help of an on-call emergency system, rather than move into retirement villages or similarly staffed facilities. They point out that their emotional goal modelling technique is particularly well suited to most socio-technical and domestic systems. In the domain of the case study, previous alarm systems tried by participants in the study, involved two devices: a pendant or wristband to be warned at all times, with a button on it to push in emergencies to alert a call centre that assistance is required (e.g. a fall they cannot get up from); and a wellbeing checking device that the elderly person is required to press within a fixed time period each day, to indicate to a carer/relative that all is going well. The design of these traditional alarms in no way included the emotions of people involved. As such, many elderly people viewed wearing the pendant as a stigma and sign of old age, while the well-being check-in, they saw as an infringement of their independence.

The authors demonstrate, by the inclusion of emotional goals as a design criteria, how much better they are able to gather requirements, analyse the problem, and design a more appropriate solution. For example, the wellbeing checking device they come up with, is not a button, but a touchscreen connected to the relative or carer, on which they receive photos each day (e.g. of a grandchild, say), and that by simply touching or commenting on it, it becomes an implicit wellbeing check-in that is positively accepted into their lifestyle.

They use goal models (drawing quality goals and emotional goals from the requirements gathering phase), and identify the various roles played in using such a system. They draw upon several deep veins of research for their methodology: role and goal models from the agent-oriented software engineering field; and viewpoint analysis from requirements engineering. They also use Scenarios with the various stakeholders in a project, to flush out the required functionalities, and pick-up any missing details from the role and goal models – much as scenarios are used in Human Computer Interface (HCI) to analyse and design systems.

The real innovation in this approach is in identifying emotional goals and placing them on an equal footing with other quality metrics such as performance and reliability of software engineering systems: "*It can be argued that emotional goals are different from traditional quality goals such as performance and reliability, because they are properties of the user rather than the system. Emotional goals are subtle, ambiguous, and difficult to measure.*" This is in line with the approach that Marshall takes in Chapter 8 in the digital media design area, which lead to the notation used for emotional goals here.

While their methodology is within the field of software engineering, typically where a team of people including stakeholders: determine the requirements for a new system, analyse, design and then build/or have it built. There is people-oriented method within an overall software engineering methodology, by way of the emotional goals being included: "*Emotional goals are linked to roles, which represent stakeholders in the system, and specify a desired state of emotion or wellbeing of an agent playing those roles. Emotional goals represent how people feel, so are a property of people, not of the system."*

One of the observations during the case study, is just how easily the non-technical stakeholders in the project, readily took up and used the emotional goal models, to converse and explain their particular viewpoints in the project. Furthermore, the use of role models from the Agent-Oriented paradigm were also readily identified with and taken up by both technical and non-technical stakeholders.

Their modelling and methodology is extensive, as can be clearly seen in this chapter, with 34 figures representing the models used to bring the new system in the case study into existence. However, the Scenarios figures are all textural and easily understood. Many of the visual models are equally as easy to comprehend. Nonetheless, what is evident in this chapter is a tendency for software engineering to lead to over specification of a system, from a people-oriented method point of view – something also recognised in Chapter 7.

One way that complexity and heavy specification is alleviated, is through the development of new software development *tools*, and indeed several of the authors of this chapter and Chapter 7 are involved in just that: improving their methodology by developing new tools and refining the visual notations used. At some stage in the near future, their approach is likely to become a fully people-oriented *methodology*. They also encourage other developers of tools and applications, to fold emotional goals into their existing processes, to improve their outcomes. We only have to look back at the four chapters in Section 1, to see that it has been innovation in the tools themselves since about 2007 forward, specifically in the integrated programming environments (IDE) rather than in the syntax of programming languages, that has put coding within range of most school children.

This chapter could have been placed in Section 2 given the significant amount of people-oriented method within it, but it is doubly useful here in this section on *theory*, as it gives some good backgrounding to the agent-oriented goal and role models used, and also shows how and why emotional goals have been folded into a software engineering methodology. It also reminds us that many applications should and will remain in the software engineering realm. Emergency alarms for elderly people wanting to continue living independently at home for as long as possible, is a safety critical situation, and not something you want tinkered into existence. And, as is emphasised in the fourth element of the People Oriented Programming paradigm at the outset, the highly usable end-user development tools that are required for the paradigm to succeed, also need to be well-engineered.

SECTION 4: PERSONALIZED LEARNING ENVIRONMENTS AND THE PEOPLE-ORIENTED PROGRAMMING PARADIGM

We saw in Section 1 a lot of the exciting developments in POP is in new programming environments for coding, and these coding environments are often much more than programming editors. Several of them including Scratch and Greenfoot, are prime examples of learning environments with large communities of likeminded people. In the recent book *Lifelong Kindergarten: Cultivating Creativity through Projects, Passion, Peers, and Play* (Resnick, 2017) the author and the prime-mover behind Scratch, Mitchel Resnick, outlines his reasons for being a strong advocate for teaching all young people to become fluent in coding: *"Most people won't grow up to become professional programmers or computer scientists, but learning to code fluently is valuable for everyone. Becoming fluent, whether with writing or coding, helps you to develop your thinking, develop your voice, and develop your identity."* While coding is only one aspect of learning in the modern school curriculum, there is considerable scope for coding activities and computational thinking in many other subjects that make up a comprehensive curriculum. For these reasons we include two chapters on Personalised Learning Environments (PLE) in this volume.

In the Editorial Preface by the guest editors for a special issue on Personalised Learning, Judith Good and Ben de Boulay (2014) characterized personalized learning learning in the following way:

Personalised learning, or the tailoring of curriculum, pedagogical approaches and the learning environment to each individual, provides a greater focus on the individual than any earlier approach to learning. In doing so, it has been concerned with adapting learning experiences and resources based on a wide variety of factors, including personal learning history, current location and context, available interactive devices, cultural preference, personality, learning preferences and gender, amongst others. A dominant source of personalisation derives from cognitive differences between individuals, whether in terms of their approaches to learning or, more commonly, what knowledge has already been acquired, and what skills have so far been mastered.

Additionally, new generation learners often like to customise their learning content and learning spaces/locales. They will personalise their interactions in the learning process, expressing themselves with their own user generated content, as much as the technology allows. And given fewer constraints than tradition learning has afforded them, they will learn whatever, wherever and whenever they desire, usually intermingled with other non-learning activities.

Personalised Learning Environments (PLEs) include technical environments which encourage and support personal learning. In a sense, several of the coding environments covered in Section 1 could be described at some level as PLEs. For example Scratch now has in excess of 20 million online projects, with commenters, collaborators and followers, within which a person learning to code, can call upon and borrow from, *whenever* and from *wherever* they desire.

However, the two chapters that follow are more focused on generic PLEs – those in which support for an individual learner of any subject (*whatever*) can be facilitated.

In Chapter 11 titled 'Intertwining E-Learning Technologies and Pedagogies at the System Design Stage: To Support Personalized Learning', George Weichhart and Chris Stary explore the issue of how a learning management systems (LMS) might be evolved so that it could explicitly incorporate different pedagogical models, depending on the individual student and teacher (or mentor). In doing so, however, they are careful to propose a model where the pedagogical aspects of the LMS remain decoupled from its technical aspects, so that different pedagogies might be applied in different circumstances, or a particular pedagogy shared across different e-learning platforms and tools. This chapter outlines many of the technical requirements that would enable interoperability across the different system components needed to support interchangeable pedagogy models.

In Chapter 12, I make the case that the future of learning environments lies in the merging of the better aspects of Learning Management Systems (LMS), with those popularised in Social Networking platforms, to enable the personalization of the individual learning experience. The resulting system is a PLE (Personal Learning Environment). After examining the details of a particularly flexible LMS, followed by the investigation of several key data structures behind the Facebook social networking platform, this chapter then demonstrates how such a merging can be done at the conceptual schema level, and presents a subset list of the novel features that it then enables.

It is unclear how LMSs and PLEs will evolve as larger percentages of current and future young students become fluent in coding in one of more of the languages covered in Section 1. However, the glimpses we see in the collaborative learning communities, such as those within Scratch and Greenfoot, are inspiring. There is even potential for those learning communities to use their knowledge gained within those empowering environments, to expand their projects and tutorials to envelop subjects in the wider curriculum of their immediate educational organisations. If the maker movement is anything to go by, should young coders in the midst of that movement, move their innovative focus towards the local curricula, beyond just coding and foundational computational thinking, the synergy arising from a pairing of the People-Oriented Programming paradigm (POP) and newly evolving

Personalised Learning Environments, could transform secondary education at the very least into a learning hothouse.

As noted earlier in the introduction of Chapter 9 with its focused upon identity, the large corporate social network platforms, as well as the niche social websites (and apps) such as the biodiversity citizen science communities, are transitioning us all into an increasingly global community, one that needs to be more functional rather than less. Empowering individuals and raising global consciousness, are it seems, two sides of the one coin. Just as Preece (2017) emphasised a limited area of endeavour (in terms of one's full identity) targeted at making a positive difference and acting locally - in that case saving species and maintaining as much biodiversity as possible by contributing in some small way to the management of the biosphere – the pairing up of POP with personalized learning environments (PLE), aimed at local curricula and local civic problems, but drawing on an online community of like-minded, collaborative peers and mentors as needed, would be an admirable application domain for developing the future of the People-Oriented Programming paradigm. Advanced PLE platforms operated by the safe sets of hands that belong to currently committed educationalists, is a good and familiar place, domain and cohort for researchers and academics in the POP space, to concentrate much/more of their future efforts.

Steve Goschnick
Swinburne University of Technology, Australia

REFERENCES

Banks Gatenby, A. (2017). Developing Critical Understanding of Computing With the Raspberry Pi. *International Journal of People-Oriented Programming*, *6*(2), 1–19.

Good, J. & de Boulay. (2014). Guest Editorial Preface. *Special Issue on Personalised Learning. International Journal of People-Oriented Programming*, *3*(2).

Goschnick, S. (2009). People-Oriented Programming: from Agent-Oriented Analysis to the Design of Interactive Systems. *Proceedings, HCI International*. 10.1007/978-3-642-02574-7_93

Graham, C., & Goschnick, S. (2006). Augmenting Interaction and Cognition using Agent Architectures and Technology Inspired by Psychology and Social Worlds. *Universal Access in the Information Society*, *4*(3), 204–222. doi:10.100710209-005-0012-x

Preece, J. (2017, March-April). How two billion smartphone users can save species! *Interaction*, *24*(2), 26–33. doi:10.1145/3043702

Resnick, M. (2017). *Lifelong Kindergarten: Cultivating Creativity through Projects, Passion, Peers, and Play*. Cambridge, MA: MIT Press.

Sterling, L., & Taveter, K. (2009). *The Art of Agent-Oriented Modelling*. Cambridge, MA: MIT Press.

Section 1
Programming Environments for People–Oriented Programming

Highly usable and well-engineered development tools are required for People-Oriented Programming so that the end-user can design, code, configure, make or mashup solutions to their own problems, either afresh or customised from solutions to similar problems or needs. This section is made up of four chapters that together present the state-of-the-art of the programming languages and coding environments of the People-Oriented Programming paradigm.

Chapter 1
Novice Programming Environments:
Lowering the Barriers, Supporting the Progression

Judith Good
University of Sussex, UK

ABSTRACT

In 2011, the author published an article that looked at the state of the art in novice programming environments. At the time, there had been an increase in the number of programming environments that were freely available for use by novice programmers, particularly children and young people. What was interesting was that they offered a relatively sophisticated set of development and support features within motivating and engaging environments, where programming could be seen as a means to a creative end, rather than an end in itself. Furthermore, these environments incorporated support for the social and collaborative aspects of learning. The article considered five environments—Scratch, Alice, Looking Glass, Greenfoot, and Flip— examining their characteristics and investigating the opportunities they might offer to educators and learners alike. It also considered the broader implications of such environments for both teaching and research. In this chapter, the author revisits the same five environments, looking at how they have changed in the intervening years. She considers their evolution in relation to changes in the field more broadly (e.g., an increased focus on "programming for all") and reflects on the implications for teaching, as well as research and further development.

DOI: 10.4018/978-1-5225-5969-6.ch001

INTRODUCTION

In 2011, an article I wrote, entitled, "Learners at the wheel: Novice programming environments come of age" was published in the International Journal of People Oriented Programming (IJPOP). It is interesting to see how things have evolved in the intervening six years. In some cases, there have been substantial advances in terms of novice programming environments, as well as the computational thinking agenda and computer science education in general, whilst in others, the issues identified as relevant then are equally relevant now.

In the original article, I stated:

Over the past few years, a number of programming environments for novices have moved out of the research lab and into the public domain. Many of these environments are available free for download, and learners can begin using them to create simple programs in a matter of minutes. This is an exciting trend for a number of reasons: firstly, the environments have increased significantly in terms of their sophistication, combining programming languages (either graphical or text-based) with 2D and sometimes 3D graphical execution environments to form fully fledged integrated development environments (IDEs). Secondly, the IDEs themselves are often embedded in what could be considered a broader ecosystem, comprising online peer support facilities, educational resources for both teachers and learners, and mechanisms for sharing the programs that one has created with other learners. And finally, many of these environments, whilst being open-ended in scope, and allowing for user creativity, are nonetheless grounded in motivating activities such as game making, animation, storytelling, etc. This is not to suggest that novice programming environments are a new phenomenon; indeed, Guzdial (2004) provides an overview of their history since the 1960s, while Kelleher and Pausch (2005) have developed one of the most extensive taxonomies to date. However, because of the ease with which the World Wide Web can make such programming environments and their associated infrastructures so freely accessible, environments of this type are much more ubiquitous, with sites such as Scratch (http://scratch.mit.edu/) reporting over half a million registered users, and over one million uploaded projects.

In particular, children and young people are finding themselves willingly engaged in programming in the pursuit of other creative activities such as making games, interactive stories, simulations or animated films. While they would not classify themselves as programmers, nor would many consider pursuing a career in computer science, they nonetheless enjoy the creative process of designing an artefact and bringing it to life, as it were, by giving it interactivity and, at a later stage, sharing it with one's peers, both locally and remotely, often with great enthusiasm. As such, these environments have opened up new worlds to novice programmers and, more informally, to "unwitting end user programmers" (Petre & Blackwell, 2007). Whereas end user programmers do not program on a regular basis, but might occasionally write a small program to achieve a particular goal, unwitting end user programmers may be unaware that what they are doing is even programming at all, a phenomenon also observed by Resnick et al. (2009) in the case of young people using Scratch.

What is perhaps most exciting about these novice programming environments is that, examined in a broader context, they may offer some answers to questions currently being posed by educators, namely, with computation becoming ever more ubiquitous and pervasive, how do we ensure that future generations are conversant with computational tools, not just as consumers, but as producers? Although learning to think 'computationally' has long been recognised as important (Papert, 1980), the recent computational thinking drive has refocused attention on this as a significant issue in modern society (Wing, 2006). There is broad agreement that it is important to teach computational thinking skills from a young age, and to people who may never learn to program (Guzdial, 2008; Fletcher & Lu, 2009), but deciding which specific skills should be taught is still an emerging endeavour.

In this article, I will argue that current novice programming environments, and in particular, the ways in which they have already been appropriated by young people, may provide some ideas for educators interested in looking at how to teach computational skills to people outside of traditional computer science disciplines. I describe the current state of the art in programming environments for novices by considering five such environments. The aim is not to provide an exhaustive review, but to highlight various features which promote learning, ease of use and engagement. I go on to discuss the features they share, and highlight some of the implications of these environments for both teaching, and research.

In this chapter, I will revisit the five novice programming environments described in my original article: Scratch, Alice, Looking Glass, Greenfoot and Flip. All have evolved substantially in the intervening years, and all are still in current use (with the exception of Flip which, while it would be technically possible to use, has suffered from being tied to a commercial games engine which is now outdated, as well as from a lack of follow up funding). Indeed, in terms of those environments which continue to receive funding, their growth and reach has increased dramatically: to date, over 20 million Scratch projects have been shared by young people through the Scratch online community (Resnick, 2017). The infrastructure around these environments has also expanded significantly, with the environment now just one element of a comprehensive set of resources for both educators and learners, as well as opportunities to become part of virtual communities, join discussions, share creations, etc.

In addition to revisiting the five environments above, I will also, briefly, consider new novice programming environments which have become available in the intervening years.

NOVICE PROGRAMMING ENVIRONMENTS

In this section, I consider five very different programming environments for novices: Scratch, Alice, Looking Glass, Greenfoot and Flip. All vary quite significantly on a number of aspects, and as such, have differing strengths and weaknesses. Only a cursory overview can be provided for each environment, however as most of the environments are quite well established, full references are given for each (including links to websites) so that they can be followed up if the reader so wishes. I consider basic information about the environment, such as the age range for which it was designed, the programming language on which it is built (if relevant), and whether it has evolved from previous versions or other languages. I then look at the *process* of creating a program in the environment, describing a typical program creation session. I also discuss, for each environment, any special features which mark it out from the others, and extra support and community features which enhance the standard programming environment. Finally, I consider the ways in which each environment is currently being used in the wild.

Scratch

Scratch (http://scratch.mit.edu/) is a programming environment designed to allow novices to manipulate media through programming activities (Maloney et al., 2008), with a primary audience aged between 8 and 16 (Resnick et al., 2009). Scratch 2, the current version of Scratch, was released in 2013, with Scratch 3 expected in 2018. Scratch has evolved from, and been inspired by, a number of other languages and environments developed in the MIT Media Lab, and is designed in such a way as to promote playful tinkering and exploration. Compared to the other environments surveyed, Scratch allows a younger age range to begin experimenting with programming concepts. An additional programming environment, ScratchJr (released in 2014), has been designed to further lower the age barrier for computing, and is aimed at children aged 5-7. Although ScratchJr shares some features with Scratch, it crucially does not require reading skills in order to write programs. A fuller review of the ScratchJr environment can be found in (Goschnick, 2015).

The Scratch interface (Figure 1) comprises a blocks pane, in the middle of the interface, with ten different categories of colour coded programming blocks shown at the top of the pane (with Scratch 2 having introduced the ability to create custom blocks). The blocks themselves snap together to create a program, with shape being indicative of function, e.g. a "forever" block will fit round a set of commands and cause those commands to run indefinitely. Programs are created by dragging blocks from the blocks pane in the middle to the scripting pane on the right-hand side of the screen. The scripting pane can accommodate multiple sets of blocks, thus creating de facto concurrent programs with ease.

On the top left-hand side of the interface is the stage, which can be maximised once a project is finished. Sprites (selected from the sprites pane) appear on the stage, and their behaviours are governed by the programs created in the scripting pane. In contrast to previous versions of the interface, the Scratch 2 interface has been streamlined to allow more space for creating programs, with blocks, costumes and sounds accessed via tabs in the middle part of the interface.

The concept of an online community of users has been central to Scratch from its inception, with the idea of sharing programs given the same importance as creating them in the first place. The Scratch website acts as a vibrant online space in which learners can share projects they have created with others, who can rate those projects, download them, remix them, and re-upload them if they wish. In a very novel approach to fostering the collaborative aspects of code reuse, and ensuring that

Figure 1. The Scratch interface

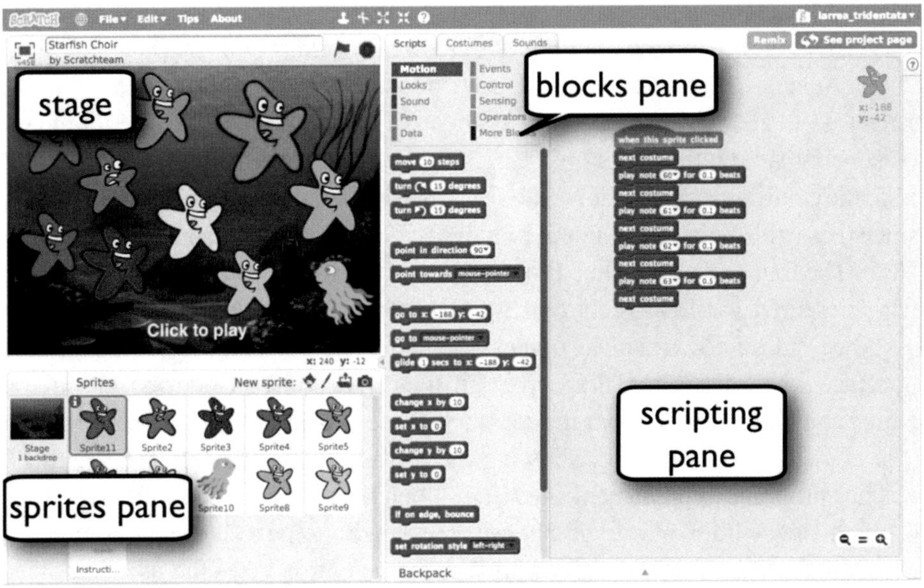

the original authors retain credit, the Scratch website includes a "remix tree", which allows users to see who has remixed their project and in what ways and, similarly, how their remixed project was subsequently remixed by others (Resnick, 2014).

Teachers wishing to use Scratch also have access to their own online community, ScratchEd, where they can ask questions and get advice. Additionally, the Scratch website provides numerous lesson plans, projects and educational resources which can be freely downloaded.

Interestingly enough, studies of young people using Scratch show that, despite the absence of formal instruction or even mentors experienced in computer science concepts, they still produce projects which contain many of the hallmarks of traditional programs, e.g. conditionals, variables and Boolean logic (Maloney et al., 2008). Despite this, when interviewed, they do not consider themselves to be "programming", although the term 'coding' is becoming used more frequently to denote these types of informal programming activities. Recent research has also shown the viability of Scratch as an effective platform for teaching important computer science concepts, even if students experience difficulties with concepts such as variables, concurrency and repeated execution (Meerbaum-Salant et al., 2013). Although originally designed for young people of school age, research using Scratch at university level suggests that it increases students' self-efficacy, and leads to much greater success when students go on to learn object-oriented programming in CS1 (Rizvi et al., 2011).

Alice

Alice (http://www.alice.org/) is a development environment designed to teach programming through the building of 3D virtual worlds (Cooper, Dann & Pausch, 2003; Adams, 2014). Alice can be used by students in middle school (typically 11 years old and upwards) through to university as it supports the development of reasonably substantial programs, e.g. 3000 lines of code (Kelleher et al., 2002). Like the environments mentioned above, Alice has been in continuous development since it was released, with Alice 3.3 being the current version at the time of writing. Note: The founder of the Alice Project at Carnegie Mellon was Dr. Randy Pausch, who presented The Last Lecture in 2007, a year before his death.

Alice is designed around an object-oriented paradigm, and uses a drag and drop interface where users can drag program tiles (now called Controls) into a code editor and parameterise them if necessary. Once a program has been constructed, it is executed in a 3D world, allowing the learner to very quickly see whether or not her program implemented the desired behaviour. In the top left panel is the Camera view with two overlaid buttons: the Run button executes the programmed animation as it currently stands; while the Scene button takes the user into Scene

Editor mode, depicted in Figure 3. The opening interface is dominated by the Edit panel (right) itself split in two with Alice code in the left half, and the equivalent Java code displayed in the right half. This ability to display the Java code equivalent is a non-default option, included by the Alice developers to help coders transition from the drag and drop Alice code, to a mainstream commercial programming language. The Edit panel has tabbed panes where different parts of a program are created and edited. Code Editor mode also has a Methods panel (bottom left) and a Controls panel (along the bottom right). The Methods panel has two tabs, one for Procedures and the other for Functions. Alice differentiates the two as follows: *Procedures* perform actions on or by an object; while *Functions* ask a question of the user or compute a value and so on. In Java, both are just called methods.

When Alice is first started with a new project template, the Camera is the current object, representing the Camera view currently displayed in top right of Figure 2. Different objects within the scene can be selected and worked on, for example, an object called Penguin is currently being edited. All objects in Alice have a method called *myFirstMethod* (the main method defined for a scene), which is the default open tab in the Edit panel as depicted in Figure 2.

Code is developed by dragging and dropping the pre-built Procedure and Function templates from the Methods panel into the Edit panel, and then populating those methods further by dragging and dropping *Controls* from the Control panel. Each control has some parameters within it that can be edited by the coder. In this sense, the Alice controls are very similar to the blocks in Scratch.

Alice was an early example of a programming environment that provided a motivational "hook", namely the ability to create one's own 3D animations. In addition, it gave learners a very tight visual feedback loop: it was very clear from the way the characters in the environment behaved (or not), whether the program created had had the desired effect, and its animated output was more compelling than a standard debugger.

Alice has evolved substantially over the years: as shown in Figure 2, it can now show the Java code side by side with the original Alice code, however, the Java code in the right-hand panel cannot be edited. In addition, the Controls themselves can be turned into Java equivalents (of the Alice controls), so that these 'Java controls' can be dragged and dropped into the methods. Furthermore, Alice 3 can be used with NetBeans, via a plugin, to convert Alice files in Java, and allow users to continue working on their programs in Java. However, once the Java code has been modified in NetBeans, the changes cannot be brought back into Alice – it is a one-way migration.

From a visual perspective, Alice 3 incorporates extensive 3D content and assets from the hugely popular Sims™ II video game, making learners' creations more similar in look and feel to the games that many of them regularly play. This

Figure 2. The Alice 3 interface

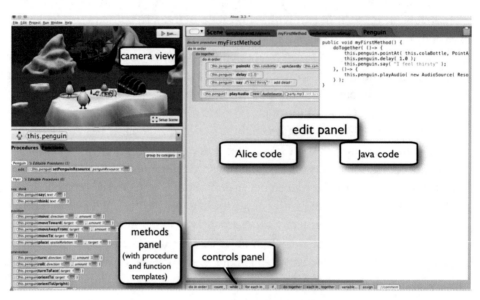

extensive gallery of objects is selectable via the five tabs in the bottom panel of the Scene Editor (see Figure 3). The included gallery is necessarily large, as each object comes pre-programmed with a set of Method and Function templates, such as the *moveForward* template for Penguin, which the coder can select then modify and expand as needed. The coder can also add new procedures of their own to an object (although this gets considerably more complex). The objects from the Sims are sophisticated in that they often have skeletal systems (e.g. the humans and animals), and the movement of the individual body-parts can be programmed although the coding to do so is, again, quite complex.

The Scene Editor makes it very easy to create 3D scenes and populate them with numerous objects from the Gallery. The placement, rotation and resizing of each object is very intuitive, making good use of both mouse and keyboard, while displaying visual handles to facilitate making the desired changes. The Scene Editor and the Code Editor are very complementary tools, for example: the hierarchy of the classes in the current project is accessible from the Code Editor (via the drop-down button that precedes the tabs in the Edit panel, and shown in Figure 4); while the hierarchy of instantiated objects in the Scene is accessible in the Scene Editor.

And similarly to the other environments described in this chapter, the Alice IDE is just one component, albeit the core one, of a substantial set of resources, including how-tos, exercises and projects, textbooks, a teacher listserv and an open forum. In the time that has passed since my earlier paper, both the terminology used within

Figure 3. The Scene Editor in Alice

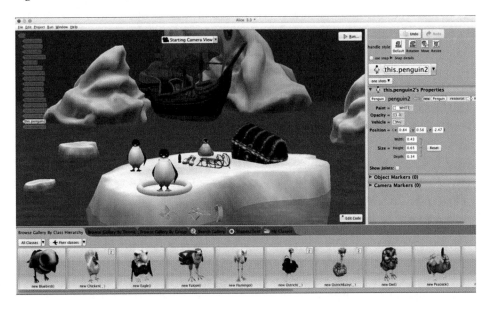

Figure 4. The Code Editor in Alice in Class mode, note: Methods Panel becomes class hierarchy

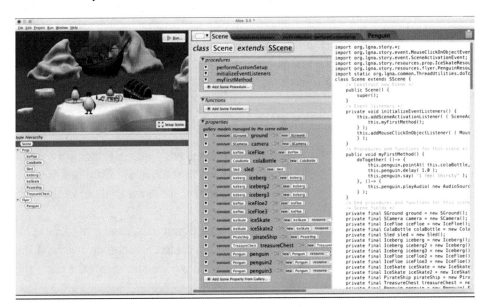

the interface and the inclusion of the view of the Java code behind the scenes, has gravitated Alice towards mainstream programming a little, by facilitating a transition for those first-time coders in Alice 3 who then wish to pursue coding in a mainstream object-oriented language within a mainstream IDE, namely Java in NetBeans.

Looking Glass

The Looking Glass IDE is the successor to Storytelling Alice, which was itself based on Alice 2.0. Whereas Alice relies on the creation of animations as its motivational hook for learning programming, Looking Glass is designed specifically with the aim of helping middle school girls (aged approximately 11-14 years) to create (non-interactive) stories in a 3D world, with the rationale that they will be sufficiently motivated by the activity to tackle the programming aspects as a result. This aim is set in the broader context of the large gender disparity in undergraduate computer science, and the need to address this gap as computing becomes ever more pervasive in society. Although the typical response has been to increase the use of video games in the undergraduate curriculum, Kelleher and Pausch (2007) have argued that this does not typically address female interests.

In order to provide support for storytelling activities, Alice was adapted in a number of ways. The resulting system contains animations which are specifically social and interactional (e.g. "look at", "touch" rather than "orient to"), 3D characters and objects designed to promote ideas for stories, and tutorials which use story-based examples rather than generic programming ones (Kelleher, Pausch & Kiesler, 2007).

The Looking Glass development environment consists of an Action Editor and a Scene Editor. In the Action Editor, learners can choose actions from the action list for each character (including the overall scene), drag the actions into the story pane, and set parameters for the actions, effectively creating the program (shown in Figure 5).

The Looking Glass IDE is built upon Alice, and has a Scene Editor very similar to that of Alice (see Figure 3). As noted above, in the Scene Editor, learners can choose 3D characters and objects from the gallery, and arrange them in the scene view in order to create their stories.

Like Scratch and Alice, Looking Glass promotes remixing, and provides explicit support for doing so. Learners can load a world created by another user, and then use video editing style controls to step through the code and select the parts they wish to retain (see Figure 6).

Again, like the other environments, Looking Glass has extensive accompanying resources and community features. In addition, the Looking Glass team have expended significant research effort into looking, in depth, at the best ways of scaffolding learning. For example, the team has looked at how tutorials can be automatically

Figure 5. The Looking Glass Action Editor

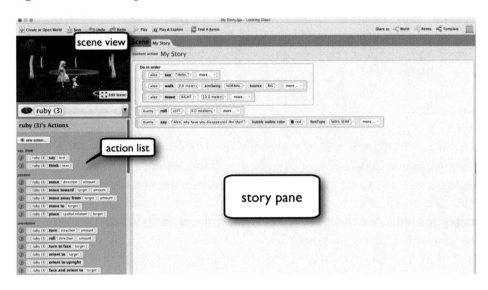

Figure 6. Support for remixing in Looking Glass

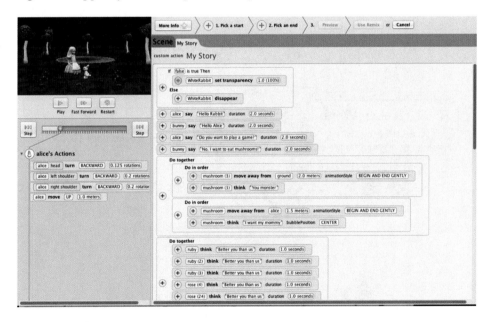

generated from code snippets selected by a learner online, therefore allowing them to learn independently (Harms et al., 2013). They have also looked at how interfaces can support students to reuse code written by others (Gross et al., 2010), as well as considering the effectiveness of learning through code completion puzzles (Harms et al., 2015).

Greenfoot

Greenfoot (http://www.greenfoot.org/) is an educational IDE which started development in 2004 and was published in 2006 (Kölling, 2015). Greenfoot was designed to teach young people to learn to program through the creation of games and simulations (Kölling & Henriksen, 2005). As it is based on Java, there is no upper age limit, however the recommended lower limit is 14 years because of possible difficulties with syntax. Thus, its target audience centres on high school and beginning university students. Code written in the Greenfoot IDE executes in the Greenfoot world, which is a 2D interactive, graphical environment (see Figure 7). The Greenfoot world is inhabited by "actors": in order to get the actors to carry out a behaviour, students program the actor's "act" method. Clicking on the "Act"

Figure 7. The Greenfoot interface

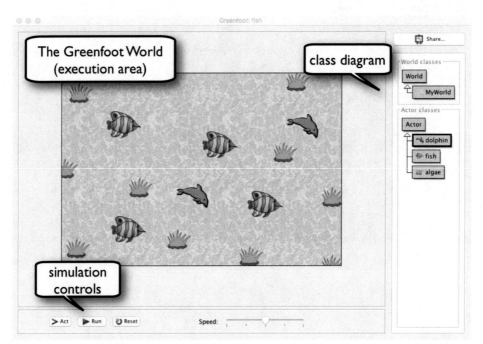

button will call this method once, while clicking on the "Run" button will call the method indefinitely.

In earlier versions of Greenfoot, young people wrote their code in Java. Whilst this is still possible, Greenfoot 3 provided additional possibilities for coding with the introduction of the Stride programming language and, more importantly, a frame-based editor for writing Stride code (see Figure 8).

The frame based editing environment allows novice programmers to write code by selecting from a series of frames using keyboard shortcuts (shown on the right). Frames often contain slots, which can be completed with further frames (e.g. in the case of, say, a nested if statement) or by typing in text, such as object names, etc. Within the frames, the Stride editor allows code to be inserted using code completion, where typing the first letters of, say, a method, will generate a list of methods starting with that prefix. The use of frames allows the system to use contextual cues in generating possible completions.

These particular features of the frame-based editor aim to reduce syntax errors. At the same time, programming in Stride allows students to learn the semantics of Java programming before moving to programming in Java. The Greenfoot environment allows code to be converted from Stride to Java, and vice versa, providing support for the transition from a more tightly constrained language (Stride) to one which has similar semantics, but requires syntactical knowledge (Java).

Figure 8. Frame based editing in Greenfoot

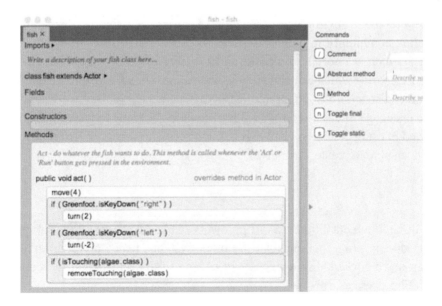

In terms of its motivational hook, Greenfoot is perhaps more domain agnostic than some of the other environments described in this chapter. Although it can support the creation of games, and its creators recognise the pull of games for some students, it is positioned more as a "micro-world meta framework" (Kölling, 2010) which allows for a variety of micro-worlds to be created, spanning a range of domains from games to simulations and visualisations. As such, it can cater for students with diverse interests, and can be applied to topic areas for which games may not be the most appropriate form of interaction.

In terms of pedagogical model, Greenfoot takes a very different approach to the teaching of programming, where it is common to have students write a very small program and observe the results. Instead, Greenfoot students are given a pre-implemented and compiled scenario. They can begin by executing the scenario to see how it works, and then augment the scenario by creating objects and adding them to the world. Doing so allows a number of fundamental OO concepts to be introduced prior to having students actually write code, an approach akin to "game first programming" (Goschnick & Balbo, 2005). At a later stage, students can go on to write their own scenarios in either Java or Stride.

Greenfoot has a number of strengths, which stem primarily from its adaptability. Because it is based on Java, it has both speed and power, runs on hardware typically available in classrooms, is multi-platform, and can benefit from the infrastructure which already exists for Java. Again, because it is Java based, young people are unlikely to "grow out of it" as quickly as some other development environments and when they do, they may be able to transition to other Java based IDEs if they wish to continue to learn to program, having already gained a certain fluency with Java.

Greenfoot has a number of features which provide a sort of "ecosystem" around the development environment itself, and have allowed for the development of an online community in much the same way as Scratch. In addition to standard materials such as tutorials, a website and a textbook (Kölling, 2016), learners can upload scenarios which can be rated by other users, who can also leave comments. Greenfoot also provides support for instructors in the form of the *Greenroom*, where they can engage in discussions and share scenarios, thereby reducing the overhead involved in using Greenfoot, and giving them access to scenarios that they may not have been able to create themselves.

Flip

The Flip environment (http://www.flipproject.org.uk/) takes a very different approach to introducing programming than the other systems, hence a certain amount of background knowledge is necessary in order to fully understand the context in which Flip operates.

Context of Flip

Rather than a standalone IDE, Flip is a programming environment which integrates with an existing game creation toolset, which itself fits within an existing commercial game. Compared to the other environments described in this chapter, this sets it apart, and gives it distinct advantages and disadvantages, described below.

The development of Flip took place within the context of our research on game creation by young people. Our initial game creation research took place using a commercial game, Neverwinter Nights (released in 2002). Flip was designed to integrate with Neverwinter Nights 2 (or NWN2), the successor to the original game, released in 2006. NWN2 is a third person perspective role playing game (RPG) based on Dungeons and Dragons rules[1]. Players explore a large fantasy world and take part in a complex interactive story with multiple branching plots and subplots. Although the game has battle scenes and fights, the narrative component of the game is a prominent and important element, and as the story progresses, the choices that the player makes will have an effect on how the plot unfolds at any given point.

The interesting thing about NWN2 from our perspective was that it shipped with the Electron toolset, a professional quality game development application which was used by the developers, Obsidian Entertainment, to build the game itself. Games enthusiasts used the toolset to create modules for the game, which other players could then download and play, a practice called modding. Because they were using the developers' own tools and resources to design new 3D worlds and adventures, their modules could potentially have a professional quality that is indistinguishable from the content originally contained in the commercial game, and for many, this was a huge motivation.

We used the Electron toolset with hundreds of young people aged 10-16 years old over a number of years and in a number of contexts (school computing lessons, after school clubs, summer holiday workshops, etc.) to help them create their own 3D role playing games. The games created involved significant effort on the part of the young people, with very sophisticated (and often quite humorous) plots, often with hundreds of lines of dialogue for their characters. Because the stories are interactive, character actions and behaviours required some programming. As such, this opened up opportunities for learning both about story creation and programming.

During that period, our research focussed on the learning benefits which could be gained from empowering young people to create their own commercial quality video games. In addition to programming (Howland, Good & Robertson, 2006), we had a particular interest in the ways in which interactive storytelling, of the type found in these role-playing games, could be used to foster young people's narrative development (e.g. Robertson & Good, 2005; Robertson & Good, 2006) and specific literacy skills (Howland, Good & du Boulay, 2008).

However, despite all of the advantages offered by working with a commercial toolset, the primary disadvantage was that it was not designed for young users, nor was it designed for educational purposes. Nonetheless, the Electron toolset, in addition to being available to the public, was a very open-ended system, which included a plugin interface: essentially, the toolset's capabilities can be extended through plugins written in C#. This led us to develop a whole series of plugins designed specifically to help young people with game creation tasks:

- Adventure Author, which can support the creative task of game design (Robertson & Nicholson, 2007);
- Narrative Threads, a suite of tools to support young people's narrative development through game creation (Howland, Good, & du Boulay, 2013);
- Flip, which supports programming tasks, described in this chapter (Howland & Good, 2015; Good & Howland, 2017).

In the next section, I will illustrate the initial stages of creating a game with the Electron toolset, prior to using Flip. I then go on to describe the Flip programming language, and how it integrates with the toolset environment.

Creating a Game Using the Electron Toolset

The Electron toolset is a graphical environment which provides a grid representation of the 3D game world, and a number of tools for creating a working game. The first step in creating a game involves choosing a setting (referred to as an 'area'). NWN2 allows one to create indoor and outdoor areas and, by customising them, transform them into forests, deserts, castles, dungeons, etc. At a later stage, game designers can add additional areas to their game, and link them together, creating a large world of different types of areas which the player will be able to explore.

Figure 9 shows an area in creation. Various mouse controls allow one to zoom in and out of the area, rotate the area, and pan across it. A new area, at least an exterior one, is a flat, featureless piece of land, so the next stage in game creation is typically to "terraform" or landscape the area: creating mountains and gulleys, and adding landscape features. Once this has been accomplished, discrete objects such as trees, houses, walls, fences etc. can be added by selecting them from the blueprints pane on the bottom right-hand side and dropping them into the area.

The next step is usually to add characters to the area. The toolset provides a wide range of characters, including animals, monsters, mythical creatures and humans. At this stage, the game has the look and feel, if not the interaction, of a commercial game, and young game designers are often keen to view their work in the 3D game

Figure 9. The Electron Toolset with a game being created

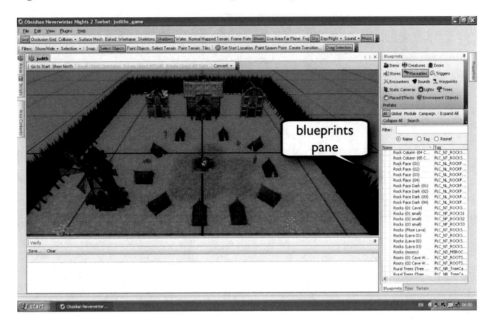

world. The game in creation in Figure 9 is shown in Figure 10 as it appears in the game world.

Once characters have been added to the game, conversations can be created for them, and here is where the real creativity of the game creators can begin to shine. Conversations are written as exchanges between the player and any non-player character (NPC). Conversations can be branching, in other words, the game designer can write conversations in which the player, when he or she plays the game, has a choice of responses to give to the NPC. These responses will, in turn, determine how the NPC responds. When the game is being played, the player can approach a character and click on the character to start conversing with it. The example below, written by Zoe, a 10 year old game designer, will help illustrate the concept. Figure 11 shows the conversation as written in the toolset. The conversation is represented as a tree structure, with the indentation representing the conversational turns that can take place between the player and the NPC. Note that turns at the same level of the tree will be represented as choices that the player can choose between in the game world (as shown in Figure 12).

Figure 12 shows part of the conversation as it appears to the player in the game world.

Although the toolset allows for the creation of games of commercial standard and complexity, learners only need around 5 minutes of instruction to begin working

Figure 10. The game as it would appear when being played

Figure 11. Zoe's conversation in the toolset

NPC: *Hello Abigail Shephard, my name is Legend. Why on earth have you come into my territory? You don't belong here!*

Player: *Okay Legend, you don't understand that you don't have everything to yourself! This is mine too and you're not going to stop me from tresspassing!*

NPC: *Well I am afraid Abigail, that you can't for it is mine!*

Player: *Hmmph! I don't think so Legend!*

NPC: *Oh I do think so Abigail! You are most rude you know, one cannot talk to you without being answered back! And there is a most dreadful tone in you're voice! Calm down girl!*

Player: *Why should I talk to you, know-it-all? You're so posh and polite and it bugs me! I hate goody-two-shoes! Bug off!*

Player: *... Was that my phone ringing? I am sorry I gotta go... Ahh!* [END]

on their own 3D worlds, complete with landscaping, props, characters and other points of interest. However, perfecting one's game can take many hours, days, or weeks, in fact, as much time as one wishes to spend on the task. As such, it is an ideal illustration of the "low floor/high ceiling" effect (Papert, 1980), where access to the toolset is within the reach of all young people who attempt it, thus, it has a low floor, but the fact that it is a professional toolset means that young people are

Figure 12. Zoe's conversation in the game world

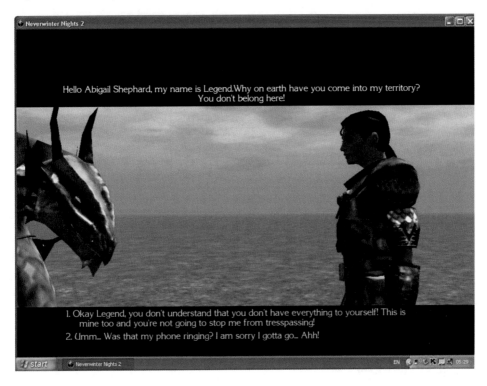

unlikely to reach its ceiling, in other words, that they will have goals that they wish to accomplish that the toolset cannot support.

As can be seen above, and in contrast to the programming environments examined earlier in this chapter, it is not necessary to start with programming in order to create a basic game. The design of an area, and any objects and characters in it, can be carried out in a primarily graphical way, by dragging and dropping items, and changing their properties, similar to the drag and drop component of many standard GUI (graphical user interface) tools. Conversations can be written and then attached to characters. Because we are using a commercial games engine, characters already have a number of basic pre-scripted behaviours, for example, walking, running, fighting, attacking, conversing. It is only when sequences of such events need to be set up, when the game designer wants to attach behaviours that are different from those already attached to a particular character, or when she wants to include novel behaviours that programming becomes necessary. Unfortunately, the toolset's inbuilt scripting language, NWScript, is very similar to C in terms of syntax and complexity (see Figure 13 for an example). As such, young people are almost invariably intimidated and frustrated by this element of the game creation process, and are unable to proceed without substantial help from experts.

Figure 13. An NWScript example

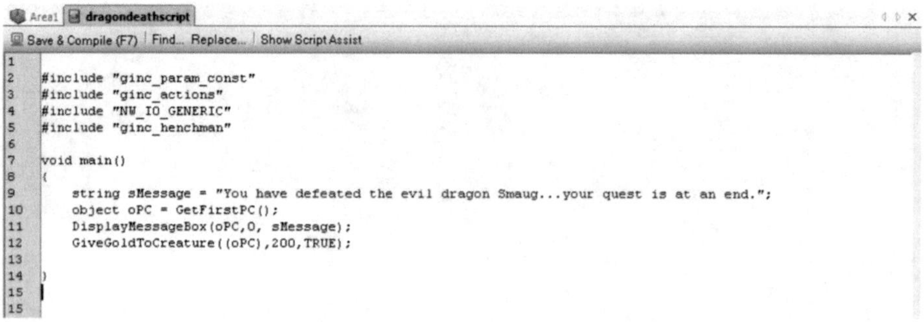

```
Area1   dragondeathscript                                                    ⬧ ⬧ ✕
  Save & Compile (F7)  Find... Replace...  Show Script Assist
1
2    #include "ginc_param_const"
3    #include "ginc_actions"
4    #include "NW_IO_GENERIC"
5    #include "ginc_henchman"
6
7    void main()
8    {
9        string sMessage = "You have defeated the evil dragon Smaug...your quest is at an end.";
10       object oPC = GetFirstPC();
11       DisplayMessageBox(oPC,0, sMessage);
12       GiveGoldToCreature((oPC),200,TRUE);
13
14   }
15
15
```

On the other hand, the fact that the need for programming occurs comparatively late in the game creation cycle is invaluable for motivation, and gives users the incentive to persevere with the activity. When they ultimately do need to begin programming, their investment in their game world and the narrative they are constructing gives them some drive to try to achieve programming outcomes. After all, a quest to steal the dragon's treasure is not much fun if the dragon hasn't been programmed to defend it!

The Design of Flip

Through the numerous game creation events we have run, we have observed that young people can specify computational rules whilst describing narrative gameplay elements in the context of an informal conversation. However, users often require prompting before they can fully and completely specify the event which might trigger the action, the conditions upon which it is dependent, stopping conditions in the case of a loop, etc., meaning that they face difficulties even before they hit the barrier of NWScript's intimidating syntax. Flip is designed to support young people in moving from their intuitive understanding of narrative events in gameplay towards a computational understanding. In this way, we introduce computational concepts through a motivating activity, and offer a route to computation through the narrative understanding which users have already developed about their game.

A key requirement for Flip was that young people without programming experience should be able to use it to create the events they wanted in their games. However, empowering them to achieve their game creation goals would not, by itself, be sufficient. The environment should also improve users' understanding of the computational processes and concepts which underlie those events.

One of the important features of Flip, and which distinguishes it from other programming languages for novices, is its use of a natural language representation alongside a blocks-based representation. Whilst we employ programming blocks similar in style to those used in Scratch and Alice, we aimed to capitalise on our learners' intuitive understanding of the story events which they were building into their games. We hoped that providing our learners with a dynamically updating natural language description of their computational events might give them a bridge between the narrative description of their story events, and the computational specification of these events, which is necessary for their execution in the game world. Our initial design work therefore focused on the graphical programming blocks, and the functionality of the natural language representation.

Flip was designed using a participatory design methodology, involving learners from the very start. Our approach was based on the CARSS framework (Good & Robertson, 2006), which helps researchers to conduct participatory design by considering the *context* in which the software is to be used, the *activities* which can be carried out during the design phase, the *roles* which the design team members must take on, the necessary *skills* which the team members must possess, and the *stakeholders* involved in the project.

We carried out an extensive range of participatory design activities, focussing on different aspects of the Flip environment, which we describe briefly below. In terms of the graphical programming blocks, we designed a low-fidelity prototype of the Flip language and carried out user testing with young people from a local high school and in a summer holiday workshop context (Good & Howland, 2017). We also asked young people to design their own visual representations for different rule elements (Good & Howland, 2017). When designing the natural language representation element of Flip, we observed non-programmers as they used Inform 7 (Nelson, 2006), a natural language based programming environment for writing interactive fiction (Good & Howland, 2017). We also gathered data on the way in which young people naturally describe game-based events which involve computational concepts, by asking them to observe game sequences and write rules to describe the behaviour that they observed (Good, Howland & Nicholson, 2010). Taken together, we used this data to develop a set of design principles which informed the design of the Flip language, described in (Good & Howland, 2017).

The Flip Language

As described above, the Flip language is a plugin to the existing Electron toolset and replaces the need to use NWScript, the inbuilt scripting language. Flip essentially acts as an overlay to NWScript, whereby scripts written in Flip are translated into NWScript and subsequently interpreted by the game engine and executed in game.

So while young people continue to create areas and customise them with objects and characters using the toolset, they use Flip to add custom behaviours and events to their games.

Flip is an event based language, a commonly used paradigm for developing interactive, game-based applications. All programs must start with a trigger, for example, "When game starts", "When creature is killed". This can then be followed by a single action or a series of actions, which can incorporate typical programming structures such as Boolean logic, conditionals, etc. Figure 14 shows an overview of the Flip interface (note that the script shown is functionally equivalent to the one shown in Figure 13).

On the top right-hand side, the 'block box' contains the blocks used to create scripts, organised by computational category (and colour-coded by type): Actions, Conditions, Events, Booleans and Control. When one of these categories is selected by the user, it is highlighted, and the available blocks in that category are displayed in the bottom right pane (in the example in Figure 14, possible 'Actions' are displayed).

Most blocks have slots, which must be filled by objects of a certain type. These slot fillers are usually objects in the user's game, for example, creatures, items or

Figure 14. The Flip interface

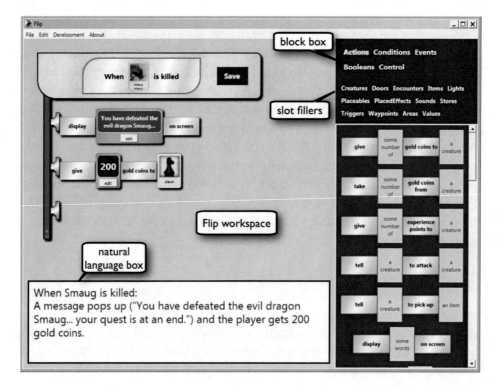

the player. The slots are similarly colour coded to indicate what types of slot fillers are permissible, with empty slots showing, in natural language, the specific type of slot filler required (which effectively constitutes a sort of type system). The choice of slot fillers is shown just below the five computational categories. Although the number of choices may seem elaborate, and the categories confusing, it was necessary to maintain coherence with the NWN2 categories used in the Electron toolset, so young users will be familiar with these category names through the use of the toolset earlier on, when they constructed their areas and populated them with objects.

The Flip workspace is shown on the left-hand side of Figure 14. Scripts in Flip always start with an event block, which contains an event slot to specify the conditions under which the script will execute. The Spine is where the script is composed, by attaching block to the pegs. As blocks are added, the spine can be extended indefinitely to accommodate further blocks.

Just under the workspace is the natural language (or 'plain English') box. As the learner builds up a program in the workspace, a natural language description of the program appears here, and is dynamically updated with each change to the program. Given that learners will have, at the outset, imagined their story event in natural language, we designed the natural language box to act as a bridge to the computational world, allowing learners to check, in natural language, that their program will function as intended. Although, our original aim had been to allow learners to edit both the blocks-based and the natural language descriptions, our participatory design work highlighted a number of issues inherent in using natural language for program generation, described in detail in (Good & Howland, 2017).

Figure 15 shows an example of a program with an "if… then…else" statement containing a Boolean conjunction. Control blocks snap onto the spine in the same way as action blocks. In this screenshot, the 'items' category is highlighted in the slot filler pane, meaning that all of the items which have been placed in the user's game also appear here, available for use in Flip scripts.

Only those blocks attached to the spine will execute when the game is loaded and run. This means that learners can experiment with programming blocks in the workspace, dragging out various ones and playing around with them before deciding whether or not to incorporate them into their scripts by snapping them onto the spine. Any elements attached to the spine will be shown in natural language in the 'plain English' box, even if the script is incomplete.

Unlike the other environments described in this chapter, and as mentioned previously, Flip was designed to work in conjunction with a pre-existing game creation environment and game engine. This has placed constraints on the design of the language, both in terms of the types of programming structures that are supported by the existing language, and in terms of the types of scripts that young people are likely to naturally write in the course of creating games of this type.

Figure 15. A Program in Flip

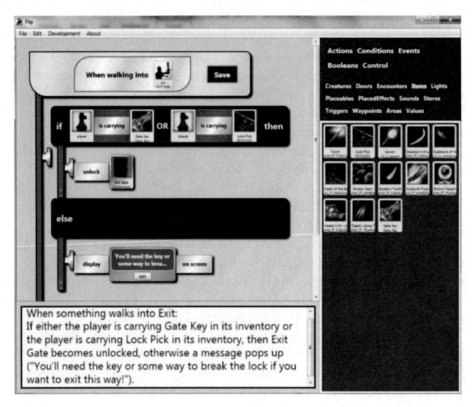

An example of the former concerns the distinction between event triggers and conditionals. At first glance, they may seem quite similar, and indeed in some cases, can act as alternative ways of describing the same event (e.g. "when the dragon is killed", "if the dragon is dead"). If we were unconstrained by the execution environment, we could have made the decision about how to best represent events and conditionals from a purely pedagogical perspective, i.e. in terms of what might be the most comprehensible to novices writing their first programs. In reality, NWN2 and NWScript operate with a number of predefined event hooks (e.g. *OnDeath*, when a creature dies, or *OnClientEnterScript*, when a game area is entered). In order for us to be able to attach Flip scripts to the appropriate script slots so that they would work in game, we needed to create equivalent Flip events for the predefined event hooks in NWScript.

We were also led, to a certain extent, by the types of programming constructs which are likely to occur naturally when young people create games of this type. While we see game construction as an ideal opportunity to engage young people in basic scripting tasks, we were also wary of turning it into an artificial programming

24

activity, and trying to impose programming tasks in the environment which might somehow break the flow of the narrative goals which young people might be trying to achieve. Loops are one such example. Currently, most of the narrative activity in the game has been focused on the interaction between the player and non-player characters (NPCs), and the need for loops does not arise. Although this means that the programming language is, in some sense, fit for purpose, it does mean that Flip can only cover the introductory elements of a computational curriculum.

We carried out a number of evaluations of Flip, reported in full in (Howland & Good, 2015; Good & Howland, 2017). A two-hour observational study in a secondary school involving 21 pupils allowed us to look in depth at the ways in which users interacted with the Flip interface, and how the features identified as important in our design principles were used by our target users (Good & Howland, 2017). A second, longitudinal study looked at the use of Flip over the course of a game creation project in two contexts: a holiday workshop and a secondary school setting (Good & Howland, 2017). There were differences in results across the two contexts (which was to be expected, given that participation in the holiday workshop was voluntary, while the school study was part of the curriculum for all pupils). However, results were positive overall in terms of ease of use (as evidenced by usage logs as well as interview and survey data), with most learners able to show evidence of an understanding of the role of the various aspects of the Flip interface, as well as the underlying computational concepts. One interesting finding concerned the natural language box, where it was used by individual learners to read the natural description and check whether the script described their intentions accurately. Some learners mentioned that it was particularly useful for more complex scripts. In other cases, the natural language box was used in collaborative settings, with learners paraphrasing the contents in order to explain their script to a teacher or peer or, conversely, with learners first reading another person's natural language description in order to understand the code and help them to debug it.

In a further longitudinal study with 56 secondary school pupils, reported in (Howland & Good, 2015), we again found that the majority of pupils were able to use Flip to create scripts to create interactive events in their games. Furthermore, we examined the impact of using Flip on pupils' computational understanding outside of the game creation environment, and found a significant improvement in their ability to express computational rules and concepts after using Flip (as measured by a pre-/post-test). A further, interesting finding was that girls wrote more, and more complex, scripts than did the boys, most likely because their narratives were more developed and therefore required the scripting of more complex behaviours as a result.

Finally, we were encouraged by teacher comments which suggested that, not only were pupils starting to learn some basic computational skills, but that the natural language box allowed pupils to better understand the scripts they created, and supported them as they worked collaboratively on tasks such as debugging:

There were a lot of kids talking about it [the output of the plain English box], but the times that stick in my mind were when things weren't working. It was quite often when kids were trying to solve problems or they were helping each other out. They looked and they read what that was saying or would speak, "Oh look, look what you're doing". And quite often, the kid helping the other kid would actually look at the English box first, as if they were trying to figure out what they were wanting to do and then looking up to see what they'd done.

Although the teacher acknowledged that blocks-based programming languages are designed to be user friendly, he nonetheless felt that a natural language equivalent may boost learners' confidence in their scripting ability:

There still may be the underlying lack of confidence in creating the programming structure, even though it's blocks, and using the English as that confirmation to say, "Yes, that is what I want to see."

The teacher also felt that the natural language box might have further, more generalizable benefits in helping pupils gain skills in using computational terminology:

It was really useful to be able to do these more technical aspects of creating a game without actually them realising they're programming and scripting, but also them developing the language and confidence to say, 'Oh, if I do this, then I'll have to do that' and them actually using the terminology without thinking about it.

I think generally just the comfort with using some technical terms and language, because I was able to direct people to set menus and things without really having to describe it. It was actually a greater confidence in using the language.

NOVICE PROGRAMMING ENVIRONMENTS COMPARED

The programming environments above span a range of genres and, in some sense, provide good complements to each other. In terms of age, all target a range of late childhood to early adulthood, with Scratch targeting the youngest users (and, with the advent of ScratchJr, even younger users), and Greenfoot the oldest. Syntax appears to be one of the factors which determines the appropriateness of language to age range: the closer the language is to a fully-fledged programming language, the less appropriate it will be for younger users. ScratchJr removes the concept of variables from Scratch in order to service even younger users.

The environments also differ in terms of their relationship to existing programming languages. Although built on NWScript, which is similar to C, Flip is not designed to be a first step to a general-purpose programming language, nor is Scratch (although in many current computing curricula, it is often used as the first language that pupils encounter, before moving to more traditional languages). Alice and Looking Glass model OO concepts, and Alice at least is designed as a precursor to Java, with the latest version of Alice having the ability to show the generated Java code in a window alongside the Alice code. Furthermore, an Alice plugin for the NetBeans IDE allows an Alice 3 project to be transferred to NetBeans where it can be enhanced by editing the converted Java code. Programming in Greenfoot can be carried out in both Java and in Stride (the Java-like language included with Greenfoot's frame based editor). As such, Greenfoot provides both the most direct link to a general-purpose programming language, and the most support for making that transition.

Some of the designers of these systems, such as the authors of Greenfoot, have consciously set out with a list of design goals which have helped focus the design and implementation of their system, for example, "support engaging functionality", in other words, allow learners to implement features in their programs which they find compelling, such as sound, graphics and animation, or allow social interaction and sharing (Kölling, 2010). Other researchers (Good & Robertson, 2006) have remarked on the sorts of motivational and learning affordances which existing systems seem to offer young users, often unintentionally, a point also highlighted by Resnick (2017). Still others (Petre & Blackwell, 2007) have examined the patterns of activity engaged in by young users, noting those which, although occurring in informal contexts, are nonetheless characteristic of software development. In some cases, researchers have looked at how they can enhance the success of existing systems, such as Alice, or Neverwinter Nights 2, to offer further improvements, either in terms of motivation for specific user groups, in the case of Looking Glass, or further pedagogical support, in the case of Flip. What is reassuring is that for all of the environments described above, the effects which have been designed for appear to be playing out in practice. What is also interesting is that although the environments described above may differ, the benefits they offer are remarkably similar.

Finally, there is the question of domain, or the purpose for which the languages can be used. None of the programming environments are designed to be truly general purpose, rather their aim is to provide a "motivational hook" which can encourage learners to engage with programming more as a means to an end, rather than an end in itself.

REFLECTIONS ON ENVIRONMENTS

Below I reflect on a few of the themes which cut across the environments described in this chapter before going on to consider possible implications for teaching, research and further development in the area. It is interesting to note that the three themes identified in 2011 remain just as relevant today.

Learner-Centred and Learner-Led

The designers of all of these programming environments share a common vision that the environments will, or at the very least can, be used in a way that is learner-centred and learner-led, rather than curriculum-driven. As such, they are likely to be more motivating than traditional methods of teaching programming. As du Boulay (personal communication, 12 November 2014) notes, "The problem with programming is that you have to convince people that they want to solve problems that they haven't yet imagined, and then you give them a tool to solve these problems that they didn't actually have before." In contrast, in the environments described above, learners can start with a topic of personal interest, and use this interest to motivate their learning, bringing in computing topics on an "as needed" basis, rather than in a strict order. Resnick et al.'s (2009) example of the learning of variables in order to keep score in a game is a good example of this type of learning. To take an example from Looking Glass, a young person may be switched on to programming by a peer, and decide to give it a go because she is motivated by the idea of making her own story-based movie. She chooses the focus for her story, and is able to search for code snippets that will accomplish the behaviours that she requires for her project. Better still, rather than generic tutorials describing the functionality of Looking Glass, any tutorials she requires will be specifically tailored to the code snippets she is working on at that particular point in time. The contextual nature of this use of support materials is compatible with the way modern programmers work with online documentation, where languages such as Java and C# have thousands of classes and interfaces, and many more methods.

Rapid Pay Off

In all of the environments, seeing a very quick return on investment seems key in establishing and maintaining motivation. In 1993, in a debate entitled, "Should we teach students to program?", Soloway and Guzdial described difficulties in learning to program as follows:

Learning to express oneself in a GPPL [General Purpose Programming Language], as they are currently conceived, requires a steep learning curve: writing a 100-line program is much harder than writing a 10-line program; writing a 1,000-line program is much, much harder than writing a 100-line program. And, let's be honest, to make the computer truly sing and dance, one needs to write significantly sized programs. What practical program can someone who finishes -- even successfully -- Computer Science 101 actually write? (Soloway, 1993, p. 22)

The picture had already changed significantly in 2011, and it continues to change. Young people can now easily write a small program to make a computer sing and dance, quite literally, in a few minutes. The "computational floor" has been lowering dramatically, allowing easier access to programming for learners. And yet, the ceiling has stayed high, meaning that the challenges available to learners as they grow in competency have remained. Armed with initial feelings of success, young people are more likely to continue into the complexities of programming with greater confidence, and persevere when things become difficult.

Rapid Feedback Loop

As has been mentioned, all of the environments described in this chapter comprise a programming language which is tightly integrated with an execution environment, either 2D or 3D. Because of this, it's very easy to (literally) see whether a program is behaving as intended (or not), and make any necessary changes. Although this is only anecdotal, I would suggest that the ludic nature of the execution environments probably encourages a wider range of hypothesis testing than would normally be the case with traditional programming languages (e.g. "Ok, now the dragon attacks the giant whenever he gets near the treasure chest. But what would happen if a rogue bear arrived on the scene and stole the chest before the giant arrived?"). These types of scenario are easy (and fun) to try out, and many systems, for example, Scratch, have been set up explicitly to encourage this sort of tinkering (Maloney et al., 2010).

Creation of a Valued Artefact

Constructionism is built on the premise that learning takes place in, and is almost a by-product of, contexts in which one is engaged in the building of a public entity or artefact (Papert & Harel, 1991). It stands to reason that motivation can only be heightened when the artefact being built has a particular meaning for the individual and their immediate peer group. Kelleher has engaged with this issue from a gender perspective, arguing that storytelling has a particular resonance with girls, and is likely to inspire girls to take an interest in programming. Kölling has taken a different tack by trying to maximise personal choice, recognising that not every young person will be motivated by creating a game, and should have a broader arena of possible choices. In all of the novice programming environments described however, the assumption is that young people will be able to start from the perspective of their own interests, and have the ability to create and/or make use of their own media so as to produce something that they and their peers will find to be of value. In this respect, novice programming has come a long way from the days of "Hello world" and the Fibonacci sequence.

Recognition of the Importance of Peers

In all of the environments described, peers play an important role. Not only can the development of programs itself be a highly social process, there is something intrinsically motivating about building something that you can share with your peers once it is completed. In addition to local communities of friends and fellow learners, the internet has made it easy to form virtual communities which are every bit as powerful in their support. As learners develop and share their programs, they are also gaining an appreciation of the intrinsic value of a community of users, and recognising the contribution of individual users' skills. This in turn can foster an appreciation for teamwork and collaboration in multiple guises. I don't think we have begun to scratch the surface of examining the types of collaboration which exist between learners, and the types of learning benefits which can accrue as a result, and I therefore consider how this might be more fully supported in the section on "Implications for Teaching, Research and Further Development".

Changing Times

In 2011, I noted that novice programming environments seemed to have "come of age", in that they "are freely available to young people across the globe, and have broad fan bases, who enthusiastically share not only their latest creations, but also their knowledge and understanding with others." Since that time, the use of novice programming environments has only increased, in some cases, seemingly exponentially. As an example, community statistics for Scratch (https://scratch.mit.edu/statistics/) show that in the month of January 2011, the number of new projects created was 56,575, while in the month of September 2017, 703,883 new projects were created. It is an open question whether the introduction of programming in school curricula worldwide is the main significant contributing factor (e.g. the English national curriculum introduced statutory computing programmes of study for all educational key stages, i.e. from age 5 to 16 (Department for Education, 2013).

Indeed, since 2011, computing for novices, particularly children, has increasingly taken centre-stage. Computing features much more prominently in the school curricula of many countries (see the special issue in ACM's Transactions on Computing Education, entitled, "Computing Education in K-12 Schools from a Cross-National Perspective", 14(2), for some examples), and there has been a proliferation of new programming environments for novices. Many of these environments stem from Blockly (https://developers.google.com/blockly/), which itself borrowed heavily from Scratch's codebase. Such environments include MIT's App Inventor (http://appinventor.mit.edu/explore/), and Code.org (https://code.org/).

Perhaps one of the biggest developments in recent times is the rise of hybrid environments, with environments providing increasing support for viewing and/ or manipulating code in more than one format. As we have seen in this chapter, advances in Greenfoot allow users to program in both Stride and Java, potentially supporting a progression from learning Java semantics in Stride before encountering Java syntax. Alice 3 similarly aims to support progression by allowing learners to view the Java version of their Alice code, and then transfer their Alice code into Java. On a slightly different tack, Flip provides a natural language view of the code which, whilst not manipulable, aims to provide an additional representation which can support computational understanding. This focus on supporting progression between different languages (in particular, moving between blocks based and text based languages) is also evidenced in environments such as PencilCode (Bau et al., 2015), Tiled Grace (Homer & Noble, 2014) or DrawBridge (Stead, 2016).

Implications for Teaching, Research and Development

In 2011, I suggested that, from a teaching perspective, "the lessons to be learned from these environments would suggest fitting the curriculum to the experience of building a reasonably large sized project, rather than the other way round". I will revisit the two specific issues I identified under this heading: that of focusing on projects, rather than topics, and considering the processes involved in project based work, rather than just the outcomes. In so doing, I will consider the extent to which these topics are addressed in current methods of teaching programming.

1. Projects, not Topics

It is easy to fall into the trap, when planning a new course in computing, of focusing on a list of topics that need to be covered in a linear order. In many cases, it would seem that a behaviourist mode of curriculum-centred instruction is still de rigueur in many institutions, and it is not surprising that many students fail to find computing motivating or relevant. The environments described in this chapter all facilitate an approach whereby a curriculum could be designed around student-led projects, with curriculum topics introduced when required, and evidence of learning gathered from the projects themselves, rather than from a decontextualised, standardised test at the end. Certainly the research described by Resnick et al. (2009) suggests that core computing topics do get covered in the course of project work. Of course, based on their observations, and those of Petre and Blackwell (2007), this approach begs the question, "If students don't know they're programming, does it count?" I would argue that the instructor's role would then become, rather than directly instructing students on topics, one of drawing out the implicit knowledge that the learners have acquired, helping them to reflect on it, and to see how it might apply in other situations. At the same time, there are real concerns as to whether such an approach is sustainable within the strict confines of school curricula, which are increasingly focussed on testing and results. As Resnick (2017) notes, even in the early years curriculum, there is an increasing focus on instruction rather than exploration, with today's kindergartens sometimes referred to as "literacy boot camps". Interestingly, Fincher (2015) considers the parallels between approaches to traditional literacy and the current call for "computer literacy". She describes the many examples of failed initiatives to increase literacy, and suggests that, in considering computer literacy, we should learn from these examples, starting by first articulating what it means to be "literate" and ensuring that our approaches are based on considerable research.

2. Processes and Products

The project based approach, advocated above, leads to a tangible outcome, which has important benefits for students, not least in terms of motivation. However, in addition to outcome, it is equally important to look at the *processes* involved in arriving at that outcome, as they may be equally worthwhile in learning terms. Again, a behaviourist view of learning would suggest that our hopes for our students can be neatly encapsulated in a set of learning outcomes (themselves ideally expressed in ways that can be measured and assessed). However, many of us would agree that the activities involved in computing are broad and far reaching. They involve design and planning, testing and rethinking. We have evidence to suggest that young people willingly engage in these activities in the environments described in this chapter, and it would be worth putting more thought into how we can capture evidence of these activities in an ecologically valid way in pedagogical contexts rather than, again, looking to measure understanding through testing. As a way of stimulating thinking on the sorts of things we might want to look for, I include Petre and Blackwell's intriguing observations on children engaged in informal programming activities, who state that they are:

… able to discuss their goals, actions and artefacts. They can identify and adapt components for re-use; recognize and generalize from patterns in different examples and explain what things do, what they are for, and why they are designed that way (although the explanations may not be in conventional language). …they are able to reason about modifications and consequences, and about interactions between components. They are able to diagnose unexpected behaviours by systematic reasoning and experimentation. Occasionally, they encounter the need to restructure programs. They spontaneously introduce disciplines such as version control, naming conventions, design for re-use and systematic debugging. (Petre and Blackwell, 2007, p. 241)

There is certainly a focus on methods for assessing computational thinking skills (see, e.g. (Grover, Cooper & Pea, 2014)) but, again, Resnick (2017) warns against overly simple quantitative measures of achievement and, instead, advocates a more holistic approach to achievement in line with project-based activities, where we "focus on what's most important for children to learn, not what's easiest for us to measure" (Resnick, 2017, p. 148).

Implications for Research and Development

So what are the implications of these novice programming environments from a research and development perspective? In 2011, I identified three themes. Firstly, I suggested that our research focus should be on investigating the particular characteristics and combinations of features and modalities inherent in modern IDEs, rather than just comparing programming languages (e.g. "visual vs. textual"). Secondly, I noted that modern novice programming environments offer ideal playgrounds for studying collaboration "in the wild". Finally, I suggested that, in conjunction with a focus on collaboration, we should nonetheless continue to study environment development from a cognitive perspective, with a view to best supporting the tasks that individual learners hope to accomplish.

In this chapter, I take a slightly different perspective on these same themes. Firstly, I consider the renewed debate around "blocks based vs. text-based" and whether we might more usefully be focussing on the "space between" and on how to support transition between languages, but also on the particular properties of each IDE in more detail. Secondly, I look at different forms of collaboration in more detail, and consider how they might best be supported. Finally, given the increase in complexity of novice programming environments, at least from a representational perspective, I renew the call for considering the cognitive aspects of accomplishing tasks in such environments, and in ensuring that the respective representations are working together to best support learners.

1. "Visual vs. Textual" Is No Longer a Useful Distinction for Programming Languages, but Neither Is "Blocks-Based vs. Textual"

Having carried out research on visual programming languages back in the day, this feels like rather a bold claim to make. In the 1980s and 1990s, there was a much clearer demarcation between textual programming languages and visual programming languages (even if a fair bit of the debate on comp.lang.visual focused on what exactly qualified as a visual programming language). In the 1990s, a number of empirical studies of visual programming languages were carried out in order to ascertain whether they made the task of programming, and program comprehension easier, particularly for novices (see, e.g. (Blackwell et al., 2001) for a summary of this debate). Today, the focus is much less on programming languages per se, and more on integrated development environments, and these are much more likely to be hybrids, with a mix of text and graphics co-existing quite happily. However, much of the debate around programming languages continues to be focussed on the high-level "blocks vs. text" distinction. Although this is a useful way of categorising languages on a first pass, I maintain that our research needs to be carried out at a finer level of granularity. I made the point in (Good & Howland, 2017) that blocks-based (or visual) languages offer an inherently high level of constraint as compared to textual languages to the extent that programming using graphical languages involves choosing from existing statements, whereas programming using textual languages often involves creating these statements from scratch. Therefore, it may be that any ease of use attributed to graphical languages results from their constrained nature, rather than their graphicacy per se. Greenfoot's frame-based editor offers some of these same constraints and, as such, would provide an excellent testbed for untangling some of the claims around blocks-based vs. text-based languages.

2. Current Environments Are Ideal Playgrounds for Studying Different Types of Collaboration

In each of the environments described above, there has been a focus on the beneficial nature of collaboration for learning, an issue which Resnick (2017) considers in some depth in relation to Scratch. Part of the power of these online environments derives from their ability to offer extensive opportunities for collaboration and sharing in a way which is different from the "enforced" collaboration sometimes associated with more traditional educational configurations. Resnick et al. (2009) have already pinpointed a number of different collaborative relationships which children enter into, and partnerships which they are able to negotiate, including forming online "companies". Wenger's model of communities of practice (Wenger, 1999) could very usefully be applied to the sorts of activities which are occurring on a daily basis on sites such as the Scratch website.

Petre and Blackwell also note the importance of social networks not just as ways of engaging in collaborative or cooperative programming, but even as "a mechanism for adjusting understanding and correcting conceptual and operational models" (Petre and Blackwell, 2007, p. 242). If one wished to take a more formal pedagogical approach, it would be possible to look at such practices through the lens of the Zone of Proximal Development (Vygotsky, 1978), looking for instances where children are being aided by their peers in mastering concepts which would have otherwise been just slightly out of their reach. Ironically, the educational field is rife with examples of situations where collaboration has been "engineered in", often unsuccessfully: the environments described in this chapter offer rich opportunities for looking at how it arises organically, and how it is sustained.

At the same time as these environments have opened up tremendous *opportunities* for collaboration, it's also important to look at how we might provide non-intrusive *support* for collaboration, both remote and co-located collaboration. One of the unanticipated benefits of Flip's natural language box was that it offered this type of support: by giving young people a language to describe computational concepts as well as their specific programs, it opened up opportunities for spontaneous collaboration and peer support. It would be good, in future, to look at how we can build on such initiatives.

3. However, the Collaborative Shouldn't Crowd Out the Cognitive

Although I have suggested we might fruitfully examine the patterns of activity which occur between learners, this is not to suggest that we do so at the expense of individual cognition and, in particular, at looking at how these novice programming environments function as external representations in supporting cognitive activity. In 2011, I wrote that "there is a need to continue to conduct studies which examine the ways in which learners use such environments, including the ways in which they interact with multiple external representations, move between their code and the execution environment, and generally make sense of multiple data streams". This is all the more important now, given that an increasing number of programming environments offer multiple representations of programming code (e.g. Alice/Java in Alice, Stride/Java in Greenfoot). Not only must leaners be able to understand the mappings between these multiple representations, but they must also be supported to develop what Stead & Blackwell (2014) term "notational expertise".

CONCLUSION

This article has considered the state of the art in novice programming environments, looking at five such exemplars: Scratch, Alice, Looking Glass, Greenfoot and Flip. Although different in many ways, all of the designers share a common aim in involving learners in building and manipulating computational artefacts, and in a way that motivates and empowers them. A number of changes in recent years, both technological and cultural, have led to these environments being truly "people oriented", with young people engaging in programming activities and with each other, in ways that (even) the tool designers may not have been able to fully envisage. While they offer stimulating virtual playgrounds for students to try out creative ideas, I have argued that they also offer rich new tools for educators and researchers alike, and the hope is that innovative pedagogy and research will be built upon these environments.

ACKNOWLEDGMENT

I would like to thank, first and foremost, Kate Howland and Keiron Nicholson, my research fellows on the Flip project and all of the young people and teachers who willingly helped us design and test Flip. I am also thankful to Steve Goschnick and to colleagues at the University of Sussex who helped me hone some of the reflections presented in this chapter. The Flip project was funded by the UK Engineering and Physical Sciences Research Council (EPSRC), EP/G006989/1, I am very grateful for their support.

REFERENCES

Adams, J. (2014). *Alice 3 in Action: Computing Through Animation*. Cengage Learning.

Bau, D., Bau, D. A., Dawson, M., & Pickens, C. (2015). Pencil Code: Block code for a text world. In *Proceedings of the 14th International Conference on Interaction Design and Children* (pp. 445-448). ACM. 10.1145/2771839.2771875

Blackwell, A. F., Whitley, K. N., Good, J., & Petre, M. (2001). Cognitive factors in programming with diagrams. *Artificial Intelligence Review*, *15*(1), 95–114.

Cooper, S., Dann, W., & Pausch, R. (2003). Teaching objects-first in introductory computer science. *Proceedings of the 34th SIGCSE Technical Symposium on Computer Science Education* (pp. 191-195). New York: ACM Press. 10.1145/611892.611966

Department for Education. (2013). *The National Curriculum in England: Computing programmes of study.* Available from: https://www.gov.uk/government/publications/national-curriculum-in-england-computing-programmes-of-study

Fincher, S. (2015). What are we doing when we teach computing in schools? *Communications of the ACM, 58*(5), 24–26. doi:10.1145/2742693

Fletcher, G., & Lu, J. (2009). Human computing skills: Rethinking the K-12 experience. *Communications of the ACM, 52*(2), 23–25. doi:10.1145/1461928.1461938

Good, J., & Howland, K. (2017). Programming language, natural language? Supporting the diverse computational activities of novice programmers. *Journal of Visual Languages and Computing, 39*, 78–92. doi:10.1016/j.jvlc.2016.10.008

Good, J., Howland, K., & Nicholson, K. (2010). Young people's descriptions of computational rules in role-playing games: An empirical study. In *2010 IEEE Symposium on Visual Languages and Human-Centric Computing (VL/HCC)* (pp. 67-74). IEEE. 10.1109/VLHCC.2010.18

Good, J., & Robertson, J. (2006). CARSS: A framework for learner-centred design with children. *International Journal of Artificial Intelligence in Education, 16*(4), 381–413.

Goschnick, S. (2015). App Review: ScratchJr (Scratch Junior). *International Journal of People-Oriented Programming, 4*(1), 50–55. doi:10.4018/IJPOP.2015010104

Goschnick, S., & Balbo, S. (2005). Game-first programming for information systems students. In *Proceedings of the Second Australasian Conference on Interactive Entertainment* (pp. 71-74). Creativity & Cognition Studios Press.

Gross, P. A., Herstand, M. S., Hodges, J. W., & Kelleher, C. L. (2010). A code reuse interface for non-programmer middle school students. *Proceedings of the 14th International Conference on Intelligent User Interfaces* (pp. 219-228). New York: ACM Press. 10.1145/1719970.1720001

Grover, S., Cooper, S., & Pea, R. (2014). Assessing computational learning in K-12. In *Proceedings of the 2014 Conference on Innovation & Technology in Computer Science Education* (pp. 57-62). ACM.

Guzdial, M. (2004). Programming environments for novices. In S. Fincher & M. Petre (Eds.), *Computer Science Education Research* (pp. 127–154). London: Taylor & Francis.

Guzdial, M. (2008). Paving the way for computational thinking. *Communications of the ACM, 51*(8), 25–27. doi:10.1145/1378704.1378713

Harms, K. J., Cosgrove, D., Gray, S., & Kelleher, C. (2013). Automatically generating tutorials to enable middle school children to learn programming independently. In *Proceedings of the 12th International Conference on Interaction Design and Children* (pp. 11-19). ACM.

Harms, K. J., Rowlett, N., & Kelleher, C. (2015). Enabling independent learning of programming concepts through programming completion puzzles. In *Proceedings of the 2015 IEEE Symposium on Visual Languages and Human-Centric Computing (VL/HCC)* (pp. 271-279). IEEE. doi:10.1145/2485760.2485764

Homer, M., & Noble, J. (2014). Combining tiled and textual views of code. In *2014 Second IEEE Working Conference on Software Visualisation (VISSOFT)* (pp. 1-10). IEEE. 10.1109/VISSOFT.2014.11

Howland, K., & Good, J. (2015). Learning to communicate computationally with Flip: A bi-modal programming language for game creation. *Computers & Education, 80*, 224–240. doi:10.1016/j.compedu.2014.08.014

Howland, K., Good, J., & du Boulay, B. (2008). A game creation tool which supports the development of writing skills: Interface design considerations. In *Proceedings of Narrative and Interactive Learning Environments (NILE 08)*, 23-29.

Howland, K., Good, J., & du Boulay, B. (2013). Narrative Threads: A tool to support young people in creating their own narrative-based computer games. In *Transactions on Edutainment X* (pp. 122–145). Berlin: Springer. doi:10.1007/978-3-642-37919-2_7

Howland, K., Good, J., & Nicholson, K. (2009). Language-based support for computational thinking. In *Proceedings of the 2009 IEEE Symposium on Visual Languages and Human-Centric Computing (VL/HCC)*, (pp. 147-150). IEEE. 10.1109/VLHCC.2009.5295278

Howland, K., Good, J., & Robertson, J. (2006). Script Cards: A visual programming language for games authoring by young people. In *Proceedings of the 2006 IEEE Symposium on Visual Languages and Human-Centric Computing (VL/HCC)* (pp. 181-184). IEEE.

Kelleher, C., Cosgrove, D., Culyba, D., Forlines, C., Pratt, J., & Pausch, R. (2002). Alice 2: Programming without syntax errors. In *Proceedings of the 2002 Conference on User Interface Software and Technology*. Available from: https://uist.acm.org/archive/adjunct/2002/pdf/demos/p35-kelleher.pdf

Kelleher, C., & Pausch, R. (2005). Lowering the barriers to programming. *ACM Computing Surveys, 37*(2), 83–137. doi:10.1145/1089733.1089734

Kelleher, C., & Pausch, R. (2007). Using storytelling to motivate programming. *Communications of the ACM, 50*(7), 58–64. doi:10.1145/1272516.1272540

Kelleher, C., Pausch, R., & Kiesler, S. (2007). Storytelling Alice motivates middle school girls to learn computer programming. In *Proceedings of the SIGCHI Conference on Human Factors in Computing Systems* (pp. 1455 - 1464). New York: ACM Press. 10.1145/1240624.1240844

Kölling, M. (2010). The Greenfoot programming environment. ACM Transactions of Computing Education, 10(4), Article 14.

Kölling, M. (2015). Lessons from the Design of three educational programming environments: Blue, BlueJ and Greenfoot. *International Journal of People-Oriented Programming, 4*(1), 5–32. doi:10.4018/IJPOP.2015010102

Kölling, M. (2016). *Introduction to Programming with Greenfoot: Object-Oriented Programming in Java with Games and Simulations* (2nd ed.). Pearson.

Kölling, M., & Henriksen, P. (2005). Game programming in introductory courses with direct state manipulation. In *Proceedings of the 10th ACM–SIGCSE Annual Conference on Innovation and Technology in Computer Science Education* (pp. 59-63). New York: ACM Press. 10.1145/1067445.1067465

Maloney, J., Peppler, K., Kafai, Y. B., Resnick, M., & Rusk, N. (2008). Programming by choice: Urban youth learning programming with Scratch. In *Proceedings of the 39th SIGCSE Technical Symposium on Computer Science Education* (pp. 367-371). New York: ACM Press. 10.1145/1352135.1352260

Maloney, J., Resnick, M., Rusk, N., Silverman, B., & Eastmond, E. (2010). The Scratch programming language and environment. *ACM Transactions on Computing Education, 10*(4), 16:2-16:15.

Meerbaum-Salant, O., Armoni, M., & Ben-Ari, M. (2013). Learning computer science concepts with scratch. *Computer Science Education, 23*(3), 239–264. doi:10.1080/08993408.2013.832022

Nelson, G. (2006). *Natural Language, Semantics Analysis and Interactive Fiction.* Available from: http://inform7.com/learn/documents/WhitePaper.pdf

Papert, S. (1980). *Mindstorms: Children, computers, and powerful ideas.* New York: Basic Books.

Papert, S., & Harel, I. (1991). Situating constructionism. In S. Papert & I. Harel (Eds.), *Constructionism.* Norwood, NJ: Ablex Publishing Corporation. Available from: http://www.papert.org/articles/SituatingConstructionism.html

Petre, M., & Blackwell, A. F. (2007). Children as unwitting end-user programmers. In *Proceedings of the 2007 IEEE Symposium on Visual Languages and Human-Centric Computing* (pp. 239 – 242). IEEE.

Resnick, M. (2014). Give P's a chance: Projects, peers, passion, play. In *Constructionism and Creativity: Proceedings of the Third International Constructionism Conference.* Austrian Computer Society.

Resnick, M. (2017). *Lifelong Kindergarten: Cultivating Creativity Through Projects, Passion, Peers, and Play.* MIT Press.

Resnick, M., Maloney, J., Monroy-Hernández, A., Rusk, N., Eastmond, E., Brennan, K., ... Kafai, Y. (2009). Scratch: Programming for all. *Communications of the ACM, 52*(11), 60–67. doi:10.1145/1592761.1592779

Rizvi, M., Humphries, T., Major, D., Jones, M., & Lauzun, H. (2011). A CS0 course using scratch. *Journal of Computing Sciences in Colleges, 26*(3), 19–27.

Robertson, J., & Good, J. (2005). Story creation in virtual game worlds. *Communications of the ACM, 48*(1), 61–65. doi:10.1145/1039539.1039571

Robertson, J., & Good, J. (2006). Supporting the development of interactive storytelling skills in teenagers. In Z. Pan, R. Aylett, H. Diener, X. Jin, S. Göbel, & L. Li (Eds.), Technologies for E-Learning and Digital Entertainment. Edutainment 2006 (pp. 348–357). Lecture Notes in Computer Science Springer; doi:10.1007/11736639_46.

Robertson, J., & Nicholson, K. (2007). Adventure Author: A learning environment to support creative design. In *Proceedings of the 6th International Conference on Interaction Design and Children* (pp. 37 - 44). New York: ACM Press. 10.1145/1297277.1297285

Soloway, E. (1993). Should we teach students to program? *Communications of the ACM, 36*(10), 21–24. doi:10.1145/163430.164061

Stead, A., & Blackwell, A. F. (2014). Learning syntax as notational expertise when using DrawBridge. In *Proceedings of the Psychology of Programming Interest Group Annual Conference (PPIG 2014)* (pp. 41-52). Academic Press.

Stead, A. G. (2016). *Using multiple representations to develop notational expertise in programming.* University of Cambridge, Computer Laboratory, Technical Report, (UCAM-CL-TR-890).

Vygotsky, L. S. (1978). *Mind and society: The development of higher psychological processes.* Cambridge, MA: Harvard University Press.

Wenger, E. (1999). *Communities of practice. Learning, meaning and identity.* Cambridge, UK: Cambridge University Press.

Wing, J. (2006). Viewpoint-Computational Thinking. *Communications of the ACM, 49*(3), 33–35. doi:10.1145/1118178.1118215

ENDNOTE

[1]   Note that a successor to Neverwinter Nights 2 was not released.

Chapter 2
Blue, BlueJ, Greenfoot:
Designing Educational Programming Environments

Michael Kölling
King's College London, UK

ABSTRACT

Educational programming systems are booming. More systems of this kind have been published in the last few years than ever before, and interest in this area is growing. With the rise of programming as a school subject in ever-younger age groups, the importance of dedicated educational systems for programming education is increasing. In the past, professional environments were often used in programming teaching; with the shift to younger age groups, this is no longer tenable. New educational systems are currently being designed by a diverse group of developing teams, in industry, in academia, and by hobbyists. In this chapter, the authors describe their experiences with the design of three systems—Blue, BlueJ, and Greenfoot—and extract lessons that they hope may be useful for designers of future systems. The authors also discuss current developments, and suggest an area of interest where future work might be profitable for many users: the combination of aspects from block-based and text-based programming. They present their work in this area—frame-based editing—and suggest possible future development options.

DOI: 10.4018/978-1-5225-5969-6.ch002

INTRODUCTION

In the last ten years or so, educational programming environments have become very popular for the teaching and learning of introductory programming. This was not always the case: while there have been educational systems for a long time, they were considerably fewer early in this century than today, and older systems were considerably simpler, often consisting of compilers or libraries, rather than complete programming environments. Long and heated debates used to rage among educators about the respective benefits of teaching with dedicated educational versus industry-strength tools. These debates usually remained unresolved.

In the last decade, the situation has shifted, due to a combination of factors which we discuss below, and educational programming environments have taken a much more prominent role. They are more used, more accepted, and simply many more in number, than ever before. As a result, the design of educational environments has become a topic of considerable interest.

In this chapter we describe experiences with the design of a sequence of educational environments dating back more than 20 years. These systems are Blue (Kölling, 1999a), a programming language and development environment for teaching and learning object-oriented programming in a single, integrated system; its successor BlueJ (Kölling, Quig, Patterson, & Rosenberg, 2003), a similar environment using the Java Programming Language; and a third pedagogical system called Greenfoot (Kölling, 2010). Blue was relatively short-lived, but is of interest here because it heavily influenced the design of its successor, BlueJ. BlueJ and Greenfoot are both systems with significant user communities built up over a number of years (and still very much in use today), and have undergone many changes and adaptations since their first publication.

In this chapter we present a short history of these systems and discuss the goals and design rationale for each, their respective target groups and how these influenced design decisions, and their scope and application. Most importantly, we discuss lessons learnt from their use with actual users, and how those lessons shaped the design of the later systems, and later versions. We also discuss their relation to other educational programming systems, similarities, possible sequences of use, and future developments. The emphasis is not on providing a complete description of each system, but to identify the trends and goals at the time of their design, and how these have changed over time. Overall, we present some lessons we learnt along the way that we hope may be of use to designers of future systems.

A SHORT HISTORY OF EDUCATIONAL PROGRAMMING

Educational software tools are nearly as old as programming as a discipline. Ever since computer scientists started teaching others about programming, they started thinking about tools to support this challenge. In the early days, there was no difference between the tools used by professionals and the ones taught to newcomers. However, pretty soon systems started to be developed that were designed partly or primarily with beginners as users in mind.

We will not give a complete history of educational software here; instead, we mention just a few influential early systems to arrive quickly at our destination: educational development environments for object-oriented programming. This is where we will slow down and start discussion in more detail.

The first pedagogically oriented software tools were programming languages and their associated compilers. Among the early ones, BASIC (1964), Logo (1967), Pascal (1970), and Smalltalk (1972) stood out as the most used and most influential—all aiming at learners as their primary target group. The goal of these languages was partly *simplification*: taking known concepts and avoiding the complications that could arise in other existing languages at the time. BASIC and Pascal were part of this movement, introducing more rigid structure and creating higher abstraction levels in programming in the process. The other part was the introduction or appropriation of concepts and abstractions that might be more accessible to learners: micro-worlds in the case of Logo (Papert, 1980), and the adaptation of object orientation (a reasonably obscure programming paradigm at the time, introduced a few years earlier in the Simula language (Dahl, Myhrhaug, & Nygaard, 1967)) in the case of Smalltalk.

In parallel, a small number of libraries were being developed for similar purposes, aiming at programming education that was (or later became) language independent. In the 70s and 80s, a few of these dominated the educational space. One of the most successful was *Turtle Graphics*, a library first developed by Seymour Papert and others for the Logo language (Papert, 1980), and later re-implemented for countless other educational languages (Caspersen & Christensen, 2000; Python Software Foundation, 2012; Slack, 1990). Turtle graphics introduced the concept of a micro-world, together with a single actor, which could produce movement and leave graphical traces as output[1].

In 1981, Pattis expanded on this idea with the widely used *Karel The Robot* system (Pattis, 1981), which again was ported to numerous languages (Bergin, Pattis, Stehlik, & Roberts, 1997; Bergin, Stehlik, Roberts, & Pattis, 2005). With Karel, students programmed a software robot that could move through a grid-based world, collect "beepers", and avoid obstacles. In each of these systems, students could gain experience with fundamental programming concepts and constructs within a carefully controlled and contained problem domain.

In the early 1990s, one of the most relevant developments—even though not aimed primarily at teaching—was the advent and rise of GUI builders. In 1991 Microsoft released Visual Basic, a new system to replace their previous environment, QuickBasic. While QuickBasic was text-based, Visual Basic's main feature was the central role of its integrated GUI builder. Similarly, Borland released Delphi in 1995, a GUI-focused development environment based on Pascal. Professional IDEs with GUI builders were sometimes used in teaching. However, since their professional focus and the dominance of GUI building (usually with automated code generation) did not easily aid the learning of foundational principles, these attempts to start programming teaching with GUI building ultimately led to a widely-held view against IDEs in programming education in general. We will come back to this below.

With the popularization of object orientation in introductory teaching from the late 1990s, the existing educational libraries were adapted to this new paradigm, and new teaching tools started to appear. By the end of the 1990s, however, the choice of educational systems was still fairly limited. Educational software in this time mostly consisted of libraries of this kind, while educational programming languages were being displaced in most teaching institutions by new, industry-strength languages. C++ (Stroustrup, 1986), Visual Basic, and Java (Gosling, 2000) were the languages of choice in introductory courses at this time—all systems developed for professional software engineers. By the turn of the century, full dedicated pedagogical development environments were still very rare[2].

However, this lack of educational environments was about to change.

Within the next 10 years, a substantial number of pedagogical systems were developed and published. Many of these introduced concepts not previously available in educational contexts, such as improved support for interaction and experimentation, and the use of rich media.

An early example was Blue (Kölling & Rosenberg, 1996), published in 1995, followed by BlueJ (Kölling, Quig, Patterson, & Rosenberg, 2003) and GameMaker (Overmars, 2004), both published in 1999. This was quickly followed by the publication of Alice 2 in 2000 (Cooper, Dann, & Pausch, 2003), DrJava in 2002 (Allen, Cartwright, & Stoler, 2002), and Jeroo (Sanders & Dorn, 2003) in 2003. 2005 saw the publication of Scratch (Maloney, Resnick, Rusk, Silverman, & Eastmond, 2010), followed by Greenfoot in 2006 (Henriksen & Kölling, 2004), StarLogo TNG in 2007 (Begel & Klopfer, 2007) and Kodu in 2009 (MacLaurin, 2009). After this, development accelerated even more, with numerous systems being published within a small number of years. One aspect that supported this proliferation was the publication of libraries specifically for the development of educational block languages, such as OpenBlocks (Roque, 2007) and Blockly (Fraser, 2013). BYOB/ Snap (Harvey & Mönig, 2010, Harvey & Mönig, 2015), Pencil Code (Bau, Bau, Dawson, & Pickens, 2015), Grace (Black, Bruce, Homer, Noble, Ruskin, & Yannow,

2013), and App Inventor (Wolber, Abelson, Spertus, & Looney, 2011) are some of the more recent examples, and more are being developed.

For this chapter, we will now concentrate on the development of Blue, BlueJ and Greenfoot, and our experiences with their designs.

BLUE AND BLUEJ: PROGRAM STRUCTURE VISUALIZATION AND INTERACTION

We will start our discussion of the development of the Blue and BlueJ environments with a description of various aspects of their creation, arranged roughly in chronological order, but selected for their relevance to the ultimate goal: the extraction of a set of generic lessons drawn from our experience, presented at the end of this section. The aspects discussed are those that motivate and explain our design choices and illustrate what we have learned in the process of this work.

The First Goal: An Educational Programming Language

In 1993, we began investigating how object-oriented languages might be taught, and how this teaching might be supported by a programming language. The initial idea was to create something like a "Pascal for object orientation". Pascal was one of the most successful teaching languages ever created, and it had instigated immense progress in structured programming: not only was it used to teach countless beginners, but it had a lasting influence on the design of programming languages, helping to make structured programming the dominant paradigm at the time. With object orientation on the rise, we were looking for a similar language for this paradigm.

Our intended target group was first year university teaching. Object orientation at the time was—if it was taught at all—often seen as an advanced subject taught in higher level courses. However, the idea to start teaching with an object-oriented language in first year was slowly gaining traction among some educators and we were interested in this approach.

We started by formulating our goals and requirements (Kölling, Koch, & Rosenberg, 1995; Kölling, 1999b), and evaluating existing systems against them. The big contenders at the time were C++, Smalltalk (Goldberg & Robson, 1983) and Eiffel (Meyer, 1988) with Java following soon after, and a long list of smaller, less popular languages. As with Pascal before us, we had goals motivated by pedagogy: we wanted a clear and consistent representation of programming concepts, clear and readable syntax, good error messages, little redundancy, a small language core, and good support for program structure. When evaluating existing candidates, they all fell short. Some came closer than others (Eiffel was the language that came closest to our wish list), while the most popular object-oriented language at the time, C++, scored worst. C++ was popular in many teaching institutions because it was seen as authentic: it was heavily used in industry, and many departments saw this as an advantage. Use in industry was not one of our goals: in our view, using a dedicated teaching language for the first year was perfectly acceptable—Pascal had demonstrated this principle—and might even be preferable. Our goal was that students would be proficient in an industry-strength language when they graduated (after three years of study), but not necessarily after the first year. The goal of the first year was to learn foundational principles, not industry-relevant syntax. This meant necessarily that the syllabus included a switch of programming language at some stage. While this creates a pedagogical overhead, we considered this necessary anyway: any university level computer science education should include proficiency in more than one language. But it also meant that ease of transfer to other commonly used languages was explicitly included in the criteria for evaluating target languages.

This issue—transferability of learning to potential successor systems that students might use—will surface again in later discussions in this paper. It is one of the core principles of the design of educational systems, and we will come back to it below.

The other issue that is a constant in discussions of educational programming systems is syntax; we will have a lot more to say about this in our discussions below. At this point, we were calling for an "easy, readable syntax" similar to what Pascal or Eiffel were using. We were thinking in terms of traditional, text-based syntax forms. Other systems later would make much more radical advances in this area by introducing block-based programming, and with that they changed the syntax question fundamentally. We will come back to this below.

For us, probably the most important insight from this evaluation was that one aspect was more important and more influential than any other single issue: the programming environment.

The Importance of the Environment

When we started formulating criteria for assessing suitability of languages for introductory teaching, we were initially thinking about language characteristics. In evaluating a number of systems, it became clear to us very quickly that the development environment in which a language was used had a major impact on the outcome. So much so, that the quality and nature of the environment had—in our view—a stronger influence than any single characteristic of the language (Kölling, 1999c).

As a result, we made the design of the development environment one of the primary goals of our project. This design had to address novel problems in teaching caused by the switch to object orientation: more complex program structure and higher level abstractions.

The Problem: Object-Oriented Structures

In the time before object orientation, most departments used structured (procedural) or functional languages in their introductory courses. The source code for typical beginners' programs was usually contained in a single file, program execution could relatively easily be traced on paper, and use of a stand-alone text editor and command shell for execution was the most common mode of work.

With the advent of object orientation, this changed.

Even small programs now consisted of multiple classes—and with this, multiple files—and both abstractions and practicalities became more complex. On the practical side, students had to deal with multiple source files and dependencies (the Java CLASSPATH setting was an example that caused regular problems), and maintaining an overview of a complete program source became more difficult. But more importantly: no support existed to understand and manage the increased complexity of abstractions inherent in these new systems. We now had classes and objects, instantiation, object interaction, and control flow across multiple source files. Both the static and the dynamic aspects of programming had become more complicated, yet the tools had not evolved.

A common complaint of teachers at the time was that students found it very difficult to understand the difference between a class and an object. This was not surprising: since common programming environments concentrated on displaying lines of source code, students were thinking about lines of code. Little support was given in existing environments to understand or interact with class or object structures.

This—the object model, not the syntax—turned out to be the most difficult aspect of the new form of programming.

The Solution: Visualization and Interaction

Our attempt to address this challenge was the design of an integrated language and environment that explicitly supported an object-oriented model, and provided visualization and interaction functionality to investigate and experiment with the underlying abstractions. We started work on such a system, named Blue (Kölling, 1999a) in 1994 (see Figure 1).

First, we made the decision to concentrate on an integrated environment, rather than separate editing, compiling and runtime tools. This reflected our view about the importance of the development environment in teaching and learning: only if we controlled the environment could we achieve the full pedagogical benefit we were aiming for.

One advantage was that an integrated development environment (IDE) made it possible to overcome many of the practical problems: compilation and execution

Figure 1. The original Blue environment (circ. 1994). The main part of the window shows the class diagram; along the bottom, objects are displayed on the object bench.

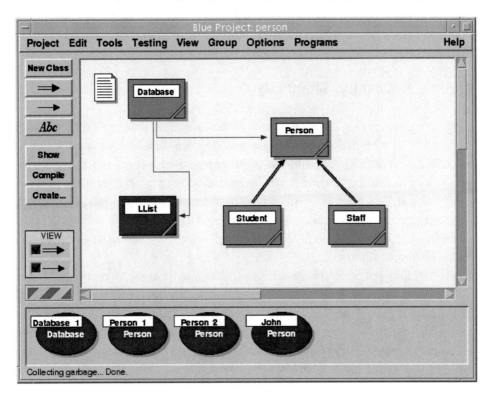

dependencies could be managed automatically, and various practical issues could be avoided.

More important, however, was the ability to provide tools for visualization and interaction: class structures were visualized in a diagram, objects could be selectively instantiated and methods could be interactively invoked with no need to write test drivers[3].

Putting the class diagram at the center of the system, in front of the eyes of users before they could see lines of source code, reflected our belief that the truly important (and more difficult) aspects of object-oriented programming were not syntax, but program and object structures. In our system, users could not avoid seeing structure and thus were encouraged to think about it.

By allowing and visualizing interactive instantiation, and by showing objects graphically as separate from classes, we encouraged construction of mental models of program execution that are otherwise difficult to convey.

Overall, the tools for visualization and interaction were the most important contribution of the Blue system. At the base of this was a belief in *active learning*: that the act of experimentation with small parts of code—single methods in our case—and quick turnaround in the edit-compile-run cycle made the most significant contribution to a thorough understanding of programming concepts.

Another Necessity: Simplicity

Integrated environments were not new at the time; many were in use, including environments for object-oriented languages. What was new was a dedicated, object-oriented development environment *for teaching*. And one of the most obvious distinctions to existing environments was the simplicity of its interface.

Existing IDEs were usually designed for professional developers. They offered large amounts of sophisticated functionality, which was useful and important in professional contexts. Most of them had well over 200 buttons and menu items visible in their main interface.

For teaching purposes this power of functionality becomes a problem.

We wanted to teach students about programming concepts, not about the IDE. By far the largest part of the IDEs would never be used by students in an introductory course, and the presence of these functions becomes a hindrance. Students needed to use only a few of these functions, but they often did not know *which* ones they should know about.

Professional IDEs looked intimidating and students often did not become comfortable in the environment before the course ended.

One design goal for Blue was to create a simple looking interface. We worked very hard to have very few buttons and menu items initially visible. Simple does not mean simplistic: the environment had some sophisticated functionality, but the interface for the user had to be as simple as we could make it.

This completes the three main principles that survive until today and which formed the primary guidelines for all extension and development that came later: visualization, interaction, and simplicity.

Other projects attempted to achieve similar simplicity by cutting down existing professional environments for beginners. This would have the advantage of having a simple environment for beginners, which could then be extended into a full professional environment by uncovering more advanced tools, without necessitating a change of environment. Gild for the Eclipse IDE (Storey *et al*, 2003) and Visual Studio Express (Microsoft, 2016) were examples of such projects. Ultimately, though, these efforts failed; the systems were discontinued or did not manage to achieve significant traction in programming education. We believe that the primary reason that they did not succeed is that they viewed a beginners' environment as a subset of a professional environment. Blue, on the other hand, was not a subset of any existing environment. We not only needed *fewer* tools, we needed *different* tools. Pedagogically motivated tools, such as direct interaction and visualization, were just not available in commonly used IDEs at that time.

Integrated Environments and the Acceptability of Black Boxes

In the second half of the 1990s, when Blue was published, a heated debate raged for quite a few years among teachers of introductory programming courses: should students use an IDE, or should they use a stand-alone text editor and a command line environment?

Proponents of the editor/command line argued that only with this tool set would students properly understand how programming works. Using these lower-level tools was somehow "good for the soul". In using an IDE, some teachers argued, too many important steps were hidden, too much code automatically generated, and students would not properly learn all the necessary steps and gain a thorough understanding of important detail. Teaching with IDEs, it was feared, would turn out students who could somehow produce a small working program, but without deep understanding of the principles.

In this argument, "using an IDE" was often conflated with "using a GUI builder", since the most famous IDEs at the time often had a GUI builder as their most prominent tool. This is where the argument about auto-generated code originated, and it is, of course, a fallacy: IDEs do not need to include GUI builders (and Blue quite consciously didn't).

The side arguing for IDEs, which included our group, argued that there is no such thing anymore as seeing "how it really works". Using a compiler for a high-level language in itself is an abstraction hiding multiple layers of lower level technology. Deciding what the right abstraction level is for introductory object-oriented teaching should be a pedagogical decision, not an accident of history. Do all students need to know the command line for their first programming encounter? Do they all need to know Assembler? Machine language? Processor and other hardware details?

Arguing that various layers below could be treated as black boxes, but that using a separate editor and command line was essential, seemed arbitrary, and we argued strongly for the use of integrated environments. With these, we were convinced, if the toolset was right, students would learn more, not less.

Time has since intervened to answer this question: almost all introductory courses (and professional developers) use IDEs today, and any remnant of this discussion has disappeared. In the late 90s, however, it was still a much-debated issue.

The Switch to Java: BlueJ

Blue was first published in 1995 and used for introductory teaching at our computer science department at Sydney University (and—to our knowledge—never used with students anywhere else). In the same year, the Java Programing Language was published.

Blue had started as an academic project (a PhD), and by the end of the decade, when the PhD had ended, we had to decide whether and how to continue. While Blue was attracting supportive comments in some academic circles, it was clear that it would be hard to develop and support it to a level where it might be widely adopted. The "team" still consisted of one (former) PhD student and a supervisor.

JIn the meantime Java gained popularity very quickly. It obviously met a need in the market (the need for a simple, free, internet-ready, Unicode-based, well supported modern object-oriented language) and was very well supported by a large company, Sun Microsystems. We were still convinced that Blue had advantages over Java in some specific aspects; we preferred its syntax and some language constructs, but most importantly: Java did not have a visual, integrated environment for teaching and learning.

We faced a decision: we could continue what we were doing with Blue, and remain a small research project noticed by a handful of academics, or we could throw away half of our project—the Blue language—, use Java instead, and continue working on the programming environment as our contribution to the state of the art. This way, we would give up some of our work, but may have the chance to have the other part—the environment—potentially adopted by actual users. We chose the latter path. It seemed the more interesting opportunity.

In March 1999, we released the first version of BlueJ, a re-implementation of the Blue environment for the Java language (see Figure 2). BlueJ not only supported Java as the user level language, it was also implemented in Java itself (while Blue had been implemented in C++). The promise of cross platform development that Java brought to the table, with its virtual machine architecture and just-in-time compilation, turned out to be vital for us: over the following years, we managed to support BlueJ on a number of different operating systems with a very small team. This would not have been possible without a cross-platform implementation language.

Changing to Java as the language was comparatively easy. Blue and Java had a lot in common. The object models were quite similar, and all relevant major abstractions matched very well. This meant that the environment could be recreated for Java without any significant design changes.

The change to Java was successful in creating more interest in actual adoption of our system. Soon after publication, other departments started adopting it for their introductory courses.

Figure 2. The BlueJ environment. The class diagram is similar to that in the Blue environment. As in Blue, objects are shown on the object bench and methods can be invoked by right-clicking on the object.

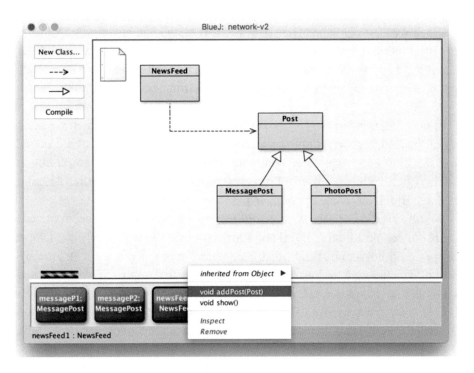

The Importance of Material

The single most important aspect of the design of the Blue/BlueJ environments for us was that they allowed a different pedagogical approach to teaching programming. It allowed a focus on the important fundamental principles—objects and classes— first, before getting bogged down in syntax and incidental detail. This aspect was so important to us that we made "Objects First" the title of a series of seminars we offered (Kölling & Rosenberg, 2000)—a term novel at the time that later came to be widely used to represent this general approach to teaching object-oriented programming (as opposed to the *objects-late* approach favored by other educators—a related, but separate, ongoing debate (Astrachan, Bruce, Koffman, Kölling, & Reges, 2005)).

When BlueJ started to be adopted by other teachers, however, we made a surprising (to us) discovery: many educators still started by using and teaching Java's *public static void main* method, using a single class and only static methods (or often: a single static method) for their entire project. In other words: they started with exactly those concepts and constructs we had intended to avoid: syntax, obscure magical incantations of advanced concepts presented for incidental reasons, and small scale statements ignoring objects. That BlueJ allowed teachers to circumvent this standard Java trap and discuss (and experiment with) more important constructs first seemed to have little impact. Many teachers ignored these features. The question was why.

When we first published Blue and then BlueJ, we had a somewhat naïve view of how adoption might work. We had designed an environment to allow a different pedagogical approach to teaching which we thought preferable, and we assumed that teachers would see its value, adopt the environment and follow this teaching approach.

In practice, this did not happen, at least not to the extent to which we hoped it would. Instead, a good number of teachers started to use BlueJ, but did not adapt their teaching approach. They continued to teach structured programming, now in Java, often with examples and projects ported directly from earlier Pascal or C versions. BlueJ was used, but *objects-first* was ignored.

We observed this phase with mixed feelings. It was good to see an increasing number of people adopting BlueJ and starting to teach an object-oriented language, but we could not avoid feeling that *they were doing it wrong*. For us, the whole point of developing BlueJ was to allow an objects-first approach, with interaction, experimentation and concepts before syntax. Instead, many lecturers adopted BlueJ because it was easy to install, had an easy-to-use editor and good tool integration. They used it as they would use any other environment, but ignored what we thought of as the most important features.

We were not sure about the reasons: did these lecturers not know how to use (and teach with) object interaction, or did they disagree with this approach and chose not to? In any case, we realized that to get our message across, making the software available is not enough. We needed to talk more explicitly about pedagogy.

We spent the next few years delivering a series of workshops and seminars, and eventually publishing a textbook (Barnes & Kölling, 2002). The seminars were largely successful—a good share of participants adopted an objects-first approach and BlueJ—but did not achieve significant scale. The book managed to reach a much larger audience. After the publication of the textbook (in 2002), adoption of BlueJ with an objects-first teaching approach increased substantially[4].

Later Extensions

With increasing numbers of users came an increasing number of suggestions and requests for additional features and functionality. While many of the suggestions were sensible, taken together they would have entirely ruined one of the most important aspects of BlueJ: the small size of the system and simplicity of the interface.

We established criteria for selecting areas of functionality that we did consider for inclusion: the feature had to be useful and widely used for introductory teaching at first-year university level (our target user group). We did not aim at supporting later work, more advanced workflows, or program sizes beyond what one might encounter in a first-year course. In practice, there was an additional, highly subjective, criterion: we had to be able to envision ourselves using it in our own course.

While we made many and frequent changes and improvements to the system (we typically released two or three updates per year), additions of larger areas of functionality were very conservatively controlled. The main ones were: the addition of explicit unit testing support in 2003 (Patterson, Kölling, & Rosenberg, 2003), ad-hoc single-statement evaluation (a *read-eval-print-loop*) in 2004, and support for repository-based team work tools in 2007.

The Lessons Learned

So far in this paper, we have presented a lengthy discursive history of our Blue and BlueJ projects. The purpose is to extract some lessons that may be useful in a more general context. Before we go on to describe development from this point forward, we will summarize the main lessons we learned from our experiences to this point.

- **Visualization, Interaction, Simplicity:** The most important aspects of our system, which were crucial to its success, are these three overarching design goals: visualization, interaction, and simplicity. For any educational programming environment, designers should identify the main concepts to be learned by the users, and make those visible as first class entities in the user interface. They should then design interactions that illustrate the characteristics of these conceptual abstractions and allow users to experiment with them. This has to be balanced with a simple, clear interface. Every other design goal and design decision has to become subordinate to these goals.
- **Know Your Target Group:** One of the most important aspects to be clear in the minds of the designers are the characteristics of the system's target user group. This sounds obvious when stated explicitly, but is nonetheless easy to lose track of. Many competing ideas will have to be weighed, each competing for attention, interface space, and development time. It is easy to get excited by an idea, and be tempted to add it, because it is clearly useful to someone. The crucial question to ask is: is it important *for our target group*? Many ideas are good ideas but still do not belong in your system.
- **Do One Thing Well:** The narrower the user group chosen, the better job the system can do to serve it. Once you have chosen your well-defined user group and application area, build the best tool you can *for that group*, to the

exclusion of everyone else. It is tempting—but counter-productive—to try to be everything for everyone.

- **Beware Feature Creep:** Very closely related to the two previous points is the importance of saying no. As soon as you have a useful and successful system, someone will start using it for application areas at the edge or outside of your envisioned domain. They will ask for additional features and extensions to support their tasks. Often, these are very reasonable and interesting ideas, and would extend the usefulness of your systems to new users. Going down this path, however, always opens the danger of unintended consequences. Feature creep—while very hard to avoid—is the mortal enemy of simplicity. And simplicity, as mentioned earlier, is one of the fundamental, immovable goals. Often, in the years of leading the development of BlueJ, one of our most important tasks for the project has been to say no to people. A good idea might be a good idea, and still not fit well with *this* project. When in doubt, leave it out. Features can always be added later, but it is nearly impossible to ever remove them to regain simplicity.

- **Do not Be Afraid to Make Decisions:** Often, when designing a system, design decisions have to be made. Sometimes, two competing options seem equally good, or might be a matter of preference of different users. A common response is to allow both versions, for example having individual preference settings for system look or behavior, or allowing alternative syntax for a language construct.

In education systems, this is a fundamental mistake. Every additional alternative forces users to make a choice. Beginners often do not have the knowledge to make an informed choice, or do not care. We are not doing users a favor by asking them to make a decision about an aspect that they either don't know or don't care about. In addition, every possible variant complicates the development of teaching material.

Your job as a designer of an educational system is to make the choice. If some users do not like it—bad luck. The system will be more usable and users more productive if the system is clearer and simpler.

- **Availability:** It is important that a system is easily available, both to institutions and individuals. This means that it has to run on multiple popular operating systems, and be affordable. (The most affordable price, of course, is free.) Whether the system needs to be open source, however, is much less clear. BlueJ was initially free, but not open source. We received regular complaints from users who demanded an open source system, and stated that they need to make source amendments. We eventually open-sourced the system, mostly to allow inclusion into Linux repositories and distributions that would not consider closed-source systems. There are, however, no contributors to the BlueJ source code outside of our team, and open-sourcing seems to have made no practical difference other than silencing those people demanding it on principle.

- **Support Material Matters:** A software system—no matter how well designed—does not, by itself, make an impact in education. What actually drives adoption is an ecosystem of support material. This can take different forms: a textbook, as in the case of BlueJ, or an active, supportive user community (as we discuss below). In any case, what makes teachers adopt a new system is—by and large—not the software itself, but the opportunity to teach differently. To make teachers see these opportunities, context is required that shows them what is possible. They may watch online videos, read the textbook, or exchange resources in a shared community. The software and the pedagogical material are both equally necessary—one without the other will fail.

GREENFOOT

In 2004 we started work on a new system named Greenfoot (Henriksen & Kölling, 2004) (see Figure 3), which was first published in 2006. A number of different developments led to the decision to work on a new design. The two main motivations came from two different directions: one was technical, the other was driven by a change in the user group. We discuss both in turn.

Object Look and Behavior

In BlueJ, classes could be instantiated and the objects were visualized as red rectangles with rounded corners on the object bench. When the objects in question were representing graphical entities, a disconnect developed. We had, for example, one project frequently used in early teaching that showed graphical shapes (see Figure 4), which could be displayed in a separate window and be manipulated via method calls. The manipulation (i.e., interactive method calls), however, had to be done on the object bench, while the visible effect occurred in the separate window. Every object was duplicated and had two representations. This was irritating.

We started to think: what if the objects on the object bench could change their appearance, or their position? What if they could react directly and visibly to interactive method invocations?

Figure 3. The main window of the Greenfoot environment. The class diagram is on the right; the main part of the window is used to show the world.

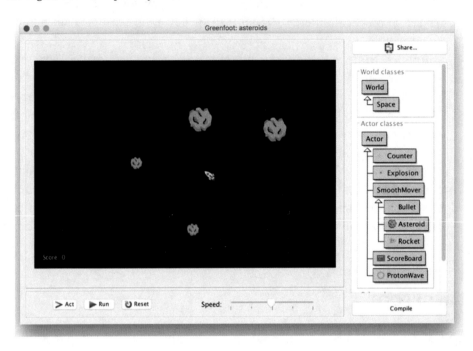

Figure 4. The BlueJ environment with the figures example. Objects are represented on the object bench, and then again graphically in a separate window.

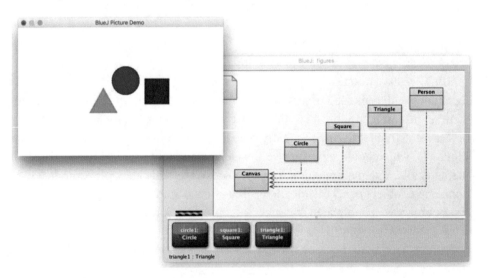

Changes in the Novice Programmer Population

At the same time, over a number of years, a fundamental shift happened in programming education: for more and more students the introductory university course was not the first point of contact with programming. Many beginners were encountering programming at school age, often in formal school instruction and sometimes on their own. Concurrently, in the first half of the 2000s, enrolment numbers in computer science courses were declining in many western countries.

We were always interested in the teaching of initial programming, and supporting that area of instruction as well as we could. When we worked on Blue and BlueJ, the context in our mind had been the introductory university course.

Now we were in a situation where pupils encountered programming—and then often decided that they were not interested in studying it further—well before they came to us in our university departments. If we really wanted to influence early learning of programming, we had to target school age learners.

BlueJ at the time had a significant user base in schools, mostly in the last two or three years of school education: about a quarter of our users were in schools, the rest mostly at universities. However, even though some teachers thought it worked well for them, we felt that this was not the right system for the initial programming experience at school.

New Target Group, New Goals, New Design

The changed target group—school pupils instead of university students—changed our goals, and with it, our design. The most fundamental question we asked ourselves was: what is the most important thing we are trying to achieve? And that question had different answers for the two different age groups we addressed. For BlueJ, our goal was to teach the fundamental concepts of object-oriented programming well. We wanted students to develop a clear and consistent understanding of the most important and useful concepts. For Greenfoot, it was different: the main goal was motivation.

The Importance of Motivation

The most important difference between the two target groups—secondary school and first-year university—is that the latter is a selective group. All the students have chosen to be there, so a certain level of motivation can be assumed. Students generally have an interest in the subject.

This is not true in secondary school. Programming there is presented to the complete population, and many of the pupils were—by default—not interested.

This does not even have to do with the manner in which programming is presented: strong pre-conceived opinions often existed about programming and programmers—even among those who had never practiced it—and the aversion was already well established *at the start* of programming instruction.

This means that the first and most fundamental problem of a programming tool dedicated to this age group was not to teach them something, but to *get them interested*. Generating motivation—and achieving this quickly—became the main goal.

Plus Ça Change, Plus C'est La Même Chose

These two strands of thinking—the importance of motivation, and aiming for a more visual object bench—merged into the design of Greenfoot, a new environment aimed specifically at school age users.

To increase motivation, we decided to concentrate on very visual, graphical, animated examples, where it is quick and easy for beginners to create a first interesting looking program. This had to include the ability to easily make use of graphics, animation, sound, and keyboard control, so that interactive games become achievable as a first example. This approach, called "Game-first programming" by Goschnick and Balbo (2005) had shown to be effective in increasing motivation, but had been impossible in BlueJ.

To achieve the goal of a more individual object representation, we decided to push the class diagram, which dominated the interface of BlueJ, to one side, and make the object bench the central part of the user interface (see Figure 5). This object bench was now called the *world*, could be styled with a custom background, and objects were given individual appearance, location, and rotation. They could then be programmed to alter their location and appearance, and this change could be automatically visualized. With this, we arrived at a well-known destination: micro-worlds.

In a sense, we had come full circle: we were doing things very similar to what Turtle Graphics and Karel the Robot had done decades before. In fact, both Turtle Graphics and Karel the Robot became very easy-to-implement examples in Greenfoot. But Greenfoot was more: Firstly, the micro-world characters could not only be programmed, they could also be interactively manipulated. Characters could be instantiated easily, placed, methods invoked, state inspected, all without writing code. This allowed experimentation to support understanding of the system.

Secondly, more characters could be created. While Turtle Graphics and Karel provided exactly one programmable actor, Greenfoot could produce any number of actors. This is one of the advantages of object orientation.

Thirdly, Greenfoot was not a library, but a complete development environment. It included an editor, runtime system, debugger, graphics library, and more.

Programming and execution was more flexible, practicalities easier to handle, and interaction more interactive.

But most importantly, Greenfoot was not a micro-world, but a *micro-world meta framework*. While Turtle Graphics and Karel (and many others over time) presented a single world with a fixed set of possible actors, Greenfoot was not a micro-world; Greenfoot allowed the creation of endless numbers of micro-worlds, each with any number of actors.

The design was carefully devised to be generic enough to allow the creation of any program whose output was primarily two-dimensional graphics. Possible projects included micro-worlds and birds-eye-view games, but also other examples such as platform-style games, simulations of ant colonies, a playable on-screen piano, simulations of solar systems, physics simulations, and many more.

In short, while Greenfoot restricted the application domain to two-dimensional graphical applications, it was still a generic programming environment.

The Next Lessons Learned

After more than ten years of continued development, releases, user feedback and maintenance of the Greenfoot system, we can again summarize the major lessons

Figure 5. Greenfoot with the shapes example. Objects have a single representation that is both graphical with custom appearance and interactive.

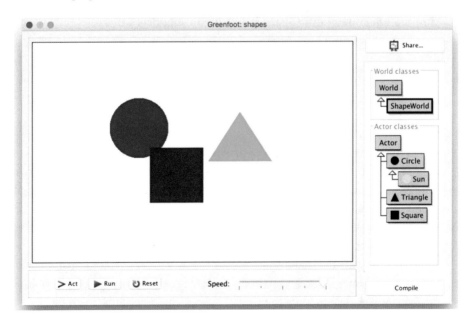

we learned from this experience. Again, most of these are not new insights, others have learned and expressed some of the same lessons before, arrived at the same conclusions from different directions. Still others may find some of these obvious, but we hope identifying what we consider to be the most important points might help to *prioritize*: there are numerous demands and goals for the design of educational development systems, and our contribution is to suggest that these are the ones that are fundamental to an extent that they should take precedence over competing alternatives.

- **Motivation:** The most important lesson for us from our experience with Greenfoot is the power of motivation. As university teachers, when we started out in our designs of educational systems, we were very much concerned with *What to teach* and *How to teach*. The Blue design reflected this thinking.

With Greenfoot, we concentrated on creating motivation and a sense of ownership. The goal was to get users into a situation where they *want to learn*—if we can achieve that, we can teach them anything. For us, this constituted a significant shift from a teacher perspective to a learner perspective. This also meant that self-directed learning (and use of the system without a teacher present) became a significant design goal. These goals shaped the design decisions and functionality of the system.

Other systems—most notably Scratch—started with this insight from the beginning. Their designers knew what we took a long time to learn: that in the learning process the learner is more important than the teacher. We will come back to this below.

Almost all the other points listed below are in support of this one: they are more concrete aspects helping to increase learner motivation.

- **Taking Control:** To allow users to become self-motivated, it is important to put them in a position where they can take control and ownership of a project quickly.

In programming, this is not easy. Since novices at the beginning usually do not know any programming constructs, they can often only do what they are shown to do. In many introductory approaches, this leads to a fairly mechanical observe-and-copy methodology, where students re-create code shown to them by an instructor (or a book, or a video), and then create minor variations (e.g. in parameter values). To create true motivation, this is not enough.

The goal of a well-designed system must be to get users into a position where they can set their own goals and then try to achieve them as soon as possible. For this, aspects of the system have to be easily changeable, and discoverable.

Most block-based systems achieve this very well by presenting block palettes and a mechanism to try out blocks very quickly and easily. This supports discoverability and recognition of language elements not present in text-based languages, and supports self-directed learning. In text-based systems, this is harder: language constructs are not easily discoverable and typically require explanation; syntax must be learned.

In Greenfoot, which initially provided only one language, Java, with a traditional text-based editor as a user language, we tried to overcome these difficulties by adding other opportunities for taking control. Even before knowing much about programming, users can change images and sounds, and easily create and arrange additional actors. This often leads to widely different background stories for early programming examples, even though the programming constructs used are very similar.

When introducing programming to groups of teenagers we often see projects of, for example, rabbits eating pizza, space craft picking up astronauts, or cars racing each other. In a typical case, a teenager saw an image of a wasp in the built-in icon library and was immediately excited to create a project with a "Hunger Games" theme (a popular book and movie at the time, where killer wasps feature in one of the story lines). Even though the programs pupils created are near-identical from a programming point of view (they all concerned one or more keyboard controlled actors moving across the screen and interacting with another kind of actor), each of the users had their own story that they had decided on themselves.

Sounds also had a very powerful effect on the sense of ownership: the easy ability to record and add sounds to projects (which allows pupils to add their own voices to their games) led to much excitement and engagement.

In short: any environment should strive to let users take control as early and as far as possible, and the extent to which this can be done will greatly influence motivation, and with that, acceptance.

- **Visualization and Experimentation—Again:** Greenfoot again reinforced our belief in the importance of visualization and support for experimentation. Greenfoot is more visual than BlueJ and—especially for younger learners—this was an important characteristic.
- **Visualization of Program Execution:** In addition to visualizing the program components (classes and objects), Greenfoot also visualizes the execution of the program. While the program is running, actors can be seen to move on screen. When the program contains an error, this is often immediately obvious in the unexpected behavior of a visible actor. This visualization of the program as it is running is a very fundamental tool that aids greatly in the construction and understanding of programs.

This is the fundamental design idea that Turtle Graphics popularized in the 1960s and 70s, and it is inherent in all micro-world related environments. Many later systems, however, do not make use of this, so we feel it is worth reiterating here.

- **The Power of Community:** In 2007, one year after the initial publication of Greenfoot, we added an export feature that allowed users to upload their projects to a public website, where others could then execute, download, and comment on these projects. Scratch, independently, added a similar feature in the same year. In the Scratch community, this is taken a step further: users are encouraged to "remix" projects (upload a modified version), and these remixes are tracked and attributed. Remixing, for the Scratch community, turned out to be a powerful motivator for engagement. In each of these communities, members can build a reputation by providing useful content or helping others.

These user communities have a high impact. They work in two distinct ways: they serve to provide help and guidance when users have questions or problems, and they greatly increase motivation by giving an opportunity to share and publish projects, and by receiving feedback and encouragement from others. Both aspects are strong drivers of motivation and engagement.

- **Teacher Communities:** In support of teaching with Greenfoot, we created the Greenroom (Fincher, Kölling, Utting, Brown, & Stevens, 2010), a community for teachers. As opposed to the Greenfoot user community, the teacher community is not public and not anonymous—teachers have to apply for access, and we ensure that members actually are who they say they are. The Greenroom provides resources for teaching and learning, and a discussion forum for members.

The advantage of excluding public access is two-fold: firstly, tests, examinations and projects for assessment can be published here with solutions, without pupils having access to them. And secondly, teachers can talk much more freely, admit more easily when they have problems, and ask for help in the knowledge that they are talking to their peers without being overheard.

When creating this community site, we evaluated various existing platforms, but decided eventually to create our own. Aspects influencing this decision included questions of resource curation, access control, and encouragement of participation. These aspects are further discussed in (Brown & Kölling, 2013).

The Greenroom plays a significant role in the pedagogical support of the system, by providing teaching material and support, much beyond what we could provide directly ourselves. For us, coming from a teaching-oriented perspective, this was a natural development. Other systems, such as Scratch, which developed from a more learner-centric view, also moved in this direction. Scratch was initially designed with self-directed learners in mind, consciously assuming that a teacher might not be present. However, as Scratch became widely used, it was also often used in classrooms, and many teachers started to look for support and material. Providing support for instructors will be crucial for every popular system.

- **Programming Language:** The programming language used within Greenfoot is Java. (A second alternative, Stride, has recently been added, discussed below.) Java is a traditional, text-based language originally designed for professionals. This has a major influence on usability and potential target groups.

Using a language such as Java imposes a hard limit on the lower age bound of potential users. For Greenfoot, we aim at users aged from 13 upwards. Below this age, many children do not have the necessary typing and abstraction capabilities to cope with the text-based editor and resulting syntax errors. Languages avoiding this type of syntax, most notably block-based languages, are usable at a much lower age range and can better focus on the initial learning of fundamental concepts. Using a standard text-based language has an advantage only when the learning of syntax and text-based programming is an explicit goal of the learning process.

For us, the choice of Java as the user language was pragmatic: as a team, we did not have the capacity to design and implement a language including all necessary libraries at the same time as developing the environment. Blue, for example, never had the scope of libraries that were now routinely expected in modern systems, and we did not want to spend multiple years on implementing a new language. Choosing Java allowed us to reuse significant portions of the implementation of BlueJ and made the project possible, even though it created limitations in its potential use. The choice, however, also has positive aspects: while it imposes a lower age boundary, it removes the limit at the other end. Since the system is full, standard Java, and is executed on a standard Java VM, very complex and sophisticated projects can be created and run efficiently. As a result, Greenfoot is occasionally used, for example, in artificial intelligence courses for the implementation of sophisticated AI algorithms.

Overall, the most important aspect of programming language choice is to be aware how the style of syntax and language limits the potential user groups, and to ensure that the language is appropriate for the target group of the system.

RELATION TO OTHER ENVIRONMENTS

Our environments were not developed in a vacuum, and many other learning environments were published at the same time. In this section, we briefly discuss selected aspects of some other systems, and how they relate to our environments.

The Rise of Blocks

Arguably the most significant impact on early learning of programming is made by the availability and popularity of block-based programming systems, a modern incarnation of a Visual Programming Language (VPL). Visual programming languages have a long history, starting with early graphical systems such as Sutherland's Sketchpad in the 1960s (Sutherland, 1963) and going through many iterations and variants (Boshernitsan & Downes 2004). However, only with the development of modern block-based education environments did these systems escape a niche existence where they are not only of interest to researchers and hobbyists, but achieved large scale adoption by practitioners in programming teaching.

Block-based systems, by side-stepping most syntactical problems, have greatly shifted the possible starting age of programming learners downwards. Seven- or eight-year olds can comfortably use some of these systems and learn fundamental programming concepts in the process.

The early block-based languages, such as Alice and Scratch, were embedded in environments that offered a host of other advantages as well: visual micro-worlds, simple execution models, block palettes that made language constructs discoverable, easy experimentation, engaging context, and user communities. Later systems, such as App Inventor (Wolber, Abelson, Spertus, & Looney, 2011), added development for mobile devices as an additional motivator.

hile we cannot fully separate visual from textual programming—Good (2011) quite justifiably stipulates that "'Visual vs. Textual' is no longer a useful distinction for programming languages" since each makes significant use of elements of the other—the terms *block-based* and *text-based* programming are sufficiently clearly understood to form a useful distinction in the discussion of educational systems. The impact of this aspect is, in fact, so fundamental and so lasting that in any categorization of educational programming environments today the division into to block-based and text-based environments might be the first, top-level category choice.

Block-based systems have, over the last ten years, managed to bring programming to large groups of users that were previously considered too young. Text-based systems, at the same time, continue to thrive, with the change to text-based programming currently seen as an important step towards a fuller programming education.

In the remainder of this section, we briefly discuss some aspects of selected block- and text-based systems where they relate to our own environments.

Selected Other Systems

Scratch

Maybe the most interesting system to discuss in comparison with Greenfoot is Scratch. Scratch and Greenfoot were designed and published at about the same time, and thus developed independently. An interesting aspect is that—despite significant differences in many details—many design decisions follow very similar paths and arrive at similar solutions, despite the difference in target group and concrete functionality.

Scratch started with a learner centric view that placed discoverability and experimentation at the center of the design5. It uses a custom block-based language and a concurrent, object-based programming model. In these aspects it differs from Greenfoot. However, many underlying design goals align: the use of a micro-world to visualize execution, the goal of supporting easy experimentation, the value of simplicity over extended functionality, the importance of community, and the clear sense of target group. Scratch could have equally been used as an example to illustrate the main conclusions of this paper.

The different age of the target group leads to very different concrete design choices in many cases, and in some aspects—such as the simplification of syntax—Scratch goes much further than Greenfoot. However, it is interesting to observe that the fundamental principles are constant. The two systems illustrate two different implementations of similar design principles for different age groups and different contexts, thus providing two examples of similar abstract ideas.

Because of their similarity of many important aspects, Scratch and Greenfoot form a possible sequence for learners as successive systems, that works well.

Alice

Alice is notable as one of the early successful block-based systems that attracted a large user base in many schools and with many individual users. It has some unique characteristics: firstly, it uses a three-dimensional (instead of a 2D) world. The Alice team has argued that the 3D nature of the system adds to its attraction and creates engagement. On balance, evidence for this assertion is thin. Anecdotal evidence points both ways: some teachers report positive comments from users, while others question the benefit in light of increased complexity. Successor systems developed later do not provide much support for this argument: 3D systems have not become more popular than their 2D competitors. Despite the open question of impact of this particular design decision, it is interesting to note yet again the same underlying goal: increasing motivation and engagement. Another interesting observation has to do with breadth of target group. Alice 2, the popular version early in this century, focused on its own block-based language for implementation. In 2007, the Alice team released a major new version, Alice 3, that added programming in Java as one of the major named goals. Alice 3 was intended to be usable for a very wide age group, starting in primary school and reaching into university level education. However, it failed to gain the same level of traction that Alice 2 had achieved earlier. Today, almost 10 years later, a significant share of the Alice user base still prefer to use Alice 2 with its more limited functionality. This may be an example how targeting a narrower user base may lead to a more successful system than attempting to offer more functionality.

Processing

Processing (Reas & Fry, 2003) is another environment that uses a variant of Java as its user language. It is interesting in our context because it presents another example of a successful educational system that makes use of a pre-existing programming language not originally developed for education. It is also interesting because it represents another example of a different concrete realization of the same design goals: leading to learning by creating engagement. Processing offers the ability to very easily and quickly create graphical programs with very responsive visual feedback. In doing this, it combines motivation with learning of a traditional, text-based language and shows an alternative to creating engagement.

CURRENT TRENDS

Earlier in this chapter, we have mentioned an "easy, readable syntax" as a goal in the initial design of our early systems. While our own systems have migrated to a language with traditional, C-style text syntax for pragmatic reasons, block-based systems have introduced an entirely new syntactic form that presents significant advantages and disadvantages.

The advantage of blocks for beginners are significant: The language is more discoverable, statement syntax needs neither to be learned nor memorized, many common errors are avoided, leading to fewer frustrations, and experimentation is quick and easy. Disadvantages, however, also exist: Once a user knows what they need to do, manipulation is slower and more cumbersome than text (to the extent that experienced users often feel that the system is holding them back in their productivity), programs often become unreadable once they grow beyond a small size, and tracing program execution can be difficult. All these make the development of larger programs unattractive. And "large" in this context does not mean professional size: Even mid-size programs of a few thousand lines—a size that learners often achieve after a year or two—count as "large" in block-based systems.

In addition, the necessary transition from blocks to text with the necessary shift in syntactic treatment has renewed our focus on syntax.

Transition Issues: From Blocks to Text

The success of these two classes of educational environments—block-based for early learners and text-based for a slightly older age group—leads to a relatively new phenomenon: learners that transition from one to the other. Viewing these systems, and their respective successes, in isolation, is not enough anymore. With the earlier encounter of programming, often in primary school, many learners will now transition through multiple educational systems, and the combination, sequence, and transition between these should be planned in context.

One of the transition points generating most interest is the one from blocks to text (Armoni, Meerbaum-Salant, & Ben-Ari, 2015; Dorling & White, 2015; Hundhausen, Farley, & Brown, 2009; Powers, Ecott, & Hirshfield, 2007; Price & Barnes, 2015; Weintrop & Wilensky, 2015a; Weintrop & Wilensky, 2015b). Recently, teachers have discovered that this transition can create significant problems for learners, and that the added complexity of text-based systems—even when familiar with foundational programming concepts—can present a difficult hurdle (Powers, Ecott, & Hirshfield, 2007; Price & Barnes, 2015).

Blocks vs. Text: A Brief Comparison

Above, we have briefly mentioned some beneficial and some problematic aspects of block-based and text-based programming environments.

Three aspects emerge as the main areas of consideration:

- **Representation:** Includes the appearance of the program at various scales, from the visual appearance of a single instruction to the representation of larger structures such as control structures, classes, or modules. Representation is crucial for program comprehension and readability.
- **Manipulation:** Describes all aspects of program entry and editing, including ease of entry and deletion of program constructs, making changes ranging from small scale edits to large refactorings, and extending existing program source.

- **Error Rate:** Refers to the rate of errors an average programmer makes, or the number of errors that can be made in a system. As we have discussed, a significant number of syntactical or type errors can be avoided in some systems.

Using these three areas of consideration, which class of system—block-based or text-based—is better for any given user?

For *novice programmers* at the very beginning of their experience, block-based environments have a lot to offer:

- They provide a clearer, easier to interpret *representation* of individual program statements and their semantics;
- They allow easier *manipulation* of program elements, to a large extent because of the recognition-over-recall characteristic of entering program code; and
- They lead to a significantly lower *error rate*, eliminating many syntax errors outright.

For a typical ten-year-old novice, block-based systems win on all counts—a finding confirmed by several recent blocks versus text comparison studies (Price & Barnes, 2015; Weintrop & Wilensky, 2015b).

Once a novice advances in their proficiency, text-based systems have some distinct advantages:

- For a trained reader of a programming language, text provides a more concise, more readable *representation* than blocks;
- *Manipulation* in standard text editors is faster and more flexible than in block-based systems—viscosity is significantly lower; but
- Text-based environments still allow a higher *error rate*, and even proficient users will make some errors which would not be possible in direct manipulation systems. Many of these errors will be slips and typographical errors, which are quickly fixed by practiced programmers; however, they still have the potential to interrupt workflow and cognitive processes.

Overall, for proficient programmers, typical text-based environments are clearly preferable. And the level of proficiency required for this shift to take effect is not far in the future for novices: We believe that a typical 16-year-old, having programmed for two or three years with Scratch or App Inventor, will normally have reached a level of expertise and expectation where she is more efficient and productive with a typical text-based system. For adults, with their higher ability of dealing with abstraction and notation, the time of usefulness of block-based systems is shorter still (and may be near zero for some novices with good technical and abstraction background).

As a result, designers have started to look at blocks and text in combination.

Combining Blocks and Text

The most common approach to try to support this transitional step is by providing a dual system: the programming system is able to present the same program both as blocks or as text, and users are able to switch between these two representations, or to view both of them side-by-side. Alice 3 introduced a "Java Code on the Side" feature, which displays block based code under construction as Java code (see Figure 6). Only the blocks can be edited; the Java code is read-only. *Tiled Grace* (Homer & Noble, 2014) is an environment for the Grace language (Black, Bruce, Homer, Noble, Ruskin, & Yannow, 2013)—originally designed to be text-based—that can show the same program alternatively as blocks or as text, with the ability to edit either representation, and offering an animated transition between them. Pencil Code is another system that allows this, either in its online environment (Pencil Code, 2016) or in the Droplet editor (Bau, 2015). Other systems, such as App Inventor (Wolber, Abelson, Spertus, & Looney, 2011) and a reusable library derived from it, Blockly (Fraser, 2013) offer similar functionality.

All these examples are based on a common assumption: that seeing blocks and text side-by-side (or alternately), of the same program in each, can aid in the learning of textual programming languages.

We believe, however, that this approach—though popular—is not an ideal solution to the problem, and that we can do better. Instead of offering blocks and text as

Figure 6. The Alice 3 environment with side-by-side view of blocks on the left and Java code on the right. (Source: Cooper, S., Dann, W. (2015) The Role Of Programming In A Non-Major CS Course, ACM Inroads 6, 1).

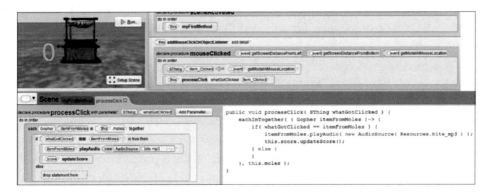

alternatives, and transitions between them, we propose to offer a *single system* that combines aspects from both blocks and text. This then can serve as a stepping stone between the two worlds.

Frame-Based Editing: The Motivation

In Greenfoot 3, published in 2015, we introduced a new language called *Stride*, and a new editor to manipulate programs in it. In 2017, Stride support was also added to BlueJ.

The main contribution in this work is not the language itself, but its *frame-based* editor. Stride, as a language, it very similar to Java, with only minor variation in its constructs and underlying object model. The editor interactions, however, are quite different: the innovation in Stride is not the program a user writes, but what interactions are available to create and manipulate the program.

Two observations led us to this work: Firstly, when offering Greenfoot programming workshops with young learners, we observed that the Java syntax and its text-based editor were the most fundamental hurdle in mastering the system. Young enthusiasts (at, say 12 or 13 years old) could often clearly understand the model and the concepts. They would know what they wanted to do, and had a reasonable plan for how to do it. However, they got stuck with the syntax. Often, they accidentally deleted one of the closing scope brackets, and could not recover. Various aspects contributed to compound this problem:

- The purpose of a closing bracket alone on its line at the end of a method or class is not clear to young beginners.
- Users at this age are often not skilled typists, and single characters are easily deleted by accident.
- Beginners at this age usually do not maintain clear indentation of their code, obscuring these structural errors and making them hard to spot.
- The Java compiler will report errors of this kind in a misleading way: The message is often unhelpful ("End of file detected while parsing") and the indicated error location far removed from the actual source of the error.

This situation is made even more infuriating when thought about in combination with a second observation: Manipulating syntax at this level is neither valuable nor necessary. It is not valuable, because at this stage—teaching fundamental programming concepts to a general population—the aim of our instruction is to illustrate the power and limitations of programming: We want to create motivation, show how a computer works, instill computational thinking, discuss problem solving, show the main aspects and limits of programming. In short, it is about concepts, not syntax.

And it is not necessary, because much of the problem can indeed be automated: If a development environment knows the correct indentation (and they do: there is an "auto-layout" function), why can a programmer ever do it wrong? Why does a programmer need to manipulate layout, spell out keywords correctly, memorize punctuation of for-loops, manually manage line breaks in long lines, and so on?

All this can be automated. And block-based systems have given us one example of what this can look like. Our goal, therefore, was to combine the best aspects of block-based and text-based systems into a single system that combined the best of both worlds (Brown, Altadmri, & Kölling, 2016). From blocks, we aimed at emulating the following aspects:

- We wanted to reduce the error rate by eliminating some of the common errors beginners make. And this does not mean to produce better error messages. It means making it impossible to make the error in the first place. For example, it should not be possible to have half an *if*-statement that is missing the closing bracket of its body.
- We wanted to make program statements more visible to support discoverability.
- We wanted to improve the representation of control statements, such as conditional statements and loops, to make code structure clearer.
- And we wanted to make some selected operations quicker and easier to achieve, such as moving statements to other locations, which can be achieved by dragging with a mouse.

But we also wanted to preserve important aspects of text:

- Larger programs have to remain readable. In fact, we thought we could improve on readability of larger text-based programs.
- We wanted to maintain the flexibility and efficiency of manipulation and navigation. This meant that it should be possible to use the system driven entirely via the keyboard (since this can achieve quicker interaction for proficient users), and offer editing and navigation options at least equivalent in efficiency to traditional text-based systems.

The result of these aims is the frame-based editor, which combines these aspects.

Merging Blocks and Text

- **Frames:** The frame-based editor (see Figure 7) presents a program as a set of nested frames. Each program construct (class, method, statement) is

Figure 7. Greenfoot's frame-based editor with the Stride language. The source code is on the left; a clickable cheat sheet is shown on the right. Statements are represented by frames with colored background. Frames are entered with a single keypress.

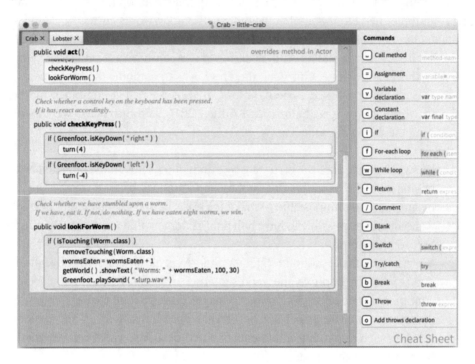

presented by a frame, which is shown with distinct background color. This presentation makes scopes more easily recognizable.

Frames are inserted and deleted in an atomic operation: a single keypress inserts the entire frame; no half statements can ever exist. This is similar to block systems. There are, however, some differences. Firstly, a softer, less saturated color palette is used with fewer distinct colors and without the 3D shadow and bezel effects of most block systems. Single-line frames, for example, (representing simple statements) have a common background color and no border, so that they appear similar to normal text programs. This makes longer program text more readable. Secondly, the editor has a *frame cursor* (see Figure 8). This blue line can be moved between frames with the keyboard and supports keyboard control for navigation and manipulation. A single keypress inserts a frame at the location of the frame cursor (pressing "i" inserts an *if*-frame, "w" inserts a *while*-frame, and so on). Thus, normal operation of the editor is via the keyboard.

Figure 8. A frame cursor marks the editing locus within the nested frames. It is represented by a blue horizontal line.

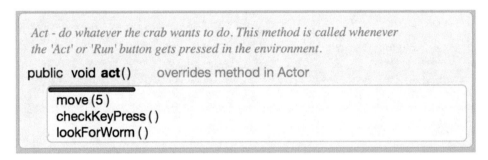

- **Slots:** Frames may have *slots*. Most frames require elements to be filled in to provide detail. An *if*-frame, for example, needs details for its condition and the contents of its body; these are provided in slots. Text-slots allow the entry of expressions (which are not frames), and frame-slots allow entry of additional frames (see Figure 9).

The two different kinds of slots provide different editing functionality, and they are indicated by displaying different kinds of cursors: in frame slots, the frame cursor is as shown earlier, while text slots provide a standard text cursor (see Figure 10). This allows faster entry of identifiers and expressions than is possible in block-based systems, while maintaining syntactic structure at the statement level.

- **Manipulation:** Frames are first class entities in the user interface. While they can be manipulated with the keyboard, they can also be dragged with the mouse like other interface objects, and they provide a context menu to

Figure 9. Frames may contain slots. Text slots are filled by entering text with the keyboard, while frame slots receive frames, either through key commands or mouse actions.

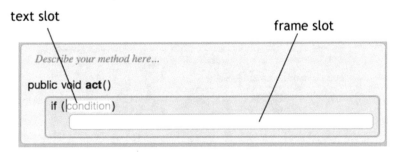

Figure 10. The frame cursor (left) for entering frames, and the text cursor (right) for entering text.

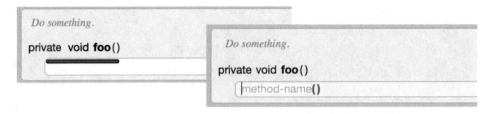

offer operations. When drag-and-drop operations are performed, frames can be dropped only at syntactically valid locations (see Figure 11). This makes some restructure operations much quicker and easier to perform.

- **Layout and Presentation**: When creating Stride programs, users create the program structure, and the system manages the presentation. Layout, indentation, line breaks, and other display issues are not the responsibility of the user—they are managed automatically and cannot be incorrect. This reverses the technique used in standard text editors: While in a standard IDE the user creates the representation of the program, and the system extracts its structure from this representation, in Stride the user creates the structure, and the system generates the representation. This has two advantages: The user is relieved from a number of unnecessary tasks (such as typing out keywords and punctuation, or managing indentation and layout), and richer presentation elements can be used to improve readability.
- **Discoverability**: One of the big advantages of block-based systems is their discoverability: blocks are shown in block palettes, and users can get an

Figure 11. Frames in the Stride editor are user interface elements: they can be dragged or selected, and they have a context menu with frame operations.

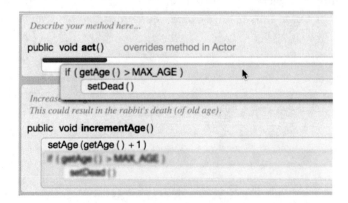

overview of all available commands. In Stride, we attempt to achieve some of these benefits by allowing the display of the "Cheat Sheet" (see Figure 7). This optionally displayed pane shows a list of all available frames that can be inserted, together with their keyboard shortcuts. This differs from block palettes in that is shows only different *kinds* of frames. While block systems effectively list all available methods, Stride shows a "method call" as a single option. The reason is the different scale of these systems: while commands in block systems typically number in the low hundreds, the number of methods available to a Java program is typically in the tens of thousands.

An advantage is that the number of different *type* of statement is very limited: all statements can be shown in a small amount of space. (The list visible in Figure 7 is complete—these are all available statements.) Display of a choice of individual available methods is then left to a code completion mechanism similar to standard IDEs.

The Cheat Sheet is context sensitive; its content depends on the current location of the cursor.

- **Localized Editing:** Since all editing takes place in slots, there is opportunity for better support in some situations. Every slot has a separate undo-stack that is available to display the most recently used values of that slot (see Figure 12). This allows local undo-operations: Changes can be reverted even after other edits have been made elsewhere—a common situation that typically prevents the use of undo in traditional systems in many cases.

Editing in slots also greatly improves error reporting. While error messages are not always accurate or specific, the *location* of the error is much more accurate than in standard text editors. It always knowns in which slot an error occurs in. This

Figure 12. The current slot showing recent values that are offered up for selection by the user

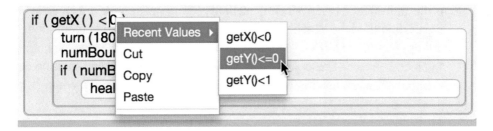

Figure 13. Disconnecting code presentation from sequential text allows several innovations e.g.: here, the method name is pinned to the top of the pane as the body of the method is scrolled beyond the pane

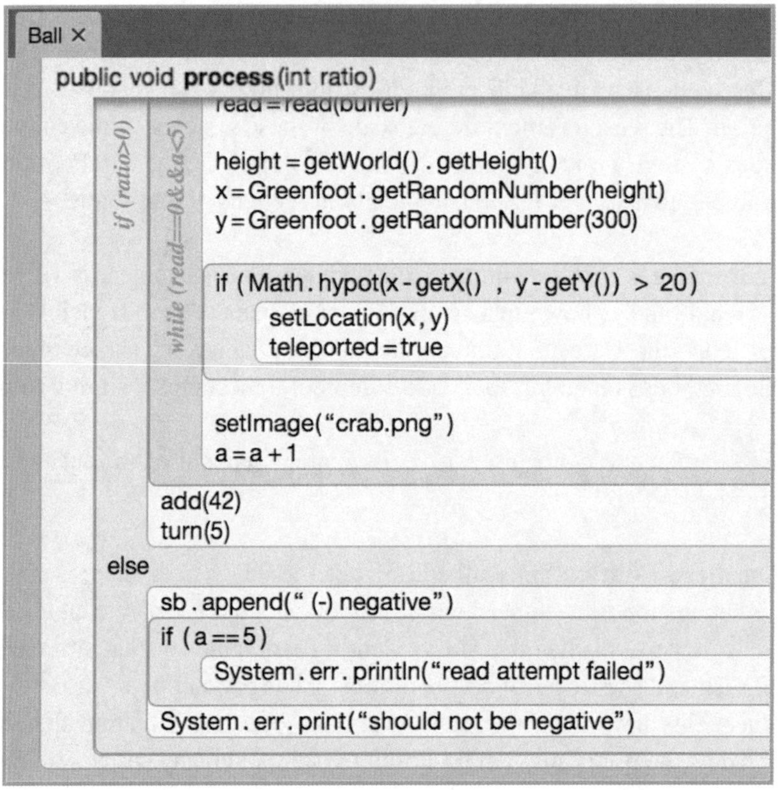

completely avoids the typical case where a compiler reports an error at the end of a method or the end of a file, when the origin of the error is actually much earlier.

- **Presentation Advantages:** The fact that the presentation of the program is generated and does not rely on pure text for its representation allows a wide variety of display improvements that serve to provide better information to the programmer. Figure 13 shows two examples: The method name is pinned to the top of the screen when a method scrolls up, thus keeping valuable information in view. When the start of long control statements (conditionals or loops) scrolls out of view, their heading is displayed in the side area of the statement's frame. These are two examples how program representation can be improved when leaving behind pure text as the presentation medium.

Other examples are the opportunity to provide guidance as to what type of information is expected in empty slots (see Figure 14), or information about actual parameters in method calls (see Figure 15). The first case is helpful for novices unsure about program structure, while the second remains useful for programmers of all ability levels when calling methods.

A more detailed description of the full functionality of Stride's frame-based editor is presented in Kölling, Brown, & Altadmri (2017).

Motivation Through Frustration Removal

We see our work on frame-based editing as a continuation of our early goals of presenting fundamental structure and increasing motivation. Program structure is emphasized more than in standard text-based systems, while motivation is increased by removing hurdles to success and experiences of frustration, which regularly develop when beginners get stuck because of syntax errors. We aim to remove accidental complexity, while exposing and bringing to the forefront the fundamental principles.

We are not alone in the belief that combining aspects of these two types of system can bring benefits. Mönig, Ohshima, & Maloney (2015), for example, are working on a new language called GP, which has a similar goal. This is interesting especially since these authors are designers of existing successful block-based languages (BYOB/Snap and Scratch among them), and are thus approaching the

Figure 14. Frames: context-sensitive prompt messages are put into the frame closest to the input slot

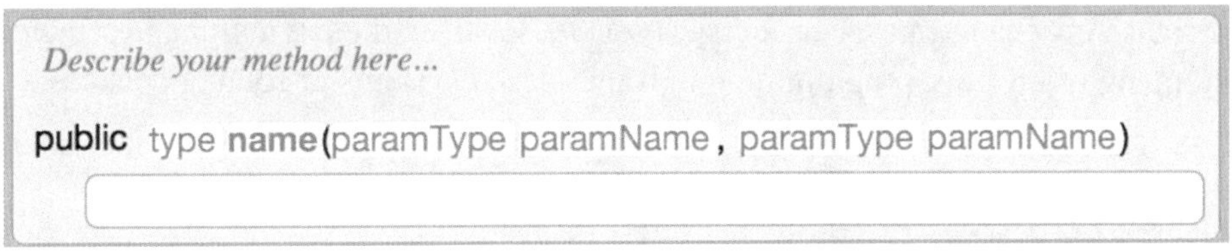

Figure 15. Frames: context-sensitive balloon message about the method parameters expected

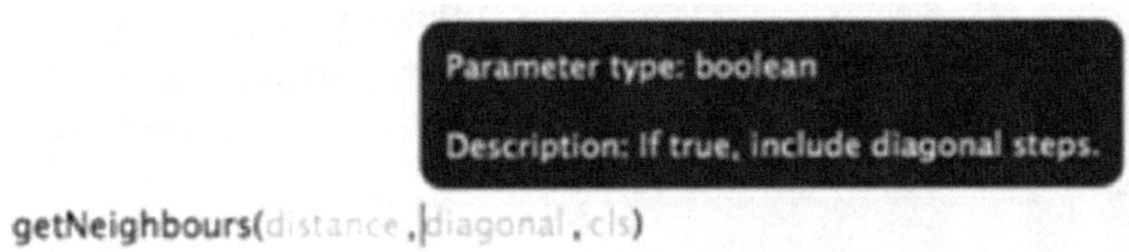

target from the other side: while our experience is with textual languages, and our work adds block-like aspects to those, their background is with blocks, which are now receiving some text-related features. It may be that we meet in the middle with systems that share some commonalities. The most interesting observation, though, is the joint belief that the future of environments supporting the transition lies not in dual systems that offer blocks and code, but in systems offering new functionality combining aspects of the two worlds in a single representation. How these kinds of system can actively support the transition from blocks to text is discussed in more depth in Kölling, Brown, & Altadmri (2015).

On the Obsoleteness of Text

Frame-based editing, should it become successful, will not replace block-based systems.

Block systems have their well-deserved place as programming environments for young (i.e. primary school) novice learners. For that target group, they are—and will remain for the foreseeable future—the most appropriate system.

Text-based editing, however, is much less defensible. Frame-based programming is—in principle—superior to text-based programming in just about every aspect. When implemented well, it is more readable, quicker and easier to edit, leads to fewer syntax errors, and is easier to process and build good tools for, than text. In theory, although our current implementation is in an educational system, it could be implemented for standard programming languages in professional IDEs.

The replacement of text by frames—should it ever happen at all—will not be quick. The existing tool chain of software development tools, with its plethora of different software systems, currently relies on plain program text as a common interchange format. Any change must be necessarily slow. However, there is nothing in principle stopping us all from programming in frame-based systems in coming decades.

CONCLUSION

The popularity of educational programming environments has boomed in the last ten years. More systems have been published than ever before, and more are being developed. Programming as a subject is currently being strengthened or introduced (or re-introduced) at school level in many countries (Brown, Kölling, Crick, Peyton Jones, Humphreys, & Sentance, 2013), and this development is again increasing the interest in these types of people-oriented systems. Many environments are currently under development, and more will follow.

In designing these environments, there are many possible paths that can be taken and many design decisions to be made. In this paper, we have described our experiences with the design and support of three systems, Blue, BlueJ and Greenfoot, and attempted to extract some general design principles that are fundamental, system independent, and that can guide the development of other innovative systems in future. We believe that awareness of these principles can improve the design of such systems.

In addition, we have highlighted one area of development that we think will be relevant to many teachers in the near future, and where significant improvements can be made: the combination of block-based and text-based programming modes. Frame-based editing, as implemented in the most recent Greenfoot and BlueJ systems, is one possibility of how these two types of system can be successfully combined.

NOTE

This chapter presents lessons from two decades of work, and many people were involved in the projects discussed here over time. I am grateful to everyone who made contributions to this work—too numerous to exhaustively enumerate—and to the many users who provided feedback. The principal contributors to the systems described here are named at the end of this chapter.

This work is an extended version of the paper Kölling, M.: Lessons from the Design of Three Educational Programming Environments: Blue, BlueJ and Greenfoot, *International Journal of People-Oriented Programming. 4*, 1, p. 5-32, 2016.

ACKNOWLEDGMENT

Many people have contributed great amounts to the systems discussed in this chapter. John Rosenberg was my PhD supervisor during the creation of the Blue project, and also closely involved in the creation of BlueJ. Without him, none of this would have happened. Many people have contributed to the implementation of BlueJ and Greenfoot, to varying degrees. The most significant contributions here are from Bruce Quig, Andrew Patterson, Davin McCall, Poul Henriksen, and Neil Brown, all of whom are fantastic programmers. David Barnes is my co-author for the BlueJ book and with this contributed immensely to BlueJ's success; without him this book may never have been written. Finally, Sun Microsystems, Oracle Inc, and Google have supported the projects over the years; I am very grateful for their continued support for our projects in particular and to the computer science education community in general.

REFERENCES

Allen, E., Cartwright, R., & Stoler, B. (2002). DrJava: A lightweight pedagogic environment for Java. *Proceedings of the 33rd SIGCSE Technical Symposium on Computer Science Education, 34*(1), 137-141. 10.1145/563340.563395

Armoni, M., Meerbaum-Salant, O., & Ben-Ari, M. (2015). From scratch to "real" programming. *ACM Transactions on Computing Education, 14*(4), 25. doi:10.1145/2677087

Astrachan, O., Bruce, K., Koffman, E., Kölling, M., & Reges, S. (2005). Resolved: Objects early has failed. *ACM SIGCSE Bulletin, 37*(1), 451–452. doi:10.1145/1047124.1047359

Barnes, D., & Kölling, M. (2002). *Objects First with Java - A Practical Introduction using BlueJ*. Prentice-Hall.

Bau, D. (2015). Droplet, a blocks-based editor for text code. *Journal of Computing Sciences in Colleges, 30*(6), 138–144.

Bau, D., Bau, D. A., Dawson, M., & Pickens, C. (2015). Pencil code: block code for a text world. *Proceedings of the 14th International Conference on Interaction Design and Children*, 445-448. 10.1145/2771839.2771875

Begel, A., & Klopfer, E. (2007). StarLogo TNG: An introduction to game development. *Journal of E-Learning*.

Bergin, J., Pattis, R., Stehlik, M., & Roberts, J. (1997). *Karel*. Wiley.

Bergin, J., Stehlik, M., Roberts, J., & Pattis, R. (2005). *Karel J Robot: A gentle introduction to the art of object-oriented programming in Java*. Dream Songs Press.

Black, A. P., Bruce, K. B., Homer, M., Noble, J., Ruskin, A., & Yannow, R. (2013). Seeking Grace: a new object-oriented language for novices. *Proceeding of the 44th ACM technical symposium on Computer science education*, 129-134. 10.1145/2445196.2445240

Boshernitsan, M., & Downes, M. (2004). *Visual Programming Languages: A Survey*. Technical report No. UCB/CSD-04-1368, December 2004, Computer Science Division (EECS) University of California Berkeley.

Brown, N., Altadmri, A., & Kölling, M. (2016). Frame-Based Editing: Combining the Best of Blocks and Text Programming. *Proceedings of the Fourth International Conference on Learning and Teaching in Computing and Engineering*. 10.1109/LaTiCE.2016.16

Brown, N., & Kölling, M. (2013). A Tale of Three Sites: Resource and Knowledge Sharing Amongst Computer Science Educators. *Ninth Annual International Computing Education Research Conference (ICER)*, 27-34. 10.1145/2493394.2493398

Brown, N. C. C., Kölling, M., Crick, T., Peyton Jones, S., Humphreys, S., & Sentance, S. (2013). Bringing computer science back into schools: lessons from the UK. *Proceeding of the 44th ACM technical symposium on Computer science education*, 269-274. 10.1145/2445196.2445277

Caspersen, M. E., & Christensen, H. B. (2000). Here, there and everywhere–on the recurring use of turtle graphics in CS1. *Proceedings of the Fourth Australasian Computing Education Conference* (ACE 2000), 34-40. 10.1145/359369.359375

Cooper, S., Dann, W., & Pausch, R. (2003) Teaching objects-first in introductory computer science. *Proceedings of the 34th SIGCSE Technical Symposium on Computer Science Education (SIGCSE 2003)*, 191-195. 10.1145/611892.611966

Dahl, O. J., Myhrhaug, B., & Nygaard, K. (1967). *Simula 67 common base language*. Academic Press.

Dorling, M., & White, D. (2015). Scratch: A way to logo and python. *Proceedings of the 46th ACM Technical Symposium on Computer Science Education*, 191-196. 10.1145/2676723.2677256

Fincher, S., Kölling, M., Utting, I., Brown, N. C. C., & Stevens, P. (2010). Repositories of Teaching Material and Communities of Use: Nifty Assignments and the Greenroom. *Proceedings of the Sixth international workshop on Computing education research*, 182-196. 10.1145/1839594.1839613

Fraser, N. (2013). Blockly: A visual programming editor. *Google developers*. Retrieved Feb 14, 2016 from: https://developers.google.com/blockly/

Goldberg, A., & Robson, D. (1983). *Smalltalk-80: the language and its implementation*. Addison-Wesley Longman Publishing Co., Inc.

Good, J. (2011). Learners at the Wheel: Novice Programming Environments Come of Age. *International Journal of People-Oriented Programming*, *1*(1), 1–24. doi:10.4018/ijpop.2011010101

Goschnick, S., & Balbo, S. (2005). Game-first programming for information systems students. *Proceedings of the second Australasian conference on Interactive entertainment*. Creativity & Cognition Studios Press.

Gosling, J. (2000). *The Java language specification*. Addison-Wesley Professional.

Harvey, B., & Mönig, J. (2010). Bringing "no ceiling" to Scratch: Can one language serve kids and computer scientists. *Proc. Constructionism,* 1-10.

Harvey, B., & Mönig, J. (2015). Lambda in blocks languages: Lessons learned. *IEEE Blocks and Beyond Workshop (Blocks and Beyond)*, 35-38. 10.1109/BLOCKS.2015.7368997

Henriksen, P., & Kölling, M. (2004). Greenfoot: combining object visualisation with interaction. *Companion to the 19th annual ACM SIGPLAN conference on Object-oriented programming systems, languages, and applications,* 73-82.

Homer, M., & Noble, J. (2014). Combining tiled and textual views of code. *Software Visualization (VISSOFT), 2014 Second IEEE Working Conference on Software Visualization,* 1-10.

Hundhausen, C. D., Farley, S. F., & Brown, J. L. (2009). Can direct manipulation lower the barriers to computer programming and promote transfer of training?: An experimental study. *ACM Transactions on Computer-Human Interaction, 16*(3), 13. doi:10.1145/1592440.1592442

Ingalls, D., Kaehler, T., Maloney, J., Wallace, S., & Kay, A. (1997). Back to the future: The story of Squeak, a practical Smalltalk written in itself. *ACM SIGPLAN Notices, 32*(10), 318–326. doi:10.1145/263700.263754

Kay, A. (2005). *Squeak Etoys Authoring & Media.* Viewpoints Research Institute.

Kölling, M. (1999a). *The Design of an Object-Oriented Environment and Language for Teaching* (Ph.D. thesis). Basser Department of Computer Science, University of Sydney.

Kölling, M. (1999b). The Problem of Teaching Object-Oriented Programming, Part 1: Languages. *Journal of Object-Oriented Programming, 11*(8), 8–15.

Kölling, M. (1999c). The Problem of Teaching Object-Oriented Programming, Part 2: Environments. *Journal of Object-Oriented Programming, 11*(9), 6–12.

Kölling, M. (2010). The Greenfoot Programming Environment. *ACM Transactions on Computing Education, 10*(4), 182-196.

Kölling, M., Brown, N., & Altadmri, A. (2015). Frame-Based Editing: Easing the Transition from Blocks to Text-Based Programming. *Proceedings of the 10th Workshop in Primary and Secondary Computing Education,* 29-38. 10.1145/2818314.2818331

Kölling, M., Brown, N., & Altadmri, A. (2017). Frame-Based Editing. *Journal of Visual Languages and Sentient Systems, 3.*

Kölling, M., Koch, B., & Rosenberg, J. (1995). Requirements for a First Year Object-Oriented Teaching Language. *Proceedings of the 26th SIGCSE Technical Symposium on Computer Science Education*, 173-177. 10.1145/199688.199770

Kölling, M., Quig, B., Patterson, A., & Rosenberg, J. (2003). The BlueJ system and its pedagogy. *Computer Science Education*, *13*, 249–268. doi:10.1076/csed.13.4.249.17496

Kölling, M., & Rosenberg, J. (1996). An object-oriented program development environment for the first programming course. *ACM SIGCSE Bulletin*, *28*(1), 83–87. doi:10.1145/236462.236514

Kölling, M., & Rosenberg, J. (2000). Objects first with Java and BlueJ (seminar session). *ACM SIGCSE Bulletin*, *32*(1), 429. doi:10.1145/331795.331912

MacLaurin, M. (2009). Kodu: End-user programming and design for games. *Proceedings of the 4th International Conference on Foundations of Digital Games*, 2. 10.1145/1536513.1536516

Maloney, J., Resnick, M., Rusk, N., Silverman, B., & Eastmond, E. (2010). The Scratch programming language and environment. *ACM Transactions on Computing Education*, *10*(4), 16. doi:10.1145/1868358.1868363

Meyer, B. (1988). Eiffel: A language and environment for software engineering. *Journal of Systems and Software*, *8*(3), 199–246. doi:10.1016/0164-1212(88)90022-2

Microsoft. (2016, February 14). *Visual Studio Express*. Retrieved from https://www.visualstudio.com/en-us/products/visual-studio-express-vs.aspx

Mönig, J., Ohshima, Y., & Maloney, J. (2015). Blocks at your fingertips: Blurring the line between blocks and text in GP. *Blocks and Beyond Workshop (Blocks and Beyond)*, 51-53. 10.1109/BLOCKS.2015.7369001

Overmars, M. (2004). Learning object-oriented design by creating games. *Potentials, IEEE*, *23*(5), 11–13. doi:10.1109/MP.2005.1368910

Papert, S. (1980). *Mindstorms: Children, Computers, and Powerful Ideas*. New York, NY: Basic Books, Inc.

Patterson, A., Kölling, M., & Rosenberg, J. (2003). Introducing Unit Testing With BlueJ. *Proceedings of the 8th conference on Information Technology in Computer Science Education (ITiCSE 2003)*, 11-15.

Pattis, R. E. (1981). *Karel the Robot: A gentle introduction to the art of programming*. New York: John Wiley & Sons, Inc.

Pencil Code. (2016, February 14). Retrieved from https://pencilcode.net

Powers, K., Ecott, S., & Hirshfield, L. M. (2007). Through the looking glass: Teaching CS0 with Alice. *ACM SIGCSE Bulletin*, *39*(1), 213–217. doi:10.1145/1227504.1227386

Price, T. W., & Barnes, T. (2015). Comparing Textual and Block Interfaces in a Novice Programming Environment. *Proceedings of the eleventh annual International Conference on International Computing Education Research*, 91-99. 10.1145/2787622.2787712

Python Software Foundation. (2012). *Python standard library: Turtle graphics for tk*. Retrieved May 08, 2015 from http://docs.python.org/library/turtle.html

Reas, C., & Fry, B. (2003). Processing: A learning environment for creating interactive Web graphics. *ACM SIGGRAPH 2003 Web Graphics, 1*-1.

Roque, R. V. (2007). *OpenBlocks: An extendable framework for graphical block programming systems* (Doctoral dissertation). Massachusetts Institute of Technology.

Sanders, D., & Dorn, B. (2003). Jeroo: A tool for introducing object-oriented programming. *Proceedings of the 34th SIGCSE Technical Symposium on Computer Science Education*, 201-204. 10.1145/611892.611968

Slack, J. M. (1990). *Turbo Pascal with turtle graphics*. St. Paul, MN: West Publishing Co.

Storey, M. A., Damian, D., Michaud, J., Myers, D., Mindel, M., German, D., ... Hargreaves, E. (2003). Improving the usability of Eclipse for novice programmers. *Proceedings of the 2003 OOPSLA workshop on eclipse technology eXchange*, 35-39. 10.1145/965660.965668

Stroustrup, B. (1986). *The C++ programming language*. Pearson Education India.

Sutherland, I. B. (1963). Sutherland, I. B. SKETCHPAD, a man-machine graphical communication system. *Proceedings of the Spring Joint Computer Conference*, 329–346.

Weintrop, D., & Wilensky, U. (2015a). To block or not to block, that is the question: students' perceptions of blocks-based programming. *Proceedings of the 14th International Conference on Interaction Design and Children*, 199-208. 10.1145/2771839.2771860

Weintrop, D., & Wilensky, U. (2015b). Using commutative assessments to compare conceptual understanding in blocks-based and text-based programs. *Proceedings of the Eleventh Annual International Conference on International Computing Education Research, ICER 15*, 101-110. 10.1145/2787622.2787721

Wolber, D., Abelson, H., Spertus, E., & Looney, L. (2011). *App Inventor*. O'Reilly Media, Inc.

ENDNOTES

[1]   In Logo's case, this also involved physical "turtles"—robots in the real world, while later micro-worlds were often software simulation only.

[2]   Smalltalk was an exception: it provided a fully integrated development environment. It had, however, failed to get traction in programming education and was rarely used for introductory teaching.

[3]   This functionality has been described in some detail elsewhere (Kölling, 1999a; Kölling, Quig, Patterson, & Rosenberg, 2003).

[4]   In 2001, BlueJ was downloaded just over 100,000 times; in the following years, growth was exponential for some time and this number doubled every two years, exceeding 2.5 million downloads per year by 2010.

[5]   Some earlier systems, such as Squeak (Ingalls, Kaehler, Maloney, Wallace, & Kay, 1997) and Etoys (Kay, 2005) were based on a similar approach, but failed to achieve the same impact as Scratch.

Chapter 3
UAPPI:
A Platform for Extending App Inventor Towards the Worlds of IoT and Machine Learning

Antonio Rizzo
University of Siena, Italy

Francesco Montefoschi
University of Siena, Italy

Maurizio Caporali
University of Siena, Italy

Giovanni Burresi
University of Siena, Italy

ABSTRACT

This chapter describes the opportunities offered by an extension of MIT App Inventor 2 named UDOO App Inventor (UAPPI). UAPPI aims to facilitate learning in programming the behavior of objects in the physical world (e.g., internet of things). In addition, UAPPI offers the opportunity to experiment with the emerging field of interactive machine learning. Two case studies devoted to different user groups are described to illustrate these opportunities. In the first, dedicated to middle school students, a door is made interactive; in the second, aimed at interaction designers, a light source is controlled by the blink of the eyes and the smile intensity.

DOI: 10.4018/978-1-5225-5969-6.ch003

INTRODUCTION

Most common visual programming environments for youths and newcomers to the computing world (for example, Scratch, Alice, Greenfoot, AgentSheets) provide solid platforms for creative activities such as designing games, animating interactive stories and running simulations. However, much of the activity is confined to a computer screen and limited to the programming the behavior of pixels. App Inventor is a programming environment that provides an important step toward programming real-world tools.

App Inventor was designed to make the development of mobile applications easy and rewarding (Wolber et al, 2015). Today's mobile devices are better equipped to interact with the physical world than a computer thanks to, for example, GPS, magnetometers, gyroscopes, accelerometers, near-field communications and so forth. App Inventor offers a specialized environment for programming real-world tools, which in turn makes programming more attractive to novices.

In what follows, we present an extension of the App Inventor 2 (AI2) Integrated Development Environment (IDE): the UDOO App Inventor (UAPPI for short; available at http://appinventor.udoo.org in a beta version). This extension transforms App Inventor into an environment for programming not only smartphones and tablets but also physical objects, by integrating microcontroller-managed sensors and actuators onto a UDOO board running Android (http://www.udoo.org; Palazzetti, 2015). UDOO App Inventor aims to gently introduce beginners to the intriguing world of the Internet of Things (IoT), a fast-growing frontier of computing that is transforming everyday objects into human-centered interactive systems (Kortuem et al, 2010).

Below, we briefly introduce App Inventor and two of its key features, live programming and event-driven programming. We then explain how UDOO for App Inventor works and the range of incentives that it offers novices of any age, acquainting them with coding by addressing real world issues with innovative solutions right from the start including the intriguing world of Machine Learning (Amershi et al., 2014).

APP INVENTOR

App Inventor for Android is a visual programming platform for creating mobile applications (apps) for Android-based smartphones and tablets. It was developed at Google Labs by a team led by Hal Abelson on sabbatical from MIT (Abelson, 2009). Today, App Inventor runs as a web application administered by staff at MIT's Center for Mobile Learning - a collaboration of MIT's Computer Science and Artificial Intelligence Laboratory and the MIT Media Lab. The App Inventor source code is available under an open-source license, allowing anyone to deploy App Inventor servers. In 2014, MIT hosted the web IDE, servicing 87,000 users per week, with a total of over 2.2 million registered users who developed 5.5 million apps (Schiller et al, 2014). Today this free online app development environment serves more than 6 million registered users, who have created almost 22 million apps (http://appinventor.mit.edu/explore/about-us.html)

App Inventor is similar to Scratch (http://scratch.mit.edu) and Alice (http://www.alice.org) in that they revolve around block-based languages. Developing apps in App Inventor or these other languages does not require writing textual code. The look and behavior of the app is developed visually, using a series of building blocks for each intended component. Like its competitors, App Inventor aims to make programming enjoyable and accessible to novices.

Of all these programming platforms, however, only App Inventor allows the creation of apps for smartphones and tablets. Given the increasing popularity and ubiquity of these and other mobile devices, App Inventor has enormous potential for attracting newcomers of any age to computing, coding and computational thinking. In a very short time (for example, a few days), beginners can build apps that are not only fun, but have real-world utility. "App Inventor allows creative people to transform their ideas into working, interactive apps that can be taken up by large companies, used by non-profit organizations and turned into startups" (Wolber, 2011).

App Inventor lets users create apps with real life impact, yet its learning curve is gentle. The visual nature of its language reduces the syntax problems common among programming beginners first starting to design an app. Even more important are two key features of the programming environment, namely live programming and event-driven programming. These features help beginners address the formidable challenges of developing a robust programming logic and specifying interactive behavior with a static, graphic language. They are instrumental to the UDOO App Inventor extension.

Live Programming

A traditional program development cycle involves four phases: development, compilation, execution and testing. Debugging sometimes alters the cycle by changing the execution mode, including breakpoints, single-stepping, etc. Programmers may spend hours working on code before they can verify that it actually works. Consequently, a key skill in traditional programming is the capacity of a programmer to simulate computing in his or her head.

Live programming is a concept with origins in the earliest days of computing (http://squeak.org), but one that has long lain dormant. Recently, the prevalence of asynchronous feedback in programming languages, as well as advances in visualizations and user interfaces, have led to a resurgence of interest in live programming in domains, such as online educational communities (https://www. khanacademy.org) and experimental IDEs (http://lighttable.com).

In a live programming environment, code changes are immediately and continually reflected in a constantly running program. Liveness makes program development more interactive by incorporating the effects of code changes more quickly than they are incorporated in the traditional edit-compile-run-test approach. Live programming environments not only integrate debugging into editing, but also permit an expansion away from the limits of a computer into the kind of dialogue a craftsman would conduct with his materials.

Live programming offers immediate feedback, which translates into concrete value, as follows (Tanimoto, 2013):

- It minimizes the latency between a programming action and its effect on program execution.
- It allows performances in which programmer actions control the dynamics of the audience experience in real time.
- It simplifies the "credit assignment problem" faced by a programmer when some programming actions induce new runtime behaviors (such as a bug).
- It supports learning (hence the early connections between liveness and visual programming and program visualization).

Initially, the introduction of live programming in App Inventor happened by chance but lead to an original implementation mode. In App Inventor, the IDE runs in a web browser within which a user specifies the components and behavior of an app to be executed on a real or emulated Android device. Live programming is implemented by means of a special app running on the target device, the App Inventor Companion. Although apps can ultimately be compiled to produce ordinary installable apk files, browser interaction during live development is accomplished by the Companion, which serves as an interpreter for the App Inventor code. In other words, the App Inventor Companion is an app onto which the user incrementally builds and modifies components, properties, procedures, variables and events. The Companion also manages the connection between the browser and an external device with the aid of a rendezvous server and allows users to probe the running app on the mobile device.

In addition, there is a functionality (Do It, see Figure 1) that immediately executes any block in the context of the running app and assesses the value, if any, produced by that execution on the app running on the device (see Figure 2).

New and seasoned App Inventor programmers alike often remark that live development mode is one of the most important features of App Inventor. Using the browser to interactively develop and test a running app on an Android device connected via Wi-Fi is an experience that many users describe as "magical" (Schiller et al, 2014). Live programming is a feature that is essential for attracting novices to the computing world in general and for encouraging them to program real-world objects in particular. Usually, hardware and software development are managed with independent tools, making it cumbersome to synchronize progress. With UDOO App Inventor, these incongruities are reduced.

Event-Driven Programming

Historically, novices were introduced to programming by executing a main program with a single entry point or by evaluating expressions in an interpreter (Turbak, 2014). Interaction with the user or relationships with events were only considered later, a reasonable approach in the early days of computing when most software programs were batch jobs consisting of data processing tasks like sorting large data

Figure 1. By right clicking on the component, a pop up menu appears from which we select the "do it" option

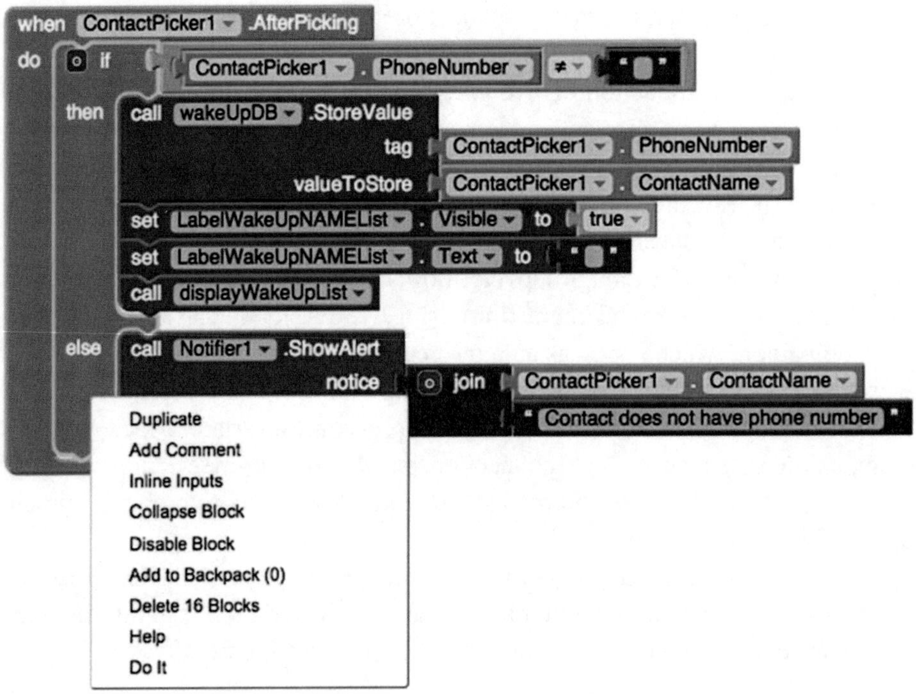

Figure 2.

files. In these systems --known aptly as time-driven-- the system state changes in tandem with changes to the time-based instructions.

In event-driven systems, on the other hand, the state changes when certain conditions occur, such that it is possible to associate one event with every system status transition, as occurs in most of the web applications and mobile apps we interact with every day (e.g., a key being pressed, a phone call arrives, a timer rings, specific values are read by a sensor, etc.). Programming this kind of applications relies on event-driven programming, an approach that was broadly introduced with graphical user interfaces (GUIs) and other types of interactive applications (Philip, 1998; Lee, 2011). In event-driven programming all the defined external events are detected either by listening for an interrupt request or via a polling technique. In the latter case, the system executes an infinite-instructions loop of which a sub-set verifies the presence of an event to be processed. In most applications, these two techniques are combined. Most event-driven applications are composed of one dispatcher and many shorter sub-programs called event handlers. The event handlers are executed when external events occur, and the dispatcher performs the call using a queue. The queue contains all the occurred events still to be processed. Today, with the prevalence of mobile and web platforms, events are becoming a central concept in computer science (Turbak, 2014).

Event-driven programming encourages programmers to use flexible and asynchronous techniques and as few bonds as possible. Moreover, it promotes a simpler architecture by decoupling the sender and receiver objects.

An event-driven approach meets the development needs of most common Android applications. Most of the Android apps are GUI based and therefore designed to react to external events or to user actions, such as the pressing of a button; however, they also need to manage external events like network calls or phone events. Being able to program real-world apps is highly motivating to students and is key to providing a successful first engagement (Wagner, 2013).

In App Inventor, all the computation occurs in response to an event. As an event occurs, the application reacts by calling the associated event handlers.

Events can be classified into two categories: user-initiated and automatic. The first ones are fired when the user interacts somehow with the GUI: a button is clicked, or a contact is selected from the address book (as in Figure 1). The latter are generated by the App Inventor runtime, for example when the text-to-speech completes a message or a clock reaches the repetition period.

In App Inventor, users can discover the events to which a component is sensitive by clicking on the component instance on the Blocks editor. These events can be bound to handlers, which activate one or more blocks containing logical and arithmetical instructions.

Live programming lets users add the main reaction to the event handlers and then quickly refine the handler, for example by adding more blocks like logic conditionals. Each of these blocks can generate other events and activate further blocks. They can be grouped and integrated into sets of macroblocks. The nature and graphical formulation of the IDE promotes the emergence of block groups. The host computer screen has finite dimensions as does the IDE screen, such that it is not possible to create an App Inventor program in a large, monolithic block. App Inventor allows for grouping and for the creation of procedures which make the graphical language more accessible.

GGrouping blocks encourages the creation of modules that reflect the functional role the user wants to attribute to the group. The improvement of the design of existing code may appear worthless. However, the refactoring process is essential to improving the simplicity and clarity of the internal structure (Fowler, 2009). App Inventor inherently promotes basic methods of refactoring, such as function extraction.

UDOO: An Enabling Platform for App Inventor

UDOO is a single-board computer with two different ARM processors embedded on the same printed circuit board (PCB). The main processor is a dual or quad core NXP i.MX 6 Cortex- A9 with a 1GHz clock. This unit can run various Linux distributions and Android. The second chip is a Cortex-M3 microcontroller, the same as that used in the Arduino DUE board. These two processors are connected by an UART serial and via a USB OTG bus, in the same way an Arduino is connected to a PC.

Since the stand-alone Arduino board is powered only by a microcontroller, it has limited computational power and cannot manage complex tasks, like GUIs, networking, storage, etc. Whereas UDOO, by providing both a microcontroller and a microprocessor, is a more apt platform for building custom physical computing projects that require interactions with the physical world and more computational power than an Arduino provides. In addition, compared to a computer, UDOO reduces power consumption, is less expensive and is easier to install in space-constrained environments. It is the first prototyping board with a powerful ARM CPU and a microcontroller that are fully accessible to users and that comes with the support of the extensive community of Arduino users.

UDOO runs Android and has all the most useful features of an Android tablet (camera, touch-screen, audio input/output, Wi-Fi connection), as well as direct access to the Arduino microcontroller. UDOO "was developed with the aim of supporting the education of computer science and R&D projects related to IoT" thanks to "the ability to get information from sensors and interact with the actuators" (Isikdag, 2015, p. 49). UDOO boards offer to App Inventor a great opportunity to be applied to the world of Internet of Things.

A Component to control Lego Mindstorm is available for App Inventor; this solution, however, is limited to the provided Lego sensors and actuators. UDOO bundles the resources provided by the Arduino community, significantly increasing the number of sensors and actuators available on App Inventor. Moreover, as we explain in the following sections, UAPPI provides even more flexibility, since it can run the Android app and the microcontroller on the same or on separate devices. Mindstorm requires a separate Android device since it cannot run Android by itself.

UAPPI, the UDOO App Inventor Extension

UAPPI is a modular, flexible, low-cost system aimed at scholars, youths, makers and designers. UAPPI aims to give novice users the tools to develop applications by providing must-have functionalities like GUI, network access and storage on databases and by supporting the popular Arduino sensors.

Tutorials on Arduino and its sensors abound on the Internet. Almost any consumer sensor or actuator has a working Arduino library. Without resorting to shields, however, Arduino sketches cannot provide GUIs, network, storage and the like. Such constraints are foreign to the Android world, where these features are standard. App Inventor provides all of them. UDOO App Inventor integrates these two worlds, adding components to the App Inventor palette.

Furthermore, we are currently exploring the possibility to make available a Machine Learning module to enable users to play with this new way to program human-computer interaction.

Machine Learning (ML) is a research field at the intersection of statistics, artificial intelligence, and cognitive science. Nowadays ML has reached an all-time high, and this is evident by considering the increasing number of successful start-ups, applications and services in this domain (Jordan and Mitchel, 2015). From automatic recommendations of movies to watch, what food to order or which products to buy, to personalized online radio and recognizing your friends in your photos, many modern services and devices have ML algorithms at their core. Although humans are an integral part of the learning process, traditional ML systems used in these applications are agnostic to the fact that inputs/outputs are from/for humans. Furthermore, even though human application of ML algorithms to real-world problems requires embedding the algorithms in systems of some sort, and the form and usability of these systems impact the feasibility and efficacy of applied ML work, research at the intersection of HCI and ML is still rare.

he integration of ML libraries into App Inventor allows one to rapidly create prototypes of applications able to identify and classify scenarios according to values measured by sensors in the environment.

The UDOO Components for IoT and ML

App Inventor IDE is made from several parts. In the center is a simulated screen that represents the application running on the Android device. On the left there is the palette listing components the users can combine to develop their app.

UAPPI adds a new category of components to this palette, UDOO (see Figure 3), that lets App Inventor users access the Arduino-side of the UDOO board, vastly simplifying the use of sensors. Component blocks mask the complexity of the C/C++ sensor libraries needed in the Arduino IDE. Furthermore, we are developing components based on Machine Learning algorithms.

UAPPI's components embody the App Inventor philosophy, simplifying the use of sensors for novices via plug-and-play blocks, while also providing flexibility for more experienced users. To this end, low-level calls to Arduino functions (e.g., digitalWrite) can be used to develop applications with the same freedom that the Arduino IDE would provide.

The UDOO palette is composed of several Arduino-related components: UdooQuadDual, UdooCamera, UdooColorSensor, UdooServo and UdooTempHumSensor. The UdooQuadDual establishes a connection with the Arduino-side of the board (more details are provided in the next section).

The other components are used to access and operate Arduino sensors and actuators connected to the board. For instance, the UdooServo component can be used to control servo-motors (small motors able to rotate a shaft to a precise angular position).

Figure 3. The elements of the UDOO component in UAPPI

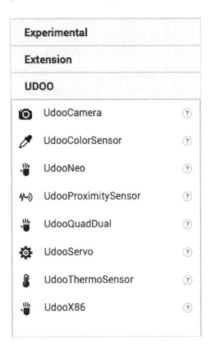

The UdooTempHumSensor component reads the data registers of two of the most used, lowest-cost digital temperature and humidity sensors, the DHT11 and DTH22 ("How to pick the best temperature sensor", 2015). Since each temperature sensor provides its own API, the read must be carried out by a custom block (ReadSensor). According to the event-driven principle, instead of blocking the app execution until the data read from the sensor is ready, the component provides an asynchronous event (DataReady), which can be used to update the user interface with the temperature value.

In order to design Android apps interacting with sensors and actuators, UAPPI users need only add those components to the project and call up the available methods, the signatures of which are often the same as in Arduino API. Having the same Arduino API helps users coming from the Arduino IDE world to develop Android apps using UAPPI, without having to learn a new interface from scratch.

Our extensions meet both Arduino and App Inventor standards. Users immediately know what to do with a component. On the Blocks editor, a panel shows all the properties, methods and events for each component (no need to read API manuals) ensuring a gentle learning curve. In addition, UDOO components are continuously improving and expanding; users can regularly find new methods and events added directly to the Blocks editor.

Beside the UDOO component that allow one to extend sensors and actuators we are also experimenting with a Machine Learning component. ML offers great opportunities to exploit sensors and actuators available in the IoT contexts for generating embedded interactions. To enable users to create such interactions, we added a ML component to the palette that includes UdooSVM and UdooVision. The first allows one to train a ML model from examples of sensors values. The latter follows a different path, using a pre-trained model. Here we focus on UDOOVision since it is simpler to use and offers straight away a clear example of the advantages of introducing Machine Learning modules in designing new kind of interactions. The UdooVision components integrates the Google Vision ("Mobile Vision", 2015) framework, which is able to find objects in photos and video, using real-time on-device vision technology. The mobile face API ("Android com.google.android.gms. vision.face APIs", 2015) finds human faces in photos, tracks positions of facial landmarks (eyes, nose, and mouth) and provides information about the state of facial features -- are the subject's eyes open? Are they smiling? Using the UDOO 5MP Camera Module, the UdooVision component can detect the prominent face in the frame. The component exposes values between 0 and 1 proportionally to how much the eyes are open and how much the person is smiling (0 means closed eyes / no smile; 1 means eyes fully opened / full smile).

UAPPI: Working Examples

Different application scenarios were devised to promote and test the design of the UAPPI system. All of them were devoted to novices of any age from K12 children to Interaction Design students.

The empirical evidence reported below was produced following the Research through Design (RtD) approach. Research through Design in Human-Computer Interaction (HCI) is a practice focused on improving the current state-of-the-art by enabling new behaviors and interactions between humans and technology. In RtD, researchers are pro-active constructors of the world they desire, makers of a better world (Zimmerman and Forlizzi, 2014). RtD also addresses a paradoxical challenge already reported in the early days of HCI by Carroll and Kellogg (1989), namely, that in HCI, theories follow things instead of driving the design of new things.

In order to formalize RtD, Zimmerman et al. (2007) proposed that this approach satisfy well established key features of the scientific endeavor such as, reproducibility of the research process and cumulative knowledge production. Specifically, interaction designers should describe and document the process used, so that it can be reproduced and/or build on top of existing knowledge. To this aim, the full source code used to build the UAPPI IDE is available on GitHub (Montefoschi, 2015). The git repository also contains the UAPPI development history documenting how we incorporated and expanded upon previous research, as well as how we modified the product on the basis of feedback from field testing.

The field tests were carried out via tutorials to facilitate reproducibility. In the following section, we report on how feedback coming from simple IoT projects carried out by children, and designers with no prior programming or electronics experience working contributed to UAPPI's design.

These two application scenarios are examples of everyday objects and related activities that rely on consolidated ways of interacting and can be transformed by merging physical objects with digital technology. Below, we focus on one example for children, *Magic Door;* and one for interaction designers, *At a Glance*, to illustrate how UDOO App Inventor works, how it was received by novices, whether children or adults, and how we exploited the feedback from these field test.

Magic Door

This exercise is what we could call a "Hello World" application in UAPPI. We tested it with children aged 10-14 at a two-hour workshop conducted at *Maker Faire Rome 2015* ("UDOO - Developing an App for IoT", 2015) and in Arezzo at *TimeLine Past 'n future Exhibition* (2015*)*. Below, we describe the steps included in the Magic Door exercise, which aims to teach students to program a smart door system and set a custom sound/voice feedback. The door is simulated using a piece of cardboard and the lock mocked with a servo-motor.

The login phase was executed by all students autonomously. After login, we briefly described the App Inventor interface, explaining the differences between the two main windows, Designer and Blocks editor and their relationships with the UDOO board. Then we invited the students to open the Companion app running on the UDOO device. On the web IDE running on the host PC, they selected "AI Companion" from the "Connect" menu to establish a link between the devices via a six-character code. After a few seconds, a white screen app appeared on the monitor connected to the UDOO board.

Given that we had no information about the technical skills of the students, we started the workshop with a simple warm-up to let participants discover the immediate relationship between actions performed in the Designer and appearance of elements on the UDOO board screen. The children immediately understood the distinction between the programming environment and the device on which the actions have an effect. Then we explained how to associate a behavior with objects using the Block editor.

The first task was changing the text of a label after clicking a button. Another was getting the text from an input box. By clicking on a button, the text was copied from the text box to the label. Later, the participants played with the TextToSpeech provided by Android OS, a step which proved important for continuing to engage their interest and participation. After this warm-up, we started on the heart of the Magic Door exercise.

The first challenge was for the students to select the most appropriate sensor for detecting a knock, from among an accelerometer, a microphone and a piezoelectric disk. These three sensors collect different types of information. The accelerometer sensor receives vibrations and stresses that occur on the door, but also involuntary movements. Microphones receive knocks but also other hit-like sounds that may be heard in the room. The piezo alone can distinguish the other vibrations from a knock on the door. After a few attempts, each student identified the correct sensor and started to build the knock-event listener and its derivative actions (e.g., greet with the TextToSpeech).

The piezoelectric disk generates a small voltage upon the compression due to the knock vibration. The picked-up signal must be amplified by a provided mini-circuit, so it can be sent as a high pulse in a GPIO pin. Within the UDOO palette, there is a component called UdooQuadDual that allows users to access the board's microcontroller, thereby making it possible to control basic GPIO functions and to read analog inputs.

UdooQuadDual component is at the core of the added value UAPPI provides to App Inventor 2. In the above exercise, we used a GPIO in input mode to detect the piezo trigger.

The UdooQuadDual component also provides a block event called "UDOO Connected" that is launched every time the connection between App Inventor and the Arduino microcontroller is established and can be used to configure the pins, like the setup() function in Arduino sketches.

When the piezo sensor detects a voltage spike, signaling a vibration of the door, it sends a message to the GPIO of the board for further processing. To this end, an attachInterrupt block was added to the UDOO Connected event handler (see Figure 4) so that an InterruptFired event is dispatched when the piezo generates a signal. All the blocks to be executed upon knock detection were inserted into this event

Figure 4. The pin #6 is initialized to detect interrupt signals when the Android app connects to the Arduino microcontroller

handler, as follows (see Figure 5). From the Designer, a TextToSpeech component was added to the main screen while a corresponding block was dragged from the Blocks editor into the InputFired handler.

The TextToSpeech component can be used to read a text. In our case, it was used to read a welcome greeting at a knock on the door. The students were invited to try the app on the board. When they knocked on the table where the piezo was located, the knock was detected and the app welcomed them.

To simulate the door unlocking, we added the UdooServo from the Designer section and configured a dedicated pin number from the component's properties. From the Blocks editor, the attach method was plugged into the UDOO Connected event by initializing pin #2 to work with the servo-motor. Then the write method was used to set the angular position of the servo arm. Using 0 degrees as an argument resets the arm position, locking the door. Another write block can be put inside the InterruptFired event, but with 90 degrees as the argument so that, when a knock was detected, the door was unlocked. Thanks to the live programming and without the obstacle of source code syntax, the students started autonomously tinkering with the app, chang- ing blocks like the TextToSpeech message or the servo-motor angular positions.

During the exercise one of the hardest concepts to understand was the interrupts. The UdooQuadDual component API, which comes untouched from Arduino, is provided in order to offer flexibility. However, in simple situations like this one, it is more effective to provide an abstraction which hides the internal technical implementation. After this workshop, we developed a UdooTrigger component, which internally sets an interrupt when the Arduino link is established and fires an event when there is a voltage change on the GPIO.

At a Glance

The second example of UAPPI applied to real-world challenges is *At a Glance*. In this scenario we addressed with four students of an Interaction Design class, the issue of

Figure 5. When a knock is picked by the piezoelectric disk, the InterruptFired event is fired and a "welcome" message pronounced by the TextToSpeech component

facilitating the interaction with everyday objects for people with different abilities. In particular for persons who can interact with the surrounding world only with their face, as in the case of ASL syndrome or in cases of drastic, albeit temporary, reduction of limb mobility. In this example the students were already literate in App Inventor, but this was their first time in the use of UAPPI. The exercise started by logging in the UDOO App Inventor platform using their Gmail account. Then they were introduced in the UDOO components (see above) and in the Machine Learning component. The ML component was illustrated by a walkthrough on the associated Blocks (Figure 6).

The walkthrough was also an opportunity to introduce with some details the salient features of Google vision, like finding human faces in live streams, tracking positions of facial landmarks such as the eyes, nose, and mouth. In the current version of the ML component, only the two eyes and the smile were made available. After this introduction, a scenario was defined where the user could control an object like a lamp or the doorbell by eyelash beats and smiles. The setup for implementing such

Figure 6. The first set of Machine Learning blocks. The first block executes some code after UdooVision takes a picture. The function blocks (in purple) start and stop the component or take an image from the video camera. The value blocks (in green) report the state of the related variables.

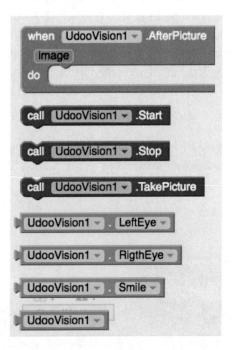

scenario consisted of a UDOO Quad running the UAPPI Companion. The board was equipped with the 7 inches LVDS touch-screen and the 5MP Camera Module. An LED connected to a GPIO mocked the lamp.

After the setup a simple interface for the *At a Glance* app was designed by the students to turn ON and OFF the LED (Figure 7).

App's interaction was defined through the Block Editor (see Figure 8). The behaviour of the two simple buttons controlling the LED and the same appearance of the buttons according to the state of the light was easily defined by the students with only some doubts about the use of digitalWrite and analogWrite to control the state of the LED. As mentioned before, UAPPI exposes the original Arduino API, where it is possible to call both digitalWrite and analogWrite on a digital pin, albeit with different results. The digitalWrite function sets the pin value into a specific state (HIGH or LOW), and that value is kept until digitalWrite is called again. Instead, the analogWrite function activates the PWM output: the value of the pin oscillates continuously between high and low, with a ratio proportional to the function argument (0 means always low, 255 is always high, 128 half the time high, etc.). Powering repeatedly the LED up/down for small amounts of time, creates an optical effect that modulates the visible light. Even if the PWM idea is not trivial for newcomers, the students ended up to use both methods.

At this point the challenge was to call the TurnON and TurnOFF functions by mean of the resources available in the Machine Learning component. For the students the hardest step was to define the event that should call the detection of the state of the eyes and the smile. The key to solve their doubts was to reflect on the kind of sensor that should trigger the event. The sensor in this case is given by

Figure 7. The simple interface to control the LED status

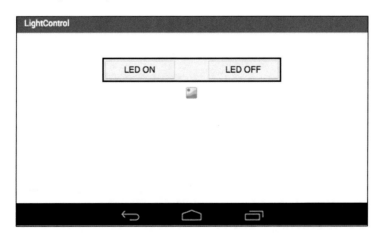

Figure 8. When the app starts (UDOO connected event) the GPIO 13 is set in output. When the function TurnON and TurnOFF are called, the value of the GPIO is set respectively at the HIGH or LOW value. Note that it is possible to use either analog or digital write.

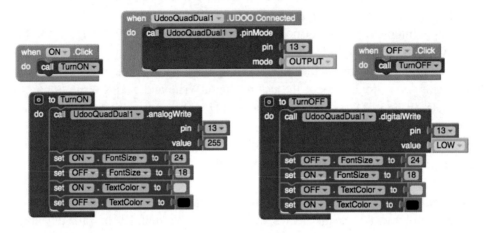

a combination of resources, the camera plugged in the board and the Google Vision ML model, a synthetic sensor. An issue was that it was not needed to recruit the Camera sensor from the sensors palette, since the UdooVision component accesses the camera automatically. This was not clear from the available documentation. A second issue was that the sensor did not produce an event by itself. To access the vision variables, it was necessary to probe the state by mean of another sensor. By browsing the Sensor components, the students had no problem to select and use the Clock sensor. Figure 9 reproduce the first solution they came about. They complemented the event handler UDOOConnected with the call of the function UdooVision Start, and produced the new event handler related to the Clock sensor

Figure 9. The code for controlling the LED status by blinking the eyes and smiling

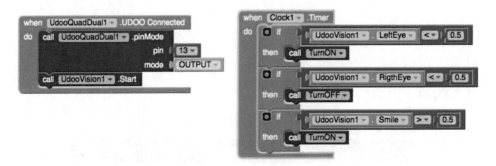

for checking the state of the three variables UdooVision control, LeftEye, RightEye and Smile. This was all needed to implement e control of the LED status by facial movements.

However, at that moment students started to refine a little more their solution. The first thing they made was to provide a feedback to the user about the receptive field of the sensor, by showing the images captured by the camera in a frame. It was located just next to the TurnOn and TurnOff Buttons. The second was to differentiate the use of the left eye blinking and the smile. Initially both turned the light on, in the following they turned on the light with different intensity (see https://youtu.be/yIK4VPk6KI4 and https://youtu.be/2BOyZ5hn4Cs for a reproduction of the student's solutions). Figure 10 reports the final state of the blocks code produced for this first exploration of the ML component with Interaction Design students. The feedback received pointed out the need to introduce at least two refinements in the design of

Figure 10. The whole final solution designed by the Interaction Design students at the end of their first session using UDOOVision

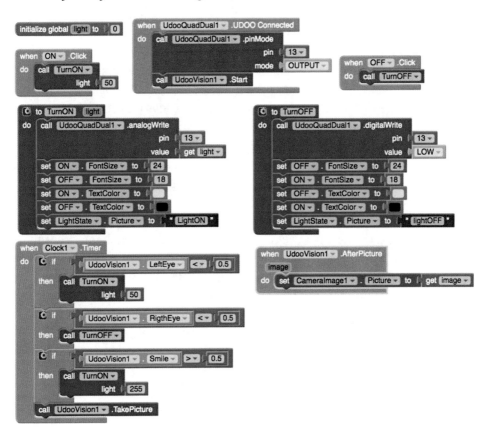

the ML component. The first is to document in the pop up window related to the UdooVision component that it is a synthetic sensor based on the data produced by the Camera and that UdooVision recruits the Camera component automatically. The second is more complex and we have not yet found a sound solution. It is related to the synthetic sensor concept. At present, to trigger an event related to this component, the most effective way is to call it from within another component's event handler, as the Clock used in the above example. This makes the computational management of the Google Vision API simpler, but does not fit well with the mental models the users have of a sensor component.

CONCLUSION

Coding is a competence of growing relevance in our society, a key component of computational thinking (Wing, 2006), which is considered the crucial skill for the third millennium. Providing opportunity for novices to the computing world to create applications with a real-world impact motivates and rewards them (Seaton et al, 2014). MIT App Inventor 2 (AI2) is a successful platform that is already adopted within educational curricula at different levels, K-8, high schools and universities all over the world. AI2 offers the opportunity to program from the start real apps for smartphones and tablets, exploiting the larger selection of sensors and connections these devices offer with respect to a personal computer. UAPPI makes App Inventor 2 work for the new generation of computing boards. Today these boards are popular in the maker community and are facilitating the transition from general purpose computing systems to cyber-physical systems and to the next frontier of computing, the Internet of Things. Computer screens were the first context for playing with code, but now, the entire world has become a potential playground for coding. To this end, on the one hand, we exploited the special architecture of a prototyping board, UDOO, which combines the world of microcomputers based on Android with the world of microcontrollers; on the other, we relied on two key features of the App Inventor 2 programming environment (live programming, event-driven programming) and on the opportunities offered by on-line Android services. These are all essential components in making the programming of physical objects in the real world affordable (Rizzo et al, 2005). In particular, live programming allows users to monitor the impact of their code as it evolves. Event-driven programming encourages thinking about the behavior of objects in their relationship to the environment and to users. Android makes powerful computation services easily accessible. UAPPI integrates all of these benefits with the versatility Arduino provides in interfacing with the physical world through the specific architecture of the UDOO boards.

Today programming IoT interactions resting only on traditional coding resources is not enough. Machine Learning is changing the rules of the game. The heart of every IoT solution are sensors and ML is a powerful tool for transforming data from them, into computational models that can drive user-managed applications. ML models enable new ways to design emerging behaviors in the interaction between humans and their environment. These interactions can concern either the use multimodal data as input to produce desiderated outputs, or the generation of new patterns of interactions that exploit the huge amount of data made available by cyber-physical systems. The integration of ML models in UAPPI allows even novices to play with these new powerful resources. In particular, for readily available models such as Google Mobile Vision, UAPPI users are only required to take some creativity and to imagine an application that can exploit the potentialities of the features detection implemented in ready to use models. Making more algorithms/models available in UAPPI will increasingly allow users to experiment. This is the main road that we will privilege for the future development of UAPPI. From one side, to make even simpler the connection and the use of sensors and actuators in the physical world; from the other side, integrating more open source ML models to allow students, makers and interaction designers to easily envision and implement new modality of interactions with the environment.

REFERENCES

Abelson, H. (2009, July 31). App inventor for android. *Google Research Blog*.

Amershi, S., Cakmak, M., Knox, W. B., & Kulesza, T. (2014). Power to the people: The role of humans in interactive machine learning. *AI Magazine*, *35*(4), 105–120. doi:10.1609/aimag.v35i4.2513

Android com.google.android.gms.vision.face APIs. (2015). Retrieved from https://developers.google.com/android/reference/com/google/android/gms/vision/face/package-summary

Carroll, J. M., & Kellogg, W. A. (1989). Artifact as Theory-Nexus: Hermeneutics Meets Theory based Design. In *Proceedings of the Conference on Human Factors in Computing Systems* (pp. 7–14). ACM Press. 10.1145/67449.67452

Fowler, M. (2009). *Refactoring: improving the design of existing code*. Pearson Education India.

How to pick the best temperature sensor for your Arduino project. (2015, February 16). Retrieved from http://www.intorobotics.com/pick-best-temperature-sensor-arduino-project/

Isikdag, U. (2015). Internet of Things: Single-Board Computers. In Enhanced Building Information Models (pp. 43-53). Springer International Publishing.

Jordan, M. I., & Mitchell, T. M. (2015). Machine learning: Trends, perspectives, and prospects. *Science*, *349*(6245), 255–260. doi:10.1126cience.aaa8415 PMID:26185243

Kortuem, G., Kawsar, F., Fitton, D., & Sundramoorthy, V. (2010). Smart objects as building blocks for the internet of things. *IEEE Internet Computing*, *14*(1), 44–51. doi:10.1109/MIC.2009.143

Lee, K. D. (2011). Event-Driven Programming. In Python Programming Fundamentals (pp. 149-165). Springer London. doi:10.1007/978-1-84996-537-8_6

Mobile Vision – Google Developers. (2015). Retrieved from https://developers.google.com/vision/

Montefoschi, F. (2015, March 06). fmntf/appinventor-sources: MIT App Inventor Public Open Source. *GitHub*. Retrieved from https://github.com/fmntf/appinventor-sources

Palazzetti, E. (2015). *Getting Started with UDOO*. Packt Publishing Ltd.

Pedell, S., Vetere, F., Miller, T., Howard, S., & Sterling L. (2014). *Tools for Participation: Intergenerational Technology Design for the Home*. Academic Press.

Philip, G. C. (1998). Software design guidelines for event-driven programming. *Journal of Systems and Software*, *41*(2), 79–91. doi:10.1016/S0164-1212(97)10009-7

Rizzo, A., Marti, P., Decortis, F., Rutgers, J., & Thursfield, P. (2005). Building narrative experiences for children through real time media manipulation: POGO World. In Funology (pp. 189-199). Springer Netherlands.

Schiller, J., Turbak, F., Abelson, H., Dominguez, J., McKinney, A., Okerlund, J., & Friedman, M. (2014, October). Live programming of mobile apps in App Inventor. In *Proceedings of the 2nd Workshop on Programming for Mobile & Touch* (pp. 1-8). ACM. 10.1145/2688471.2688482

Seaton, D. T., Reich, J., Nesterko, S. O., Mullaney, T., Waldo, J., Ho, A. D., & Chuang, I. (2014). *6.00x Introduction to Computer Science and Programming MITx on edX Course Report*. Academic Press.

Tanimoto, S. L. (2013, May). A perspective on the evolution of live programming. In *Proceedings of the 2013 1st International Workshop on Live Programming (LIVE)* (pp. 31-34). IEEE. 10.1109/LIVE.2013.6617346

TimeLine Past'n Future Exhibition. (2015, October 27). Retrieved from http://hub.garden/timeline

Turbak, F., Sherman, M., Martin, F., Wolber, D., & Crawford Pokress, S. (2014, June). Events-first programming in APP inventor. *Journal of Computing Sciences in Colleges, 29*(6), 81–89.

UDOO - Developing an App for IoT with App Inventor and UDOO. (2015, October 16). Retrieved from http://www.makerfairerome.eu/en/events/?ids=544

Wagner, A., Gray, J., Corley, J., & Wolber, D. (2013, March). Using app inventor in a K-12 summer camp. In *Proceeding of the 44th ACM technical symposium on Computer science education* (pp. 621-626). ACM. 10.1145/2445196.2445377

Wing, J. M. (2006). Computational thinking. *Communications of the ACM, 49*(3), 33–35. doi:10.1145/1118178.1118215

Wolber, D. (2011, March). App inventor and real-world motivation. In *Proceedings of the 42nd ACM technical symposium on Computer science education* (pp. 601-606). ACM. doi:10.1145/1953163.1953329

Wolber, D., Abelson, H., & Friedman, M. (2015). Democratizing computing with app inventor. GetMobile. *Mobile Computing and Communications, 18*(4), 53–58. doi:10.1145/2721914.2721935

Zimmerman, J., & Forlizzi, J. (2014). Research through design in HCI. In *Ways of Knowing in HCI* (pp. 167–189). Springer New York; doi:10.1007/978-1-4939-0378-8_8

Zimmerman, J., Forlizzi, J., & Evenson, S. (2007, April). Research through design as a method for interac- tion design research in HCI. In *Proceedings of the SIGCHI conference on Human factors in computing systems* (pp. 493-502). ACM. 10.1145/1240624.1240704

Chapter 4
From Natural Language to Programming Language

Xiao Liu
Pennsylvania State University, USA

Dinghao Wu
Pennsylvania State University, USA

ABSTRACT

Programming remains a dark art for beginners or even professional programmers. Experience indicates that one of the first barriers for learning a new programming language is the rigid and unnatural syntax and semantics. After analysis of research on the language features used by non-programmers in describing problem solving, the authors propose a new program synthesis framework, dialog-based programming, which interprets natural language descriptions into computer programs without forcing the input formats. In this chapter, they describe three case studies that demonstrate the functionalities of this program synthesis framework and show how natural language alleviates challenges for novice programmers to conduct software development, scripting, and verification.

INTRODUCTION

Programming languages are formal languages with precise instructions for different software development purposes such as software implementation and verification. Due to its conciseness, the absence of redundancy causes less ambiguity in describing problems but on the other hand, reduces the expressiveness. Since the early days of automatic computing, researchers have considered the shortcomings

DOI: 10.4018/978-1-5225-5969-6.ch004

that programming requires to accommodate the precision with the adoption of formal symbolism (Myers, Pane, & Ko, 2004). They have been exploring techniques that could help untrained and lightly trained users to write programming code in a more natural way, and natural programming is then proposed (Biermann, 1983; Pollock, Vijay-Shanker, Hill, Sridhara, & Shepherd, 2013).

Natural language, on the contrary, is excessive but in its expressiveness lacks precision (Biermann, Ballard, & Sigmon, 1983). Describing problems in natural language gives a considerable freedom in clarifying requirements closer to practice, but specifications will contain ambiguities which are fatal to problem-solving. The errors result from two perspectives: structural errors and descriptive errors. Structural errors are caused by language designs. For instance, "then" is used for describing sequential events but is considered only as the "consequence" construct in those programming languages (Pane et al., 2001). Descriptive errors are those brought by participants in specific problem descriptions which contain errors and ambiguities as well.

To achieve a balance between programming languages that contain rigid symbolism and syntaxes and natural language that contains ambiguities. We discuss the question of what is natural to end-users by reviewing a few papers on the language features in non-programmers' descriptions to problem-solving. On top of the central finding on these features, we proposed a general framework for understanding natural language descriptions and automatically synthesizing programs for different software engineering purposes. With the implications of the proposed general framework, we take a closer look at different scenarios and conduct case studies on synthesizing a few domain specific languages. At the last, we discuss the potential limitations of the current framework and propose future works, before drawing a few conclusions.

BACKGROUND

Natural Programming, according to the definition from Brad Myer is "working on making programming languages, APIs, and environments easier to learn, more effective, and less error-prone". To achieve the goal, researchers have conducted studies on various methods to make the programming process more natural. But what is natural to end-users? A few terms, including closeness of mapping (Green & Petre, 1996) and cognitive dimension (Bonar & Soloway, 1985) were created to evaluate the learnability of a programming environment or its language syntax. The closer a programming method is to the problem world, the easier the solution can be composed.

Natural language programming is one of the significant directions being discussed that creates an easier way for people to compose the solutions for a programming task with limited programming experience. Great efforts have been made by researchers and some new language syntaxes have been created during the past two decades. In spite of the features of these new syntaxes, we are interested in essentially how natural they are when fitted into practical problem-solving. We ground our analysis in findings on vocabulary and structure features and discuss the implications for future designs of end-user programming environments.

PROGRAMMING PARADIGMS

On practical problem-solving, a recent study (Pane et al., 2001) reveals a preference for event-based descriptions such as statements that start with *if* or *when*. Meanwhile, a remarkable number of other paradigms are also observed such as constraint programming, declarative programming and imperative programming. Language paradigms are often discussed by researchers about their privileges and people are creating new programming environments for their specific domain of uses. We will get a closer view on these paradigms with a literature walk-through.

In event-based programming or event-driven programming, the program state goes to an event queue to find the next event and then calls some code to process that event (Lee, 2011). This paradigm is widely adopted in programming for graphical user interfaces and game designs due to its naturalness in describing the state machine transitions. E.g., Node.js, the popular cross-platform runtime environment for developing server-side Web applications is event-based. Many end-user programming environments also take this paradigm as their main feature. Pane et al. proposed HAND (Pane, Myers, & Miller, 2002), which is event-based, motivated by his findings. In recent studies, this paradigm is more popular in the domain of Internet of Things where IFTTT (If-this-then-that) recipes are created the most by users (Tibbets, 2010). Their preference to use event-based descriptions in this domain is confirmed with Blackwell's findings with an empirical field study as well (Perera, Aghaee, & Blackwell, 2015). Imperative language is one of the earliest paradigms in the programming history that uses statements to change a program's state. Typical programming languages that are considered imperative include Fortran, C, and Shell programming. LOGO (Feurzeig & Papert, 1967) is a successful and popular language for children to draw graphics. LOGO is based on Lisp and the imperative style of it enables users to describe a procedure of a Turtle movements. The imperative style programming is incorporated in some educational languages, such as Alice (Dann, Cooper, & Pausch, 2011), Looking Glass (Kelleher, 2008), and Moodie (Lieberman & Ahmad, 2010), which are designed for storytelling. These environments share a common feature that users have the solutions/algorithms in detailed procedures before they start to program.

Declarative language describes a problem rather than defining a solution, which is opposite to the imperative paradigm. SQL is an example of declarative languages that specifies the results one requires instead of the method to get it. The constraint-based style is a special kind of the declarative paradigm and Prolog may be the most famous representative. By specifying the true assertions in facts and rules, the logic system can solve problems automatically for users. There are also some end-user development environments use this kind of approach, mostly for the domain of testing and debugging. Burnett (Burnett et al., 2003) proposed an assertion-based method for spreadsheet debugging which allows users to find errors in spreadsheets by continuously adding constraints to cells. It is later improved by Erwig (Abraham & Erwig, 2008) with a more powerful reasoning system. These systems provide users an easier way to solve a problem with knowledge/facts but not reasoning/algorithms.

Programming environments with other styles, e.g., object-oriented (Price et al., 2000), runtime coding (Rode & Rosson, 2003), interactive programming (Liu & Wu, 2014), are proposed by researchers for different domains of uses. Hot topics including spreadsheet programming (Gulwani & Marron, 2014), web application development (Chang & Myers, 2014), and data modeling (Sarkar et al., 2014) have been touched in recent years. One apparent reason that so many languages exist is that it is difficult to decide how to evaluate programming languages, let alone which individual to evaluate. There is no single better language paradigm, just those more suitable for ones purpose. Therefore, it is of critical importance to analyze the domain of use and possible users' preference with empirical studies before designing a new environment. A good way to start any implementations is to collect some user descriptions of domain problems within a small-scale lab study or experimental walkthrough.

PROGRAMMING WORLD VS. REAL WORLD

Pane et al. (2002) observed some interesting findings on the distinctions between the programming world and real life from users' problem-solving descriptions. Based on our analysis, these distinctions can be categorized into four levels from the natural language perspective: word, sentence, abstraction, and precision. To create a successful natural programming environment, the first step is to correctly understand users' expressions and these cases should be handled appropriately.

Word-level distinctions are mostly observed in users' descriptions. A word can be used with a different meaning in users' descriptions compared with its definition in the programming world. For example, "then" is treated as an adverb for connecting two events in sequence by users which is consistent with its usage in daily life. But as a programming term, it means consequently and usually goes along with the term IF...THEN... The word "and" is another example which is a Boolean operator in programming but used as a sequence word quite often in users' descriptions. In addition to the distinctions between the programming world and real world, Ko et al. (2006) also point out a large number of variations among different users according to his analysis of people's descriptions of software problems, especially for noun words.

For the word-level distinctions, both rule-based and statistical-based NLP methods are adopted as solutions. In rule-based methods, the basic idea is to process words or sentences with same meanings according to a pre-defined dictionary, such as WordNet (Miller, 1995) which is a general synonym dictionary. Statistical methods usually look for some surrounding words as the context. It will pick up the closest semantic meaning for a word with the highest probability with the co-occurred words (Wang, Berant, & Liang, 2015).

Sentence-level distinctions are the differences in the structures of sentences with a same semantic meaning. For example, some users would say "if A do something unless B" while the others prefer "if A and not B do something". These distinctions come from different user habits and the various natures of programming tasks. Similar as the word-level distinctions, sentence-level distinctions can also be analyzed with natural language processing techniques. Dictionary-based techniques are widely used in early artificial intelligence, e.g., Eliza (Weizenbaum, 1966) and IBM Watson (Wikipedia, 2016). The pre-defined grammars in the dictionary are usually constructed by experts through empirical studies on the regularity of sentences. Recently, gradually more end-user programming systems tend to process natural language descriptions with statistical methods such as FlashFill (Gulwani & Marron, 2014) that enables end-users to program in a spreadsheet in natural language. Primary NLP models, such as SVM, are good enough for handling the sentence-level distinction problems (Mihalcea, Liu, & Lieberman, 2006).

Abstraction-level distinctions usually happen in describing an operation on some objects. Programs use data structures to organize objects in a programming task, which are usually defined by default. However, users are more accustomed to the data structures that are closer to life. For example, when applying the operation "cut" to a bag of apples, users are more likely to say "cut the bag of apples" rather than "pick an apple and cut it, do this for all apples in the bag". A natural programming design should appeal to these data abstractions that are more often used in real-life scenarios.

To tackle the problem from Abstraction-level distinctions, ideas from the programming language community can be borrowed. As a part of programming language designs, libraries are built for different usages. The same idea applies to end-user programming environments. A general library with programming data structures will be supported by default. Both designers and users can extend the library with new abstracted data structures and operations which are more natural to them if necessary.

Precision-level distinctions are the last kind of distinctions we want to discuss. It represents the distinctions caused by users' coarse expressions. Similarly, Ko et al. (2006) also report the inaccuracy in verb usages in his study. The implicit descriptions can cause problems like range with holes or overlaps which seems a minor issue, but will lead to big problems such as overflows. Many reasons account for these distinctions and the most significant one may be the difference between symbolic expressions and literal expressions. End-users prefer literal expressions in most cases, while programs only take in symbolic expressions. Literal expressions are more expressive than symbols but lose precision to some extent.

For the precision-level distinctions, one solution is making the environment interactive. Whenever the system gets a sentence that it cannot parse or an implicit expression contains ambiguities, it will interactively clarify the requirements with users' additional response. A basic type of interactions can be a reported exception or warning. To make it more user-friendly, a dialog-based interface will be a better choice.

GENERAL FRAMEWORK

On top of these requirements, we proposed a general framework that synthesizes programs from natural language descriptions based on Eliza. Eliza, a primitive prototype of natural language processing, plays the role of a therapist to communicate with patients (Weizenbaum, 1966). The input sentences are processed with a pre-defined script, where there are two basic types of rules: the decomposition rules and the reassemble rules. Decomposition rules are made up of different combinations of keywords and for each decomposition rule, there are a couple of reassemble rules corresponding to it. When a sentence is typed in, it will be decomposed into pieces according to the decomposition rules and then based on one of the reassemble rules, answer in natural language will be generated automatically. Following is an example of how Eliza works (Table 1).

Table 1.

Input It seems that you hate me.
Decomposition Rule (Any Words) (you) (Any Words) (me).
Decomposition (1)It seems that (2)you (3)hate (4)me.
Reassemble Rule (What makes you think I) (3) (you).
Output What makes you think I hate you?

Although Eliza belongs to the first-generation NLP techniques using a rule-based method to understand users, it works quite well in specific domains. The proposed general framework works as in Figure 1. We encode the Decomposition Rules as the Tokenizer which breaks down the sentences into chunks. The mechanism is similar to conventional tokenizer in modern compilers. With preset regular expressions for string matching, we extract valid tokens and construct the symbol sequence that represents the given sentence. In order to get the semantics, the predefined rules will catch the sequential tokens and accurately locate the semantics with provided reassemble methods. After analysis on the selected reassemble method, the analyzer will generate the Intermediate Representation (IR) and it will then be ported to any specific domains with the assistance of the domain interpreter.

The proposed framework allows any kind of translation between natural language descriptions and formal languages. For different domains, we are supposed to analyze the possible descriptions and construct the domain-specific modules. The general framework has been applied in a few practical tools that serve different software engineering purposes, including the software implementation, scripting and verification. In the following part of this paper, we will discuss the functionality of the general framework and special defined modules with domain studies.

CASE STUDY

In this section, we will discuss specific designs which implement the general framework for different software engineering purposes. PiE (Liu & Wu, 2014) is an educational programming tool that synthesizes programs to draw graphs; Natural Shell (Liu et al., 2016) is an enabling tool that assists with scripting in various platforms; and EasyACL (Liu, Holden, & Wu, 2017) functions for constructing and verifying access control list for both Cisco and Juniper systems. The abovementioned tools are designed based on translating natural language descriptions into programming languages. We will detail the motivations, implementations and conducted studies as follows.

Figure 1. General framework for program synthesis

PiE

Aiming at lowering the entrance bar for novice programmers or children, we proposed a domain-specific program synthesis system called Programming in Eliza (PiE), with which, only the conversations in natural language with the computer are required. PiE is capable of synthesizing programs in the LOGO programming language, to draw graphs from the English conversation between Eliza and users. The system consists of three parts: Eliza, PiE script, and LOGO. The core lies in the PiE script which can be seen as a connector between the other two. This script processes the natural language descriptions from users and synthesizes programs in the LOGO programming language which will be executed by the LOGO module. Meanwhile, it provides feedback in natural language to users via the Eliza module.

A user starts with a conversation with our prototype system, PiE (Programming in Eliza) by telling what she would like to code, and at the end of the dialogue, the system outputs a program. We started with the LOGO programming language. Our prototype system is based on Eliza, a primitive AI prototype. Original Eliza was designed to be a therapist. We make it a programming robot. A set of rules is developed for accepting LOGO commands in natural languages, and after a conversation, a LOGO program that draws a turtle graphics picture is produced.

Our study starts from a collection of 877 use descriptions of LOGO commands. The descriptions are collected from a lab study. The commands from the sampling cover all the implemented LOGO instructions. By analyzing the existing descriptions, combined with basic paraphrase assumptions, we implemented the basic library of decomposition rules which can catch 88.4% success ratio when applied to a larger data set which is consisted of 1,877 natural language descriptions. The implemented prototype is currently adopted as an assisting tool for introductory programming courses (Liu & Wu, 2016).

We choose a popular example: the Koch Curve among many latest drawings from users who draw with Turtle on the website, papertlogo in your browser. The input natural language is not case-sensitive and by using the regular expression matching, the system can tolerate some spelling mistakes as well. This demonstration is designed to show that PiE can handle complex tasks. The program goes a little bit further than a beginner can understand, but with a designed algorithm in hand, he could make simple conversations with PiE and draw a Koch Curve without much difficulty.

The interaction between the user and the PiE system is in Table 2 and the output graph is in Figure 2. The Koch Curve, also known as Koch snowflake (Von Koch, 1993), is one of the earliest fractal curves. It demonstrates a normal pattern which adopts the idea of recursion in the drawing. Table 2 shows the dialogs between the

Figure 2. Koch Curve

user and PiE system together with the LOGO program generated. Learners can parallel their natural language commands and this helps a lot since these abstract syntaxes are not easy to learn at the very beginning.

Our system can take in sentences in natural language with few constraints. Phrases like "move ahead 100 steps", "Go on 100 steps", "draw a line 100 inches long" will all be recognized and translated to the same LOGO command "FD 100". In fact, there are still three statements and one loop in the natural language descriptions according to the user, but for beginners, they may focus more on how to design the "process" which can be seen as the algorithm but not the rigid syntax of a specific language at the very beginning.

We proposed PiE to alleviate the anxiety and enhance the learning experience with dialog in natural language. Without the necessity to remember a lot of command syntaxes, it will make the learning experience less stressful compared with traditional introductory programming courses. It will streamline students learning efficiency by teaching algorithm which is the intrinsic in programming but not the various standards. Meanwhile, it will create a lot of fun during the learning process as students can try anything they want to draw without the interruptions from many

Table 2. Transcripts of Using PiE for synthesizing LOGO programs to draw Koch Curve

User Descriptions [PiE Start]	PiE Response	LOGO Program
> Let's first draw a line	Thanks for trying PiE. How can I help you?	
> Oh, I mean, to define a function called line	Okay, what is the length of that line? I see, what are the arguments of the function Line?	to line :count :n
> They are count and n	Okay, I have designed a function called Line with input arguments called count and n. Then?	ifelse :count = 1 [fd :n]
> let the turtle move ahead n steps when the count equals to one	Okay, if the Count is 1, turtle will forward N steps	
> In other cases, do the following things:	I see. do what else?	make "count :count - 1
> let count decrease by one	Okay, Count equals to Count -1	line :count :n
> repeat the line function with new count	I see. Function Line is called with the new argument count	lt 60
> turn left 60 degrees	Okay, the turtle turns 60 degrees to the left	line :count :n
> repeat the function line	Okay, Function Line is called	rt 120 line :count :n
> turn right 120 degree and repeat function line	I see, the turtle turns 120 degrees to the right. Function Line is called.	lt 60 line :count :n
> Again turn but left 60 degrees and repeat the function line	Okay, the turtle turns 60 degrees to the left. Function Line is called	end
> That is all for the function	I see, Function Line is end. end	
> Start another function called Koch	I see, what are the arguments of the function Koch?	to koch :count :n
> still count and n	Okay, I have designed a function called Koch with input arguments called count and n. Then?	rt 30 line :count :n
> first turn right 30 degrees and execute the function line	I see. The turtle turns 30 degrees to the right. Function Line is called.	rt 120 line :count :n
> turn right 120 degrees and execute the function line	I see. The turtle turns 120 degrees to the right. Function Line is called.	rt 30 line :count :n
> repeat the last command	I see. The turtle turns 120 degrees to the right. Function Line is called.	
> Let's call it Koch	I see, Function Koch is end. end	end
> Clear everything	Okay, the canvas is clean.	clear
> let the turtle start from point (45,370)	I see, turtle is moved to point (45,370).	setxy 45 370
> Begin the function Koch	Okay, but what are the arguments?	
> count is 5 and n is 5	Okay, function Koch is called with the argument Count=5 and n=5.	koch 5 5
> Quit	Okay, Done! Done	Done

compiler errors and warnings. Consider the education use of the PiE system, when using this system to learn how to program, the non-experienced learners, especially for the young children, may experience a better interaction other than coding directly on their own.

To demonstrate its educational use, we built a web application as shown in Figure 3 and composed a complete introduction tutorial for entry-level programming courses. During a two-week summer school for high school students, PiE was adopted as a section for an introduction to different programming languages, i.e., Turing Machine, Python, and Prolog. During each lesson, a new programming language was introduced and students were exposed to a few labs to experience how to program with these languages. At the end of the summer school, students were encouraged to provide reflections on these different programming languages and how the interactions were with different environments. According to students' reflections, the experience with PiE-LOGO brought a new understanding of programming language. Students are in favor of PiE-LOGO comparing with the others as one of them commented,

Figure 3. Web App for PiE. (1) Drawing Canvas: The output of executing the synthesized command. (2) Feedback Box: The feedback from the chatbot in response to the natural language commands. (3) Natural Command Box: Type in your natural language commands here. (4) Execute Button: Try your natural language commands. (5) Instruction Panel: Instructions including tutorials for using PiE, some incorporated libraries, history commands, and challenge examples are shown here.

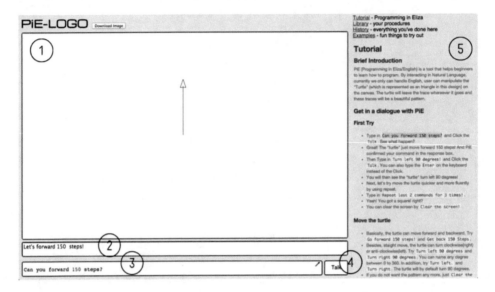

My favorite parts of the course were PiE-LOGO. I enjoyed PiE-LOGO because it was the easiest to understand and I enjoyed the challenges to create the different shapes. I believe I learned a lot in the two weeks, especially since everyone at my school who takes computer science or AP computer science talks about how tough it is. I thoroughly and genuinely enjoyed the course, and I would not change anything about it.

NATURAL SHELL

Natural Shell is a new interface for users to interact with system kernel functions, within the design of a local desktop application. Instead of the numerous command line tools that have a dark background and over-simplified imperative functionality, Natural Shell is more user-friendly, with an interface more akin to a modern application program, as can be seen in Figure 4. There are three main boxes in our design, which are the Natural Command Box, Uni-Shell Command Box and Execution Result Box.

Figure 4. User interface of Natural Shell. (1) Syntax Button: Choose the target syntax. (2) Execute Button: Try out your natural language commands. (3) Export Button: Export the commands in target syntax as a local script. (4) Quit Button: Quit the application. (5) Natural Command Box: Type in your natural language commands here. (6) Uni-Shell Command Box: The synthesized commands are shown here. (7) Execution Result Box: Both the natural language feedback and execution return values are shown here.

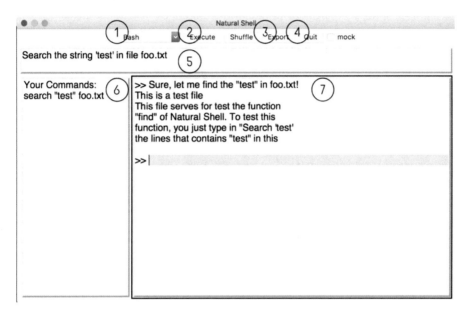

There are two modes of operation: Novice mode and Apprentice Mode. For novices who are not familiar with any shell syntaxes, Natural Shell enables them to harness the system functions using natural language commands. In this mode, the "natural command box" accepts the user's natural language descriptions, which either can be a single-line command or multi-line scripts. Unlike the original shell commands, there is no syntax restriction on the natural language inputs, which provides users with more flexibility in composing commands and generates fewer errors as well. After typing in their natural language commands, the user can expect: (1) commands in the Natural Shell syntax which are presented in the "Uni-Shell command box"; (2) natural language feedback that confirms the entered commands which are shown in the "execution result box"; and (3) return values from execution of the synthesized script commands which is also shown in the "execution result box". However, some users may have gained familiarity with Uni-Shell and it may be redundant for them to start with natural language descriptions. Therefore, in the

Apprentice Mode, these users can directly compose their script in Uni-Shell syntax inside the "Uni-Shell command box" and they can either execute the script in Natural Shell or export the script to local storage in any target syntax.

To demonstrate the ability of our system for end-users to write shell scripts/batch files, we show two examples for users in different scripting skill levels: a non-experienced user only knows basic file operations in Windows; and an experienced cross-platform user knows a few scripting languages. We provided them with descriptions of the script functions in natural language or demonstrate by operations and what they were supposed to do step by step. We assigned them with 2 different tasks and recorded their behaviors, including (1) can they write the task scripts? (2) how can they understand the given materials? and (3) do they refer to any additional materials? We built our system to create a dialog-based scene for users and outputs the final scripts in a text file as well as execution.

In the first case, the user had no previous knowledge of any scripting languages, including the shell for Unix and batch for Windows, but he was asked to write a batch file with a series of basic file operations in the Windows operating system. We provided him a copy of instructions of a task in which, there were only a few conditions and several file operations like creating a folder or deleting a folder. We obtained this piece of script from a shell scripting online forum and it served for deleting current directory entries except for specified files. Before scripting, we taught the user some basic concepts like arguments, labels and directories. Then he was allowed to describe the commands in natural language unrestrictedly and interactively with the system but one after another in case of some conflicts. The interaction was conducted by the user under the supervision of an expert. During the interaction, he asked about the meaning of "shift" and "display". As a result, he generated the target batch file which is shown in Table 3 along with the interaction transcript. The task was completed without any syntax errors in the batch file. The user found our tool helpful, with which the process developed his interest in learning how to use scripts for file operation automation.

In the second case, the user was familiar with both the Windows and Unix operating systems and had written scripts in a few common-used scripting languages like Bash, WinBat and Tcsh. But he cannot remember the syntax quite well which leads to frequent reference on manual books. We retrieved a case from recent problem list on a shell programming online forum (Ramirez, 2015) which asked for getting the list of unique entries from different files and their counts. The questioner also provided a few input and output examples to detail the requirements. We asked the user to write a script in bash with and without our tool. After the task, we measured both the generated scripts and the behavior when he was conducting the task. He composed the scripts function correctly in both cases. However, we noticed that he referred

Table 3. Interaction of the use-case scenario

User Transcript	Response From Natural Shell	Batch File
If there is no specified file name, end the script	> Okay, Let's end the scripts when no argument specified for the file names.	IF "%1" == "" GOTO END
Create a directory called SAVE	> Okay, Let's create a directory called SAVE.	MD SAVE
Label the following as MOVE-FILE	> Okay, Let's label this part as MOVE-FILES	:MOVE-FILES
Copy the specified files to the SAVE folder	> Okay, Let's copy the files specified to the folder called SAVE.	XCOPY %1 SAVE
Shift to the next specified file	> Okay, Let's consider the next file.	SHIFT
If no files specified, then go to FILE-DELETE	> Okay, Let's do FILE-DELETE of no files specified	IF "%1"=="" GOTO FILE-DELETE
Else, go back to MOVE-FILE	> Okay, else we go back to the MOVE-FILES.	GOTO MOVE-FILES
End this part	> Okay, Let's end MOVE-FILES.	
Label the following as FILE-DELETE	> Okay, Let's label this part as FILE-DELETE.	:FILE-DELETE
Delete all the files in current folder	> Okay, Let's delete all files in current folder.	DEL .
End the FILE-DELETE	> Okay, Let's end FILE-DELETE.	
Please move all the files in SAVE to current folder	> Okay, Let's move all files in folder SAVE to current folder.	MOVE SAVE˙ .
Delete the directory called SAVE	> Okay, Let's delete the folder called SAVE.	RD SAVE
Label here as the END	> Okay, Let's label here for the ending.	:END

to the manual four times searching the usage of certain commands like "sed" and "wc", which did not happen when he was assisted by Natural Shell. Additionally, he claimed that taking advantage of our tool, it saved a lot of time from the worries about command options.

One of the students commented on Natural Shell as "Toy Scripting". She just started to learn Java and had no experience with shell scripting. She said, "*I will never use shell scripting without Natural Shell because the original syntax is too complex*". The simplicity of Natural Shell commands will be the most reason that novices will try scripting or she would prefer conducting the system tasks without a script. Her voice represents most of the non-experienced participants in our study and we believe that Natural Shell can encourage students to try system scripting which will enhance their daily working efficiency. Another student commented that "*It is great to know that there is no syntax for a programming language. According to my previous experience, only how to print 'hello world' can be remembered during the first round going through the manual book of any programming languages.*" As described by these students, Natural Shell will assist their experience with scripting in the first a few weeks as an introductory. It will be easier for novices to start with compared with any syntax provided by the system.

EasyACL

To lower the bar of entry for network administration training and reduce the configuration complexity, we also propose EasyACL, a tool that synthesizes ACL configuration commands for different platforms directly from natural language descriptions. To overcome the challenge from option specifications, we introduce a natural language interpretation system which accepts descriptions in a considerable flexibility and synthesize the target commands directly by extracting the semantics with a rule-based natural language processing method. To avoid redundant training processes, EasyACL can port the synthesized commands to different platforms, namely, Cisco and Juniper, for the current stage.

With an empirical analysis over the configuration process plus a thorough survey with network administrators in our department, a few complications are the main trouble-makers. The misuse of configuration options is one of the main issues that were brought up. For ACL configuration commands, options are critical which enlarge the semantic sets with succinct syntax. However, the large number of abbreviated options are disturbing for network administrators, especially those who are not apprenticed. Take the IP permit command for example; there are in total six options that it would accept. To permit the network flows of a specific type needs a few options filled out by the administrator who is required to read the specification carefully to avoid possible mistakes.

To write a correct permit, commands are difficult with these complex options to consider. Additionally, the command is case-sensitive, therefore, it is very likely for a careless administrator to misuse an option or two. On the other hand, the platform dependency of syntax makes the case more complicated. Network companies hold their own operating systems and with the design of platform-directed syntaxes, the ACL configurations are entirely different. Cisco and Juniper are two main network device manufacturers and they have their own configuration syntaxes respectively. If one wants to "permit HTTP traffic from IP 172.21.1.1 to IP 172.21.1.15", the Cisco configuration and Juniper configuration are as follows:

```
# Cisco command
permit tcp host 172.21.1.1 host 172.21.1.15 eq 443

# Juniper command
filter 1 {
```

```
term T1 {
    from {
        source-address {
            172.21.1.1/32; }
        destination-address {
            172.21.1.15/32; }
        protocol tcp;
        destination-port 443; }
    then {
        accept; }
    }
}
```

As demonstrated in this example, the syntax of Cisco ACL configuration commands is distinct from what Juniper system adopts. While Cisco commands are designed to be imperative, Juniper's are object-oriented (Davies et al., 2012). Because of these distinctions, people have to learn different syntaxes when they change platforms which brings more hurdles to the networking engineering training process.

Troubleshooting is one of the main motivations that we propose EasyACL. This tool will handle natural language descriptions with no ambiguity and then make interpretations. Therefore, we can leverage this feature for troubleshooting. To be more specific, when we find any errors in the network, such as no connectivity, we can describe the requirements in natural language and re-implement an access control list quickly. Problems should be resolved if it is simply an implementation error; otherwise, it should be a design problem. Next, we present an analysis of a practical implementation error (Orbitco, 2015).

If the configuration requires: any tcp traffic from hosts 192.168.1.0/8 should be permitted through the telnet port; all ip traffic are permitted.

As shown in Figure 5, there is an error in the access control list implementation: Host 192.168.1.4 has no telnet connectivity with 192.168.3.6. It is a common mistake that many network engineers may encounter, because the router processes ACLs from the top down, statement 1 denies host 192.168.1.4, so statement 20 does not get processed. To troubleshoot this problem, we asked a network administrator to try with our proposed method.

He tried with feeding our system with the natural language descriptions one sentence after the other. And EASYACL synthesized the commands:

```
1 permit tcp 192.168.1.0
  0.0.0.255 any eq telnet
2 deny tcp 192.168.1.0
```

Figure 5. Example of Using EasyACL for ACL verification

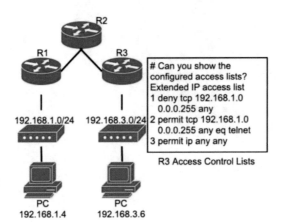

```
   0.0.0.255 any
3 permit ip any any
```

Comparing the synthesized commands and the original implementation, statement 1 and 2 are reversed. The last line allows all other non-TCP traffic that falls under IP (ICMP, UDP, and so on). The network administrator corrected the implementation right away and claimed it a nice tool for network troubleshooting.

DISCUSSION

We have proposed a general framework that synthesizes programming languages from natural language descriptions. The proposed framework serves for various software engineering purposes, including development, scripting, testing, and verification. But essentially, we are providing more natural interfaces for cases where formal languages were adopted previously. Compared against tutorial-style training process, our framework has some key advantages. Most importantly, it conveys the meaning of programming concepts in plain language. The translation makes the training contents closer to users' daily language and it reduces the cost in debugging an incorrect command with syntactic errors. However, the end-users learn a substitution instead of original development. Therefore, they cannot learn a programming language if they cannot assign semantics to commands. Without such an understanding end-users are less able to remember syntax or make adaptations.

In addition to ensuring that the end-user understands the meaning of tasks in a programming language, the use of natural language translation also reduces the time it takes to learn. The casual and conversational dialogue included in our framework allows the end-user to transition from English to programming syntax at his or her own pace. Natural Shell and EasyACL both provide an intermediate phase, which accepts the formally defined language for users to switch to. Although, it is the syntactic sugar for the original development language, this intermediate representation has two benefits. First, the intermediate representation is platform-independent. That is to say, the commands can be ported to any platforms with same functionalities, i.e., Bash, Csh and Winbat for Natural Shell; Cisco and Juniper systems for EasyACL. Second, it allows users to adopt the syntaxes which are more natural towards themselves. Taking advantage of the function define in PiE, users can customize the languages caters to their daily uses.

Furthermore, because the generated framework responses in natural language and program syntax, the end-user is always able to easily refer between the two, should they become confused. Synthesizing programming language from natural language descriptions has been discussed widely. While natural language translation is largely advantageous over tutorial or training software as a method of programming education, there are some drawbacks of natural translation, as well as some instances where a tutorial-model is more effective. If an end-user is not sufficiently attentive, a natural language translation and program synthesis system has the potential to be too overly flexible, such that it prohibits learning. For example, if an end-user can use a wide range of natural language commands to synthesize a target program, and he or she is not attentive to recognize the associated program syntax, this may inhibit their learning by not directly forcing them to learn the syntax. Because tutorial software most often attempts to mimic real programming scenario, it does not typically have this issue.

CONCLUSION

Programming is difficult. We analyzed what is more natural to end-users with respect to language features and on top of the central finding on these features, we proposed a general framework that builds a bridge between the natural language and the programming language. Based on this framework, we conducted three case studies with our deployments for different software engineering purposes, including software development, scripting and verification. We discussed the motivations, functionalities of these studies and evaluated user reflections in practice. Our approach has shown a great improvement in terms of efficiency and usability, across all three case studies.

REFERENCES

Abraham, R., & Erwig, M. (2008). Test-driven goal-directed debugging in spreadsheets. *2008 IEEE Symposium on Visual Languages and Human-Centric Computing*, 131–138. 10.1109/VLHCC.2008.4639073

Biermann, A. W. (1983). Natural language programming. In *Computer Program Synthesis Methodologies* (pp. 335–368). Springer. doi:10.1007/978-94-009-7019-9_10

Biermann, A. W., Ballard, B. W., & Sigmon, A. H. (1983). An experimental study of natural language programming. *International Journal of Man-Machine Studies*, *18*(1), 71–87. doi:10.1016/S0020-7373(83)80005-4

Bonar, J., & Soloway, E. (1985). Preprogramming knowledge: A major source of misconceptions in novice programmers. *Human-Computer Interaction*, *1*(2), 133–161. doi:10.1207153270511hci0102_3

Burnett, M., Cook, C., Pendse, O., Rothermel, G., Summet, J., & Wallace, C. (2003). End-user software engineering with assertions in the spreadsheet paradigm. *Proceedings of the 25th International Conference on Software Engineering*, 93–103. 10.1109/ICSE.2003.1201191

Chang, K. S.-P., & Myers, B. A. (2014). Creating interactive web data applications with spreadsheets. *Proceedings of the 27th Annual ACM Symposium on User Interface Software and Technology*, 87–96. 10.1145/2642918.2647371

Dann, W. P., Cooper, S., & Pausch, R. (2011). *Learning to Program with Alice*. Prentice Hall Press.

Davies, J. N., Comerford, P., Grout, V., Rvachova, N., & Korkh, O. (2012). An investigation into the effect of rule complexity in access control list. *Радіоелектронні І Комп'ютерні Системи*, (5), 33–38.

Feurzeig, W., & Papert, S. (1967). LOGO. *ODP-Open Directory Project*.

Green, T. R. G., & Petre, M. (1996). Usability analysis of visual programming environments: A cognitive dimensions framework. *Journal of Visual Languages and Computing*, *7*(2), 131–174. doi:10.1006/jvlc.1996.0009

Gulwani, S., & Marron, M. (2014). NLyze: Interactive programming by natural language for spreadsheet data analysis and manipulation. *Proceedings of the 2014 ACM SIGMOD International Conference on Management of Data*, 803–814. 10.1145/2588555.2612177

Kelleher, C. (2008). Using storytelling to introduce girls to computer programming. *Beyond Barbie & Mortal Kombat: New Perspectives on Gender and Gaming, 247*–264.

Ko, A. J., Myers, B. A., & Chau, D. H. (2006). A linguistic analysis of how people describe software problems. In Visual Languages and Human-Centric Computing (VL/HCC'06) (pp. 127–134). Academic Press. doi:10.1109/VLHCC.2006.3

Lee, K. D. (2011). Event-Driven Programming. In *Python Programming Fundamentals* (pp. 149–165). Springer. doi:10.1007/978-1-84996-537-8_6

Lieberman, H., & Ahmad, M. (2010). *Knowing what you're talking about: Natural language programming of a multi-player online game. In No Code Required: Giving Users Tools to Transform the Web.* Morgan Kaufmann.

Liu, X., Holden, B., & Wu, D. (2017). Automated Synthesis of Access Control Lists. In *Software Security and Assurance (ICSSA), 2017 International Conference on.* IEEE.

Liu, X., Jiang, Y., Wu, L., & Wu, D. (2016). Natural Shell: An Assistant for End-User Scripting. *International Journal of People-Oriented Programming, 5*(1), 1–18. doi:10.4018/IJPOP.2016010101

Liu, X., & Wu, D. (2014). PiE: Programming in Eliza. In *Proceedings of the 29th ACM/IEEE International Conference on Automated Software Engineering* (pp. 695–700). ACM.

LiuX.WuD. (2016). *PiE-LOGO.* Available: http://bambool.github.io/pie-logo/index.htm

Mihalcea, R., Liu, H., & Lieberman, H. (2006). NLP (natural language processing) for NLP (natural language programming). In *International Conference on Intelligent Text Processing and Computational Linguistics* (pp. 319–330). Academic Press. 10.1007/11671299_34

Miller, G. A. (1995). WordNet: A lexical database for English. *Communications of the ACM, 38*(11), 39–41. doi:10.1145/219717.219748

Myers, B. A., Pane, J. F., & Ko, A. (2004). Natural programming languages and environments. *Communications of the ACM, 47*(9), 47–52. doi:10.1145/1015864.1015888

Orbitco. (2015). *What is ACLs Error? Solutions to ACLs errors Examples.* Retrieved from http://www.orbit-computer-solutions.com/network-troubleshooting-access-control-lists-errors/

Pane, J. F., Myers, B. A., & Miller, L. B. (2002). Using HCI techniques to design a more usable programming system. In Human Centric Computing Languages and Environments, 2002. Proceedings. IEEE 2002 Symposia on (pp. 198–206). IEEE. doi:10.1109/HCC.2002.1046372

Pane, J. F., Ratanamahatana, C. A., & Myers, B. A. (2001). Studying the language and structure in non-programmers' solutions to programming problems. *International Journal of Human-Computer Studies, 54*(2), 237–264. doi:10.1006/ijhc.2000.0410

Perera, C., Aghaee, S., & Blackwell, A. (2015). Natural Notation for the Domestic Internet of Things. In *International Symposium on End User Development* (pp. 25–41). Academic Press. 10.1007/978-3-319-18425-8_3

Pollock, L., Vijay-Shanker, K., Hill, E., Sridhara, G., & Shepherd, D. (2013). Natural language-based software analyses and tools for software maintenance. In *Software Engineering* (pp. 94–125). Springer. doi:10.1007/978-3-642-36054-1_4

Price, D., Rilofff, E., Zachary, J., & Harvey, B. (2000). NaturalJava: a natural language interface for programming in Java. In *Proceedings of the 5th International Conference on Intelligent User Interfaces* (pp. 207–211). Academic Press. 10.1145/325737.325845

Rode, J., & Rosson, M. B. (2003). Programming at runtime: requirements and paradigms for nonprogrammer web application development. In *Human Centric Computing Languages and Environments, 2003 IEEE Symposium on* (pp. 23–30). IEEE.

Sarkar, A., Blackwell, A. F., Jamnik, M., & Spott, M. (2014). Teach and try: A simple interaction technique for exploratory data modelling by end users. In *2014 IEEE Symposium on Visual Languages and Human-Centric Computing (VL/HCC)* (pp. 53–56). IEEE. 10.1109/VLHCC.2014.6883022

Tibbets, L. (2010). *IFTTT the beginning*. Available: https://ifttt.com/blog/2010/12/ifttt-the-beginning

Von Koch, H. (1993). On a continuous curve without tangents constructible from elementary geometry. In *Classics on Fractals*. Westview Press.

Wang, Y., Berant, J., & Liang, P. (2015). Building a semantic parser overnight. Association for Computational Linguistic (ACL). doi:10.3115/v1/P15-1129

Weizenbaum, J. (1966). ELIZA. *Communications of the ACM, 9*(1), 36–45. doi:10.1145/365153.365168

Wikipedia. (2016). *IBM Watson*. Author.

Section 2
New Methods for the People–Oriented Programming Paradigm

As with the programming languages and environments covered in Section 1, a similar rate of progress has been made to help along with the third element of People-Oriented Programming: employing self-ethnography, which may include the use of sensors (informational probes), to define and refine the individual's requirements and clarify the context. This is being enhanced with ongoing improvements and innovations in new methods for: requirements gathering, analysis, through to the design of applications - for individuals and around an individual's situatedness.

Chapter 5
Cultural Probes as a People-Oriented Method

Connor Graham
National University of Singapore, Singapore

Mark Rouncefield
Lancaster University, UK

ABSTRACT

This chapter reflects on some of the methodological aspects of the use of cultural probes (or probes) and the extent to which they constitute a people-oriented method. The authors review different kinds of probes, documenting and analyzing two separate deployments—technology probes and informational probes—in a care setting. They suggest that probes, when deployed in this fashion, reflect a "post-disciplinary" era of "messy" data and a shift of attention beyond "the social" to greater concern with individual variation, personal aggregated datasets in technology design, materiality, and the visual. The authors also suggest that in an era of big data, through considering everyday development in terms of personhood, everyday technology and practice, probes can play an important role in providing insights concerning the product of people-oriented programming and, potentially, its process.

INTRODUCTION

This chapter involves a somewhat nostalgic revisiting of some of our early research in the general area of technology-assisted living and some of our very first deployments of Cultural Probes (or Probes) as a method for gaining some understanding, some basic awareness, of what might be termed a 'sensitive setting' as a precursor to design

DOI: 10.4018/978-1-5225-5969-6.ch005

work. We were, and are, both enthusiastic ethnographers, believing in its ability to make visible the 'real world' sociality of a setting; to produce detailed descriptions of the 'workaday' activities of social actors within specific contexts (Hughes et al 1992) and to present a portrait of life as seen and understood by those who lived and worked within a domain or setting – our archetypal 'users'. As Fielding puts it: "The concern to balance detailed documentation of events with insights into the meaning of those events is the enduring hallmark of ethnography" (Fielding 1994: 154). But research methods and orientations are often, perhaps disappointingly, subject to academic fashion. So today the fashion seems to be engaging possibilities through, for example, design fiction, (e.g. Lindley and Coulton 2015) to which we might respond that the probable is challenging enough to discover. To quote Harold Garfinkel, the founder of ethnomethodology:

Immortal ordinary society evidently, just in any actual case … is only discoverable. It is not imaginable. It cannot be imagined but is only actually found out, and just in any actual case. The way it is done is everything it can consist of and imagined descriptions cannot capture this detail. (Garfinkel 1996: 7-8)

Nevertheless, this research took place at a time when the initial popularity and enthusiasm for ethnographic approaches, although increasingly becoming mainstream and commercialized (e.g. through contextual enquiry (Beyer and Holtzblatt, 1998), was simultaneously being questioned, particularly in terms of both its general applicability and its design relevance (e.g. Plowman et al., 1995). Cultural probes appeared to be one possible response to some of these criticisms: a way by which we might see everyday, mundane activities as social actions embedded within some socially organised domain and accomplished in and through the day-to-day activities of participants, providing access to the ways in which participants understand and conduct their lives. The move towards the adoption and use of cultural probes also seemed to resonate with some of Grudin's (1990) observations, who in his historical account of the evolution of interface research, points to transformations in focus with regard to principal users, 'parent' disciplines, research methods, units of analysis and the precision and generality of studies. Grudin's argument is indicative of the focus of computing research and development changing as "the interface" has abstracted further and further away from low-level circuitry to being situated in particular places with particular "social" features, and even retreating and disappearing altogether (Weiser, 1991; Norman, 1998). The shift Grudin describes changes the interface problem space to consider the broader, social aspects of computing beyond the hardware, software and even beyond usability. It also suggests a shift in the "principal user" base, the methods and metrics used to investigate these users and what we can draw from such investigations. Thus users have changed in character from highly trained engineers and programmers to, in his terms, "groups of end users" or, in terms pertinent to this edited volume, ordinary people. In other words he is arguing that there has been a shift of low-level activities such as programming away from 'the user' of the final product or interface. In parallel, methods and metrics have shifted from an almost universal adoption of laboratory experiments deploying quantitative measures hoping for mass generalization to more eclectic approaches, including 'softer', ethnographic methods that generate findings more particular to people and the settings in which they interact. A more recent shift still is towards the collection of very large data sets autonomously through which specifically designed interfaces can be used to draw inferences regarding people's behaviour en masse (Kitchen, 2014). Thus, it seems, the product of programming, the interface, has also shifted to encompass more aspects of people's lives. This move towards 'the person' or 'people' is something we comment on in this chapter.

In parallel to the shifts Grudin describes, from the late 1970s and 1980s, 'programming' has broadened its audience to include various 'end users' such as children (e.g. through Logo and Basic – Papert (1980), and Scratch – Resnick et al. (2009)), young "digital natives" (Prensky, 2001), non-'experts' and everyday technology users. The development of the digital literacy movement (e.g. http://www.ictliteracy.info/) has placed technology skills at the heart of education programs, where, "...digital fluency requires not just the ability to chat, browse, and interact but also the ability to design, create, and invent with new media..." (Resnick et al., 2009). Most recently, the ready availability and relatively low barrier to entry for Web 2.0 technologies such as web applications, mashups etc. via authoring tools and content management systems (e.g. Drupal - http://drupal.org/) has narrowed the gap between (and perhaps converged) the 'traditional' skills required to generate content and the digital skills required to make it available. These movements, as well as themselves constructing and differentiating specific user populations, create opportunities to investigate people's use of technology as they toggle between creation and use. This can be achieved through, at least in part, drawing on the data they automatically generate from 'the moment' (e.g. pathways of use 'through' the Internet and social and authoring technologies, specifically emails, text messages, posts, digital photographs, videos and the orchestration of these different fragments of media across different platforms) and what they, more reflectively, observe about what they do (e.g. through blogs, annotating and structuring photo streams, commenting and making public these fragments in various ways). The first category of data, the orchestration of different fragments in particular, collapses authoring and interacting. While not programming in the strictest sense, it engages specific skills and expertise, comprising and making visible interactions with others as well as a certain authoring of the self. The second category of data engages people reflexivity generating accounts of their own lives. These two categories, as well as providing insights into different people's interactions through digital and physical spaces and across different scales, in the terms of Churchill (2017), can be understood as 'big' and 'small' data. Big data is "data about people's behaviours online and offline...in many different formats" that aggregates and correlates, "rendering it visible and interrogable" while small data is lesser in scale and at finer granularity that develops different and more nuanced understanding of people's behaviour (ibid). We argue, like Churchill that neither of these means of gaining access into people's lives eclipses the other but instead that they are complementary: "The essence of ethnography is the mixing of the qualitative and the quantitative, and the embracing and connecting of very different representations from disparate sources at multiple levels of granularity."

These shifts are relevant for People-Oriented Programming because, as Goschnick (2009:837) explains, this term focuses on the individual user in three main ways: "as the central focus of a customised software system addressing heterogeneous needs"; "as a self-ethnographer...gather[ing] their own very-specific data (including in the domestic space)" and; "as end-user developers, coming up with their own solutions to match their personal needs, utilising well-engineered software toolkits."[1] In this chapter we wish to focus on the first two aspects of Goschnick's four-pronged definition of People-Oriented Programming and consider particular methods that leverage and/or make available a whole raft of data on the individual person. But here we also wish to remark upon the terms "person" and "people" as being quite distinct from "user" or even "social actor" and "population". "Personhood" is suggestive of a distinct, individual identity and "'sense of self'" (Durrant et al., 2017) that is not static but may be subject to transformation over time (Kerrigan and Hart, 2016). In addition, a person's being is, although not tied exclusively to the use of digital technology (or surveillance by it), increasing connected and associated with it. The exclusive association of 'the person' with digital technology is surely the mistake that much literature on 'digital personhood' makes. These aspects of personhood are notably distinct from, if complementary to, those described by Dennett (1976, cited in Meese et al., 2015) and Tehranian (2011, cited in Meese et al., 2015) as involving rationality, consciousness and an ability to communicate.

One research approach that has been distinct in its treatment of the individual person and particular populations of people widely adopted and adapted in the Human-Computer Interaction and Design communities is that of Probes. Graham et al (2007:29) note how: "The notion of a 'probe' can refer to a number of things – and all of these versions, or aspects of them, can and have appeared in HCI research." Boehner et al. (2007:1077), describe the original version, Cultural Probes as: "designed objects, physical packets containing open-ended, provocative and oblique tasks to support early participant engagement with the design process."

Thus Probes, like surgical biopsies, unmanned spacecraft and investigations into criminal activity are deliberately constructed collections of materials and strategies used to explore and discover more; in this case, more about people's lives (Gaver et al. 1999b; Graham et al., 2007). Our primary aim here then is to argue that Probes as a method can help us to understand what programming might achieve in people's lives in the broadest sense and how it might engage (digital) personhood, as the computer reaches out to more and more aspects of these people's lives – family, friendship, leisure, politics, citizenship etc.

The popularity of Probes exposes the eclecticism of particular research communities in computing with regard to method (Boehner et al., 2007) but, we believe, is also indicative of a retreat in the wider computing space from singular commitments to particular methodologies. Avison and Fitzgerald (2003) argue that we have entered a 'post-methodology' era where diversity is key and fitness to purpose and flexibility are critical. They also argue that we need to be careful not to interpret a willingness to adapt and move from one single methodology as "the death of methodology". In a similar fashion we argue here that one of the reasons that Probes have been so successful and spawned so many versions or "'x' probes" (Boehner et al., 2007) – "methods inspired by probes which replace the 'cultural' of cultural probes with another topic of interest or to indicate a different style" (Boehner et al., 2007) – is their openness to appropriation by the many different communities related to computing. For example, the 'softer' "Cultural Probes" (Gaver et al., 1999b) that produce fuzzier 'inspiration' for interpretation have appealed to the creative design community (e.g. Mattelmäki, 2005) while the 'harder' Technology Probes that produce more objective 'data' appeal to the computing design community (e.g. Hutchinson et al., 2003). Thus different Probes can embrace quite different traditions in design – from creative design to engineering design to systems design.

We also argue that Probes suggest four additional shifts in methods, design, use and datasets in computing. These shifts are towards the individual person (albeit as positioned in particular communities and society at large), to the material (through acknowledging the sheer amount of and increasing impact of 'stuff' in people's lives), to the visual (through utilizing the increasing availability and reduction of cost and barriers to entry for photographic and video technologies) and towards individuated and aggregated datasets (through automated collection of online interactions and analytical tools supporting multiple views at different scales). Thus in this chapter our focus on People-Oriented Programming regards methods that can support the development of people-oriented programs. At the end of the chapter we consider the possible relevance of these methods to People-Oriented Programming because of the convergence of programming with everyday computing use. In this, at least initially, we deliberately shift away from concerns regarding the design of programming languages and environments toward what such languages might both draw on for their design and exactly what they might build.

PROBE 'VARIETALS'

There are several critical reviews of Probes already available. Boehner et al (2007) describe ten Probes varietals/blends or "'x' probes", eight of which we do not describe in any detail here: Empathy Probes (e.g. Mattelmäki and Battarbee, 2002), Digital Cultural Probes (Iverson and Nielsen, 2003), Identity Probes (Candy, 2003), Mobile Probes (Hulkko et al., 2004), Urban Probes (Paulos and Jenkins, 2005), Value Probes (Voida and Mynatt, 2005), Domestic Probes (Vetere et al., 2005), and Cognitive Probes (Mamykina et al., 2006). These different Probe varietals suggest there are certain common features (Graham et al., 2007): they involve particular ways of capturing different aspects of people's lives (e.g. self-photography); they generate (auto) biographical accounts of individual people; they make particular things in people's lives (e.g. actions, places, people) visible; they focus on the participant as an expert in their own lives and; they start a dialogue between observers and participants. This focus on the individual and the various aspects of people's lives is, we believe, important for People-Oriented Programming. Indeed, the original Cultural Probes were initially deployed as part of the Presence Project (Gaver et al., 1999b) across three very distinct communities of older people (Bijlmer, a housing development in the Netherlands; Majorstua, a district in Oslo; and Peccioli a small village in near Pisa) to get at "people's emotional, aesthetic, and experiential reactions to their environments, but in open-ended, provocative and oblique ways" (Gaver et al., 1999b).

This somewhat careful engagement with particular communities is consistent with two other Probe varietals – Technology Probes (Hutchinson et al. 2003) and Informational Probes. Technology Probes were first used as part of the interLiving project: "working with diverse families from Sweden, France and the U.S. to design and understand the potential for new technologies that support communication among diverse, distributed, multi-generational families" (ibid). Informational Probes (Crabtree et al., 2003) were deployed in the context of the Digital Care experience (https://en.wikipedia.org/wiki/Digital_health), part of the interdisciplinary Equator Project (https://en.wikipedia.org/wiki/Equator_IRC) in the UK. This 'experience' was concerned with developing appropriate assistive and enabling technologies across a number of residential care settings: a hostel for former psychiatric patients; a number of elderly people living at home; and a stroke victim and her family.

These three particular Probe varietals are useful in community and domestic settings because they have centred on previously neglected user populations while capturing a range of less considered aspects of personhood, such as who individuals in these populations actually were and a sense of how others, including family members, related to this individual self. They constitute a 'people-oriented' method if not a methodology. For example, Cultural Probes focused on older Bijlmer residents' concerns regarding security via a map of the area with extensive notes on "junkies and thieves" (ibid) while Technology Probes examined cross-generational interaction through collecting data concerning the kinds of everyday messages that are exchanged across a distance between different family members at different times and with varying frequency. Informational Probes focused on design for those typically excluded from the design process – for example, people with disabilities – and in gaining insights into their "abiding concerns" (Crabtree et al., 2003:8). These kinds of Probes were concerned with 'getting at' a sensitive setting where any disruption (through standard ethnographic work for example) had to be carefully considered. In addition, as Gaver et al. (2004:55), suggest, these Probes were not aimed at generating a single, static, unchanging, understanding of the individual person:

Rather than producing lists of facts about our volunteers, the Probes encourage us to tell stories about them, much as we tell stories about the people we know in daily life. At first, these stories can reflect dismissive stereotypes ("she's a dumb media wannabe"). But stories are provisional. Our interpretations are constantly challenged: by the returns themselves, by the differing interpretations of colleagues, by our own changing perceptions. Over time, the stories that emerge from the Probes are rich and multilayered, integrating routines with aspirations, appearances with deeper truths. They give us a feel for people, mingling observable facts with emotional reactions.

The Technology Probes deployed in the interLiving Project allowed for the ongoing capture of ethnographic style data (through logging) from within, while the same technology was appropriated and domesticated. The Informational Probes in the Digital Care project supported an ongoing engagement with individuals from description of the setting to design and evaluation for the setting and beyond, as we shall present below.

Another important aspect of these three different Probe varietals is that they engaged participants differently with different physical materials. Both the Cultural and Informational Probe packs comprised packs of carefully selected and/or designed *things* that were circulated in particular ways: postcards with questions concerning participants' lives; maps asking participants to highlight particular areas in their environment; cameras and photo albums with instructions asking participants to photograph particular things; dictaphones and; diaries of some kind. The "messageProbe" system deployed in the interLiving Project also had a physical component – a writeable LCD display that was placed in people's homes. This Technology Probe comprised a simple application that enabled participants to communicate using digital Post-It notes in a zoomable space. Despite the commonality of having a particular physical form these Probes varied in the kinds of participation and engagement they required. For instance, Gaver et al's (1999b) Cultural Probes asked participants to record a vivid dream upon waking using a dictaphone and when, where and in whose company participants used media in diaries while Crabtree et al's (2003) Informational Probes required residents to record a diary of their activities, ideas and thoughts using a dictaphone and daily activities using a personal diary. Hutchinson et al (2003)'s messageProbe system simply required participants to use and even innovate with it. Across these different Probes people participated in different ways – Cultural Probes required imaginative and playful participation while Informational Probes required more investigative participation. Technology Probes required participants, on the other hand, to react in some way to the disruption that the new, albeit simple, design required.

These Probes also directly engage with the process of design, despite there being some controversy concerning exactly how. Gaver et al (2004:56) note:

Sometimes the trajectory from Probes to designs is relatively straightforward, and design ideas can clearly be traced back to Probe returns...Most of the time the relationships between Probes and proposals are more complex and difficult to trace.

Yet Gaver and Dunne (1999) also describe in detail how the Cultural Probe returns were used in the Bijlmer project: to generate a set of loose design proposals and then to present these proposals back to the participants and their colleagues. Design concepts were integrated into a final proposal in this second stage. They also note how they used particular techniques to generate their design ideas: brainstorming; concept development; 'storybook' impressionistic images such as collages; and interactive simulations. These fed off the insights that the Probes provided. For instance, the Bijlmer residents' concerns regarding security were reflected in a design idea of a community radio device plugged into a power socket, helping older people become more aware of their neighbours. The coupling between the Informational Probe returns and the resulting designs seemed to more of a "straightforward" trajectory however. These Probes helped establish that care work at the setting could be endangered through poorly designed, unstable (although, perhaps, highly innovative) technology and processes, establishing a central requirement for dependability. More specifically the description of participants' major preoccupations with safety and security, managing medication and the coordination of activities resulted in the designs of a prototypical medication management application and an implemented messaging system, SPAM (see below). However, these designs were developed through using the Probe returns as resources supporting cooperative analysis and to focus and facilitate user workshops. Hutchinson et al's (2003:18) Technology Probes married data collection focused on use with support for design:

Technology probes are a particular type of probe that combine the social science goal of collecting information about the use and the users of technology in a real-world setting, the engineering goal of field-testing the technology, and the design goal of inspiring users and designers to think of new kinds of technologies to support their needs and desires.

Thus their "messageProbe" may have been an intuitive, learnable and minimally designed system embedded within the research setting that supported data collection concerning messaging practices but it was also "different enough from commonly available technologies" to "provoke families to consider how they do or don't fit into their lives" (Hutchinson et el. 2003). Thus insights on individuals' lives were closely coupled with insights about design.

There are also notable differences concerning how users of Probes deploy or regard the resulting data. Boehner et al's (2007) examination of the uptake of Probes within Human-Computer Interaction suggests that there is an unhealthy decoupling between method and methodology, the means of engaging users and any epistemological position:

Our reading of the use of probes points to a tension between, on the one hand, the appeal of the approach in finding a new way to engage with users around topics that traditional HCI methods have frequently left unexplored, and, on the other hand, a set of epistemological constraints that are implicit in the traditional HCI toolkit...The value of probes may eventually turn out to be less in the forms of inquiry and procedure that they open up, but in the fundamental epistemological commitments that they challenge and represent.

Thus, Boehner et al (ibid) argue for Probes exposing assumptions and commitments to particular approaches to design and knowledge production. Crabtree et al. (2009:884), on the other hand, critique particular uses and characterizations of Probes as over-emphasising the role of interpretation by 'cultural commentators':

...new approaches to ethnography muddle what ethnography is in design and what it does for design. Ironically, nowhere is the muddle more evident than in efforts to clarify how cultural probes work, most notably in the suggestion that

interpretation rather than facts are key to ethnography, participatory design and cultural probes alike...

Thus, Crabtree et al (ibid) voice concern over the characterization of ethnography as 'cultural interpretation' *by observers* against the hard-won generation of accounts of naturally occurring situated action *from the observed* when linking users with design.

The view presented here does not aim to be as complete or critical but instead aims to target commonly used Probe varietals and examine the evidence, the facts about them in some detail and consider their utility and 'fit' as a method for People-Oriented Programming on the basis that the tools of data collection should be 'fit for purpose'. This view progresses the argument presented in Graham et al. (2007) by moving beyond an exploration of how Probes work to the kinds of work that different Probes draw attention to and how these kinds of work relate to People-Oriented Programming. This treatment will, as with Boehner et al's (2007) review, briefly consider specific instances of how they have been taken up, adopted and adapted. It will also, like Crabtree et al (2009), critically consider Probes and the kinds of 'social facts' they uncover (or fail to uncover). In this treatment we wish to be fair to Probes and avoid the kind of entrenched bluster that impedes inquiry by considering the broader context in which Probes have been deployed.

TWO PROBE DEPLOYMENTS

In this section we consider the adapted, testing-oriented and design-oriented Technology Probes (Hutchinson et al., 2003) and more ethnographically oriented Informational Probes (Crabtree et al., 2003) through focusing on our own work at a community residential care setting: a charitable trust in a large town in the North of England. These Probes exhibit a distinct approach to methods, data and data's coupling with design and support a discussion of recent disagreement about methods in computing. They also permit us to explore the opportunities Probes present for People-Oriented Programming as a people-oriented method. We base our analysis on actually having got our hands dirty with Probes, offering a view based on "perceptions...personal experiences, and...hard-won analyses" (Glaser and Strauss, 1968:225) not a "ready-made" perspective (Bowers, 1991).

At the time of the study, the community health care setting we describe here was based at two sites and supported ex-psychiatric hospital patients suffering from a variety of conditions. One site was a converted house (or "residential hostel" – Cheverst et al., 2007) and was the larger facility with individual rooms and shared spaces for residents. It was staffed by shift staff around the clock. The other site comprised a series of flats: small, self-contained units that supported semi-independent living for 17 people with support from staff. The two sites were about one kilometre apart. Previous work (Crabtree et al., 2003) had focused on the residents but the participants in the Probe deployments we describe here comprised approximately ten full-time and part-time staff (carers and a manager) employed across the two sites at the time of the study. Staff's primary activity was the everyday care of residents across the two sites forming the organisation. This activity, as described below, involved other clusters of activities such as: visiting, spending time and interacting with residents; manual labour; and clerical duties (Graham et al., 2006). Staff tended to have work experience from unrelated fields and had a varying degree of experience with technology and computers. Staff education varied from high school education (Certificate of Secondary Education (CSE) qualifications in England) to university degrees. Approximately half the staff were female.

The nature of the setting meant that there were considerable constraints governing data collection. These included concerns over confidentiality and alarming the residents through the data collection process and the appearance of 'strangers' where they lived. With these concerns in mind, earlier work at this setting (e.g. Crabtree et al., 2003) led to the design and deployment of the SPAM (SMS Public Asynchronous Messaging) system, developed to support communication and coordination involving staff across the two facilities. The SPAM system (Figure 1) ran an SMS messaging application, allowing staff at the two sites to communicate easily by composing text messages using an on-screen keyboard displayed on a touch sensitive screen (Crabtree et al., 2003). Each SPAM unit contained a prepaid SIM card and corresponding telephone number and thus messages were sent between the two locations via the service provider's GSM network. Given this, the units could also receive messages from other sources (e.g. a mobile phone) although they were not widely used in this way. When a message sent from one unit was opened through the other unit an acknowledgment or 'receipt' was sent back to the originating unit confirming the message had been read. One SPAM unit was deployed at each office in October 2002 and since then the units had been used regularly.

SPAM use was assessed (see below) through being a Technology Probe. This assessment was followed up with a Design Workshop focusing on the design of a public display at the setting and then by Informational Probes focusing on the use and exchange of photographs and messages (see below). Thus the deployments we describe here were part of an extended process of engagement with a 'sensitive setting' (Crabtree et al., 2003) through which people-oriented technologies were suggested proposed, designed, deployed and evaluated. Both deployments were instances of 'small data' in that their scope was limited, centred on on particular

Figure 1. SPAM display 'on location' at the setting[2]

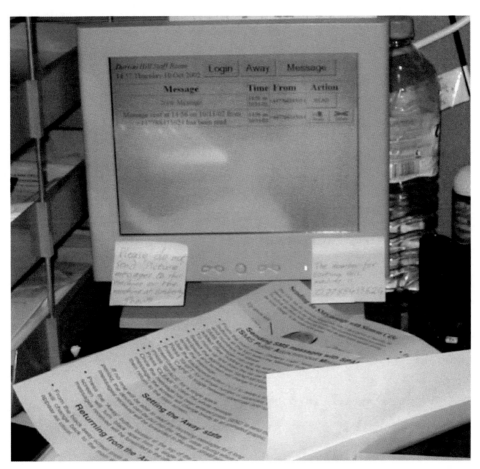

aspects of people's lives and not readily viewed or analysed using visualisation tools (although in the case of the Technology Probe these views were constructed). Instead of supporting inferences based on extensive data they made individual people's lives accountable through limited, if specific and rich views (Graham et al, 2007:34). Yet the two deployments differed in that the Technology Probe data resembled, and could even be considered a precursor to, the kinds of big data that are readily generated and inferred from today.

SPAM as a Technology Probe

The SPAM system itself comprised logging functionality (see Figure 2) within to enable us to monitor its use in the form of locally stored text files. Although

Figure 2. Parsed text log from SPAM[4]

```
Attempting to Send: can you repy to this to: 07766333000 (BB)
--
ACK received at 13:01:30 on 04/01/06
--
Attempting to Send: please contact house to: 07766333000 (BB)
--
ACK received at 16:36:42 on 04/01/07
--
Attempting to Send: all man u fans aresuckers to: 07766333000 (BB)
--
ACK received at 17:33:46 on 04/01/07
--
Attempting to Send: liverpool 10  chealse 0 to: 07766333000 (BB)
--
ACK received at 17:59:33 on 04/01/07
--
sender: +447766333000 (BB)
date: 04/01/07
time: 18:11:25
message: check your spelling
--
ACK sent at 18:11 on 07/02/04 to: +447766333000 (BB)
--
Attempting to Send: i have the wireless on, would u like the scores as they come in? to: 07766333000 (BB)
--
ACK received at 20:21:39 on 04/01/07
--
sender: +447766333000 (BB)
date: 04/01/07
time: 20:22:37
message: we have got sky on
--
Attempting to Send: liv 0 chel o to: 07766333000 (BB)
--
ACK received at 20:23:28 on 04/01/07
--
ACK sent at 20:22 on 07/02/04 to: +447766333000 (BB)
--
Attempting to Send: mu  1  bol  0 to: 07766333000 (BB)
--
ACK received at 20:26:34 on 04/01/07
--
Attempting to Send: liv 1  ch 0   cheriou to: 07766333000 (BB)
```

it is not always apparent what should be captured in such logs from the outset, given previous work on analyzing text messages and messaging (e.g. Grinter and Eldridge, 2003), it seemed important to capture the content of the message and information on the source and timing in order to obtain a view on 'threads' of communication through SPAM. Although the logs initially also captured system state information (e.g. debug output from communication with the GSM terminal) not all this information was required to support the examination of dialogue between the SPAM units (and therefore setting sites). Thus, Dan Fitton, who built SPAM, wrote parsing programs, stripping out information irrelevant to the understanding of these threads of communication and dialogues. These programs outputted the telephone number of the sender, the date and the time of receipt and information concerning whether a 'receipt' for the message had been sent or not (Figure 2)[3]. Crabtree et al., (2006) discuss the problems with working with such text logs in more detail.

Some of our analysis of this Technology Probe data is presented below (see also Cheverst et al., 2007). Specifically, we report on 164 messages sent between 6th February 2004 and 23rd March 2004. We used techniques drawn from Grounded Theory (Glaser & Strauss, 1968) in this analysis to evolve a series of categories descriptive of the messages in the SPAM logs. Using a spreadsheet to support our work (see Figure 3)[4], we coded 142 messages with a primary (most relevant) category and 58 messages with a secondary category-sub-category pairing if relevant – a total of 200 applications of category-sub-category pairings. For example, we coded the message "*we have got sky on*"[5] (message 7, Figure 3) with a *primary category*-**sub-category** pairing of *Social Interaction*-**sharing info & resources** and a *secondary category*-**sub-category** pairing of *Managing Distribution*-**resource sharing**. We did not code 22 messages – 13 were incomprehensible (e.g. "*waht o erslut si ahtt lufl mite*"), six were duplicate messages (i.e. the same message produced twice in the logs for an unknown reason), and three were initial messages testing the system (e.g. "*Test message from BB-spam is now working!*").

The data produced by the Probe initially appeared nonsensical but through the analysis, which was supported by visits to the setting, interviews (Graham et al., 2006) and a review of relevant literature, a series of super-categories (e.g. "COMMUNICATION AND COORDINATION), categories (e.g. "*Managing distribution*") and sub-categories (e.g. "**Resource sharing**") emerged, relating to the use of SPAM to facilitate ongoing work and communication and how interactions through SPAM related to the core activities operating across the sites. Figure 4 shows a snapshot of the frequency of different categories and sub-categories and the perceived relationship among them – indicated through double-ended arrows, dotted boxes for primary vertical groupings and grey polygons for secondary horizontal groupings. We describe the categories and sub-categories in more detail beneath the figure.

Figure 3. Spreadsheet supporting the grounded analysis of the SPAM text logs

No	Day/Date	From	To	Message	Analysis: Primary Category	Analysis: Secondary Category
1	Fri 06/02	DH	BB	can you repy to this	Outeraction - ongoing interaction	
2	Sat 07/02	DH	BB	please contact house	Outeraction - ongoing interaction	
3	Sat 07/02	DH	BB	all man u fans aresuckers	Social interaction - playful abuse & sarcasm	
4	Sat 07/02	DH	BB	liverpool 10 chealse 0	Social interaction - humour	
5	Sat 07/02	DH	BB	check your spelling	Social interaction - playful abuse & sarcasm	
6	Sat 07/02	DH	BB	i have the wireless on, would u like the scores as they come in?	Social interaction - sharing info & resourc	Managing distribution - resource sharing
7	Sat 07/02	BB	DH	we have got sky on	Social interaction - sharing info & resourc	Managing distribution - resource sharing
8	?	DH	BB	liv 0 chel o	Social interaction - sharing info & resourc	Managing distribution - info exchange
9	Sat 07/02	DH	BB	mu 1 bol 0	Social interaction - sharing info & resourc	Managing distribution - info exchange
10	Sat 07/02	DH	BB	liv 1 ch 0 cheriou	Social interaction - humour	Managing distribution - info exchange
11	Sat 07/02	DH	BB	ars 1 leeds0	Social interaction - sharing info & resourc	Managing distribution - info exchange
12	Sat 07/02	BB	DH	excellent you spelled it rignt	Social interaction - playful abuse & sarcasm	
13	Sat 07/02	DH	BB	mu 2 bol 2 cheeky	Social interaction - humour	Managing distribution - info exchange

Figure 4. SPAM use categories developed through the log analysis

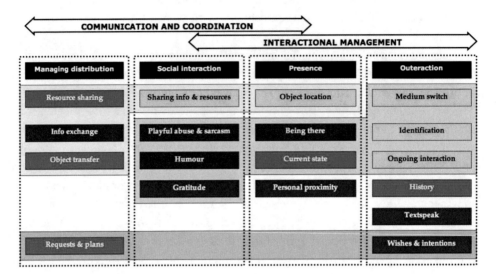

Managing Distribution

This category describes interactions that occurred specifically because the care work occurred across two sites. Some interactions described by this category were indicative of care workers' movement between the two sites e.g. when a request was made for something to be done at the site being moved to e.g. putting on the kettle.

Resource sharing describes interactions that involved sharing of a remote resource, such as offering to share a resource such as a diary or a computer with others. **Info exchange** describes work-related interactions that involve the exchange of information, including specific queries and news, schedules running at the different sites and urgent situations. **Object transfer** is closely related to **Resource sharing** above and describes requesting the transfer of particular objects (e.g. *"please can u send the overtime sheet for feb"*) or to inform others about the transfer of objects. **Requests & plans** describes asking others to do some work or making arrangements of some kind: both emerged from the need to coordinate. These interactions often involved explicit requests or creating contingency plans while moving or asking others to make arrangements e.g. *"could you put diary for someone on sunday early to take <a resident> to st pauls 10.30 please df"*.

Social Interaction

Social interaction describes non-work related communication, or communication that obliquely supported work. Although the exchange of football scores may support social cohesion in the workplace, the mapping of these communications onto 'core' care work at the setting is not direct.

The **Sharing info & resources** sub-category described messages sharing information (such as football scores – *"newcastle 1 man u o chelsea 4 leicster 0"*) or a source of information or alternative medium (e.g. radio and television) and messages requesting non-work related information. **Playful abuse & sarcasm** describes messages making fun of past interactions via SPAM (e.g. *"are u drunk orjust silly"*) or individuals (e.g. *"<name of person> smells of pee"*). The **Humour** sub-category describes messages that had a limited work function, but were very important function in maintaining optimism and cohesion. These varied from exchange of fallacious football scores to jokes about others to plain old jokes. The **Gratitude** category describes messages indicating gratitude to another party. Such messages indicated the end of a block of interaction.

Presence

The presence sub-category describes messages communicating information about availability, state or proximity of self, others or objects.

The **Object location** sub-category relates to the *Managing distribution-***Object transfer** category-sub-category pairing. This describes messages communicating the location of particular objects or things. Thus, these messages were less focused on sharing and more on locating. These interactions were brief, consisting of a question and answer, or simply a question or statement. **Being there** describes messages to people either indicating their own presence, asking about others' presence (e.g. *"is there any body out there"*) or indicating awareness of others (e.g. *"Do you realise that all these messages are looked at Lancaster university"* *"ooh im scared"*). This sub-category reflected the physical self being tied to a particular location or other people's physical selves in association with a particular location or an awareness of an audience for the messages. The **Current State** sub-category described messages asking about others' condition (e.g. *"helo to you too! hws life down there in the wulderness???"*) or communicating concerning their own state (e.g. *"we are 2 busy to play with the spam"*). Implicit in this communication was a query concerning their own and others' availability for further communication (see *Outeraction* below). A series of interactions occurred due to interactants having **Personal proximity** to a location. This proximity was stated in temporal terms (e.g. *"If i am not thdre by 9 30 you might have to ring a taxi..."*). Thus, in this example, due going to a site, an interactant makes a request.

Outeraction

Outeraction is taken from Nardi et al (2000): it describes interaction about interaction or the process of how interaction is managed using communication. This could involve "negotiating conversational ability" (ibid:82-4), "establishing social connection" (ibid:82) and needing to "preserve a sense of conversational context" (ibid) and "manage the communication situation as it unfolds" (ibid).

The **Medium switch** sub-category described instances when SPAM supported switching to a different medium of communication, often the telephone (e.g. "*pp can you ring when not busy*"), but on one occasion the fax machine. Email was referred to once, but not with regard to switching communication medium. Much of the time the medium switching involved only two parties and involved a direct request regarding a switch from SPAM to telephone. However, in some cases others were involved: in one case SPAM was used to note that someone else had called or that s/he should be contacted. The **Identification** sub-category describes the identification of an individual or individuals. Identification was important to sustain ongoing interaction. Sometimes, in order to contextualize past interactions, it was also important to identify a particular person e.g. "*that's me*". Most interactions did not include any identification of individuals. This may have been due to staff knowing who was on duty at a particular location or them being familiar with communication styles. **Ongoing interaction** describes when SPAM was used to maintain communication that may or may not involve using SPAM. This includes efforts to maintain communication using SPAM itself, particularly after there were communication breakdowns of some kind or to initiate communication using other media, particularly the telephone e.g. "*<name of person> WILL CALL YOU BACK IN ONE HOUR. YOUR PHONE IS CONSTANTLY ENGAGED*". This theme is often clustered with **Medium Switch** – SPAM was often used when other mediums were unavailable. **History** describes messages referring to past interactions often to sustain and manage a phase of communication. Thus interactants would refer to information already passed on or to features of past communication. **Textspeak** describes messages about messages that involved the use of commonly used texting abbreviations or 'textspeak'. This happened only once: most interactants seemed comfortable with texting abbreviations (such as "u" for "you") although there were 31 individual uses of "you" against 14 of the abbreviation "u" in the logs. The **Wishes & intentions** sub-category describes wishes and intentions of interactants with regard to communication e.g. "*will ring asap*".

Overall Comment

The SPAM logs also supported numerical analysis, particularly of the frequency of particular categories and sub-categories (Figure 5). This showed that *Social Interaction* was the most frequently occurring category. *Social Interaction* type messages describe over 40% (42.3%) of all SPAM messages. *Presence* and *Outeraction* described just over a fifth each of all messages (21.8% and 23.2% respectively) while *Managing Distribution* described 12.7%. These figures consider primary categories only. The most frequently applied single *category*-**sub-category** pairing (when considering primary *and* secondary categories) was *Managing distribution*-**Info exchange**, followed by *Social Interaction*-**Humour** and *Social Interaction*-**Sharing info.** Sixty percent of **Info exchange** messages were as a secondary sub-category, not as a primary sub-category so, although there was an element of information exchange in many interactions, it is not solely descriptive of many messages. The three sub-categories of the *Social Interaction* category, **Humour**, **Sharing info** and **Playful abuse** accounted for 30% of all primary and secondary category-sub-category pairings applied. The importance of these sub-categories is reinforced by the finding that SPAM was not used a great deal for planning or scheduling or even to communicate about planning or scheduling. The **Requests & plans** sub-category of *Managing distribution* only described 4.5% of all messages.

Figure 5 presents a different view on the messages sent/received between the two sites during the period of the log analysis by day of the week. It presents a raw view of the messages sent/received between the two sites during the period of the log analysis. This is an approximate view of the timing of all the messages as it was very hard to determine what week some messages belonged to and on what day they were sent. This figure shows most messages were sent during the first, second

Figure 5. Frequency of SPAM's primary categories (left) and temporal analysis of SPAM messages over the 7 weeks of the log analysis (right)

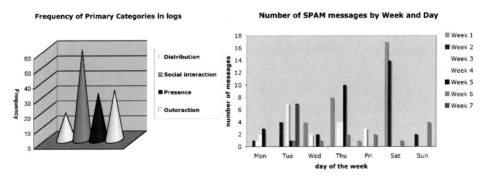

and fifth weeks. It also shows that, in general, most messages were sent/received on Saturdays and Thursdays, two days when soccer matches are played in England.

As Technology Probes automatically capture data about use they therefore simply require participants to use the technology. In this case this capture and 'monitoring' was used to support description and evaluation, redesign and the generation of new designs. SPAM firstly provided insights into the fabric of local culture – what people exchanged messages about as well as the work and events at the setting. The logs examined before this analysis resulted in two specific modifications to SPAM: blocking functionality (to prevent the sending of inappropriate texts) and a smaller font for messages (to prevent easy reading of messages by residents). As Hutchinson et al (2003) suggest such deployments can support envisaging new technologies. In this case SPAM's deployment led to a more general interest in the design and deployment of situated displays (Taylor et al, 2007; Taylor et al., 2009). This 'bridge into design' (Hughes et al., 1993) is described in more detail below.

Informational Probes

Following the deployment of the SPAM system we became interested in the possibilities of designing a situated display for use in the setting and so wanted to know more about current practice. Our Probe pack considered the "information work" (Strauss et al., 1985:251) of the staff focusing on communication and use of visual material among staff members and residents. We were interested in finding out about the particular detail of how staff exchanged messages and how they used pictures and photos as part of their everyday work: we wanted them to describe their current practice through the probe packs. Elements of this probe pack were diary-like in character (cf. Brown et al., 2000; Palen & Saltzman, 2002) – the booklet was designed as a journal and all the materials included supported the construction of a detailed picture describing the role of messages, photographs and pictures in participants' everyday working lives by the participants themselves for the participants themselves. The Probe pack comprised: a structured journal booklet; a Polaroid camera; a disposable camera; PostIt notes, glue and pens. The booklet was divided into three parts (a Photo Diary, a Message Book and an Ideas Book). The Probe pack comprised: a structured journal booklet; a Polaroid camera; a disposable camera; PostIt notes, glue and pens. The booklet was divided into three parts (a Photo Diary, a Message Book and an Ideas Book). We focus on the Photo Diary returns of one participant, Sam, as our main aim here is to exemplify the kinds of insights Informational Probes can provide. After we collected and reviewed the probe packs we interviewed Sam, using the probe pack as a prompt. Figures 6 – 8 show the photographs and hand-written captions in this probe return.

Figure 6. Probe entries grouped under Notices on walls and Pictures on walls

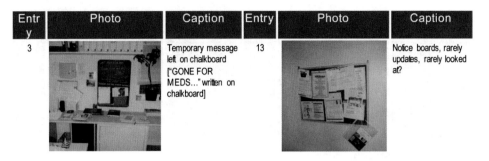

Notices on walls type entries (Figure 6) depicted the main noticeboard for staff (Entry 13). Sam also wrote "Whiteboard listing name of residents in each flat/ bedsit, their GP's name and their consultant name" in Entry 5. These entries show that staff used a chalkboard and whiteboard to make the location of particular staff (Entry 3) and particular resident information visible for the staff working there. Sam, when interviewed, noted how the chalkboard in the office (Entry 3) was useful for indicating where each staff member was (e.g. "I'm in flat...") and where particular important objects were (e.g. "the medication is on the..."). He also described how staff stuck PostIt notes to the chalkboard and that he might place PostIts on the office computer, on the desk and or hand them over in person at handover and/or pass the message on verbally. He described how "the system works quite well" and noted that sometimes information from the previous day was passed on this way. Sam also noted that PostIt notes were used for "short-term" purposes as opposed to daily reports that were used for more "long-term" purposes.

Sam's Entry 13 promoted some discussion about notices and communication: Sam noted how he would go around to tell people about public events and sometimes would put fliers through people's doors. He described how some residents would rarely visit the office and that they would "live their own lives". Sam also described how a list of telephone numbers would be useful – so he just needed to glance up to get information. He also described how staff stuck photos on the wall of the office. He noted that one edited photo, depicting some staff as "the four witches", had been stuck to the wall of the office as part of the "fun and banter" there.

As shown in Figure 7 entries grouped under *Visible artefacts* depicted notes on paper (Entry 1), a medication file (Entry 4), staff drawers for passing information on (Entry 5), a phone number book (Entry 6), a Diary and Communication Book (Entry 7). The Communication book from the Flats was "...taken to the Hostel every night in case staff need to pass on information to the Flats' day staff" (Entry 7). Other visible artefacts included SPAM (Entry 10), CCTV for monitoring the setting (Entry 11) and an Intercom (Entry 14). Thus the visible artefacts from

Figure 7. Probe entries grouped under Visible artefacts

Entry	Photo	Caption	Entry	Photo	Caption
1		Notes written on paper used to pass information from telephone conversations onto other staff	4		Medication file. Signed when medication is secondary dispensed to residents when do not self medicate
5		Each member of staff at the project has a pigeon hole where information is left so they will receive it	6	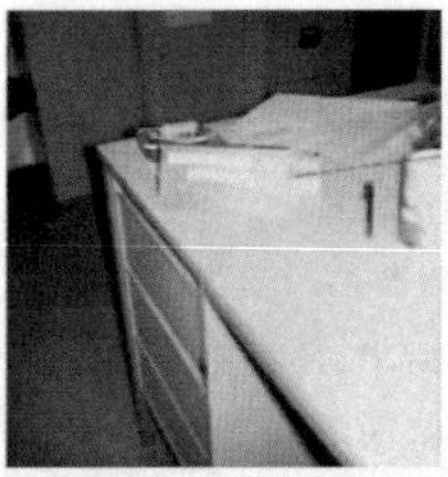	Phone numbers kept in this book for quick reference. Book always kept in top drawer of desk
7		Large desk diary...used everyday each day entry ticked when completed...infor mation written in here to pass on messages etc.	10		Spam, Spam, Spam, Spam, Spam, Spam, Spam, Spam everybody loves Spam
11		CCTV monitor staff noticed an unsavoury character visiting a resident	14		Intercom from main door, each bedsit also has intercom to front door.

the probe returns mainly assisted with the communication of information and the monitoring of residents. ***Invisible artefacts***, on the other hand, described pictures of things that were generally kept hidden away in cupboards and cabinets such as hard copies of client files.

In the interview about his Probe returns Sam described, when referring to his Entry 1 (Figure 7), how information was passed among people "all the time" and how information was "flying backwards and forwards". Sam then described how medication was "all confidential" and information about this was not kept on the

Figure 8. Probe entries grouped under People portraits and People working

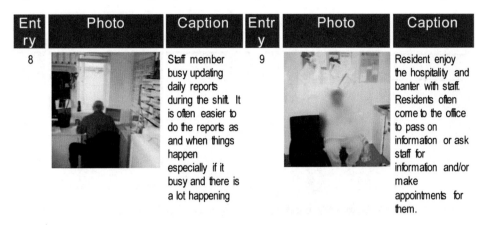

Entry	Photo	Caption	Entry	Photo	Caption
8		Staff member busy updating daily reports during the shift. It is often easier to do the reports as and when things happen especially if it busy and there is a lot happening	9		Resident enjoy the hospitality and banter with staff. Residents often come to the office to pass on information or ask staff for information and/or make appointments for them.

walls. He also described how notes about residents were confidential and how only initials were used to represent residents. When referring to Entry 6 (Figure 7) Sam noted how staff used the telephone to contact "the pharmacy" and make certain appointments for residents at the setting. Having ready access to these telephone numbers was important. When discussing Entry 11, Sam described how the CCTV was being used to monitor who was visiting the residents. He gave the example of one person who had tried to sleep on a resident's couch. This could be a problem as this person could exploit the resident.

People portraits and *People working* included photos of staff and residents (Figure 8). When discussing *People portraits* Sam noted that staff liked to talk about the staff rota – they asked who was on. He also described how the residents have "favourites" and this affected whether they come to the office or not (as in the above photo).

Workplace views, where the ecology of the setting was depicted, also included *People working* on two occasions. Sam's photo depicting the Flats' office attracted the following entry: "THE NERVE CENTRE!!!" (Figure 9). During the interview Sam noted how a member of staff's shopping was included in Figure 9. He also described how the office environment had lots of paper, describing how the amount of stuff on paper and PostIt notes was "unreal". He noted again that PostIt notes were used a lot, mainly for messages and how it was "a handy thing to do" as a pen and PostIt noted were "easy and accessible" and that information on PostIt notes was sometimes transferred to daily reports, depending on how important it was. Sam also noted that he stuck these notes on the office computer or on the desk. Staff passed these notes on physically when handing over information or communicated the information verbally.

Figure 9. Sam's 15th Entry – "THE NERVE CENTRE"

PACK SECTION 1: Photo Diary

DAY 6:

THE NERVE CENTRE ! ! !

DISCUSSION

We deployed both these Probe deployments in a sensitive setting as part of research that required successfully negotiating a series of complex design, as well as social and ethical, issues. Firstly, they supported our initial access to and acceptance in the setting. Secondly, they supported data collection over an extended period – in the case of the Technology Probes over years – that would have been hard to secure otherwise. They also enabled us to gain particular, situated views on the setting – both sets of Probes told a story about "information work" (Strauss et al., 1985:251-60) and "information flows" (Sheller & Urry, 2006:1), drawing attention to the particular ecology and important objects. They both also produced insights into work such as "sentimental work" (e.g. showing interest, building trust, reassuring – Strauss et al. (1985:129-39)), "comfort work" (Strauss, 1985: 99-128) and, as noted by others at different settings (e.g. Bardram and Bossen, 2005), "articulation work" (Strauss, 1985) or the aligning of different streams of work. Both Probes engaged participants and started a dialogue with them about design. The Technology Probes supported an ongoing dialogue that focused on evaluating SPAM: before the analysis reported on here the design of the original SPAM system had changed, as already noted. A number blocking function had been added after misuse of SPAM and a smaller font implemented on the display to support the reading of confidential messages by staff only. These design features marked a move to a more restricted user population for SPAM for very good reasons concerning the care and well-being of residents. The analysis of both Probes' 'returns' also supported a dialogue about the design of a public display at the setting both during a subsequent design workshop and beyond. This is where the differences between Technology and Informational Probes start to become clear. What these different Probes suggested that any such display should respond to at the setting was different.

One of the surprising outcomes of the analysis of the Technology Probe data, given the nature of the work at the setting, was the extent to which SPAM seemed to have a social affordance that facilitated "lightweight" interaction (Whittaker et al., 1994). The exchange of football scores (***Social interaction*-Sharing info & resources**) was not directly work-related and reflected the dislocation between two sites: these interactions seemed an attempt to narrow the one kilometre gap. These findings resonate with Nardi et al.'s (2000:82, 84) work on the expressive nature of Instant Messaging and the notion of "communication zones" for intermittent conversations and Perry et al's (2001:341) finding that mobile phones were used to maintain informal awareness of the social aspects of the workplace: "Such phone calls also had an element of social banter that helped to maintain the social connection at work while callers were away from the office…". Again, in line with Nardi et al's (2000) work, people also used SPAM to support *"quick questions and clarifications"* (Nardi et al., 2000:81) through the messages grouped under ***Managing Distribution*-Info Exchange** and to support plans formulated on-the-fly. SPAM afforded particular forms of interaction and given that it was embedded in an ecosystem of technologies that the staff inhabited. Thus, the SPAM logs also gave some indication of the different technologies that the staff moved from and to. For instance, the message *"pp can you ring when not busy"* suggests moving from using SPAM to using the telephone and suggests particular affordances of each technology.

Abstract, numerical views on the categories of data (e.g. Figure 8) also produced supported an indication of the temporal rhythms (Zerubavel, 1985) at the setting – that, for example, people sent a lot of messages on a Saturday. Examining the messages on the Saturday of the first week the day with the most messages sent/ received over the whole 7-week period analysed shows that 14 of the 17 messages concerned Social Interaction. In addition, of these eight were either **Playful abuse & sarcasm** or **Humour** with the other six being **Sharing info & resources**. Thus this 'view' was surprisingly *personal* and *individual*, despite the generic, abstract statistics and visuals generated and given the SPAM displays were so public to particular audiences. This was because the capture mechanism, SPAM, despite its simplicity, supported capturing individual text messages and even text exchanges. Very importantly, SPAM was also appropriated by the staff at the setting through being gradually embedded into the workplace and carefully evaluated. In addition, the analytical work that produced descriptive abstractions describing what people used SPAM for (e.g. Figure 4) actually supported narrowing in on the personal, dialogic nature of this work.

The Informational Probe showed how work, particularly "information work" (Strauss et al., 1985:251), was orchestrated through the particularities of the locality of a place (e.g. the position of a chalkboard, the conventions regarding use of abbreviations), the particular mobilities of objects (e.g. PostIt notes), the physicality of people (e.g. the location of staff) and how work is achieved through particular media with particular affordances and expressiveness. It also indicated the importance of considering the visibility and availability of these same objects to particular people within the context of the social world (Strauss, 1978) in which they operate. That there are "information flows" (Sheller and Urry, 2006:1) at the setting through the mobility of objects (e.g. PostIt notes) became evident through the interview with Sam in particular. Sam writing "THE NERVE CENTRE" and taking a photo of the office at the Flats (Figure 9) reflected how important he regarded this area as a nexus for message exchange and, more generally, the importance of a particular place configured in a particular way. However, despite this focus on information, a central background concern was residents' care and ongoing relationships with them (Figure 8, Entry 9). This Probe also revealed the importance of the everyday banter in the workplace and of very ordinary routines, such as going shopping and visits. Thus, these Probes exposed material and visual aspects of the workplace *from the participant's point of view for a particular audience*. Thus these Probes also exposed the boundaries between different social worlds, boundaries that were important to maintain appropriately.

What is evident from the brief discussion of the findings above is that although both Probes deployed particular 'kit', the composition and use of that kit varied and this was important for the stories that they told. These 'stories' generated insights into the kinds of expertise that people at the setting deployed both through specific technologies like SPAM, the telephone and paper files and through moving among and across them. New, even if minimal and potentially throw-it-away, digital artifacts were embedded in the setting via the Technology Probe and therefore impacted work practices on a more direct and ongoing basis. This Probe converged data capture with technical experimentation: it was not packed with functionality and highly determined but was open-ended and ambiguous enough to inspire new uses among participants (e.g. telling jokes) and new design concepts among designers (e.g. a public display as described below). In this way it supported participants expressing their individual personhood e.g. through telling jokes. In contrast, the 'analogue' Probes were only deployed for a matter of weeks and, although they supported reflection on work, they were not an integral part of the setting where the work occurred. These Probes concentrated on data capture, although they certainly impacted the awareness of particular work practices, causing Sam to comment on how information was "flying backwards and forwards" at the setting. Thus the Informational Probes primarily enabled the care workers to describe their current practice in an analytical, if reflexive manner through which the relational aspects of their work, such as interacting with specific residents, became visible. There was a strong sense they were designed for this particular use even if that use was supportive of design. Put in other terms, the Technology Probes required a reactive and adaptive participation while the Informational Probes encouraged investigative and reflective participation (Graham and Rouncefield, 2008). Both forms of participation made available description about people, data that acted as a resource for design. The former automated the generation accounts of interaction in which individuals became visible, if anonymous. Through the latter the individual person's sense of self and relations to others became available. The resultant data was, in the case of the Technology Probe, temporal and thematic while, for the Informational Probe, data was more spatial and episodic.

However, we are the first to acknowledge that this 'resource for design' notion is a vague one and, as already noted, one that has provoked all sorts of debate in HCI and CSCW about how to interpret Probes or if they should be interpreted at all. One characterization of the disagreement has been in terms of Probes providing "comprehensive information" against "inspirational responses" (Gaver et al., 2004:53). Boehner et al. (2007:1081) characterize this debate:

Whereas the original cultural probes created a funnel that started from the narrow end with very specific stories and fragments and moved toward a broad set of interpretations and resulting design space to explore, probes for information tend to reverse the funnel and move from a broad collection of data to a small, well-defined set of requirements, themes, or insights which then are used to inform design.

In Gaver et al.'s (2004:56) terms, the suggestion here is that the path from Probes to design can be "straightforward" or "more complex and difficult" deploying "a combination of conceptual interests, technological possibilities, imaginary scenarios and ideas for how to implement them" (ibid). Crabtree et al (2009:885) suggest however that there is some "muddle" in this argument and instead emphasise the role of fieldwork in explicating users to designers:

Ethnographic studies of work have been employed to 'bridge' between users and designers...enabling the designer to understand what people do in a setting and how they organize their activities...In other words, ethnographic studies of work bridge between users and design by explicating the interpretive framework of users in methodical detail.

In the case of deployments described here the Technology Probe data was used directly in a Design Workshop to assist with participants remembering situations of past technology use. This interdisciplinary workshop involving staff at the setting and people with a design interest from Lancaster University, including both authors, happened after an initial examination of the Technology Probes and before the Informational Probe data had been collected. At the workshop one group seeded the design of a large, flat touchscreen placed in a communal area. Both the Technology Probe and Informational Probe data then informed the development of this design idea by us. For example, the importance of social interaction between staff garnered via the Technology Probes suggested the need for an area supporting the posting of messages and digital photographs. The Informational Probe data emphasized the importance of making staff rota information available and visible for residents and other staff alike via the display reacting to staff changeover for example through updating the digital photographs of staff on duty. We then developed this idea through a simple design sketch (see Graham et al., 2006). This progression was less about 'broad' and 'narrow' design spaces than about responding to the key staff and resident concerns at what was a "sensitive setting" (Crabtree et al., 2003). In this process, we were less concerned with engaging "users" i.e. users of technology than people with individual identities and awareness of themselves and their work practice.

As this setting was sensitive, ethical issues were particularly important. These concerns regarded appropriate access to the setting, the confidentiality and use of the data collected and the impact and dependability of any new technologies introduced. These concerns were addressed through carefully negotiating access, de-identifying Probe logs and photographs and carefully co-realising and evaluating proposed new technologies. Yet different kinds of Probes afford different kinds and awareness of disclosure. The conscious disclosure afforded through the deliberate capture via photographs in Informational Probes contrasted with the automatic capture of Technology Probes, even though this 'capture' was directed at particular things such as SPAM message content and time of sending. Yet, examining particular Probe data illustrates a perhaps surprising lack of concern over these issues in the case of the Technology Probe – consider the *"ooh im scared"* message. This is not to suggest that soliciting appropriate consent and managing participant awareness of data collection, as had been done in the case of SPAM, is not important but instead to suggest that as a technology is embedded in a setting over time and trust accumulates, concerns over inappropriate surveillance diminish. In the example provided, the Manager at the setting, with whom one of the authors regularly discussed the research, managed this awareness among staff. We can also argue this kind of data has greater value because it is less constructed and assembled for the particular public or 'observer' than the case of the Informational Probe described. Thus, the kind of shaping for a particular audience by a particular participant that the Informational Probe returns described here afforded, differs starkly from the automatic, even if carefully considered, negotiated, designed and configured, logging mechanisms deployed through Technology Probes. Such issues emphasise the importance of considering, discussing and exploring the composition and access of individual populations for Probes.

We suggest that both deployments described above point to the particular strengths of Probes as a people-oriented method. Both were part of a process of engagement with a real and 'sensitive' setting for the purposes of design. Both Probes converged actual work for participants and a process of discovery for us, a process that helped us engage with participants meaningfully without disrupting their 'safety critical' work and as importantly, not irritating them. We have shown how interactions at the setting, through Technology Probe data in particular, extend beyond traditional notions of work to include lightweight interactions, awareness of others, comfort work, reflexive interactions and even interactions about interactions and jokes. These various kinds of work through 'conversational' exchanges would have been hard to capture otherwise in this particular setting. Beyond this, as shown by the Informational Probes, through Probes we can acknowledge "the user" not only as a content producer but also as a diarist, photographer, cultural commentator etc. in a material place and, as a person who exhibits their identity and self through physical and digital spaces. Through presenting actual visual data from an Informational Probe return, we have shown the value of allowing a participant to engage in these roles, 'walking through' their everyday working life, capturing and organising the kinds of 'stuff' and constellations of material things that are important to them. This account is not only populated by materials, but also by key relationships between people, 'work' and these materials. This engagement of the visual also extends to how we can present Technology Probe data in terms of the frequency and temporal rhythms of certain kinds of messages. We have shown that these views are not only beneficial for the observers. The kinds of insights such as Sam's realization concerning the amount of information work and the movement of objects and communication at the setting can be valuable for participants too. Overall, the discussion has supported the argument that Probes have common features (Graham et al., 2007) – the deployment of particular capture mechanisms, generation of accounts of individual's lives through making particular things visible and the ability to start a dialogue between observers and participants.

CONCLUSION

In my world, where we strive to understand not just how and when people use technologies, but also why, an ethnographic perspective on multi-faceted data is the path forward to bringing not just good products and services, but valued and valuable ones. (Churchill, 2017)

Pursuing any ethnographic approach in a range of (largely domestic) settings inevitably raises both practical (logistical) and important ethical challenges. Cultural probes offer a relatively unobtrusive, perhaps harmless, way of providing some insight into exactly how technology could fit (and why it sometimes does not fit) into any particular setting. The point we have made in this chapter is that two different kinds of Probes, as part of an ethnographically informed approach to research and design, are a people-oriented method that can help us understand people's lives in the broadest sense. They both focus on and help us understand the ways in which everyday or mundane activities are achieved and how discrete expertises are expressed. Probes can describe or explicate the various forms and features of everyday 'work' in people's lives, including work involving the orchestration and organization of different technologies with different (social) affordances.

We wanted to peer outside the microcosm of the disciplines in which Probes have been utilised and consider both the shifts in methods that Probes are indicative of and the more general insights they can provide for the three main elements of People-Oriented Programming, focusing on the person in two main ways: "as the central focus of a customised software system addressing heterogeneous needs"; "as a self-ethnographer...gather[ing] their own very-specific data (including in the domestic space)". We have argued this move is particularly important in a time of "the fetishization of large data sets of aggregated information about consumers" (McAfee et al., 2012, cited in Kerrigan and Hart, 2016). The discussion above has continually highlighted the value of recognizing and exploiting the material form of Probes, that Probes are made up of various material 'stuff': to engage participants in responding to new technologies and systems and in reporting their lives to us; to garner personal, naturalistic and generally reflective accounts of individuals' lives as they happen and; to exploit the visual through various views on textual interactions and photography. The Technology Probe data in particular has shown that 'probing' involving automatically collected datasets of different scales and specificity can happen in parallel with people's domestication of a technology and illustrated how we might gain detailed views on interactions at a setting and reason about them while maintaining confidentiality, respecting participants' privacy rights and being minimally disruptive.

The literature we have reviewed, in particular the description of the various "x-probes", their similarities and differences, and the particular deployments of Probes has also shown that in general Probes, like the particular Technology Probes described here, have also been 'domesticated' (Silverstone et al., 1992) in particular ways by particular research communities and individuals within those communities. Probes are pliable enough to fit to the purpose and emphasis of different communities while keeping at the minimum some attention on those being designed for, and ideally enlisting participants into the design enterprise as 'co-designers' in the widest sense of the word. But they are not simple or easy, they are 'messy', they encourage what Law (2004) would call 'mess' in social research that parallels the 'mess' in people's lives; they require working out by participants and ethnographers, designers etc. alike and, at least in how they have been appropriated, often are distanced from the epistemology they were originally grounded in. This 'working out' whilst in the midst of doing research is part of a process of organizing and deciding what is important about a setting. Yet there is a commonly understood (if somewhat general) notion of what they are. These features, far from undermining them as an approach, position them ideally for interdisciplinary work and a post-methodology era. These features also make them amenable as a method for this community of people: People-Oriented Programming.

As a point of comparison, more recently, the ATHENE project developed a version of the Cultural Probe, named the 'Home and Life Scrapbook' asking participants to report on seven activities to help capture detailed information on their physical, emotional, social and environmental factors related to health and independence at home (Wherton et al. 2012). The research suggested that providing care at home through the use of various forms of assistive technology was not a simple matter of providing the technology but required a subtle understanding of the complex and diverse living experiences and care needs of *individual* older people. It was this subtle understanding that the Probes attempted to uncover and unpack, based on the belief that if the needs of older people are to be met, then technology suppliers, as well as health and social care providers must devote more resources to understanding and supporting individual older people's impairments and 'ageing in place' as it is mundanely achieved in the course of everyday life. The Probes and other accompanying research activities identified how ageing in place is individually, socially and collaboratively accomplished – 'co-produced' – by the efforts of both formal and informal networks of carers – with a special emphasis on family and friends as part of a process of 'bricolage' whereby new and old technology got reconfigured and customised and by informal support networks, including family members and neighbours. They revealed who the participants were as people and their, at times fading, sense of themselves and their lives.

Drawing on Churchill (2017), we can understand the deployments of Probes described here as instances of what we might term 'small big data' and 'small data'. Each has their value. The Technology Probe gave us insights into both the patterns and general character of digital interactions at the setting. This, in turn, helped us reason about how people expressed their individual identities and their sense of self in the workplace. Despite the public, situated nature of the display, particular messages had an individual character that helped form the culture of the workplace. In this way, because of the inbuilt logging capacity of this Probe, we were able to observe not only what a simple technology gave channel to expressing, but also infer how it shaped everyday work e.g. in terms of how it became part of an expert repertoire of collaborative, distributed work practices. The Informational Probe was informed by this 'small big data' in terms of its focus. But it also informed and made sense of the 'small big data', helping to, in the terms of Churchill (2017), triangulate the findings from more 'traditional' ethnographic work. Taken together, these two Probes gave us access to the multi-sited nature of the setting, and the bodily work and interaction there as well as the digital interactions becoming part of these working people's lives.

The discussion of Probes presented here also has implications for the third aspect of Goschnick's (2009:837) definition of People-Oriented Programming that considers people "as end-user developers, coming up with their own solutions to match their personal needs, utilising well-engineered software toolkits." Although programming is still often highly specialized work, programming-like activities have entered, even sneaked, into many people's everyday lives. There is a raft of everyday, unnoticed work that people do to configure, administer, tailor and even create and publish through computing systems. As Edwards and Grinter (2001) observe, work to maintain the technical order of domestic technologies, for example, has now filtered down to individual, non-'expert' household members through system administration work and, more broadly, what Tolmie et al (2010) refer to as "digital plumbing" or "the actual work of installing digital technologies in a setting" that ensures newly installed technologies "'fit' with a whole constellation of pre-existing organisational arrangements, both physical and social" (ibid:181). Taking this to the level of the individual, and drawing on the work of the ATHENE project (Wherton et al., 2012), the individual person is increasingly subject to and responsible for the work of maintaining their own digital personhood.

Beyond administration, home users can also upgrade, tailor, purchase and even develop new domestic software and hardware solutions that contribute to the socio-technical order of their households. Thus, the specialist work of programming professionals is now transferable to domestic life through more intentional, creative work. This, in the case of the home, is achieved through configuring and tailoring various technical domestic systems, by developing new ways of accessing and consuming domestic media through a bespoke home network for example. The Probes we have described here acknowledge the importance of this kind of work: the Informational Probe as a method afforded obtaining a personal view on otherwise unnoticed "information work" (Strauss et al., 1985:251) and even the technical work of taking photographs; the Technology Probe as a method afforded disrupting the setting to make this work more visible, specifically how it enters into, transforms and becomes integral to the character of work. For example, the importance of maintenance work and individual responsibility for it became visible when SPAM broke down.

Considering these developments on the level of the individual person, the growing amount of data on self (some might say narcissism) that was then available about everyday interactions through "mundane technologies" (Dourish et al., 2010), such as mobile phones and the services that these technologies supported (e.g. texting), has continued to grow through increasingly integrated cross-device services and data-related technologies. These technologies, as Michael (2003:131) comments "are now fully integrated into, and are an unremarkable part of, everyday life". Everyday development brings with it a different level of engagement with such technologies and services that potentially means the increased logging, even surveillance of everyday behaviour that may well go unnoticed. In addition, today the availability, interrogatability and volume of the 'mundane data' tracing and tracking everyday behaviour is notable. The pertinent questions now are what we can (ethically) do with such data and how we can make sense of it.

The methods discussed here provide some perspectives on these questions. They acknowledge the importance of taking seriously the relationships between individual people and the material artifacts that produce this data, exemplified through, for example, practices. These practices and materials evolve and change as they converge and not only produce data that is readily reducible to text but a variety of visual materials that requires a different analytical approach. Considering the ***Medium Switch*** sub-category and the "information flows" (Sheller and Urry, 2006:1) exposed through the different Probes here seems to suggest the importance of illuminating people's pathways around, between and through particular technologies. Views on pathways generated via Probes promise to inform us, as visualizations are generated, about how people are living their lives digitally, how they achieve technology configurations, the troubles they are having with technologies, as well as how they appropriate technologies over time. As with Crabtree et al's (2006) work, we see opportunities to develop digital records assembled from various recorded sources, mashed up into a summative view or even post-event replay. As the kind of everyday work we describe above persists, the kinds of data people generate also has the potential to show everyday users of technology how and by whom something was accomplished (e.g. fixed) 'the last time'. In an era where the home user is a 'digital plumber' (Tolmie et al., 2010) and solutions to problems with domestic technology may be forgotten or discarded, this promises to be useful. Beyond insights into everyday debugging Probes also have the potential to highlight how everyday developers' own practices, in the process of e.g. articulation work, are spread across different materials, particular to the individual. This is the kind of information and insight that would indeed help 'everyday development' both for individuals themselves and the broader community of people struggling with the same kinds of problems (consider e.g. http://www.instructables.com/). Thus, Probes can potentially tell us more about 'everyday development' both for the 'developers' themselves, those who study them and the associated community of practice (Wenger, 1998) while, as with the deployments in the 'sensitive' setting above, being tuned to the boundaries between, members of and participation in these different social worlds.

Yet the introduction of the category of "everyday development" and the transfer of expertise that it involves is not unproblematic as our experiences with these two Probe deployments have shown. The category brings forth four important questions specifically centred on everyday development with relation to personhood, mundane technology and practice:

1. *Whose responsibility is it?* Whose responsibility is it to maintain mundane technologies? To what extent is this work central to and focused on the individual person e.g. the expression and knowledge of self? To what extent is it a collective achievement?

2. *What is made visible?* What do mundane technologies reveal about the individual person? How is s/he engaged with and in control of the new visibilities that it enforces? What is the effect of these visibilities?
3. *Where is it performed?* In what spaces (digital or physical) is the data produced by mundane technologies situated with relation to the individual person? Given this locatedness, who owns it? What are the implications of this ownership with relation to e.g. rights?
4. *What expertise is required?* What are the different levels of expertise and knowledge required to sensibly engage in answering questions 1. – 3.

Given the kinds of views on an organization's and on individuals' lives provided by these Probe data sets, there seems, in the spirit of 'total capture' (Bell and Gemmell, 2009) and big data developments, opportunities to make such probing autonomous and complete. Yet, as these four questions show, this approach, at least for People-Oriented Programming, seems both overly simplistic and to miss the point entirely. What we choose to collect through Probes is informed and selective and helps drive how we 'make sense' through selection, extraction and presentation of the data we collect. In addition, what people effortfully collect and choose to put on display (e.g. with Informational Probes) is of some importance to us (Graham et al., 2009) and with such 'work' automated this no longer becomes effortful. There is a strong sense that different Probe varietals shape the choices that people make about what they disclose about themselves through a variety of materials, textual, visual and otherwise. These kinds of choices are neither banal nor overly problematic but instead informative concerning individual perspectives on particular situations. In addition, there are real ethical concerns with automating the display (as opposed to capture as with Technology Probes) of individual data to others because 'leaving the human out' also denies them awareness concerning what they are disclosing. This seems especially problematic when the distribution and possible identification of such data sets is considered. With observation, for example, someone 'being there' at some stage in the investigative process reminds people about being observed although, of course, a desirable state of affairs is that participants forget about the observer and get on with their work. Yet perhaps the greatest concern of all is that too much unconsidered autonomy in data collection creates a morass of data that cannot be easily reasoned about. As we have pointed out here, appropriately designed Probes can circumvent this problem by acknowledging the capacity for non-reductionist visualizations and of people themselves to organize views on what is important that both provide new, summative views of and supplements existing observations.

Whilst not explicitly talking about the use of Probes we suggest that Churchill's (2017) comment also summarizes what we expect (and get) from probes as a 'people-oriented-method': "Only by looking for meaning in the data traces, the data "fumes", will we be able to understand what is of value to people, and able to create lasting services that people value. To be able to do this well, to do this better than we are currently doing it, we need better tools for dealing with data at all scales and granularities—from collection to curation to manipulation to analysis to the drawing of defensible insights and conclusions. We also need innovative techniques and tools to better support data triangulation focused on producing high quality, interpretive work". We have further argued that questions of responsibility, visibility, performance and expertise are essential to ethically understand and develop the potential of new forms of probing for People-Oriented Programming.

ACKNOWLEDGMENT

This research was supported by a Microsoft European Research Fellowship (Social Interaction and Mundane Technologies), the EPSRC funded PLATFORM: Social Analysis in Systems Engineering project (grant ref: R97726/01), the EPSRC funded CASIDE project (grant ref: EP/C005589) and a Nokia University Donation (Mobile Phones as Probes, Props and Prototypes For Life Change). We thank all five reviewers for their constructive critique. This paper has been a result of work with our friends and colleagues Keith Cheverst, Dan Fitton (who built SPAM) Martin Gibbs and Frank Vetere so we thank them for their ongoing support and input. Special thanks too to Bill Gaver for his comments on Cultural Probes and our participants for their help and support with the research.

REFERENCES

Avison, D. E., & Fitzgerald, G. (2003). Where Now For Development Methodologies. *Communications of the ACM*, *46*(1), 79–82. doi:10.1145/602421.602423

Bardram, J., & Bossen, C. (2005). Mobility Work: The spatial dimension of collaboration at a hospital. *Computer Supported Cooperative Work*, *14*(2), 131–160. doi:10.100710606-005-0989-y

Bell, G., & Gemmell, J. (2009). *Total recall: How the e-memory revolution will change everything*. New York: Dutton.

Beyer, H., & Holzblatt, K. (1998). *Contextual Design: Defining Customer-Centered Systems*. San Francisco: Morgan Kaufmann.

Boehner, K., Vertesi, J., Sengers, P., & Dourish, P. (2007). How HCI interprets the Probes. In *Proceedings of the 2007 SIGCHI Conference on Human Factors in Computing Systems* (pp. 1077-1086). New York, NY: ACM. 10.1145/1240624.1240789

Bowers, J. M. (1991). The Janus face of design: some critical questions for CSCW. In J. M. Bowers & S. D. Benford (Eds.), *Studies in Computer Supported Cooperative Work* (pp. 333–350). Amsterdam: Elsevier Science Publishers.

Brown, B. A. T., Sellen, A. J., & O'Hara, K. P. (2000). A diary study of information capture in working life. In *Proceedings of the 2009 International Conference on Human Factors in Computing Systems* (pp. 438-45). New York, NY: ACM Press. 10.1145/332040.332472

Candy, F. J. (2003). The fabric of society: a proposal to investigate the emotional and sensory experience of wearing denim clothing. In *Proceedings of the 2003 International Conference on Designing Pleasurable Products and Interfaces* (pp. 28-33). New York, NY: ACM. 10.1145/782896.782904

Cheverst, K., Dix, A., Fitton, D., Rouncefield, M., & Graham, C. (2007). Exploring awareness related messaging through two situated-display-based systems. *Human-Computer Interaction*, 22(1), 173–220.

Churchill, E. (2017). The Ethnographic Lens: Perspectives and Opportunities for New Data Dialects. *EPIC2017*. Retrieved from https://www.epicpeople.org/ethnographic-lens/

Crabtree, A., French, A., Greenhalgh, C., Benford, S., Cheverst, K., Fitton, D., ... Graham, C. (2006). Developing digital records: Early experiences of Record and Replay. *Computer Supported Cooperative Work*, 15(4), 281–319. doi:10.100710606-006-9026-z

Crabtree, A., Hemmings, T., Rodden, T., Cheverst, K., Clarke, K., Dewsbury, G., ... Rouncefield, M. (2003). Designing with care: Adapting Cultural Probes to inform design in sensitive settings. In *Proceedings of the 2003 Australasian Conference on Computer-Human Interaction* (pp. 4-13). Brisbane, Australia: Ergonomics Society of Australia.

Crabtree, A., Rodden, T., Tolmie, P., & Button, G. (2009). Ethnography considered harmful. In *Proceedings of the 2009 International Conference on Human Factors in Computing Systems* (pp. 879-88). New York: ACM.

Dennett, D. (1976). Conditions of Personhood. In A. O. Rorty (Ed.), *Identities of Persons* (pp. 175–196). Berkeley, CA: University of California Press.

Dourish, P., Graham, C., Randall, D., & Rouncefield, M. (2010). Social Interaction and Mundane Technologies. *Theme Issue of Personal and Ubiquitous Computing, 14*(3), 171–180. doi:10.100700779-010-0281-0

Durrant, A., Kirk, D., Pisanty, D. T., Moncur, W., Orzech, K., Schofield, T., ... Monk, A. (2017). Transitions in Digital Personhood: Online Activity in Early Retirement. In *Proceedings of the 2017 CHI Conference on Human Factors in Computing Systems (CHI '17)* (pp. 6398-6411). New York: ACM. 10.1145/3025453.3025913

Edwards, K., & Grinter, R. (2001). At home with ubiquitous computing: Seven Challenges. In G.D. Abowd, B. Brumitt, & S.A. Shafer (Eds.), Lecture Notes In Computer Science: Vol. 2201. *Proceedings of the 3rd international Conference on Ubiquitous Computing* (pp. 256-272). London: Springer-Verlag. 10.1007/3-540-45427-6_22

Fielding, N. (1994). Ethnography. In N. Gilbert (Ed.), *Research in Social Life.* London: Sage.

Garfinkel, H. (1996). Ethnomethodology's Program. *Social Psychology Quarterly, 59*(1), 5–21. doi:10.2307/2787116

Gaver, B., Dunne, T., & Pacenti, E. (1999b). Cultural probes. *Interactions: New Visions of Human-Computer Interaction, 6*(1), 21–29. doi:10.1145/291224.291235

Gaver, W., Boucher, A., Pennington, S., & Walker, B. (2004). Cultural probes and the value of uncertainty. *Interactions: New Visions of Human-Computer Interaction, 11*(5), 53–56. doi:10.1145/1015530.1015555

Gaver, W., & Dunne, A. (1999). Projected Realities: Conceptual Design for Cultural Effect. *Proceedings of the 2003 SIGCHI Conference on Human Factors in Computing Systems* (pp. 600-7). New York, NY: ACM. 10.1145/302979.303168

Gaver, W. H., Hooker, B., & Dunne, A. (1999a). *The Presence Project.* London: Department of Interaction Design.

Glaser, B. G., & Strauss, A. L. (1968). *The discovery of grounded theory: Strategies for qualitative research.* New Brunswick, London: Transaction Publishers.

Goschnick, S. (2009). People-Oriented Programming: from Agent-Oriented Analysis to the design of interactive systems. In J.A. Jacko (Ed.), Lecture Notes In Computer Science: Vol. 5610. *Human-Computer Interaction: New Trends. Proceedings of the 13th International Conference of HCI International* (pp. 836-845). Berlin: Springer-Verlag. 10.1007/978-3-642-02574-7_93

Graham, C., Cheverst, K., & Rouncefield, M. (2006). Technology For The Humdrum: Trajectories, Interactional Needs and a Care Setting. *AJIS. Australasian Journal of Information Systems*, *13*(2). doi:10.3127/ajis.v13i2.43

Graham, C., & Rouncefield, M. (2008). Probes and Participation. In *Proceedings of the Tenth Anniversary Conference on Participatory Design 2008 (PDC '08)* (pp. 194-197). Indianapolis, IN: Indiana University.

Graham, C., Rouncefield, M., Gibbs, M., Vetere, F., & Cheverst, K. (2007). How probes work. In *Proceedings of the 2007 Australasian Conference on Computer-Human Interaction: Entertaining User Interfaces* (pp. 29-37). New York, NY: ACM.

Graham, C., Rouncefield, M., & Satchell, C. (2009). Blogging as 'therapy'? Exploring personal technologies for smoking cessation. *Health Informatics Journal*, *15*(4), 1–15. doi:10.1177/1460458209345897 PMID:20007652

Grinter, R. E., & Eldridge, M. (2003). Wan2tlk?: Everyday text messaging. In *Proceedings of the 2003 SIGCHI Conference on Human Factors in Computing Systems* (pp. 441-448). New York, NY: ACM.

Grudin, J. (1990). The Computer Reaches Out: The Historical Continuity of Interface Design. In J. C. Chew, & J. Whiteside (Eds), *Proceedings of the 1990 SIGCHI Conference on Human Factors in Computing Systems: Empowering People* (pp. 261-268). New York, NY: ACM. 10.1145/97243.97284

Hughes, J. A., Randall, D., & Shapiro, D. (1993). From Ethnographic Record to System Design: Some Experiences from the Field. *Computer Supported Cooperative Work*, *1*(3), 123–141. doi:10.1007/BF00752435

Hulkko, S., Mattelmäki, T., Virtanen, K., & Keinonen, T. (2004). Mobile probes. In *Proceedings of the Third Nordic Conference on Human-Computer Interaction* (pp. 43-451). New York, NY: ACM. 10.1145/1028014.1028020

Hutchinson, H., Mackay, W., Westerlund, B., Bederson, B.B, Druin, A., Plaisant, C., … Eiderbäck, B. (2003). Technology probes: Inspiring Design for and with Families. In *Proceedings of the 2003 SIGCHI Conference on Human Factors in Computing Systems* (pp. 17-24). New York, NY: ACM.

Iversen, O. S., & Nielsen, C. 2003. Using digital cultural probes in design with children. In S. S. MacFarlane, T. Nicol, J. Read, & L. Snape (Eds.), *Proceedings of the 2003 Conference on Interaction Design and Children* (pp.154-154). New York, NY: ACM. 10.1145/953536.953564

Kerrigan, F., & Hart, A. (2016). Theorising Digital Personhood: A Dramaturgical Approach. *Journal of Marketing Management*, *32*(17-18), 1701–1721. doi:10.10 80/0267257X.2016.1260630

Kitchen, R. (2014, April). Big Data, New Epistemologies and Paradigm Shifts. *Big Data & Society*, 1–12.

Law, J. (2004). *After Method: Mess in Social Science Research*. Oxon, UK: Routledge.

Lindley, J., & Coulton, P. (2015). Back to the Future: Ten Years of Design Fiction. In *Proceedings of the 2015 British HCI Conference* (pp. 210-211). New York, NY: ACM. 10.1145/2783446.2783592

Mamykina, L., Mynatt, E. D., & Kaufman, D. R. (2006). Investigating health management practices of individuals with diabetes. In *Proceedings of the 2006 SIGCHI Conference on Human Factors in Computing Systems* (pp. 927-36). New York, NY: ACM. 10.1145/1124772.1124910

Mattelmäki, T. (2005). Applying Probes – From Inspirational Notes to Collaborative Insights. *CoDesign*, *1*(2), 83–102. doi:10.1080/15719880500135821

Mattelmäki, T., & Battarbee, K. (2002) Empathy Probes. In *Proceedings of the 2002 Participatory Design Conference* (pp. 266-271). Palo Alto, CA: CPSR.

McAfee, A., Brynjolfsson, E., Davenport, T. H., Patil, D. J., & Barton, D. (2012). Big Data. The Management Revolution. *Harvard Business Review*, *90*(10), 61–67. PMID:23074865

Meese, J., Nansen, B., Kohn, T., Arnold, M., & Gibbs, M. (2015). Posthumous Personhood and the Affordances of Digital Media. Mortality. *Promoting the Interdisciplinary Study of Death and Dying*, *20*(4), 408–420.

Michael, M. (2003). Between the mundane and the exotic: Time for a different sociotechnical stuff. *Time & Society*, *12*(1), 127–143. doi:10.1177/096146 3X03012001372

Nardi, B., Whittaker, S., & Bradner, E. (2000). Interaction and Outeraction: Instant Messaging in Action. In *Proceedings of the 2000 ACM Conference on Computer Supported Cooperative Work* (pp. 79-88). New York, NY: ACM.

Norman, D. (1998). *The invisible computer: Why good products can fail, the personal computer is so complex and information appliances are the solution.* Cambridge, MA: MIT Press.

Palen, L., & Salzman, M. (2002). Voice-mail diary studies for naturalistic data capture under mobile conditions. In *Proceedings of the 2002 ACM Conference on Computer Supported Cooperative Work* (pp. 97-95). New York, NY: ACM. 10.1145/587078.587092

Papert, S. (1980). *Mindstorms: Children, Computers, and Powerful Ideas.* New York, NY: Basic Books.

Paulos, E., & Jenkins, T. (2005). Urban probes: encountering our emerging urban atmospheres. In *Proceedings of the 2005 SIGCHI Conference on Human Factors in Computing Systems* (pp. 341-50). New York, NY: ACM. 10.1145/1054972.1055020

Perry, M., O'Hara, K., Sellen, A., Brown, B., & Harper, R. (2001). Dealing with mobility: Understanding access anytime, anywhere. *ACM Transactions on Computer-Human Interaction, 8*(4), 323–347. doi:10.1145/504704.504707

Plowman, L., Rogers, Y., & Ramage, M. (1995). What are Workplace Studies For? In *Proceedings of the Fourth European Conference on Computer-Supported Cooperative Work ECSCW '95* (pp. 309-324). Dordrecht: Kluwer Academic Publishers, Springer.

Prensky, M. (2001). Digital Natives, Digital Immigrants. *On the Horizon, 9*(5), 1–6. doi:10.1108/10748120110424816

Resnick, M., Maloney, J., Monroy-Hernández, A., Rusk, N., Eastmond, E., Brennan, K., ... Kafai, Y. (2009). Scratch: Programming for all. *Communications of the ACM, 52*(11), 60–67. doi:10.1145/1592761.1592779

Sheller, M., & Urry, J. (2006). Introduction: mobile cities, urban mobilities. In M. Sheller & J. Urry (Eds.), *Mobile Technologies and the City* (pp. 1–17). London: Routledge.

Silverstone, R., Hirsch, E., & Morley, D. (1992). Information and communication technologies and the moral economy of the household. In R. Silverstone & E. Hirsch (Eds.), *Consuming Technologies: Media and Information in Domestic Spaces* (pp. 13–58). London: Routledge. doi:10.4324/9780203401491_chapter_1

Strauss, A. (1978). A Social World Perspective. *Studies in Symbolic Interaction, 1*, 119–128.

Strauss, A., Fagerhaugh, S., Suczek, B., & Weiner, C. (1985). *Social Organisation of Medical Work.* Chicago: University of Chicago Press.

Taylor, N., & Cheverst, K. (2009). Social interaction around a rural community photo display. *International Journal of Human-Computer Studies*, *67*(12), 1037–1047. doi:10.1016/j.ijhcs.2009.07.006

Taylor, N., Cheverst, K., Fitton, D., Race, N. J., Rouncefield, M., & Graham, C. 2007. Probing communities: study of a village photo display. *Proceedings of the 2003 Australasian Conference on Computer-Human Interaction* (pp. 17-24). New York, NY: ACM. 10.1145/1324892.1324896

Tehranian, J. (2011). Parchment, Pixels & Personhood: User Rights and the IP (Identity Politics) of IP (Intellectual Property). *University of Colorado Law Review*, *82*(1), 1–84.

Tolmie, P., Crabtree, A., Egglestone, S., Humble, J., Greenhalgh, C., & Rodden, T. (2010). Digital plumbing: The mundane work of deploying UbiComp in the home. *Personal and Ubiquitous Computing*, *14*(3), 181–196. doi:10.100700779-009-0260-5

Vetere, F., Martin, R., Kjeldskov, J., Howard, S., Mueller, F., Pedell, S., Mecoles, K., & Bunyan, M. (2005) Mediating intimacy: designing technologies to support strong tie relationships. In *Proceedings of the 2005 SIGCHI Conference on Human Factors in Computing Systems* (471-80). New York, NY: ACM. 10.1145/1054972.1055038

Voida, A., & Mynatt, E. D. (2005). Conveying user values between families and designers. In *CHI '05 Extended Abstracts on Human Factors in Computing Systems* (pp. 2013–2016). New York, NY: ACM. doi:10.1145/1056808.1057080

Wenger, E. (1988). *Communities of Practice: Learning, Meaning and Identity*. Cambridge, UK: Cambridge University Press.

Wherton, J., Sugarhood, P., Procter, R., Rouncefield, M., Dewsbury, G., Hinder, S., & Greenhalgh, T. (2012). Designing Assisted Living Technologies 'In the Wild': Preliminary Experiences with Cultural Probe Methodology. *BMC Medical Research Methodology*, *12*(1), 188. doi:10.1186/1471-2288-12-188 PMID:23256612

Whittaker, S., Frohlich, D., & Daly-Jones, O. (1994). Informal Workplace Communication: What Is It Like and How Might We Support It? In *Proceedings of the 1994 ACM Conference on Computer Supported Cooperative Work* (pp. 131-7). New York, NY: ACM.

Zerubavel, E. (1985). *Hidden Rhythms: Schedules and Calendars in Social Life*. California: University of California Press.

ENDNOTES

[1]   Goschnick (ibid) also suggests that a final way of characterizing the individual user through people-oriented programming is via "the cognitive models behind the tools, techniques and frameworks upon which the user toolkits are built."

[2]   This photograph first appeared as Figure 5 in: Cheverst, K., Dix, A., Fitton, D., Rouncefield, M., and Graham, C. (2007). Exploring awareness related messaging through two situated-display-based systems. Human Computer Interaction, 22(1), 173-220. It is reproduced here with the permission of the publisher (Taylor & Francis Ltd, http://www.tandf.co.uk/journals).

[3]   All logs have been anonymised through parsing out identifying information through e.g. find and replace functions.

[4]   We have removed identifying information from the figure.

[5]   "*Sky*" refers to the UK broadcasting company of the same name.

Chapter 6

A Design Method for People–Oriented Programming:
Automating Design of Declarative Language Mashups on the Raspberry Pi

Steve Goschnick
Swinburne University of Technology, Australia

ABSTRACT

The miniature Raspberry Pi computer has become of interest to many researchers as a platform for building sociotechnical IoT systems for end-users; however, for the end-user to design and build such apps themselves requires new people-oriented tools and design methods. This chapter describes a people-oriented design method called TANDEM and demonstrates the use of it in detail, by way of a case study— the design of a mashup of services and local data stores—that solves the so-called movie-cinema problem. An implementation of the newly designed movie-cinema app is then built within the DigitalFriend, an end-user programmer IDE. Furthermore, a significant part of the TANDEM design method is then automated within the development tool itself. This automation removes the most skilled task required by TANDEM of the end-user: the automation of the process of data normalization. The automation applies data normalization to the initial model of components and data sources that feed into the mashup. The presentation here relies on some understanding of data normalization, so a simple example is presented. After this demonstrated example of the method and the implementation, the authors discuss the applicability of a model achievable by end-users using TANDEM coupled with the automated normalization process built into the IDE vs. using a top-down

DOI: 10.4018/978-1-5225-5969-6.ch006

model by an experienced information analyst. In conclusion, the TANDEM method combined with the automation as demonstrated does empower an end-user to a significant degree in achieving a workable mashup of distributed services and local data stores and feeds. Such a powerful combination of methods and tools will help the Raspberry Pi to become a significant people-oriented platform, beyond just a platform for teaching novices to code. Furthermore, the TANDEM method does have broader applicability to designing a broad class of logic programs, complementing the use of collected patterns in logic programs.

INTRODUCTION

With 14 million plus units of the Raspberry Pi having sold (up to mid 2017 and growing: Cellan-Jones, 2017) it is not only a formidable platform for makers and to teach school kids something of coding and computer science, but is also a fully functional Linux machine with desktop level tools together with low level interfaces to all sorts of sensors and physical world devices to be controlled. Single board computers like the Raspberry Pi, have become of interest to many researchers as a platform for building sociotechnical IoT systems (Rizzo et al, 2018), for end users, by end users. It is with this in mind that we have ported the DigitalFriend (Goschnick, 2006) to the Raspberry Pi. Using the DigitalFriend, end-users are able to build mashups of REST and SOAP web services, together with local resources and processes, and information sources including IoT sensors and devices, into newly envisaged and often personalised applications (Figure 1).

While the tools that end-users may use have increased in number and accessibility over the last decade, the methods and design techniques that are targeted at end-user programmers and novice coders, have not followed suit. This chapter describes an end-user-friendly method called TANDEM (Goschnick et al., 2006) and demonstrates the use of it in detail, by way of the design of a mashup of services that solves the so-called movie-cinema problem. An implementation of the newly designed movie-cinema app is then built within an end-user-friendly development environment called the DigitalFriend. While many publications targeted at end-user programmers making mashups, have promoted imperative programming languages for the task, such as JavaScript, PHP and Python (e.g. Orchard, 2005; Feiler, 2008), the DigitalFriend uses CoLoG, a built-in logic programming language. CoLoG features overlap a substantial subset of the Prolog language (Sterling & Shapiro, 1994; Colmerauer & Roussel, 1993), together with added extra-logical predicates concerned with character-based I/O and the GUI interface in order to interact with an end-user, together with some features of a Constraint Logic Language (Marriott & Stuckey, 1998). The use of logic languages is more often associated with AI (Artificial

175

Figure 1. A mashup app of services, data stores and feeds, in the DigitalFriend on a Raspberry Pi

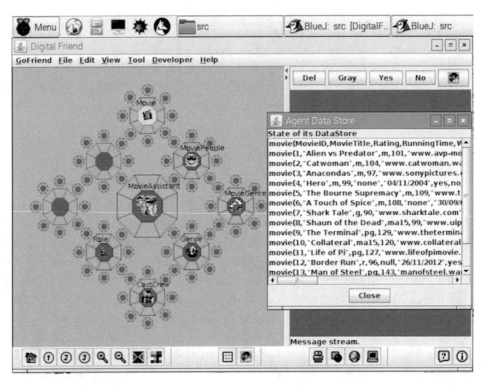

Intelligence) and agent-oriented (AO) software development environments, then it is with IDEs (Integrated Development Environments) targeting end-user programmers; nonetheless, logic languages could have a big role to play in end-user programming, hopefully foreshadowed by the approach taken here. And although the DigitalFriend is usable as a multi-agent system (MAS), it was envisaged from the outset of its development, as an IDE targeted at end-user programming (Goschnick, 2006), via a methodology grounded upon people-oriented programming (Goschnick, 2009).

Even from the early days of Prolog it was recognized as a language that could be used to bring together code, additively over time, that included both descriptive logic (data structures) and procedural logic (algorithms), as Ceri & Gottlob (1986) noted: "Prolog makes possible an integrated description of data structures ('facts') and algorithms ('rules'), where the algorithms are produced and presented additively, as small 'granules' of the overall system." Although the authors went on to describe incremental development on one computer, the quote remains descriptive of how we use CoLoG today, to bring together data records (facts) from multiple local and distributed web-based sources, including Relational DBMS, often in real-time, and combine them with rules that have been devised for the purpose of a mashup, in the DigitalFriend IDE. And the technology that comes within and on the low-cost Raspberry Pi computer, including Java and the BlueJ development environment (Kölling, 2018), is more than adequate to run the DigitalFriend efficiently.

Given that logic programming is not widely used as compared to imperative programming (e.g. JavaScript, Python, PHP), particularly with respect to making mashups, and that some appreciation of the highly compact expressive-power of it, is useful to the reception of this chapter, two small sample logic programs written in CoLoG are given here: one sporting procedural logic, and the second one mostly descriptive logic. This first example given in Figure 2 is all procedural in its logic and quite cryptic, as procedural logic often is. Whereas the second example given in Listing 1 is mostly descriptive logic and hence much less cryptic, is made up by a single procedural rule at the top that is supplemented by the many facts (hundreds of data records), coming from various data sources, that follow it. Note: Those lines in Listing 1 consisting of an ellipsis only (...), indicates the omission of many more similar facts, for example the lines starting with *countryCurrency* each represent one country, and there are 248 such lines in the full program, needed to cover all countries.

The example in Figure 2 implements the often used mortgage calculator, useful when dealing with compound interest rates on loans from banks. The algorithm comes from Marriott & Stuckey (1998: p.178). The query or goal that it is currently answering, put into English is: "I initially borrowed $148,000 at a compound interest rate of 7.5%, and so far I have made 180 monthly payments of $1250 each, so what is the current Balance I still owe?" And the program answers: $40,388.51. The figure is a screenshot of the user-interface to the CoLoG interpreter built into the DigitalFriend. It has three multi-line textfields titled: *Program, Query* and *Results.* The first six lines in the Program textfield are just comments describing the 5 variables, represented by capital letters P,T,I,R and B, that are the parameters in the predicate called *mortgage* at the head-of-the-rule (Left-Hand-Side - LHS - of the symbol <++ which itself represents 'IF'). The total program is only 6 lines in length, consisting of 2 rules, both with the same predicate called mortgage. A rule ends with the character ';' and can flow over multiple lines. The body-of-the-rule is on the Right-Hand-Side (RHS) of the symbol <++ and is made up from a number of clauses separated by commas. And these commas ',' each represents a logical AND. The # symbol represents assignment here, such that #(T,0) equates to the more familiar: T=0. Commas inside brackets are just separating different terms, and not acting as logical ANDs as per the use of them outside of brackets. Terms can be either: variables, literals, integers or real numbers. Variables always start with a capital letter, while literals start with a lowercase character or are surrounded in quotes like this one: "Fred Ng".

Figure 2. A small logic program running in the DigitalFriend

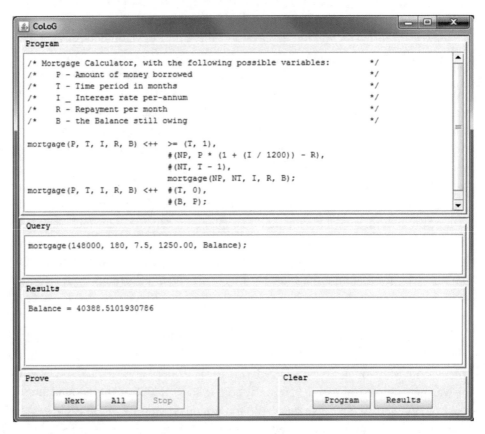

```
/* Mortgage Calculator, with the following possible variables:    */
/*     P - Amount of money borrowed                                */
/*     T - Time period in months                                   */
/*     I _ Interest rate per-annum                                 */
/*     R - Repayment per month                                     */
/*     B - the Balance still owing                                 */

mortgage(P, T, I, R, B) <++  >= (T, 1),
                             #(NP, P * (1 + (I / 1200)) - R),
                             #(NT, T - 1),
                             mortgage(NP, NT, I, R, B);
mortgage(P, T, I, R, B) <++  #(T, 0),
                             #(B, P);
```

Query

```
mortgage(148000, 180, 7.5, 1250.00, Balance);
```

Results

```
Balance = 40388.5101930786
```

Prove   Next All Stop   Clear   Program Results

Programs in Prolog (and CoLoG) set about proving things. The head on the LHS is true, IF the tail on the RHS is provable. Rules in Prolog/CoLog can call themselves recursively, RHS to LHS, which gives the language both its power, but also often contributing to its cryptic nature. The scope of a variable is just within the current rule of which it is a part, explaining why a single program can define the same predicate on the LHS - such as mortgage - more than once, with different tails on the RHS. If the first rule fails, the language interpreter moves on to the second rule, if there is another with that name, and so on. Hence such rules are logically OR'ed together in the way they work.

The second example (Listing 1) is much less cryptic but there is much more of it. Luckily, it is typical of the programs for mashups that an end-user programmer will most often build in the IDE. This logic program called CostingMyWishlist represents a mashup application that sources the price of any book in a user's wishlist, priced at the current list-price, but then converts it into any currency the user desires, at the current currency conversion rates. It is an example mashup used throughout the paper (Goschnick, 2006), and was also programmed in the DigitalFriend IDE, albeit an earlier version.

This example has a single, simple logic rule at the top of it with a predicate on the LHS called book. The user can Query the program for any book in their wishlist, by replacing the variable Title with a book's actual title, such as "Life of Pi". Regardless of where the book's price is sourced (i.e. via multiple Web services), or in what currency it is returned in, the user can choose the currency of the country where they currently are. E.g. the current Query in Listing 1, is down at the last line, namely:

book("Life of Pi",australia,Cost,aud)

which requests the cost of "*Life of Pi*" in Australian dollars, which has the currency code *aud*. Note: some countries allow multiple currencies as legal tender, and multiple countries use the aud, thus requiring both literals australia and aud to get a single solution.

In the first example we saw that each rule ends with a ';' which technically marks the end of an axiom in CoLoG. Logic programs may have two sorts of axioms - rules and facts - and a logic program is simply a list of these two sorts of axioms. Facts are like this:

countryCurrency(at,austria,eur,euro);

where, *countryCurrency* is called a predicate, while at, austria, eur and euro are four terms, each is a literal value in this case, together called a tuple. The brackets are defining a structure, a compound term, in logical programming terminology. If you are more familiar with database terminology, you can see that each of these *countryCurrency* facts are just like database records. Table 1 shows some overlapping meanings between the terminologies of the database world and the logic programming world, which should help orientate some readers.

For example, the version of currencyConversion(CurrencyCode1,CurrencyCode2, Rate) that appears in the rule part of the program - all the terms of which, start with a capital letter, and are thus variables - is the equivalent of a relation-schema, if you were declaring such a table in a Relational DBMS.

However, there are many differences between the paradigms, for example: terms can be lists (none, in the two example programs given) defined with square brackets [mylist], allowing for recursive structures such as trees, which are difficult to emulate in relational DBMS; universal facts are compound terms where some of the terms remain as variables; etc. Nonetheless, most relational database concepts can be very easily accommodated in logic programs.

Listing 1. CoLoG logic code for a Book Wishlist Mashup

```
/* The Program: CostingMyWishlist */
/* The Mashup Rule:  */
book(Title,Country,Cost,Currency) <++
     bookWishList(ISBN,Title,Year),
     quote(ISBN,CurrencyCode2,Amount,Vendor),
     currencyConversion(CurrencyCode1,CurrencyCode2,Rate),
     countryCurrency(CountryCode,Country,CurrencyCode1,Curren
cy),
     #(Cost,  (Rate)*(Amount));

/* Coming from a Quotation Web Service: */
quote(0156027321,usd,11.15,nobleAndBarnes);
quote(0316206849,usd,15.50,nobleAndBarnes);
quote(0316017930,usd,10.20,nobleAndBarnes);
quote(0811871258,usd,42.98,nobleAndBarnes);
quote(0262133415,gbp,78.50,nobleAndBarnes);
quote(0321537351,gbp,83.25,nobleAndBarnes);
quote(0465067107,gbp,12.70,nobleAndBarnes);
quote(0321751043,gbp,158.48,nobleAndBarnes);
...
/* Non-volatile data held in a local datastore: */
countryCurrency(af,afghanistan,afn,afghani);
countryCurrency(al,albania,all,lek);
countryCurrency(dz,algeria,dzd,algerian_dinar);
countryCurrency(as,american_samoa,usd,us_dollar);
countryCurrency(ad,andorra,eur,euro);
countryCurrency(ao,angola,aoa,kwanza);
countryCurrency(ai,anguilla,xcd,east_carribbean_dollar);
countryCurrency(ag,antigua_and_barbuda,xcd,east_carribbean_
dollar);
countryCurrency(ar,argentina,ars,argentine_peso);
countryCurrency(am,armenia,amd,armenian_dram);
countryCurrency(aw,aruba,awg,aruban_guilder);
countryCurrency(au,australia,aud,australian_dollar);
countryCurrency(at,austria,eur,euro);
...
countryCurrency(gb,united_kingdom,gbp,pound_sterling);
countryCurrency(us,united_states,usd,us_dollar);
```

continued on following page

Listing 1. Continued

```
...
/* Coming from the CurrencyConversion Web service: */
currencyConversion(usd,aud,0.76);
currencyConversion(aud,usd,1.32);
currencyConversion(gbp,aud,0.56);
currencyConversion(aud,gbp,1.79);
...
/* Coming from local datastore holding users wishlist: */
bookWishList(0156027321,"Life of Pi",2003);
bookWishList(0316206849,"The Cockoos Calling",2013);
bookWishList(0316017930,"Outliers: The Story of Success",2011);
bookWishList(0811871258,"Rebus",2011);
bookWishList(0262133415,"Programming with Constraints: An
Introduction",1998);
bookWishList(0321537351,"Designing the User Interface",2009);
bookWishList(0465067107,"The Design of Everyday Things",2002);
bookWishList(0321751043,"The Art of Computer
Programming",2011);
bookWishList(0932633420,"The Psychology of Computer
Programming",1998);
bookWishList(1451648537,"Steve Jobs",2011);
...
/* The Query / Goal  */
book("Life of Pi",australia,Cost,aud);
```

Table 1. Overlapping meanings between the terminologies of the database world and the logic

Relational Model	Database System	Logic Programming
relation name	table name	predicate
relation	table	set of facts
attribute	column name	term
relation-schema	table-schema	functor /compound term
value / instance	value	atom / ground term
tuple	row/record	ground compound term

Note: It is perhaps not a simple coincidence that Codd's Relational model (Codd, 1970) and Prolog (Colmerauer & Roussel, 1993; Kowalski, 1988), both came into existence around the same year or so, 1970. They represent parallel advances made in the same short period of innovation in Computer Science, as is often the case in Science in general.

Traditionally, logic programs have their list of axioms collected together in an editor or an IDE. In the DigitalFriend the list of axioms that makes up a CoLoG program, come from numerous sources and are dynamically updated - rewritten at discrete points in time - with the fast-changing ones (described as: highly volatile) coming from web services (including REST services). E.g. the logic program in this second example is made up of 5 blocks of code, that are each sourced differently:

- The first part with the book predicate at its head, is the rule and does not change.
- Next is a block of facts, each with a predicate name quote, comes from a Web service called Quotation (it is polled at a regular interval, as set by the DigitalFriend end-user).
- The third block of facts, each with the predicate name *countryCurrency* comes from a local datastore represent 248 countries, each record with the appropriate 2-letter country code, and 3-letter currency code. Much less volatile - i.e. the list of countries changes about one per year.
- The fourth block of facts, each with the predicate name *currencyConversion*, comes from a Web service called CurrencyConversion, that is regularly polled to retrieve current exchange rates.
- The fifth block of facts, each with a predicate name *bookWishList* are coming from a datastore on the local end-user's device, which simply holds the list of books that they currently have on their personal wishlist of books on their Raspberry Pi, updated by the user as they see fit.

The DigitalFriend dynamically updates the program in the mashup, each time one of the service feeds is polled for an update, or when a local datastore is updated with a new or a modified record, (including from sensors, if the app uses them attached to the Raspberry Pi). I.e. the program in Listing 1 gets rewritten very often, and generates notifications to the end-user that an update has occurred. For example, the currency conversion service is polled every 20 minutes - if it was a currency-trading mashup, real-time currency feeds would be cost-justified, but as a book wishlist an update three times an hour is ample and inexpensive.

The Need for a Design Method

As already pointed out, the rule at the top of the program includes predicates (c/f relation-schemas) that fit these different feeds of facts coming from distributed sources, combined in some way (mostly via logical ANDs), that is the heart of the mashup. The design of such rules, as in, devising good, functional and even optimal rules, presents the need for a *design method*. It becomes the most critical aspect of building such mashups in IDEs that conscript logic languages for the computational tasks.

When we first developed the DigitalFriend V1, complete with a logic language interpreter at its heart (Goschnick, 2006), we went in search of design methods for logic programs to address this great need, and were quite surprised and impeded by a lack of such methods. Sterling (2002) gives us a definition of a good logic program as one that is: 'declarative, easily understood, and able to efficiently solve the problem at hand'.

In the classic text on the logic language Prolog, within the chapter on program development, Sterling and Shapiro (1994) reflect that the design of a good logic program is generally achieved through rapid prototyping, evolving it through rewriting and extension. Some years later, Sterling applied the concept of patterns to logic programs (Sterling, 2002), and identified two classes of patterns, namely *skeletons* and *techniques* – the first class is to do with program control flow, and the second targets generalized, method-like operations, that have a wide range of applicability.

He notes

Despite attractive features, Prolog has not been widely adopted within software engineering. Standard development practices have not been adapted to Prolog. A major area of weakness is design... Nothing analogous to design techniques, such as structure analysis for procedural or object oriented design for object-oriented languages, have been developed for logic languages.

He then includes the two design patterns of skeletons and techniques into a method of design called *stepwise enhancement*, which is a more refined and formal specification of the rapid prototyping approach in the earlier mentioned work. A part of that formalism involves listing predicates and their terms, but no specific method is advocated for identifying the correct, best or most useful predicates and their terms, beyond the 'experience of the programmer', and predicate refinement via iteration in the design approach. Later again, advances in the knowledge of patterns used in the related field of agent-oriented software design, are catalogued here (Oluyomi et al., 2007).

While the pattern-oriented approach to designing logic programs is indeed useful to regular or advanced logic programmers and analysts, there is much less benefit in the methodology to the logic language novice looking to put together information feeds such as described in the example mashup above. Algorithms and patterns are most useful in logic programs that are heavily procedural logic, of which the mortgage example in Figure 2 is but a simple yet useful case. Devising the arrangement of predicates of compound terms and choosing their constituent terms, such as in the second example logic program in Listing 1, is *not* addressed at all in the patterns approach to a design method. Although Listing 1 has a very small procedural part at the end of the rule, alluding to some role for *patterns* in mashups that are more computationally complex.

Having uncovered such a significant gap in logic programming design methods, we developed TANDEM, first presented in a short three-page paper here (Goschnick et al., 2006). TANDEM does address the need to choose appropriate predicates together with the best arrangement of compound terms, for an efficient and flexible solution to many novel problems. As such it does fill that gap, by addressing an essentially unlimited set of problems, way beyond a fixed set of patterned usage. TANDEM is fully detailed below, in the next section titled THE TANDEM DESIGN METHOD, where we step through a specific example - a solution to the movie-cinema problem - in enough detail to understand the proper and constructive use of the method.

In the section titled IMPLEMENTING THE DESIGN USING THE DIGITALFRIEND we take the design devised in section THE TANDEM DESIGN METHOD and implement it as a working solution, using the DigitalFriend IDE, exploiting the CoLoG language interpreter supplied within that tool to good effect, as a proof of the worth of TANDEM.

Despite this advance, a significant weakness in TANDEM with respect to end-user usage, is the need to perform Data Normalization - a technique drawn from Codd's original theory for relational databases and extended with Boyce (Codd, 1970; Codd, 1971; Kent, 1983) - on the assembled data and data-feeds, identified in a Task Analysis. So, in the following section we addressed that weakness by *Automating the Data Normalization* process, using an algorithm from (Bernstein, 1976; Beeri & Bernstein, 1979) to do it. The algorithm automates so-called 1st, 2nd and 3rd Normal Forms, as well as Boyce-Codd Normal Form, given raw input of entities and attributes. Furthermore, a paper from 1986 details in full, a Prolog program that fully implements Bernstein's algorithm to automate data normalization (Ceri & Gottlob, 1986). Given that CoLoG is a substantial subset of Prolog, a conversion of their code is relatively straightforward. A more recent paper also documents the automation of data normalization, but in this second paper the tool used is Wolfram's Mathematica, using the internal language of that product (Yazici, & Karakaya, 2007), together with some Java. I went with the Ceri & Gottlob technique and converted their code, given that their solution is in Prolog and that it is functionally complete. This allows for the automation of the data normalization part of TANDEM, to be incorporated directly into the IDE we use: into the DigitalFriend IDE itself. Note: As some understanding of Data Normalization is useful to understanding this section, a brief overview of the concept, why it is useful and how it is done, is included in this section to help with this presentation.

Then in *Discussion* we examine what has been accomplished with respect to information modeling more generally, and identify and address a number of perceived weaknesses to the approach. While in *Conclusion* there is a summary of what advances have been made in this reported research.

THE TANDEM DESIGN METHOD

This section presents a detailed case study of applying the *TANDEM design method* to a mashup problem, by way of introducing the method. It is used to derive logic predicates and rules, to be used in an IDE or other application development tool, that incorporates a logic language. It combines a *Task Analysis* (Annet, J., 2004; Balbo, S., 2004) and the *N*ormalization technique from entity relation (ER) analysis (Codd, 1970), into a logic language *DE*sign *M*ethodology (hence the acronym *TANDEM*). Although the example here is applied to a mashup, targeting a Prolog/CoLoG enabled IDE, the method is applicable to a broad range of domain problems, using any of a number of logic languages. Having identified a gap in the provision of logic language methods, and given the significant conceptual correlation between database *relations* and *predicates* in logic languages as described in the Introduction, we recognized the value that data normalization could bring to designing well-formed predicates in logic languages, and so incorporated it within TANDEM.

The analysis begins with the collection of all possible candidate *entities* that a requirements gathering exercise uncovers. Entities are usually a specialization of either a: Person (e.g. *patient*), Place (e.g. *cinema*), Object (e.g. *vehicle*), Event (e.g. *enrollment*) or Concept (e.g. *account*). Further along in the actual implementation of a distributed application, information representing these entities identified in the analysis, will often be sourced from a number of unrelated web services, distributed across the Internet, together with some other sources resident in a client machine's storage, as was the case with the user's book wishlist in the earlier example, or via attached sensors (e.g. IoT). Nonetheless, the initial conceptual ER diagram is modeled as if it were going to be implemented in a single system. I.e. a *conceptual* model is best achieved, by temporarily disregarding the eventual implementation technology and configuration specifics. Those specifics are addressed later on, in the physical implementation. See Figure 3 for a conceptual ER model, for the example problem described in the next section.

Figure 3. A conceptual ER (entity relation) model for the movie-cinema problem

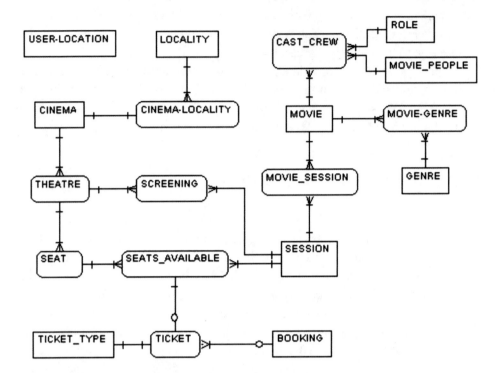

The Movie-Cinema Problem

- **The Problem:** The client, a movie cinema operator, wants a mashup accessible by movie-going customers via the Internet, one which will allow users of smart handheld devices, to search for specific movie screening details, ultimately leading to the booking of cinema tickets. The business rules and app requirements:
- The client has a number of cinemas across the state, with names that reflect their locations e.g. 'City Centre' is the name of the cinema within the city itself, while 'Chadstone'is the name of the cinema at the Chadstone Shopping Centre. They have many such cinemas, but never more than one per location;
- When the user has a smart device capable of determining their current location, they should be informed of the closest cinemas;
- When the user has chosen a cinema, they should be shown the movies currently playing there. When they have chosen a movie, they should be shown which cinemas are playing it;

- Each cinema has a number of theatres at which movies are viewed. There are three types of theatre, namely: Standard, Luxury (e.g. lounge chairs), and Art-house (where they show less commercial movies, and serve drinks and food) to the seated movie-goers. A selected cinema may for example have: 8 standard theatres, 2 art-house theatres and 1 luxury theatre, but these numbers vary from cinema to cinema. Each theatre has a number of seats, which can be selected when a customer buys a ticket online. A seat is identified by its seat row (A to Z) and its seat number within that row;

- The client wants to make available details on the movies that are currently playing, including: title, rating, director, length (i.e. running time), main cast members (i.e. known stars), rating (i.e. G, PG, M, MA, R), genre (e.g. drama, horror, comedy), official movie web- site, release date (when the movie was first released on to the marketplace). If an alternative service can be found that can provide this information dynamically, then that would be preferable, to fast-track the project;

- A movie can be screening (shown) in one or more theatres consecutively. A movie will usually be screened during one or more sessions within a given day. Details about each session include: day, start-time, number-of-features (i.e. One session can screen either one movie, or two movies – called a double-feature). Operationally, the system never needs to hold more than seven days-worth of *sessions* – i.e. the movies that are screening from 'today', forward one week;

- Both *available* and *allocated* seats should be displayed on a graphic image of the theatre plan, allowing the user to self-select consecutive seats during a booking, as required;

- Ticket types can be either: *Adult, Student, Child, Pensioner* or *Senior Citizen*. Each ticket-type has a different cost. However, the cost of a given type (e.g. Student) remains the same across all movies at all cinemas that the client owns and operates.

Once a movie-going customer purchases a ticket, full ticket details are provided including: Cinema, Movie title, day, start-time, ticket-type, cost, seat row and seat number. (Note: the recreational end-user programmer would not normally have access to this level of requirements document - this issue is addressed in the section addressing Automating the Normalization, further down.)

Phase 1: Applying Task Analysis (TA)

Task Analysis identifies users' goals and the procedure or steps needed to achieve them. It includes the process of analyzing the structure of a task and decomposed the task into related sub-tasks. Some of the tasks identified for the users of the envisaged system, were extracted using a task analysis and are listed below as verb-first directives, a TA convention:

Task 1: Cinema-Oriented Search

- Determine which recent movies are playing in a cinema.
- Determine which cinemas are playing a specific movie.
- Find what ticket types are available at a specific theatre.
- Find the cost of a specific ticket type.

Task 2: Movie-Oriented Search

- Find all recently released movies.
- Find all movies within a particular genre.
- Find which movies feature a specific actor.
- Find all movies by a specific director.

Task 3: Location-Oriented Search

- Find all cinemas within a given radius of the current user's position.
- Find all cinemas within the locality of a specific user postcode/zipcode.
- Calculate the distance to the nearest cinema where a specific movie is playing.

Task 4: Seat-Oriented Search and Ticket Allocation

- Select unallocated seats for movie, theatre and cinema of choice.
- Select ticket type/s.
- Enter name and payment method.
- Allocate the booked seats.

These four groups of tasks and sub-tasks - represent the first step in a hierarchical task modelling exercise (Annet, J., 2004).

This task modeling phase may employ any of a number of task analysis notations, as described by Balbo et al. (2004) – who review six well-known and widely used task notations. However, for our purposes in the design method in this chapter, we do not need to proceed further with task analysis, as the logic rules we derive from the method, are able to answer the many diverse tasks in our problem above, and more, as we shall see.

Phase 2: Applying ER Normalization

In database applications a technique for designing new systems that is widely used and widely taught in Information Systems, Computer Science and Business Schools, is *entity relation* (ER) modeling (Ramakrishnan & Gehrke, 2003). And further, the aforementioned technique of Data Normalization is applied to such ER models to get the model into an ideal form - a form equally suited to all manner of SQL-based queries and updates put to the implementation, and one that is most flexible with regard to future change requirements (Codd, 1970). What is not appreciated by a lot of students (and some instructors and books authors too), is that data normalization is also a powerful bottom-up design heuristic. Bottom-up methods are especially useful when the information analyst is working in a domain area, that they have not faced before - something that happens frequently, in consulting. Bottom-up methods gather those artifacts and details that seem relevant, and distill models from them, using various heuristics. In this sense, TANDEM is a bottom-up method.

[Very briefly, referring to some of the notation in Figure 4, the visual notation is called Information Engineering (IE), or colloquially, crows-feet notation. It was identified as the predominantly used notation, in a sample of over 480 of the thought leaders and preeminent practitioners world-wide, in the field of Data Modeling (Simsion, 2006). The PK stands for Primary-Key - a unique record identifier in

Figure 4. The fully-keyed entity relation model in 3NF

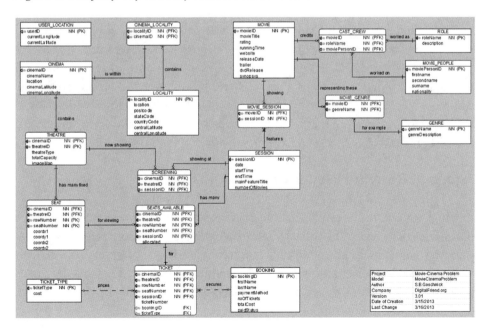

a database table. FK stands for Foreign-Key - a redundant copy of the PK from another table, stored in the second entity to enable meaningful links between related records. PFK indicates a PK that is also an FK. While this terminology is specific to database modeling, and not necessarily a part of a logic program, the concept and usage of database keys, turns out to be analogous to the way that logic languages unify across predicates - more of this further down.]

In the next main section, I describe the process of automating normalization in the DigitalFriend, where further explanation of data normalization is also given. However, here, we proceed with the TANDEM method, with a given normalized model of the entities and their attributes, in this case, depicted as a so-called fully-keyed relational database model as shown in Figure 4.

Once we have the entity relation model in 3NF, the next step required is the division of the ER diagram into appropriate sub-areas, which in turn can be implemented as sub-applications (often termed sub-agents). We do this by identifying *logic flow lines* as depicted in Figure 5. These lines are mapped by taking the four high level tasks identified in the Task Analysis above, and then identifying which of the entities in the ER diagram are involved in each task - without breaking the line.

The reason for not breaking the line, is that logic languages, during the process of unification (Marriott & Stuckey, 1998), dynamically join each predicate expressed in a rule, wherever there is a commonly named attribute/term between them – in order to satisfy a query. The major difference with respect to a standard SQL relational database management system (RDBMS), is that the RDBMS only joins entities (i.e. predicates), on common attributes, where specified by the developer. A logic language will find all possible joins automatically and systematically, often building a huge space state, finding all possible solutions, one after the other. The relationships between entities in Figures 3, 4 and 5 (the straight lines), each infer a common attribute between the pair of entities at both ends of a given line. The curved lines in Figure 5, identify just those entities that we will group together in a sub-model. Hence, to break the line – meaning to have two entities which have no relationship line between them - would prevent a logic program from successfully answering many queries via unification.

Phase 3: Deriving Well-Formed Logic Rules

In a logic program, the predicate at the head-of-the-rule is a template for many of the queries that can be answered by the whole program. The total set of such rules, gives the templates for all queries that are answerable by the complete system. In the DigitalFriend implementation, these rules and their associated logic is distributed between the various sub-agents, and the entity data is sourced from different distributed information sources.

Figure 5. Logic flow lines matching the needs of the four high-level Tasks

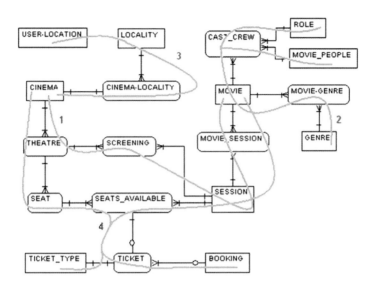

In the design solution, five rules are derived and explained in the next four sub-sections, with the following five head-of-the-rule predicates:

```
cinemaAssistant(CinemaName, Location, TheatreType, MovieTitle,
GenreName, Rating, Date, StartTime)
movieAssistant(MovieTitle, Rating, GenreName, RunningTime,
DvdRelease, RoleName, FirstName, Surname)
localityAssistant(Distance, Radius, Location, TownSuburb,
Postcode, CinemaName)
seatSelection(CinemaName, Location, TheatreID, ImageMap,
MovieTitle, Date, StartTime, RowNumber, SeatNumber, CoordX,
CoordY, allocated)
ticketAssistant(CinemaID, TheatreID, Date, StartTime,
RowNumber, SeatNumber, TicketNumber, TicketType, Cost,
BookingID, FirstName, LastName, PaymentMethod, PaidStatus)
```

The terms within the brackets of the predicate, all begin with a capital letter, to indicate that they are all variables. A query is constructed by replacing one or more of those variables with a specific instance, for example, a query in English:

What movies feature Matt Damon as a star?

would be specified to the CoLoG program as the following Query or Goal:

movieAssistant(MovieTitle, Rating, GenreName, RunningTime, DvdRelease, star, matt, damon)?

It can also be specified with under-scores in place of the variable names we have no interest in, leaving only the need to supply the literals (individual terms), as follows:

movieAssistant(MovieTitle, _, _, _, _, star, matt, damon)?

Note: The underscore character _ is used in many logic languages to represent so-called anonymous variables - they do the job of the normal variables they stand in for, without us wanting or needing to specifically name them. The analogy of anonymous variables in natural languages are pronouns.

In the TANDEM method we first decide on all the head-of-rule predicates that will be necessary to answer all of the tasks extracted via the Task Analysis. The four groupings of primary tasks, told us that we needed the four predicates as detailed above. We simply settled upon the four predicate names - *cinemaAssistant, movieAssistant, localityAssistant* and *ticketAssistant* - as meaningful names that characterized the typical tasks they would each address, and are the names utilized within the DigitalFriend implementation, outlined in Section 3.

Deriving the Cinema Assistant Rule

To identify the actual terms needed by each compound-term predicate, we use a more detailed diagram than the ER diagram depicted in Figure 5. So, we now refer back to the fully-keyed ER model in Figure 4, choosing just those entities and their respective attributes identified by a logic flow line in Figure 5. The sub-model of just those entities touched by logic flow line 1 is isolated in Figure 5 for clarity in the following rule construction.

The constituent terms within each predicate rule are then determined by the atomic tasks that made up the high-level task for which the predicate was instigated. Task 1 - Cinema-oriented search - is addressed first, by devising Rule 1 below.

The second stage of this phase involves identifying the best configuration of predicates on the right hand side of each rule in turn:

Figure 6. The entities and attributes that fall on logic flow line 1

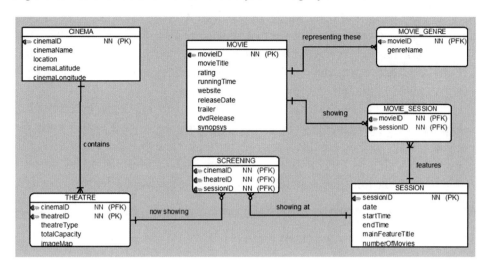

Rule 1

```
Head of the Rule:
cinemaAssistant(CinemaName, Location, TheatreType, MovieTitle,
GenreName, Rating, Date, StartTime) ←
Requires the following Predicates (from the normalized ER
diagram) on the right-hand side of the implies (←):
cinema(CinemaID, CinemaName, Location, CinemaLatitude,
CinemaLongitude),
theatre(CinemaID, TheatreID, TheatreType, TotalCapacity,
ImageMap),
session(SessionID, Date, StartTime, EndTime, MainFeatureTitle,
NumberOfMovies),
movie(MovieID, MovieTitle, Rating, RunningTime, Website,
ReleaseDate, Trailer, DvdRelease, Synopsys),
movieGenre(MovieID, GenreName)
screening(CinemaID, TheatreID, sessionID),
movieSession(MovieID, SessionID);
```

Note 1: From here onwards, these predicates on the LHS are called the body of the rule.

  Note 2: The commas between predicates, are conjunctions (logical ANDs).

These required predicates making up the body of the rule, are identified via their member terms within the entity. I.e. Each entity in Figure 6 that has a member attribute which corresponds with a term within the head-of-the-rule predicate, is then included as a rule body predicate. These matching member attributes are highlighted in bold-italic font above. The multiple rule body predicates are ANDed together via the ',' as noted in the Introduction above.

Note that the last two predicates have no such matching terms in the head-of-rule predicate, but are there as connective predicates, between the other necessary predicates. That is, they provide a path - in the logic flow line - for the search-space constructed within an executing logic program, to include all necessary terms, in order to satisfy the rule. In ER models such connective relations are called associative entities.

Deriving the Movie Assistant Rule

Figure 7 depicts the sub-model entities involved in the *movieAssistant* rule. Again, all of the appropriate entities have been identified for this sub-model, by following the appropriate logic flow line in Figure 7. The entities are all to do with movies, and nothing to do with cinemas or locations. A user could simply use a Query which uses this rule, to enquire details about a movie, whether or not they ever intended to go and see it in a cinema, or not. I.e. it could enable a useful standalone app by itself, given appropriately populated information feeds; or conversely, it might well be sourced from an existing service.

Figure 7. The entities and attributes that fall on logic flow line 2

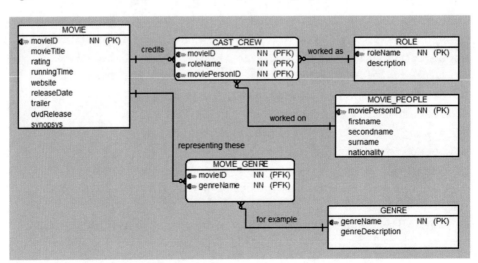

Thus Rule 2 addresses Task 2 - Movie-oriented search.

Rule 2

```
Head-of-the-rule:
movieAssistant(MovieTitle,Rating,GenreName,RunningTime, DvdRele
ase,RoleName,FirstName,Surname) ←
It requires the following predicates in the rule body, via
the normalized entities, represented with their attributes/
compound-terms in Figure 7.
movie(MovieID, MovieTitle, Rating, RunningTime, Website,
ReleaseDate, Trailer, DvdRelease, Synopsys),
moviePeople(MoviePersonID, Firstname, Secondname, Surname,
Nationality),
movieGenre(MovieID, GenreName),
genre(GenreName, GenreDescription),
castCrew(MoviePersonID, MovieID, RoleName),
role(RoleName, Description);
```

Deriving the Location Assistant Rule

Figure 8 depicts the sub-model entities involved in the *localityAssistant* rule. As before the appropriate logic flow line 3 identifies the necessary entities for this sub-model. The rule for Task 3 - Location-oriented search is then determined accordingly.

Rule 3

```
Head-of-the-rule:
localityAssistant(Distance,Radius,Location,
TownSuburb,Postcode,CinemaName) ←
Requires the following Predicates in the rule body, via
normalized ER diagram:
cinema(CinemaID, CinemaName, Location, CinemaLatitude,
CinemaLongitude)
locality(LocalityID, TownSuburb, PostCode, StateCode,
CountryCode, CentralLatitude, CentralLongitude),
cinemaLocality(cinemaID, localityID),
userPosition(CurrentLatitude, CurrentLongitude);
Plus, the addition of the following predicate together with
```

Figure 8. The entities and attributes that fall on logic flow line 3

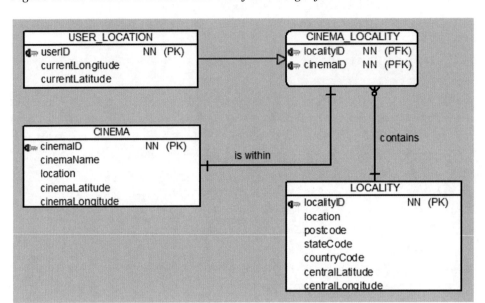

a little extra logic in CoLoG syntax, to get the desired
functionality:

```
distanceBetween(Distance, Longitude1, Latitude1, Longitude2,
Latitude2)
#(CurrentLongitude = Longitude1),
#(CurrentLatitude = Latitude1),
#(CinemaLongitude = Longitude2),
#(CinemaLatitude = Latitude2),
#(Distance <= Radius);
```

The *distanceBetween* predicate is not in the ER diagram, so where does it come from in the method? Via the need for distance in the rule head, and by observing that we have terms for longitude and latitude in both the cinema and the user-location relations in Figure 8. In the implementation it will need to be provided with some extra logic, or via a wrapped web service that is able to calculate the distance between two global coordinates.

The four lines of code below *distanceBetween* simply assign the appropriate terms from cinema and *userPosition*, as the two global coordinates that will be used to calculate a distance.

The other predicate in the tail of Rule3 is *cinemaLocality* which is another connective predicate, the need for which was discussed above in deriving Rule1.

Deriving the Ticket Assistant Rules

Figure 9 depicts the sub-area entities involved in the *ticketAssistant* rule. The logic flow line in Figure 5 which identifies the necessary entities for the sub-area, branches in two directions, at both ends. This is partly due to the dual need to select unallocated seats in a theatre and session of choice, and book and pay for the seats that are ultimately chosen by the user. Consequently, we decided to satisfy the various sub-tasks that the Ticket Assistant agent is involved in, with two logic rules.

Rule 4

The attributes/terms within this head-of-the-rule predicate are the things a customer would like to know after they have decided on the movie to see, and on the cinema in which to see it, such as which seats are available in what session. The client for the mashup wanted an interface that displays a graphic 2D plan of the theatre, showing both: the seats that are already allocated, and the seats that are still available. The design caters for this by including an image-map of the theatre plan in the Theatre

Figure 9. The entities and attributes that fall on logic flow line 4

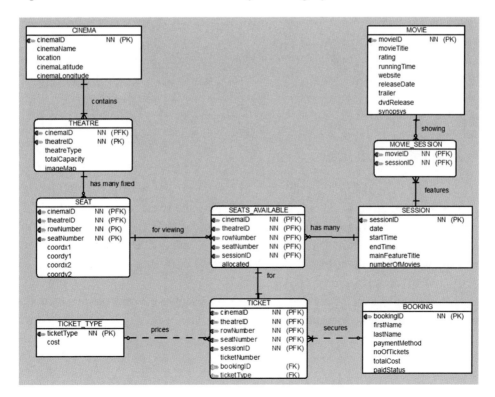

entity, and by storing the (x,y) pair of coordinates of each seat, in the Seat entity. Note: seat row and number were insufficient as coordinates, as the seats are often in a curvilinear layout punctuated by doorways, rather than a simple linear formation. So, in addition to the various movie and cinema text fields, the head-of-the-rule also has the name of the image-map file, and the seat (x,y) coordinates, which are relative to that image origin (0,0), which the sub-agent then presents to the system, and the implemented system will need to display to the user for interaction. The head-of-the-rule is as follows:

seatSelection(CinemaName, Location, TheatreID, ImageMap, MovieTitle, Date, StartTime, RowNumber, SeatNumber, CoordX, CoordY, allocated) ←

It requires the following predicates in the rule body, via normalized fully-attributed entities in Figure 7:

```
cinema(CinemaID, CinemaName, Location, CinemaLatitude,
CinemaLongitude),
theatre(CinemaID, TheatreID, TheatreType, TotalCapacity,
ImageMap),
seat(CinemaID, TheatreID, RowNumber, SeatNumber, CoordX,
CoordY),
seatsAvailable(cinemaID, theatreID, rowNumber, seatNumber,
sessionID, allocated),
session(SessionID, Date, StartTime, EndTime, MainFeatureTitle,
NumberOfMovies),
movieSession(MovieID, SessionID),
movie(MovieID, MovieTitle, Rating, RunningTime, Website,
ReleaseDate, Trailer, DvdRelease, Synopsys);
```

This rule is used to return all seats in a session, and whether or not they are currently allocated. It is also capable of returning the seats coordinates within the returned *ImageMap* filename. The implementation of the Ticket Assistant sub-agent can then use these returned tuples, to display an interactive image of the theatre seating, with which the user interacts, to select the seats they want to book. It uses extra-logical methods to do the GUI interface.

A second rule is then used that takes the user's seat selection from the agent that encapsulates Rule4, to forward payment details. The necessary logic rule follows:

Rule 5

```
ticketAssistant(CinemaID, TheatreID, Date, StartTime,
RowNumber, SeatNumber, TicketNumber, TicketType, Cost,
BookingID, FirstName, LastName, PaymentMethod, PaidStatus) ←
```

It requires the following predicates in the rule body, via the normalized, fully-attributed entities in Figure 9:

```
ticketType(TicketType, Cost),
ticket(CinemaID, TheatreID, SessionID, RowNumber, SeatNumber,
TicketNumber, TicketType, BookingID),
booking(BookingID, FirstName, LastName, PaymentMethod,
NoOfTickets, TotalCost, PaidStatus);
```

The agent that wraps the ticket predicate, gets its values for *CinemaID*, *TheatreID*, *SessionID*, *RowNumber*, *SeatNumber* and *TicketNumber* from the interaction surrounding the seatsAvailable rule. It then requires interaction with the user, to determine the *TicketType* of each ticket - again requiring extra-logical methods.

The last predicate - booking - will need to be encapsulated by a web service agent, that is capable of accepting payment, and returning the *BookingID* and *PaidStatus* values/terms, not implemented in the example yet and again, requiring extra-logical GUI methods.

IMPLEMENTING THE DESIGN USING THE *DIGITALFRIEND*

The DigitalFriend (Goschnick, 2006) is an end-user-friendly IDE with a multi-agent system (MAS) theoretical foundation (Wooldridge, 2009), one that also employs user-agents as a visual interface metaphor. It was the tool used to implement the design. It is especially good at incorporating any number of agents and sub-agents in a hierarchically ordered manner – including an agent type which is able to wrap a web service (Goschnick & Sterling, 2003) thus enabling web services to be brought into a mashup.

The hierarchical view of the various agents and sub-agents in an end-users's digital-friend is displayed via an octagonal-tile interface, which is recursively deep, but displays a lens of three consecutive levels of the hierarchy at any one time. The user may zoom back and forth through the hierarchy. There are three related windows visible in Figure 10, the deepest one (top-left) shows the hierarchy focused in upon the implemented MovieAssistant agent. The five head-of-rules devised in Section

Figure 10. The MovieAssistant built in the DigitalFriend IDE on the Raspberry Pi

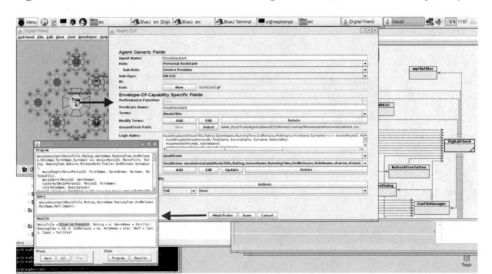

2.4 lead to five such assistant agents in the build: *MovieAssistant*, *CinemaAssistant* and *LocalityAssistant*, *TicketAssistant* and *SeatingAssistant*.

MovieAssistant is called an EOC-agent within the DigitalFriend - meaning that it encapsulates an Envelope-of-Capability. An EOC agent encompasses a number of sub-agents and the logic that binds them together, each of which in turn can recursively have more sub-agents as needed (Goschnick, 2001; Goschnick & Sterling, 2003). MovieAssistant addresses the sub-tasks in Task 2 in the analysis described in Section 2.2, and implements the second rule that was derived in Section 2.4, matching the head-of-the-rule predicates.

In the figure we can see that the sub-agents of MovieAssistant are called Movie, MoviePeople, MovieGenre, Genre, CastCrew and Role – that together exactly matches the list of predicates in the tail-of-the-rule for the movieAssistant rule, in Section 2.4.

Both EOC agents and non-EOC sub-agents encompass predicates, which are created within the DigitalFriend interface via interactive GUI property dialog boxes. The second window in Figure 10 represents the property dialog box for the MovieAssistant agent.

There are four main sub-areas of input/edit fields in this dialog: role and identity fields (under the label 'Agent Generic Fields'); predicate and term related fields and buttons for interaction (under the label 'Envelope-Of-Capability Specific Fields'); logic rules and a series of predefined/saved goals/queries for the agent; and under the label 'Communicates with' an inter-agent communication language section (agent communication languages are beyond the scope of this chapter).

The rule for movieAssistant – Rule 2, as designed in Section 2.4 – has been entered by the end-user into the field 'Logic Rules'. The currently saved query will return any movies involving the actress Sharon Stone as star, or indeed in any other role, as it goes about solving its current goal. The query can easily be modified interactively with the full flexibility of Prolog/CoLoG, and saved afresh, as we will see.

Each of the predicates in the rule body are represented by a sub-agent. These agents may be of various types including: agents which wrap a web service; DB-lookup (local/ client-side database) agents; SQL-based agents (client and/or server-side); java-coded agents (as is needed for the TicketAssistant agent) and reminder-agents that provide specific notifications. These types are each discussed elsewhere (Goschnick, 2006), but for space requirements and clarity sake with regard to the design method presented here, we will just look at how the EOC agent combines the sub-agents within the mashup.

The third window opened in Figure 10 (bottom-left) occurs when the user clicks on the [Mind Probe] button in the property dialog window of the EOC agent, in this case, metaphorically 'the mind of' the MovieAssistant user-agent. This opens up an interaction dialog with the Prolog/CoLog code itself. I.e. while it does show the current-state of the underlying code in the top sub-window labelled 'Program', the user can also modify the current goal in the 'Query' sub-window, push the [Next] button below the 'Prove' label, and get the program's output in the 'Results' sub-window. E.g. in this figure it is clear that the user altered the Goal/Query to search for all movies in which Matt Damon was a member of the cast. The Results sub-window shows the movie that he has starred in: Alien vs Preditor.

Although only a small portion of the code can be seen in the Program sub-window, it actually runs to several hundred lines of logic predicates, which is partly expanded upon in Listing 2.

As in Listing 1, Listing 2 shows different chunks of code - ground predicates; rules - that are sourced from the distributed resources encapsulated by sub-agents, in a dynamic manner. I.e. the CoLog program in Listing 2 is just a snapshot in time of a dynamically changing, orchestration of code, albeit updated via discrete, often periodically-timed events. The /* comment */ lines were added for clarity.

The rule, as derived using the TANDEM method, only occupies the first 5 lines of code, whereas, the rest of the program consists of base/ground compound terms, or, as more commonly recognized, as data records using database terminology.

Sub-agents that retrieve data records/ground-terms from Web-services are represented in the rule by a predicate with a list of terms. They also have timers, set to retrieve new information at regular intervals, and they update datastores of ground-terms that they maintain. The user sets the timer intervals via the GUI interface to the sub-agent within the DigitalFriend. I.e. The DigitalFriend is more

Listing 2. A snapshot in time of the logic within MovieAssistant

```
movieAssistant(MovieTitle,Rating,GenreName,RunningTime,DvdRele
ase,RoleName,FirstName,Surname) <++ movie(MovieID, MovieTitle,
Rating, RunningTime,Website,ReleaseDate,Trailer,DvdRelease,Syn
opsys),
    moviePeople(MoviePersonID, FirstName, Secondname, Surname,
Nationality),
    movieGenre(MovieID, GenreName),
    castCrew(MoviePersonID, MovieID, RoleName),
    role(RoleName, Description);
/* Coming from sub-agent MoviePeople, sourced via a web-service
*/
moviePeople(1,lance,null,henriksen,usa);
moviePeople(2,halle,null,berry,usa);
moviePeople(3,sharon,null,stone,usa);
moviePeople(4,jet,null,li,hong_Kong);
moviePeople(5,ziyi,null,zhang,china);
moviePeople(6,tony,null,leung,hong_kong);
moviePeople(7,maggie,null,cheung,hong_kong);
moviePeople(8,matt,null,damon,usa);
moviePeople(9,will,null,smith,usa);
moviePeople(10,robert,null,de_Niro,usa);
moviePeople(11,angelina,null,jolie,usa);
moviePeople(12,renee,null,zellweger,usa);
moviePeople(13,simon,null,pegg,uk);
moviePeople(14,nick,null,frost,uk);
moviePeople(15,tom,null,hanks,usa);
moviePeople(16,catherine,null,zeta-jones,usa);
moviePeople(17,tom,null,cruise,usa);
moviePeople(18,michael,null,mann,usa);
moviePeople(19,steven,null,spielberg,usa);
...
/* Coming from a Web Service of Movies*/
movie(1,"Alien vs Predator",m,101,"www.avp-movie.
com","30/09/2004",yes,no,"An international team of scientists
and security experts encounters mysterious aliens and predators
in the Antarctica");
...
movie(11,"Life of Pi",pg,127,"www.lifeofpimovie.
```

continued on following page

Listing 2. Continued

```
com","21/11/2012",yes,yes,"A young man survives a sinking ship
only to share a lifeboat with a Tiger, with whom he finds
something in common");
movie(12,"Border Run",r,96,null,"26/11/2012",yes,yes,"An
American reporter searches for her missing brother around US/
Mexico border insurgency");
movie(13,"Man of Steel",pg,143,"manofsteel.warnerbros","14/
06/2013",yes,yes,"A young worker confronts his secret alien
heritage when earth is invaded by members of his race");
movie(14,"Iron Man 3",pg,130,"marvel.com/ironman3","03/05/2013"
,yes,yes,"Tony Starks world is torn apart by a terrorist called
Mandarin. After rebuilding he seeks retribution");
movie(15,"Les Miserables",pg,158,"www.lesmiserablesfilm.
com","25/12/2012",yes,yes,"A minor lawbreaker becomes a
fugitive and a respectable mayor, until tracked down by a
dogged policeman");
movie(16,"Lincoln",pg,150,"www.dreamworksstudios.com/films/linc
oln","09/11/2012",yes,yes,"President Lincoln fights within his
own as the civil war rages around slavery");
...
/* Coming from sub-agent MovieGenre, built from a web-service
*/
movieGenre(1,thriller);
movieGenre(2,action);
movieGenre(2,adventure);
movieGenre(3,thriller);
movieGenre(4,action);
movieGenre(4,adventure);
movieGenre(5,action);
movieGenre(5,adventure);
movieGenre(5,thriller);
movieGenre(6,drama);
movieGenre(6,art-house);
movieGenre(7,family);
movieGenre(8,comedy);
movieGenre(8,thriller);
movieGenre(9,drama);
movieGenre(9,comedy);
```

continued on following page

Listing 2. Continued

```
movieGenre(10,thriller);
movieGenre(11,adventure);
movieGenre(11,drama);
movieGenre(11,fantasy);
movieGenre(12,crime);
movieGenre(12,thriller);
movieGenre(13,action);
movieGenre(13,adventure);
movieGenre(13,fantasy);
movieGenre(14,action);
movieGenre(14,adventure);
movieGenre(14,sci-fi);
movieGenre(15,drama);
movieGenre(15,musical);
movieGenre(15,romance);
movieGenre(16,biography);
movieGenre(16,history);
movieGenre(16,drama);
...
/* Coming from local datastore holding Genre names and
descriptions, via sub-agent genre: */
genre(action,"Films with lots of physical stunts and activities
to generate tremendous impact and continuous high energy");
genre(adventure,"Exciting stories with exotic experiences or
locales designed to provide action-filled and energetic viewing
experiences");
genre(comedy,"Light-hearted dramas designed to elicit laughter
and provoke enjoyment");
genre(crime,"Films that portray the actions of criminals or
gangsters or bank robbers or murderer or other lawbreakers");
genre(drama,"Stories that portray realistic characters in
conflict with themselves or others or forces of nature");
genre(epic,"Films that glorify an historical or imagined event
or a legendary or heroic figure");
genre(horror,"Films designed to frighten and panic and to cause
dread and alarm");
genre(musical,"Films that emphasize and showcase full-scale
song and dance routines");
```

continued on following page

Listing 2. Continued

```
genre(sci-fi,"Scientific or imaginative stories that are often
set in a future time");
genre(war,"Films that acknowledge the horror and heartbreak of
war by portraying combat fightings or conflicts");
genre(western,"Films that portray the conquest of the
wilderness or a goal of maintaining law and order on the
frontier");
genre(fantasy,"Magic and the supernatural are used as a primary
theme or part of the plot");
genre(thriller,"Stimulates the viewers mood by experiencing a
rush of emotions, through highs and lows");
genre(romance,"A search or encounter with romantic or pure
love, is a central theme");
genre(drama,"Both fiction and non-fiction where the story takes
place in the 20/21st centuries");
genre(biography,"Based on the true story around a particular
individual");
genre(history,"Factually accurate story on a significant event
or period in history");

/* Coming via local datastore maintained by sub-agent CastCrew
*/
castCrew(1,1,star);
castCrew(25,1,director);
castCrew(2,2,star);
castCrew(3,2,star);
castCrew(4,4,star);
castCrew(5,4,star);
castCrew(6,4,star);
castCrew(7,4,star);
castCrew(24,4,director);
castCrew(8,5,star);
castCrew(23,5,director);
castCrew(9,7,star);
castCrew(10,7,star);
castCrew(11,7,star);
castCrew(12,7,star);
castCrew(21,7,director);
```

continued on following page

Listing 2. Continued

```
castCrew(22,7,director);
castCrew(13,8,star);
castCrew(14,8,star);
castCrew(20,8,director);
castCrew(15,9,star);
castCrew(16,9,star);
castCrew(19,9,director);
castCrew(17,10,star);
castCrew(18,10,director);
castCrew(26,11,director);
castCrew(26,11,producer);
castCrew(27,11,star);
...
/* Coming from non-volatile datastore, maintained by sub-agent
Role */
role(star,"A draw card actor");
role(director,"The main manager of the making of a movie");
role(producer,"Puts up the money for a movie");
role(screenwriter,"Writes or adapts the storyline");
role(writer,"Writer of the original book-story");
```

than just an IDE, it is also a constantly running agent system, much like an email program runs 24/7 fielding updates.

The DigitalFriend dynamically collects all rules, predicates and ground terms for an EOC agent and its sub-agents, and effectively combines them into a logic program in the internal CoLoG language – built and fired as necessary. Many of the resultant terms are passed to other agents – as specified via the inter-agent communication language in CoLoG – and many are passed as notification messages for the user's attention, in the right-hand side of the background of Figure 1, i.e. the Message Stream pane.

Clearly, these inner dynamically constructed Prolog/CoLoG programs can run to thousands of lines of code, largely consisting of ground/base data. The efficiency of it, as compared to a performance driven DBMS, is not a big issue on modern client machines including desktops, touch-pads and mobile phones, as they invariably have hundreds of MBytes of memory and more, such that the computation happens in-memory. I.e. traditional database systems are computationally efficient with regard to secondary-storage (usually, hard disk drives), employing memory-based indexes (on key identifiers) to make them so. Conversely, in-memory datastores of thousands or even tens of thousands of lines of data, can now be handled efficiently on such modern client smart devices, without the need for such indexes to secondary storage. Note: While the Prolog/CoLoG does not build indexes on key identifiers explicitly, it does use common attribute-names that appear across multiple relations, to join them logically, much as the SQL language does with keys in relational DBMS. SQL traditionally requires the programmer to identify the attributes (usually keys) on which multiple tables are going to be joined; whereas, Prolog automatically finds like-named terms across numerous relations, and joins them systematically in a process called unification.

In the case of an EOC agent such as *MovieAssistant* that wraps data-feeds and datastores, the only CoLoG code that the end-user has to conceive and enter into the DigitalFriend is Rule 2. It is entered via the 'Logic Rule' field in the property dialog in Figure 10. All other details have been created via less textual GUI interaction involving buttons and single name screen-input fields. The Rule is where the end-user developer needed some automated support, and the reason why the TANDEM design method was developed. And since TANDEM in-turn relies on the concept of Data Normalization, I have also set about automating that process as much as possible, as described in the next section.

AUTOMATING THE NORMALIZATION

So far this chapter has been concerned with using a normalized ER model in the process of finding well-formed predicates for better logic programs, for a specific mashup application; and then showing how that translates readily into an implementation, when the tools at hand are appropriately end-user-friendly. However, in addressing the movie-cinema problem we began with a previously normalized entity relation model of the various entities needed and their attributes, leaving the specific details of Normalization until now. So, how do end-user programmers get a normalized data model for their novel mashup?

Anecdotally, in my long experience in information modeling, in both consulting and in teaching, it is a minority of practicing analysts who understand that Data Normalization is a powerful tool for bottom-up design. Many more simply tick-off the '3NF-done' box inside a quality-process, performed well into the SDLC (software development lifecycle). So, a legitimate question at this stage is: If the data normalization process has been either too tedious or not well enough understood by many information/data analysts, what hope is there for the end-user to take it up successfully in a design method? There-in lies the need for some significant automation in achieving that goal.

It turns out, that in earlier times, not very long after logic language compilers were first developed, algorithms were devised (Bernstein, 1976; Lucchesi & Osborn, 1978; Beeri, & Bernstein, 1979; Beeri, 1980; Tsou & Fischer, 1982; Loizou & Thanish, 1983) and programs were written (mainly in Prolog), to significantly automate the process of Data Normalization itself (Bernstein, 1976; Bouzeghoub et al., 1985; Fagin, 1977; Kerschberg, 1984; Lee, 1985; Potter, 1984; Ceri & Gottlob, 1986). Those authors back then were predominantly concerned with the design of relational database systems which were relatively new at the time, or simply embarked on the academic exercise, rather than conceiving it as an aid to designing logic programs themselves, which is the purpose of TANDEM. I.e. they designed logic programs to do data normalization, while we are using those logic programs to design other logic programs.

In other words, by combing such algorithms and logic programs from that research, with the TANDEM method described above, and implementing it within an IDE that incorporates a built-in logic language interpreter, such as the DigitalFriend, we arrive at a situation where the resultant system can devise well-formed predicates, largely by itself - with just a bit of interaction and reflection from the user. The well-formed entities from the normalization process directly represent the predicates in the tails-of-rules, and also map into the heads-of-rules of an unfolding application using TANDEM as demonstrated earlier in Section 2. The inputs to such a system are simply: some base entities and their candidate attributes from the artifacts gathered during a requirements gathering exercise at the planning stage of a new application or mashup. (Note: in Section 2, we started with the list of requirements, for brevity sake.)

The main algorithm used here is from (Bernstein, 1976; Beeri & Bernstein, 1979). Their algorithm takes a relation to 3rd Normal Forms (3NF). The algorithm for finding all the keys of a relation is from Lucchesi & Osborn (1978). While the algorithm for getting a relation into Boyce-Codd Normal Form (BCNF) is from Tsou & Fischer (1982). Ceri and Gottlob (1986) wrote a Prolog program, that fully implements those three algorithms. Given some raw input in the form a few entities and their constituent attributes, coupled with some user-identified functional dependencies, the program normalizes them into BCNF. And since CoLoG is a substantial subset of Prolog, I was able to convert their code into the CoLoG used within the DigitalFriend.

To present the rest of this chapter effectively, a good understanding of the process of data normalization and the original problems that Codd addressed with it, is required (Codd, 1977; Kent, 1983). Therefore, to facilitate this presentation an introduction or a recap of Data Normalization up to 3NF and including Boyce-Codd Normal Form (BCNF), is provided here, together with an illustrative example using it as a bottom-up design technique. Note: There are rarer normal forms that are much less frequently a concern, including 4NF and 5NF (Kent, 1983), not covered below.

Data Normalization and Bottom-Up Design

At the heart of the process of data normalization is the concept of functional dependencies between attributes within a proposed entity. It is simply that concept of the same name that we probably all first met in mid-school regarding mathematical functions:

$X \to Y$ means: X determines Y, or Y is a function of X, like this: $Y = f(X)$. For any given value of X there is only ever one value of Y, for all possible values of X and Y. E.g. if $Y = X^2$ and we plug the value of 2 into X, then that determines $Y = 4$, since Y is functionally dependent on X. The reverse does not hold true. E.g. if $Y=4$ then that alone cannot determine the value of X. E.g. $X = -2$ also determines $Y=4$.

These functional dependencies also hold between attributes of a relation (or columns of a database table), and the attributes do not have to be numeric, they are simply any properties of the entity. E.g. If we have a database of motor vehicle records, with the license-plate number/code in there as an identifier, along with other vehicle details such as: make, color, owner, owner-address - then there are also some functional dependencies between these attributes. The relation can be written as:

VEHICLE(license-plate, color, make, year, owner, owner-address)

If you witnessed a hit-and-run accident and reported that you saw a red car do it, that would not be of much help in tracking down the offender. However, if you recalled the license-plate number, the offender is as good as caught. Vehicle color does not determine license-plate number, however, license-plate number does determine vehicle color - and the vehicle's owner. I.e. in that relation license-plate is our X.

VEHICLE(license-plate, color, make, year, owner, owner-address)

In the relation above, VEHICLE is the relation-name, the identifier license-plate, is a key, the primary-key in this case (and is usually identified in some visually distinctive way, such as the underlining used here). While color, make, year, owner and owner-address are the remaining attributes. The whole line is a relation schema - a template which describes any number of actual data records that match it, but with actual values where the attributes go, such as: (XYZ-123, blue, Ford, 2012, "Fred Smith", "1 Universe Road, Utopia, CA"). Note: we could break the owner and owner-address attributes down to smaller constituent parts, which is a specific problem scoping-issue not addressed here as yet. (Note: the line-based notation of a relation schema here, is a horizontal version of the vertical depiction on an entity, in the visual notation seen in Figure 5, where a visual notation is used instead.)

Examples of the anomalies that Codd addressed are evident in this VEHICLE schema as follows. If it were to describe the whole database, then it has Insert, Modify and Delete problems: Modify anomaly: if a vehicle changes owners, we lose the details of the old owner (unless they own another vehicle). Delete anomaly: if a vehicle is removed from the database, we also lose the details of the owner. Insert anomaly: we cannot insert the details of a new vehicle owner into our database, until we also have the details of the vehicle they own.

The problem here with VEHICLE is the cross-dependency between two attributes that are not the primary-key: owner-address is functionally dependent upon owner. Codd identified this particular problem as a transitive dependency - because it exists between two non-key attributes - and he showed the solution to the problem is to take out the attributes involved and place them in a new entity, while leaving a copy of the new identifier in the original entity, so as to allow the two entities to be inter-related in future queries. E.g.

VEHICLE(license-plate, color, make, year, owner);

OWNER(owner, owner-address);

At about this point in an analysis it would be abundantly clear even to the novice data modeler that owner is not a good choice as a primary-key, as several people may well have the same name. Therefore, a numeric identifier that is guaranteed to be unique for every record, is usually introduced as a primary-key. Furthermore, the various parts of owners' names could be introduced:

VEHICLE(license-plate, color, make, year, ownerID);

OWNER(ownerID, firstname, surname, owner-address);

as could also be done with owner-address.

I.e. In reality, beyond the simplified text-book examples, the normalization of relations is correlated with little design decisions along the way, in an interaction between the analysis and the design.

Similarly, in the beginning of a mashup, in the absence of a requirements document, an end-user usually begins with some pre-existing related artifact, and oftentimes that is a spreadsheet that has been used to do some similar, but simpler manual or semi-manual record keeping together with a little computation. I.e. End-user developed spreadsheets are often the forerunners to fully-developed innovative custom information systems that follow. For an example of the use of normalization as a bottom-up design technique (as a heuristic), consider the following relation schema that represents a single table of details about movie tickets, held in a large spreadsheet, as the starting point (i.e. the starting relation schema is represented by the column headings in the spreadsheet):

TICKET(ticketID, ticketType, cost, bookingID, customerName, paid, movieTitle, rating, runningTime, cinemaName, theatreNo, row, seatNo, address, screeningDate, sessionNo, startTime, sold);

where: theatreNo is a sequential number relative to a cinema; row (from A to Z) and seatNo together identify a seat within a given theatre; sessionNo is a sequential number starting at '1' each day for a given movie at a given cinema, for multiple screenings of a specific movie.

Applying Codd's rule to remove transitive dependencies gives us the following new entities and a modified TICKET entity:

```
TICKET(ticketID, ticketType, bookingID, movieTitle, cinemaName,
theatreNo, row, seatNo, sold);
TICKET_TYPE(ticketType, cost);
BOOKING(bookingID, customerName, paid);
MOVIE(movieTitle, rating, runningTime);
CINEMA(cinemaName, address);
SCREENING(cinemaName, movieTitle, screeningDate, sessionNo,
startTime, theatreNo);
```

In this case, all the non-primary-key attributes left in the slimmed-down TICKET are all foreign-keys, meaning they are the primary-keys (or part thereof) of other relations kept here to service the various inter-relation relationships, with the exception of 'sold'. They are shown in italics here to indicate as much. The new entities are all given seemingly sensible names with respect to the domain. That naming may appear straightforward, and yet the selection of a meaningful and useful name is often harder than it sounds, when many people are involved. People generally load the meaning of a given word with their own specific meaning, which is why information analysts make a dictionary to hold the project/app specific meanings of words/terms, as a shared reference point available to all project/app stakeholders.

Another type of functional dependency that Codd identified is called a partial dependency which can only occur when a primary-key is constructed from more than one attribute, meaning: where it takes more than one attribute to uniquely identify any given row. Partial dependency refers to a situation where an ordinary attribute is functionally dependent on only part of a multi-part primary-key, rather than on all of it. When we dealt with the original TICKET relation above there was no cause to check for partial dependency, but now there are two new entities with multi-part (compound) primary-keys and one of these does have a partial dependency:

SCREENING(cinemaName, movieTitle, screeningDate, sessionNo, startTime, theatreNo);

The *theatreNo* attribute is dependent upon the *cinemaName* part of the key only, so it needs to be brought out into a new entity, leaving the remaining two as follows:

SCREENING(cinemaName, movieTitle, screeningDate, sessionNo, startTime);

THEATRE(cinemaName, theatreNo);

thereby removing the partial dependency from the model. Note: When taking out a partial dependency, it is not necessary to leave behind a foreign-key to facilitate a cross-relationship, as it already exists within the compound primary-key of the original entity.

Even though we removed the partial dependency after removing transitive dependency in our case, the removal of partial dependencies delivers a design in 2NF, while removing the transitive dependencies delivers a design in 3NF, and they are usually done in numeric order. Yet, in bottom-up analyses we often don't get many-part/compound keys until after the transitive dependencies are removed, as was the case here.

Note: 1NF is achieved by removing any repeating groups in an entity, if they exist. They do not often exist in spreadsheets, where the original table is usually flat (2-dimensional, with all cells filled). For an example of a repeating-group attribute, consider a starting entity for MOVIE that incorporates a list of genres that categorized a specific movie, such as: MOVIE(movieTitle, runningTime, genre [drama, history, biography, ...]).

Also note: Boyce-Codd Normal Form is needed when there is a reverse partial dependency: meaning that a part of a multi-part primary key is dependent upon an ordinary attribute, rather than the other way around. Examples of this are rarer, although end-users are more likely to encounter them than practicing information/ data analysts, and there is no such dependency in our example here. Nonetheless, the automation of data normalization in the next section, does enact both 3NF and BCNF.

As mentioned above, analysis and design are usually intertwined in practice in an iterative, step-wise manner. You may have noticed that one of the new entities is currently all primary-key, i.e. THEATRE. At this stage the information analyst would typically think about other useful attributes that might be added to each of the newly derived entities, that would further facilitate the functionality we are after in the complete mashup. For example, adding longitude and latitude to CINEMA would be useful in an app targeting GPS-empower smartphones and similar portable devices; adding a bitmap plan view of the seating in a THEATRE would facilitate a user-friendly interface; etc. (Remember, the casual end-user programmer will not normally be given a requirements document as a starting point). In the adding of such new attributes, the analyst is careful to be sure that they are each dependent upon 'the primary-key, the whole-key and nothing but the key', as the data modeler saying goes, in summing up the 3NF process. Reapplying normalization after the addition of new attributes to the previously extracted new entities, is always prudent.

Automating Data Normalization Using Logic

Having demonstrated manually how data normalization can be used as a bottom-up design heuristic, this section demonstrates the automation of an algorithm to do much the same. It does so using the logic programming language Prolog/CoLoG.

The Ceri & Gottlob (1986) paper includes a complete listing of their Prolog program in the appendix. It runs to more than 300 lines of complex logic programming. Rather than replicate that code here, this section looks at what the program requires from the end-user in the way of input, and shows what output is produced by a subsequent running of the program on the example TICKET schema. The output is then compared with the manual bottom-up analysis.

The program expects two types of predicate as input:

schema(relationName,[attribute1, attribute2, attribute3, ...]);

and

fd(relationName, [determinant/s], [functionalDependent/s]);

Note: The square brackets indicate the list notation used in Prolog, i.e. repeating-groups are allowed in a predicate in logic languages.

So, to use the same relation TICKET from the spreadsheet artifact as used in the manual normalization example above, the fact base required by the program as input is:

```
schema(ticket,[ticketID, ticketType, cost, bookingID,
customerName, paid, movieTitle, rating, runningTime,
cinemaName, theatreNo, row, seatNo, address, screeningDate,
```

```
sessionNo, startTime, sold]);
fd(ticket, [ticketType], [cost]);
fd(ticket, [bookingID], [customerName, paid]);
fd(ticket, [movieTitle], [rating, runningTime]);
fd(ticket, [cinemaName], [theatreNo, address]);
fd(ticket, [cinemaName, movieTitle, screeningDate, sessionNo],
[startTime]);
fd(ticket, [row], [seatNo]);
fd(ticket, [theatreNo], [row]);
```

The program has many rules within it that it uses internally, some of which are useful in their own right. The following is a list of the main ones (remember, variables in Prolog start with a capital letter):

- thirdNF(Relation): Decomposes Relation into 3NF.
- isInBCNF(Relation): Tests whether Relation is in Boyce-Codd Normal Form.
- bcNF(Relation): Decomposes Relation into Boyce-Codd Normal Form.
- minCover(Relation): Finds a minimal cover of the functional dependencies defined for Relation.
- oneKey(Relation,Key): Finds one Key for Relation.
- assertAllKeys(Relation): Determines and asserts all the keys of Relation.
- projectFDs(Rel1,Rel2): Projects the functional dependencies that hold for relation Rel1 to relation Rel2; the schema of Rel2 must be a subset of the schema of Rel1.
- minimize(Relation): Minimize the decomposition of Relation.

Each of these is detailed in Ceri & Gottlob (1986). A central algorithm used by all these rules is one that builds a minimum set of attributes from a given set. It is called closure, and in Prolog it utilizes a recursive algorithm that works much like that one back in Figure 2, for the mortgage calculator, by recursively calling itself:

```
closure(Relation, X, Result) <++ fd(Relation, LHS, RHS);
        subset(LHS, X),
        not subset(RHS, X),
        union(W, X, RHS, Relation),!,
        closure(Relation, W, Result);
closure(Relation, X, Result <++ #(Result, X);
```

Where union and subset are other parts of the total code-base, that are general-purpose, small, utility rules.

Running the program through a number of steps, until it gets all validations, returns these useful synthesized relations:

```
TICKET_a(ticketID, ticketType, bookingID, movieTitle,
cinemaName, theatreNo, sold);
Some other keys: ticketType, bookingID, movieTitle, cinemaName,
theatreNo.
TICKET_b (ticketType, cost);
TICKET_c (bookingID, customerName, paid);
TICKET_d (movieTitle, rating, runningTime);
TICKET_e (cinemaName, theatreNo, address);
TICKET_f (cinemaName, movieTitle, screeningDate, sessionNo,
startTime);
TICKET_g (cinemaName, theatreNo);
TICKET_h (cinemaName, theatreNo, row, seatNo);
```

The program does not present them in this format, but these are the relations it produces, put back into the notation used earlier in the manual normalization. Clearly, the program cannot assign meaningful relation names for the relations it synthesizes, instead just adding variations on the name of the input schema, so the end-user still needs to do that. And as already alluded to above, selecting the most meaningful name for a newly synthesized relation, is only straightforward to all, in retrospect.

After a quick look back at the earlier models, including Figure 4, to add naming consistency across this chapter, we assign the following names to those synthesized entities: TICKET to TICKET_a, TICKET_TYPE to TICKET_b, BOOKING to TICKET_c, MOVIE to TICKET_d, CINEMA to TICKET_e, SCREENING to TICKET_f, THEATRE to TICKET_g and SEAT to TICKET_h.

Overall the program produced a very good match with the manual normalization in the bottom-up design, but there are a few differences. Firstly, the SCREENING relation does not have *threatreNo* in the synthesized version. It has come about by the way that the functional dependencies were arrived at, in the manual process. I.e. it was initially assumed that *theatreNo* would be a part of the dependency for *startTime*, but on a closer examination of the definition of *sessionNo* (i.e. examining the actual business-rule based on *sessionNo*), it became clear the *sessionNo* was incremented sequentially within a Cinema, for a given Movie, on a given day/date - and so *startTime* was not dependent upon *theatreNo* at all. I.e. In practice, the same movie is made available to different sized audiences at different times of the day, by moving it about the different theatres that a Cinema complex has available. Therefore, it was a mistake in the manual normalization by the end-user in taking *theatreNo* to the SCREENING entity in the first place, and that inclusion got overlooked even after they properly understood the business rule around *sessionNo*. However, it was via that mistake that the manual process picked up the THEATRE entity via the partial dependency rule. Whereas, the automated normalization process picked up THEATRE directly, and got SCREENING correct as well.

Another difference, is that the automated process picked up the SEAT entity, and removed row and *seatNo* to this new entity. It did so because more functional dependencies were identified at the input stage of the automated process. I.e. by concentrating on the identification of functional dependencies, one-by-one, via the need to define each of them codified as input, the end-user realized that a given *seatNo* was dependent on the row it was within (e.g. taking values A-Z, say), and that row was in turn dependent upon *theatreNo*. I.e. more dependency information was input to the program, than was considered during the manual normalization process.

It is worth noting that while this SEAT entity would provide little functionality as it is, in an ensuing implementation (apart from enabling a query to tally-up the total number of seats in a Theatre or in a whole Cinema). It did turn out to be useful in the fuller design as shown earlier in Figure 4 (i.e. the given normalized model, back then). I.e. once a bitmap image of the theatre plan-view was added to THEATRE as a useful attribute - to enable user-friendly interaction for seat selection - that then required the coordinates (in pixels) of each seat within the bitmap, to be added to the SEAT entity. This latter handy use of SEAT in the bottom-up design process,

Figure 11. High-level ER model in a top-down design method

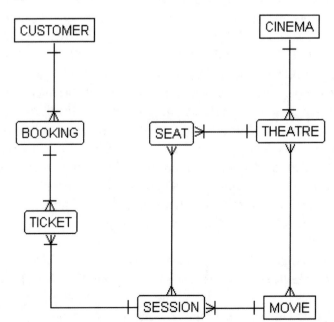

demonstrates one of the inherent values of a normalized data model: that apart from removing the Insert/Delete/Modify anomalies, it also renders the design in a state most flexible to enhancements in the future, catering for unforeseen personal end-user whims, change-requests and/or other requirements, that invariably follow a successful implementation.

DISCUSSION

The previous section finished with a discussion about the closeness between a bottom-up design model that was achieved via a manual normalization, versus the bottom-up model achieved using the automated normalization in the logic program within the IDE. They were remarkably similar, and the variations between them was adequately explained. An additional point worth making here, is that the starting set of entities and attributes that the end-user sets upon, can be played around with quite readily, given the highly interactive nature of the built-in CoLoG/Prolog language interpreter. I.e. Logic programs either prove whether goals are satisfied, or not. They are very forgiving in that regard, as new facts are added and/or new goals/queries are put to them.

Before a discussion of how effective bottom-up design using normalization is per se, and how useful the automation of that process is to end-users, we need to compare the bottom-up design example given above, with one that was arrived at via a top-down design method, an approach usually favored by experienced information analysts.

Top-Down Design

Top-down design is harder to do and harder to teach, as there are fewer heuristics available to the Information Analyst to use, than there is with bottom-up design. The analyst needs to be either: an experienced conceptual modeler; have some innate conceptualization ability (i.e. gifted); and/or be an expert in the domain area that is being modeled. An analyst doing a top-down analysis and design of the movie ticket problem would begin the model with a handful or two of the entities that seemed the most important to the problem at hand - always far more easily recognized in retrospect than in the original analysis going forward. In the movie-cinema example here, the entities depicted in Figure 11, namely: MOVIE, CINEMA, THEATRE, SEAT, CUSTOMER, BOOKING, TICKET, SESSION - represent a good example of what a top-down analysis might start with.

The analyst would have chosen these high-level entities, typically after reading over some contextual artifacts (documents; web-sites; vocabularies; ontologies; etc.).

In conjunction with reading over these, they would have held some discussions with various stakeholders (user, managers, cinema staff, etc.), tasked with assembling the so-called business rules evident in the domain area being modeled. (Note: Business Rules and their acquisition, is beyond the scope of this chapter (see: Hoffer et al., 2007). Instead, we chose a well-known domain area to compensate that exclusion, i.e. movies and cinemas are things that almost all readers know something about. However, the business rule about *sessionNo* discussed above, showed the importance of a business rule to the overall design.

Next, in the top down method, the analyst is guided by those assembled business-rules, to determine the cardinalities of the relationships between these high-level entities; specifically, whether they are: one-to-one; one-to-many; or many-to-many, as indicated by the crows-feet notation on the relationship lines in Figure 11. Of particular interest at this stage, is the identification of many-to-many relationships, as they each become entities/tables in their own right - the so-called associative entities that appear in the more detailed ER model that follows. There is one between SESSION and SEAT in Figure 11, meaning that a SESSION has many seats available, and a specific SEAT is used in multiple SESSIONs, at different times. E.g. from that many-to-many relationship in the high-level model comes the SEATS_AVAILABLE entity in the more detailed model as given earlier in Figures 3 and 4.

Another domain-specific business rule that is particularly illustrative of the impact that one such rule may have on the model, is uncovered in the answer to this question by the analyst, put to a stakeholder: 'How many movies are shown in a SESSION, only one, or sometimes more than one?' If the answer is 'only ever one', then the model in Figure 11 is sufficient, and what is called a SESSION there is the equivalent of the relation called SCREENING in the bottom-up design using normalization as the guiding heuristic. However, if the answer is 'sometimes more than one' - then the model needs to have both SCREENING and SESSION as two distinct entities, together with another called MOVIE_SESSION to accommodate multiple movies per session, as they appear back in those given models in Figures 3 and 4.

Automated Bottom-Up Modeling vs. the Top-Down Modeling

It turns out that the iterative, step-wise, intertwined analysis and design that we observed in the bottom-up analysis above, is very well serviced by the Prolog/CoLoG interpreter built into the IDE, running the code that automates the 3NF/BCNF process. However, the experienced information/data analyst, armed with data normalization as just one of their spectrum of heuristics and frameworks, and professionally-versed to seek wide-ranging input from a broad-range of stakeholders, will generally out-model the end-user using just data normalization in bottom-up analysis-design fashion, in a model quality sense. There are research studies that have set out to measure the different approaches of data modeling experts versus novices (Chaiyasut & Shanks, 1994) and to improve the quality of such models accordingly (Moody, Shanks & Darke (1998); Moody & Shanks, 2003).

Nonetheless, armed with a tool that does achieve the automation of 3NF and BCNF, this chapter claims that the end-user programmer is generally capable of achieving a reasonable design. Particularly if they are given, or face, the same set of requirements as the information analyst, and where each is constrained by a similarly limited scope of functional capability in the envisaged application.

A caveat here is that the Information/Data Analyst (or Business System Analyst - the job titles used, vary), is usually part-and-parcel of gathering the Requirements, doing so in a professionally trained manner; while the end-user developer gathers their requirements in a myriad of different ways. Given those two distinct paths, the requirements and the scope used by each, will rarely align very well, so neither will their respective models covering similar terrain at the start.

User Interface Issues

I concede that, despite the automation of data normalization demonstrated here, the end-user programmer still needs a good understanding of functional dependencies. S/he needs to at least be able to grasp the basics presented here in sub-section above *Data Normalization and bottom-up design*, but no more than that.

Furthermore, the user interface to the program that does the automated normalization could be vastly improved, as currently it just uses the CoLoG interface window shown in Figure 2. A dedicated GUI interface that specifically prompts the end-user for a starting entity and for its constituent attributes, would help. And further, a GUI that makes specific requests for user-identification of each functional dependency, attribute-by-attribute, would go a long way to easing the end-user's task of assembling the schema and fd facts needed by the automation program as outlined in sub-section above: *Automating data normalization using logic*.

Anecdotally, we noted that the concentration of an end-users mind upon each attribute in turn, improves the likelihood of getting them right. Along this line of reasoning, it is also worth noting that the other relatively recent paper that uses those algorithms assembled by Ceri & Gottlob (1986), detailed here (Yazici, & Karakaya, 2007), promotes their particular automation as an educational tool for teaching Data Normalization, as much as a modeling tool for practicing database designers. I.e. the feedback of seeing it done, from the input that the user supplies, promotes both the appreciated worth of data normalization and the method of achieving it. That in turn, heightens a user's interest in mastering identification of the functional dependencies.

Lack of Control Over Remote Computational Resources

Another aspect of the models from the view of designing a distributed application or mashups, not discussed so far, is that the structure of data available via an external web service, or via the method signatures (which are also analogous to logic predicates) available at an external API (application programming interface), is usually totally out of the control of the end-user building the distributed app or the mashup.

However, this potential problem too is amply addressed by the logic program interpreter built into the IDE. Prolog and CoLoG and other similar prolog-compatible languages, have the ability to simply project a different predicate, combining bits and pieces of other existing predicates in a logic program, via new end-user formulated logic rules. This capability allows the 'ideal' model coming from the design process, to be mapped onto the fixed external models of the remote resources employed for their capabilities. This process is akin to projecting Views (new, logical tables) in Relational DBMS. Relational Views allow the users of Relational DBMS to map new logical structures coming from design, upon fixed legacy systems that are not easily changed physically. Similarly, user-defined rules and predicates, allow users of logic programming interpreter, to map new structures coming from design, upon fixed or given remote structures, that they in-turn employ in the implementation of a distributed app or mashup.

CONCLUSION

Several interactive development environments either have internal logic languages, or can employ plug-ins to get them. The DigitalFriend IDE for example, uses the internal Prolog-like CoLoG language interpreter to glue together various sub-agents by dynamically combining predicates, rules and ground terms, from both local and remote resources. In turn, the mashup or distributed app developer, needs to be able to write well-formed logic predicates and rules, to use such systems effectively. However, there is a recognized gap in available methods for writing such predicates and rules (Sterling, 2002).

As seen in the overview of the implementation of the *MovieAssistant* in the section *Implementing the Design and using the DigitalFriend*, there is a significant and timely need for such design methods, in designing and developing mashups and distributed apps that incorporate a logic language, such as the Movie-Cinema problem covered in much detail in this chapter, not to mention that the local user platform (Raspberry Pi in our case) is capable of sourcing data from all sorts of connected sensors and devices in the users locale in addition to the internet, in an IoT future.

To compound that need, an IDE such as the DigitalFriend is aimed at the end-user programmer/developer, who will most often not be a logic language programmer at all, but who may well initially have technical skills at the spreadsheet-developer or the desktop database designer level, or the recreational programmer level, and now, novice coders too who have cut their teeth on Scratch, Greenfoot and similar languages (Good, 2018) aimed at school-age learners and beyond. This led to a requirement for strong guidance in finding appropriate predicates as early as possible, using well-tested techniques that they are either familiar with, or which can be learned in a short timeframe. The TANDEM design method came about to address that requirement (Goschnick et al., 2006).

The TANDEM method concentrates on achieving well-formed logic rules in programs that are predominantly declarative in nature (e.g. Listing 1). It does this by starting with a very basic task analysis, followed by normalization of the accrued entities, and then identification of logic flow lines, which address the primary tasks identified in the task analysis. The derivation of well-formed logic rules then becomes relatively straightforward, as demonstrated in the case study in section *The TANDEM Design Method*. Furthermore, a significant tool is given to the end-user programmer, by automating the data normalization process itself, where a logic language interpreter is available to them in the IDE. This does provide an end-user programmer/developer with a significant bottom-up design method; and a flexible tool that they can literally play with the starting entities and attributes, in an interactive, iterative and stepwise manner.

The whole process results in flexible logic programs, which can be distributed amongst sub-agents in a mashup or a distributed app, and one with IoT data streams, that can each handle specified tasks, but which also have flexible combinations of predicates and terms, to handle many new unforeseen goals. The well-formed nature of the predicates and logic rules, means that they are in a highly adaptable form, that can be modified and added to with new rules, via either easily modified existing sub-agents, or with the addition of new sub-agents and new web services, as new requirements unfold in the ongoing life of a successful application.

Furthermore, the TANDEM method does have broader applicability to designing a broad class of logic programs, irrespective of the skill of the programmer. It complements the pattern-oriented approach identified by Sterling (2002). His approach with patterns helps with logic programs that have intricate procedural logic rules (e.g. Figure 2). The TANDEM design method addresses logic programs that are more concerned with descriptive logic, but nonetheless also often require a few procedural rules (e.g. Listing 1), complementing the use of recognized patterns in logic programs, in a programming paradigm where there has been a dearth of design methods.

Perhaps the most significant outcome of this research, is the synergy achieved by combining the TANDEM method with the algorithms in a logic program that automates Data Normalization (a key process used within the method), and implementing it within an IDE, the tool used by the end-user programmer during their need of the design method. The resultant system can therefore devise well-formed predicates, largely by itself, given only some relevant starting entities and their constituent attributes – the raw data coming from modest requirements gathering exercises - together with some light-weight analysis by the user to uncover any functional dependencies between those attributes.

ACKNOWLEDGMENT

The DigitalFriend V1.0 - is a product of a development project titled The Digital Self Project funded by a Telstra Broadband Fund Development Grant, provided by Telstra Ltd (Australia). It in turn was based on the ShadowBoard architecture as the blueprint, as presented in my Research Masters thesis (Goschnick, 2001). An earlier version of this chapter, prior to movement of the whole system (DigitalFriend V2) and the accompanying research project to the Raspberry Pi platform, was published in *IJPOP* 2(1).

REFERENCES

Annet, J. (2004). Hierarchical Task Analysis. In D. Diaper & N. Stanton (Eds.), *The Handbook of Task Analysis for Human-Computer Interaction* (pp. 67–82). Lawrence Erlbaum Associates.

Balbo, S., Ozkan, N., & Paris, C. (2004). Choosing the Right Task-modelling Notation: A Taxonomy. In D. Diaper & N. Stanton (Eds.), *The Handbook of Task Analysis for Human-Computer Interaction* (pp. 445–465). Lawrence Erlbaum Associates.

Beeri, C. (1980). On the membership problem for functional and multivalued dependencies in relational databases. *ACM Transactions on Database Systems*, 5(3), 241–259. doi:10.1145/320613.320614

Beeri, C., & Bernstein, P. A. (1979). Computation problems related to the design of normal relational schemata. *Communications of the ACM*, 4(1), 30–59.

Bernstein, P. A. (1976). Synthesizing third-normal-form relations from functional dependencies. *ACM Transactions on Software Engineering and Methodology*, 1(4), 277–298.

Bouzeghoub, M., Gardarin, G., & Metais, E. (1985). Database design tools: An expert system approach. In *Proceedings of 11th International Conference on Very Large Data Bases* (pp. 82-95). Academic Press.

Cellan-Jones, R. (2017). *Raspberry Pi scores UK's top engineering award.* BBC. Retrieved from http://www.bbc.com/news/technology-40444356

Ceri, S., & Gottlob, G. (1986). Normalization of Relations and Prolog. *Communications of the ACM, 29*(6), 524–544. doi:10.1145/5948.5952

Chaiyasut, P., & Shanks, G. (1994). *Conceptual data modelling process: a study of novice and expert data modellers.* Dept. of Information Systems, Monash University.

Codd, E. F. (1970). A relational model of data for large shared data banks. *Communications of the ACM, 13*(6), 377–387. doi:10.1145/362384.362685

Codd, E. F. (1971). *Further normalization of the database relational model. Courant Computer Science Symposia 6: Data Base Systems.* Englewood Cliffs, NJ: Prentice-Hall.

Colmerauer, A., & Roussel, P. (1993). The birth of Prolog. In *Proceedings of HOPL-II The second ACM SIGPLAN conference on history of programming languages.* New York, NY: ACM. 10.1145/154766.155362

Fagin, R. (1977). Functional dependencies in a relational database and propositional logic. *IBM Journal of Research and Development, 21*(6), 534–544. doi:10.1147/rd.216.0534

Feiler, J. (2008). *How to do everything with Web 2.0 mashups.* New York, NY: McGraw-Hill.

Good, J. (2018). Novice Programming Environments: Lowering the Barriers, Supporting the Progression. In S. Goschnick (Ed.), *Innovative Methods, User-Friendly Tools, Coding, and Design Approaches in People-Oriented Programming.* Hershey, PA: Information Science Publishing.

Goschnick, S. (2006) The DigitalFriend: the First End-User Oriented Multi-Agent System. *Proceedings of the 3rd Open Source Developers Conference (OSDC-2006).*

Goschnick, S., & Graham, C. (2006). Augmenting Interaction and Cognition using Agent Architectures and Technology Inspired by Psychology and Social Worlds. Universal Access in the Information Society, 4(3), 204-222.

Goschnick, S., & Sterling, L. (2003). Enacting and Interacting with an Agent-based Digital Self in a 24x7 Web Services World. In *Proceedings, IEEE Joint Conference on Web Intelligence and Intelligent Agent Technology (WI/IAT).* Halifax, Canada: IEEE.

Goschnick, S. B. (2001). *Shadowboard: An agent architecture for enacting a sophisticated Digital Self* (Thesis). Dept. of Computer Science and Software Engineering, University of Melbourne, Melbourne, Australia.

Goschnick, S. B. (2009). People-Oriented Programming: from Agent-Oriented Analysis to the Design of Interactive Systems. *Proceedings, HCI International.* 10.1007/978-3-642-02574-7_93

Goschnick, S. B., Balbo, S., Sterling, L., & Sun, C. (2006). TANDEM - a design method for integrating Web services into multi-agent dystems. In *Proceedings, Fifth Joint Conference on Autonomous Agents and Multi-Agent Systems (AAMAS-06)* (pp.939-941). Academic Press. 10.1145/1160633.1160799

Hoffer, J. A., Prescott, M. B., & McFadden, F. R. (2007). *Modern Database Management* (8th ed.). New Jersey: Pearson Prentice Hall.

Kent, W. A. (1983). A simple guide to five normal forms in relational database theory. *Communications of the ACM, 26*(2), 120–125. doi:10.1145/358024.358054

Kerschberg, L. (1984). Expert database systems. *Proceedings, The 1st International Conference on Expert Database Systems.*

Kölling, M. (2018). Blue, BlueJ, Greenfoot: Designing Educational Programming Environments. In S. Goschnick (Ed.), *Innovative Methods, User-Friendly Tools, Coding, and Design Approaches in People-Oriented Programming.* Hershey, PA: Information Science Publishing.

Kowalski, R. A. (1988). The early years of logic programming. *Communications of the ACM, 31*(1), 38–43. doi:10.1145/35043.35046

Lee, R. M. (1985). Database inferencing for decision support. *Decision Support Systems, 1*(1), 57–68. doi:10.1016/0167-9236(85)90197-6

Loizou, G., & Thanish, P. (1983). Testing a dependency-preserving decomposition for losslessness. *Information Systems, 8*(1), 25–28. doi:10.1016/0306-4379(83)90026-1

Lucchesi, C. L., & Osborn, S. L. (1978). Candidate keys for relations. *Journal of Computer and System Sciences, 17*(2), 270–280. doi:10.1016/0022-0000(78)90009-0

Marriott, K., & Stuckey, P. J. (1998). *Programming with Constraints: An Introduction.* Cambridge, MA: The MIT Press.

Moody, D. L., & Shanks, G. (2003). Improving the quality of data models: Empirical validation of a quality management framework. *Information Systems, 28*(6), 619–650. doi:10.1016/S0306-4379(02)00043-1

Moody, D. L., Shanks, G., & Darke, P. (1998). *Improving the quality of entity relationship models: experience in research and practice. In Conceptual Modeling-ER'98* (pp. 255–276). Berlin: Springer.

Oluyomi, A., Karunasekera, S., & Sterling, L. S. (2007). A comprehensive view of agent-oriented patterns. *Autonomous Agents and Multi-Agent Systems*, *15*(3), 337–377. doi:10.100710458-007-9014-9

Orchard, L. M. (2005). *Hacking RSS and Atom*. Indianapolis, IN: Wiley Publishing.

Potter, W. D. (1984). Design-Pro: A multi-model schema design tool in Prolog. In *Proceedings, The 1st International Conference on Expert Database Systems* (pp. 747-759). Academic Press.

Ramakrishnan, R., & Gehrke, J. (2003). *Database Management Systems* (3rd ed.). New York, NY: McGraw-Hill.

Rizzo, A, Montefoschi, F., Caporali, M. & Burresi. (2018). UAPPI: A platform for extending App Inventor towards the worlds of IoT and Machine Learning. In S. Goschnick (Ed.), *Innovative Methods, User-Friendly Tools, Coding, and Design Approaches in People-Oriented Programming*. Hershey, PA: Information Science Publishing.

Simsion, G. C. (2006). *Data Modeling: Description or Design* (Doctoral thesis). University of Melbourne.

Sterling, L. (2002). Patterns for Prolog Programming. Computational Logic: Logic Programming and Beyond, 374-401. doi:10.1007/3-540-45628-7_15

Sterling, L., & Shapiro, E. (1994). *The Art of Prolog*. Cambridge, MA: The MIT Press.

Tsou, T. M., & Fischer, P. C. (1982). Decomposition of a relation scheme into Boyce-Codd normal form. *ACM-SIGART*, *14*(3), 23–29.

Wooldridge, M. (2009). *An introduction to MultiAgent Systems* (2nd ed.). John Wiley & Sons.

Chapter 7
Interdisciplinary Design Teams Translating Ethnographic Field Data Into Design Models:
Communicating Ambiguous Concepts Using Quality Goals

Jeni Paay
Swinburne University of Technology,
Australia

Sonja Pedell
Swinburne University of Technology,
Australia

Leon Sterling
Swinburne University of Technology,
Australia

Frank Vetere
The University of Melbourne, Australia

Steve Howard
The University of Melbourne, Australia

ABSTRACT

Translating ethnographic field data to engineering requirements and design models suitable for implementing socio-technical systems is problematic. Ethnographic field data is often "messy" and unstructured, while requirements models are organized and systematic. Cooperation and communication within an interdisciplinary design team makes the process even more complicated. A shared understanding between ethnographers, interaction designers, and software engineers is vital to ensure that complex and subtle social interactions present in the data are considered in the final system design. One solution for supporting team conversations uses the quality goal construct as a container for complex and ambiguous interaction attributes. Quality

DOI: 10.4018/978-1-5225-5969-6.ch007

goals in system modelling promote shared understandings and collaborative design solutions by retaining a high level of abstraction for as long as possible during the design process. This chapter illustrates the effectiveness of abstract goals for conveying complex and ambiguous information in the design of a socio-technical system supporting social interaction between couples.

INTRODUCTION

In designing socio-technical systems, it is necessary to discover what discriminates social requirements from other types of requirements. Designers need to focus on the identification of user goals, and in particular those non-work-related, non-goal-oriented interpersonal interactions that happen between individuals. An interdisciplinary team is important for the translation from ethnographic field data to requirements modelling to achieve a solution that takes account of both function and non-functional aspects of social interactions. Embracing ambiguity in requirements modelling for socio-technical systems helps withhold design commitment on social requirements for as long as possible. Recognizing and working with how models of ambiguous concepts, such as joking and play, facilitates rich conversations between ethnographers, interaction designers and software engineers with respect to the social needs and interactions of users of proposed systems. The need for the design team to create a shared understanding becomes particularly relevant when designing digital technologies for activities outside of the work domain, for example, mediating personal and intimate relationships between couples (Paay et al., 2009).

Cultural probes produce ethnographic field data that is particularly suitable for learning about intimate and personal aspects of people's lives (Gaver et al., 1999). Data generated from cultural probes can include user-generated photographs, postcards, drawings, and scrapbook entries, and can be supplemented with contextual interviews to enrich understanding. However, it is a substantial challenge to take the "messy" user data and translate it into the formal models required for system implementation. A design team needs to identify non-work-focussed and non-goal-oriented interpersonal interactions that happen between individuals, to discover social requirements of a system. These interactions, for example, flirting or joking, constitute much of what occurs between intimate couples, families, friends and social groups engaged in leisure. Ambiguity plays a vital role in maintaining openness and flexibility in the interpretation of cultural probe data throughout the design process. Ambiguity, as described by Gaver et al. (2003) becomes "a resource for design" when designing technologies to support activities outside of work. Ambiguity should be regarded as an opportunity, rather than a problem, because it allows for multiple possible meanings and individual interpretations of concepts. According to Gaver et al., ambiguity in design allows people to interpret situations for themselves, and establish deeper and more personal relations with meanings offered by systems.

Software engineering is proficient at modelling individual purposeful needs but it does not yet convincingly address requirements elicitation of non-goal-oriented social interactions. Additionally, ethnographers and interaction designers come to the design process with their own interpretations of the data and hence different implications for system design. It therefore remains an ongoing challenge to merge the differing viewpoints, skill sets and understandings of members of an interdisciplinary team, to create an effective and relevant technology solution for end users (Paay, 2008). Using ambiguity in requirements modelling can provide a solution to the problem, through the use of *quality goals* from the Agent Oriented Software Engineering (AOSE) method (Sterling & Taveter, 2009). Quality goals are essentially non-functional goals encapsulating social aspects of the context into software requirements models. They represent quality attributes that both enrich and constrain the goals and roles of a multi-agent system. This is particularly relevant when data about people's experiences are gathered using ethnographically inspired methods. The construct of quality goals, attached to functional goals in the requirements models, represent quality attributes of social interactions as abstract, ambiguous and unresolved concepts. The ability to articulate quality goals and carry them through to the design phase in an undischarged form, adds the necessary level of ambiguity for interpretation and translation of social requirements. Quality goals can carry subtle nuances of social interactions from field data through to final system design. They are able to stimulate conversations on design alternatives during collaborative conceptual design, because they remain flexible and open to interpretation. They do not need to be resolved early in the process. This is important when the team is interdisciplinary, allowing for translation of different concepts and ontologies, toward a shared understanding.

This chapter presents the development of the *Secret Touch* system, illustrating the design of a novel technology supporting flexible and meaningful social interactions between people in intimate relationships. An interdisciplinary team of ethnographers, interaction designers and software engineers modelled system requirements for *Secret Touch* collaboratively. User data was collected in a cultural probes study exploring social interactions between couples in the "Mediating Intimacy in Strong-Tie Relationships" project (Kjeldskov et al., 2005; Vetere et al., 2005). Although technological innovations are typically created to address commercial interests, technologies are often appropriated to mediate personal and intimate relationships (e.g. typewriter for love letters, telephone for maintaining personal ties, mobile phone for texting personal interactions). Rather than wait for the consequences of commercially oriented innovation to permeate personal lives, the mediating intimacy project sought to examine the design of technologies for strong-tie relationships explicitly. The project proposed a framing of intimacy that supported a design oriented discussion. Intimacy was characterised by Antecedents (pre-conditions for intimacy), Constituents (elements of the intimate acts), Yields (the consequences of an intimate exchange). The themes were used to stimulate 22 design ideas, one of which was Secret Touch which enables partners to "virtually hold hands" while physically separated. Couples exchange tactile impulses over the Internet by padding or squeezing a device in their hand or pocket. These impulses would be sensed as vibrations, heat or pressure by the partner.

The secret touch concept was explored through contextual interviews to supplement and interpret the probe data with participants. Probe data was analysed using affinity diagramming (Beyer & Holtzblatt, 1998) and scenarios were created (Carrol, 1997), before cooperative modelling by the team. Quality goals and modelling notation inspired by the ROADMAP methodology (Sterling & Taveter, 2009), were used during requirements elicitation. However, quality goals can be equally well elicited in most requirements modelling methodologies. The Prometheus methodology (Padgham & Winikoff, 2004), an AOSE methodology, inspired modelling at the design level.

The *Secret Touch* design process demonstrates the benefits of using *quality goals* during requirements modelling when using cultural probe data about the social interactions of a couple. The final design of *Secret Touch* runs on a small pocket device, communicating with a similar partner device. Couples in intimate relationships interact discretely and remotely by physically moving a device in their pocket which makes their partner's device move in an identical fashion. Detailing the design process shows how quality goals maintained ambiguity throughout the elicitation, analysis, and conceptual design stages of requirements modelling. They supported richer on-going conversations between ethnographers, interaction designers and software engineers. This shows that by combining ethnographic techniques for understanding complex and subtle human relationships with best practice from interaction design and software engineering disciplines the outcome is a socio-technological system incorporating rich, valued aspects of people's social interactions. Recognizing ambiguity in an adequate and open way is particularly relevant when developing social technologies.

This chapter presents background information on social concepts in requirements modelling, eliciting requirements from cultural probe data, quality goals in requirements modelling and ambiguity in the modelling process. The design of the *Secret Touch* system is described, with detailed requirements elicitation, analysis and design modelling, tracing the progression and resolution of ambiguous concepts through the use of quality goals, throughout the process. This is followed by a discussion on the benefits of the approach, as well as insights on how the research has influenced current methodologies in software engineering of socio-technical systems. The chapter concludes with implications of the study.

229

BACKGROUND

Software engineering has a long tradition of identifying constraints on software behaviour, representing functional services, and modelling them as functional goals that the system is expected to deliver (Jureta et al., 2006). However, with increased development of socio-technical systems supporting people's activities outside of work, such as leisure activities, functional goals are no longer sufficient to represent all system requirements. This is because people's social interactions are not easily decomposed into measurable functional requirements. Domestic and social pursuits comprise a range of purely communicative activities, not necessarily serving any external productive purpose. In designing socio-technical systems, capturing social concepts accurately but flexibly at a high level is essential, while not losing their vitality through over specification.

Social Concepts in Requirements Modelling

In software engineering requirements modelling, social issues have been considered since the early 1990's. Goguen and Linde (1993) introduced techniques for requirements elicitation acknowledging that work takes place within a social context. These techniques used concepts from ethnomethodology and sociolinguistics, including conversation, interaction and discourse analysis, to gain access to social interactions. Quality issues such as security, portability, reliability and modifiability, although not easily quantified, were identified and their imprecise nature embraced as desirable for making trade-offs during the design phase (Goguen & Linde). Other software engineering approaches including social needs modelling are: i* framework (Yu, 1995); TROPOS (Castro et al., 2001); ROADMAP (Sterling & Taveter, 2009); and the Softgoal Concept (Jureta et al., 2006). These approaches include social context but focus on coordination and collaboration tasks, which are social but with deliberative purposes, for example, arranging a time to meet.

Ethnographically inspired methods have been successfully used in Human Computer Interaction (HCI) to understanding how people interact and to gather requirements for interaction design since the mid 1990's (e.g., Hughes et al.,1995; Rouncefield et al., 2003; Sommerville, 2015). These methods include: field observations, field studies, contextual interviews and cultural probes. HCI designers want to understand the current practice of people in a particular situation in order to design technologies to support them or improve their experience of that situation. The ethnographic approach to understanding user needs puts the user firmly at the centre of data gathering. Viller and Sommerville (2000) used ethnographic studies of work to inform systems design. They demonstrated how ethnographic results could be integrated into the object-oriented software engineering (OOSE) process.

They identified use cases and generated initial use case models, using the Unified Modelling Language (UML) to represent social aspects of work. However, because their case study was in air traffic control, the focus was on defining functional requirements around distributed coordination, plans and procedures, and work awareness. They were also faced by the problem that OOSE does not explicitly encourage the inclusion of information pertinent to social contexts. According to Sommerville (2015), ethnographically inspired data collection can provide a rich source of ideas for new technological products. Especially when data is collected about a social activity, as and when it happens.

For the representation of non-functional social requirements, it is essential to capture social concepts while also communicating the rich quality of people's social interactions. Several approaches have been made in software engineering to achieve this, the most successful being the introduction of actors and agents using the AOSE paradigm. In an agent-based system, agents have characteristics of autonomy, reactivity, pro-activeness and social ability (Wooldridge & Ciancarini, 2000). The social ability characteristic allows agents to interact with other agents, and sometimes even with humans. Agents have the ability to engage in social activities. They are primarily used for cooperative problem solving and negotiation toward achieving functional goals of a system. However, the construct of the agent, and agent roles, opens up the possibilities for representing human qualities of social interactions. The AOSE paradigm is promising for supporting social concepts in software development because the characteristics of agents can be equated to human actors. Agents can exhibit human-like behaviours such as autonomy, flexibility, intelligence, learning, and dynamic adaptability to the surrounding environment, increasing their suitability for socio-technical software development. Agent-oriented concepts help design teams collaborate toward a deeper understanding of the implications of quality requirements in design, and work together to find solutions.

Constructs for capturing social concepts in requirements modelling can be found in the *i*framework* (Yu, 1995), *Gaia* (Wooldridge et al., 2000; Zambonelli et al., 2003), *TROPOS* (Castro et al., 2001), *ROADMAP* (Sterling & Taveter, 2009) methodologies. The *i* framework* approaches social concepts in requirements engineering from the broader perspective of describing a network of social dependencies among "actors" in the system. The *i*framework* inspired approaches for explicitly handling qualitative system aspects using quality requirements, often called Non-Functional Requirements (NFRs) (Chung et al., 2000). *Gaia* is an early and well-cited AOSE methodology. It takes an organisational view, describing systems in terms of the roles that agents take on. However, *Gaia* starts modelling from a requirements statement, assuming requirements have been gathered by some other process. Conversely, *TROPOS* is requirements-driven and strongly involved in the early requirements phase. *TROPOS* defines systems in terms of autonomous, intentional and social software actors, incorporating concepts from the i* framework, and focussing on social dependencies amongst actors. *TROPOS* documents requirements in a way that is compatible with a business environment and facilitates software engineering from design through to implementation. However, it is a rather formal methodology, so modelling quickly becomes quite complex. Complexity precludes it from being suitable for capturing ambiguous social concepts. *ROADMAP* (Role-Oriented Analysis and Design for Multi-Agent Programming) is an AOSE methodology that started as an extension of *Gaia*. Analysis and design in *ROADMAP* differs from the other AOSE methodologies because it enables extensive, detailed and fine-grained capture of the different roles and goals that agents have. It separates analysis and design, and is independent of design architecture and agent platform. *ROADMAP* exhibits strong flexibility, enabling uncertainty and ambiguity to be maintained during requirements elicitation. It does so through the representation of *quality goals* in goal model diagrams. Quality goals, directly associated with system goals, constrain the ways in which agents enact their roles. The flexibility of *ROADMAP* makes it particularly suitable for conveying ambiguous social concepts encapsulated in quality goals throughout system modelling.

Eliciting Requirements From Cultural Probe Data

Cultural probes are a novel data collection technique developed by Gaver et al. (1999) gaining prominence in interactive systems design (e.g., Burrows et al., 2015; Cheverst et al., 2003; Dey & De Guzman, 2006; Hassling et al., 2005; Mayasari et al., 2016; Paulos & Jenkins, 2005; Petrelli et al., 2009; Rodden & Benford, 2003; Rouncefield et al., 2003; Schorch et al., 2016; Soro et al., 2016). Cultural probes, an ethnographically-inspired method, are particularly suited to investigating people's everyday life in situations otherwise difficult to reach with traditional social science methods, such as questionnaires, interviews, focus groups or observation. Like deep sea or planetary probes, cultural probes are 'sent-out' by researchers and return fragmentary data over time. The data returned gives subjective, inspirational glimpses into the situational context and lives of participants and captures *motivations* that shape domestic life. Cultural probes are carefully designed packages of materials, including: diaries, scrapbooks, postcards, cameras, pens, pencils, glue, sticky tape and other materials. Participants use these to document everyday activities as they occur or shortly afterward, and then return them to researchers. It is left to the participants to record their own experiences. The probes both encourage and empower subjects to collect data themselves, rather than relying on the presence and intervention of a researcher (Arnold, 2004). Participants provide researchers with insight into their daily lives, but at their own discretion.

Cultural probes facilitate collection of research materials over longer periods of time and in multiple locations concurrently, compared with resource intensive observational ethnographic approaches. In particular, cultural probes garner an understanding of the playful character of human life and the multifaceted ways in which people "*explore, wonder, love, worship, and waste time*" (Gaver, 2001, p.1). The initial intention behind cultural probes was simply to inspire design, not to gather system requirements (Gaver et al., 2004). Cultural probes are looking for clues about how people get on in the world, and how technology might support their interactions with each other and their environments. They enable elicitation of information otherwise difficult to obtain about participants' habits, and emotional, aesthetic and social values (Hemmings et al., 2002). Interaction designers have embraced cultural probe data as providing rich descriptions of real social phenomena (Rouncefield et al., 2003) useful for informing technology design. However, probes, by their very nature, provide fragmentary data, making it difficult to elicit detailed requirements for systems design, since they were not designed to provide data easily transformable into technical specifications. Hence, difficulties arise when using cultural probes for requirements gathering in software engineering requirements modelling. It is because the cultural probe method is so good for learning about the subtleties of social interactions in the domestic domain, that researchers persist with it as the data gathering method of choice for the design of innovative social technologies. They provide rich information to designers about people's daily lives (Vetere et al., 2005). Cultural probe data is also useful for team design. It inspires "*interdisciplinary iterative interpretative and design work where stories are generated, renewed and reworked over time*" (Graham et al., 2007, p.35). Provocative and traceable discussion points arise within the design team as they develop a shared understanding of system requirements through insights garnered from the rich probe data.

With ethnographic field data, the problem is how to derive usable and useful system requirements while retaining the insights and inspirations collected. Eliciting requirements from probe data involves working in a way that captures concepts accurately but flexibly, at a high level, without losing their liveliness and vitality through over specification. The rich information gathered in the field needs to be transformed to fit the formalized and rigorous models of software requirements elicitation and design. The team identifies goals for the system, and then cooperatively designs how they should be operationalised. Quality goals are a necessary part of the abstraction, maintaining the richness of data while concrete system requirements are generated to support technology implementation. Quality goals are closely related to *system use* and yet are not necessarily always translated directly into system requirements. In socio-technical systems, the quality of the final design tends to be greater than the sum of the individual single functions it is composed of, that is, "*the whole is greater than the sum of the parts*" (Sterling &

Taveter, 2009, p.11). High-level quality goals associated with social activities act as a point of reference for discussing design alternatives. Quality goals function as a bridge between "messy" cultural probe data and requirements elicitation models, providing a focus for conversations within an interdisciplinary team.

Quality Goals in Requirements Modelling

Quality goals provide a constant reminder of the overall goals and intentions of people interacting in social situations. They capture the essence of human interactions better than other elicitation mechanisms found in software engineering practices, because they are more dynamic and fluid. A design team uses quality goals to understand the reasons why people do things, or the essence of a relationship, rather than the actions taken. Quality goals can be used to withhold design commitment beyond the elicitation phase, keeping quality attributes of an interaction unresolved and interpretably flexible throughout all stages of the process. From a software engineering point of view, requirements and design models enable a design team to take the outputs from a cultural probe study and use them to inform socio-technical software design. Thus taking account of the richness of human social interaction provided by the cultural probe data and encapsulating quality attributes of that interaction into quality goals in the models. These models then facilitate high-level discussions in designing a system that supports and enhances domestic social interaction. Agent-oriented modelling, in particular, facilitates the expression of non-functional requirements by attaching quality goals to goal models, and putting constraints in role models (Sterling & Taveter, 2009). Goal model diagrams specify roles required to enact a goal. Role model diagrams detail responsibilities and constraints relevant to enacting goals. These roles are consolidated into agents that form part of a multi-agent software system. The success of a design in achieving its goals can really only be confirmed after implementation. However, to build technologies that genuinely facilitate social connections and relationships, it is important to maintain an openness in the process and not resolving all aspects of requirements too early. The fact that quality goals are not directly implemented, but influence design by providing a rich picture of the social interactions of people and their domestic roles being modelled, means that openness can be achieved.

Quality goals in requirements modelling, as introduced by ROADMAP (Sterling & Taveter, 2009), represent quality attributes of the system as high-level abstractions that remain unresolved throughout the design process. Multiple interpretations and design alternatives for social aspects represented in the final product are encouraged. The quality goal container facilitates conversations between ethnographers, interaction designers and software engineers on quality attributes of social interactions, until a collaborative solution is reached. Innovation and creativity in design are stimulated, as people with different expertise and skills sets communicate their different ideas, provoke "out of the box" solutions, evaluate them as a team, and negotiate holistic solutions. The process brings together the deep social understanding of the ethnographer, the human factors and HCI expertise of the interaction designer and the abstraction and modelling expertise of the software engineer to create a technology design embedded into real social contexts. By externalizing quality attributes in quality goals, they become shared artefacts that sustain multiple interpretations across disciplines (Paay et al., 2009).

Focus on quality is a well-established aim within software and systems engineering. Software engineers realise the need to express quality attributes of software, as well as functional capabilities, as digital technologies move into the home and leisure domains. Some form of "quality attributes" are included in several modelling methodologies, using a variety of terms, including: non-functional requirements (NFRs), constraints, quality attributes, quality goals, or quality of service requirements (Gross, 2005; Kirikova et al., 2002; Reekie & McAdam, 2006; Sommerville, 2015; van Lamsweerde & Letier, 2004). Technology that supports interpersonal contact in social situations is only valuable if it fulfils the felt needs of the people acting in these environments, who will use technology to augment and support their social interactions. People's social needs are typically high-level, cognitive, emotional, and *hard to measure*. For example, playfulness, the act of engaging in an activity or expressing feelings for no functional purpose, is an important part of close relationships. Playfulness helps define the nature and closeness of a relationship (Davis et al., 2007). It is therefore important that any device facilitating interaction between close couples should be able to represent playfulness in the user experience. Playfulness encapsulated in a quality goal means that it becomes a visible part of the model, to be remembered and incorporated into the design at some point.

Quality goals are an effective container for quality attributes in requirements modelling, conveying a more positive connotation than the term "non-functional requirements". They are seen as different from functional goals, and not reduced to measureable goals. Quality goals, by their very name, infer concern with the quality of a system, and aspects of user experience that go beyond functionality. Quality goals are most effective in requirements modelling when directly paired with system goals. The direct relationship is necessary for quality attributes to be carried through the stages of the elicitation, analysis and design in an unresolved state. System goals are user goals that are satisfied by using the system and are not necessarily implemented as specific functions in the final system. Relating an abstract, unresolved quality attribute to a system goal maintains ambiguity for as long as possible within the design process. By openly defining quality goals during socio-technical system design, quality concerns are kept visible throughout the design process, ensuring they do not become an afterthought in system development.

Quality goals in a process, emphasize a more active searching for qualities of the interaction from the ethnographic data, distinct from identifying functional goals. They purposefully use words directly linked to people's interactions in social environments, such as, flirting, joking, teasing.

Quality goals are often subjective, context-specific, and imprecise (Sterling & Taveter, 2009), and hence actively promote ambiguity in the process. Quality goals that are intentionally ambiguous, represent an opportunity rather than a problem to be solved. They encompass ambiguous elements in social systems, such as flirtatiousness, fun and play, and carry them through to design in a system independent form. Delaying specification enables the design team to ideate on solutions and negotiate trade-offs while evolving the functional design. Functional goals are generally hierarchical and are decomposed into sub-goals. Quality goals are not. They require a more "holistic" design approach. Rather than specifying solutions for resolving quality goals as a set of sub-tasks, they are incorporated into the overall design through inspirational and collaborative leaps, requiring a "designerly way of thinking" (Cross, 2011; Kjeldskov, 2014).

Scenarios, used in conjunction with quality goals, are an addition to the requirements modelling process that further deepen the design teams understanding of the user's situation and help translate those goals into system design (Sterling & Taveter, 2009). Scenarios are a well-established tool for requirements engineering (Carroll, 1997; Sutcliffe et al., 1998). They are typically textual descriptions of situations of use, described from the perspective of an end user. Carroll (2000) states scenarios keep the future use of the technology in view, making the technology easier to design: "The defining property of a scenario is that it projects a concrete description of activity that the user engages in when performing a specific task, a description sufficiently detailed so that design implications can be inferred and reasoned about" (p.3). Stories enable developers to empathise with the people in the situation, which leads to questions about motivations, intentions, reactions and satisfaction. Therefore, scenarios are powerful when designing and evaluating systems with requirements that involve user engagement. While goal model diagrams are purposefully simple they are reinforced through more extensive information captured in motivational scenarios and domain models.

Motivational scenarios, in requirements elicitation, can be informed by cultural probe data. They hold more detailed information about the qualities of a system from a person-centred view and describe the roles people take on. The addition of scenarios to a modelling methodology, further socializes quality goals and deepens the richness of understanding available to the design team. Scenarios attached to quality goals help identify key steps in user interaction with the system where a particular quality attribute is important, helping the design team interpret quality goals appropriately. Domain models capture important information about the use context, for example, the home. Quality goals rely on context from domain models for the design team to understand and resolve ambiguity in quality attributes.

Quality requirements are an important part of any software project, they are a major factor in determining system success, and yet quality attributes are often forgotten about during software development (Sterling & Taveter, 2009). The ability of socially oriented quality goals to carry quality attributes as abstract and ambiguous concepts makes it possible for design teams to evaluate and resolve these concepts at any point during elicitation, analysis or design. While some quality goals, such as performance targets or system availability, are readily quantifiable, others such as a system being secure or a game being fun, are less so. Quality goals are used to define quality attributes in the data, without the need to resolve them. Resolution of quality requirements can be done while solving functional requirements, impacting the way both are resolved. Through the use of the quality goal container, quality aspects found in the data are able to influence design decisions throughout the process, because they remain visible and yet still ambiguous.

Ambiguity in the Design Process

The value of embracing ambiguity in the design process is in giving space for creativity in the design process. Gaver et al. (2003) define ambiguity *"as uncertainty in the interpretative relationship linking person and artifact"*. They identify three aspects in design where uncertainty can exist: the ambiguity of *information* or attributes of the artefact itself; the ambiguity of *context* in the sociocultural discourses that are used to interpret it; and ambiguity of relationship in the interpretative and evaluative stance of the individual or his attitude towards the artefact. Several HCI studies have investigated benefits of preserving ambiguity in design products, to give users space for their own interpretation of the artefacts (Aoki & Woodruff, 2005; Dalmau, 2003; Gaver et al., 2003). The benefits of ambiguity can equally be applied to the process of requirements modelling. However, using *"ambiguity as a resource for design"* in modelling, is most beneficial during design specification. The set of models are the design artefact where ambiguity sits, and the design team are users of those evolving models.

Although ambiguity seems antithetical to the routines of software engineering, it has always been part of it. However, software engineers typically view ambiguity as having a negative impact on development because it is a source of impreciseness that can lead to misinterpretation and incorrect formal specifications (Kamsties et al., 2001). Software engineering research has been primarily concerned with detecting ambiguity in requirements specification and dealing with it in (Blaha et al., 2005), involving either reducing it to a minimum (Tjong et al., 2007) or removing it completely (Fabrini et al., 2001). Research has explored the use of tools

(Fabrini et al.), inspection techniques (Kamsties et al.), and rules (Tjong et al.) to detect ambiguity in the design process or in requirements documents (Buckeridge & Sutcliffe, 2002). It is a generally held belief that a requirements specification is of high quality if there is no ambiguity (Fabrini et al.).

The use of natural language in requirements specification is regarded as one reason that ambiguity finds its way into the process (Berry, 2008; Kamsties et al., 2001; Tjong et al., 2007). The use of a formal requirements specification language is an often-suggested solution for removing ambiguity (Berry et al., 2003). By dealing with ambiguities in data at the informal level, before formal specifications are produced, misinterpretations and incorrect formal specifications can be avoided (Kamsties et al.; Fabrini et al., 2001). However, very few requirement documents are written in formalized language because the translation from informal natural language requirements to formal requirements documentation is difficult (Berry; Fabrini et al.; Sawyer et al., 2005). The difficulty is exacerbated by a "messy" data set informing those the requirements, for example, gathered using cultural probes or other ethnographically inspired methods, and especially within a non-work context.

Software engineering research, since the early 1990's, has used a social science perspective to recognize that models, and other documentation, are not simply feeding user data into a formal process of modelling for system design (Button & Sharrock, 1994; MacLean et al., 1990; Randall et al., 1994). They provide ways to think through problems, to reach agreements, and elaborate needs. For example, MacLean, et al., found the most useful form of design rationale was the very rough documents made early in the design process. These documents provide a resource for revisiting, used as orienting documents and artefacts later in the process. Similarly, the value of ambiguous attributes in quality goals is in giving the design team a more structured way of elaborating and confronting the complexity of the design space for socially-oriented technologies. Thus, considering not only ambiguity *per se*, but the role of models in the design process. If ambiguity is removed from the modelling process too early, designers lose clarity on where it occurred and the context of the resolution (Kamsties et al., 2001). Early disambiguation leads to unrecognized or unconsciously assumed meaning, that could be entirely wrong, finding its way into design specification (Berry et al., 2003; Gause & Weinberg, 1989). It also leads to ambiguous concepts not being represented properly in the final design, because they are resolved before their impact on the overall design is completely understood. It is difficult to detect missing non-functional attributes once a formal specification document is made (Kamsties et al.). Therefore, the essence of non-functional quality social interactions could be lost to the final design, if they are interpreted too early.

"Soft" goals, such as fun, are difficult to precisely define, independent of the domain, because these quality attributes tend to be imprecise, subjective, idealistic and context-specific (Jureta et al., 2008). Goal models are used early in design to arrive at a common understandings of system goals. There is a directive in the software engineering process to detect and resolve system issues as soon as possible, often without seeking clarification (Jureta & Faulkner, 2007; Kamsties et al., 2001). With quality goals, it is more difficult to arrive at a shared understanding early in the process. During early requirements elicitation, designers might not be able to clarify social concepts sufficiently to resolve them, therefore social goals should be kept at a high level of abstraction, even after formal specifications are written. Identifying ambiguities in social data creates awareness in the design team of the need to maintain the high level of abstraction. Team discussions around highly ambiguous complex concepts that are not easily clarified, helps complexity reduction without losing the richness of the social concepts themselves. Resolving design through discussion, embraces interpretation and openness amongst design team members and supports correlation with overall goals of the system and the context of use. Rather than eliminating ambiguity early in the process, withholding design commitment gives the design team time to discuss and clarify what it might mean to disambiguate with respect to the overall design.

Ambiguity in the requirements modelling process helps the design team to recognize, design for, and evaluate systems with the view that multiple, competing and divergent interpretations of a system can co-exist, and solutions to design problems do not need to reside in a single correct interpretation (Sengers & Gaver, 2006). The value of ambiguity is in the flexibility it provides in the design process. Ambiguity, as embodied in goal models, allows for multiple interpretations of a problem to co-exist throughout the requirements modelling and design phases. By integrating quality goals into system goal models, the ambiguous nature of social interactions is acknowledged, and can impact the final design of the system. Some ambiguity may be resolved during requirements modelling; some may be carried through to the design phase. By keeping quality goals at an informal and ambiguous level throughout the analysis and design processes, they remain available as a resource for discussion. They facilitate an interpretive relationship between team members and models and can be used to prompt and influence design decisions without the need to clarify and specify quality attributes within fixed system boundaries. These discussions around models and motivational scenarios, bring to the table as many different interpretations of the models as there are members of the design team. Conversations around complex and abstract social concepts such as "having fun" and "playing" help the design team to identify concepts at goal level and include qualities related to the achievement of those goals in the overall system.

THE SECRET TOUCH SYSTEM

The design of the *Secret Touch* system demonstrates the translation of data from a cultural probes study to system requirements and a final design of a socio-technical system. The models include a scenario to motivate the design, goals, roles and ambiguous concepts in the form of quality goals. Presentation of a sample set of models shows how quality goals contribute to the process of interpreting data for system design. By identifying important aspects of social interactions, such as "Risky" and "Playful", and representing them as quality goals associated with system goals in the models, they were made visible. The design team of ethnographers, interaction designers and software engineers had a construct for analysing, interpreting and designing around complex social concepts. The interdisciplinary design team worked together in interpreting quality attributes, resulting in a design that was more holistic in its resolution of social interactions. However, the models presented do not provide a step-by-step process for designing socio-technical systems, rather, they show the role of ambiguity within a requirements and design modelling methodology. By tracing specific quality goals through the different models, it can be seen how uncertainty, inherent in the data, is carried through the process of design. The *Secret Touch* quality goals represent information about intimate interactions that occur between couples, which in themselves are sometimes intentionally ambiguous. These quality goals actively promote and tolerate ambiguous attributes of intimate interactions, maintaining them throughout the elicitation process at a high level of abstraction. They are not discharged before they are passed to the design process, demonstrating a sensitivity to the non-functional aspects of the data, and a radical extension and application to the synthesis of probe outcomes into the technology design process. Through the processes of requirements elicitation, analysis and design, the software engineering models were used in a flexible way, acting as artefacts for discussion between team members.

Requirements Gathering

Requirements gathering for The *Secret Touch* system used the findings from the Mediating Intimacy project (Vetere et al., 2005). The study focused on supporting intimates (i.e. life partners, parents and younger children, adult offspring with dependent parents, etc.) when both co-present or separated by distance. Data gathering in the Mediating Intimacy study was a multi-method approach to understand intimate interactions between participants, extending the work of Gaver et al. (1999) by combining cultural probes, interviews, focus groups and scenario-based acting out sessions. The cultural probe data collected included workbooks and diaries produced by six couples, documenting their interactions throughout the day.

Scenarios drawn from the Mediating Intimacy data, were used to drive design ideation. A series of motivational scenarios were created, each suggesting technological solutions to assist in mediating intimacy. One of these was the *Secret Touch* scenario (see Table 1), which described a device designed to facilitate intimacy between couples by maintaining a digital connection with each other throughout the day. The *Secret Touch* scenario was chosen for design and implementation of a socio-technical device for mediating intimacy in couples.

Requirements elicitation from the data was an iterative one. Software engineers driving the requirements elicitation phase would regularly present their ideas and models through presentations, discussions and survey questionnaires to the team of six ethnographers and interaction designers, who conducted the fieldwork for the Mediating Intimacy project. The team would then discuss the abstractions being made from the data and cooperatively form revised models and design features. Through team interactions, *Secret Touch* became a robust and flexible system reflecting needs of target users. The communicative and integrated design process was able to cater for and embrace the diverse opinions within the design team about the desirability of different intelligent Secret Touch options. The process resulted in a range of different features for the system representing complex and subtle needs of end users. Table 2 contains the complete feature range, listed from the simplest to most complex activity enabled by the system.

"Flirt" is the basic feature of the Secret Touch system, where all device movements are transformed into touches. These touches are instantaneously sent to the partner's device, and received as a movement of the device. If there are simultaneous incoming and outgoing movements, the device resolves them and moves in a direction that is the vector sum of both touches, simulating a playful tug-of-war situation between users, where they can actively counteract touches from their partner.

"Discrete Flirt" enables partners to enter into a turn taking dialogue of interactions. If the user is busy, for example, attending a meeting, they can either switch their

Table 1. The Secret Touch motivational scenario generated from the Mediating Intimacy Project

Scenario: Secret Touch
Inspiration: • Couples wanting to communicate in private • Feeling each other • Being playful • Individuals like fiddling with toys
Description: They both reach in their pockets during work. She feels that he is fiddling with the device. She turns the device in the other direction, engaging into playful activity

Table 2. The Secret Touch features

Feature	Description	Details
Flirt	Risk and openness to flirtation	Open channel, full-duplex communication, i.e. always on
Discrete Flirt	Partner chooses level of accessibility	Choice of open channel or modes: ON, OFF, PASSIVE
Fiddler's Choice	Response possibly from agent	Add learning or remembering to either of the above
Guessing Game	Who or what is that?	An open, dynamic system – partners and devices change

device off, or they can set it to discretely receive touches from their partner. The discreet flirt feature collects incoming flirts, which can be replayed later when the meeting is over. The user is able to control when they are not available for flirting, or they would like to remain connected, but review collected flirts when it is more convenient.

"Fiddler's Choice" is an intelligent, learning feature of the system. When a user receives an incoming touch, but is unable to personally engage in the flirting episode, the device takes control and responds to their partner on their behalf. The feature can also be used by individuals who would like the system to actually flirt with them. An important application for personal use is in learning and behavioural education. It can be used to assist in reducing the kinds of nervous fiddling associated with anxiety or autism. Both awareness and satisfaction comes to the user by giving them a device movement in response to their fiddling.

"Guessing Game" is designed for playing "hard and fast" in personal relationships, with connectivity between groups of devices. There is no longer only a set partnership or connection between two devices. Connected devices may still be aligned with a single intimate couple, but can also involve multiple partners. It is an open, dynamic system, where devices participating in the exchange of touches can appear and disappear from the game, seemingly at random.

Requirements and Analysis Models

In requirements elicitation, requirements modelling diagrams, based on the *ROADMAP* methodology (as detailed in Sterling & Taveter, 2009), were used to elicit a set of roles, goals and quality goals from the data collected during the Mediating Intimacy project. These models offer capacities at the requirements analysis level, enabling various levels of abstraction, hiding complexity, or focussing on details of a section of the model. The models facilitate high-level abstraction, flexibility in design, and ease of use, which are important in the process of interdisciplinary design when transforming field data into system requirements. System requirements and quality constraints can be captured independent of later decisions concerning design and architecture. For the final design, modelling diagrams, based on the *Prometheus* methodology (Padgham & Winikoff, 2004), were used to create the AOSE system design for *Secret Touch*. *Prometheus* arose out of a BDI (Belief-Desire-Intention)-based agent platform *JACK* (2015), is more fully developed for design than requirements analysis, and offers a well-documented and usable set of methods for designing agent software.

Goal and Role Modelling Notation

Goal models represent system goals, in a loosely hierarchical fashion. Goal models can have quality goals associated with them, which influence how that goal should be fulfilled. Quality goals are the intangible goals of a system, such as, privacy, risk taking, and timeliness. Goal models show overall goals of a system at a high level. Quality goals make complex and ambiguous constructs visible in the models, making them available for discussion by the design team. Roles are attached to goals, and indicate who is responsible for achieving that goal. While goals retain ambiguity through quality goals, roles allow different members of the design team to identify different alternatives on how goals might be achieved, based on their own experiences. Role models comprise a name, description, list of responsibilities, and list of constraints. The concept of roles is particularly useful in modelling socio-technical systems, as an analogy can be drawn between agents and human actors. Agents take on one or more roles within the social situation being modelled and are usually responsible for a set of goals. Role models capture a lot of detail, which is an advantage when eliciting requirements and initiating discussions between ethnographers, interaction designers and software engineers about the different responsibilities and constraints of the roles that people play that in the situations being modelled.

Figure 1. Requirements and Analysis Modelling Notation: a) Goal, b) Quality goal, and c) Role

(a)	*(b)*	*(c)*
Goal: to be fulfilled by the agent system. Roles often have responsibility for specific goals.	Quality goal: or "soft" goal, are attached to goals and may be addressed by a role's constraints.	Role: has responsibility and constraints. An agent may have many roles.

The notation used includes: goals represented in diagrams as parallelograms, with goal names written in the centre (Figure 1a.); quality goals, attached to goal models, drawn as clouds, with names in the centre (Figure 1b.); and roles represented as stick figures with the name of the role written underneath it, indicating their analogy to agent/human roles (Figure 1c.). These three different constructs are connected in modelling diagrams by lines indicating their relationships to each other.

Goal Model Diagrams

The *Secret Touch* highest-level goal model diagram, *Mediate Intimacy*, is shown in figure 2. There are two sub-goals, *Flirt* and *Communicate*. The *Flirt* sub-goal (see Figure 2), has the *Partner* role associated with it, as well as the quality goals of *Risky* and *Playful*. The *Flirt* goal is achieved using the sub-goal *Initiate Flirt*. A *Touch Initiator* role describes how a flirt should be initiated, leading to the achievement of the sub-goal, *Capture Touch* which has the quality goal of being *Timely*, and constraints associated with capturing the touch defined by the *Touch Perceiver* role. Guided by the *Device Manager* role, the goal of *Translate Movement Into Touch* has the quality goal of being *Accurate*. The other outcome of a *Flirt*, (as seen in Figure 2), is that it can be responded to using a *Respond To Flirt* goal. Responding is important for the intelligently learning *"Fiddler's Choice"* feature of the system (as described in Table 2). The *Touch Responder* role is responsible for how it is done. There are two sub-goals associated with the goal, *Recognise Incoming Touch* and *Propose Touch Sequence*. A *Choreographer* role is responsible for both sub-goals. The *Choreographer* recognizes an incoming touch and proposes the appropriate counter-movement. The response must have the qualities of being *Matching* and

Figure 2. Secret Touch Requirements Model, with sub-goals Flirt and Communicate

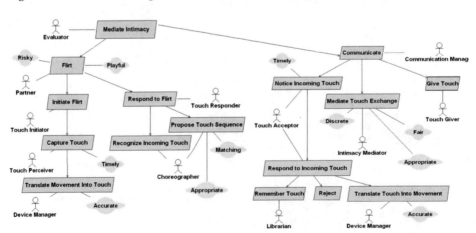

Appropriate, as it builds on habits that often develop within relationships, for example, finishing a telephone call with *"Love You"* instead of *"Bye"*.

The *Communicate* sub-goal, (see Figure 2), described in general terms, involves noticing incoming touches in a timely manner, and accepting and responding to those incoming touches. It is controlled by a communication manager. Remembering incoming touches is available only in the *"Fiddler's Choice"* design. Remembering past touches is done using a library, and based on past responses, either rejecting the touch, or responding to it by translating that touch into movement using a device manager, while ensuring that the movement response is accurate. Alternatively, the system can mediate a touch exchange, in a discrete, fair and appropriate manner, available in the *"Discrete Flirt"* feature, as controlled by an intimacy mediator. Finally, a touch can be given by a touch giver.

The goals represented in the *Secret Touch* requirements model are at a high level, but easy to understand as the goal names used are familiar social concepts. Ambiguous concepts in the social interactions, such as risky, playful, and appropriate, are captured using quality goals and are available for discussions in the design team, with respect to associated goals.

Role Model Diagrams

Role Models are specified in table form, inspired by the *REBEL* toolkit (Sterling & Taveter, 2009). These role models represented important details of envisioned system behaviour. Details of the role model for *Touch Acceptor* are shown in Figure 3. The *Touch Acceptor* role, (seen in Figure 2), is associated with sub-goals of *Notice Incoming Touch* and *Respond To Incoming Touch*, in the *Communicate* section of the requirements model. The *Touch Acceptor* role model shows the list of responsibilities required to enact accepting touches when they are noticed, and responding to them, using a "Responsibilities List" (as shown in Figure 3). These responsibilities include: "Notice incoming touch"; "Check partner availability"; "Accept/Reject/Remember a touch"; and "If appropriate, inform of touch's fate".

The "Constraints List", shown in Figure 4, is used to describe how a goal might be achieved, including: "If partner is currently openly flirting, pass touch on to be felt"; "If partner is currently interactively available, inform of accepted touch to be felt"; "If partner is currently passively available, inform of accepted touch to be remembered"; and "If partner is unavailable, reject touch". The *Touch Acceptor* role model gives the design team information needed to ideate design ideas for dealing with incoming touches, and discussing how the associated quality goal, *Timely*, might influence that design. Thus, the role model construct facilitates design team discussions around an ambiguous concept while maintaining the ability to withholding design commitment. Actions resulting from partner availability are defined, but the

Figure 3. Touch Acceptor Role Model: Responsibilities List

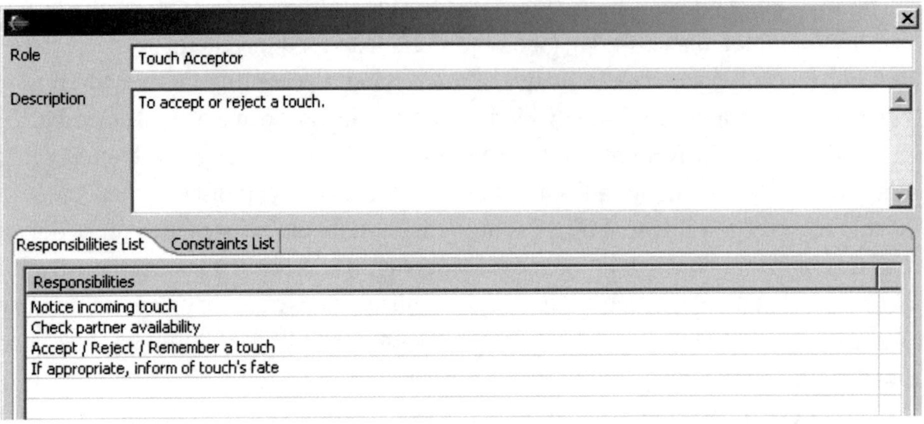

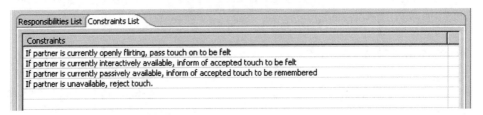

Figure 4. Touch Acceptor Role Model: Constraints List

degree of timeliness of these responses, that is, the quality of the response, remains open for alternative design solutions.

The lists of responsibilities and constraints attached to role models proved to be a useful communication tool for achieving a shared understanding between ethnographers, interaction designers and software engineers. They encouraged each team member to offer different interpretations of quality attributes and their impact on design. For ethnographers, it involved retaining strong links to social interactions observed in the field data. For interaction designers, it involved bringing human-centred design guidelines and usability considerations into the discussion. For software engineers, it involved sharing expertise on software implementation and technology capabilities. Role models, associated with goals and quality goals, acted as shared artefacts used to generate lively discussion within the design team during requirements elicitation sessions. The coming together of different disciplines, experiences and understandings, resulted in the emergence of additional quality goals.

Detailed Design

Agent-oriented design models, including scenario and agent diagrams, were used in detailed design of the *Secret Touch* system. Plans and capabilities, which are sets of functions and abilities within each agent, and any messaging internal to that agent, were created. Each plan represents a subset of functionality that becomes a chunk of code in implementation. Capabilities include the sub-capabilities, plans and messages needed for agents to fulfil their functionality. The relationship between plans and capabilities are shown in an agent overview diagram. A plan may include several alternate versions, based on different triggers or pre-conditions. The detailed design serves as instructions for implementation. As an exemplar of the detailed design modelling for *Secret Touch*, one set of high-level design diagrams are presented, including detailed design agent overview diagrams for one agent.

Design Notation

The constructs of design modelling used include: Agents, Protocols, Percepts, and Actions. Agents are the central component of an agent oriented system, represented by rectangles containing stick figures (Figure 5a.). They act as humans might, sometimes even representing the roles and behaviours of people. Protocols are represented by a double-ended arrows and define the ways in which agents communicate, containing the communication patterns between agents (Figure 5b.). Percepts and actions represent interactions with the external environment. Percepts represent interactions from the outside world that cause the system to react in some way, diagrammed as splats (Figure 5c.). Actions represent how the system acts outwardly upon the world, diagrammed as arrows (Figure 5d.). In the notation used, connecting lines indicate relationships, and arrows on the ends of connecting lines show the direction of the interactions. The models show inter-agent interactions within a system, via protocols. They also show system boundaries through actions and percepts related to each agent.

Scenario Diagrams

Scenarios have tabular constructs to represent their descriptions in design modelling. These scenarios are built from goals, actions, percepts and sub-scenarios. They are different from motivational scenarios created during requirements modelling. Actions associated with scenarios indicate how the system acts on the external world. Percepts associated with scenarios indicate how the system reacts to events in the outside world. Scenarios are useful during consolidation of roles into corresponding agents. Interactions between agents are based on scenarios. The role responsible

Figure 5. Design Notation: Agent, Protocol, Percept, Action

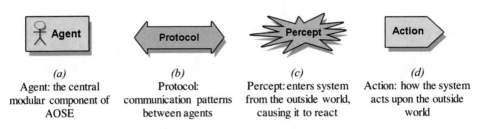

(a)	*(b)*	*(c)*	*(d)*
Agent: the central modular component of AOSE	Protocol: communication patterns between agents	Percept: enters system from the outside world, causing it to react	Action: how the system acts upon the outside world

for each step in a scenario is documented in the table. Scenarios are useful during the process of consolidating sets of roles into corresponding agents. Interactions between agents are based on scenarios, and interaction diagrams are created after coalescing roles into agents.

The *Tug-of-War* design scenario from *Secret Touch* is shown in Figure 6. The artefact was defined through discussions in the design team involving the translation of quality goals into the underlying details of these scenarios. The design team considered ambiguous concepts associated with quality goals, attached to system goals, during creation of these design scenarios. Additionally, design scenarios remain flexible, and open to change through their descriptions. At the highest level, the *Tug-of-War* design scenario consists of a back and forth between giving touches in the *Flirt* sub-scenario and receiving them in the *Feel Touch* sub-scenario, in any order, at any time. Each of these sub-scenarios is detailed in a similar form, defining related goals, actions and roles.

For example, the *Feel Touch* scenario, as illustrated in Figure 8, involves the activation of the sub-scenario of *Notice Touch*, which involves the role of *Touch Acceptor* (detailed in Figures 3 and 4). It involves the goal of *Translate Touch Into Movement*, which the *Device Manager* role is responsible for, (as seen in Figure 2). The goal of *Translate Touch Into Movement* carries with it the quality goal of *Accurate*, ensuring that touch responses are authentic and genuine. The role *Device*

Figure 6. Design Scenario: Tug-of-War, in "Flirt" feature of system

		Type	Name	Role	Description	Data
	1	Scenario	Feel Touch scenario	Touch Feeler		
	2	Scenario	Flirt scenario	Partner		
	3	"Other"			potentially infinite loop i.e. etc.	

Edit Scenario - Tug of War scenario

⬇ ⬆ Insert Step | Edit | Remove | Close

Figure 7. Design Scenario: Feel Touch, in "Flirt" feature of system

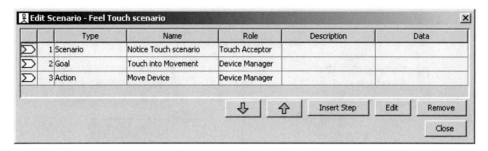

Manager is also associated with the subsequent action of *Move Device*. In the final system, when a touch is noticed by the device, it is translated into movement in an accurate manner, and the device then moves (vibrates), to indicate that a partner has sent a touch.

Using scenarios in the detailed design process ensured continuity from the requirements role and goal models, through creation of these scenarios, to defining software agents of the final system. Goals defined during requirements elicitation, and their associated quality goals, were included in the definitions of design scenarios. Thus, quality goals remained in an undischarged form and continued to represent ambiguous concepts into the final agent and interaction diagramming phases.

Agent Models

The detailed design process involved assigning roles to agents, where one agent had one or several roles. Different features of the system, as defined in Table 2, required different sets of roles and agents. During assignment, Agent-Role coupling diagrams acted as shared artefacts for design team discussions. Software engineers presented final system designs using these diagrams. Agent models were a great communication tool, as both ethnographers and interaction designers could clearly see analogies between the roles of the agents, and the roles and responsibilities of people in social interactions. Quality attributes attached to goals informed team discussions during allocation of roles to agents, enabling checking of role assignments with respect to qualities of the social interactions being modelled.

The *Secret Touch* system has four agents, each corresponding to a system interface to the external environment: *Device Handler*, *Intimacy Handler*, *Partner Handler*, and *Resource Hander*. These are required in the different system features. The simplest feature, *"Flirt"*, consists of the *Device Handler* agent interfacing to the physical device and the *Intimacy Handler* agent interfacing to the partner system. The *Intimacy Handler* agent (detailed in Figure 8) has the *Touch Accepter* role assigned

Figure 8. Agent-Role Coupling: Intimacy Handler agent

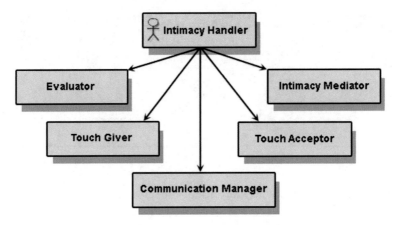

to it, because the agent is responsible for noticing touches, and ensuring that they are responded to in an *Accurate* manner. *Accurate* is the quality goal carried into agent modelling through the *Feel Touch* scenario (Figure 7), by virtue of its direct association with the *Translate Touch Into Movement* goal. The *Intimacy Handler* agent also handles the roles of *Evaluator*, *Touch Giver*, *Communication Manager* and *Intimacy Mediator*.

More complex features of the device require the other agents. The *Partner Handler* agent is used in the *"Discrete Flirt"* feature, so that the user can indicate availability to their partner. The *Resource Handler* agent is used in the intelligent feature, *"Fiddler's Choice"*, because it requires access to a library (knowledge base).

Design Model

The detailed design model of *Secret Touch* is presented in Figure 10. The coupling between agents can be seen by the links between agents via protocols, where each protocol contains the inter-agent messages for connected agents. The *Intimacy Handler* agent is at the centre of the system. The *Exchanges* protocol contains the basic inter-agent communications needed to flirt and enables interaction between the *Intimacy Handler* agent and the *Device Handler* agent. The *Discretion* protocol adds the ability to change availability, thus communicating between the *Intimacy Handler* agent and the *Partner Handler* agent. *Discrete*, an important quality goal in the requirements model associated with the *Mediate Touch Exchange* goal (see Figure 2) finds its way into the design model through the *Discretion* protocol, indicating that agents must communicate with discretion. The design model also shows the *Intelligent* protocol influencing communication between the *Intimacy Handler* agent

Figure 9. Secret Touch Design Model, with agents Intimacy Handler, Device Handler, Partner Handler, Resource Handler

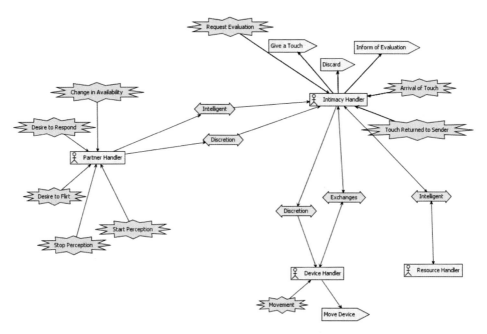

and both the *Resource Handler* and *Partner Handler*. These agents are involved in the "*Fiddlers Choice*" feature, and rely on information about partner availability or past touches when deciding how to respond. The percepts and actions in the design model represent interactions with the external environment. For example, the *Arrival of Touch* percept associated with the *Intimacy Handler* agent represents an incoming touch, while the *Give A Touch* action represents an outgoing touch. For the remainder of the process, example sequences of interactions between agents are documented using interaction diagrams, which are similar to UML interaction diagrams in OOSE. From the interaction diagrams, protocols of inter-agent messaging are built, and include all possible variations in communication between agents. The system can then be implemented from this detailed design. This part of the process has not been described here but can be found in Paay et al. (2010).

In summary, in designing the *Secret Touch* system, cultural probes were used to gather data on how people appropriate existing technologies to support their intimate relationships. A mixed team of ethnographers, interaction designers and software engineers then analysed the data. During the process of translating cultural probe data to system requirements, we found that coordinative and collaborative goals were not sufficient to model social interactions between people in the domestic space, because there are a range of purely communicative activities that do not serve any productive purpose, for example, communication for the sake of pleasure. Instead, we discovered that the use of quality goals attached to system goals enabled the design team to model social needs while keeping them at a high level of abstraction, hence ambiguous and open for conversations throughout the modelling process. Quality goals added a richness to the goal models that supported conversations about ambiguous concepts related to social interactions, throughout the design phase. In this way, ambiguity became a resource for the design team in achieving a shared understanding of user needs in the final system requirements.

PUTTING EMOTION INTO SOFTWARE ENGINEERING

Scenarios as they are currently used in software engineering lack the kinds of emotional aspects often associated with social interactions. Carrol (1997) refers to the inclusion of emotions in scenarios as "*a condition of comprehension*", rather than just something that would be nice to have. Hence, it is important when understanding the user and their intentions through scenarios, that some component representing people's emotions is incorporated into scenarios. Understanding people's emotions in a situation increases understanding of it, and hence the ability to build technologies that suit their context.

Considering emotions is particularly important when modelling social interactions in a non-work context, as in the case of Secret Touch. It is not straightforward to model emotions, however, because emotions felt by a specific user can vary based on their cultural background, age, gender, belief systems and living situations. Our experience suggests that it is better to link emotions to individual roles and goals acting within a scenario, rather than represent emotions in the scenario itself (Lopez-Lorca et al., 2014).

We have extended our experience through modelling a range of situations. The mediating intimacy project was followed by a project which developed models which guided the building of software systems to encourage grandparents and grandchildren to have fun over the internet (Davis et al., 2007). A subsequent application domain was the design of emergency alarm monitor systems to help older people wishing to live at home. In this domain, emotions of the older people are critical (Pedell et al., 2014).

Continuing from the aged care case study discussed in Pedell et al. (2014), we have used quality goals in modelling in several other domains, especially in the area of mental health. Wachtler et al. (2018) describes the development of a screening app to match people with current depressive symptoms with appropriate treatment recommendations. Thomas et al. (2016) describes the development and pilot study of a novel digital intervention to promote personal recovery in people with persisting psychotic disorders. In this case, the goal models were used during the requirements elicitation phase which involved different groups of stakeholders including mental health workers, people suffering from psychosis, psychologists and the families of the patients. The high level of abstraction of the goal models made them accessible for stakeholders without a technical background and acted as a boundary object to support interactions between the development team and clients. Sterling et al. (2017) describes the development of *SleepWell*, an app to help people with sleep difficulties. The most recent example of use was in tele-audiology as described in Sterling et al. (2018).

Quality goals and goal models are now routinely used in interaction design and software engineering teaching at tertiary education level (Marshall, 2018). The models have been incorporated with requirements elicitation methods and incorporated in agile development, within a semester-long requirements elicitation subject, and within a year-long software engineering project subject. While the models were inspired by agent concepts, students are able to understand and build the models without any special training in agents. The high-level models are intuitive and easy to understand from our experience.

CONCLUSION

Software engineering of socio-technical systems is difficult, because people's social interactions cannot be easily decomposed into measurable requirements. The domestic space gives rise to a range of purely communicative activities, which do not necessarily serve any external productive purpose. During system design, it is essential to capture social concepts accurately but flexibly at a high level, without losing the liveliness and vitality of those concepts through over specification. Modelling socially nuanced requirements while maintaining the richness of social interactions and generating concrete requirements ready for software implementation is problematic. Communicating ambiguous concepts using quality goals is an important part of solving the problem. Quality goals can remain unresolved for as long as possible, without committing to a specific design solution. Requirements and design models, incorporating quality goals and scenarios, embrace ambiguity a resource for design teams, prompting ongoing cooperation and communication around design alternatives and achieve a shared understanding of both user needs and final system requirements. In the *Secret Touch* case study presented, the ambiguous concepts were made explicit in the process and accessible for team discussion. The use of AOSE notations also supported effective communication and translation of complex and subtle social interactions into the modelling process, helping to retain the essence of a couple's intimate social interactions.

Detailed requirements, analysis and design modelling of the *Secret Touch* system illustrated how data from a cultural probes study exploring social interactions between couples, can be translated to create design requirements for a technology that supports them keeping in touch with each other. Quality goals were used to contain ambiguous concepts found in the social data. These quality goals remained visible and traceable throughout the modelling process, giving the design team focal points for discussions on representative modelling and design alternatives. By combining expertise and techniques from ethnography, interaction design and software engineering, the interdisciplinary team was well placed to translate data collected about people's appropriation of existing technologies in maintaining their close relationships, into system requirements for new and novel technology supporting social interactions.

ACKNOWLEDGMENT

The authors acknowledge the contributions of Professor Steve Howard to this chapter. He participated in the field work, analysis, and the interdisciplinary design team for this research, as well as the writing of earlier versions. Sadly, Steve passed away unexpectedly in April 2013, but lives on in his words and in the legacy of all the HCI researchers that he guided, nurtured and inspired.

This project was supported by Smart Internet CRC [project UE-06].

REFERENCES

Aoki, P. M., & Woodruff, A. (2005). Making space for stories: ambiguity in the design of personal communication systems. In *Proceedings of ACM Conference on Human Factors in Computing Systems, CHI '05* (pp. 181-190). New York: ACM Press.

Arnold, M. (2004). The Connected Home: Probing the Effects and Affects of Domesticated ICTs. In *Proceedings of PDC '04* (pp. 1-6). ACM Press.

Berry, D. M. (2008). Ambiguity in Natural Language Requirements Documents. In B. Paech & C. Martell (Eds.), *Innovations for Requirement Analysis: From Stakeholders' Needs to Formal Designs* (pp. 1–7). Berlin: Springer. doi:10.1007/978-3-540-89778-1_1

Berry, D. M., Kamsties, E., & Krieger, M. M. (2003). *From Contract Drafting to Software Specification: Linguistic Sources of Ambiguity - A Handbook Version 1.0.* Retrieved from http://se.uwaterloo.ca/~dberry/handbook/ambiguityHandbook.pdf

Beyer, H., & Holtzblatt, K. (1998). *Contextual Design: Defining Customer-Centered Systems*. Academic Press.

Blaha, K., Monge, A., Sanders, D., Simon, B., & VanDeGrift, T. (2005). Do students recognize ambiguity in software design? A multi-national, multi-institutional report. In *Proceedings of the 27th international conference on Software engineering, ICSE '05* (pp. 615-616). ACM Press.

Buckeridge, A. M., & Sutcliffe, R. F. E. (2002). Using Latent Semantic Indexing as a Measure of Conceptual Association for Noun Compound Disambiguation. *Proceedings of AICS, 02*, 12–19.

Burrows, A., Gooberman-Hill, R., & Coyle, D. (2015). Empirically derived user attributes for the design of home healthcare technologies. *Personal and Ubiquitous Computing, 19*(8), 1233–1245. doi:10.100700779-015-0889-1

Button, G., & Sharrock, W. (1994). Occasioned practices in the work of software engineers. In M. Jirotka & J. A. Goguen (Eds.), *Requirements Engineering: Social and technical issues* (pp. 217–240). Academic Press.

Carroll, J. M. (1997). Scenario-based design. In M. Helander & T. K. Landauer (Eds.), *Handbook of human-computer interaction* (2nd ed.; pp. 383–406). Amsterdam: North-Holland. doi:10.1016/B978-044481862-1.50083-2

Carroll, J. M. (2000). *Making use: scenario-based design of human-computer interactions*. MIT press. doi:10.1145/347642.347652

Castro, J., Kolp, M., & Mylopoulos, J. (2001). A Requirements-Driven Development Methodology. *Proceedings of CaiSE, 01*, 108–123.

Cheverst, K., Clarke, K., Dewsbury, G., Hemmings, T., Hughes, J., & Rouncefield, M. (2003). Design with Care: Technology, Disability and the Home. In R. Harper (Ed.), *Inside the Smart Home* (pp. 163–180). London: Springer. doi:10.1007/1-85233-854-7_9

Chung, L. K., Nixon, B. A., Yu, E., & Mylopoulos, J. (2000). *Non-Functional Requirements in Software Engineering*. Kluwer Publishing. doi:10.1007/978-1-4615-5269-7

Cross, N. (2011). *Design Thinking*. London: Bloomsbury Publishing. doi:10.5040/9781474293884

Dalmau, M. (2003). *Ambiguity as a Conceptual Framework for Design*. Technical Report: Contemporary Issues and Concepts in HCI, 7 November 2003. Retrieved from http://mcs.open.ac.uk/yr258/amb_frame/

Davis, H., Skov, M., Stougaard, M., & Vetere, F. (2007) Virtual Box: Supporting Mediated Family Intimacy through Virtual and Physical Play. In *Proceedings of the 19th Australasian Conference on Computer-Human Interaction, OZCHI '07* (pp. 151-159). CHISIG Australia. 10.1145/1324892.1324920

Dey, A. K., & De Guzman, E. (2006). From awareness to connectedness: the design and deployment of presence displays. In *Proceedings of the SIGCHI Conference on Human Factors in Computing Systems, CHI '06* (pp. 899-908). ACM Press. 10.1145/1124772.1124905

Fabrini, F., Fusani, M., Gnesi, S., & Lami, G. (2001). An Automatic Quality Evaluation for Natural Language Requirements. In *Proceedings of the Seventh International Workshop on Requirements Engineering: Foundations for Software Quality, REFSQ '01, Lecture Notes in Computer Science*. Springer-Verlag.

Gause, D. C., & Weinberg, G. M. (1989). *Exploring Requirements: Quality Before Design*. New York: Dorset House.

Gaver, B., Dunne, T., & Pacenti, E. (1999). Design: Cultural Probes. *Interaction*, 6(1), 21–29. doi:10.1145/291224.291235

Gaver, W. (2001). *Designing for Ludic Aspects of Everyday Life*. ERCIM News. No.47, October 2001. Retrieved at http://www.ercim.org/publication/Ercim_News/enw47/gaver.html

Gaver, W., Beaver, J., & Benford, S. (2003). Ambiguity as a Resource for Design. In *Proceedings of CHI '03* (pp. 233-240). ACM Press. 10.1145/642611.642653

Gaver, W., Boucher, A., Pennington, S., & Walker, B. (2004). Cultural probes and the value of uncertainty. *Interaction*, 11(5), 53–56. doi:10.1145/1015530.1015555

Goguen, J., & Linde, C. (1993). Techniques for Requirements Elicitation. *Proceedings of RE*, 93, 152–164.

Graham, C., Rouncefield, M., Gibbs, M., Vetere, F., & Cheverst, K. (2007). How probes work. In *Proceedings of the 19th Australasian Conference on Computer-Human interaction, OZCHI '07* (pp. 29-37). ACM Press.

Gross, H. (2005). *Component-based Software Testing with UML*. Springer.

Hassling, L., Nordfeldt, S., Eriksson, H., & Timpka, T. (2005). Use of cultural probes for representation of chronic disease experience: Exploration of an innovative method for design of supportive technologies. *Technology and Health Care*, 13(2), 87–95. PMID:15912006

Hemmings, T., Clarke, K., Crabtree, A., Rodden, T., & Rouncefield, M. (2002). Probing the Probes. In *Proceedings of PDC '02* (pp. 42-50). ACM Press.

Hughes, J., O'Brien, J., Rodden, T., Rouncefield, M., & Sommerville, I. (1995). Presenting Ethnography in the Requirements Process. *Proceedings of RE, 95*, 27–34.

JACK, Autonomous Decision Making Software. (2015). Retrieved at http://aosgrp.com/products/jack

Jureta, I. J., & Faulkner, S. (2007). Clarifying Goal Models: Conceptual Modeling. In *Proceedings of 26th International Conference on Conceptual Modeling, ER 2007*(pp. 139-144). Australian Computer Society.

Jureta, I. J., Faulkner, S., & Schobbens, P. Y. (2006). A More Expressive Softgoal Conceptualization for Quality Requirements Analysis Conceptual Modeling. In *Proceedings of 25th International Conference on Conceptual Modeling, ER '06* (pp. 281-295). Springer.

Jureta, I. J., Mylopoulos, J., & Faulkner, S. (2008). Revisiting the Core Ontology and Problem in Requirements Engineering. In *Proceedings of 16th IEEE International Conference on Requirements Engineering, RE '08* (pp. 71-80). Springer. 10.1109/RE.2008.13

Kamsties, E., Berry, D. M., & Paech, B. (2001). Detecting Ambiguities in Requirements Documents Using Inspections. In *Proceedings of the First Workshop on Inspection in Software Engineering, WISE '01* (pp. 68-80). IEEE Computer Society.

Kirikova, M., Grundspenkis, J., Wojtkowski, W., Zupancic, J., & Wrycza, S. (2002). *Information Systems Development: Advances in Methodologies, Components, and Management.* Springer. doi:10.1007/978-1-4615-0167-1

Kjeldskov, J. (2014). *Mobile Interactions in Context: A Designerly Way Toward Digital Ecology. Synthesis Lectures on Human-Centered Informatics.* Morgan & Claypool Publishers.

Kjeldskov, J., Gibbs, M., Vetere, F., Howard, S., Pedell, S., Mecoles, K., & Bunyan, M. (2005). Using Cultural Probes To Explore Mediated Intimacy. *AJIS. Australian Journal of Information Systems, 1*(12), 102–115.

Lopez-Lorca, A., Miller, T., Pedell, S., Mendoza, A., Keirnan, A., & Sterling, L. (2014). One size doesn't fit all: diversifying "the user" using personas and emotional scenarios. In *Proceedings of the 6th International Workshop on Social Software Engineering* (pp. 25-32). New York: ACM Press. 10.1145/2661685.2661691

MacLean, A., Bellotti, V., & Young, R. (1990). What rationale is there in design? In *Proceedings of the IFIP TC13 Third International Conference on Human-Computer Interaction* (pp. 207-212). Amsterdam: North-Holland Publishing Co.

Marshall, J. (2018). Agent-Based Modelling of Emotional Goals in Digital Media Design Projects. In S. Goschnick (Ed.), *Innovative Methods, User-Friendly Tools, Coding, and Design Approaches in People-Oriented Programming*. Hershey, PA: Information Science Publishing. doi:10.4018/978-1-5225-3822-6.ch034

Mayasari, A., Pedell, S., & Barnes, C. (2016). "Out of sight, out of mind", investigating affective intergenerational communication over distance. In *Proceedings of the 28th Australian Conference on Computer-Human Interaction, OzCHI '16 I* (pp. 282-291). New York: ACM Press.

Paay, J. (2008). From Ethnography to Interface Design. In J. Lumsden (Ed.), *Handbook of Research on User Interface Design and Evaluation for Mobile Technology*. Idea Group, Inc. doi:10.4018/978-1-59904-871-0.ch001

Paay, J., Pedell, S., Sterling, L., Vetere, F., & Howard, S. (2010). The Benefit of Ambiguity in Understanding Goals in Requirements Modelling. *International Journal of People-Oriented Programming*, *1*(2), 24–49. doi:10.4018/ijpop.2011070102

Paay, J., Sterling, L., Vetere, F., Howard, S., & Boettcher, A. (2009). Engineering the Social: The Role of Shared Artifacts. *International Journal of Human-Computer Studies*, *67*(5), 437–454. doi:10.1016/j.ijhcs.2008.12.002

Padgham, L., & Winikoff, M. (2004). *Developing Intelligent Agent Systems: a practical guide*. Chichester, UK: John Wiley & Sons. doi:10.1002/0470861223

Paulos, E., & Jenkins, T. (2005). Urban probes: encountering our emerging urban atmospheres. In *Proceedings of the SIGCHI Conference on Human Factors in Computing Systems, CHI '05* (pp. 341-350). ACM Press. 10.1145/1054972.1055020

Pedell, S., Lopez-Lorca, A. A., Miller, T., & Sterling, L. (2015). Don't Leave Me Untouched: Considering Emotions in Personal Alarm Use and Development. In M. Tavana, A. Ghapanchi, & A. Talaei-Khoei (Eds.), *Healthcare Informatics and Analytics: Emerging Issues and Trends* (pp. 96–127). Hershey, PA: IGI Global. doi:10.4018/978-1-4666-6316-9.ch006

Petrelli, D., van den Hoven, E., & Whittaker, S. (2009). Making history: intentional capture of future memories. In *Proceedings of the SIGCHI Conference on Human Factors in Computing Systems, CHI '09* (pp. 1723-1732). New York: ACM Press. 10.1145/1518701.1518966

Randall, D., Hughes, J., & Shapiro, D. (1994). Steps toward a partnership: ethnography and system design. In M. Jirotka & J. A. Goguen (Eds.), Requirements Engineering: Social and technical issues (pp. 241-254). Academic Press.

Reekie, H. J., & McAdam, R. J. (2006). *A Software Architecture Primer: A Primer*. Angophora Press.

Rodden, T., & Benford, S. (2003). The evolution of buildings and implications for the design of ubiquitous domestic environments. In *Proceedings of the SIGCHI Conference on Human Factors in Computing Systems, CHI '03* (pp. 9-16). ACM Press. 10.1145/642611.642615

Rouncefield, M., Crabtree, A., Hemmings, T., Rodden, T., Cheverst, K., Clarke, K., ... Hughes, J. (2003). Adapting Cultural Probes to Inform Design in Sensitive Settings. In *Proceedings of OZCHI '03*. Ergonomics Society of Australia.

Sawyer, P., Rayson, P., & Cosh, K. (2005). Shallow Knowledge as an Aid to Deep Understanding in Early Phase Requirements Engineering. *IEEE Transactions on Software Engineering*, *31*(11), 969–981. doi:10.1109/TSE.2005.129

Schorch, M., Wan, L., Randall, D. W., & Wulf, V. (2016). Designing for Those who are Overlooked: Insider Perspectives on Care Practices and Cooperative Work of Elderly Informal Caregivers. In *Proceedings of the 19th ACM Conference on Computer-Supported Cooperative Work & Social Computing, CSCW'16* (pp. 787-799). New York: ACM Press. 10.1145/2818048.2819999

Sengers, P., & Gaver, B. (2006). Staying open to interpretation: engaging multiple meanings in design and evaluation. In *Proceedings of the 6th Conference on Designing Interactive Systems, DIS '06* (pp. 99-108). New York: ACM Press. 10.1145/1142405.1142422

Sommerville, I. (2015). Software Engineering. Pearson Higher Ed.

Soro, A., Brereton, M., Lawrence Taylor, J., & Hong, L. A. & Roe, P. (2016). Cross-Cultural Dialogical Probes. In *Proceedings of the First African Conference on Human Computer Interaction, AfriCHI'16* (pp. 114-12), New York: ACM Press. 10.1145/2998581.2998591

Sterling, L., Lopez-Lorca, A., Pedell, S., & Goschnick, S. (2017, December). *Developing Emotionally Supportive Technology for Monitoring Sleep Disorders*. Paper presented at Design4Health Conference, Hallam, UK.

Sterling, L., & Taveter, K. (2009). *The Art of Agent-Oriented Modelling*. Cambridge, MA: MIT Press.

Sutcliffe, A. G., Maiden, N., Minocha, S., & Manuel, D. (1998). Supporting scenario-based requirements engineering. *IEEE Transactions on Software Engineering, 24*(12), 1072–1088. doi:10.1109/32.738340

Thomas, N., Farhall, J., Foley, F., Leitan, N., Villagonzalo, K., Ladd, E., ... Kyrios, M. (2016). Promoting personal recovery in people with persisting psychotic disorders: Development and pilot study of a novel digital intervention. *Frontiers in Psychiatry, 7*, 196. doi:10.3389/fpsyt.2016.00196 PMID:28066271

Tjong, S. F., Hartley, M., & Berry, D. M. (2007). Disambiguation Rules for Requirements Specifications. In *Proceedings of Workshop in Requirements Engineering* (pp. 97-106). Springer.

van Lamsweerde, A., & Letier, E. (2004). From Object Orientation to Goal Orientation: A Paradigm Shift for Requirements Engineering. In M. Wirsing, A. Knapp, & S. Balsamo (Eds.), *Radical Innovations of Software and Systems Engineering in the Future, Revised Papers from RISSEF '02, LNCS 2941* (pp. 325–340). Springer. doi:10.1007/978-3-540-24626-8_23

Vetere, F., Gibbs, M., Kjeldskov, J., Howard, S., Mueller, F., Pedell, S., ... Bunyan, M. (2005). Mediating Intimacy: Designing Technologies to Support Strong-Tie Relationships. In *Proceedings of CHI '05* (pp. 471-480). ACM Press. 10.1145/1054972.1055038

Viller, S., & Sommerville, I. (2000). Ethnographically Informed Analysis for Software Engineers. *International Journal of Human-Computer Studies, 53*(1), 169–196. doi:10.1006/ijhc.2000.0370

Wooldridge, M., & Ciancarini, P. (2000). Agent-Oriented Software Engineering: The State of the Art. In P. Ciancarini & M. Wooldridge (Eds.), *Agent Oriented Software Engineering* (pp. 1–24). Springer.

Wooldridge, M., Jennings, N., & Kinny, D. (2000). The Gaia Methodology For Agent-Oriented Analysis And Design. *Journal of Autonomous Agents and Multi-Agent Systems, 3*(3), 285–312. doi:10.1023/A:1010071910869

Yu, E. (1995). *Modelling Strategic Relationships for Process Reengineering* (PhD thesis). Department of Computer Science, University of Toronto, Canada.

Zambonelli, F., Jennings, N., & Wooldridge, M. (2003). Developing Multiagent Systems: The Gaia Methodology. *Transactions on Software Engineering and Methodology, 12*(3), 317–370. doi:10.1145/958961.958963

ADDITIONAL READING

Miller, T., Pedell, S., Sterling, L., Vetere, F., & Howard, S. (2012). Understanding socially oriented roles and goals through motivational modelling. *Journal of Systems and Software*, *85*(9), 2160–2170. doi:10.1016/j.jss.2012.04.049

Pedell, S., Miller, T., Vetere, F., Sterling, L., & Howard, S. (2014). Socially-Oriented Requirements Engineering - Software Engineering Meets Ethnography. In V. Dignum, F. Dignum, J. Ferber, & T. Stratulat (Eds.), *Integrating Cultures: Formal Models and Agent-Based Simulations* (pp. 191–210). Springer International Publishing. doi:10.1007/978-3-319-01952-9_11

Ramos, I., & Berry, D. M. (2005). Is emotion relevant to requirements engineering? *Requirements Engineering*, *10*(3), 238–242. doi:10.100700766-005-0014-5

Thew, S., & Sutcliffe, A. (2017). *Requirements Engineering*. Springer.

KEY TERMS AND DEFINITIONS

Agent: A software agent is a computer program that acts for a user or other program in a system.

Ambiguity: The quality of being open to more than one interpretation.

Cultural Probe: A technique used to gather fragmented data about people's lives, values, and thoughts for the purpose of inspiring ideas in a design process.

Ethnography: The study of people and cultures, traditionally through observational methods.

Interaction Design: The practice of designing interactive digital products, environments, systems, and services.

Interdisciplinary: Crossing traditional boundaries between academic disciplines.

Intimacy: Close familiarity or friendship.

Requirements Engineering: The process of defining, documenting, and maintaining requirements for systems and software engineering.

Socio-Technical System: Systems that include technical components but also operational processes and people who use and interact with the technical system.

Strong-Tie Relationships: Strong-tie relationships are intimate, well developed, with frequent interactions, such as experienced in families or married couples.

User-Centered Design: A design process that focuses on the end user, through understanding usability goals, user characteristics, environment, tasks, and workflow in the design of an interface.

Chapter 8
Agent–Based Modelling of Emotional Goals in Digital Media Design Projects

James Marshall
Swinburne University of Technology, Australia

ABSTRACT

The author promotes agent-oriented models to identify, represent, and evaluate high-level abstractions of digital media design projects. The models include emotional goals, in addition to functional goals and quality goals, to describe feelings such as having fun, being engaged, and feeling cared for. To establish emotional goals, digital media design methods and processes were employed including the development of emotional scripts, user profiles, mood boards and followed an iterative creative design process. Using agent-oriented models proved to be highly successful not only to represent emotional goals such as fun, tension, and empathy but also to facilitate the ideation, creation, and progressive evaluation of projects. The design process supported communication between designers, developers, and other stakeholders in large multidisciplinary development teams by providing a shared language and a common artefact. The process is demonstrated by describing the development of Aspergion, a multiplayer online role play game that promotes respect for people with Asperger's Syndrome.

DOI: 10.4018/978-1-5225-5969-6.ch008

INTRODUCTION

Human interaction with technology is ubiquitous, and the objectives of software have been widening from the utilitarian to the facilitation of rich and engaging human interactions. "Interaction with technology is now as much about what people feel as it is about what people do." (McCarthy & Wright, 2004). Computing and software is increasingly pervasive and integrated throughout our lives making the consideration of human factors fundamental to the development of successful products and systems. "We do not just admire technology; we live with it. Whether we are charmed by it or indifferent, technology is deeply embedded in our ordinary everyday experience." (Pacey, 1999).

Computing and software has moved from the workplace, into our personal lives rendering socio-cultural aspects increasingly influential (Iacucci & Kuutti, 2003). Meta-issues outside of the technical system, such as lifestyle and social structures, have become more important and need to be considered in design (Dourish, 2001b; Randall Harper & Rouncefield, 2004; Rheingold, 2003).

Realising emotional factors is fundamental to design disciplines, from industrial and communication design to architecture and fashion design. In each discipline, collaboration with manufacturing, science and engineering experts is required. A current challenge for the field of digital media design is to develop mutually beneficial partnerships with software engineering, as architecture has achieved with civil engineering, and industrial design with materials science.

As digital technologies increase in complexity and collaboration with other disciplines has become necessary, a trans-disciplinary approach for developing sociotechnical systems is required, where both digital media design practices may be incorporated into software engineering, and software engineering methods incorporated into design practice. Agent-oriented models show potential, not only to identify and realise emotional goals, but also to provide an overall progressive evaluation of these goals as will be demonstrated.

The overall objective of my research is to facilitate the creation of digital media design outcomes including sociotechnical systems that positively affect people's emotional state or wellbeing. This can be achieved by incorporating creative design processes that explicitly identify emotions as high-level goals into existing agent-oriented goal models (AOM) to provide a shared language between stakeholders and support project design, development and evaluation. A colour-coded evaluation system is used to easily communicate the progress of projects to all stakeholders and serve as a form of acceptance testing.

EMOTIONAL GOALS IN DESIGN

Sociotechnical systems may contain complex interactions between people and technology. A sociotechnical system can be defined as a system that includes hardware and software, has defined operational processes and offers an interface, implemented in software, to humans.

Sociotechnical systems exist to support human activities, such as guarding of a building, trading, planning a route, and flirting. (Sterling & Taveter, 2009)

The consideration of emotions is important in the development of many sociotechnical systems. If a computer game does not feel fun, we will not play it; if an ecommerce website does not feel trustworthy (irrespective of the actual security) we will not purchase from it; and if a social networking application does not feel engaging we will not use it. We describe these as the *emotional goals* of the system, which we define as goals that aim to affect people's emotional state or wellbeing. These include basic emotions such as happiness, sadness, fear, anger, surprise and disgust, human factors like engagement and flow and more abstract descriptions of feelings such as fresh, cool, wicked and fun.

Emotional goals, often described by designers as the *look and feel* or *values* of a product, have always played an important role in design considerations (Desmet & Hekkert, 2009). The industrial designer Hartmut Esslinger who worked on Apple product lines from 1984 to 1990 expresses the importance of considering emotions, saying that; "even if a design is elegant and functional, it will not have a place in our lives unless it can appeal at a deeper level, to our emotions […] form follows emotion" (Esslinger quoted in Demirbilek & Sener, 2003).

Apple's commitment to achieving emotional goals is expressed in an advertising campaign launched in June 2013. The Apple campaign presents a manifesto that reflects Esslinger's design philosophy "form follows emotion" in the television commercial "Our Signature" and in the motion graphic "Our Intention" quoted here:

The first thing we ask is what do we want people to feel? Delight, surprise, love, connection? Then we begin to craft around our intention. It takes time. There are a thousand no's for every yes. We simplify, we perfect, we start over, until everything we touch enhances each life it touches. Only then do we sign our work. Designed by Apple in California. (Apple Inc, 2013)

Apple exemplifies a design-led approach to developing products and services, including software, where the "feel" precedes the functional and quality goals. By identifying, valuing and satisfying the emotional goals of its customers, Apple's products and services have revolutionised the Personal Computer, Desktop Publishing, Mobile Phone, Tablet PC, Retail Space and Music Industries. In 2012 Apple became the world's most valuable company and at the time of writing in 2017 according to the Forbes Fortune 500 (Forbes Inc, 2017), Apple is still the world's most valuable company and brand. Apple is cited in this paper to demonstrate how the consideration of emotional goals may facilitate the creation of successful products and services.

As a system requirement, it is admittedly difficult, perhaps impossible, to quantify whether an emotional goal has been fully satisfied. Emotional goals depend on context, individual experiences and attitudes and are constantly changing. So even if we could quantify an emotional response at one moment in time, we could not apply it at all times. However, whilst emotional goals are qualitative and temporal they are none the less important and in sociotechnical systems are often the primary system requirement. For example, a computer game must be engaging enough that people will play it. Making a game that is fun trumps other system requirements, irrespective of whether the goal of fun is clearly definable or measurable. If no one wants to play the game, no matter how robust the code is, it has not met the primary system requirement.

Digital media design methodologies have a tradition in realising emotional goals (often referred to by designers as the look, feel, values or brand values) by using tools and processes such as: emotional colour scripts, flowcharts, rich pictures and mood boards, where "the mood board takes all structure and explicit message out [...] leaving only colour type and innuendo [...] to capture a feeling." (Daniel & Brown; 2007). Designers model emotion and communicate the *feel* to clients and to each other using this visual, and in some cases, audio and textural language.

However, digital media design lacks the modelling techniques, ontology and domain expertise required to represent and build large sociotechnical systems. A trans-disciplinary approach that encourages digital media designers and software engineers to co-create sociotechnical systems is needed. Current software engineering modelling techniques are inadequate to provide for such integration. This is recognised by Baxter and Sommerville (2011): "The abstractions currently used in technical system modelling (e.g., use-cases, objects, etc.) do not seem to us to be sufficient to represent sociotechnical considerations." The main thinking underlying this research was that if emotional goals could be incorporated into agent-oriented models complemented with digital media design process then emotional goals could be realised in sociotechnical system design.

EMOTIONAL GOALS IN AGENT-ORIENTED MODELS

Agent-oriented models provide a promising direction forward as the characteristics of agents can be equated to human actors. They are highly suitable for understanding complex topics because the concepts used in these models are suitable for expressing the behavioural aspects of individuals and their interactions (Pavon, 2008). Agents may exhibit human-like behaviours such as autonomy, flexibility, intelligence, learning, and dynamic adaptability to the surrounding environment, increasing their suitability for socially oriented software facilitating people's social interactions. Figure 1 illustrates an agent-oriented modelling conceptual space from Sterling and Taveter (2009), where on the motivation layer, goal models describe high-level abstractions. Current software engineering practices specify two types of goals. Functional goals, which describe a specific function such as performing a calculation, and quality goals that describe the systems attributes, such as the system being stable, scalable or safe.

Focusing on quality is well established within software and systems engineering. Software engineers are aware of the need to express quality attributes of software as well as functional capabilities of software. These quality attributes are referred to using a variety of terms including: non-functional requirements, constraints, quality attributes, quality goals, or quality of service requirements (Gross, 2005; Kirikova et al., 2002; Reekie & McAdam, 2006; Sommerville, 2007; van Lamsweerde & Letier, 2003). However, goal models are often perceived as useful only at the early stages of requirements analysis to arrive at a shared understanding between stakeholders (Guizzardi & Perini; 2005; Jureta & Faulkner, 2007). Following early requirements analysis the goal models are effectively discarded and the quality goals deprioritised. Furthermore quality goals do not generally have a direct relationship with functional goals (Chung et al., 2000). It is more difficult to carry them through the whole development process and so quality considerations get lost during development. Consequently, quality goals have been neglected, as they are difficult to specify, implement, and measure during development (Paay et al., 2009).

However, Sterling and Taveter use the construct of quality goals attached to functional goals to represent quality attributes of social interactions. Quality goals are formulated to encapsulate social aspects of the context into the software requirement model, thus providing a mechanism to carry subtle nuances of those social aspects through to the implementation phase. The direct pairing between system goals and quality goals opens up a variety of possible interpretations both in the design and use of the system.

Figure 1. Agent-oriented modelling conceptual space (Sterling and Taveter, 2009)

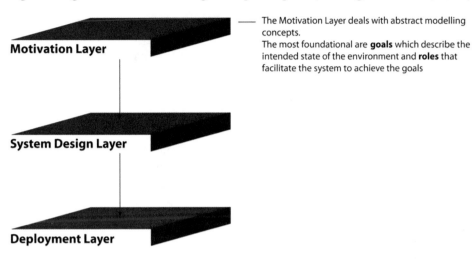

The Motivation Layer deals with abstract modelling concepts.
The most foundational are **goals** which describe the intended state of the environment and **roles** that facilitate the system to achieve the goals

In agent-oriented models, real people may be included in goal models and emotional factors may be expressed as quality goals. "We believe that agent-oriented concepts enhance the handling of quality requirements in open, distributed sociotechnical systems." (Sterling and Taveter, 2009).

Importantly, the agent-oriented models do not require that the implemented system be agent-based, instead, the agent paradigm is used to understand a domain and the activities of its people. An agent-oriented approach is again well described by Sommerville:

Agent-oriented technology is an effective way to construct sociotechnical systems, which take into account organisational and human issues as well as technical issues. Agents are a useful abstraction that helps us think about how sociotechnical systems deliver the services required by their users. We should think about this without regard to whether the agents that deliver these services are people or automated systems... (Ian Sommerville 2008 foreword page xii, in Sterling and Taveter)

Sterling and Taveter focus on how to make high-level agent-oriented models palatable to design discussions. Goal models are presented with an easy and straightforward syntax and semantics. Functional goals are represented as parallelograms, quality goals are clouds and roles are people figures. These constructs can be connected using arcs, which indicate relationships between them (Figure 5). The construct of quality goals attached to functional goals is used to represent quality attributes of social interaction as abstract, ambiguous and unresolved concepts in the models.

Proposed Method for Considering Emotional Goals

To promote the consideration of human factors, I advocate a new category of goal, called an *emotional goal*, to be modelled with equal hierarchy to functional and quality goals. By incorporating emotional goals into agent-oriented models the aim is to signal that the goal may be best realised by a trans-disciplinary approach. When these goals are encountered by software engineers they should seek a domain knowledge expert to apply creative design methodologies and processes.

An icon set was developed for these goals as illustrated in Figure 2. This includes the parallelogram and cloud icons developed by Sterling and Taveter, to signify functional and quality goals with the introduction of a heart symbol to signify emotional goals. Roles are represented by a person icon and facilitate the system to achieve goals. Agents fullfill roles and may include real people, physical devices and software agents.

To assist in the elicitation and categorisation of goals it is helpful to refer to them as 'doing', 'being', and 'feeling' goals and list them in a Goal Elicitation Table. Table 1 considers a university as a sociotechnical system and lists its high-level goals.

For most universities, the functional and quality goals will be similar, however the emotional goals will differ depending on the university's market position. Table 1 describes the type of emotional goals to which a small, mid ranking university may aspire. An Ivy League university may have emotional goals such as feeling elite, traditional, influential, distinguished and preeminent. Emotional goals are central

Figure 2. Icon set for roles functional, quality and emotional goals

Table 1. Goal Elicitation Table of a university

Functional Goals (Do)	Quality Goal (Be)	Emotional Goal (Feel)
Teach students	Equitable	Dynamic
Promote wisdom	Credible	Cool
Conduct research	Accessible	Inspiring
Engage with society	Accountable	Cutting edge
Archive knowledge	Financially Sustainable	Flexible

to design and are treated with the highest consideration often as brand values. The emotional goals of sociotechnical systems like universities should permeate though every aspect of the system, from the physical and virtual spaces to the smallest interactions such as answering the phone. This includes systems like the university's website and student management system and is therefore highly relevant to software engineers.

For digital media design projects, agent-oriented models were further adapted to include a colour-based rating scale. The aim was to provide a method of communicating project progress to stakeholders in a quick and easily understood way. A ten step colour chart, from red to green was developed to indicate whether the project goals were being met, where one (red) indicated no progress and ten (green) indicated excellent progress (Figure 3). The colour brightness and saturation of the red and green colours used in the scale are similar to ensure that text can remain single colour (black). Alternatively, if the colour brightness varied for example from white to black, the text colour would also have to change inversely to remain readable. Consequently, the colour scale must be viewed in colour, or when viewing in black and white a numbering scale may be added to each goal.

To explore the feasibly of incorporating emotional goals into agent-oriented models and rate project progress using a colour-based scale, the process was applied in the development of a sociotechnical system called Aspergion.

CASE STUDY: THE ASPERGION PROJECT

Aspergion is a learning resource for secondary school students, which promotes 'respect' for people with Asperger's Syndrome. Asperger's Syndrome is an autism spectrum disorder at the least severe, or high-functioning end of the autism spectrum. To generalise, people diagnosed with an autism spectrum disorder have behavioural, social and communication impairments. Typically, people with Asperger's Syndrome will have a special interest that they focus on in detail. These are often rule-based and predictable such as mathematics, music, computer programing and science. Some famous people diagnosed with high-functioning autism / Asperger's Syndrome include abattoir designer Temple Grandin and actress Daryl Hannah. Albert Einstein,

Figure 3. Colour rating scale for project goals

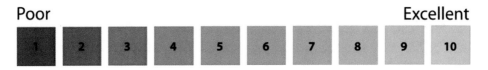

269

Wolfgang Amadeus Mozart, Thomas Edison and others that have hyper-focus in specific interests display traits of Asperger's Syndrome, however exhibiting such behavioural traits is insufficient to be diagnosed with an autism spectrum disorder.

Ten people with Asperger's Syndrome (further referred to as Asperger participants) were heavily involved in the development of the Aspergion project to give creative direction, provide domain knowledge, act as representative users, give user feedback and set the project goals. In setting the high-level project goals it was clearly stated that they did not want to create a project that provided therapy for people with Asperger's Syndrome, rather they wanted to create awareness and change of attitude in Neurotypicals (non-autistic or 'normal' people). The Asperger participants collectively set the primary project goal, which was to promote 'respect'.

Approximately 160 students developed the Aspergion project in the 3rd year of the Digital Media Design Program at Swinburne University of Technology. Aspergion was delivered as a capstone (finishing) project in the Group Research Project and Advanced Technology units, each of which had three contact and nine non-contact hours per week over a 12-week semester. There were two separate cohorts of students (approximately equal in size) that created the project over two semesters with each student working approximately 250 hours. In addition, university lecturers and domain specialists contributed to the Aspergion project bringing the total project development time to 42,550 hours as detailed in Table 2. As a digital media design university project, this is extremely large, both in the time commitment and complexity.

Incorporating Emotional Goals Into Agent-Oriented Models

The Aspergion project provided a unique opportunity to explore the feasibility of incorporating emotional goals into agent-oriented models because the high-level system requirement was to affect a real world behavioural change of respect by evoking feelings of empathy and responsibility in the player. Additionally, the system was a Multiplayer Online Role Play Game (MORPG), requiring a range of emotions

Table 2. Participants in the Aspergion project (approximate numbers)

Participants	Quantity	Semester Delivery	Hours
Student Developers	160	1, 2	40,000
Lecturing Team	12	1, 2	1,800
Aspergers Participants	10	1	300
Psychologists	4	1, 2	200
Documentary Maker	1	2	200
Script writer	1	2	50

to be realised throughout the gameplay. The game was developed in two phases by separate development teams providing an opportunity to collect systematic data on whether or not agent-oriented models affected the quality of the outcome.

The primary target market for Aspergion was Neurotypical secondary school students. To achieve the functional goal of respect, the project aimed to demonstrate that people with Aspergers could be cool and creative, through the creation of a MORPG. The game was developed in Unity 3D and has similar functions to the popular MORPG, World of Warcraft. All of the code, characters, animations, environments, attacks, spells and interface design, were developed by the digital media design students, rather than modifying an existing game. Playing the game took approximately 40 hours to complete and was resolved to a Beta stage. A screenshot of the game can be seen in Figure 4.

Aspergion is a space adventure containing ten planets that may be explored. Each of these planets was designed and developed by a team of six students and specified by one of the ten Aspergers participants. The specification included the planet's name, inhabitants, flag, environment, laws, manifesto, activities, friends and enemies, obstacles, objects, and currency. The majority of Aspergers participants used their special interest as a foundation for the planet specification. For example, the planet "Scientifica" reflected the participant's interest in science, planet "AncesTree" in genealogy, planet "Cadenza" in music and planet "Dilemmacon" reflected the participant's interest in moral dilemmas. Backstories were developed for each planet such as the following:

Figure 4. Aspergion game play

Dilemmacon is a planet of mystery and contradiction. Once having unrivalled biodiversity, the planets energy source, known as Mana, has now been plundered. In the past, this opulent planet thrived with dramatic mountain vistas, magical flowering fields and valleys of treasure. However greed and overconsumption has resulted in a dystopia. With a lack of resources for daily survival, distrust festers on Dilemmacon and caution is advised.

Students met with the Aspergers participants and communicated via email. Each week the students would send an updated design document detailing the progress of the planet development and receive feedback from the Aspergers participants. At the conclusion of the first semester delivery of Aspergion, a design document approximately 40 pages in length specified each planet.

How Agent-Oriented Models Were Used

Aspergion was developed by two separate groups of students over two semesters, each covering a different phase. In the first delivery an agent-oriented model was developed that was derived from interviews with the ten Aspergers participants to set the high-level project goals (Figure 5). This was an early exploration of using agent-oriented models to support digital media projects and the intention was to investigate the feasibility of incorporating emotional goals into agent-oriented models.

The agent-oriented model shown in Figure 5 was posted in the main development lab and the lecturers reinforced the goals to the student developers on a weekly basis. The model proved useful as a communication tool to ensure that all 80 students were aligned and working to achieve the primary functional, quality and emotional goals. In post interviews with the Aspergers participants it was clear that these goals had been addressed in the development process. Consideration of emotional goals was also evident in self and peer assessment conducted by the students and in the context of a capstone university project was successful. However, in the first semester delivery the Aspergion game was not successful. Whilst an interesting concept the game lacked an overall narrative and purpose and was not fun to play.

The Aspergion project was delivered again the following semester. To make the game fun to play a professional games scriptwriter was employed to provide expert advice. An overarching plot was developed that included the necessary conflict and character arcs that make games engaging. The plot was to save the Aspergion galaxy from being pulled into a black hole, by restoring balance to the 'VIBE'. The planets of Aspergion were out of harmony, resulting in conflict due to their inhabitants being intolerant, exclusionary and communicating poorly. The character arc enacted by solving these conflicts was to grow your avatar from being a rogue space traveller,

Figure 5. Aspergion project level agent-oriented model

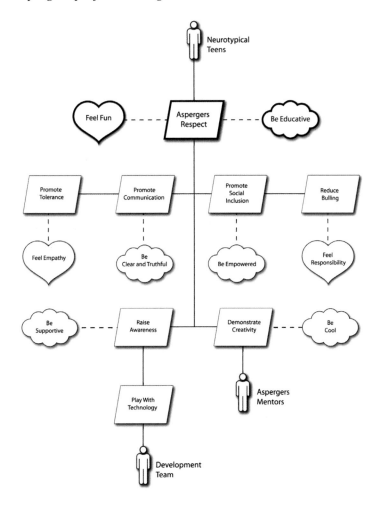

to "Aspinaut Admiral, Grand Master of the VIBE." The game introduction script provides the backstory:

In a parallel universe much like our own the Aspergion Space Architects developed the universe's ultimate energy source. By focusing their positive emotions they harnessed the virtually infinite potential of black holes. They used this power to create new and utopian worlds. As the planets grew, three space stations were constructed to focus the collective emotions of the galaxy's inhabitants. Known as VIBE, this Virtually Infinite Behavioural Energy keeps the delicate system in balance. It requires Behavioural Tolerance, Social Inclusion and Clear Communication. The VIBE is the life force on which everything depends.

On entering the game the player finds that the 'VIBE' is critically low and the Aspergion Galaxy is on the brink of annihilation. To complete the game the player must visit all ten planets and resolve a societal conflict by demonstrating tolerance, inclusion and clear communication. As previously mentioned Asperger's Syndrome is characterised by behavioural, social and communication impairments and the goals of the game encourage the user to recognise, accommodate and tolerate these.

In the first semester delivery an agent-oriented model described the entire Aspergion sociotechnical system, including the game, documentary, social network and website. The model proved useful in focusing the student developers on the project goals. In the second semester delivery of Aspergion the use of agent-oriented models was greatly extended to facilitate a coherent narrative for the game and to model the emotional goals that the developers were aiming for the player to feel. Three levels of agent-oriented models were developed, a high-level project level model (Figure 5), a game level model and a planet level model (Figure 6), with a breakdown of goals being detailed in Table 3.

The high-level project level model remained similar to the first delivery model, but was updated to focus more on achieving goals related to the Aspergion game. The game level model described the overall game goals and detailed which planets had the role of achieving these goals. Thirdly, a planet level goal model (Figure 6) described the overall conflict, the quest chains required to resolve the conflict, the characters (roles) involved and the associated emotional story and character arcs. Each level of agent-oriented model increased in complexity as illustrated in Table 3.

Figure 6. Planet level agent-oriented model (Planet Dilemmacon)

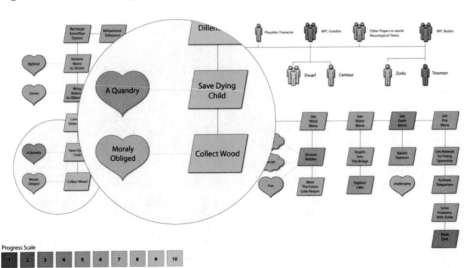

Table 3. The granularity of goals and roles across three levels of goal model

Level	Model	Roles	Functional Goals	Quality Goals	Emotional Goals
Level 1	Project	3	8	5	3
Level 2	Game	3	18	3	2
Level 3	Planet	219	363	115	97

Emotional goals were derived from the story elements. For example, on planet Dilemmacon the overarching conflict was between the native inhabitants and an alien race that was stealing the planet's precious minerals. In working to resolve the conflict the player was exposed to a series of quest chains to complete. As the name suggests Dilemmacon is a world of moral dilemmas. When playing the game, the first task you encounter on Dilemmacon is a mother who is nursing her sick child and requires wood for the fire to keep him warm. She cannot leave the child and fears that he will surely die that night of exposure if the fire goes out. You are asked to collect wood from the neighbouring houses, but the neighbours aren't home to grant you permission to take it. The moral dilemma is that to take the wood without permission would be stealing. What should you do, is it morally correct to steal sometimes and if so when? The functional goal of this task was to "save dying child" by doing "collect wood". These functional goals were linked to the emotional goals of feeling "a quandary" and of feeling "morally obliged". The narrative elements and tasks, known as quests, were developed in collaboration with a professional game scriptwriter to create emotional arcs that supported the higher-level project goal of feeling "respect" and "responsibility".

Quests are game interactions that the player undertakes to complete a larger game objective, or mission called a quest chain. For example, to complete the quest chain "Save Dying Child" the player must complete a conversation quest with the child's mother, a multi-choice question quest to resolve a moral dilemma, a search quest to collect wood and a return quest to take the wood to the child. To build emotional goals into quest chains, in addition to the environmental and character design, game patterns are used, for example battling an enemy will make the player feel *tension* and *accomplishment*.

In order to incorporate digital media design processes into the agent-oriented models, each time an emotional goal was specified it was supported with a mood board and game pattern. The emotional goals for the Dying Child quest chain were for the player to feel both "a quandary" but ultimately "morally obliged". The mood boards provided art direction for the designers by translating the emotion into a visual from. From this, the dialogue, character design, objects, environment, ambience and colour palette could be derived. By sequencing the mood boards the emotional flow was developed and refined. A similar process is used in the animation industry by companies such as Pixar, where a movie will be broken down into type of storyboard called a colour script from which the emotional arc of the movie is visible. The happy, scary, exciting and dramatic sections of the movie are evident in the colour palette.

The three levels of agent-oriented goal models provided a common language and shared artefact between the lecturing staff and student developers and the granularity of the models allowed for sufficient detail to be expressed at different levels. For example, the planet level model directly described the storyline as a series of quest chains allowing for the story and character arcs to be identified and realised.

How AOM Supported Progressive Appraisal and Evaluation

Rotating teams of approximately twenty student testers would evaluate the project goals on each project build, which occurred weekly in the last six weeks of both the semester one and semester two project deliveries. The students would assess aspects of the game that they hadn't previously worked on, which usually meant playing an Aspergion planet other than the one that they were developing. Lecturers also provided an expert evaluation. The evaluation involved giving each of the 614 project goals a ranking from 1 to 100, which was then translated to an absolute score out of ten and given a colour coding on the agent–oriented goal model. Table 4 shows the assessment of the high-level project goals in a table format, derived from the project level goal model in Figure 5. The data was collected from the student developers at the completion of the Aspergion project, where the rows are individual student evaluations of each goal. An average of these provides an empirical project evaluation by the students of 76.7% for the entire project.

The majority of the testing occurred at the planet level, where the agent-oriented models described the quest chains that the player would be required to complete such as the Save Dying Child quest. The project lecturers provided a rubric of the criteria for assessing functional goals. Firstly, did the quest chain break the game? If so it received a rating from 1-10 indicating that it required critical attention. Secondly, if the functional goal (quest chain) broke but was non-critical to the game progression, it would score 11-20. Thirdly were there major errors in continuity (21-30), fourthly spelling mistakes (31-40) etc. The majority of user testing and evaluation of functional goals was bug fixing, primarily ensuring that the game didn't break, as such it was relatively easy to develop the rubric criteria and to rate the progress of achieving the goals from 1 - 100.

The evaluation of emotional goals was more subjective than that of functional goals. Firstly this was due to the fact that emotional goals are subjective by nature and it is difficult to develop a rubric to empirically measure goals such as fun, respect and moral obligation in a consistent way. Secondly, within the scope of the project, the vast majority of the 12-week production time was spent in development and to assess the emotional goals requires a minimum level of development for example the game must be playable, should not crash and ideally should be conducted with the target market. Thirdly the scale of the project was prohibitive. It was possible to measure whether sections of the game achieved the specified emotional goals. For example, did the Save Dying Child quest chain make you feel morally obliged and how this could be improved? The higher-level emotional goals such as, was the game "fun" and did it "promote respect" for people with Asperger's Syndrome required that the game be played to completion. This took approximately 40 hours and required at least two people, a player and a facilitator to record the player's feedback on the 614 goals being assessed.

To evaluate emotional goals student testers provided a numerical rating based on their own feeling as they played sections of the game and from this assessment valuable data was gained. Where numerous tests consistently ranked an emotional goal like "moral obligation" poorly, this provided an indication that the game section required investigation and usually, further work as well. In addition, by declaring and modelling high-level emotional goals such as "fun," "cool" and "respect" with the same hierarchy as functional and quality goals, ensured that they were continuously being considered throughout the development process, even if not explicitly measured.

The data collected from student and lecturer evaluation was averaged and transferred into colours on the project agent-oriented model. In this way the student developers, lecturers and other stakeholders such as financial backers could get a fast overview of the project progress. A large print of the model (Figure 7) containing the 614 goals of the project was displayed in the main production lab and was updated after each testing phase. This also encouraged peer feedback and support where team members from successful production teams would voluntarily help the teams who were falling behind. The agent-oriented model shown describes the state of the goals at approximately three quarters of the way through the project build.

Each assessment provided a snapshot of the overall state of the project. In the first delivery fun had been specified as a high-level emotional goal. However, insufficient tools, processes and focus were employed to realise the goal of fun sufficiently. Instead the project relied on the tacit knowledge of students and lecturers, which is often the case in digital media design projects and can be successful in projects of a smaller scale. By expanding the use of agent-oriented goal models to include the planet level goals (the game play) the user interaction was evaluated at regular intervals, between 30 seconds and 5 minutes, depending on the length of the quest chain. This granularity ensured that the users didn't get bored and that the developers gave appropriate attention to the emotional goals, rather than focusing solely on the

Table 4. Assessment of the high-level project goals by student developers at the completion of the Aspergion project

Aspergers Respect	Fun	Educative	Promoting Communication	Promoting Tolerance	Promoting Social Inclusion	Reduce Bulling	Feel Empathy	Be Clear and Truthful	Be Empowered	Feel Responsibility	Be Supportive	Raise Awareness	Demonstrate Creativity	Be Cool	Play with Technology	Project Goals Total
85	85	80	85	80	80	80	100	80	75	80	80	75	90	85	80	82.5
70	80	65	7	60	60	50	70	80	70	80	70	60	70	70	90	65.75
70	80	80	80	70	60	60	70	90	90	80	70	65	80	75	70	74.375
70	60	70	70	60	50	40	50	50	80	80	60	90	10	80	90	63.125
80	60	60	80	75	90	60	60	70	85	80	95	90	90	60	70	75.3125
75	62	65	70	72	81	65	87	82	76	84	79	69	70	83	72	74.5
60	65	70	70	60	60	45	50	60	60	60	60	70	80	60	80	63.125
95	75	80	85	80	80	75	70	75	70	80	80	80	80	75	60	78.75
85	85	60	40	40	40	30	30	30	65	85	85	75	85	50	85	59.0625
90	75	75	90	80	90	75	90	80	85	90	80	90	90	85	90	84.6875
93	88	92	89	90	87	89	88	90	91	94	95	88	92	94	90	90.625
85	83	82	86	84	88	85	84	83	82	85	88	85	84	88	85	84.8125
82	80	80	82	80	79	78	80	80	79	80	80	79	85	85	81	80.625
50	75	50	75	75	75	75	75	75	75	75	75	75	75	75	75	71.875
85	80	65	85	50	90	80	90	70	90	75	80	85	90	85	90	81.875
80	85	80	85	85	85	80	85	85	80	80	85	85	80	85	80	82.8125
60	75	85	70	75	75	80	65	65	60	75	75	75	60	65	95	73.4375
70	80	60	80	75	90	50	50	80	40	50	70	20	20	60	80	60.9375
80	75	90	80	80	85	85	75	90	90	85	85	90	95	80	95	85
80	70	70	80	70	74	70	63	70	80	75	60	80	65	70	70	71.6875
70	80	80	70	70	70	50	50	90	90	90	80	90	90	80	90	77.5
85	85	75	60	60	60	75	85	80	60	75	75	90	90	70	90	75.9375
75	65	75	65	78	60	60	65	60	54	55	70	70	70	50	60	64.375
70	75	70	80	80	80	75	70	60	65	60	75	75	60	70	70	70.3125
35	40	35	50	35	40	35	40	35	50	70	60	35	80	60	60	48.75
90	50	10	80	80	80	90	70	60	50	20	30	80	40	10	70	56.875
40	60	45	65	40	40	50	40	60	35	60	50	40	80	60	80	52.8125
70	70	65	60	80	80	60	69	70	60	90	90	65	60	80	90	72.4375
70	75	70	90	80	85	70	80	90	90	80	80	70	85	85	90	80.625
85	86	90	88	80	90	75	76	85	81	90	90	86	88	85	90	85.3125
65	80	70	90	90	60	70	70	70	65	60	80	90	100	90	90	78.75
70	70	80	70	80	70	70	70	80	70	80	70	80	80	80	100	76.25
80	80	70	80	75	80	80	80	80	70	80	80	70	70	80	70	76.5625
85	85	85	85	80	75	85	85	85	80	80	80	85	85	85	85	83.125
70	80	70	85	85	85	75	70	80	85	80	75	75	77	80		78.25
90	90	80	90	100	100	100	100	90	100	100	100	80	100	100	100	95
90	90	70	80	80	70	85	80	90	90	80	70	90	80	70	80	80.9375
85	70	90	90	90	90	75	77	84	70	70	85	90	95	70	85	82.25
80	87	80	82	78	82	86	82	83	83	80	79	78	79	85	80	81.5
80	80	78	81	79	84	87	83	87	85	87	84	85	90	97	80	84.1875
80	90	99	90	85	87	87	70	99	80	99	95	90	90	99	100	90
75	80	60	75	60	60	50	80	60	50	75	80	50	90	75	100	70
80	75	90	89	80	85	90	98	100	85	80	90	85	85	100	80	88.25
75	80	70	78	74	70	76	72	69	72	79	68	73	80	72	75	73.8125
83	78	80	80	78	78	78	80	90	77	78	78	80	79	81	60	79.25
85	88	85	78	77	75	75	80	80	75	80	80	80	75	78	80	79.4375
80	85	85	85	80	85	80	85	85	85	80	85	85	85	85	65	83.75
95	85	75	90	90	95	95	95	85	70	75	85	90	95	80	90	86.875
90	90	100	100	80	90	90	100	80	80	80	90	100	90	80	90	89.375
90	80	80	85	90	75	80	80	86	85	87	85	85	90	90	95	85.1875
80	70	70	88	90	90	90	70	70	80	90	80	85	78	70	80	80.0625
76.824	**76.804**	**73.745**	**77.765**	**75.353**	**76.863**	**72.373**	**74.294**	**76.235**	**74.314**	**78.196**	**77.667**	**77.51**	**79.216**	**76.745**	**83.588**	**76.718**
8	**8**	**8**	**8**	**8**	**8**	**7**	**7**	**8**	**7**	**8**	**8**	**8**	**8**	**8**	**8**	**8**

programming. Importantly, the process of defining, modelling and evaluating goals was repeatable, both in the two development phases of the project and throughout the project, game and planet level goals.

The assessment detailed in Table 4 demonstrates that from the student developer's perspective all high-level project goals were addressed, ranging from 74% to 84% completion. The consistency of results for each goal indicates that an appropriate level of attention was given to realising the functional, quality and emotional goals and shows the value of modelling them with the same hierarchy. By using a colour-coded system any of the stakeholders could rapidly see the state of the project.

Figure 7. Agent-oriented goal model of the 2011 Aspergion project

BENEFITS FOR THE DESIGN AND AGENT COMMUNITIES

Agent-oriented goal models used in the development of Aspergion demonstrated that emotional goals could be effectively incorporated into agent-oriented models to support the development of digital media design projects and sociotechnical systems. By providing high-level abstractions that were easily interpretable, the agent-oriented models served as a common language between student developers, lecturing staff and other stakeholders. Modelling emotional goals in addition to, and with the same hierarchy as, functional and quality goals provided an appropriate focus and acted as a signalling point for digital media design processes to be employed. In this way the process supports a trans-disciplinary approach to the development of sociotechnical systems that engage people by appealing to their emotional goals. By explicitly identifying emotions using creative design processes, and incorporating them into agent-oriented goal models that were available throughout the design, development and evaluation phases of the large cross-discipline team project, we went a long way to achieving our objectives.

An important development step of Aspergion was that the game was conceptualised by people with Asperger's Syndrome, each designing a planet to be included in the game. Having asked the participants to specify planet designs, agent-oriented goal models were created to clearly communicate the planet goals, inhabitants, character arcs and overall narrative. In the second delivery of the project three levels of agent-oriented goal models were developed to communicate goals at the project level, the MORPG game level and the planet level. This significantly contributed to the development and evaluation of the project, which in past digital media projects had been tacit.

The colour-coded evaluation system that was developed ensured that all stakeholders could get an instant snapshot of the projects progress and served as a form of acceptance testing. Over 614 project goals were defined, modelled and progressive evaluated. The process was repeated to support the realisation of high-level project goals, game level goals and more granular planet level (narrative) goals. This approach of using emotional goals to model narrative introduces a new method for incorporating emotional goals into agent-oriented goal models. 614 project goals, 102 of which were emotional goals, were being evaluated on a weekly basis by teams of student user testers. Explicitly modelling emotional goals ensured a coherent narrative and also signalled when design processes should be employed to support the development.

The process described of incorporating emotional goals into agent-oriented goal models and using a colour scale to evaluate project progress, has become standard in project subjects taught in the Digital Media Design Program at Swinburne University of Technology. Between 2011 and 2017 the process has been repeated in over 200 separate projects, ranging in scale from 1 to approximately 300 developers, and at academic levels including 3rd year, Honours, Masters, Doctoral, Post-doctoral students, Industry-based and Research projects. Outcomes have included the development of software, computer games, websites, animations, services, products and more. In each case the use of goal models varied to reflect the specific project needs and focus, whether that be to tell a narrative such as in the planet level goal models in Aspergion, or to communicate a high-level abstraction of the project to stakeholders, such as in the project level goal model in Aspergion. The following three examples, Gunter's Fables, Engaging the Ageing, and Science Island show further uses of the process, demonstrating its repeatability, scalability and flexibility.

Gunter's Fables was a project that involved animating and promoting a series of story books created by the entrepreneur and sustainability activist Gunter Pauli, with the primary project goal to 'inspire kids'. Gunter's Fables was undertaken in 2012 by 75 final year Digital Media Design students, being supervised by 4 lecturers at Swinburne University of Technology and represented approximately 22,500 hours of research and development. The students were distributed somewhat evenly (18-19 per team) across four teams, each with a primary objective to animate one of Gunter's Fables and also address one of the following secondary objectives. A Publication Team was responsible for generating outputs for various platforms such as a PDF storybook, eBook, DVD and a website. An Edutainment Team developed a game for each of the 4 books being animated. A Design Team provided art direction including style guides, characters, environments, audio and visualizations. Finally, a Marketing Team was responsible for the development of a Promotional Video

Trailer, Branding and Identity, Promotional Posters, a Book and Documentary of the development process.

Gunter's Fables included an agent-oriented goal model similar in structure and detail to the Aspergion project level goal model illustrated in Figure 5, with the purpose of communicating high-level project goals to stakeholders. In addition, more detailed goal models were created for the Publication, Edutainment, Design and Marketing Teams, that were similar in the number of goals to planet level goal models in Aspergion (Figure 6). However, rather than being used to describe narrative elements such as quests and characters they specified project outcomes, such as branding, a DVD and website and served as a project management tool that communicated the project development pipeline. Furthermore, for each of the four animations produced, the primary and emotional goals described were incorporated into a new animation production process (Murdoch, 2015). Both the Aspergion and Gunter's Fables projects demonstrated the use of multi-level agent-oriented goal models in the development, management and evaluation of large group projects, however agent-oriented goal models have been used equally successfully at the single project, single developer level.

Engaging the Ageing was an individual research project undertaken by 48 final-year Digital Media Design students at Swinburne University of Technology in 2013. The project explored how to make modern technologies palpable and engaging for older adults, making use of the new opportunities these technologies present whilst catering for the specific needs of an older demographic.

Under the supervision of two lecturers, students working on the Engaging the Aging project were asked to choose from one of the following six areas as a focus for their investigation: Social interaction, mobility, life-long learning, game play, memory training and information retrieval. These were distributed across the 48 students, with approximately 7 students developing outcomes in each focus area, representing in total approximately 7,200 hours of research and development.

The outcomes of the 48 projects undertaken varied from software applications, systems and services, advertising campaigns, branding, games, websites, animations and physical products. Based on target market research and in consultation with the lecturers each of the students gathered requirements and created an elicitation (initial) agent-oriented goal model. Throughout the development process the project goals each student had specified were progressively appraised and the goal models updated to illustrate this using the colour ranking system. At the conclusion of the project, based on user feedback conducted through interviews with the target market, an acceptance testing goal model was developed that served as part of the student's formal assessment. Student feedback and assessment indicated that the agent-oriented goal models were intuitive, easy to use, provided a common artefact to communicate progress and focused students on the primary project goals.

The process of incorporating emotional goals into agent-oriented goal models is also being used in the development of Science Island, a project that promotes STEM learning (Science, Technology, Engineering and Mathematics) to children globally (aged 10 – 12) by communicating scientific principles in a "cool" and "scientifically accurate" way.

The project has two primary components. One is a free online computer game called "Science Island", accessible via the domain scienceisland.com. The second is the development of a science-based school in Uganda. Having been in development for 5 years (2012 – 2017) and with a target completion date of 2018, the Science Island project currently represents over 100,000 hours of research and development, by approximately 620 participants. In that time, the Kasese Humanist Primary School (KHPS) in Uganda has been built from the ground up and now includes an orphanage, primary and secondary school with 650+ students (of which 1/6 are orphans).

The Science Island game content includes 120 science-based questions that have been answered in the form of stories, games, songs, animations, experiments and quizzes and are distributed across the following 10 subject areas; Environment & Nature, Animals, Inventions, Space, Life & Evolution, Medicine & Health, Physics, Weather, Dinosaurs & Fossils and Mathematics. Responses to the questions are being developed by final-year Digital Media Design students in collaboration with scientists globally. The science questions were originally posed by students from KHPS.

Players (children aged 10-12) access this content by exploring Science Island, which is a dilapidated theme-park, and earn tokens for each activity that they engage with. The tokens allow the player to repair the park and go on the rides.

Science Island uses a single high-level agent-oriented goal model, with a similar number of goals to the Aspergion project level goal model in Figure 5. However, differing from other goal models described, the Science Island goal model is a hybrid that blends high-level abstractions such as *communicating science* with lower level deliverables such as *do a quiz*. In addition, each functional goal is directly linked to either a quality or emotional goal to clearly show how project components are integrated, indicating to the developers not only 'what to do' but 'why they're doing it. For example, the functional goal of *do a quiz* is linked to the goal of *being measurable*.

A more detailed discussion of Science Island, Gunter's Fables and Engaging the Ageing is described in the thesis 'Incorporating Software Engineering Models Into Digital Media Design Processes' Marshall, J. (2018). The thesis also details how goal models may be incorporated into an iterative creative design process (known as MAD, Marshall's Augmented Design process) and includes a detailed method for evaluating emotional goals.

Further research in this area should involve developing a rigorous method of categorising and evaluating emotional goals and using the process detailed in this paper to investigate whether agent-oriented models may be used to describe how game patterns elicit emotional goals.

ACKNOWLEDGMENT

I would like to thank Leon Sterling, the students and lecturers from the Swinburne University of Technology Digital Media Design program and the people with Asperger's Syndrome who participated in this project.

REFERENCES

Apple Inc. (2013). *Designed by Apple in California.* Retrieved June 30, 2013, from http://www.apple.com/designed-by-apple

Baxter, G., & Sommerville, I. (2011). Socio-technical systems: From design methods to systems engineering. *Interacting with Computers, 23*(1), 4–17. doi:10.1016/j.intcom.2010.07.003

Chung, L. K., Nixon, B. A., Yu, E., & Mylopoulos, J. (2000). *Non-Functional Requirements in Software Engineering.* Kluwer Publishing. doi:10.1007/978-1-4615-5269-7

Daniel, M. B., & Brown, D. M. (2007). Communicating design: developing web site documentation for design and planning. Berkeley, CA: Peachpit Press.

Demirbilek, O., & Sener, B. (2003). Product design, semantics and emotional response. *Ergonomics, 46*(13-14), 1346–1360. doi:10.1080/00140130310001610 874 PMID:14612324

Desmet, P. M. A., & Hekkert, P. (2009). Special issue editorial: Design & Emotion. *International Journal of Design, 3*(2), 1–6.

Dourish, P. (2001b). *Where the Action Is: The Foundation of Embodied Interaction.* Cambridge, MA: MIT Press.

Forbes Inc. (2017). *Fortune 500.* Retrieved October 14, 2017 from http://fortune.com/fortune500/apple/

Gross, H. (2005). *Component-based Software Testing with UML.* Springer.

Guizzardi, R., & Perini, A. (2005). Analyzing requirements of knowledge management systems with the support of agent organizations. *Journal of the Brazilian Computer Society*, *11*(1), 51–62.

Iacucci, G., & Kuutti, K. (2002). Everyday life as a stage in creating and performing scenarios for wireless devices. *Personal and Ubiquitous Computing*, *6*(4), 299–306. doi:10.1007007790200031

Jureta, I. J., & Faulkner, S. (2007) Clarifying goal models. *Proc. ER 2007*, 139-144.

Kirikova, M., Grundspenkis, J., Wojtkowski, W., Zupancic, J., & Wrycza, S. (2002). *Information Systems Development: Advances in Methodologies, Components, and Management*. Springer. doi:10.1007/978-1-4615-0167-1

McCarthy, J., & Wright, P. (2004). *Technology as Experience*. MIT Press.

Murdoch, S. (2015). Exploring Primary and Emotional Goals within an Agent-Oriented, Animation Production Process. *ASPERA Annual Conference 2015: "What's This Space? Screen Practice, Audiences and Education for the Future Decade"*.

Paay, J., Sterling, L., Vetere, F., Howard, S., & Boettcher, A. (2009). Engineering the Social: The Role of Shared Artifacts. *IJHCS*, *67*(5), 437–454.

Pacey, A. (1999). *Meaning in Technology*. MIT Press.

Pavon, J., Arroyo, M., Hassan, S., & Sansores, C. (2008). Agent-based modelling and simulation for the analysis of social patterns. *Pattern Recognition Letters*, *29*(8), 1039–1048. doi:10.1016/j.patrec.2007.06.021

Randall, D., Harper, R., & Rouncefield, M. (2004). *Fieldwork for design: Theory and practice*. Amsterdam: Kluwer Academic Press.

Reekie, H., & McAdam, R. (2006). *A Software Architecture Primer: A Primer*. Angophora Press.

Rheingold, H. (2003). *Smart Mobs: The Next Social Revolution Transforming Cultures and Communities in the Age of Instant Access*. New York, NY: Basic Books.

Sommerville, I. (2007). *Software Engineering* (8th ed.). Harlow, UK: Addison Wesley.

Sterling, L. S., & Taveter, K. (2009). *The art of agent-oriented modeling*. Massachusetts Institute of Technology.

van Lamsweerde, A., & Letier, E. (2003). From Object Orientation to Goal Orientation: A Paradigm Shift for Requirements Engineering. In Radical Innovations of Software and Systems Engineering in the Future, Revised Papers from RISSEF '02 (pp. 325-340). Springer.

Section 3
Theory in the People– Oriented Programming Paradigm

As previously highlighted, a new software design and development paradigm doesn't come into existence in a neat chronological order like: Theory, Tools, Methodology, Framework, Applications. And so it is with the theory part of People-Oriented Programming. However, there have been advances in the area of theory coming from disparate disciplines, that do sit well within the embryotic POP paradigm. The two chapters in this Section hold important aspects of how relevant theoretical considerations from diverse disciplines have already impacted the other areas of POP, namely, the theory behind some of the tools and the methods described in Section 2.

Chapter 9
Formation and Control of Identity:
In a Social Media World

Christine Yunn-Yu Sun
eBookDynasty.net, Australia

Steve Goschnick
Swinburne University of Technology, Australia

ABSTRACT

This chapter explores the construction of identity in online communities and websites for social purposes, and its consequences in terms of how one's online identity may be utilized to such an extent that one's real-world identity is either enforced or eroded. It does so by investigating the very nature of identity, coming predominantly from a cultural studies research and philosophical view, although it also cites some related findings and advances in computing and information systems (IS) research. The central argument across the chapter is two-fold: firstly, in promoting an initial shift in focus from the management of online identity to the nature and significance of identity itself whose construction may be conceptualized as a process of sense making and strengthening; and only then, armed with a better understanding of identity, one can focus back upon the management of it more effectively, with a view to the individual taking more control of their own identity within cyberspace, which is increasingly transitioning us all into a functioning global community, in both predictable and unforeseen ways.

DOI: 10.4018/978-1-5225-5969-6.ch009

INTRODUCTION

This chapter explores the construction of identity in online communities and websites for social purposes, and its consequences in terms of how one's online identity may be utilized to such an extent that one's real-world identity is either enforced or eroded. We also present a case study with the aim of demonstrating that an individual's identity can be methodically represented, so that they may be appropriately notified of information coming in from the online world from multiple sources; and, which may be used as both an aide in taking control of how one is represented in the online world, and in placing information in the context of one's own roles, interests and knowledge generation.

This chapter argues that identity is an imagined "site" the boundaries of which distinguish whoever is assigned within them, from those outside. Identity is flexible and ever-changing in nature, constructed on the needs of an individual to react to the demands of their political, economic, societal and cultural circumstances. As such, the formation, standardization and circulation of one's identity within society affects not only how one understands and represents oneself to others, but is also the basis of how one is recognized and treated by others accordingly. Furthermore, from the individual's point of view, having a model that represents identity, helps them stay orientated on the things that matter to them. In his book *The News: A User's Manual* philosopher Alain de Botton wrote, that immersing ourselves in the daily electronic news feeds and other news sources, is "*to raise a shell to our ears and to be overpowered by the roar of humanity*". That there is too much of it for our own good, and that we are becoming "news junkies". He suggests that one must know themselves well, to not be left disorientated and distracted by the constant flow of news and information.

To take this argument one step further, unlike the real world, the Internet is capable of enabling one to reach across nearly all political, cultural and sociological traits that are commonly used to construct one's identity as an imagined "site". What's more, the Internet (also known as cyberspace) itself is an imagined "site" whose social functions, capacities and protocols are continually expanding and regularly redefined. The imagined boundaries of the Internet are therefore considerably different from those of the real world, creating the needs, opportunities and means for one to continuously present, reproduce and dynamically manage one's online identity. Most importantly, in the case of online identity, it is more often a matter of one's choice to actively construct a specific identity than being randomly assigned an identity by others. This presents one with ample opportunity and choice not only to represent oneself but also to have a significant bearing on how one is recognized.

As a result, there is a clear and urgent need to examine the formation, standardization and circulation of one's online identity and how it impacts upon the ways in which one interacts with others on the Internet. Because of the social nature of online communities and websites, the imagined "site" that is online identity becomes even more fluid and its boundaries increasingly fragile due to a lack of protection against misrepresentation and privacy violations. At this point it is worth stating that Identity is researched, defined and managed from several different fields of study. The research behind this paper is best described as Cultural in nature. However, given the technological foundation of the Internet that enables cyberspace as we know it, Information Systems (IS) research and development also has a significant interest and research record in Identity, which we draw upon in the case study. While this paper focuses on cultural and even philosophical aspects of identity, papers in other fields including IS are cited from time-to-time as there are some parallel findings and observations across these disparate fields of study.

Additionally, when Facebook, LinkedIn, Google+ and other social network platforms are discussed further down, we will see that there is a continuing push from the technology companies behind the preeminent social networking platforms today, to mesh one's real world identity, with as many of one's online sub-identities as possible, through our various interactions spread across the Internet. Indeed, in February 2017, the Facebook founder outlined what has become known in the tech industry as the Facebook Manifesto (Zuckerberg, 2017) in an article titled – Building Global Community – in which he puts heavy emphasis on Facebook supporting (by evolving Facebook tools) real world traditional community groups, and in doing so, wooing them to come online if such groups do not already have a representation on Facebook. Zuckerberg expresses the eventual goal of forming a functioning worldwide community of sub-communities, with media, safety and recovery mechanisms, voting on community standards (initially, but later global governance), and other functionality.

At this point a useful paper from IS research by Roussos et al. (2003), titled 'Mobile Identity Management: An Enacted View', suggests three principles regarding Identity. The first two are of some use in clarifying the discussion here:

- **The Locality Principle:** Identities are situated within particular contexts, roles, relationships and communities. People will have multiple different and overlapping identities in (these) different contexts, and each of these should be respected.
- **The Understanding Principle:** In human relationships, knowledge of identities is negotiated and both sides in a relationship should know how properties that characterize identity are exchanged and used. Relationships should be symmetrical and reciprocal.

The third principle, not repeated here, is really a restatement of the second with emphasis upon mutual understanding by those in a relationship. Much of the technology and management issues around identity focus on the Locality Principle (e.g. identifiers and how they are used for particular services, while in specific contexts), whereas, the Understanding Principle as given by Roussos et al., leans much more towards a Cultural Studies approach to identity, such as the emphasis in this paper. And yet, both principles involve aspects of identity that we are all interested in, and have a particular view on, no matter what one's outer field of study.

While the technical, legal and security issues have been and will continue to be investigated from IS, sociological and psychological perspectives, this paper argues for two things: a shift in focus from the management of online identity to the nature and significance of identity itself whose construction may be conceptualized as a long process of sense making and strengthening; and then, armed with a better understanding of identity, one can focus back upon the management of it more effectively, with a view to the individual taking more control of their own identity within the technology space.

An inquiry into how one positions oneself on the Internet also helps in the estimation and measurement of the extent to which such positioning, affects what is being said by whom and for what social purposes they are saying it. Finally, we add to the current and future research on the management of one's reputation on the Internet through tactics of online identity disclosure and control. The case study we refer to, models identity and considers technology outside of and apart from the various social networks, to help an individual identify, disclose and control aspects of themselves, and to also aggregate information and assemble knowledge specific to them according to the Locality Principle, with less reliance on external filters

IDENTITY AS A SELF-PRODUCED CONTINUITY AND THE MEDIA

In his essay "Cultural Identity and Cinematic Representation" (Hall, 1989), British cultural theorist Stuart Hall proposed to define identities as being "always constructed through memory, fantasy, narrative and myths". Instead of providing "unifying and unchanging points of reference and meaning", identities are made "within the discourses of history and culture" and are therefore "not an essence but a positioning". This view supports the argument that identity is not and should not be seen as a "given fact", although the persuasiveness of a given representation may lead to this form of essentialization. Instead, it is necessary to conceptualize identity as a constructed, normalized and widely circulated cultural "norm" that has the potential to cause different positive and/or negative effects on different individuals and groups.

Hall's essay mainly deals with cinematic constructions and presentations of national identity in Caribbean countries, where new generations of native artists strove to create and express a "Caribbean uniqueness" in films that may unify their people politically and culturally against a colonized past. However, Hall's conceptualization of identity as a self-produced continuity that designates what is said by whom and for what purposes, is particularly useful for this chapter, as it attempts to understand the formation, standardization and circulation of identity through powerful social channels which includes the Internet. Hall's view is further supported by Graeme Turner who, in his essay "Media Texts and Messages" (Turner, 1997), studies the important role of the media in the promotion of a national identity in the Australian context:

While there have been plenty of nationalist arguments for the media's active collaboration in the preservation of an Australian "identity", most recent accounts accept that such an identity is an invention. By this I mean that there is no "natural" reason why all of us who live on this island continent should share the same government, the same institutions, common values or characteristics. That Australians think of themselves as doing so, "naturally", is a result of the cultural construction of the idea of the nation through language, myths and history. The "national identity" is in a sense of a "national fiction" Australians collaborate in producing everyday.

Turner suggests that the analysis of the media is important because media texts "are among the most important sites for interrogating the work of representing the nation, assessing its effects and interests, and revealing its ideological and political determinants". This is because the texts produced by the media are "crucial components in definitions of the nation which do not simply represent a 'real', national identity, but which selectively construct versions of nationhood which serve some interests, and not others". Yet, if the words "nation" and "national" are omitted from the quotations above, and if one supplants "the media" with one's personal communications via the Internet, then it becomes obvious that Turner's argument is highly relevant to an investigation on how much the construction of one's identity reveals about oneself. In this context, the political, cultural and sociological traits used by the *individual* to establish, maintain and utilize one's identity are the most important sites in which one's perceptions of oneself may be adequately explored. Particularly in communications with others for social purposes, one's identity is a form of "personal fiction" that we and those around us collaborate in producing everyday, with each intercommunication further defining, refining or rebuking minute aspects, bit by bit.

Alain de Botton (ibid) places the role in society of the media, specifically *the news*, at an even higher level of impact. He argues that the news is a major source of authority in modern technological society to the point where it has replaced religion as a dominant source of guidance to many, becoming the "prime creator of political and social reality". Little wonder the turmoil surrounding fake news involving Facebook and Google emanating from the 2016 US election (more on fake news later), where it has been revealed that more than half of the American people receive their news through Facebook. If we take the analogy made in the previous paragraph, i.e. from society to the individual, then the impact of the deluge of news on and through the Internet upon an individual, taking into consideration de Botton's well-argued view, is highly likely to affect the nature of identity further in the more-fluid direction. This may help explain the rise of social networks on the Internet – as something of a refuge from that increasing fluidity, just as they were originally something of a refuge from spam email. In this light, the rise of so-called *filter bubbles* within social networks and search engines, is not surprising. A definition of filter bubbles from Wikipedia (2017):

A filter bubble is a state of intellectual isolation that can result from personalized searches when a website algorithm selectively guesses what information a user would like to see based on information about the user, such as location, past click-behavior and search history. As a result, users become separated from information that disagrees with their viewpoints, effectively isolating them in their own cultural or ideological bubbles. The choices made by these algorithms are not transparent. Prime examples include Google Personalized Search results and Facebook's personalized news-stream.

Many have been concerned about the *political polarization* (a person's view being reinforced by an extreme counter view, without any consideration of other alternative views) and its effect on democracy that can come of filter bubbles, particular since the 2016 US election. It is one of the concerns discussed by the Facebook founder in (Zuckerberg, 2017). Since objections were first raised about personalised news feeds and search results, Facebook and others have conducted research about filter bubbles. E.g. Bleiberg & West (2015) report that "The Facebook study demonstrates that the polarization phenomenon also applies to the social network (even with personalisation filtering turned off). The study finds that roughly speaking a Facebook user has five politically likeminded friends for every one friend on the other side of the spectrum." I.e. According to the Facebook study, even in the absence of filter bubbles, people seek the articles and information that aligns with their interests and views and avoid the others, as evidence that there is nothing unique here regarding social media platforms.

Other researchers are concerned about filter bubbles with regard to the hidden algorithms selecting one's news, search results, and social network experience, and that some individuals may even have their identities socially constructed for them to some degree (Bozdag & Timmerman, 2011). After conceding the need for filtering to manage the information deluge, they state their concern is specifically related to transparency of the filtering used: "Personalized filtering is thus based on an interpretation of a user's identity. Identity refers to people's understanding of who they are over time, embracing both continuity and discontinuity. To a certain extent there is also a discontinuity of identity when a person moves from one context to the other." The filters are generally not aware of the subtleness of changing contexts. They finish with 3 guidelines for those designing personalisation filter algorithms:

1. Make sure different identities are allowed per user, which might differ per context.
2. Design for autonomy, so that the user can customize the filter, and change the identity that is formed on basis of his previous interactions.
3. Design for transparency, so that the user is aware that a filter is taking place. The user must be able to see which criteria is used for filtering, and which identity the system has of the user.

There is conflicting research about the effects of filter bubbles, and de Botton's insight coupled with the fluidity of identity backs up the idea that weighing us the pros and cons of personalised filtering is far from a simple choice situation.

Identity is an invented and/or imagined label that is open to interpretation. Because identity is developed through shared patterns of interaction, one's identity in practice alters depending on the groups of people with whom one regularly and habitually interacts. This is explicitly illustrated by Paul Macgregor as he discusses the limits of geography and ethnicity as determinants of identity:

We are part of a multiplicity of communities, and we interact with different communities on different occasions.

We thus have multiple identities, intrinsically tied to processes of shared communal activity. Depending on which community of people we are with, we change aspects of our speech, mannerisms, even, to an extent, our thoughts, to take part in the shared rituals of behavior which ties us together in temporary, yet continually repeated, gatherings of each community. We temporarily locate in a shared space, read the same newspapers, exchange according to shared patterns, then go off and join with other groups, make other patterns. (Macgregor, 1995)

What Macgregor illustrates here is the extremely complex nature of identity as an abstract construct embodied in practice, and thus given to change both historically and when it encounters all kinds of pressure within the context of an individual's or a group's everyday experience. One's identity is exhibited to a certain degree at any given moment, depending on the nature of the people with whom one interacts, the meaning of the occasion, the role one sees oneself in, and the location of the interaction. The result is that various "shared patterns" or "shared rituals of behaviour", which are always subject to change, are what constitute the flexible nature of identity in individual circumstances. This supports Hall's and Turner's conceptualization that identity is a never-ending process of positioning. More importantly, throughout this process, identity is not and should not be seen as something that is based on a mere "recovery" of the past, such as one's cultural roots which is waiting to be found, and when found, will secure one's sense of belonging. Rather, according to Hall, "identities are the names we give to the different ways we are positioned by, and position ourselves within, the narratives of the past" (Hall, 1989). In other words, identity is not only about the past, but also in the naming and the meaning attached to those names; about how one narrates and interprets such a past, in the present and in the future.

At this point some people may object somewhat to Hall's depiction of identity as 'an ongoing positioning', of being quite fluid, an identity that includes deeply held cultural and religious aspects, which they may view as definitely fixed, as 'unchanging points of reference and meaning'. It is certainly true that the majority of people do operate with a set of deeply held *core values*, but equally, most agree that other aspects and values of ones self-identity may well be subject to change, never mind their wider identity.

Helpfully, within Computing and Information Systems research, there are so-named agent-oriented (AO) systems that draw upon psychology for underlying models of the mind when building intelligent support systems (applied AI). One such AO architecture called ShadowBoard (see Figure 1), was created to help augment human abilities, particularly via the Internet. It is based on the *Theory of Sub-selves* from psychology. The theoretical source of a given *sub-agent* (embodied or enlisted software) within it, is the *sub-self*, within a hierarchical grouping of numerous sub-selves, that together make up the whole Agent (the one that augments the individual human). That psychological model fits the description of identify briefed upon in the above quote from Macgregor, quite well.

Note: The ShadowBoard agent architecture is the initial blueprint behind the software developed and used in our case study, a system that combines personal assistant agents. The overarching system is called the *DigitalFriend* (Figure 3), which we turn to, further down in the case study.

Figure 1. The ShadowBoard Agent Architecture

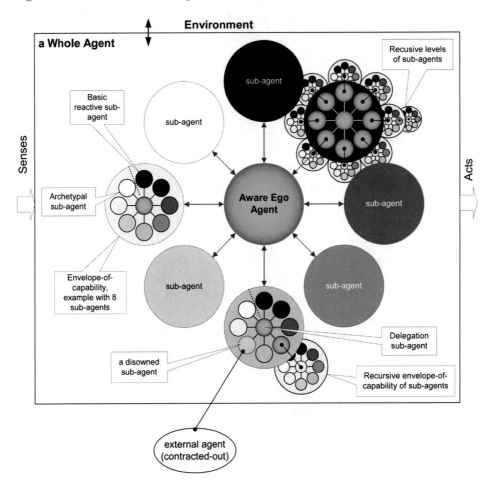

Furthermore, these sub-selves in the psychology are very often related to different roles in a given person's life (parent, daughter, manager, defender, critic, etc.), and that is where the overlap with the theory of sub-selves and the agent model in the ShadowBoard architecture, align. I.e. the sub-agents in the human-supporting technology also have *roles* – in turn supporting the roles of the person being augmented - and the *role model* that comes with the architecture, is central to a methodology (of the same name) for collecting and building sub-agents that populate and enhance one's *digital self* (Goschnick & Graham, 2006), enacted via the DigitalFriend software. See the role model in the ShadowBoard methodology in Table 1.

Returning to our discussion on the seemingly *fixed* aspects of identity: even deeply held core values are sometimes subject to change, albeit, at glacial speed

Table 1. Generic Roles and Sub-roles in the ShadowBoard methodology

Manager Benevolent Manager *(arch.)* Conciliatory Manager Planner Scheduler Coordinator Recycler Controller Decisive Manager *(reactive)*	**Protector** Safety Officer *(archetype)* Defender Risk Analyst Environmentalist Pacifier Doctor Exit Strategist *(reactive)*	**Personal Assistant** Selfless Pleaser *(archetype)* Service Provider Networker Communicator Marketer Teacher Adviser	**Initiator** Inventor *(archetype)* Success Seeker Resource Master Trouble Shooter Pusher Reminder *(reactive)*
Critic Perfectionist *(archetype)* Editor Quality Controller Doubter Cynic *(reactive)*	**Adventurer** Explorer *(archetype)* Risk Taker Traveller Vacationer 2D Situator 3D Situator Lazybones *(reactive)*	**Knowledge Seeker** Knowledge Worker *(arch.)* Concept Learner Learner Information Officer Data Miner Random Generator *(react.)*	**Intuitive** Seer *(archetype)* Mood Senser Pattern Finder Dreamer Profiler Role Keeper Core Value Bearer Affirmation Agent

or subject to seismic events in one's personal history. Consider this anecdote to underline several related points:

A Western-raised husband and a Chinese-ethnic raised wife have just seen the wife's mother off at the airport, heading home after a 6-week stay with the happy couple and their children. Husband says to wife: "The first 4 weeks was great, but nobody enjoyed the last week or two. Next time you should invite her to come for 4 weeks, it is a much better length of time, where we can focus the proper amount of attention and activity around her visit." To which the wife answers: "I can't suggest to her how long she should stay. There is no way in the world that I could ever say that to my mother! You don't do that in my culture. Its called filial piety - very high respect for ones elders." To which he answers: "I don't see what the problem is? She'd be happier with a shorter stay. You'd be happier with a shorter stay. I'd be happier with a shorter stay. She might even visit more often if that were the case. Where is the disrespect? I can't see the issue?" To which she again replies: "It is just impossible for me to have such a conversation with my mother." To which he replies: "Some years ago now, it was similarly impossible that you could or would marry a foreigner, and yet, here we are."

That they each had a different view of the identity of the other (e.g. her self-identity, versus his idea of her identity), makes the point that identity is not a fixed nor a singular thing. Furthermore, the concept of identity being fluid, a continuing positioning, does not mean all aspects of an identity are fluid to the same degree, all the time. Some aspects might stay as fixed points of reference for very long periods of time, even a lifetime.

To take this argument one step further, not only can one actively form, standardize and circulate an identity for the purpose of distinguishing one from others under all kinds of political, economic, societal and cultural circumstances, but one can also be passively assigned an identity by others for the same reason. This is because one not only positions oneself within, but is also positioned *by*, the numerous narratives and interpretations of one's surroundings that never cease re-producing and re-defining themselves. Therefore, if identity may be conceptualized as an imagined "site", then one can either actively assign oneself or be passively assigned within its boundaries. While both acts of assignment can happen at the same time, they also take place constantly and continuously, in the same way that numerous identities or imagined "sites" are subject to ongoing construction and are continually impacting on how individuals and groups interact with each other, and why for example, democracy can bring about change (hence the concerns raised above with filter bubbles). Ultimately, identity is a construction reified in practice and resembles geo-political entities such as Australia and the United States. It differs from geo-political entities insofar as it is somewhat more open-ended and subject to change.

Unfortunately, precisely because one's identity is constructed for the purpose of differentiating one from others, the boundaries of this imagined "site", though forever fluid and open to interpretation in their nature, are often considered to be as necessary and unalterable as geo-political borders that require safeguarding. Furthermore, such safeguarding is often conducted by those within or outside of the boundaries of an imagined "site" that is identity, or both, by enforcing those political, cultural and sociological traits that were used to construct this "site" in the first place. A risk thus occurs that these traits, or "shared patterns" or "shared rituals of behaviour" as referred to by Macgregor, are perceived by all involved to be as permanent and unchallengeable as the borders of geo-political entities. A highly likely result of such perception, intentional or otherwise, is the invention and prolonged utilization of all kinds of labels, or "norms", that affect the ways in which those both within and outside of the imagined "site" negotiate with each other and among themselves.

Most importantly, in the same way that the subjects of a geo-political entity such as Australia or the United States "naturally" consider themselves as belonging within its boundaries and feeling the need to distinguish themselves against those outside, those who assign themselves or are assigned by others to be within the boundaries of their identity may also feel its "binding power". That is, in spite of the fluid and complex nature of one's identity as an imagined "site", one is likely to do all that is possible to uphold and even strengthen those political, cultural and sociological traits that one considers as being essential to the continued existence of such identity or imagination, which provides one with a sense of belonging. That one "naturally" feels obliged to do so is the consequence of a long process of *sense making*. Instead of embracing all the narratives and interpretations of one's surroundings that can possibly be employed to help one position oneself, one willingly and actively chooses to acknowledge and even advocate a much lesser set that one believes are the "facts". It also involves less intellectual work. Some might call these their core values. To borrow Hall's words, the result of such an "essentialist" approach is to render identity as something concrete and permanent that provides "unifying and unchanging points of reference and meaning", whose existence cannot be neglected and whose omnipresent influence can be felt in one's life at any moment.

Such an "essentialist" approach is in sharp contrast to Turner's "non-essentialist" conceptualization of identity, "a positioning" as a form of "personal fiction" that one and those around one collaborate in producing every day. However, together, they explicitly illustrate the actual dichotomous nature of identity. Although one's identity may be formed, standardized and circulated either by oneself or by those around her for the purpose of differentiating one from others, it can easily become a self-produced continuity that grants value to one's existence and provides one with both a sense of belonging and of an evolving identity. More importantly, although one's identity is constructed using those various political, cultural and sociological traits that one is commonly associated with, these traits, or "shared patterns" or "shared rituals of behaviour", are often employed by both oneself and others as a "definite" and "necessary" means to uphold and even advocate such identity. Finally, although one's identity is flexible and always subject to some degree of change, it does have the potential to become a caricature, an identity made up of just that set of concrete "facts" that one "naturally" considers to being essential to one's existence under all kinds of political, economic, societal and cultural circumstances - something very much like a stereotype.

ONLINE IDENTITY, ITS CONSTRUCTION AND CIRCULATION

The conceptualization of identity as a "personal fiction", a "positioning", an imagined "site" whose boundaries are forever ambiguous and open to definition and interpretation by those assigned both within and outside of them - is a particularly useful idea here, with respect to exploring the construction of identity in online communities and websites for social purposes. Specifically, the formation, standardization and circulation of one's online identity -- the deliberate and active establishment of one's reputation on the Internet and its long-term management -- can have such profound consequences that one's identity in the real world may be either enforced or eroded. Indeed, in the case of online identity, rather than one being randomly assigned a username, it is more often the matter of one's choice to construct and maintain a special identity that well reflects how one positions oneself within the narratives and interpretations of the much larger and complex imagined "site" that is the Internet. Nonetheless, in the same way that identity is established to differentiate one from others under all kinds of political, economic, societal and cultural circumstances, online identity functions as a self-produced continuity that grants certain values to one's existence and provides one with a sense of belonging on the Internet, something that has a global span. Whether online identity is capable of providing one with a sense of security within and outside of the Internet is a separate matter that was discussed in an earlier related paper (Sun, 2012).

In the same way that one's identity is constructed using various political, cultural and sociological traits that one is commonly associated with, an online identity reveals varying amounts of information that help identify the characteristics of one's real-world identity, depending on whom one interacts with and for what purpose. As Dorian Wiszniewski and Richard Coyne propose in their paper 'Mask and Identity: The Hermeneutics of Self-Construction in the Information Age', one portrays a mask of one's real-world identity whenever one interacts online for social purposes. "Identity is clearly related to community. The Enlightenment promoted the concept of the individual, the lone identity, who sets herself apart from the collection of other individuals, or amongst whom she has her place, and with whom she may ultimately identify. In as much as we wear a mask, it is to assume a role in the social sphere." (Wiszniewski & Coyne, 2002). Throughout this process, at least something of the subject behind the mask is revealed by the kind of mask one chooses, whether it is by answering specific questions about one's age, gender, address and so on, in the process of registering as a member of an online community or website, or through the style of writing, vocabulary and topics one frequently uses as one interacts with others. In the words of Wiszniewski and Coyne, "the mask is an artifice, but the face behind it is subject to the same account. The question of what constitutes a mask and what is not is subject to the workings of the practical field of engagement". This observation supports Macgregor's argument that identity as a construction reified in practice is "intrinsically tied to processes of shared communal activity". Just as much online as in the real world, one changes aspects of one's speech, mannerisms and even thoughts in order to take part in the shared rituals of behavior that ties together the members of each community.

Wiszniewski and Coyne further suggest "insofar as it acts as a signifier, the mask deflects the function of the sign away from the object behind the mask to some other object". As a result, attention is deflected "away from the mask to the context, the situation in which the masking takes place". For example, if one chooses to blog about American writer Stephen King, this mask reveals an interest in horror fiction.

Even if one chooses to hide behind a completely false online identity, this in itself reveals something about a fear or perhaps a lack of self-esteem behind the false mask.

An online identity is one of the numerous "points of reference and meaning" that helps one position oneself and be positioned by others on the Internet. As one participates in different online communities and websites, one establishes different online identities, each of them being an abstract construct embodied in practice and forever subject to change in nature. It is through the process in which these online identities are formed, standardized and circulated *that glimpses of one's identity in the real world are gained*. The metaphor of "mask", in this case, may signify not only one's online identity but also one's real-world identity, both of which can also be seen as "masks" that reveal something about oneself as an individual among the numerous narratives and interpretations of one's surroundings. While a commonly accepted notion is that there is nothing behind the mask that is online identity (e.g. "On the Internet, nobody knows you're a dog", which is generally perceived as a comment on one's ability to socialize online in general anonymity), others argue there is everything behind such a self-produced mask (e.g. "On the Internet, everybody knows you're a dog", a comment created to illustrate the collective human effort in collaborated exposure and mass distribution of personal information amidst the "human flesh search" phenomenon in China, which an earlier paper discusses (Sun, 2012), strongly related to 'wisdom of the crowd' in the West). Tension inevitably arises between these two views, as the act of "masking" that is the construction and management of online identity, is scrutinized. However, it is the interaction among one's many masks both online and in the real world that is and should always be the focus of attention.

Wiszniewski and Coyne declare in their paper that "it is no longer possible to discuss identity in traditional terms. Identity is constantly in flux, the repetition of the question into identity being the only constant. By its very nature, identity is always elusive, and the notion of community follows suit". Such a view sheds light onto the significance of online identity as a self-produced continuity for social purposes, an abstract construct that grants certain values to one's existence and provides one with a sense of belonging on the Internet. Specifically, while those assigned within an imagined "site" that is identity, are distinguished from those outside of it. The two groups are also intrinsically connected via the boundary of this "site", and neither can exist without the other. This conceptualization is particularly applicable to the case of online identity because, on the Internet, the notion of self cannot make sense without that of community.

One's perception of oneself via the formation, standardization and circulation of online identity very much reflects one's awareness of the other members of the enormous imagined "site" that is the Internet. Note: further down we drawn on the ShadowBoard methodology introduced in Table 1 above, to construct a representation of a digital self on a computer, done so within the DigitalFriend (software based on the ShadowBoard Architecture shown earlier in Figure 1). This example digital self is held outside of all of one's communities on Internet, where an individual can create and 'nurture' a digital representation of their self-identity, from which facets of self (see Figure 1) can be revealed in specific online communities that they choose; but more so, it is used to store and reference information and other resources in a private space, as the individual selects and builds knowledge, through the filter of their own goals, interests, activities, interactions, capabilities and outcomes.

Finally, considering the fact that online identity is more often than not proactively established for social purposes, Coyne (2011) observes in his essay "Profile Yourself (Narcissus online)" that:

Social media encourage personal and private disclosures, or at least, the tools for presenting oneself professionally readily elide into tools for personal presentation. You have to decide whether to let your online professional persona deliver insights into hobbies, holidays and family matters. The scope of identity formation seems to be expanding, or at least changing. There will always be some group or other, no matter how small, amongst whom one can entertain unusual or idiosyncratic interests, and with whom one can readily identify. There is a group out there, possibly not yet formed, and unknown to you, amongst whom you can enjoy a ration of fame if you really want it.

Specifically, in the process of constructing one's online identity, one has "control (or at least the illusion of control)" over how one projects oneself to others (notwithstanding lone trolls and other reputation damaging entities), what one chooses to make public or private, and the extent to which one may reveal different identities in different contexts. This is a significant distinction between one's online identity and real-world identity -- this ability to control, or at least the sense of it, that enables one to choose the extent to which one reveals some characteristics of one's real-world identity to different groups on the Internet. Specifically, the imagined boundaries of one's identity as a series of political, cultural and sociological traits, are often employed by oneself or others as "definite" and "necessary" ways to uphold and even advocate such identity. In sharp contrast, one is free to establish and manage any online identity that one deems as "definite" and "necessary", as ways to uphold and advocate the kinds of political, cultural and sociological traits that one considers as representative of oneself. More importantly, as a result of constant and continuous management, one's online identity has the tendency to become a caricature of a set of concrete "facts" that one considers as being essential to one's existence *on the Internet*, as one interacts with others under all kinds of political, economic, societal and cultural circumstances. This, to a large extent, is distinct from one's real-life identity that is more fluid and subject to change - both one's self-identity and how others identify us: that two-way real-life identity. Think of a well-known author's or celebrity's online profile, maintained over a decade or two, versus their changing real life circumstances over the same time period. For some there is little difference, for others, it is greatly so.

It is this separation between one's online managed identity, and one's real world identity, that the largest social network companies, particularly Facebook, Google and Twitter, want to bring into alignment, for all sorts of reason's but mainly for capturing the advertising dollar, upon which their respective main business models are founded. They want to have the ultimate profile of an individual, all individuals. They want a complete identity, no matter how unrealistic that possibility is (i.e. the myths "We know what you want to buy before you do!" and "We know what you will do before you do?"). We will discuss this further in the next section.

SOCIAL MEDIA IDENTITY AND THE MEANING OF SELF

Since this paper investigates the complex interrelations between oneself and the communities with which one interacts, both online and in the real world, we find Yehudah Mirsky's position in his essay 'Identity = ?' (Mirsky, 2011), to be acutely helpful. Using 'Jewish identity' as an example in his discussion of what it means to be Jewish in contemporary America, Mirsky argues

instead of signifying that individuals are what they are in any fixed sense, as in x = x, 'identity' today is often used to indicate that individuals are what they will themselves to be, over time and in different ways. Resistant to classification by any external standard or institution, one's identity is, rather, a complex truth that emerges from within.

This existentialist notion that "individuals are what they will themselves to be", that identity is something that "emerges within", echoes what Coyne refers to as the decision, and often the determination as well, to "profile yourself" (Coyne, 2011). Coyne declares "part of the definition of identity involves connections with people, associating with the right group of other individuals (identifying with them), and letting it be known with whom you identify". In other words, it is not only the act of "identifying" with a community, but also that of "letting it be known" that such identification is established, that explicitly illustrates the nature and significance of online identity. The social function of online identity is thus self-evident.

Indeed, on today's Internet, particularly in Facebook, LinkedIn, Google+, other online communities, mobile apps and websites with a social aspect - one is increasingly required to "profile" oneself, to provide a series of political, cultural and sociological traits that can be used to not only identify but also verify and even solidify oneself to others, including to marketers and instruments of government. (E.g. Not only do they try to get you to use your 'Google Login' or your 'Facebook Login' on other partnering web-sites, they also try to extract the details of your contacts from your mobile phone, both to grow their membership, and to enhance their knowledge of the social network in your pocket). To make various aspects of one's real-world identity available online is to make even more elastic the boundaries of the imagined "site" that is one's self. Instead of eradicating the abstract line that distinguishes one from others, it allows personal and private disclosures that enable others to cross this line in a way, at a time and/or on an occasion that one determines and makes known. In doing so, *when appropriate safeguards are in place*, one allows such crossings to take place conditionally upon certain political, economic, societal and cultural circumstances. Throughout this process, one's sense of self can be considerably strengthened, and one's awareness of the larger imagined "site" that is the Internet can also be enhanced - *provided that the line crossings abide by one's agreed to conditions*. Unlike one's identity in the real world, which may be either self-produced or assigned by others, one's online identity is almost always proactively formed, standardized and circulated by oneself, in the first instance. However, the amassed identity behind the scenes, built up by the profiling engines behind Facebook, Google and other social network facilitators, is far more complex and detailed than that one initially outlined in the submitted profile. And they work at continually adding detail to it.

Currently, the 2 billion active users of Facebook (Constine, 2017) across the globe are 'required' to provide their true identities in terms of their basic details – name, age, gender, and so. Although there are clear violations of these Facebook designated terms by many, including the 7.5+ million children under the age of 13 with accounts even back in 2011 (Fox, 2011). The popularity and high penetration rate of this social networking platform does indicate the desire of its users to announce, affirm and promote something of their real-world identities on the Internet. This phenomenon is intriguing because it represents a large-scale attempt to merge real-world identity and online identity; or, more specifically, to "borrow" from one's real-world identity and use that as one's online identity in order to enhance one's interactions with communities both online and in the real world.

Particularly with the conceptualization of identity as an imagined "site" in mind, the Facebook phenomenon appears to suggest a tendency (willed or co-erced?) amongst the website's users to combine into one, the many imagined "sites" that they have previously constructed and assigned their identity within, including those much larger "sites" that are the greater Internet and the real world. There is also an apparent attempt by many of those users, to join together, or at least make coexistent, those many real-world and online *communities* with which one associates, which may be readily achieved through various Facebook features such as Messenger, Groups, Events, Like Pages, Share, News Feed, Notifications, Photo and Video Tagging, Status Updates, and even checking-in to Places (i.e. tying one's online Facebook identity, with one's current geographic location in the real world, and with the identities of those who you are with). Mobile social media apps have accelerated this trend, given that one's mobile phone is on or near one's person, for most of the waking hours.

Mark Zuckerberg is famously said to have "emphasized three times in a single interview" with David Kirkpatrick in his book 'The Facebook Effect: The Inside Story of the Company that is Connecting the World' (2010), "you have one identity… The days of you having a different image for your work friends or co-workers and for the other people you know are probably coming to an end pretty quickly". So, it seems safe to suggest that these words, together with Zuckerberg's observation "having two identities for yourself is an example of a lack of integrity" (Culter, Kim-Mai, 2010), explicitly illustrate Facebook's approach to providing what Hall refers to as the "unifying and unchanging points of reference and meaning" among the numerous narratives and interpretations of one's online surroundings.

In other words, in Facebook currently, the identity of each user is "essentialist", rather than one of "positioning". Although it started out with your 'friends' and 'family', it soon appropriated everyone else that it could. As each user is encouraged to allow crossings over the boundaries of the imagined "site" that is his or her self, either by agreeing to accept others as new friends or by requesting to become a friend of others, or to allow public *Follows*, it considerably essentialises one's awareness of self. This process of essentialisation also merges the online and real-world communities with which one interacts, as the "shared patterns" or "shared rituals of behaviour" that connect the members of each community, are no longer distinguished. All communities that one ever had anything to do with, are merged into one that is conceptualized by the user as a larger imagined "site" that is the Facebook universe. The jury is still out on whether Zuckerberg has identified and is servicing some new social trend in this regard for some large percentage of people, or whether his particular 20-something view back then (2010) on identity is yet to embrace the broader complexities of identity as one moves further through other parts of the life-cycle, including having one's own children, as he now has, and holding passionate time-consuming interests beyond ones immediate passion for the work currently being done. Not to mention the security and privacy issues regarding unforeseen crossing of the lines one had hoped to keep control over.

Two other social networking websites/platforms requiring users to provide their true identities are LinkedIn (bought by Microsoft in 2016 for $26 billion) and Google+. Unlike Facebook whose users are encouraged to add anyone and everyone on Facebook to their Friends Lists, to get maximum inclusion on the site, LinkedIn is (currently) mainly used for professional networking, while the 'Circles' feature of Google+ enables users to organize their 'contacts' into different groups as a first-class feature, from the ground up. Whereas *Groups* within the Facebook platform, is a relatively recent addition in its considerable lifeline (inception in 2005) as an evolving technical platform (Chai, 2010), and is currently non-hierarchical (i.e. no sub-groups of groups). It seems reasonable to suggest that in sharp contrast to Facebook's "essentialist" approach, LinkedIn and Google+ attempt to help their users better position themselves among the numerous narratives and interpretations of their surroundings by distinguishing the "professional" and "personal" aspects of their social lives on the Internet. In fact, Jeff Weiner, the Chief Executive Officer (CEO) of LinkedIn (with 7 years prior senior management experience at Yahoo, a company also heavily invested in social media), is on record as saying that he believes there are *at least* three distinct, major, social groupings that Facebook has attempted to merge into one, namely: "Personal, Professional and Family" (Weiner & Battelle, 2010) - while conceding that they overlap, more or less depending on the individual. Accordingly, LinkedIn has differentiated itself from Facebook by going for just the "professional identity".

A shift of focus is necessary here, from the notion of disclosure to that of control over disclosure. That is to say, despite the social functions of Facebook, LinkedIn and Google+, the fact that these social networking platforms enable their users to choose their own privacy settings and decide who can see specific parts of their profiles, explicitly demonstrates the resilient nature of the boundaries of the imagined "site" that is one's self. The sense of control (or at least the illusion of it, as Coyne suggests) over how one projects oneself to others, what one chooses to make public or private, and the extent to which one might reveal different aspects of one's online and/or real-world identities in different contexts, is so fundamental that Facebook has met prolonged criticism on numerous related issues since its launch in February 2004 (Wikipedia, 2017). Indeed, the aforementioned later addition of Groups (see Figure 2) to the Facebook technology platform, came about to address users expressed need to differentiate amongst their accumulated Facebook 'Friends'. This addition is expressed in the data model part of the overall Facebook data model, that caters for Groups. Note: a *Group* is expressed as a first-class entity that a number of *Users* can join, represented in the *Member* many-to-many entity (i.e. a Group can have many Users as Members, while a User can also be a Member of many Groups). In addition to sharing general Facebook *Posts* via the *Group-Feed*, these individuals can also share other *Files* and even collaboratively edit shared documents (see the *Group_Doc* entity in Figure 2).

Google+, launched in 2011, which came after the addition of the Groups feature in Facebook (in October, 2010), picked up on that much needed feature, calling

Figure 2. That part of the Conceptual Data Model dealing with Facebook Groups (from figure 1.6, Goschnick (2014))

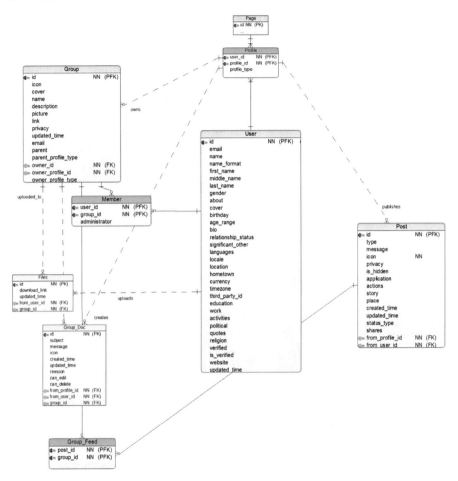

their approach 'Circles' and embedding it into the opening user interface in a much more intuitive and usable manner than Facebook did with their Groups feature. Even LinkedIn, which so far has been considered by many as having "a solid track record of taking user privacy seriously", faces questions of how to protect the data of its users from being accessed by third parties (Sampson, 2011). Indeed, some of their business model revolves around providing paid access to various details of people beyond those an individual has listed as their immediate 'Connections', via an annual subscription fee to 'LinkedIn Premium'.

What is worth noting here is the ambiguous nature of the boundaries of the imagined "site" that is one's self on the Internet. On the one hand, one actively forms, standardizes and circulates an online identity by disclosing and distributing one's personal and private information, an act that Yehudah Mirsky and the social network industry in general refers to as 'opting-in' that not only is 'meaningful' but also helps "realize the significance of today's personal freedom" (Mirsky, 2011). On the other hand, one constantly fears the discovery and disclosure of such personal and private information by others without one's permission, and/or in ways not originally foreseen, such as by potential employers far in the future. Consider the following legal terms designated by Google when it launched Google+, with regard to the content one submits, posts or displays on or through its numerous services:

You retain copyright and any other rights you already hold in Content which you submit, post or display on or thorough the Services. By submitting, posting or displaying the content you give Google a perpetual, irrevocable, worldwide, royalty-free, and non-exclusive license to reproduce, adapt, modify, translate, publish, publicly perform, publicly display and distribute any Content which you submit, post or display on or through the Services. This license is for the sole purpose of enabling Google to display, distribute and promote the Services and may be revoked for certain Services as defined in the Additional Terms of those Services. (Google, 2011)

It seems highly unlikely that a sane person would sign a contract giving someone such free range with his or her intellectual property if they consider it to have any value. However, according to Google's then CEO Larry Page, within just three weeks of the launch of Google+ in its invite-only "field testing" phase on June 28, 2011, there were already more than 10 million users sharing and receiving more than a billion items each day (Matthews, 2011). While not all of these items may be of a private nature, and many of these people were probably early-adopters of technology for the sake of evaluation, the need for users of supposedly free social networking websites such as Google+ to disclose and distribute personal information to each other is evidently overwhelming - enough to overcome terse conditions of usage. As one makes these boundaries of the imagined "site" that is one's online identity, extremely flexible, the risk that others can cross these boundaries in ways, at times and/or on occasions that one may not be able to anticipate or control nor even be aware of, apparently becomes an almost insignificant personal consideration to many, when signing on to these so-called 'free' services. This well demonstrates the perceived nature and significance of online identity as a self-produced and community-oriented continuity.

There are earlier precedents of 'service providers' taking many more benefits than their 'users', in such provider-consumer arrangements, that hold forewarnings for both parties in the current use of social networking websites/platforms. In Satchell et al's paper 'Knowing Me, Knowing You: End User Perceptions of Identity Management Systems' (2006), the authors set out in an IS research project, to determine people's views and reactions to, what is called *Federated Identity*. The concept of Federated Identity, although used across inter-related organizations in the past (e.g. using Microsoft Passport), to provide 'one login' (i.e. username and password authentication), has been more recently subscribed to by Facebook and other Internet based companies. E.g. third-party Facebook developers can allow their users to in turn use their Facebook login, to access the 3rd party site in question, and use various services there (such as posting a facebook Like against content on that site, which shows up in the news feeds of the user's friends, etc.). What Satchell et al found with Federated Identity, was that the benefits were very much in the providers favor and not in the end users favor much at all - apart from the convenience of that single login.

However and more importantly, they found that when the "options to control and personalise" ones data was out of the end users hands, and very much in the providers hands, users usually provided as little information about themselves as possible. E.g. one user informated "I separate or compartmentalise my personal information when I don't know the source of who is asking for them." and "if all information is kept under one banner it could be accessed by the wrong person (or people)." Satchell et al concluded: "failure to provide control (to end users) results in the erosion of trust between users and the provider and culminates in a culture of use where the user aims to suppress rather than reveal information." Anecdotally, that is certainly the way that many people have adapted their usage of Facebook, Google+ and other social networking websites in more recent times, as control and disclosure mechanisms are perceived to be further out of users hands than they had thought when they first signed on, not to mention the ramification eminating from the fake news and political polarisation issues for Facebook, Twitter and Google in particular, being researched and examined since the 2016 US election (Allcott & Gentzkow, 2017).

The number of users of these sites is significant. While Facebook has gone on to 2 billion users, Google+ has struggled with 395 million active accounts in 2017, but with only 34 million of them visiting per month (https://www.statisticbrain.com/google-plus-demographics-statistics/). However, Google's YouTube site has 1.5 billion active monthy users, and numerous other social media sites have gained significant numbers, particular via mobile apps (Constine, 2017): WeChat with 890 million (mainly China), Twitter 328 million, SnapChat 255 million, Line 217 million (mainly Japan), KaKaoTalk 43 million (South Korea), and Facebook-owned WhatsApp 2 billion (its not clear how many of these are also Facebook users). LinkedIn has 470 million users with 106 million of the active per month (https://www.linkedin.com/pulse/linkedin-numbers-2017-statistics-meenakshi-chaudhary)

Table 2. Action Types that third-party Facebook Developers can use (Facebook, 2017)

Name	Description
apps.saves	An action representing someone saving an app to try later.
books.quotes	An action representing someone quoting from a book.
books.rates	An action representing someone rating a book.
books.reads	An action representing someone reading a book.
books.wants_to_read	An action representing someone wanting to read a book.
fitness.bikes	An action representing someone cycling a course.
fitness.runs	An action representing someone running a course.
fitness.walks	An action representing someone walking a course.
games.achieves	An action representing someone reaching a game achievement.
games.celebrate	An action representing someone celebrating a victory in a game.
games.plays	An action representing someone playing a game. Stories for this action will only appear in the activity log.
games.saves	An action representing someone saving a game.
music.listens	An action representing someone listening to a song, album, radio station, playlist or musician
music.playlists	An action representing someone creating a playlist.
news.publishes	An action representing someone publishing a news article.
news.reads	An action representing someone reading a news article.
og.follows	An action representing someone following a Facebook user
og.likes	An action representing someone liking any object.
pages.saves	An action representing someone saving a place.
restaurant.visited	An action representing someone visiting a restaurant.
restaurant.wants_to_visit	An action representing someone wanting to visit a restaurant
sellers.rates	An action representing a commerce seller has been given a rating.
video.rates	An action representing someone rating a movie, TV show, episode or another piece of video content.
video.wants_to_watch	An action representing someone wanting to watch video content.
video.watches	An action representing someone watching video content.

Interestingly, LinkedIn also has 10,000 employees worldwide, which makes it a very significant commercial organisation in scale. For comparison, Facebook had 19,000 employees by March 2017 (https://qz.com/975081/facebook-fb-is-adding-employees-at-a-faster-clip-even-as-revenue-growth-slows/).

Also demanding attention is that one's sense of self on the Internet inevitably comes under the influence of the communities with which one *interacts*, both online and in the real world. While LinkedIn may have borrowed that part of our professional identity that was traditionally captured on the 'business cards' that people physically share, now that it is in an electronic and social form, it balloons in scope and blends with other sites, at a scale not before seen in professional identity management. For an example of that increased scope, LinkedIn offers "Hiring Solutions at massive scale" (Weiner & Batelle, 2010). As an example of blending, LinkedIn integrates with Twitter to some degree - the *Comments* in one can be automatically passed on to the other. Similarly, the "Like" button on websites external to Facebook, allows external political, commercial, cultural and sociological promotion, to enter the Facebook universe with ease (Facebook, 2011), in a similar manner to the Federated Identity approach discussed above, in past identity management systems. In linking and blending such websites and the related new functionality, the boundaries of the imagined "site" that is one's online identity are increasingly blurred, causing one to constantly re-define and re-interpret the meaning of privacy. And *Like* is just the first verb that Facebook appropriated for its representation of one's identity through *structured interaction*. It has appropriated other verbs for use on similar buttons and in other ways, to represent other activities such as *Eating, Watching, Reading* and *Running* (Geron, 2011), in what it terms 'frictionless sharing'. See table 2 for the current *Action Types* that Facebook has available to third party developers. Clearly, these verbs were chosen as significant handles that the advertising dollar can use.

Facebook on Building a Global Community in the Near Future

According to the aforementioned Facebook manifesto (Zuckerberg, 2017), Facebook now intends to dramatically expand its Groups feature ("social infrastructure for communities"), towards a platform capable of supporting a Global Community. In what seems to be a new recognition of the need for diversity and multiple identities of individual users, Zuckerberg lays down a blueprint of what Facebook thinks is needed, and what its already doing about it. That is, to turn their platform into one that will support a truly Global Community, effectively etching out a real world global community (connected, voting, caring through action – since global problems require global solutions) in the absence of one that includes the individual participants themselves (i.e. not just one's representative in the UN). In the online article:

- He makes a pitch for traditional communities ("Whether they're *churches, sports teams, unions or other local groups,* they all share important roles as social infrastructure for our communities…") to join up, offering them technology-enabled functionalities that come with the social network platform, to help traditional groups arrest "their declining memberships in recent times". Zuckerberg calls these groups "very meaningful groups". I.e. the sort that Mirsky (ibid) positions one as: "identifying" with a community, and also that of "letting it be known" that is where I stand.

- At the same time he pitches to people to join existing virtual Facebook Groups, and to would-be leaders to create new virtual communities on common interests, that can aspire to the sociability that those real world traditional communities already have: "These communities don't just interact online. They hold get-togethers, organize dinners, and support each other in their daily lives".

- On the Global Community front, he shows a careful eye to the importance of balance in benefits between *service provider* and *user* that Satchell (ibid) highlighted, as he outlines the benefits that a global community in a single social network would reap: "Problems like terrorism, natural disasters, disease, refugee crises, and climate change need coordinated responses from a worldwide vantage point ... There is a real opportunity to build global safety infrastructure, ... the *Facebook community is in a unique position* to help prevent harm, assist during a crisis, or come together to rebuild afterwards ... When a child goes missing, we've built infrastructure to show *Amber Alerts* ... To *rebuild* after a crisis, we've built the world's largest social infrastructure for collective action. A few years ago, after an earthquake in Nepal, *the Facebook community raised $15 million to help people recover and rebuild...*"

- He also has an eye on the new revenue stream that would come of it, with those same structured 'actions' in mind as depicted in table 2, coming into play: "We can *look at many activities* through the *lens of building community*. Watching video of *our favorite sports team or TV show, reading our favorite newspaper*, or playing our *favorite game* are not just entertainment or information but *a shared experience ...*", but it is a learned eye that concurs with Macgregor's (ibid) argument discussed earlier, that identity as a construction reified in practice is "intrinsically tied to processes of shared communal activity".

- To counter the *fake news* issues that have dogged Facebook recently, he turns to advancing AI techniques to identify it, and to increasing Facebook's fact checking ability.

- To counter the *filter bubble* concerns of critics outlined above, he discussed the complexity of the issue, then to disarm the polarisation of opinions, he suggests "A more effective approach is to show a range of perspectives, let people see where their views are on a spectrum and come to a conclusion on what they think is right" and to do enable that: "*A strong news industry is also critical to building an informed community.* Giving people a voice is not enough without having people dedicated to uncovering new information and analyzing it". As mentioned above, more than 50% of the US population admit to getting their news through Facebook, and now Facebook looks like doubling-down on traditional/partnered news outlets for more professional collection and analysis of news intermixed within the people's personal news feeds. Interestingly, de Botton (ibid) thinks that "proper" investigative journalism should "start with an all-encompassing interest in the full range of factors that sabotage group and individual existence", including health, family structures, relationships, architecture, leisure time, and so on – all the complexities of modern life. Social media in general and Facebook in particular, are in an excellent position to do that with news if they so wish, beyond just the advertising opportunities.

- A lot of people and companies see a lucrative future for electronic voting systems. Zuckerberg sees that future too. He sees a way that brings cultural diversity into those new 'meaningful groups' (e.g. traditional communities) in Facebook. By allowing them to vote on their own 'community standards'. "The guiding principles are that *the Community Standards should reflect the cultural norms of (the) community,* that each person should see as little objectionable content as possible, and each person should be able to share what they want while being told they cannot share something as little as possible…" In addition to voting, AI will be used to apply the results to the group as a whole, or customised for the individual within that group: "The approach is to combine creating a large-scale democratic process to determine standards with AI to help enforce them. The idea is to give everyone in the community options for how they would like to set the content policy for themselves. Where is your line on nudity? On violence? On graphic content? On profanity? What you decide will be your personal settings… For those who don't make a decision, the default will be whatever the majority of people in your region (sub-community) selected. Of course, you will always be free to update your personal settings". That, becomes a compelling reason to provide even more profile information to Facebook.

- Beyond voting within respective 'meaningful groups' Zuckerberg has a global scale voting technology in mind: "Building an inclusive global community requires establishing a new process for citizens worldwide to participate in community governance. I hope that we can explore examples of how collective decision-making might work at scale."

In other words, in that new future Facebook, the identity of each user will serve as both "essentialist" *and* "positioning". Where he has people "positioning" beyond just family and friends via the melding of Facebook with traditional and other "meaningful" groups; while the "essential" identity of each user, is both centred on an 'authentic' Facebook profile – a much expanded profile via the voting upon numerous community standards options that may be expanded by the service provider into the future - and upon a new Global Citizenship. While Zuckerberg never mentions the UN at any point in the article, his musings are in that same sphere of governance, but the one he envisages involves mass participation, through Facebook technologies.

Zuckerberg's article outlines an audacious plan in a mid-way career built on audacious plans. Given the current 2 billion users of Facebook and a market value hovering around $400 billion in 2017, the article/plan is worth a full read and should not be dismissed lightly in any discussion on the future of identity and the impact upon it by social media.

Echoing Mersky's observation above is Danah Boyd's assertion that "cyberspace is not our utopian fantasy; many of the social constraints that frame physical reality are quickly seeping into the digital realm" (Boyd, 2011). Boyd's observation of the differences between social interaction on the Internet and that in the real world is worth quoting at some length:

The underlying architecture of the digital environment does not provide the forms of feedback and context to which people have become accustomed. The lack of embodiment makes it difficult to present oneself and to perceive the presentation of others. As people operate through digital agents, they are forced to articulate their performance in new ways. Additionally, the contextual information that they draw from does not have the same implications online. Situational context can be collapsed with ease, thereby exposing an individual in an out-of-context manner. Unlike physical architecture, the digital equivalent is composed of bits, which have fundamentally different properties than atoms. The interface to the digital world is explicitly constructed and designed around a user's desires. As with any fundamental differences in architecture, there are resultant differences in paradigms of use, interpersonal expectations, and social norms. Performing online requires that people be aware of and adjust to these differences so as to achieve the same level of social proficiency that they have mastered offline.

That Facebook has invested heavily in Virtual Reality (VR) technology via its Occulus Go technology (ABC, 2017), is an investment in adding embodiment to the virtual world.

The whole approach at Facebook to building global community is often in stark contrast to other existing (potentially) global communities, such as some of the citizen science projects with inclusive social network functionality, as alluded to by Preece (2017) in an article appropriately titled: *How two billion smartphone users can save species*. For example, the iNaturalist.org site. The push in that article is one of global responsibility via local action, in the form of collecting data to be used by scientists to record changes in the population and distribution of species, "enabling us" (global citizens) to take action to help save threatened species in particular (of which is a lot) and maintain biodiversity (of the planet). The biodiversity data is typically *"collected using smartphones can include photos, comments, numerical data, video, and sound, together with metadata (e.g., time, date, and geolocation logging)"*. The focus of citizen science is on the real world, using the virtual world in a crowd sourcing manner. These citizen science biodiversity projects are interested in using people's smartphones as information probes to collect data around the individual, while building participant commitment, enthusiasm and community for a cause. While Facebook is more interested in the data from the same devices that can add detail to the profile of the individual. Citizen science projects are happy with a slice of an individual's life and attention, often focusing on pressing issues facing humanity. Facebook wants the lot. Wants to do the lot, global platform wise. However, both Zuckerberg and Preece (ibid) make a play for attracting would-be leaders in creating new 'meaningful groups'. In Preece's case, to members of the HCI community to start new biodiversity maintaining initiatives, lending their unique skillset to make citizen science a more effective vehicle for global health – and making HCI even more relevant. In Facebooks case 'think of a meaning group' – making Facebook even more relevant. Facebook assumes it will gather all of your identity information; citizen science projects just want a slice of your time and resources, and to focus your passion on a particular scientific quest, for humanity – a slice of your identity.

Boyd's study, titled "Faceted Id/entity: Managing representation in a digital world", specifically focuses on one's ability to maintain control of personal representation and identity information. While she too argues for "a design approach that will aid sociable designers in developing human-centred technologies that allow for individual control over personal identity", it is equally important that one is constantly aware of the flexible nature of identity as one interacts online for social purposes, as well as the positive and negative consequences such interaction may have on one's reputation both on the Internet and in the real world. Only a full awareness of identity can empower one with a desire to appropriately control it.

A CASE STUDY IN REPRESENTATION AND CONTROL OF IDENTITY AND PRIVACY

That future Facebook realised, or not, one's sense of community is changing, as a result of different online communities being introduced within the confines of one larger imagined "site" that is the Internet, which increasingly causes the distinct "shared patterns" or "shared rituals of behaviors" of each community to impact upon each other. Empowered individuals are increasingly becoming global citizens at some level of their identity. This forces the commonly accepted notion of privacy to become open to interpretation, depending on the nature of the community with whom one interacts, the meaning of the occasion, and the location of the interaction not only online but also in the real world.

As Mirsky observes, the construction of identity "involves not just trying out, or trying on, a random set of 'shifting, syncretic, and constructed' accoutrements that 'can be re-forged under new circumstances' but assuming real, durable responsibilities" (Mirsky, 2011). In the context of the Internet, where many traditional structures of the real world appear to have dissolved for a time, such "real, durable responsibilities" entail the ability to remain aware of the fact that one's online identity is simply an imagined "site", and then being rather proactive in positioning one's self among the numerous narratives and interpretations of numerous much larger imagined "sites" that are the online communities with which one interacts. The flexibility of the boundaries of these "sites" very much depends on whether a fine balance can be achieved throughout this process of positioning between the disclosure and control of personal and private information for social purposes. However, much like the assumption that people read the legal conditions when signing up to a so-called 'free' service such as Google+ or Facebook, to assume that people will really embrace such a responsibility en mass, is a big and probably unrealistic Ask - or whether they even can if they wished to. This question of balance between disclosure and control - whether it can realistically be achieved within these new overlapping, interrelated technologies - still has a long way to run. At stake is mass trust in the service providers of these new social media and search platforms. Also at stake is the last interior privacy firewall of Self.

A REPRESENTATION OF A DIGITAL SELF IN THE DIGITALFRIEND

Where better to create a digit self, a digital representation of one's self-identity, than on a personal computer (PC)? However, the question then quickly moves to a technical one, of what constitutes one's personal computer these days? Is it a laptop, a desktop, a tablet, a smart phone or some other mobile device? Or a virtualisation that materialises on all of the above, when summoned, as needed? We are going to leave that technical question out of this discussion while we briefly present a working example of a such a digital representation of a self-identity, one that does run on many platforms, but in this case (Figure 3) on a personal desktop computer.

Figure 3. Interface of the DigitalFriend representing a Digital Self

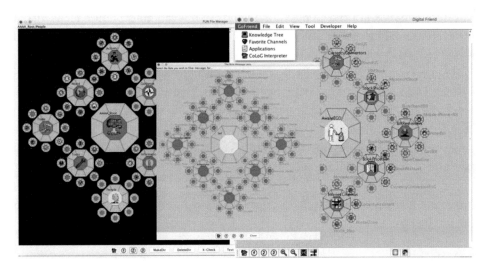

However, before describing what is represented in this figure, we return to Mirsky's notion that "individuals are what they will themselves to be", that identity is "resistant to classification by any external standard or institution, one's identity is, rather, a complex truth that emerges from within". The approach taken in this case study, is that rather than have one's identity either: classified by some external entity, or floating around in mind where it is perhaps stronger on a good day than not, or that can perhaps be somehow gleaned from a super-set of all those on and off-line communities pronouncements and activities – the best thing to do once one knows themselves well, is to build a computer model of it on one's private personal computing device. The DigitalFriend is like a living diary for both building and maintaining such a representation. As Satchell et al (ibid) concluded: "failure to provide control (to end users) results in the erosion of trust between users and the provider and culminates in a culture of use where the user aims to suppress rather than reveal information." We are yet to see an online system or social network where the user is both aware of the full model of themselves that has been built up behind the scenes, nor one where the user can control such a model, in particular, who has access to it, for what purposes, now and in the future. Keeping the most complete model themselves, of themselves, and deciding themselves on which information goes to which provider, is the most obvious solution to having providers get the best reveals of accurate information for the actual service they are providing. It is the individual's Identity, after all. It seems that the citizen science communities assume this, while the large social media platforms, fight it.

Furthermore, by having a deliberative and reactive system (i.e. applied AI), that can store, retrieve, notify and monitor all sorts of relevant information feeds, makes for a representation of identity that is live, that is running in real time with the user, and even as they sleep, and in many ways, can augment their cognitive functions.

Figure 3 represents a person's digital self, built and maintained in the DigitalFriend system. There are currently 3 windows open in the figure, representing 3 interrelated hierarchies, that are displayed in such a way as to instantiate the underlying architecture represented back in Figure 1. The middle hierarchy instantiates the generic role model represented in Table 1. The initial model in the table is a starting point only, as the individual user then customises it into a role model that matches the actual roles in their life. This live role model alerts and notifies the user about important messages and data feeds, ones that they have prioritised as important to them (Goschnick, 2006).

The hierarchy on the left is the user's custom Knowledge Tree, where personal files and all sorts of data is stored. Again, the methodology used with the DigitalFriend provides a starting personal ontology as a default structure (Goschnick, 2005), which the user can modify or completely replace, as their personal ontology deems necessary over time. The user can store their photos, videos, documents and files of all sorts into this hierarchy, where they can easily relocate them any time. Other sorts of data that is deposited into this personal ontology, are the newsfeeds coming from RSS aggregators (news feeds) and various types of web services. Bozdag & Timmerman (2011) argued that the good that comes of having information can only be obtained by individuals if they rely on filtering technology of some sort, due to the enormous increase in the information supply – hence the complexity around the discussion on filter bubbles mentioned above. As de Botton (2014) tells us, the way to deal with the excessive amounts of information available via the Internet, is to 'know yourself well' and use those biases as the filter. By having both a personal role model, a goal model, and a personal ontology structure to receive the information, the individual is in control of what information they gather and store for future use. Bozdag & Timmerman (ibid) also identified three important criteria in the design of personalization systems: autonomy, identity and transparency. The DigitalFriend has all three very well covered.

The hierarchy to the right is the configuration of the user's personal assistant agents. These are running processes, either receiving information from the internet, from sensors in an IoT way (Internet of Things), or using stored data within the Knowledge Tree, or computing new information possibly from those other sources. These running agents are interlinked in such a way that they can achieve user goals (computational plans), and even carry out some of their forward intentions (e.g. sending a message off to the outside world, when a desired condition has been met).

Figure 4. Meta-model of the DigitalFriend, V1

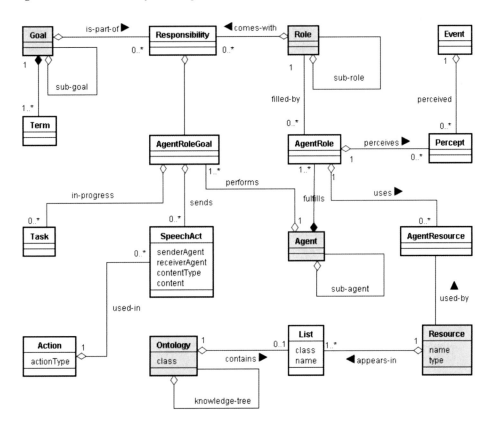

The conceptual model in Figure 4 is a structural model for the first version of the DigitalFriend. We have advanced it considerable since then. The conceptual model in Figure 5, taken from and explained more fully in Goschnick et al. (2015), is the model of the second version of the DigitalFriend, currently in beta. One small detail to note here: the SocialWorld hierarchy in the right middle of the figure -- it enables a structure of sub-communities within communities, to any depth -- the sort that Zuckerberg (2017) alludes to in a future Facebook. Where the V1 model had 4 interrelated hierarchies, the V2 model has 8 interrelated hierarchies. (Note: These extra levels of complexity add to the functionality and sophitication but don't need to add to complexity in the user interface – the reverse is often the case in software. For example, there are many more levels of complexity behind the user interface in an iPad than there are in a Windows XP interface, and there are many more levels of complexity in the Windows XP interface than there are in the harder to use character-based interface of Microsoft DOS)

Figure 5. Meta-model of the DigitalFriend, V2

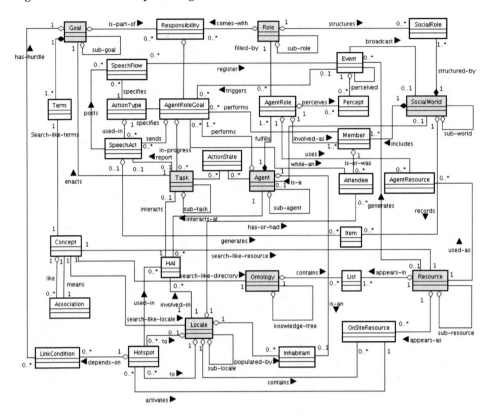

That is all the explanation of the DigitalFriend we give in this chapter – it is presented here to demonstrate what is possible regarding a self-managed computational representation of identity (a digital self). It is well documented in the references already given above. This example of one's digital self is held on a private personal computer, outside of all of one's communities on the Internet. The individual has full autonomy and control over it, where they can create and evolve a digital representation of their self-identity. From it, sub-sets of information about their identity can be put out into specific online communities. Furthermore, it is used to store and reference information and other resources, as the individual goes about their life building knowledge through the filter of their own interests, activities, interactions, capabilities, goals and their outcomes.

CONCLUSION

This chapter has explored the fundamental nature of identity and how identity can be constructed in online communities, with respect to how one's online identity may reflect and affect one's real-world identity. In summary, in the first section *Identity as a Self-Produced Continuity and the Media* we considered the traditional views of identity in the context of the media, particularly with regard to the News. A dichotomy of 'essence' and 'positioning' within Identity is uncovered and discussed. We considered the new concept of the *filter bubble*, and whether it is a new effect or whether one's daily dose of selective news and views has long been the case. We also briefly introduced a software architecture based on the psychological theory of sub-selves, that closely matches a construct of identity by the cultural theorists introduced. We argued that one's identity is flexible and subject to change in the real, non-Internet world, but that perceived identity by the individual, is often a caricature in the form of a set of concrete "facts" that one considers essential to one's existence there. We point out that even the 'essentialist' core values of an identity, are also subject to change, sometimes.

In section *Online Identity, Its Construction and Circulation*, we note that while identities on the Internet and in the real world are both of a flexible and ever-changing nature, serving as a point of reference among the many narratives and interpretations of one's surroundings, online identity is far more proactively constructed and managed for social purposes. In the same way that one's identity can be conceptualized as an imagined "site" whose boundaries are those political, cultural and sociological traits commonly that one commonly subscribes to, one's online identity also reveals various amounts of information that help identify the characteristics of one's real-world identity, depending on whom one interacts with and on what occasion. There is a clear and present risk that the boundaries of both real-world identity and online identity are perceived to be as permanent and unchallengeable as the borders of geo-political entities, which in turn prompts the invention and prolonged utilization of all kinds of labels, caricatures and "norms", that affect the ways in which those within and outside of these imagined "sites" interact with each other and among themselves, in our daily lives.

In section *Social Media Identity and the Meaning of Self* we outline how one can 'position' oneself in both the online world and in the real world, by identifying with communities, in a 'let it be known' way. In early social media platforms we are free to present and manage what one considers to be the current best representation of oneself if one wills it so (e.g. LinkedIn is for a professional identity) - with better control over the disclosure of personal and private details at a time, in a way and on an occasion that one sees fit.

However, after discussing several different platforms that use the Internet -- namely, Facebook, LinkedIn and Google+ -- it becomes clear that personal control over one's Internet identity has been significantly loosened. The individual needs to be aware and on guard that the timely disclosure and personal control over one's private information used for social purposes in the online communities they interact with, is paramount to being able to manage one's online identity. Platforms such as Facebook have continued to try and meld one's online identity with real world identity, with plans to bring in many more traditional communities, where peoples 'essentialist' identities are likely to reside, together with your 'positioning' identities, such as your professional network. As incentive to get people to meld their identities in Facebook, they make a pitch with their unprecedented infrastructure and toolset to build a truly global community. Meanwhile, certain citizen science communities (e.g. those dedicated to maintaining biodiversity), demonstrate how authentic global communities, are being built through local action for (up to) global responsibilities. We looked at lessons from earlier research on 'federated identity' in IS, and apply them to Social Media ambitions.

Awareness of identity as an imagined "site" helps in managing all crossings over its boundaries, but if one can personally facilitate much of the traffic between this "site" and other larger imagined "sites" that are the communities in which one interacts both online and offline, then one can ensure a balanced control of the fluidity of the borders. If one cannot do so through a lack of proper control over such deliberate disclosures then ones reputation, opportunities and even safety may at times be at risk. Mass erosion of trust in the mainstream service providers may well then follow. People need to be fully aware of what Identity is and the issues that surround it, to be empowered rather than disempowered by these increasingly sophisticated social media platforms.

In *A Case Study in Representation and Control of Identity and Privacy* we present an innovative approach to dealing with the issues and actions that revolve around the control and disclosure of identity, outlined above. Initial emphasis is placed on 'knowing yourself well' through one's interests and roles in life. We present two conceptual models of the technology used to instantiated a digital-self, running on a personal computing device, that helps a person manage and evolve their own identity, as they interact in the online world, both through social media and the greater Internet.

In this chapter we urge a careful re-evaluation of the nature of online identity and a comprehensive comparison between its formation, standardization and circulation and that of identity in general. The central argument that runs across this chapter is two-fold, firstly, we promote and indeed demonstrate an initial shift in focus from the management of online identity to the nature and significance of identity itself, whose construction may be conceptualized as a process of sense making and strengthening.

We demonstrate with theory, an example technology and a methodology, how this can be assisted at the individual level. Then, armed with a better understanding of identity, one can focus back upon the management of it more effectively, with a view to the individual taking more control of their own identity, particularly with regard to privacy. We emphasise the importance of this, as the technology space (most notably but not limited to, social media, search engines, and mobile apps) is increasingly transitioning us all into members of a global community, that needs to be functional not dysfunctional. It is important that we are each represented in this community as authentically as possible while also only revealing as much of ourselves that we agree to, in each sub-community in which we have a role. Gaining proper permission from each individual, and revealing transparency (to each person) regarding the storage and usage of identity data by service providers and their communities, is necessary for the sake of both individual privacy and reputation, and for gaining and maintaining trust in service providers, community organisations, and their governance. The larger the community, the more important these issues are.

REFERENCES

Allcott, H., & Gentzkow, M. (2017). Social Media and Fake News in the 2016 Election. *The Journal of Economic Perspectives*, *31*(2), 211–236. doi:10.1257/jep.31.2.211

Anderson, B. (2006). *Imagined Communities: Reflections on the Origin and Spread of Nationalism*. London: Verso. (Original work published 1983)

Bleiberg, J., & West, D. M. (2015). *Political Polarization on Facebook*. Retrieved Nov 30, 2017 from https://www.brookings.edu/blog/techtank/2015/05/13/political-polarization-on-facebook

Boyd, D. (2011). *Faceted Id/entity: Managing representations in a digital world* (Master's Thesis). MIT Media Lab's Sociable Media Group. Retrieved on July 17, 2011 from http://smg.media.mit.edu/people/danah/thesis/thesis/

Bozdag, E., & Timmerman, J. (2011). Values in the filter bubble Ethics of Personalization Algorithms in Cloud Computing. In *Proceedings, 1st International Workshop on Values in Design – Building Bridges between RE, HCI and Ethics* (pp. 7-15). Lisbon, Portugal: Academic Press.

Chai, D. (2010). *New Groups: Stay Closer to Groups of People in Your Life*. The Facebook Blog. Retrieved April 2, 2013 from http://blog.facebook.com/blog.php?post=434700832130

Constine, J. (2017). *Facebook now has 2 billion monthly users... and responsibility.* Retrieved on 30 Nov 2017, from https://techcrunch.com/2017/06/27/facebook-2-billion-users/

Coyne, R. (2011). *Profile yourself (Narcissus on line).* Retrieved February 20, 2013, from http://richardcoyne.com/2011/02/12/narcissus-on-line/

Culter, K.-M. (2010). Why Mark Zuckerberg needs to come clean about his views on privacy. *SocialBeat.* Retrieved on July 15, 2011 from http://social.venturebeat.com/2010/05/13/zuckerberg-privacy/

De Botton, A. (2014). *The News, A User's Manual.* Penguin.

Facebook. (2017). *Open Graph Reference Document.* Retrieved from https://developers.facebook.com/docs/reference/opengraph

Fox, J. (2011). *Five million Facebook users are 10 or younger.* ConsumerReports.org. Retrieved on July 15, 2011 from http://news.consumerreports.org/electronics/2011/05/five-million-facebook-users-are-10-or-younger.html

Geron, T. (2011). *Facebook Moves Beyond 'Like'--To Listen, Watch, Eat, Run.* Retrieved on March 20, 2012, from http://www.forbes.com/sites/tomiogeron/2011/09/22/facebook-moves-beyond-like-to-listen-watch-eat-run/

Google. (2011). *Google Terms of Services.* Retrieved from http://www.google.com/accounts/TOS

Goschnick, S. (2005). *The FUN File Manager.* Accessed Nov 30, 2017 from http://digitalfriend.org/knowledge-tree/know.html

Goschnick, S. (2006). *The DigitalFriend: The First End-User Oriented Multi-Agent System.* OSDC 2006, the third Open Source Developers Conference, Melbourne, Australia.

Goschnick, S. (2014). Facebook From Five Thousand Feet: a visual mapping from conceptual model down to ground level graph api data. eBookDynasty.net.

Goschnick, S., & Graham, C. (2006). Augmenting Interaction and Cognition using Agent Architectures and Technology Inspired by Psychology and Social Worlds. *Universal Access in the Information Society, 4*(3), 204–222. doi:10.100710209-005-0012-x

Goschnick, S., Sterling, L., & Sonenberg, L. (2015). Modelling Human Activity in People-Oriented Programming with Metamodels. International Journal of People-Oriented Programming, 4(2), 1-24. doi:10.4018/IJPOP.2015070101

Kirkpatrick, D. (2010). *The Facebook Effect: The Inside Story of the Company that is Connecting the World*. Simon & Schuster.

Macgregor, P. (1995). Chinese? Australian? the limits of geography and ethnicity as determinants of cultural identity. In J. Ryan (Ed.), *Chinese in Australia and New Zealand: a multidisciplinary approach* (pp. 5–20). New Delhi: New Age International.

Matthews, L. (2011). Google CEO confirms Google+ has more than 10 million users. *International Business Times*. Retrieved from http://www.ibtimes.com/articles/180869/20110715/google-google-google-circles-google-1.htm

Mirsky, Y. (2011). Identity =? *Jewish Ideas Daily*. Retrieved on March 17, 2013 from http://www.jewishideasdaily.com/839/features/identity/

Preece, J. (2017, March-April). How two billion smartphone users can save species! *Interaction*, *24*(2), 26–33. doi:10.1145/3043702

Roussos, G., Peterson, D., & Patel, U. (2003). Mobile Identity Management: An Enacted View. *International Journal of E-Commerce*, *8*(1), 81–100.

Samson, T. (2011). *Will Linkedin Suffer Facebook's privacy problems?* Retrieved on Nov 30, 2017, from http://www.infoworld.com/t/internet-privacy/will-linkedin-suffer-facebooks-privacy-problems-677

Satchell, C., Shanks, G., Howard, S., & Murphy, J. (2006). Knowing me, knowing you: end user perceptions of identity management systems. *Proceedings of the 14th European Conference on Information System (ECIS 2006)*, 795-806.

Sun, C. Y. (2012). Something Old, Something New, Something Borrowed, Something Blue: The Construction of online Identity and Its Consequences. *International Journal of People-Oriented Programming*, *2*(1), 53–73. doi:10.4018/ijpop.2012010103

Weiner, J., & Battelle, J. (2010). A Conversation with Jeff Weiner. *Web 2.0 Summit 2010*. Retrieved from http://www.youtube.com/watch?v=R1yNDDLiHyY&feature=player_embedded

Wikipedia. (2017). *Criticism of Facebook*. Retrieved on Nov 30, 2017 from http://en.wikipedia.org/wiki/Criticism_of_Facebook

Wiszniewski, D., & Coyne, R. (2002). Mask and Identity: The Hermeneutics of Self-Construction in the Information Age. In Building Virtual Communities: Learning and Change in Cyberspace (pp. 191-214). Cambridge University Press.

Zuckerberg, M. (2017). *Building Global Community*. Retrieved on Nov 30, 2017 from https://www.facebook.com/notes/mark-zuckerberg/building-global-community/10154544292806634/

Chapter 10

Adding Emotions to Models in a Viewpoint Modelling Framework From Agent-Oriented Software Engineering:
A Case Study With Emergency Alarms

Leon Sterling
Swinburne University of Technology, Australia

Alex Lopez-Lorca
University of Melbourne, Australia

Maheswaree Kissoon-Curumsing
Deakin University, Australia

ABSTRACT

In modern software development, considering the viewpoints of stakeholders is an important step in building the right system. Over the past decade, several authors have proposed solutions to capture and model these viewpoints. While these solutions have been successful, emotions of stakeholders have been largely ignored. Considering the emotional needs of stakeholders is important because both the users' perceptions of a product and their use of a product are influenced by emotion as much as cognition. Building on recent work in modelling the emotional goals of stakeholders, the authors extend an existing viewpoint framework to capture

DOI: 10.4018/978-1-5225-5969-6.ch010

emotions, and to use emotions in models from early-phase requirements to detailed software design. They demonstrate the models and framework with a case study of an emergency alarm system for older people, presenting a complete set of models for the case study. The authors introduce recent experience in using emotional models in requirements elicitation within an agile process.

INTRODUCTION

Building interactive systems has never been more challenging with the increasing need to understand the social requirements of users. Most people-oriented systems involve a number of stakeholders. Each stakeholder has their own perspective of how the system should be developed. The differing views of stakeholders often conflict (Easterbrook & Chechik, 2001) and no set of requirements exists to satisfy all stakeholders. To accommodate social requirements and meet customer demands, many organisations are looking for innovative ways to change their strategic business processes (Baxter & Sommerville, 2011; Cernosek, 2004; Demoly, Monticolo, Eynard, Rivest, & Gomes, 2010). Andrade et al. (2004) state that to solve a complex problem, we first need to understand the problem through acquisition and conceptualisation activities. That is, we need to start by gathering as much information as needed about the context and then organise or model the information to provide a meaningful picture of the problem at hand. The resulting *conceptual model of the problem* represents the problem from the viewpoint of the *problem owner* (Andrade et al., 2004). Since there are multiple stakeholders in projects, there may be different, and possibly conflicting, models representing the different viewpoints of the multiple stakeholders. It is important to ensure that the conceptualisation process considers everybody's views and addresses any discrepancies that emerge.

Viewpoint modelling has been a technique commonly used by software professionals to resolve discrepancies during the requirements specification process. Viewpoint modelling enables the specification of a complex system by providing different viewpoints, facilitating communication with stakeholders at different stages (Andrade et al., 2004; Enders, Heverhagen, Goedicke, Tröpfner, & Tracht, 2002; Finkelstein, Kramer, Nuseibeh, Finkelstein, & Goedicke, 1992). In (Sterling & Taveter, 2009) a viewpoint framework is proposed based on agent-oriented models. The framework provides models at different stages of the software life cycle starting with the early-phase of requirements elicitation. In previous work (Lopez-Lorca, Miller, Pedell, Sterling, & Kissoon-Curumsing, 2014; Miller et al., 2014; Miller, Pedell, Sterling, Vetere, & Howard, 2012; Pedell, Lopez-Lorca, Miller, & Sterling, 2014), we have used the agent-oriented models proposed by Sterling and Taveter (2009) to present systems pertaining to different domains and involving different stakeholders. For example, Miller et al. (2012) use the models to illustrate a socially oriented system involving interactions between grandparents and grandchildren who are separated by distance.

In recent work, we have investigated the use of *emotional goals* to model the emotional viewpoints of different stakeholders in a project (Miller et al., 2014). Emotional goals are linked to *roles*, which represent stakeholders in the system, and specify a desired state of emotion or wellbeing of an agent playing those roles. Emotional goals represent how *people* feel, so are a property of people, not of the system. In a case study of an emergency alarm system for older people (Pedell et al., 2014), we demonstrated that by failing to consider the emotional goals of users, modern emergency alarm systems failed in their objective of keeping older people safe, despite being well-engineered and highly reliable systems. For example, many older people choose not to wear their emergency alarm pendant, due to the emotional stigma attached to it, so in an emergency they could not get help. We designed and implemented part of an emergency alarm system, a wellbeing monitoring system, based on our findings and trialled the wellbeing monitoring system in the homes of nine older people. Our findings showed better user experience over existing emergency alarm systems.

More recent work (Lopez-Lorca, Miller, Pedell, Sterling, et al., 2014) has extended emotional goals to the models of Sterling and Taveter (2009). We demonstrate how to model emotional goals in early phase requirements, and to carry these emotional goals through to detailed design. The extensions support straightforward traceability of emotional goals through the development lifecycle.

This paper extends our previous work on emotional modelling. While previous publications illustrated some of the agent-oriented models developed to describe the personal alarm system problem (Lopez-Lorca, Miller, Pedell, Sterling, et al., 2014; Miller et al., 2014; Pedell et al., 2014), a comprehensive set of models of the alarm system has not been made available before. The contributions are twofold. First, a complete set of models is presented for the emergency alarm system, from early-phase requirements to detailed design. We briefly discuss which models were most useful in the case study and why. Second, we demonstrate how to use the viewpoint framework proposed by Sterling and Taveter (2009) to capture the viewpoints of stakeholders, in particular emotional aspects, throughout the entire process from early-phase requirements to detailed design. We claim that the early-phase models are the most useful and least time consuming of all of the models, which we attribute to the early phases being the most critical in terms of capturing user needs.

The Literature Review section that follows, discusses existing relevant work. The section after that presents details of the emergency alarm system Case Study followed by the entire set of models for the emergency alarm system. Then, in Discussion we outline what we learnt from this exercise, and how we have applied it other socio-technical and domestic systems. In the concluding section we reflect on what was achieved in this research; and emphasise that our approach with modelling emotions from the requirements phase of a project, forward, adds little to no cost to any existing methodology used by developers, lowering the barrier in giving it a go in parallel with what they do now.

LITERATURE REVIEW

This section provides an overview on viewpoint methodologies, user emotions and the use of smart home technologies by older adults.

Viewpoint Methodologies

Viewpoint methodologies have been used by several researchers to represent the different views of stakeholders (Darke & Shanks, 1996; Easterbrook & Chechik, 2001; Sommerville, Sawyer, & Viller, 1998; Sterling & Taveter, 2009). According to Darke and Shanks (1996), a viewpoint can be represented using informal, formal and semi-formal techniques. For example, text, pictures and animations fall under the category of informal ways to represent the viewpoints of stakeholders. On the other hand, a formal representation would consist of logic-based languages while a semi-formal representation would include models such as dataflow diagrams and entity-relationship diagrams. Over time, the viewpoint approach has been used in different methods such as CORE (Mullery, 1979), SADT (Marca & McGowan, 1988), VOSE (Finkelstein et al., 1992) and VORD (Kotonya & Sommerville, 1996). Darke and Shanks (1996) compile a list of viewpoint development approaches used over time.

Table 1. The viewpoint framework (Adapted from Sterling and Taveter (2009))

Viewpoint Models Abstraction Layer	Viewpoint Aspect		
	Interaction	**Information**	**Behaviour**
Conceptual domain Modeling	Role models and organisation models	Domain models	Goal models and motivational scenarios
Platform-independent computational design	Agent models and acquaintance models, interaction models	Knowledge models	Scenarios and behaviour models
Platform-specific design and implementation	Agent interface and interaction specifications	Data models and service models	Agent Behaviour specifications

Controlled Requirements Expression (CORE) defines viewpoints informally and considers each viewpoint as sources or sinks of data. The main objective of this approach consists of producing a requirements specification which comprises different, non-conflicting views of a system which when viewed together provide a comprehensive description of the system. The Structured Analysis and Design Technique (SADT) also considers viewpoints as sinks or sources of data and makes use of a graphical notation to portray a decomposed view of the system using both data and activity models (Darke & Shanks, 1996). Viewpoint-Oriented Systems Engineering (VOSE) on the other hand, acknowledges the use of different system models by engineers during system specification and design. This method aims at resolving the conflicts that may arise due to the use of different models. Viewpoint-Oriented Requirements Definition (VORD) makes use of an object-orientation approach to analyse viewpoints and focuses mainly on the link that exists between the system and the entities in its environment.

Different agent-based approaches have also been proposed over time by several researchers to handle the complexity involved during the requirements specification phase (Bresciani, Perini, Giorgini, Giunchiglia, & Mylopoulos, 2004; Gilbert & Terna, 2000; Munroe et al., 2006; Sterling & Taveter, 2009; Yu, 2002). All strongly argue that agent-oriented methodologies provide more flexibility and a higher level of abstraction compared to the previous paradigm of object orientation, especially when it comes to people-oriented systems. Viewpoint frameworks which use agent-oriented models, specifically the Information Systems Architecture framework, the Reference Model for Open Distributed Processing, the Enterprise Model, and the process modelling framework (Sterling & Taveter, 2009) use different abstraction layers whereby each layer portrays the perspective of a particular audience such as the designers, builders or owners of the system. Even though these frameworks allow for different viewpoints to be represented, Sterling and Taveter (2009) argue that they cannot be used to depict open distributed systems that span heterogeneous networks. For instance, a smart home device such as an emergency alarm system for older adults requires local area networks, global cable and wireless networks to allow the adults to communicate with the service providers, emergency services and their relatives. Sterling and Taveter (2009) therefore proposed a new viewpoint framework in the form of a matrix which consists of the three rows and three columns depicted in Table 1. The three rows portray three abstraction layers: *conceptual domain modelling*, *platform-independent computational design* and *platform-specific design and implementation*. The three columns on the other hand represent three viewpoints: *interaction*, *information* and *behaviour*. Each cell in the matrix in Table 1 depicts a particular viewpoint which can be represented through the use of the models specified in the cell. For example, the models in the first abstraction layer, also known as the *motivation layer*, present how the system is motivated and its overall purpose; those in the second abstraction layer, also known as the *design layer,* show how the system is designed; while the models in the third layer, also known as the *deployment layer,* express how the system is situated in its environment. The models in the *conceptual domain modelling* and the *platform-independent computational design* layers are not only independent of particular hardware and software platforms but also architecture-independent unlike those at the *platform-specific design and implementation* layer. That is, the models in the lowest layer depend largely on the platform that is used to implement the system and therefore have to be developed accordingly.

Sterling and Taveter (2009) dedicates a whole chapter to describing and mapping different agent-oriented methodologies to their proposed viewpoint framework. The methodologies include Gaia (Zambonelli, Jennings, & Wooldridge, 2003), Tropos (Bresciani et al., 2004), Prometheus (Padgham & Winikoff, 2003), ROADMAP (Juan, Pearce, & Sterling, 2002; Wooldridge, Jennings, & Kinny, 2000) and RAP/AOR (Taveter, 2005). Even though these methodologies consist of different processes, they use common concepts such as agents/roles and goals (Miller et al., 2012; Sterling & Taveter, 2009). The agents/roles are used to represent interactions between people and systems while the goals refer to functional requirements which describe the intended behaviour of the system. Quality goals are used to denote the non-functional requirements.

Gaia uses an organisational abstraction to model both social and agent internal aspects of a system consisting of different agents. It focuses mainly on the interactions that exist between roles within a system. The Gaia methodology uses five models relating to the analysis and design phases. According to Sterling and Taveter (2009), these models can be easily mapped to their proposed viewpoint framework. Two of the Gaia models from the analysis stage namely the role and interaction models fall under the category of conceptual domain modelling while the remaining three from the design stage namely the agent, service and acquaintance models fit under the platform-independent design layer. Gaia does not provide any models for the requirements gathering phase, being only applied to the analysis and design phases once the requirements are gathered.

Tropos, on the other hand, covers the complete software life cycle starting with early requirements phase through to design, implementation and testing. The methodology makes use of the concepts of actor, goal and dependency to model the early and late requirements as well as architectural and detailed design based on the *i** framework proposed by Yu (1997). The *i** framework was designed to focus mainly on early-phase requirements engineering. It uses two models, a strategic dependency model and a strategic rational model, to look into dependency relationships that exist among the actors within the system and how the interests and concerns of the stakeholders can be addressed by the configurations of the system.

When mapped to Sterling and Taveter's proposed viewpoint framework, the actor diagrams and goal diagrams of the Tropos methodology fit within the conceptual domain modelling layer while the refined goal diagrams fit within the platform-independent design layer. The platform-specific design and implementation layer consist of the agent interaction diagrams, UML class diagrams, capability diagrams and the plan diagrams.

Prometheus, another agent-oriented methodology, emphasises three phases of the software development life cycle - specification, design and implementation. Different methods are advocated to develop artefacts at each of these stages. The Prometheus models consisting of analysis overview diagrams, system roles diagrams, goal overview diagrams, functionalities and scenarios fit within the conceptual modelling layer. Agent acquaintance diagrams, interaction diagrams, protocol diagrams, system overview diagrams, data coupling diagrams and agent descriptors fit within the Platform-independent Computational design layer. The Platform-specific design and implementation layer comprises the event descriptors, data descriptors, agent overview diagrams, process specifications and capability overview diagrams.

Sterling and Taveter (2009) describes the ROADMAP and RAP/AOR methodologies together as the two methodologies complement each other. The ROADMAP methodology was initially proposed as an extension of the Gaia methodology and provides more explicit models to cover the requirements elicitation phase. RAP/AOR was more geared towards distributed agent-oriented systems. Sterling and Taveter (2009) map the models from both methodologies to their viewpoint framework. The role models, domain models and goal models from the ROADMAP methodology map to the conceptual domain layer along with the interaction-frame diagrams from the RAP/AOR methodology. The second layer consists of four models from the RAP/AOR methodology - interaction-sequence diagrams, agent diagrams, scenarios and AOR behaviour diagrams. The platform-specific design and implementation layer is also made up with models from the RAP/AOR methodology namely the UML class and sequence diagrams.

Even though these methodologies provide artefacts to look into the complexity of the requirements specification process, there are very few methodologies that focus on capturing user emotions. The next subsection highlights the importance of user emotions and some of the methodologies that have touched upon this concept.

User Emotions

Our previous work (Lopez-Lorca, Miller, Pedell, Sterling, et al., 2014; Miller et al., 2014) highlighted the importance of considering user emotions during software development. According to our analysis, even though most of the functional and non-functional requirements of a system are met, many users may be left unsatisfied if their emotional expectations were not taken into consideration. A detailed literature review on emotions and emotions in software engineering has been given in previous work (Kissoon-Curumsing et al., 2014). In that paper, we discussed methods for evaluating emotions. They are akin to methods for measuring emotions in product design as described in (Desmet, 2005).

User emotions may be characterised as soft goals (Thew & Sutcliffe, 2008) but are only indirectly represented using traditional software engineering methods and are typically ignored even if raised. Explicit emotional goals are discussed by Marshall (2018) as separate from other quality goals to represent emotional expectations of users. It can be argued that emotional goals are different from traditional quality goals such as performance and reliability because they are properties of the user rather than the system. Emotional goals are subtle, ambiguous, and difficult to measure. An example of an emotional goal from our case study of emergency alarm systems described in Section 3.1 is that the relatives of older people want to *feel reassured* that their relative is safe. Relatives feeling reassured is hard to consider being a property of the system. Measuring such feelings requires us to measure the emotional state of people (e.g. representative users) unlike other qualities; for example, performance, which can be measured directly, or even usability, which can often be measured using well-defined metrics and qualitative observation from system logs. We advocate that emotional goals be regarded as first-class objects in software engineering and be treated separately from other quality goals.

Miller et al. (2014) differentiates emotional goals into personal emotional goals and system-dependent emotional goals. A personal emotional goal is defined as the way a person wants to feel such as feeling loved, safe or angry, and is independent of the existence of a system. A system dependent emotional goal is defined as the way a person feels about a system for example, feeling engaged or frustrated with the system. Emotional goals are important in people-oriented systems such as smart home technologies for elderly people (Demiris et al., 2004; Pedell, Sterling, Keirnan, & Dobson, 2013).

Use of Smart Home Technologies by Older People

The rapid increase in the older adult population has led to a growing interest in the design of technologies for the ageing generation to reduce the escalating health costs faced by governments all round the world (Demiris et al., 2004; Morris et al., 2012; Pedell et al., 2014; Selwyn, Gorard, Furlong, & Madden, 2003). The Australian government is concerned about the quality of life of older people and seeks technological solutions to improve the lives of its older citizens (CoA., 2011). Many elderly people want to live independently at home despite having health problems such as dementia, poor eyesight and depression (Pedell et al., 2014). Researchers

331

feel that the adoption of technological devices by older people can improve their quality of life and increase their self-confidence (Heo, Kim, & Won, 2011; Kim, 2012; Russell, 2011; Zimmer & Chappell, 1999).

According to (Burns, Gassert, & Cipriano, 2008; COBALT, 2013; Hanson & Magnusson, 2011), in order to encourage older people to adopt technological solutions, the solutions have to be designed so that they suit the needs of users, are easy to use and are cost effective. Even though many technological solutions have been proposed over time (Demiris et al., 2004; Hanson & Magnusson, 2011; Mynatt, Rowan, Craighill, & Jacobs, 2001), many senior citizens are reluctant to use technological devices (Gray, 1985; Selwyn, 2004; Zimmer & Chappell, 1999). According to Burns et al. (2008), the important factors determining the successful adoption of technology by older adults consist of willingness and enthusiasm for acquiring new knowledge. However, such feelings are rarely expressed by older people when it comes to using a system which is linked with a stigma.

A study on the use of the personal alarm pendant conducted by Peeters (2000) revealed that some of the older people refused to use the pendant simply because of its visibility to others. Another study with users of the emergency alarm pendants by Pedell et al. (2014) found that some users did not wear the pendant because it was viewed as a sign of and stigma of old age. These studies concluded that the non-adoption of the personal alarm was linked to the way users perceived technology from an emotional aspect. Many negative emotions were identified during the study, including lack of independence, loneliness, disappointment, confusion and embarrassment. Another reason identified for the non-use of the personal alarm system is that people feel uncomfortable to wear it at night hence placing themselves at great risk when they get up in the middle of the night to go to the bathroom (De San Miguel & Lewin, 2008).

Hence, when it comes to designing technological solutions such as personal alarm pendants, it is important to consider the feelings of the people using those alarms along with the functionalities that best suit their needs.

USING THE CONCEPTUAL FRAMEWORK TO REPRESENT AN EMERGENCY ALARM SYSTEM

This section introduces a case study of the modelling of elements of a personal emergency alarm system provided to older adults who live independently at home. A comprehensive set of agent-oriented models for the emergency alarm system is presented. The models are placed within the viewpoint framework proposed by Sterling and Taveter (2009).

Emergency Alarms

Emergency alarm systems are designed to support people, particularly elderly adults, who live on their own while having some physical or mental health issues such as dementia, diabetes, heart problems and osteoarthritis (Chung-Chih, Ming-Jang, Chun-Chieh, Ren-Guey, & Yuh-Show, 2006). The living situation may trigger an emergency. In general, emergency alarm systems are comprised of two components: 1) an *emergency alarm* used by the older person to alert the authorities when emergency assistance is required; and 2) a *wellbeing check* to ensure that the older person is doing well. The emergency alarm mechanism is typically implemented as a pendant or wristband that should be worn at all times. The device has a button that, upon being pressed, immediately establishes connection with the service provider to ask for help. The coverage area of the emergency alarm is normally limited to the older adult's home. The wellbeing check typically consists of a base station, which is connected to a landline. The elderly person is required to press a button on the base station on a regularly basis, usually daily, within a fixed time window to inform the service provider of their wellbeing. If no signal is received during the specified time window, the service provider calls the older person to check whether they need help.

Emergency alarm systems are designed with reliability and robustness as priority concerns. However older persons' emotional needs are completely ignored, as are many aesthetical considerations. Consequently, many users have serious reservations regarding the use of emergency alarm pendants (Demiris et al., 2004; Heo et al., 2011; Pedell et al., 2014). For instance, some older adults refuse to wear the pendant in public since they think it makes them look old and frail; they feel stigmatised and dependent on others (Pedell et al., 2014). Relatives of the pendant wearers highlighted the stress that its use entailed.

We conducted a field study to understand the emotional needs of older adults in order to develop a better set of requirements for emergency alarm systems, with the expectation of better acceptance by older adults. We interviewed users, relatives and non-users. Based on their responses, agent oriented models were built. The field study has been reported in (Pedell et al., 2013 and Pedell et al., 2014).

Agent-Oriented Models

This subsection presents the models for the emergency alarm system, structured according to the viewpoint framework proposed by Sterling and Taveter (2009) that sets the theoretical basis of this chapter. The three abstraction layers defined

Table 2. Modifications made to existing models to include emotional modelling

Abstraction Level	Model	Emotions
Conceptual domain modelling (a sub-section below)	Role model	Included as new sections for *Personal emotional goals* and *System-dependent emotional goals*
	Organisation model	Not included
	Domain model	Not included
	Goal model	Included as new symbols (hearts) attached to functional goals
	Motivational scenario	Included as a new row namely *Emotional description*
Platform-independent modelling (a sub-section below)	Agent model	Not included
	Acquaintance model	Not included
	Interaction model	Included as annotations for the relevant interactions
	Knowledge model	Not included
	Scenario model	Included as new rows to describe generally the emotional goals achieved by the scenario and as new columns for each activity to highlight the relevant emotions
	Behaviour model	Included as annotations for the relevant states

by the viewpoint framework that contain the models are the *conceptual domain modelling*, *platform-independent computational design* and *platform-specific design and implementation*. In each layer models are presented from interaction, information and behaviour viewpoint aspects. Emotional goals are included in the models along with goals and quality goals, which extends the models presented in (Sterling & Taveter, 2009). Table 2 summarises how the models have changed to include emotion modelling. Models belonging to the platform-specific layer are not included in Table 2 as the appropriate design decisions should cater for emotions being manifest in the implementation models.

Conceptual Domain Modelling

The conceptual domain modelling layer, also known as the motivation layer, depicts the overall view of the system being designed and implemented. Sterling and Taveter (2009) propose the use of *role* models and *organisation models* from an *interaction* viewpoint aspect; *domain models* from an *information* viewpoint aspect; and *goal models* and *motivational scenarios* from a *behaviour* viewpoint aspect.

Interaction Viewpoint Models

The role model provides an overview of the different roles involved in the system by listing responsibilities, constraints and emotional goals associated with each role. Six roles have been identified for the emergency alarm system: 1) the older person (Figure 1); 2) the carer/relative (Figure 20 in the Appendix); 3) the service provider (Figure 21 in the Appendix); 4) the technician (Figure 22 in the Appendix); 5) the in-touch monitor (Figure 23 in the Appendix); and 6) the alarm monitor (Figure 24 in the Appendix).

In this case study, as depicted in Figure 1, the older person is an adult who lives on their own at home and who uses the emergency alarm system to support their wellbeing (*description*). Responsibilities of the older person include interaction with the service provider to personalise the system based on their needs, communication with the system on a regular basis to keep in touch with their carer or relative, activation of the alarm in case of emergency and deactivation of the alarm in case of a false alarm (*responsibilities*). To ensure proper functioning of the system, the older person is required to carry the emergency alarm device with them at all times (*constraints*). The older adult expects to feel cared about, safe, independent, in touch and unburdened of the obligation of routinely get in touch with their relative/carer (*personal emotional goals*). Additionally, they want a system that feels integrated in their life and they also want to feel in control of the system (*system-dependent emotional goals*).

Figure 1. Role Model – Older Person

Role ID: R1
Name: Older Person
Description: The older person is an adult that lives independently in their own home and adopts the use of the emergency alarm system to support their wellbeing.
Responsibilities:
1.   Take responsibility in maintaining their wellbeing.
2.   Collaborate with the service provider to personalise the system.
3.   Periodically communicate with the system to keep in touch with their carer/relative.
4.   Activate the alarm in case of emergency.
5.   Deactivate the alarm in case of a false alarm.
Constraints:
1.   The older person must carry the emergency alarm device with them at all times.
Personal Emotional Goals:
1.   The older person wants to feel cared about.
2.   The older person wants to feel safe.
3.   The older person wants to feel independent.
4.   The older person wants to feel in touch with their relatives and carers.
5.   The older person wants to feel unburdened of the obligation of routinely get in touch with their relative/carer.
System-related Emotional Goals:
1.   The older person wants a system that feels integrated in their life.
2.   The older person wants to feel in control of the system.

The *organisational model* depicts the relationship(s) that exist between the different roles. In our case, control and peer relationships have been identified, as illustrated in Figure 2. A peer relationship means that the roles involved have the same level of authority within the system and these roles do not control each other. For instance, the older person shares a peer relationship with the carer/relative and the service provider. This means that neither the older person nor the carer/relative nor the service provider can control each other. A double arrow is used to depict a peer relationship. On the other hand, a control relationship means that a particular role controls another role. For example, the service provider has control over the technician as depicted by the arrow pointing towards the technician.

Information Viewpoint Models

The *domain model* provides information about the environment in which the agents of the system will be situated. In our case study, the older person lives in their own home and surrounds, for example a garden around the house. The older person carries and uses the alarm monitor which monitors the emergency call activator. The latter covers the home of the older adult and its surrounds. Figure 3 is a domain model illustrating this information.

Behaviour Viewpoint Models

The *goal* model represents the functional goals of the system to be developed along with any quality and emotional goals linked to the functional goals. The main functional goal of the emergency alarm system consists of providing technology-supported care to older persons and the roles which are responsible for achieving this goal are relatives, service providers and older persons as shown in Figure 4. The model also identifies the quality goals and emotional goals attached to each particular functional goal. These are represented as clouds and hearts respectively. Each functional goal can further be decomposed into sub goals. For example, the *"provide technology-supported care"* goal is decomposed into 1) Introduce emergency alarm system (see Figure 17 in Appendix), 2) I'm in touch (see Figure 18 in Appendix) and 3) Call for help (see Figure 19 in Appendix).

The *Motivational Scenario* provides a high-level description of the purpose of the system in terms of functional, quality and emotional goals. It reflects how the agents enacting a particular role can achieve the goals assigned to them. We present only one scenario of the emergency alarm system in this section in Figure 5. The remaining set of scenarios is available in the Appendix from Figure 25 to Figure 27.

Figure 2. Organisational Model

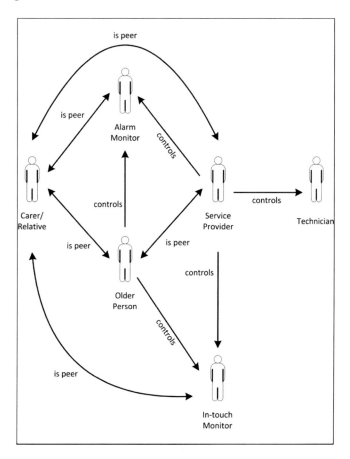

Platform-Independent Computational Design

The platform-independent computational design layer, also referred to as the design layer consists of models required for designing a system. The models presented in the first abstraction layer of the framework represent the problem domain in abstract terms which are easily understandable to customers and external stakeholders. System designers, however, need a different view of the system in order to be able to design the system. Sterling and Taveter (2009) recommends the use of *agent, acquaintance* and *interaction models* from an *interaction* viewpoint aspect; *knowledge models* from the *information* viewpoint aspect; and *scenarios* and *behaviour models* from the *behaviour* viewpoint aspect. The specific models are described in the rest of this section.

Figure 3. Domain Model

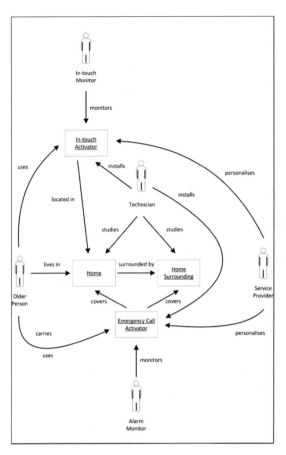

Interaction Viewpoint Models

The *agent model* is used to map abstract constructs from the analysis stage to design constructs known as agent types. In the agent model, each role identified in the role model is mapped to one or more agent types whereby the agent is responsible to fulfil certain roles. The agent model for the emergency alarm system is illustrated in Figure 6. In our case study the mapping is straightforward with each role identified earlier mapped to an agent type in a one-to-one relationship. For example, the role of the *older person* is mapped to the agent type *older person*, and the role of the *service provider* is mapped to the agent type *service provider* and so on.

The *acquaintance model* complements the agent model by outlining interaction pathways between the agents of the system. The acquaintance model for the emergency alarm system is shown in Figure 7. For example, the carer/relative interacts with the

Figure 4. Goal Model

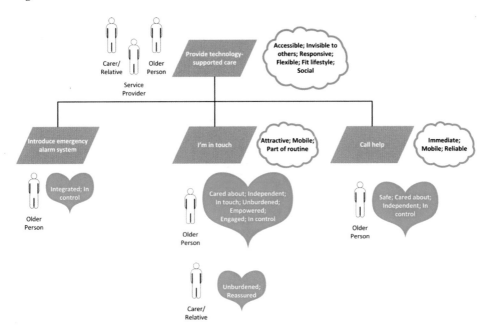

Figure 5. Motivational Scenario – Provide technology-supported Care

Scenario name	Provide technology-supported care
Scenario description	Neighbours and relatives keep an eye on a person who lives at home to ensure that everything is fine. Technology-supported care is added to these mechanisms to further support the person's wellbeing. The technology-supported care consists of a keep in touch activity that the older person performs periodically, and an emergency alarm that can be activated by the older person when in need of help.
Quality description	The system must be accessible to the older person and invisible to everyone else. The system must be responsive and flexible to adapt to the specific needs of the older person, in particular it must fit in their lifestyle.
Emotional description	The relative wants to feel reassured that the older person's wellbeing is maintained. The older person wants to feel that the system is integrated in their life and under their control. The system will help maintaining the feeling of independence for the older person. By using the system, the older person will feel safe, cared about and in touch with their carers/relatives. Both, the carer/relative and the older person want to feel unburdened of the obligation of getting in touch to instead enjoy doing it.

service provider since the carer/relative is responsible for liaising with the service provider to install the emergency alarm system.

The *interaction model* represents a set of interactions existing between the different agents within the system. Several interaction models for a particular system are expected where each model represents a particular scenario or functionality of

Figure 6. Agent Model – mapping roles to agent types

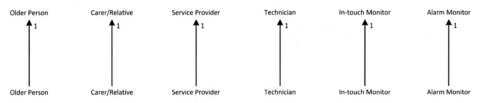

Figure 7. Acquaintance Model

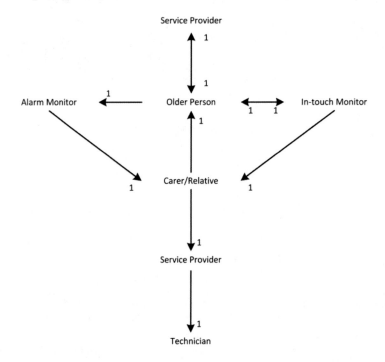

the system. The interaction models for the emergency alarm system are illustrated in Figures 8, 9 and 10 representing diagrammatically three major functionalities of the system, introduction of the system, and the in-touch and the emergency alarm mechanisms. Along with seeing the flow of interactions between agents, software practitioners can identify how the emotional goals associated with each agent can be achieved. For example, Figure 8, which demonstrates a scenario of the introduction of the emergency alarm system, also shows how certain interactions can make the older person feel in control and feel that the system is integrated in their life.

Information Viewpoint Aspect

At this second abstraction layer, more concrete knowledge about the agents involved in the system is required. The *knowledge model* is a model which represents the knowledge that agents have about their environment and about themselves. Two approaches have been proposed by Sterling and Taveter (2009) to present knowledge models: 1) using ontology-like notation and 2) using UML-like notation. In both cases, information about the agent and the agent's environment are identified. For instance, the knowledge models for the emergency alarm system provided in Figure 11 and Figure 12 both provide the same set of information about the older person including their *details*, their *emergency contact list*, the *current time* and the time during which they must contact the in-touch monitor. The same information is also known to the in-touch monitor. The alarm monitor on the other hand is only aware of the older person's *details* and *emergency contact list*. The two approaches to depicting the knowledge model illustrates the flexibility of the models to adapt to different modelling styles. The ontology-like style uses semantic relationships, whereas the UML-like style borrows elements from UML class diagrams to express relations in a manner more oriented for development.

Behaviour Viewpoint Aspect

A *scenario* is a behaviour model which represents a collective activity that models how a particular goal is achieved by agents enacting particular roles. A system can have more than one scenario depending on its complexity and number of functionalities involved. Each scenario provides information about a particular functionality by identifying the associated quality and emotional goals, the initiator of the function, how the function gets triggered and the set of activities linked with the function. A complete set of scenarios for the emergency alarm system is provided in Figure 28 to Figure 34 in the appendix.

A *behaviour model* focuses on what individual agents do within the system. There are two kinds of behaviour models - *behavioural interface models* and *agent behaviour models*. The *behaviour interface model* for the emergency alarm system is depicted in Figure 13, which displays the different behavioural units (*activity*) and interface (*trigger, pre-condition and post-condition*) for each unit. The *agent behaviour model* describes the behaviour of an agent in terms of rules and triggering messages. The agent behaviour model for the emergency alarm system is provided in Figure 14 which highlights how the agents of the system behave in different situations.

Figure 8. Interaction model – Introducing the emergency alarm system

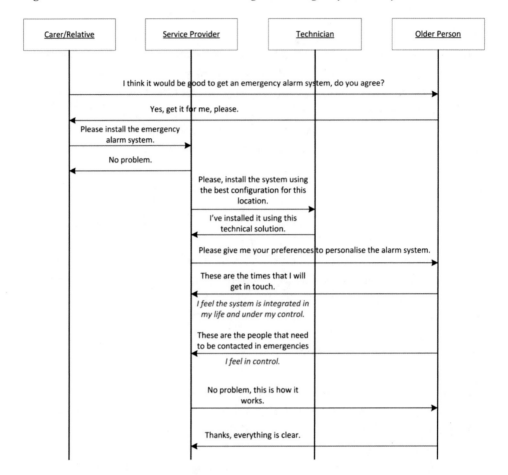

Platform-Specific Design and Implementation

The platform-specific design and implementation layer, also known as platform-dependent, refers to the deployment layer. Models developed at this stage rely heavily on the technology that is used for the implementation of the system (Sterling & Taveter, 2009). A number of solutions can be adopted to implement the final system, and the models to describe them will vary accordingly. Sterling and Taveter (2009) mostly focus on the transition from computation-independent models to platform-independent models, as this is the pain point ignored by other disciplines which could benefit the most from agent-oriented modelling concepts. In contrast, the transition from platform-independent models to platform-dependent models has been well explored by disciplines such as Model Driven Architecture (Kleppe, Warmer,

Figure 9. Interaction Model – I'm in touch

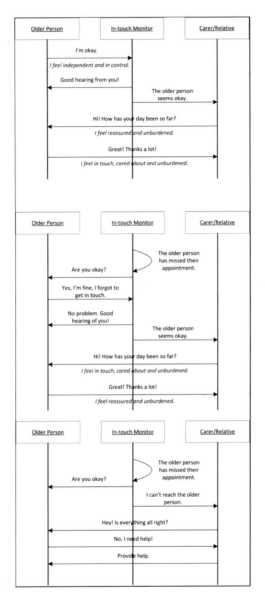

& Bast, 2003). In this level, the models proposed by Sterling and Taveter (2009) are the *agent interface* and *interaction specification* from an *interaction* viewpoint aspect; the *data* and *service models* from the *information* viewpoint aspect; the *agent behaviour specifications* from the *behaviour* viewpoint aspect. These models

Figure 10. Interaction Model – Call for help

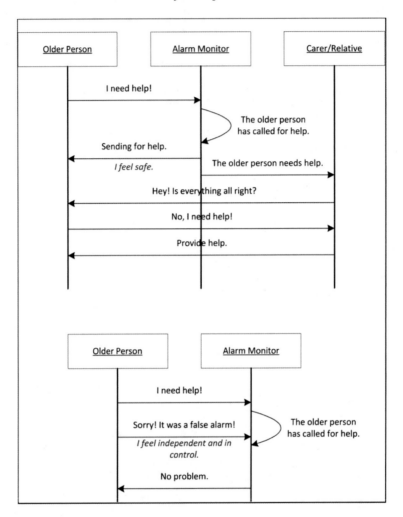

are mostly placeholders for technology-specific models, such as UML models for object oriented developments.

Our purpose in this case study was not to build models that could be translated directly to code. Our aim was to develop a set of computation-independent and platform-independent models to allow the designing of a solution that considered the emotional needs of older adults. However, for the sake of completeness, we illustrate platform-specific models that could be used to implement part of the emergency alarm system. Harnessing the emotional knowledge captured in the models for the emergency alarm system, we have chosen to implement the in-touch mechanism

Figure 11. Knowledge Model – Ontology like notation

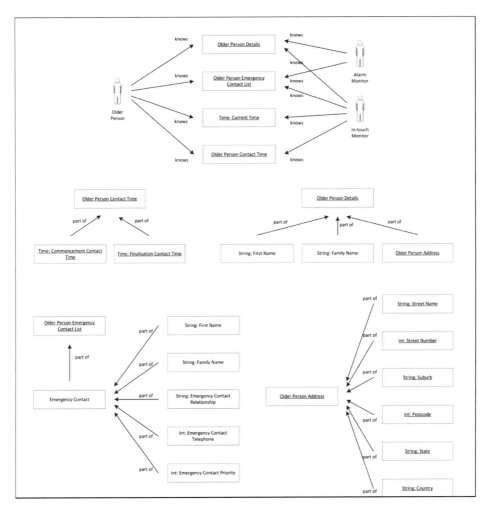

in a manner that is flexible and integrates into the lifestyle of the older adults that makes them feel cared about and in touch.

A key design decision has been to envision the wellbeing check as a touchscreen to a digital picture frame rather than an impersonal check-in button. Carers or relatives would send the older adults pictures that convey positive emotions, such as pictures of grandchildren, memories of their wedding day, or sharing special moments from holidays. The older adult would see the picture in the tablet. They would touch it, comment or reply to its caption or simply look at it and move it away to display a different one. Any of these actions have a meaning for the older person and are interpreted by the system as an implicit *well-being check*. Seeing

Figure 12. Knowledge Model – UML like notation

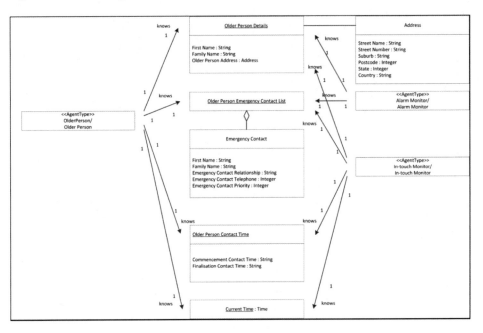

Figure 13. Behaviour Interface Model

Activity	Trigger	Pre-condition	Post-condition
Introduction of the emergency alarm system	The carer/relative is concerned about the wellbeing of the older person.	One service provider has been selected by the carer/relative as the most suitable for the older person.	The emergency alarm system is installed at the older person's home.
			The older person knows how to operate the system.
			Due to its personalisation, the older person feels the system is integrated in their life and under their control.
I'm in touch	It is time for the older person to get in touch with their carer/relative.	The older person has the in-touch activator within reach.	The carer/relative feels reassured that the older person is okay and unburdened.
			The older person feels in touch, cared about and unburdened.
Call help	The older person needs help.	The older person has the alarm activator within reach.	The older person receives help.
			The older person feels safe and cared about.

Figure 14. Agent Behaviour Model

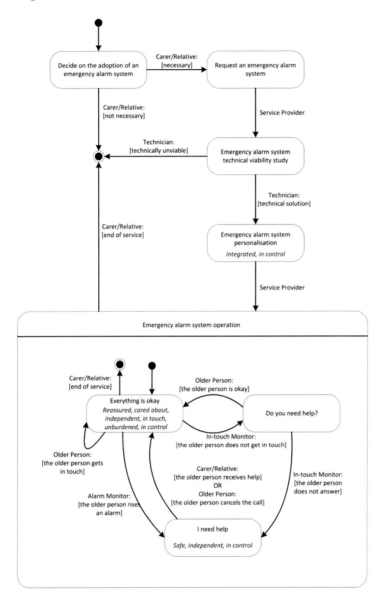

a meaningful picture has added value for the older person rather than pressing a nondescript button.

We have chosen to model the digital picture frame using object-oriented technology. UML class and interaction sequence diagrams are used to guide coding. The class diagram portrays all three viewpoints namely the *interaction*, *information* and *behaviour* viewpoints. The interaction sequence diagram is used from an *interaction* and *behaviour* viewpoint.

The UML class diagram provides a static view of the system by representing the system's structure in terms of classes. Information about each class is provided in terms of a set of attributes and operations. The relationship that exists between the different classes is also represented in the class diagram thus reflecting the possible interactions that exist between the classes. The class diagram for the emergency alarm system is depicted in Figure 15. In this diagram, the operations and attributes identified for each class mainly relate to the in-touch mechanism.

The interaction sequence diagram represents a set of interactions that occurs between different objects of the system in a sequential order within a particular scenario. This diagram is helpful to portray which objects interact with other objects and which object is responsible to trigger communication within a particular scenario. Different sequence diagrams are used to depict different scenarios within a system. The sequence diagram for the in-touch scenario of the emergency alarm system is shown in Figure 16. In this diagram, the communications that exist between the carer, older person and different components of the system are portrayed in a chronological order.

Figure 15. Class Diagram for emergency alarm system with implicit well-being check

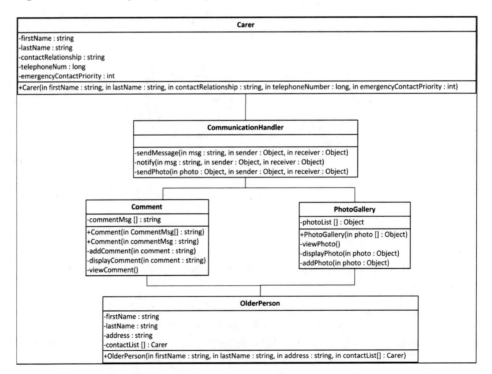

DISCUSSION

While constructing the models for the emergency alarm system described in this paper, we found that the models lend themselves to a seamless transition between layers. The concepts used in higher abstraction layers are easily transformed into equivalent ones at lower abstraction layers, i.e. closer to implementation. For instance, the role model, defined in the conceptual domain modelling layer, provides basic information about the different roles involved in the system, human or otherwise, and highlights their responsibilities. The equivalent constructs one layer lower, are agents, which aggregate roles according to their capabilities as concrete agent types. At this stage, the agent model still includes both human and man-made agents. However, in the lowest level of abstraction, the platform-dependent layer, only the man-made agents are codified as software entities.

It is worth noting that even though we discuss an agent-oriented approach to modelling, it is not essential to produce agent-oriented models within the platform-dependent layer. The final product might be more suitable for other approaches

Figure 16. Interaction Sequence Diagram for implicit well-being check

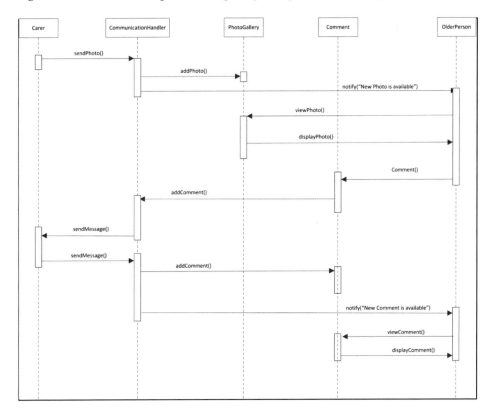

such as object-oriented. Even though Sterling and Taveter (2009) proposes a list of agent-oriented models at different layers of the viewpoint framework, software professionals have the flexibility to use only those models which best suit their project and toolset. Additionally, the models can be tailored as per the needs of the system.

In a previous paper, Pedell et al. (2014), describe a method which was used to inform the design of technology-based systems that take into account emotional goals of users. This method consisted of three main steps namely: 1) applying content analysis techniques to classify important topics from the ethnographic data, in particular emotional related topics; 2) model building using similar models proposed in this paper; 3) validation of models with stakeholders to ensure that the developers have a proper understanding of the stakeholders' needs.

Using the approach from (Pedell et al., 2014), two prototypes were designed to allow elderly people to interact with their loved ones through photos and text messages. The idea behind both prototypes is the promotion of connectivity between the elderly people who live on their own and their close family and friends. The first prototype was tested with nine elderly adults over a period of two weeks. A questionnaire was used to evaluate the emotional expectations of the users.

The second prototype was an app called TouchFrame which was available as an app in the App store. There was a companion app called TouchFrame Connect which made it easy for family and friends to send pictures. TouchFrame was trialled in the homes of seven elderly adults for a period of two to three months. It was originally intended for the trial to run over the course of the year. However some difficulties emerged, including recruitment of participants, network connectivity and family dynamics. Looking at the data generated, it was decided to end the trial after three months. A companion app, called TouchFrame Carer was built by a team of nine Master of Software Engineering students at the University of Melbourne as a year-long capstone project. The system was tested on data from the TouchFrame trial.

The modelling approach from Pedell et al. (2014) is applicable in any domain where emotions are relevant. Socio-technical and domestic systems are particularly suitable as the role of people is more prominent and their engagement with the system can influence its success. However, even traditional business systems can be affected by stakeholders' emotions as illustrated by Ramos, Berry, and Carvalho (2005) in their paper where they highlight the impact of a change in management decision on the emotions of the employees.

Continuing from the aged care case study discussed in this paper, we have applied the modelling approach in several other domains, especially in the area of mental health. (Wachtler et al., 2018) describes the development of a screening app to match people with current depressive symptoms with appropriate treatment recommendations. (Thomas et al., 2016) describes the development and pilot study of a novel digital intervention to promote personal recovery in people with persisting psychotic disorders. In this case, the goal models were used during the requirements elicitation phase which involved different groups of stakeholders including mental health workers, people suffering from psychosis, psychologists and the families of the patients. The high level of abstraction of the goal models made them accessible for stakeholders without a technical background and acted as a boundary object to support interactions between the development team and clients. (Sterling et al, 2017) describes the development of SleepWell, an app to help people with sleep difficulties. The most recent example of use was in teleaudiology as described in (Sterling et al, 2018).

Goal models are now routinely used in teaching, both in Digital Media Design at Swinburne University of Technology (Marshall, 2018), and Software Engineering at the University of Melbourne. The models have been incorporated with requirements elicitation methods and incorporated in agile development, within a semester-long requirements elicitation subject, and within a year-long software engineering project subject. While the models were inspired by agent concepts, students are able to understand and build the models without any special training in agents. The high level models are intuitive and easy to understand from our experience.

CONCLUSION

This paper has presented a complete set of models for an emergency alarm system for older people. We demonstrated how the models fit within the conceptual framework proposed by Sterling and Taveter (2009). The models described have arisen from our research on modelling emotional goals of stakeholders (Lopez-Lorca, Miller, Pedell, Sterling, et al., 2014; Miller et al., 2014). Combining the concepts of emotional goals and viewpoint modelling, we captured the viewpoints of multiple stakeholders, including their emotional needs. The paper demonstrates that the viewpoint framework proposed by (Sterling and Taveter (2009)) is flexible and can be adapted by software practitioners as needed. The models helped guide the development of two prototypes that have been tested in people's homes allowing older people to keep in touch in a positive way.

While using the models in different domains and with different target groups, we found that the models in the first two layers have proven to be useful for communicating with a non-technical audience. At the conceptual domain modelling layer, the goal model provides valuable information to stakeholders allowing them to better understand the problem. In the case of the emergency alarm system, the goal model proved useful to initiate discussions and identify confusing requirements at the very initial stages of the project. Furthermore, the role models and motivational scenarios were particularly helpful to identify the roles and responsibilities of the different agents involved in the system and how the responsibilities are achieved. Stakeholders found it easy to relate to their specific goals and easily highlighted missing and confusing goals.

At the platform-independent computational design layer, the interaction models were used to identify different interactions that exist between the different agents of the system. It allowed designers to understand the link that exists between the interactions and the emotional goals. The scenarios also proved useful at this stage as they provided additional information on how the different functionalities need to be designed thus ensuring that the system caters for all the goals identified in the goal model.

The use of these models ensures a system that is better aligned with the emotional needs of the users. Making the emotional goals explicit encourages developers and designers to consider emotions while designing and developing the system. The models are at a high level of abstraction and are useful to discuss with non-technical stakeholders. They are simple and quick to draw and can be built collaboratively with the client. We are not dogmatic about the application of these models, and recommend that developers choose any models that are appropriate in the context of a specific project. Interestingly, there are no major costs involved with this approach as the models can be drawn in parallel with other requirements engineering activities.

REFERENCES

Andrade, J., Ares, J., Garcia, R., Pazos, J., Rodriguez, S., & Silva, A. (2004). A methodological framework for viewpoint-oriented conceptual modeling. *Software Engineering. IEEE Transactions on, 30*(5), 282–294.

Baxter, G., & Sommerville, I. (2011). Socio-technical systems: From design methods to systems engineering. *Interacting with Computers, 23*(1), 4–17. doi:10.1016/j.intcom.2010.07.003

Bentley, T., Johnston, L., & Von Baggo, K. (2002) Putting some emotion into requirements engineering. *Proc. of the 7th Australian Workshop on Requirements Engineering*, 227-244.

Bresciani, P., Perini, A., Giorgini, P., Giunchiglia, F., & Mylopoulos, J. (2004). Tropos: An Agent-Oriented Software Development Methodology. *Autonomous Agents and Multi-Agent Systems, 8*(3), 203–236. doi:10.1023/B:AGNT.0000018806.20944.ef

Burns, L., Gassert, A., & Cipriano, P. (2008). Smart technology, enduring solutions. *Journal of Healthcare Information Management, 22*(4), 24–30. PMID:19267016

Cernosek, G. (2004). *The Value of Modeling*. IBM.

Chung-Chih, L., Ming-Jang, C., Chun-Chieh, H., Ren-Guey, L., & Yuh-Show, T. (2006). Wireless Health Care Service System for Elderly With Dementia. *Information Technology in Biomedicine. IEEE Transactions on, 10*(4), 696–704.

CoA. (2011). *Don't fall for it. Falls can be prevented!* Canberra: Commonwealth of Australia.

COBALT. (2013). *Older people have a thirst for technology*. The University of Sheffield. Retrieved 20 November, 2013, from http://www.shef.ac.uk/news/nr/older-people-and-technology-1.275964

Darke, P., & Shanks, G. (1996). Stakeholder viewpoints in requirements definition: A framework for understanding viewpoint development approaches. *Requirements Engineering, 1*(2), 88–105. doi:10.1007/BF01235904

De San Miguel, K., & Lewin, G. (2008). Brief Report: Personal emergency alarms: What impact do they have on older people's lives? *Australasian Journal on Ageing, 27*(2), 103–105. doi:10.1111/j.1741-6612.2008.00286.x PMID:18713202

Demiris, G., Rantz, M. J., Aud, M. A., Marek, K. D., Tyrer, H. W., Skubic, M., & Hussam, A. A. (2004). Older adults' attitudes towards and perceptions of 'smart home' technologies: A pilot study. *Informatics for Health & Social Care, 29*(2), 87–94. PMID:15370989

Demoly, F., Monticolo, D., Eynard, B., Rivest, L., & Gomes, S. (2010). Multiple viewpoint modelling framework enabling integrated product–process design. *International Journal on Interactive Design and Manufacturing, 4*(4), 269–280. doi:10.100712008-010-0107-3

Desmet, P. (2005). Measuring Emotion: Development and Application of an Instrument to Measure Emotional Responses to Products. In M. Blythe, K. Overbeeke, A. Monk, & P. Wright (Eds.), *Funology* (Vol. 3, pp. 111–123). Springer Netherlands. doi:10.1007/1-4020-2967-5_12

Easterbrook, S., & Chechik, M. (2001). A framework for multi-valued reasoning over inconsistent viewpoints. *Software Engineering, 2001. ICSE 2001. Proceedings of the 23rd International Conference on.*

Enders, B. E., Heverhagen, T., Goedicke, M., Tröpfner, P., & Tracht, R. (2002). Towards an integration of different specification methods by using the Viewpoint Framework. *Journal of Integrated Design & Process Science, 6*(2), 1–23.

Finkelstein, A., Kramer, J., Nuseibeh, B., Finkelstein, L., & Goedicke, M. (1992). Viewpoints: A framework for integrating multiple perspectives in system development. *International Journal of Software Engineering and Knowledge Engineering*, *2*(01), 31–57. doi:10.1142/S0218194092000038

Gilbert, N., & Terna, P. (2000). How to build and use agent-based models in social science. *Mind & Society*, *1*(1), 57–72. doi:10.1007/BF02512229

Gray, J. A. (1985). The whole and its parts: Behaviour, the brain, cognition and emotion. *Bulletin of the British Psychological Society*, *38*, 99–112.

Hanson, E., & Magnusson, L. (2011). The role of ICT support services to promote ageing in place: The ACTION service. *Eurohealth (London)*, *17*(2-3), 24–26.

Heo, J., Kim, J., & Won, Y.-S. (2011). Exploring the Relationship Between Internet Use and Leisure Satisfaction Among Older Adults. *Activities, Adaptation and Aging*, *35*(1), 43–54. doi:10.1080/01924788.2010.545975

Juan, T., Pearce, A., & Sterling, L. (2002). *ROADMAP: Extending the Gaia Methodology for Complex Open Systems*. Paper presented at the First International Joint Conference on Autonomous Agents and Multiagent Systems, AAMAS 2002, Bologna, Italy. 10.1145/544741.544744

Kim, K. O. (2012). *The emotional responses of older adults to new technology (Ph.D.)*. University of Illinois at Urbana-Champaign.

Kissoon-Curumsing, M., Pedell, S., & Vasa, R. (2014). Designing an Evaluation Tool to Measure Emotional Goals. International Journal of People-Oriented Programming, 3(1), 22-43.

Kleppe, A. G., Warmer, J. B., & Bast, W. (2003). *MDA explained: the model driven architecture: practice and promise*. Addison-Wesley Professional.

Kotonya, G., & Sommerville, I. (1996). Requirements Engineering With Viewpoints. *Software Engineering Journal*, *11*(1), 5–18. doi:10.1049ej.1996.0002

Lopez-Lorca, A. A., Miller, T., Pedell, S., Mendoza, A., Keirnan, A., & Sterling, L. (2014). One size doesn't fit all: diversifying "the user" using personas and emotional scenarios. *Proceedings of the 6th International Workshop on Social Software Engineering*. 10.1145/2661685.2661691

Lorence, D., & Park, H. (2006). New technology and old habits: The role of age as a technology chasm. *Technology and Health Care*, *14*(2), 91–96. PMID:16720952

Marca, D. A., & McGowan, C. L. (1988). *SADT: Structured analysis and design technique*. New York, NY.

Marshall, J. (2018). Agent-Based Modelling of Emotional Goals in Digital Media Design Projects. In S. Goschnick (Ed.), *Innovative Methods, User-Friendly Tools, Coding, and Design Approaches in People-Oriented Programming*. Hershey, PA: IGI Publishing. doi:10.4018/978-1-5225-3822-6.ch034

Miller, T., Pedell, S., Mendoza, A., Keirnan, A., Sterling, L., & Lopez-Lorca, A. A. (2014). *Emotionally-driven models for people-oriented requirements engineering: the case study of emergency systems*. Academic Press.

Miller, T., Pedell, S., Sterling, L., Vetere, F., & Howard, S. (2012). Understanding socially oriented roles and goals through motivational modelling. *Journal of Systems and Software*, *85*(9), 2160–2170. doi:10.1016/j.jss.2012.04.049

Morris, M., Ozanne, E., Miller, K., Santamaria, N., Pearce, A., Said, C., & Adair, B. (2012). *Smart Technologies for older people*. Retrieved 20 February, 2014, from http://broadband.unimelb.edu.au/resources/Smart-technologies-for-older-people.pdf

Mullery, G. P. (1979). CORE - a method for controlled requirement specification. *Proceedings of the 4th international conference on Software engineering*.

Munroe, S., Miller, T., Belecheanu, R. A., Pechoucek, M., McBurney, P., & Luck, M. (2006). Crossing the agent technology chasm: Lessons, experiences and challenges in commercial applications of agents. *The Knowledge Engineering Review*, *21*(04), 345–392. doi:10.1017/S0269888906001020

Mynatt, E. D., Rowan, J., Craighill, S., & Jacobs, A. (2001). Digital family portraits: supporting peace of mind for extended family members. *Proceedings of the SIGCHI Conference on Human Factors in Computing Systems*. 10.1145/365024.365126

Padgham, L., & Winikoff, M. (2003). Prometheus: A Methodology for Developing Intelligent Agents. In F. Giunchiglia, J. Odell, & G. Weiß (Eds.), *Agent-Oriented Software Engineering III* (Vol. 2585, pp. 174–185). Springer Berlin Heidelberg. doi:10.1007/3-540-36540-0_14

Pedell, S., Lopez-Lorca, A., Miller, T., & Sterling, L. (2014). Don't Leave me Untouched: Considering Emotions in Personal Alarm Use and Development. In *Healthcare Informatics and Analytics: Emerging Issues and Trends*. IGI Global.

Pedell, S., Sterling, L., Keirnan, A., & Dobson, G. (2013). *Emotions around emergency alarm use: A field study with older adults: Report for smart services crc*. Swinburne University of Technology.

Peeters, P. H. F. (2000). Design criteria for an automatic safety-alarm system for elderly. *Technology and Health Care*, 8(2), 81–91. PMID:10955763

Ramos, I., Berry, D. M., & Carvalho, Á. (2005). Requirements engineering for organizational transformation. *Information and Software Technology*, 47(5), 479–495. doi:10.1016/j.infsof.2004.09.014

Russell, H. (2011). Later life ICT learners ageing well. *International Journal of Ageing & Later Life*, 6(2), 103–127. doi:10.3384/ijal.1652-8670.1162103

Selwyn, N. (2004). The information aged: A qualitative study of older adults' use of information and communications technology. *Journal of Aging Studies*, 18(4), 369–384. doi:10.1016/j.jaging.2004.06.008

Selwyn, N., Gorard, S., Furlong, J., & Madden, L. (2003). Older adults' use of information and communications technology in everyday life. *Ageing and Society*, 23(05), 561–582. doi:10.1017/S0144686X03001302

Sommerville, I., Sawyer, P., & Viller, S. (1998). Viewpoints for Requirements Elicitation: A Practical Approach. *Proceedings of the 3rd International Conference on Requirements Engineering: Putting Requirements Engineering to Practice.* 10.1109/ICRE.1998.667811

Sterling, L., Lopez-Lorca, A., Pedell, S., & Goschnick, S. (2017). Developing Emotionally Supportive Technology for Monitoring Sleep Disorders. In Proc. Design4Health Conference. Swinburne University.

Sterling, L., & Taveter, K. (2009). *The Art of Agent-oriented Modeling*. The MIT Press.

Taveter, K. (2005). Towards Radical Agent-Oriented Software Engineering Processes Based on AOR Modeling. In H.-S. Brian & G. Paolo (Eds.), *Agent-Oriented Methodologies* (pp. 277–316). Hershey, PA: IGI Global. doi:10.4018/978-1-59140-581-8.ch010

Thew, S., & Sutcliffe, A. (2008). *Investigating the Role of 'Soft Issues' in the RE Process*. Academic Press.

Thomas, N., Farhall, J., Foley, F., Leitan, N., Villagonzalo, K., Ladd, E., ... Kyrios, M. (2016). Promoting personal recovery in people with persisting psychotic disorders: Development and pilot study of a novel digital intervention. *Frontiers in Psychiatry*, 7, 196. doi:10.3389/fpsyt.2016.00196 PMID:28066271

Van Lamsweerde, A., Darimont, R., & Letier, E. (1998). Managing conflicts in goal-driven requirements engineering. *Software Engineering. IEEE Transactions on*, *24*(11), 908–926.

Wooldridge, M., Jennings, N., & Kinny, D. (2000). The Gaia Methodology for Agent-Oriented Analysis and Design. *Autonomous Agents and Multi-Agent Systems*, *3*(3), 285–312. doi:10.1023/A:1010071910869

Yu, E. (1997). Towards modelling and reasoning support for early-phase requirements engineering. *Paper presented at the Requirements Engineering, 1997, Proceedings of the Third IEEE International Symposium on.*

Yu, E. (2002). Agent-Oriented Modelling: Software versus the World. In M. Wooldridge, G. Weiß, & P. Ciancarini (Eds.), *Agent-Oriented Software Engineering II* (Vol. 2222, pp. 206–225). Springer Berlin Heidelberg. doi:10.1007/3-540-70657-7_14

Zambonelli, F., Jennings, N. R., & Wooldridge, M. (2003). Developing multiagent systems: The Gaia methodology. *ACM Transactions on Software Engineering and Methodology*, *12*(3), 317–370. doi:10.1145/958961.958963

Zimmer, Z., & Chappell, N. L. (1999). Receptivity to new technology among older adults. *Disability and Rehabilitation*, *21*(5/6), 222–230. PMID:10381234

APPENDIX

Goal Models

See Figures 17-19

Role Models

See Figures 20-24

Figure 17. Goal Model – Introduce emergency alarm system

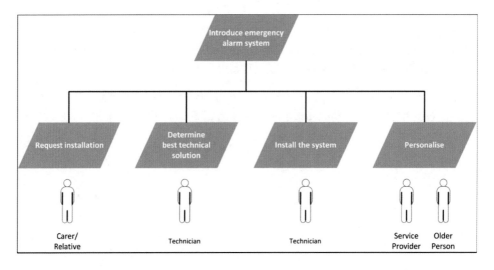

Figure 18. Goal Model – I'm in touch

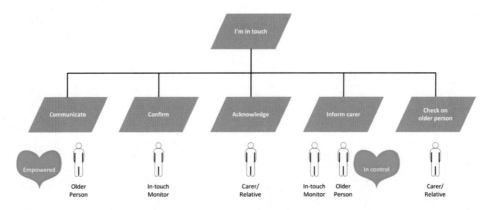

Figure 19. Goal Model – Call Help

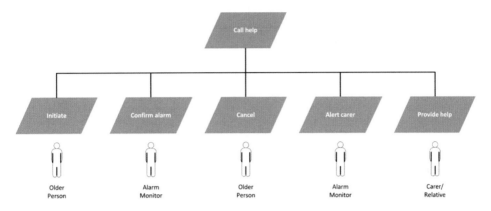

Figure 20. Role Model – Carer/relative

Role ID: R2

Name: Carer/Relative

Description: The carer seeks the wellbeing of an older person (often a relative) who adopts the use of the emergency alarm system to stay at home.

Responsibilities:

1.   Support the wellbeing of the user of the emergency alarm system.

2.   Request the installation of the emergency alarm system at the older person's home.

3.   Make the older person feel cared about by interacting with them during the periodic "keep in touch" activity.

4.   Check on the older person when their status is uncertain.

5.   Provide help to the older person when in distress.

Constraints: N/A

Personal Emotional Goals:

1.   The carer/relative wants to feel reassured that the older person is safe at home.

2.   The carer/relative wants to feel unburdened of the obligation of routinely get in touch with the older person.

System-related Emotional Goals: N/A

Motivational Scenarios

See Figures 25-27

Scenarios

See Figures 28-34

Figure 21. Role Model – Service Provider

Role ID: R3
Name: Service provider
Description: The service provider supports the wellbeing of the older person by providing the necessary technical and human resources.
Responsibilities:
1.   Provide a mechanism to contribute to the wellbeing of the older person by supporting them to regularly get in touch with their carer/relative and monitoring emergency alarms.
2.   Liaise with the older person to personalise the emergency alarm system installed at their home.
Constraints:
1.   The technology-supported care system must be accessible for the older person.
2.   The technology-supported care system must be invisible to others than the older person.
3.   The technology-supported care system must be responsive.
4.   The technology-supported care system must be flexible to adapt to the older person's needs.
5.   The technology-supported care system must fit into the lifestyle of the older person.
6.   The keep in touch mechanism must be integrated in the everyday routine of the older person.
7.   The emergency alarm system must be mobile.
Personal Emotional Goals: N/A
System-related Emotional Goals: N/A

Figure 22. Role Model – Technician

Role ID: R4
Name: Technician
Description: The technician is a person who has technical expertise and who is associated with the service provider.
Responsibilities:
1.   The technician studies the older person's home to determine the best technical solution given the particularities of the building.
2.   The technician installs the emergency alarm system at the older person's home.
Constraints: N/A
Personal Emotional Goals: N/A
System-related Emotional Goals: N/A

Figure 23. Role Model – In-touch Monitor

Role ID: R5
Name: In-touch Monitor
Description: The in-touch monitor maintains awareness of the status of the older person's keep in touch mechanism and acknowledges its activation.
Responsibilities:
1.   Give feedback to the older person that the periodic keep in touch procedure has been successfully initiated.
2.   Advise the carer/relative that the older person was out of reach and may need help.
Constraints: N/A
Personal Emotional Goals: N/A
System-related Emotional Goals: N/A

Figure 24. Role Model – Alarm Monitor

Role ID: R6
Name: Alarm monitor
Description: The alarm monitor maintains awareness of the status of the older person's emergency alarm system and reacts to its activation.
Responsibilities:
1.   React to the activation of the alarm by notifying the older person that help is coming.
2.   Alert the carer/relative that the older person needs help.
Constraints:
1.   The alarm monitor must be able to react immediately to the older person's request for help.
2.   The alarm monitor must be capable of handling alarms 24/7.
Personal Emotional Goals: N/A
System-related Emotional Goals: N/A

Figure 25. Motivational Scenario – Introduce the emergency alarm system

Scenario name	Introduce the emergency alarm system
Scenario description	The emergency alarm system is introduced to the older person's home. The carer/relative agrees with the older person on the need of getting an emergency alarm system. The technician determines the best technical solution for the older person's home and installs the system. The service provider personalises the system according to the older person's requirements.
Quality description	N/A
Emotional description	By personalising the system according to their needs, the older person feels that it is integrated in their life and under their control.

Figure 26. Motivational Scenario – I'm in touch

Scenario name	I'm in touch
Scenario description	The older person periodically uses the system to keep in touch with their carers. The older person interacts with the system to indicate that everything is fine. When the carer receives notification from the system contacts the older person for a more personalised and human exchange.
Quality description	The keep in touch mechanism must be designed in such way that is part of the older person daily routine.
Emotional description	The older person wants to feel cared about, independent and in touch. The carer/relative wants to feel reassured. By using the functionality of getting in touch the carer/relative and the older person want to feel unburdened of the responsibility of routinely contacting each other.

Figure 27. Motivational Scenario – Call help

Scenario name	Call help
Scenario description	The older person raises an alarm as a response to an emergency situation. The alarm monitor receives the distress signal and contacts the older person's carers. The carers provide help to the older person. The alarm can be cancelled by the older person if it was accidentally initiated.
Quality description	The alarm trigger must be mobile to adapt to the older person movement. The alarm monitor must be active 24/7 and react immediately to alarms.
Emotional description	The older person wants to feel safe, independent and cared about.

Figure 28. Scenario – Provide technology-supported care

Scenario			1				
Functional goal			Provide technology-supported care				
Quality goal			Accessible				
			Invisible to others				
			Responsive				
			Flexible				
			Fit lifestyle				
			Part of routine				
			Immediate				
			Mobile				
			Reliable				
Emotional goal			Reassured				
			Cared about				
			Safe				
			Independent				
			In touch				
			Unburdened				
			Integrated				
			In control				
Initiator			Carer/Relative				
Trigger			The carer/relative suggests the older person the use of technology-supported care.				
Condition		Step	Activity	Roles	Resources	Quality goals	Emotional goals
Sequential	Interleaved, repeat	1	Introduction of the technology-supported care system in the older person's home.	Older Person, Carer/Relative, Service Provider, Technician	In-touch activator, Emergency call activator	N/A	Integrated, In control
		2	The older person uses the system to get in touch with the carer/relative.	Older Person, Carer/Relative, In-touch Monitor	In-touch activator	Part of routine	Reassured, Cared about, Independent, In touch, In control, Unburdened
	Optional	3	The older person calls help in case of emergency.	Older Person, Alarm Monitor	Emergency call activator	Immediate, Mobile, Reliable	Safe, Cared about, Independent, In control

Figure 29. Scenario – Introduce emergency alarm system

Scenario		2				
Functional goal		Introduce emergency alarm system				
Quality goal		-				
Emotional goal		Integrated				
		In control				
Initiator		Carer/Relative				
Trigger		The carer/relative is concerned about the older person's wellbeing.				
Condition	Step	Activity	Roles	Resources	Quality goals	Emotional goals
Sequential	1	The carer/relative suggests the older person getting an emergency alarm system.	Carer/Relative	-	-	-
	2	The older person agrees to the suggestion of getting the system.	Older Person	-	-	-
	3	The carer/relative requests the service provider the introduction of the system.	Carer/Relative	-	-	-
	4	The service provider accepts the request.	Service Provider	-	-	-
	5	The service provider asks the technician to install the system at the older person's home taking into account the technical constrains.	Service Provider	-	-	-
	6	The technician studies the older person's home to determine the best technical solution.	Technician	-	-	-
	7	The technician installs the system.	Technician	In-touch activator, Emergency call activator	-	-
	8	The technician reports back to the service provider.	Technician	-	-	-
	9	The service provider asks the older person their preferences to personalise the emergency alarm system.	Service Provider	-	-	-
	10	The older person gives the service provider their preferred contact times to get in touch.	Older Person	-	-	Integrated, In control
	11	The older person gives the service provider the list of their emergency contacts.	Older Person	-	-	In control
	12	The service provider uses the older person's preference to personalise the system.	Service Provider	-	-	-
	13	The service provider explains the older person how to operate the system.	Service Provider	-	-	-

Figure 30. Scenario A – I'm in touch

Scenario			3a				
Functional goal			I'm in touch				
Quality goal			Accessible				
			Invisible to others				
			Responsive				
			Flexible				
			Fit lifestyle				
			Part of routine				
Emotional goal			Reassured				
			Cared about				
			Independent				
			In touch				
			Unburdened				
			In control				
Initiator			Older Person				
Trigger			It is time for the older person to get in touch with their carer/relative.				
Condition		Step	Activity	Roles	Resources	Quality goals	Emotional goals
Repeat	Sequential	1	The older person operates the in-touch activator to signal that everything is okay.	Older Person	In-touch activator	Accessible, Invisible to others, Flexible, Fit lifestyle	In control, Independent
		2	The in-touch monitor detects that the older person has initiated communication and informs the older person that this action has been registered and a response is being processed.	In-touch Monitor	-	Responsive	-
		3	The in-touch monitor informs the carer/relative that the older person has established communication.	In-touch Monitor	-	-	Reassured
		4	The carer/relative establishes a dialog with the older person to confirm that everything is going well.	Carer/Relative, Older Person	-	-	Cared about, In touch, Unburdened

Figure 31. Scenario B – I'm in touch

Scenario		3b				
Functional goal		I'm in touch				
Quality goal		Accessible				
		Invisible to others				
		Responsive				
		Flexible				
		Fit lifestyle				
		Part of routine				
Emotional goal		Reassured				
		Cared about				
		In touch				
		Unburdened				
Initiator		Older Person				
Trigger		The older person forgets to get in touch with the carer/relative during the established period.				
Condition	Step	Activity	Roles	Resources	Quality goals	Emotional goals
Sequential	1	The in-touch monitor detects that the older person did not get in touch within the established period.	In-touch Monitor	-	-	-
	2	The in-touch monitor asks the older person whether everything is okay.	In-touch Monitor	-	-	-
	3	The older person confirms that everything is fine.	Older Person	In-touch activator	Accessible, Invisible to others, Flexible, Fit lifestyle	-
	4	The in-touch monitor informs the older person that the communication with the carer/relative is being prepared.	In-touch Monitor	-	Responsive	-
	5	The in-touch monitor informs the carer/relative that there is an established communication with the older person.	In-touch Monitor	-	-	Reassured
	6	The carer/relative establishes a dialog with the older person to confirm that everything is going well.	Carer/Relative, Older Person	-	-	Cared about, In touch, Unburdened

Figure 32. Scenario C – I'm in touch

Scenario		3c				
Functional goal		I'm in touch				
Quality goal		-				
Emotional goal		-				
Initiator		In-touch Monitor				
Trigger		The older person is unwell and cannot get in touch with the carer/relative during the established period.				
Condition	Step	Activity	Roles	Resources	Quality goals	Emotional goals
Sequential	1	The in-touch monitor detects that the older person did not get in touch within the established period.	In-touch Monitor	-	-	-
	2	The in-touch monitor asks the older person whether everything is okay.	In-touch Monitor	-	-	-
	3	The in-touch monitor does not get a response from the older person.	In-touch Monitor	-	-	-
	4	The in-touch monitor informs the carer/relative that the older person failed to establish communication.	In-touch Monitor	-	-	-
	5	The carer/relative establishes a communication with the older person to check whether everything is okay.	Carer/Relative	-	-	-
	6	The older person confirms that they need help.	Older Person	-	-	-
	7	The carer/relative provides help.	Carer/Relative	-	-	-

Figure 33. Scenario A – Call Help

Scenario		4a				
Functional goal		Call help				
Quality goal		Immediate				
		Mobile				
		Reliable				
Emotional goal		Cared about				
		Safe				
Initiator		Older Person				
Trigger		The older person is alone at home and needs help.				
Condition	Step	Activity	Roles	Resources	Quality goals	Emotional goals
Sequential	1	The older person operates the emergency call activator.	Older Person	Emergency call activator	Mobile	-
	2	The alarm monitor notifies the older person that help is coming.	Alarm Monitor	-	Immediate, Reliable, Responsive	Cared about, Safe
	3	The older person confirms that everything is fine.	Older Person	In-touch activator	Accessible, Invisible to others, Flexible, Fit lifestyle	-
	4	The carer/relative establishes a communication with the older person to confirm that they need help.	Carer/Relative	-	-	-
	5	The older person confirms that they need help.	Older Person	-	-	-
	6	The carer/relative provides help.	Carer/Relative	-	-	-

Figure 34. Scenario B – Call Help

Scenario		4b				
Functional goal		Call help				
Quality goal		Immediate				
		Mobile				
		Reliable				
Emotional goal		Independent				
		In Control				
Initiator		Older Person				
Trigger		The older person is alone at home and everything is okay.				
Condition	Step	Activity	Roles	Resources	Quality goals	Emotional goals
Sequential	1	The older person accidentally operates the emergency call activator.	Older Person	Emergency call activator	Mobile	-
	2	The alarm monitor notifies the older person that help is coming.	Alarm Monitor	-	Immediate, Reliable, Responsive	Cared about, Safe
	3	The older person realises that the emergency call has been made accidentally and cancels it.	Older Person	-	-	Independent, In Control
	4	The alarm monitor confirms the older person that the emergency procedure has been cancelled.	Alarm Monitor	-	Responsive	-

Section 4
Personalized Learning Environments and the People–Oriented Programming Paradigm

We saw in Section 1 that a lot of the exciting developments in POP are in new programming environments for coding, and these coding environments are often much more than programming editors. Several of them including Scratch and Greenfoot, are prime examples of learning environments with large communities of likeminded people. In the recent book Lifelong Kindergarten: Cultivating Creativity through Projects, Passion, Peers, and Play the author and the prime-mover behind Scratch, Mitchel Resnick, outlines his reasons for being a strong advocate for teaching all young people to become fluent in coding: "Most people won't grow up to become professional programmers or computer scientists, but learning to code fluently is valuable for everyone. Becoming fluent, whether with writing or coding, helps you to develop your thinking, develop your voice, and develop your identity." While coding is only one aspect of learning in the modern school curriculum, there is considerable scope for coding activities and computational thinking in many other subjects that make up a comprehensive curriculum. For these reasons we include two chapters on Personalized Learning Environments (PLE) in this volume.

Chapter 11

Intertwining E–Learning Technologies and Pedagogies at the System Design Stage:
To Support Personalized Learning

Georg Weichhart
Johannes Kepler University, Austria

Chris Stary
Johannes Kepler University, Austria

ABSTRACT

Although a large number of e-learning systems for individual learning support exist today, many of them still deal with pedagogical issues in an isolated way. In contrast, intertwining interactive system features with educational concepts allows pedagogical designs that may be considered according to their educational rationale. However, pedagogical approaches also do not provide requirements for technologies; they rather consider tools and features as predefined design parameters. Taking an interoperability point of view allows focus on the interaction between the pedagogical and the technological systems. By interpreting technology and didactic approaches as systems and ensuring their interoperability, educators are able to adapt learning experiences and technological features in a way that the overall learning system becomes personalized. A key element of the described work is an architecture that captures the design elements from both progressive education focusing on individual learning support, and the enabling web-based e-learning technologies.

DOI: 10.4018/978-1-5225-5969-6.ch011

INTRODUCTION

Today, e-learning systems are developed to support the independent and individual acquisition of knowledge (Friedman & Deek, 2003). Individual and group learning processes may be facilitated through dedicated e-learning designs and implementations (Aqda, Hamidi & Ghorbandordinejad, 2011, Auinger & Stary, 2005). This includes didactic designs according to pedagogical objectives, as well as technological designs. However, recent research reveals a gap between the feature-oriented approach to e-learning software development, and education viewing technology as a black box (cf. Casanova, Moreira & Costa, 2011).

Designing and developing an e-learning system requires a team of developers that is not only capable of producing software, but needs to "be aware of process of curriculum development, technical pedagogical knowledge, (TPCK), content knowledge, the place for designing and delivering the course, the learners." (Assareh & Hosseini Bidokht 2011, p.792). Although a large number of different pedagogical approaches have been developed so far, educators still need to acquire know how on software development to design a learning support system that grounds technological features on reflected didactic instruments (cf. Anderson, 2004, Pan et al., 2010). In the following an approach to bridge conceptual gaps between technology developers and educators is developed for designing individual learning support systems in a mutually informed way. It is based on identifying interoperable components that may be arranged according to certain situational contexts and designer needs.

Interoperability focuses on the interface and interaction between two and more independent systems that together form a larger system (Naudet et al., 2010; Guédria & Naudet, 2014). Although these system elements are not dependent on each other, all elements contribute to a greater common functionality of the larger system. Integrated systems, in contrast to interoperable systems, have a functional dependence, where the entire system fails as soon as a single element fails. Hence, in an integrated system the sub-systems are not independent. Interoperable systems are contrary to compatible systems, as these latter types of systems do not interfere with each other and therefore do not contribute to some higher larger system functionality or goal (Panetto, 2007).

In order to support the structured implementation of pedagogical approaches in e-learning, explicit representations of didactically valid designs and software features allow for transparent mutual relationships. While multiple approaches exist for the representation of such systems, to reach our objectives an approach providing an overview of modules and interfaces on both levels, the e-learning/ pedagogy level and the software technology level, is required. We make use of an Enterprise Architecture language, as it promotes a layered and contextual perspective on usage- and stakeholder-relevant processes supported by software technologies.

ArchiMate (www.archimate.org; Iacob et al. 2012; Jonkers and Proper, 2009) allows the modelling of an abstract architecture pinpointing essential system parts and their relationships, including their refinement from domain or business structures to system functions to be executed by IT. Moreover, ArchiMate allows inclusion of interoperability aspects (Guédria et al. 2013).

In the following sections we introduce an interoperability model that has been designed to support educators in the structured and context-aware development of web-based, personalized e-learning systems. The approach is based on interoperable design elements that encode progressive education concepts for informed personalization. First, we give definitions of core concepts used throughout this paper. This section is followed by a discussion of State-of-the-Art features and systems for technology-supported learning. Then, we review recent architectures of Learning Content Management Systems (LCMS) and reveal their limitations taking into account pedagogical systems and design elements. After elaborating the requirements from the pedagogical perspective, we show various degrees of support, ranging from integrated to compatible systems, and exemplify their design benefit for a specific pedagogical approach. It is based on building systems, and using these systems for creating content according to educational principles, such as finally exemplified for a selected pedagogical approach to personalized learning.

CONCEPTS

In this part we address all core concepts relevant to this contribution. First, we elaborate on the specific type of socio-technical system under consideration, as it constitutes the universe of discourse. These explanations are followed by a brief conceptualization of interoperability, as it is a key element to the system approach in our work.

Learning Environments as Socio-Technical Systems

The system addressed in this article is a socio-technical system. Teachers are responsible for providing a learning environment (technical system) that supports students in their acquisition of knowledge. The technical system is not constrained to computer support - it includes all (constructed) tools to achieve that objective.

Applying constructivism to learning (Glasersfeld 1989) shows that students actively construct their own knowledge. This knowledge is a subjective mental model. Objective "wisdom" is not simply handed over by teachers using books (Dewey 1938).

Several educationalists have designed approaches which suite the core constructivist principles and additionally provide practical ideas and means on how to design and implement learning environments, putting emphasis on enabling individual acquisition processes of students. The selected approaches have been developed before the theory of constructivism has been developed and are labelled "progressive education".

Within each selected progressive education approach, technical instruments have been developed according to certain pedagogical principles, in order to meet the intention of the educational objectives. In this category of approaches a well-known example, is Maria Montessori (Lillard 2007, Montessori 1917), who designed learning materials that allow students to individually master knowledge acquisition by using graspable materials according to given rules.

Besides cognitive dimensions, learning has a social aspect, where students are observing, socializing with, and imitate behaviour of peers (Bandura, 1976). Again, progressive education has explicitly emphasised elements in the design of learning environments that facilitate this kind of learning. In this view the technical learning system is only part of a larger learning environment. It will not determine the learning results, but the technical system aims at enabling students and teachers to reach their goals with respect to knowledge acquisition by supporting the active acquisition process[1].

In some cases, independently of existing didactical designs for learning environments, technology has been created to support self-driven knowledge acquisition in groups. Modern web-based technologies have provided facilities for students to adapt their tools and in this way, the process of learning, too (Hadjerrouit, 2005). Recent empirical findings indicate that the trend emphasising self-regulation in e-learning environments will continue (Eichelberger and Laner, 2010).

Interoperability of Systems

Along the dimension of interoperability there is a continuum between two extremes. In the following list the first and the last element do not comply with the concept of interoperability.

- **Integrated Systems (not Interoperable):** The systems functionally depend on each other. Once one of the systems fails, the overall system fails.
- **Integrated Interoperable Systems:** The systems share the same meta-model. While remaining independent systems, the syntax and semantics of the exchanged information are well defined and may be exchanged seamlessly.
- **Unified Interoperable Systems:** Here an abstract layer is introduced in the communication. Referring to elements on that layer requires abstracting from

individual details. However, the individual systems are free to modify their own syntax or semantics as long as it is possible to relate information to the abstraction layer commonly agreed upon.

- **Federated Interoperable Systems:** This is the loosest interoperable approach. It allows, but at the same time also requires, negotiating in an ad-hoc manner with respect to exchanged information syntax and semantics.
- **Compatible but not Interoperable Systems:** Compatible systems exist next to each other, but no meaningful information is exchanged between them. These systems do not interfere with each other. However, it is not possible to provide greater functionality through a meaningful combination of the individual system's functions.

E-Learning Systems

Technologies and services for supporting learning have matured to a stage in which e-learning has become a mainstream activity (Hung, 2012). Currently, the support of learning with technologies is researched from multiple scientific domains, ranging from social science disciplines like psychology, and pedagogy, to technical disciplines like software engineering and artificial intelligence. The user's perspective to technology-supported learning has been researched from different domains like medicine, engineering education, mathematics education and many others.

Consequently, different views on e-learning can be taken, and multiple definitions of the term e-learning exist. In the context of this paper we consider e-learning systems as "web-based learning" and "digitally delivered content with services" (cf. Assareh & Hosseini Bidokht, 2011; Hung, 2012; Yau, Lam & Cheung 2009). Two extreme approaches to these types of e-learning systems exist. With the first approach, independently developed Web 2.0 tools, such as blogs, wikis, chat rooms and video streaming are used in web-based learning settings (Yau, Lam & Cheung 2009; Alario-Hoyos et al., 2013). The second approach is to make use of, or create an, integrated learning (content) management system (Khalid, Basharat, Shahid & Hassan, 2009).

Focusing on digital content delivery, e-learning systems can have the capability to support the management of learning content (Khalid et al., 2009). These types of systems provide a tight integration of features for authoring, content navigation and course management. A large number of systems of this type exist, exhibiting the benefit of having an integrated tool-set. However, the effort to integrate (and maintain the integration of) third party tools developed in separate and isolated projects is high. Therefore supporting another pedagogy beyond that initially designed for, is not a straightforward task, if not impossible.

The approach of using existing tools provides the opportunity for learners and teachers to make use of software they know and allows them to deliberately choose tools depending on the situation and personal preferences. However, this freedom comes at the cost of managing multiple accounts per user. More important, these tools are agnostic to any pedagogic activity, and thus cannot be easily tuned to meet pedagogical objectives (Alario-Hoyos et al., 2013).

Although pedagogically-driven approaches exist, their embodiment requires a flexible and open software architecture, enabling software developers to implement (separate) pedagogical modules representing the various educational approaches.

E-Learning System Architectures

In this section we show that existing architectures do not tackle either the interface to a pedagogical model nor provide an explicit architecture for interoperability, and accordingly, do not allow elaboration on how to interface a pedagogical model, except for Intelligent Tutoring Systems. The following sub sections are based on a literature search for existing contributions containing 'e-learning' and 'architecture' in title, abstract, or keywords.

Knowledge Based E-Learning Architectures

An e-learning architecture striving for knowledge innovation with a strong focus on project-based learning has been proposed in (Zahn & Chengyang, 2008). In particular it makes use of a collaborative learning environment which allows learners to solve real problems and generate new knowledge through collaboration in projects. It uses AJAX (Asynchronous JavaScript and XML (Leonard, 2010)) for dynamically updating relevant parts of the user interface in the users' browser. A knowledge processing layer identifies whether created information is new knowledge or not. The knowledge is accessed and stored through a knowledge access layer in a knowledge base, a project and task base, and a resource base. This architecture focuses on the creation of knowledge and only provides limited possibilities outside of the collaboration in a project scope. It is not detailed how this architecture handles content, course management tasks, a.t.l., nor how pedagogic approaches could be integrated.

Another e-learning architecture focusing on knowledge engineering technologies is FekLoma (Li et al., 2009). It makes use of Semantic Web technologies like OWL (Web Ontology Language) for enhancing the use and re-use of Learning Objects. Learning Objects are packaged information for (re-)use when learning. A well-known standard for Learning Objects is SCORM (Sharable Content Object Reference Model) (ADL 2012). The ROLE project combines cloud services and ontologies for allowing self-organized learners to personalize content and navigation re-using learning objects provided by cloud services (Mikroyannidis, Lefrere & Scott, 2010). Supporting self-organized learners includes the possibility to flexibly adapt the user interface to the learner's computer skills (Nagasaki & Nagasaki, 2007).

For the knowledge based e-learning architectures focusing on Learning Objects' re-use, it has not been detailed how to implement a course following a particular didactic approach. It is assumed that the learning objects' meta-data together with the ontologies contain sufficient information for enabling the assembly of learning objects according to a specific pedagogy. So far, transferring pedagogical concepts into Learning Objects has not been addressed.

Intelligent Agent-Based E-Learning Architectures

An architecture based on standard web-services and intelligent agents has been proposed in (Hussain & Kahn, 2005). The intelligent agents help students and teachers to find required information. On the client side of the distributed infrastructure, these agents may be configured to suit the needs of different devices. These agents make use of SOAP (Simple Object Access Protocol) message calls to web service-based agents on the server side. These server side agents describe their functionality using standard WSDL (Web Services Description Language) files. Making use of agents allows this architecture to also provide information for users when offline. The server side agents make use of educational services which are published in an UDDI (Universal Description, Discovery and Integration) registry. These educational services may provide Learning Forums, SCORM compliant Learning Object Repositories, Virtual Classrooms, among others. A similar architecture is described by (Wei & Yan, 2009). It additionally includes a content delivery service where content agents deliver content to the students. Both architectures allow, through the use of agent technology, to integrate other services at a later time.

A Multi Agent System (MAS) where agents make use of intelligent Blackboards has also been researched (Hammami, Mathkour & Al-Mosallam, 2009). The goal of this architecture is to facilitate learning through the use of intelligent agents' adaptability and intelligence features. An interface MAS interacts with the users. A learning MAS is responsible for the learning process. An authoring MAS supports authors in providing content. An interaction MAS supervises the interaction between the different agents. The system has been enhanced through the use of web-services and an ontology service to provide a distributed infrastructure which is used by agents to search for learning resources (Al Muhaideb, Hammami & Mathkour, 2010).

For each of the above described agent-based systems, it has not been detailed how the agents are prepared, for example, how the data used by the pedagogic agent to reason over pedagogical issues (like the next activity a learner should do) is provided.

Workflow-Based E-Learning Architectures

In order to support the activities of learners a workflow based e-learning architecture has been proposed in (Weining, Junzhou & Tiantian, 2005). A learning path is a designed workflow of learning activities by students and teachers. Services are used to provide Learning Objects (LO) which in turn may be reused. These LO Services are the lowest layer of the workflow-based learning architecture WELA (Weining, Junzhou & Tiantian, 2005). The next layer is composed of a PathGenerator tool which enables the creation of a BPEL workflow course template, where the users specify explicitly the required LOs, which are retrieved from a Service Registry. These workflows are published through a registry, whereby they can be found by students. A standard Workflow Engine is used to execute the BPEL workflows.

From the description provided, it cannot be determined how elements of the architecture support teachers in providing pedagogical knowledge.

Modular Web 2.0-Based Architectures

The E-School System Architecture (Pandit et al., 2010) follows the Model View Controller Paradigm. It incorporates different layers for presentation, common services (e.g. authorization), e-learning specific services and the database layer. Across these layers different modules are provided: Information Management System, E-Learning System, Test and Assignment Management System, and Result Management System. The description of the architecture provides requirements for each module. However, each module is discussed in an isolated fashion and the points of interaction between the modules remain unclear. Missing here is a dedicated component w.r.t. pedagogy, as the e-learning system only provides access to course material and personal notes, and provides means for interaction between users (like discussion forums and blogs).

Intelligent Tutoring Systems

Intelligent Tutoring Systems (ITSs) as computer-based instruction tools attempt to provide individualized instructions based on the learner's educational status. Recent development frameworks recognize the value of explicitly representing and mapping various categories of knowledge to specifications (cf. Badaracco et al., 2011, Wenger, 2014). From an architecture perspective computer-based instructional systems require components:

1. To collect information about a learner's learning status
2. To utilize this information to adapt the instruction to meet the learner's needs

3.   To predict learner behaviour (cf. Latham et al., 2012).

Although there is no standard architecture for Intelligent Tutoring Systems, several logical components are common to many ITS architectures (cf. Butz et al., 2006). They are mutually related, with the communication module providing a direct interface to the learner:

- The expert model is intended to capture knowledge about the learning domain. It should process learner data, in order to rate potential misconceptions and provide proper explanations.
- Student models record learner behaviour information as the learner interacts with the ITS. Each activity is logged, referring to affected content, learning steps, and the degree of understanding.
- The pedagogical module has the objective of implementing instruction methods. When kept independently, the format of instruction using an ITS can be completely changed through using another pedagogical model. This module is connected with the expert and student model, as it needs domain structures for content preparation and presentation, and activities from learners.
- The communication module is required for content presentation and the capture of learning data in the course of interacting with the ITS.

For implementation, a layered, 3-tier architecture has turned out to be effective. It is based on the user interface on top of a middle layer, termed the core, on top of a knowledge base (cf. Gonzalez-Sanchez et al., 2011 p3ff):

- 'The knowledge base (KB) includes data structures and databases responsible for putting into the computer system the information instructed by the ITS. The process of putting data in KB is called "authoring". Authoring involves a human expert interacting with an authoring tool to provide this knowledge.'
- The 'user interface includes graphical interfaces (windows, buttons, text and so on) and interaction mechanisms (from simple keyboard events to more complex interfaces, such as motion capture, voice recognition, brain-computer interface and so on).'
- The 'core implements ITS behavior. While Knowledge Bases and User Interfaces are highly different from one ITS to another, the behavior of all of them is quite similar and the next components can be identified: (1) Task Selector provides a Task (problem or activity) the student must solve; (2) a Tool or Environment presents the information that the student must know to complete the activity; (3) Step Analyzer methodically examines and measures

the performance of the student and provides that information to the Assessor and the Pedagogical module; (4) Pedagogical Module provides support (hints and feedback) to make the student successfully complete the task; (5) Assessor learns from the student (how many hints he needed, how skilled was in the topic, how much time he used to go from one step to another in order to solve the task, etc.) and then stores this information in what is called a Learner Model.'

Oulhaci et al. (2013) have proposed a multi-agent architecture for ITSs maintaining didactic aspects and enriching it with serious gaming and evaluation functionality. Hereby, a simulation function based on a multi-agent system simulates the behaviour of the scenario's non-playing actors. The evaluation function is based on interacting agents taking care of data sources (e.g., missions), indicators to compute or to select the appropriate information for learner evaluation, and other evaluation using these indicators. The results are fed into the pedagogical module which represents a virtual tutor accompanying the learner when using the ITS. Recent work in this context, e.g., Gross et al., (2013) emphasize the domain-independence of ITS, complementing the aforementioned didactic independence achieved in varying the format of instructing learners.

Conclusive Summary

A prerequisite for successful and effective implementation of e-learning systems is careful consideration of underlying pedagogy. However, incorporating pedagogical approaches during the development of web-based educational systems today remains an issue. (Zardas 2008, p 884)

For the above analysed architectures it can be concluded that their focus is on software features rather than pedagogical interfaces. For some approaches it remains open whether they show interoperability with pedagogical concepts at all.

Progressive Education

Constructivist learning approaches and progressive education approaches seem (*per se*) well suited for e-learning (Aqda, Hamidi & Ghorbandordinejad, 2011; Auinger & Stary, 2005; Weichhart 2014). Both theories focus on the individual learner and the individual and group learning processes (see above). Learning systems designed according to these theories put emphasis on instruments that make the individual processes transparent and also facilitate communications between all participants of the learning processes.

Approaches

In order to understand pedagogical interfaces, we have analyzed several approaches which are classified as progressive educational approaches. The approaches have been selected based on the knowledge and experiences the authors gained through theory and practical application of the didactical designs.

Approaches that conform to constructivist learning principles, first of all, have to encourage active learning and support active learners (Aqda, Hamidi & Ghorbandordinejad, 2011). In constructivist learning and progressive education, knowledge is created through interaction in groups of collaborating, self-organized learners who solve complex problems (Stary & Weichhart, 2012). Teachers provide a positive learning environment and are facilitators and not controllers of the individual learning processes.

An e-learning system is part of a positive socio-technological learning system. The technology has to support the following general progressive educational requirements, in order to be interoperable with the approaches described in the following (Stary & Weichhart, 2012; Eichelberger et al., 2008):

- Focus on the individual learning styles of the student
- Have a prepared, motivating learning system
- Emphasize self-organized, social learning

These three properties make progressive education well suited for e-learning support, as students in distance education are under no direct supervision, but have to be self-organised in their work. E-learning technology is facilitating individual approaches to knowledge acquisition (Auinger & Stary, 2005).

We have examined several progressive educational approaches. The basis of our analysis included: general introductions (e.g. Skiera 2003), special literature (e.g. Eichelberger et al. 2008), and practical experiences in the application of progressive education (e.g. Stary 2009, Stary and Weichhart 2012, Weichhart 2012).

For representing the core elements of each approach, we have used Concept Maps following the mapping approach of Novak and Cañas (Novak & Cañas 2008). This mapping process has been developed to support the externalisation of knowledge. It depicts individual mental models. Each map consists of two elements "concepts" and "propositions". A concept is visualised as a labelled rectangle. Here a concept is a subjective system element which might be represented using more than one word. A proposition is visualised as "concept linking-phrase concept". While for the construction of the maps a process is described by Novak and Cañas (Novak & Cañas 2008), neither linking-phrases nor concepts are restricted to predefined categories.

The following Concept Maps are conceptualisations of different progressive education approaches.

Maria Montessori has developed one of the most well-known progressive education approaches. One cornerstone of her pedagogy is the physical learning materials that have been developed (Lillard 2007, Montessori 1917). These materials may be used by the students at any time, as students work self-organized in Montessori classes. Classes are composed of students at different ages, and older members may teach younger ones in the usage of the material. Emphasis is placed on structure and order in the learning system.

John Dewey was an American Philosopher, who puts emphasis on educating children using democratic principles, and educating them to acquire experimental, self-organized learning capabilities which allow them (later) to support the development of the overall society (Dewey, 1938).

Helen Parkhurst was an US-American Teacher who appreciated Montessori and Dewey. She developed an approach that allows a teacher to guide students. The developed pedagogy is centred on two instruments, which allow the provision of guidance and progress monitoring. Assignments do not provide the details on how to solve a task but rather scaffolds (Parkhurst 1923, 2010). The progress of the

Figure 1. Conceptualisation of Montessori's pedagogy

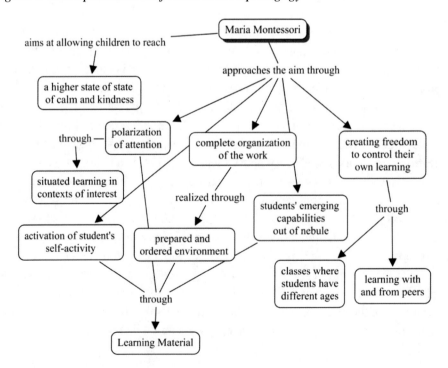

Figure 2. Conceptualisation of Dewey's pedagogy

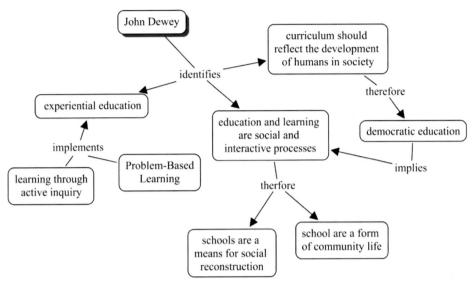

students along these scaffolds is monitored. In addition, group work and cooperation are of crucial importance.

Célestin Freinet also made use of assignments. However, in this pedagogy assignments are written by students themselves (Skiera 2003). The class counsel (composed of students) is responsible for setting learning goals. Of importance to the realization of these goals are ateliers which allow students to work and learn self-organized. Ateliers (rooms prepared for particular types of tasks) provide the organizational and areal frame for self-organized learning. Results are documented in texts which are printed using a manual printing press. The published texts document the learning process and are also used to communicate with students from other Freinet schools.

The pedagogy developed by Martin Wagenschein emphasizes the creation of significant examples. The challenge is to identify the important core of a topic and use examples to transfer the core ideas (Eichelberger 2003).

Peter Petersen aimed at transforming schools, while relying on core elements of the above approaches. He considered schools as social systems where pupils live.

Rudolf Steiner's Waldorf principles have a wider range than the above mentioned pedagogies (Kiersch 2007). His contributions include school architecture and health theories in addition to child development theories. Emphasis is put here on a friendly, organic system, allowing individual children to develop on the basis of their own free will.

Figure 3. Conceptualisation of Parkhurst's pedagogy

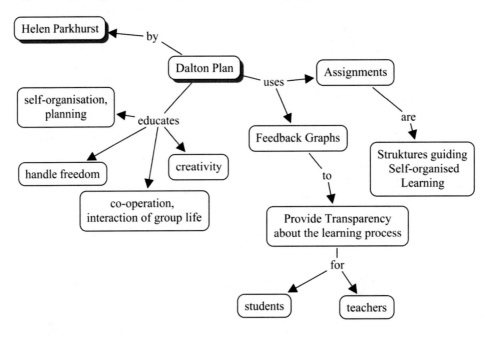

Figure 4. Conceptualisation of Freinet's pedagogy

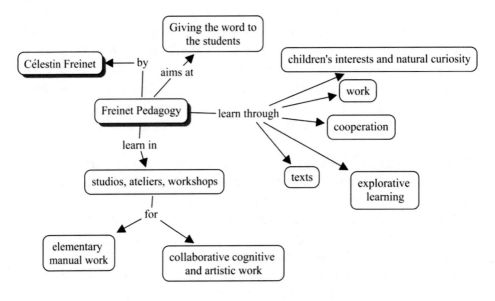

Figure 5. Conceptualisation of Wagenschein's pedagogy

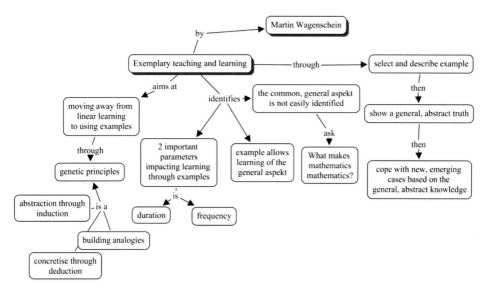

Figure 6. Conceptualisation of Petersen's pedagogy

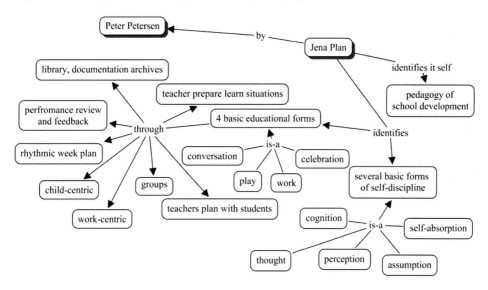

Figure 7. Conceptualisation of Steiner's pedagogy

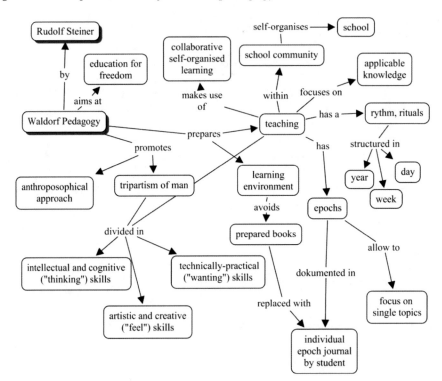

INFORMED REQUIREMENTS SPECIFICATION

In the following we combine parts of the above concept maps of the individual pedagogies, to provide an aggregated view on progressive education. In order to allow the identification of the source the concepts and links, these have different styles where every educationalist has a unique form, line, shadow, etc. as shown in the following figure. Concepts having a rectangular shape represent the core concept of the particular map.

First, the aims and objectives of the approaches above are identified and put together in the following map (Figure 9). Giving individual students the freedom to self-control their learning is a prominent aim of progressive education. The school's organization reflects society and allows students at least to influence the learning goals.

The following two maps (Figures 10 & 11) show educational principles used in order to develop a certain set of skills and capabilities.

Figure 8. Coding of educationalists

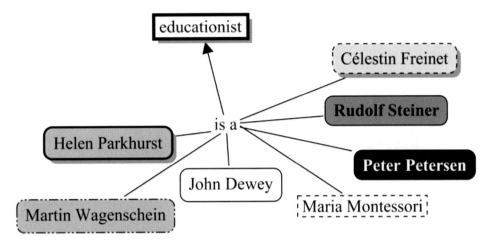

Figure 9. Aims of progressive education

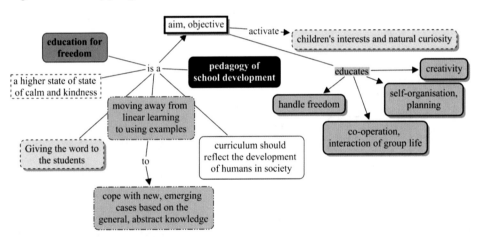

The analysed approaches require students to handle the freedom in a responsible manner. They are not free to do what they want, but need actively to explore problems. The required problem-solving capabilities include analytical thinking, creativity, practical abilities, and social capabilities, since learning occurs in groups.

Finally, the individual approaches are analysed for their requirements on the learning system. The learning system here includes the organization of schools. The following concept map (Figure 12) shows the concepts a learning environment needs to provide in facilitating the learning processes according to the above mentioned principles, and in order to reach the initially listed goals.

Figure 10. Educational principles

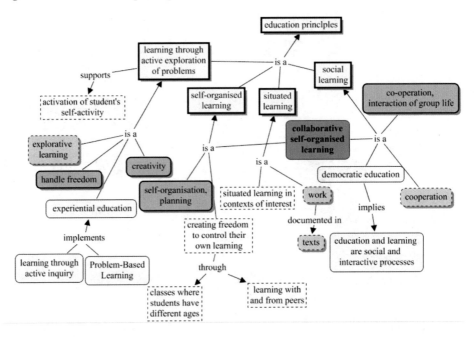

Figure 11. Skills and capabilities developed

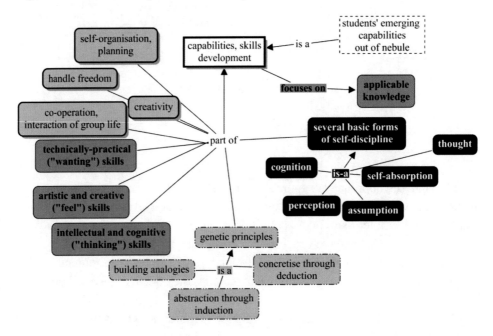

Figure 12. Prepared Progressive Education Learning System

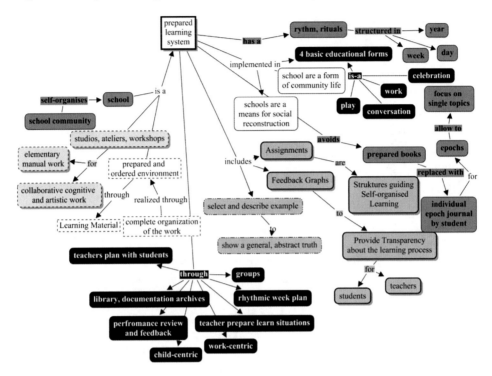

SUPPORTING INTEROPERABILITY OF PROGRESSIVE EDUCATION AND E-LEARNING SYSTEMS

In this section we first present a conceptual design of the overall learning system. We make use of an enterprise architecture language. Enterprise Architectures separate the end-user system and the technical system. By doing so, the interfaces between different sub-systems are identified and clarified. The second part of this section initially presents the concept of interoperability before giving three examples on how pedagogy and technology could work together. In these examples the pedagogical and the technological subsystem are modified to various degrees, effort, and effect.

Model of the Overall Learning System

For the discussion of the system and the social and technological sub-systems, we use the ArchiMate language. ArchiMate (Iacob et al. 2012; Jonkers and Proper, 2009) is an Enterprise Architecture (EA) diagrammatic language, which consists of three interlinked layers as discussed below. This EA language is designed to give an overview on the interplay between the social system and the technical system. It captures user and process aspects in the business layer and technical aspects in the software layer. We make use of this approach as it allows discussion of software features without detailing them, while showing software support services that meet requirements from the pedagogical and user points of view. Finally, the software architecture allows us to organise the pedagogical concepts from a more technical point of view.

The symbols used for diagrammatic representation are shown in Table 1.

The technological infrastructure layer additionally consists of a network and multiple devices.

Figure 13 shows the process of creating a software architecture from the pedagogical concepts identified above. As such it is only of temporary interest and aims at highlighting the areas which are affected by different pedagogical concepts. For clarity Figure 14 shows just the result of this process.

The *Services* on the *Business Layer* are concepts from the "Aims of Progressive Education" concept map above. The *functions* and *processes* concepts originate from the concept map entitled "Learning Principles". All *objects on the application layer* stem from concepts of the "Learning Environment" concept map.

- **User Roles, Processes (Top Layer, Yellow):** This Layer shows Users, Roles and (Business) Services provided by the Organization. These Services are realized through (Business) Functions and Processes. This layer shows the services (denoted as boxes with round left/right sides) provided by students and teachers. In order to implement these services, several functions (rectangular shapes with an upwards directed arrow) and processes (rectangular shapes with horizontal arrow) are needed. Software services are used to provide the required functionality.

Table 1. Core Concepts ArchiMate (Iacob et al. 2012)

ArchiMate Symbols	Semantics
	... Services are the "functional interface" to the next higher level.
	... Role of a User
	... Processes describe behaviour as a coordinated series of activities
	... Functions describe behaviour
	... Software Component that provides one or more software services
	... Data Structure used to handle and store Information

- **Software Application, Modules, Data (Middle Layer, Light Blue):** The Software application shown on this layer provides (Software) Services (ellipses) to support the business processes and functions. Software Services access Data Structures (rectangles with a dark blue bar on top) and are provided through Software Components/Modules (rectangles with 2 smaller rectangles on the left side). The software requires an existing infrastructure to be executed.
- **Technical Infrastructure (Bottom Layer, Green):** The bottom Layer is the technical infrastructure required to make the application work. In this concrete case we only represent the existence of a network of connected devices.

In the following we focus on the interface between the business and software layer. Here the technology meets the users, in order to support the user's learning process. For making use of a software feature in a concrete learning situation, sub-systems have to be adapted. Either the pedagogy has to be adjusted to make use

Figure 13. Creating a software architecture from pedagogical requirements

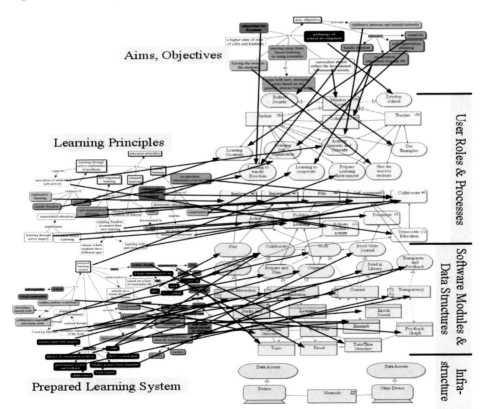

Figure 14. System elements relevant for Pedagogical Technologies in Progressive Education

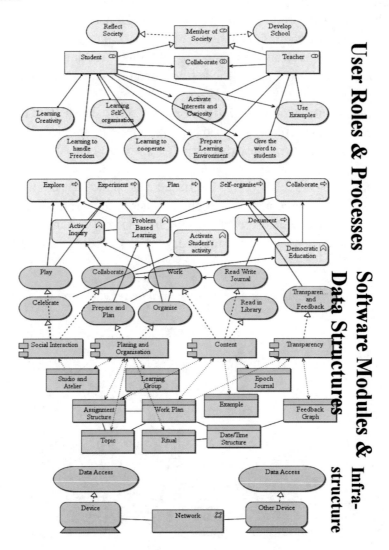

of software, or the software has to be tuned to support the pedagogy. It might be required to adapt both, the social and the technical system.

Interoperability in E-Learning

According to the above described understanding of interoperability, we now describe three cases of e-learning systems where the pedagogy and the technological system have been adjusted to be interoperable to various degrees.

We demonstrate this using the ideas developed by Helen Parkhurst in her Dalton Plan (Parkhurst 1923, 2010). The Dalton Plan makes use of two instruments: *Assignments* and *Feedbackgraphs.* Assignments according to the Dalton Plan are detailed forms that provide a motivation and a description of concrete goals. Assignments require that the process of documentation is given, but not a detailed description of how a solution is to be found. The Dalton Plan is rather clear in its aims requiring students to have a high degree of freedom for organising their work in order to meet the objectives given explicitly in the assignments. The feedback graphs are drawn lines on a form sheet by teacher and students, making the knowledge acquisition progress of students explicit. When students complete a learning tasks, they discuss matters with teacher and peers. The teacher notes the progress on the graph form. In this way both the teacher and the students understand who has made progress where, and how much is missing to complete the assignment.

This paragraph above captures the pure pedagogical point of view. We make use of this concept in the following three sub-sections to demonstrate the realisation of interoperable e-learning support involving the pedagogical & social system and the technological system (i.e. the "e" and the "learning" part of e-learning).

Integrated E-Learning (Sub-)Systems

The integrated support is implemented as a Dalton Plan module in an existing e-learning system. The process of gathering pedagogical requirements, transferring these into technical design elements and then implementing the features in order to realise an e-learning platform that integrated the Dalton Plan instruments has been described elsewhere (Weichhart 2014). Yet it is important to understand that the effort of understanding pedagogical requirements and transferring these into technical requirements has been considerable. The process has taken roughly 1.5 person years. For the implementation of the module (without the learning environment) 6.963 lines of code have been produced. The overall lines-of-code for the e-learning system (called nymphaea) is 190.862. The module therefore provides 3.6% of the overall system. The module reuses as much as possible of the existing code and approaches. The implemented functions are accompanied with existing communication support through bulletin boards and conferences.

Support is focusing on the teacher's point of view. Figure 15 shows the Assignment Editor (mainly for teachers) embedded in the web 2.0 learning environment.

Figure 15 shows the nymphaea assignment editor, allowing the user to provide content for all parts given by Dalton Plan assignments. The editor has a button bar providing features with drop down boxes for selecting and navigating the environment and assignments below these (1). Part (2) of the view shows content for which the assignment is created. This part of the view may be resized or hidden. It supports

Figure 15. Integrating the pedagogical system in a technical system (Weichhart, 2014)

teachers in reflecting given content and e.g. to synchronise wording between assignment and content. Part (3) of the view is the on-line form for the Dalton Plan assignment. It is followed by a view part that shows discussion forums for the given lecture, used to replace face to face meetings (4). Part (5) is a search area to access existing assignments.

Figure 16 shows two screen-shots of a particular assignment from the students' perspective. This is content-wise a "read-only" perspective. However, the e-learning system allows students to highlight part of the text using a virtual marker. The marked text is placed on a virtual notes layer (like a transparency / overhead slide). Students may additionally leave textual comments on this notes layer. This notes layer may be shared by a group of students and discussed in the forum. It may also be kept private for individual learning purposes.

Following the Parkhurst pedagogical model, the integrated e-learning system nymphaea also provides feedback graphs shown in the following Figure 17.

The change of the learning system, from a mainly social system with limited "technological" support using paper-based feedback graphs, to a learning support system which has a social and a larger technical sub-system, required several (minor)

Figure 16. Student view of assignment on mobile device (left) and on the desktop (right)

Figure 17. Feedback-graphs nymphaea (Weichhart, 2014)

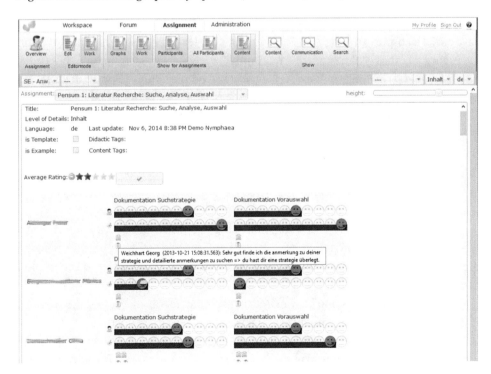

justifications for the pedagogy. In the original version of the Dalton Plan teacher and student met personally to discuss matters and produce a line on the graph form sheet. In the web 2.0 version of the feedback graphs, interaction is asynchronous. In the above figure for each student the upper graph shows the student's self-assessment and the lower part shows the teacher's assessment of the student's work. In addition, as mentioned above, the usage of the bulletin sections and the conferences sections has been transferred to digital counterparts.

The specific nature of the above presented implementation required major software implementation effort. This is not only true for writing the software for the Dalton Plan module, but also when functionality is to be reused, or new functionality is required, namely for a different pedagogical approach. The targeting of a specific pedagogical approach, with the aim of supporting it in a most effective manner, hinders straightforward reuse of the developed components.

Interoperable E-Learning

In the following a technical system is described, which also aims at supporting the Dalton Plan pedagogy. However, instead of developing software that provides specific features supporting the creation and use of the Dalton Plan instruments, a state of the art web-portal has been customised. The portal is based on Liferay[2], a Java based web-portal framework. This particular e-learning system is named aeolion.

Figure 18 shows the student "read-only" view of an assignment. Since it is based on a generic content management system, no particular learning features are available. However, support for mobile devices is available out of the box.

From a teachers' perspective, there is a need for an editor to support authoring of assignments, and such a tool does not exist upfront. Assignments are created using the given Rich-Text (HTML) editor. Each section of the Dalton Plan is a paragraph in the Text. Linking the bulletin or a conference section can be achieved by using "generic" http-links copy & pasting these from the forum area to the content area (see Figure 19).

The usage of assignments for students using aeolion does not vary significantly from the nymphaea approach. However, as there is no specific support for teachers preparing the assignments available, the task of authoring is harder to accomplish because of the generic nature of the tools.

With respect to the second Dalton Plan instrument, feedback graphs, the situation is more difficult as there is no direct generic corresponding functionality to create feedback graphs. However, the content management system allows polls to be conducted. This allows a partial realisation of feedback-graphs. Self-assessments are implemented using the polling module. Students answer on a 5 point Likert scale, a question concerning the perceived state of their work.

Figure 18. Assignments in aeolion on a mobile device (left) and on the desktop (right)

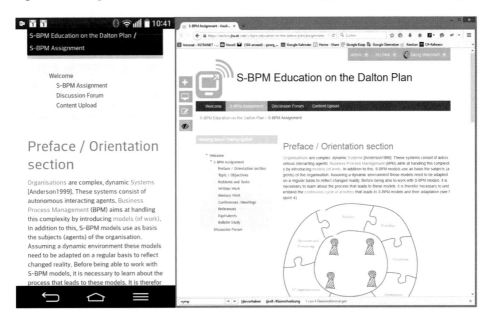

Figure 20 shows such self-assessment results. In contrast to the tailored and integrated system, the results are ordered along the score. The bar graph shows how many students have chosen a particular answer with respect to assessing the quality of their work.

Below the bar chart, the result for each student is visible. However, no direct (visual) comparison with the teacher's assessment (again in contrast to the integrated system) is possible.

There is no additional effort for coding Dalton Plan support, as standard components provided by a generic content management are used. The estimated effort for administrating and configuring the e-learning environment is roughly equal. The teachers' effort in using the interoperable system (aeolion) is higher compared to the integrated system (nymphaea) which provides concrete and targeted support for the specific pedagogical approach.

With respect to transferring an e-learning system support from one pedagogic approach to another, the effort is also different when contrasting a system with integrated pedagogics to a system made interoperable to a pedagogical approach. To reach the same level of support, the integrated system needs to be implemented based on the available features. Depending on the differences between the approaches this effort may sum up to a new implementation from scratch of all relevant features. With respect to the interoperable approach and the "limited" support for a particular

Figure 19. Editing assignments in aeolion

pedagogical approach, this effort is (by definition) low. It sums up to configuration of the e-learning system and aligning needs with existing functionality.

Compatible Systems

Interoperability research discusses multiple qualities of the degree of interoperability between systems (Naudet et al. 2010). The degree ranges from integrated over interoperable to compatible. In this category of interoperability multiple systems co-exist. They do not show particular interaction, and do not disturb each other.

Above we have contrasted two e-learning system approaches. In the integrated case we have shown a specific implementation integrating the Dalton Plan pedagogics. In the interoperable case, we have shown a standard content management system customised to provide as much support as possible for the Dalton Plan pedagogics. In the following we consider existing, cloud-based technical systems, which may

Figure 20. Self-assessments in aeolion

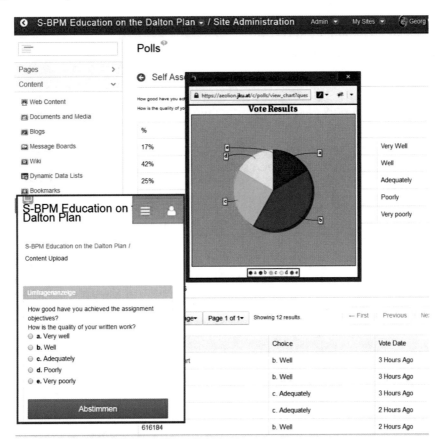

be used for e-learning, but which cannot even be configured and have to be used as provided.

When using existing technical systems like twitter, google docs and the like, no implementation, or configuration is required, as these systems are provided in the cloud. However, users have to be registered with accounts for all used tools. This may involve privacy issues.

While the technical effort is reduced, much of the preparation burden is shifted to teachers. Teachers have to understand and evaluate the provided functionality of multiple systems. Based on their understanding of the pedagogical approach, one or more (technical) systems need to be selected to achieve the technical support. For instance, J. Hart has conducted a survey and compiled a list of the top 100 technological systems supporting learning ranging from online tools over videos to offline software (http://c4lpt.co.uk/top100tools/; Hart, 2014). In the 2014 ranking the top 5 tools are:

- Twitter (twitter.com)
- Google Drive (drive.google.com)
- YouTube (youtube.com)
- PowerPoint (Microsoft.com)
- Google search (google.com)

Found down at only place #12 was moodle (a classic widely used platform, see: moodle.org) as the highest ranked e-learning system.

A teacher's deep pedagogical understanding and technical creativity is required for effective use of existing tools. For instance, feedback graphs could be implemented using google docs' spreadsheet implementation. Links between a google hangout and google docs could be established through copying / pasting hypertext links. Alternatively, in the specific case of the Dalton Plan, the comment feature is helpful for facilitating communication in a group of students.

It is the teacher's responsibility to find a good mix of tools that support the pedagogical system. Figure 21 shows a Dalton Plan assignment "realised" in google docs. Figure 22 shows a comment to the right and a dialog for linking to another hypertext page, on a mobile device.

Figure 21. Editing and commenting on assignments in google docs

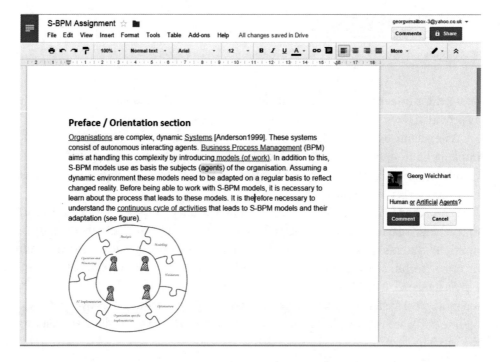

Figure 22. Mobile Device interface to assignments in google docs including a comment (right)

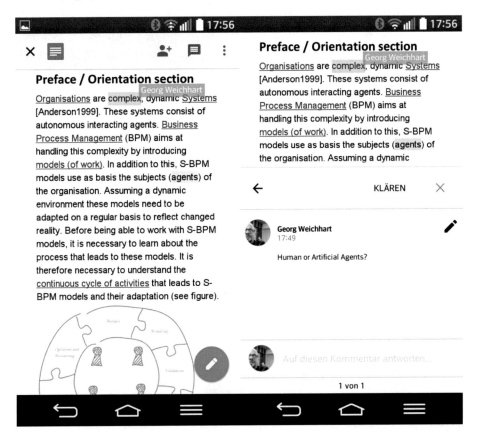

Regular, automated updates or changed privacy policies will have an impact on the course and eventually the pedagogy. In the worst case scenario a "show-stopping" update (with an essential feature missing/broken) will be (automatically) installed in the middle of a course. The teacher is no longer in control of this part of the learning environment.

CONCLUSION

With the advent of social and semantic technologies the design space of e-learning environments can be continuously enriched. However, existing architectures are still focused on technological features rather than interfaces or interoperability concepts to make educational principles work in line with the technical system.

We have analysed several approaches from progressive education supporting personalized learning processes, in order to understand in which cases technological support by e-learning systems is feasible and useful. Based on a general understanding of progressive education, its aims, principles and requirements for a correspondingly adjusted learning environment, we have developed and demonstrated three approaches to designing and implementing the technical system. In order to demonstrate the pros and cons of approaches ranging from integrated over interoperable to compatible architectures, we have shown the various degrees of support for a specific pedagogical system.

For tailoring the overall socio-technical learning system to make use of different pedagogical approaches supported by technology, the approach of creating an interoperable learning system (aeolion in this case) is the most promising. It consists of a generic technical system, adapted to the pedagogics. However, for meeting the demands of the pedagogical system, the supporting technical system needs to be flexible and adjustable to allow a customised configuration interoperable with the pedagogy. Implementations are kept to a minimum which impacts the degree of support for the teachers and students.

In contrast to the targeted, but most effective integrated approach, the interoperable approach is more flexible. In contrast to the compatible approach of using pre-existing tools with no a-priory customisation to meet pedagogical requirements, it reduces the teacher's effort considerably. The mere provision of software shifts the overall burden to the teacher, inflating their overall effort.

The research shown here provides a generic "systems to systems" perspective. This point of view serves as a basis for further research on a method to provide a structured way for linking a pedagogical system to a technical system.

ACKNOWLEDGMENT

The research leading to these results has received funding from the European Commission within the Marie Curie Industry and Academia Partnerships and Pathways (IAPP) programme under grant agreement No 286083. For more information on the IANES project see http://www.ianes.eu.

REFERENCES

ADL. (2012). *Sharable Content Object Reference Model (SCORM)*. Retrieved from http://www.adlnet.org

Al Muhaideb, S., Hammami, S., & Mathkour, H. (2010). Towards a Distributed Architecture for Adaptive E-Learning System. *Int. Conf. On Advanced Learning Technologies*, 632-636. 10.1109/ICALT.2010.180

Alario-Hoyos, C., Bote-Lorenzo, M. L., Gómez-Sánchez, M. L., Asensio-Pérez, J. I., Vega-Gorgojo, G., & Ruiz-Calleja, A. (2013). GLUE! An architecture for the integration of external tools in Virtual Learning Environments. *Computer Education*, *60*(1), 122–137. doi:10.1016/j.compedu.2012.08.010

Anderson, J. (2005). IT, E-Learning and Teacher Development. *International Education Journal*, *5*(5), 1–14.

Aqda, M. F., Hamidi, F., & Ghorbandordinejad, G. (2011). The impact of constructivist and cognitive distance instructional design on the learner's creativity. *Procedia Computer Science*, *3*, 260–265. doi:10.1016/j.procs.2010.12.044

Assareh, A., & Hosseini Bidokht, M. (2011). Barriers to e-teaching and e-learning. *Procedia Computer Science*, *3*, 791–795. doi:10.1016/j.procs.2010.12.129

Auinger, A., & Stary, C. (2005). Didaktikgeleiteter Wissenstransfer - Interaktive Informationsräume für Lern-Gemeinschaften im Web Deutscher Universitäts-Verlag. GWV Fachverlage GmbH.

Badaracco, M., & Martínez, L. (2013). A fuzzy linguistic algorithm for adaptive test in Intelligent Tutoring System based on competences. *Expert Systems with Applications*, *40*(8), 3073–3086. doi:10.1016/j.eswa.2012.12.023

Bandura, A. (1976). *Social Learning Theory*. Englewood Cliffs, NJ: Prentice Hall.

Beetham, H. (2005). e-Learning research: Emerging issues? *Research in Learning Technology*, *13*(1). doi:10.3402/rlt.v13i1.10976

Butz, B. P., Duarte, M., & Miller, S. M. (2006). An Intelligent Tutoring System for Circuit Analysis. *IEEE Transactions on Education*, *49*(2), 216–223. doi:10.1109/TE.2006.872407

Casanova, D., Moreira, A., & Costa, N. (2011). Technology Enhanced Learning in Higher Education: Results from the design of a quality evaluation framework. *Procedia: Social and Behavioral Sciences*, *29*, 893–902. doi:10.1016/j.sbspro.2011.11.319

Dewey, J. (1938). Experience and Education. *Touchstone (Nashville, Tenn.)*.

Eichelberger, H., & Laner, C. (2010). *Unterrichtsentwicklung via eLearning*. München: Oldenbourg. doi:10.1524/9783486704754

Eichelberger, H., Laner, C., Kohlberg, W. D., Stary, E., & Stary, C. (2008). *Reformpädagogik goes E-Learning – neue Wege zur Selbstbestimmung von virtuellem Wissenstransfer und individualisiertem Wissenserwerb*. Oldebourg.

Fisher, P. T., & Murphy, B. D. (2010). *Spring Persistence with Hibernate*. Apress. doi:10.1007/978-1-4302-2633-8

Friedman, R. S., & Deek, F. P. (2003). Innovation and Education in the Digital Age: Reconciling the Roles of Pedagogy, Technology, and the Business of Learning. *IEEE Transactions on Engineering Management*, *50*(4), 403–412. doi:10.1109/TEM.2003.819650

Gonzalez-Sanchez, J., Chavez-Echeagaray, M. E., Vanlehn, K., & Burleson, W. (2011). From behavioral description to a pattern-based model for intelligent tutoring systems. In *Proceedings of the 18th Conference on Pattern Languages of Programs* (paper 26). ACM. 10.1145/2578903.2579164

Gross, S., Mokbel, B., Hammer, B., & Pinkwart, N. (2013). Towards a domain-independent its middleware architecture. In *13th International Conference on Advanced Learning Technologies (ICALT)*. IEEE.

Guédria, W., Gaaloul, K., Naudet, Y., & Proper, H. (2013). A Modelling Approach to Support Enterprise Architecture Interoperability. In Y. T. Demey & H. Panetto (Eds.), *OTM 2013 Workshops, LNCS 8186* (pp. 189–198). Heidelberg, Germany: Springer Berlin. doi:10.1007/978-3-642-41033-8_27

Guédria, W., & Naudet, Y. (2014). Extending the ontology of enterprise interoperability (ooei) using enterprise-as-system concepts. In *Enterprise Interoperability VI. Proceedings of the I-ESA Conferences* (*vol. 7*, pp. 393–403). Springer International Publishing Switzerland. 10.1007/978-3-319-04948-9_33

Hadjerrouit, S. (2005). Learner-Centered Web-based Instruction in Software Engineering. *IEEE Transactions on Education*, *48*(1), 99–104. doi:10.1109/TE.2004.832871

Hammami, S., Mathkour, H., & Al-Mosallam, E. A. (2009). A multi-agent architecture for adaptive E-learning systems using a blackboard agent. *Int. Conf. On Computer Science and Information Technology*, 184-188 10.1109/ICCSIT.2009.5234741

Hart, J. (2015). *2014 Top 100 Tools for Learning*. Available at http://c4lpt.co.uk/top100tools/

Hung, J. (2012). Trends of e-learning research from 2000 to 2008: Use of text mining and bibliometrics. *British Journal of Educational Technology*, *43*(1), 5–16. doi:10.1111/j.1467-8535.2010.01144.x

Hussain, N., & Kahn, M. K. (2005). Service-Oriented E-Learning Architecture Using Web Service-Based Intelligent Agents. *Int. Conf. On Information and Communication Technologies*, 137-143. 10.1109/ICICT.2005.1598570

Iacob, M., Jonkers, H., Lankhorst, M., Proper, H., & Quartel, D. (2012). *ArchiMate 2.0 Specification*. The Open Group.

Jonkers, H., & Proper, H. A. (2009). *TOGAF and ArchiMate: A Future Together*. White Paper W192. The Open Group.

Khalid, S. U., Basharat, A., Shahid, A. A., & Hassan, S. (2009). An adaptive E-learning Framework to supporting new ways of teaching and learning. *Int. Conf. On Information and Communication Technologies*, 300-306. 10.1109/ICICT.2009.5267175

Kiersch, J. (2007). *Die Waldorfpädagogik*. Verlag Freies Geistesleben.

Latham, A., Crockett, K., McLean, D., & Edmonds, B. (2012). A conversational intelligent tutoring system to automatically predict learning styles. *Computers & Education*, *59*(1), 95–109. doi:10.1016/j.compedu.2011.11.001

Leonard, A. (2010). *JSF 2.0 Cookbook: Over 100 simple but incredibly effective recipes for taking control of your JSF applications*. Packt Publishing Ltd.

Li, Y., Chen, Z., Huang, R., & Cheng, X. (2009). New e-Learning system architecture based on knowledge engineering technology. *IEEE Int. Conf. On Systems, Man and Cybernetics*, 5140-5144. 10.1109/ICSMC.2009.5346013

Lillard, A. S. (2007). *Montessori – The Science behind the Genius*. Oxford Press.

Mikroyannidis, A., Lefrere, P., & Scott, P. (2010). An Architecture for Layering and Integration of Learning Ontologies, Applied to Personal Learning Environments and Cloud Learning Environments. *Int. Conf. on Advanced Learning Technologies*, 92-93. 10.1109/ICALT.2010.33

Montessori, M. (1917). *The advanced Montessori method - The Montessori Elementary Material*. Frederick A. Stokes Company.

Nagasaki, H., & Nagasaki, M. (2007). A system architecture model for web-based adaptive e-learning systems. *Proceedings of the 14th European conference on Cognitive ergonomics: Invent! Explore!* 129-132. 10.1145/1362550.1362576

Naudet, Y., Latour, T., Guédria, W., & Chen, D. (2010). Towards a systemic formalisation of interoperability. *Computers in Industry*, *61*(2), 176–185. doi:10.1016/j.compind.2009.10.014

Novak, J. D., & Cañas, A. J. (2008). *The Theory Underlying Concept Maps and How to Construct and Use Them*. Retrieved from http://cmap.ihmc.us/Publications/ResearchPapers/TheoryUnderlyingConceptMaps.pdf

Oulhaci, M. H. A., Tranvouez, E., Espinasse, B., & Fournier, S. (2013). Intelligent Tutoring Systems and Serious Game for Crisis Management: A Multi-agents Integration Architecture. In *22nd International Workshop on Enabling Technologies: Infrastructure for Collaborative Enterprises (WETICE)*. IEEE. 10.1109/WETICE.2013.78

Pädagogisches Institut f. d. deutsche Sprachgruppe. (2015). Retrieved from http://blikk.it

Pan, N., Lau, H., & Lai, W. (2010). Sharing e-Learning Innovation across Disciplines: An Encounter between Engineering and Teacher Education. *Electronic Journal of e-Learning, 8*(1), 31-40.

Pandit, S., Acharya, H., Sanvedi, A., Nahar, P., Soni, S. K., Saxena, P., & Ramani, A. K. (2010). An architecture solution for E-Learning System ESSA. *Int. Conf. On Technology for Education*, 56-62.

Panetto, H. (2007). Towards a classification framework for interoperability of enterprise applications. *International Journal of Computer Integrated Manufacturing, 20*(8), 727–740.

Parkhurst, H. (2010). *Education On The Dalton Plan*. Nabu Press. (original publication 1923)

Simuth, J., & Sarmany-Schuller, I. (2012). Principles for e-pedagogy. *Procedia: Social and Behavioral Sciences, 46*, 4454–4456. doi:10.1016/j.sbspro.2012.06.274

Skiera, E. (2003). Reformpädagogik in Geschichte und Gegenwart: Eine kritische Einführung, R. *Oldenburg Verlag, 2003*, 514.

Stary, C. (2009). The Design of e-Learning Contracts: Intelligibility Catchers in praxis. *IEEE/WIC/ACM International Joint Conferences on Web Intelligence and Intelligent Agent Technologies, WI-IAT '09, 3*, 203-206. 10.1109/WI-IAT.2009.263

Stary, C., & Weichhart, G. (2012). An e-Learning Approach To Informed Problem Solving. *Knowledge Management & E-Learning International Journal (Toronto, Ont.), 4*, 195–216.

von Glasersfeld, E. (1989). Constructivism in Education. In T. Husen & T. N. Postlethwaite (Eds.), *The International Encyclopedia of Education* (Vol. 1, pp. 162–163). Oxford, UK: Pergamon Press.

Walls, C. (2008). *Spring im Einsatz.* Hanser.

Wei, X., & Yan, J. (2009). An E-learning System Architecture Based on Web Services and Intelligent Agents. *Int. Conf. On Hybrid Intelligent Systems*, 173-177. 10.1109/HIS.2009.147

Weichhart, G. (2012). *S-BPM Education on the Dalton Plan: An E-Learning Approach.* S-BPM ONE – Education and Industrial Development.

Weichhart, G. (2013). The Learning Environment as a Chaotic and Complex Adaptive System. *Systems, 1*(1), 36-53. Available at: http://www.systems-journal. eu/article/view/130/138

Weichhart, G. (2014a). *Der Dalton Plan im E-Learning: Transformation einer Reformpädagogik ins Web.* Trauner Verlag.

Weichhart, G. (2014b). Learning for Sustainable Organisational Interoperability. *Proceedings of the 19th IFAC World Congress, International Federation of Automation and Control (IFAC).*

Weining, K., Junzhou, L., & Tiantian, Z. (2005). A workflow based e-learning architecture in service environment. *Int. Conf. On Computer and Information Technology*, 1026-1032. 10.1109/CIT.2005.56

Wenger, E. (2014). *Artificial intelligence and tutoring systems: computational and cognitive approaches to the communication of knowledge.* San Francisco: Morgan Kaufmann.

Yau, J., Lam, J., & Cheung, K. S. (2009). A review of e-Learning Platforms in the Age of e-Learning 2.0. *Hybrid Learning and Education, Lectur Notes in Computer Science, 5685*, 208–217. doi:10.1007/978-3-642-03697-2_20

Zahn, Q., & Chengyang, C. (2008). A Study of E-Learning Architecture Based on Knowledge Innovation. *Int. Conf. On Computer Science and Software Engineering*, 781-784.

Zarandi, M. H. F., Khademian, M., Minaei-Bidgoli, B., & Türkşen, I. B. (2012). A Fuzzy Expert System Architecture for Intelligent Tutoring Systems: A Cognitive Mapping Approach. *Journal of Intelligent Learning Systems and Applications, 4*(1), 29–40. doi:10.4236/jilsa.2012.41003

Zardas, G. (2008). The Importance of integrating Learning Theories and Pedagogical Principles in AHES (Adaptive Hypermedia Educational Systems). *Int. Conf. On Advanced Learning Technologies.* 10.1109/ICALT.2008.204

ENDNOTES

[1]   See also http://blikk.it/blikk/angebote/reformpaedagogik/rp10030.htm for information, however, mainly in German but also in English (Pädagogisches Institut f.d. deutsche Sprachgruppe 2015).

[2]   www.liferay.org

Chapter 12
Merging Social Networking With Learning Systems to Form New Personalized Learning Environments (PLE)

Steve Goschnick
Swinburne University of Technology, Australia

ABSTRACT

The future of learning environments lies with the merging of the better aspects of learning management systems (LMS), with those popularized in social networking platforms, to personalize the individual learning experience in a PLE (personal learning environment). After examining the details of a particularly flexible LMS, followed by the investigation of several key data structures behind the Facebook social networking platform, this chapter demonstrates how such a merging can be done at the conceptual schema level, and presents a list of novel features that it then enables.

INTRODUCTION

This paper investigates the fusion of *social networking* capabilities with those from a fine-grained Learning Management System (LMS), into a *personalised learning environment* (PLE), described largely in terms of a design expressed as a conceptual schema. The social network platform investigated is Facebook, which perhaps surprisingly, has several of the necessary generic structures already in place, should that company choose to pursue the emerging personalised learning environment

DOI: 10.4018/978-1-5225-5969-6.ch012

marketplace. However, an LMS could equally be evolved, taking on some aspects popularised by social networking platforms, in new ways that personalise a learner's experience.

Some General Background

In situating the research in this chapter it is first worth noting that learning systems have advanced in parallel with similar strides in learning theory, and those in ICT (Information Communication Technology) in general. Although they are interrelated, we concentrate here on the technology side, with brief reference to some theory in learning, only when it is useful to the main research direction. We are primarily concerned with personalised learning environments (PLEs) – which are predicated on putting the student into a more central and active role in their own learning, both with regard to the design of learning materials, and the learning path or trajectory they take in using them. Such an underlying basis of PLEs makes them both more personalised and more adaptive than the typical LMS (Learning Management Systems – such as WebCT, Blackboard and Moodle, and many lesser-known platforms) that thousands of universities and schools have used for up to a decade now.

Tsolis et al (2011) state that '*A traditional LMS offers to all its users the same services and content, meaning that all learners taking an LMS-based course, regardless of their knowledge, goals and interests, receive access to the same educational content and the same set of tools, with no further personalized support.*' Some envisage PLEs as an approach that will replace (or at least speed-up the evolution of) the LMS (Downes, 2010; Trolis et al, 2011). According to Downes: '*the typical LMS is static, declarative, authority-based*' whereas '*a personal learning environment is learning through community; a PLE is a technological tool that allows us to do (that)*'. According to Trolis et al: they are '*extending the capabilities of a traditional open source LMS (Moodle), into (their) proposed OWLearn system … an adaptive, personalized and open source e-Learning system*' – yet that paper is little more than a wish-list of the features they want to see realised in it, with little in the way of design or specification toward achieving it. Others see a merging of PLEs and LMS into something new beyond either (Mott, 2010). According to Mott: '*the LMS has become a symbol of the status quo that supports administrative functions more effectively than teaching and learning activities*'; and that '*PLEs offer an alternative ...but with their own limitations*' including security and reliability. Mott believes the two approaches should and can be mashed up into '*open learning networks*'. Mott presents a good comparison of the strengths and weaknesses of both the LMS and the PLE, as he sees them.

The concept of a PLE preceded the arrival of well-endowed tools to demonstrate it, and as such there is some variation around the edges of what a PLE is, or should be. Attwell (2007) believed that the tools were already available. He believed that the software applications many people use regularly, together with the services they call upon, could be aggregated to enact a PLE just by changing the mindset of both students and teachers toward personalised learning. His example application tools included: the word processor, Keynote (for presentations), Net Newsreader, Garage Band (for podcasts) and iMovie (for video editing). While his example range of existing services that could be folded in included: Skype, Delicio-us (for sharing bookmarks), Flickr (for sharing photos), and Joomla (for creating web sites). '*It was not a software application, instead it was more of a new approach to using technologies for learning... by the net-generation*'.

Downes (2005) was happy with the blogging tools of the day – e.g. Blogger and WordPress – but he saw a further need for some automation in the way that these *page islands* of output by creative, active learners could be interrelated. Initially, the RSS aggregator (of newsfeeds from blogs in RSS format) was Downes' early answer to that automation, in what Mott called '*the PLE (is) the educational manifestation of the webs "small pieces loosely joined"*' - incorporating a quote from Dave Winer, the inventor of RSS.

Some researchers took that early optimism about available tools and services, and put it upon their 'net-gen' students to '*put students in a more central position in the learning process by allowing them to design their own learning environment*' (Valtonen et al, 2012). They embedded this in the running of actual vocational courses in Finland, across a range of disciplines. Valtonen et al asked themselves '*what kinds of personal learning environments would (the) students produce*'. The feedback was mixed, with many students expressing the negative impact of the learning of the tools needed, against what they actually needed to learn in their respective subjects (i.e. catering services, international business, health care, computer science, engineering, massage therapy). Valtonen et al cite their experience in retrospect as '*romantic constructionism*'. One of their conclusions is that instead of focusing on technology '*the emphasis ought to be on the pedagogical demands of PLEs in education*', and interestingly, that '*with adequate pedagogical support from teachers, students can potentially make use of PLEs for learning and thus develop their metacognitive and self-regulative skills*'.

Beyond the use of mundane (everyday) software applications and existing services by net-gen learners to spontaneously create or *mashup* effective PLEs, the two other approaches advanced in the research thus far to achieve a PLE are: to evolve an existing LMS towards a PLE; or thirdly, to create a new PLE unrelated to any founding LMS. A fourth approach is considered in this chapter: to examine what would be necessary to evolve an existing social network platform into a PLE.

So, what features set a PLE apart from an LMS? Personalised learning includes both personalisation to suit the individual learner – this often requires a much more detailed profile than in a typical LMS, with tagging (i.e. assigning *keywords*) to highlight an individual's interests and also a similar set of tags to represent their existing knowledge. Personalisation includes adaptability of the learning materials presented, and also allows or empowers the student to be more pro-active in creating learning material themselves, often in a collaborative way with participating peers. The adaptability achieved through techniques such as tagging, can be manual or automated in some manner. Some automation of the personalisation and any automation of the adjustable learning content, added to a PLE beyond adjustments in a more manual manner, either by the student or the teacher, are also increasingly possible.

Within learning technologies, the now well-used traditional LMS are generally characterised with features that do *not* lend themselves well to personalisation and adaptability to individual learners, such that those taking such a route are on a difficult path to achieve their goal - unless the LMS has more flexibility than most, or the necessary changes are coming via the LMS vendor. The open source LMS, Moodle, gains some such flexibility by way of the open source approach to its licensing, allowing others to add plugins to it in the form of apps, a route that a number of the researchers of papers cited in this chapter, have taken or are in the process of taking. There are other LMSs that have considerable flexibility in their initial design, such as the one described in following section.

In a significant contrast to the Valtonen et al (2012) approach of putting the onus on 'net-gen' students to come-up with their own novel PLEs, Limongelli et al (2011) take the third approach to having a PLE: creating a new one from technologies unrelated to a traditional LMS. Adding to the contrast, they put emphasis on helping the *teachers role* (by adding some smarts via some automation) in providing a PLE experience to students. The basic technology they do call upon in the absence of an LMS, is the use of planner technology based on *Linear Temporal Logic* (Mayer et al, 2007) from AI, and the way they use it serves as a useful illustration in applying a formulaic approach to adaptive learning:

From the adaptive learning perspective, *Lecomps5* (their system) is for creating *learning paths* through a sequence of *Learning Objects* (LO) that have metadata added to each, which they then call *Learning Components* (LC). Their system allows for two types of such sequences: one where the sequencing is performed at the beginning (by the planning software), and the second, an adaptive step-by-step sequencing, following the student during their path through the graph of Learning Components. Both types use quizzes to fuel the decision points in the planning software. The metadata is added to the Learning Objects by the teacher and includes two sets of tags (either from formal ontologies, or else any other terms): concept prerequisites are set as a series of *Required Knowledge* (RK) tags – just identifiers representing a set of concepts; and the concepts-to-be-acquired as a series of

Acquired Knowledge (AK) tags. Each of those two series of tags represent a set of like *knowledge items* (*ki*).

As a learner moves through a course (a sequence of LCs), their Cognitive State (CS) is represented by a subset of *ki* from the pool of LCs (plus any ki's they had previously acquired as prerequisites relevant to the current course). The Lecomps5 system also provides for different learning styles (LS) of students (initially four styles: *intuitive-visual, intuitive-verbal, sensing-visual, sensing-verbal* – adapted from Felder & Silverman, 1988), by having four different versions of the LCs (specifically, variations of the instructional content within them). They then consider they have a relatively simple student model (SM): Cognitive State (CS) and the LS measure of the learner i.e. SM = CS + LS (Note: they allow the teacher to put weights against the four learning styles for the one student, as a vector that can be adjusted over time). A traditional LMS requires a significant amount of work on the part of the teacher to manually select and sequence the learning content and activities, so the Lecomps5 system is focused on lightening that load on the teacher considerably.

Their approach to adding smart technology into the learning process does put focus back on learning theory (which as already stated, is not the focus of this chapter). However, a learning framework by Luckin (2008) is specifically aimed at using technologies and other resources beyond the desktop, as a scaffold (meaning *tutorial assistance*) for learning. It is called *The Learner Centric Ecology of Resources*. It helps design learning experiences that matches up available resources to the needs of the learner. The underlying premise is that the learner needs to be in a collaborative environment, where a more abled participant can step in when need be, to occasionally guide the learner, who is otherwise advancing at their own pace. The aim of most smart learning technology is usually to be a part of that assistance, and/or facilitate it from other human participants. Luckin's framework sets about making that possible: *"For technology to provide software scaffolding the system needs a model of its learners"*. The PLE developed by Limongelli et al (2011), as we have seen, has a simple Learner model (SM), one that includes their knowledge state and learning style. However Luckin's approach is much more detailed and based on well-accepted learning theory.

The PLE developed by Limongelli et al (2011) is described by them as providing '*automated production and adaption of personalized courses*', but it has no features that enhance collaboration or that enables learners to author their own content, nor any use of social software to make up for those gaps in a PLE feature set. Nonetheless, they inform the reader that in another research effort they are integrating their approach with Moodle – presumably for its administrative and other functions, including the feature that allows it to have plugins from the community around that particular open source LMS.

In a strong sense, the focus and tool development on automating *teacher tasks* by Limongelli et al, and the focus of Valtonen et al (2012) upon the *learner tasks* with the tools at hand, are near the two extremes of the envelope of features and focus that a PLE can have. Our research is looking toward a good balance somewhere in the middle.

What Follows in This Chapter

In the next section describes in detail a pioneering online education content and delivery system developed at the University of Melbourne (by a company then wholly owned by the University) in 1997-98 which foreshadowed the presentation of learning objects we now see in iBooks on the Apple iPad. It was more flexible and adaptive than most mainstream LMSs then and now. As well as describing the Creator LMS, we look at key structures in that system which lend themselves to similar usage in a PLE. It was also early in employing 'smart' technology in an LMS, in the form of intelligent software agents, to seek out a certain form of specific data across the web – again, a technique and tool that could be much more broadly applied in a PLE future.

In the section *Conceptual Models from a Social Networking Platform* we look at structures underpinning the Facebook social network platform, from research that infers a *conceptual data model* from the textual programming API (Graph API V2.0) that Facebook makes available to third party developers. We do this with the aim of uncovering aspects of a social network platform that will add user-friendly proactive content creation features to a smart PLE, where a student may create, curate, participate and share such content with peers and friends, regardless of context, mobile or otherwise.

In Section 4 we draw from the models and experience presented in Sections 2 and 3, with a view to putting some combination of them together in the one PLE system, in particular with an emphasis on what would be needed to turn the existing Facebook conceptual model into a Personal Learning Environment (PLE), as one such future possibility.

TECHNICAL PARALLEL BETWEEN AN OLD AND A NEW LEARNING SYSTEM

What first sparked this research was an observation of a direct parallel in the technologies used to deliver online course material to the browser within an earlier pioneering educational content creation and management system, with a much more recent need to deliver personalised educational content to tablets and large-format smartphones such as Apple iOS devices. This new need requires high fidelity presentation and fine-grained delivery of educational content down to the page level, and even multiple learning objects on such a tablet displayed page. The earlier system was called Melbourne IT Creator and was briefly introduced in Goschnick (1998).

The *authoring* tools in the Creator platform were delivered in a technology open to *most* teachers, academics and other content creators, including students using the premier cross-platform language of that time (the Java language on the desktop). We chose HTML V4, CSS V1 and the JavaScript language to *deliver the content* to students using almost any computers available (all those with a web browser). The HTML mark-up code allowed broad student access via all the major web-browsers, while the then lesser known CSS V1 was used to place *learning objects* (any presentation/interactive technology that could be presented on the screen upon a rectangular sub-area) within the HTML rendered page, at an absolute location (x,y, width, height) in the browser window. This choice of underlying technology gave content developers WYSIWYG (what-you-see-is-what-you-get) delivery, which was deemed particularly important by our designers and multimedia artists. The JavaScript language was used to retrieve and manipulate server-side stored content, and create the needed CSS and HTML code to render it as intended.

When investigating the iPad much more recently as the target device for personalised, dynamically configurable content, the *Page* was once again seen as the fundamental unit of both design and delivery to the learner. The iBook format – itself based on EPUB3 (V3) – was identified as an attractive format for the purpose. For example, Adobe *InDesign,* a page mark-up tool used by many page design professionals, can output in the EPUB3 format, as can a number of open-source tools, which can in turn be directly imported into iBookstore on the iPad. A significant goal in the later project was to find a good balance between: professionally designed and built learning objects, and professionally designed page renditions that house those objects; or alternatively, end-user developer pages and media content, and a smart personalised system that can dynamically select the particularly learning-objects most applicable for the individual learners' (and their peers') current circumstance. EPUB3 is basically *HTML5* (with a formal index-page structure) – which is a term generally used interchangeably with three closely integrated standards used in the web browser, namely: *HTML V5* mark-up, *CSS V3*, and *JavaScript* (W3C, 2014) – i.e. these are simply later versions of the same three technologies used to deliver Creator content in the web-browser, 15+ years earlier. That being the case, the design and conceptual data model behind Creator lent itself to further investigation, as an eminently suitable one for storage and retrieval of learning-objects in a newly envisaged personalised learning environment (PLE).

Description and Conceptual Model of Creator

The earlier online education system presented in this section was called *Melbourne IT Creator* (Goschnick, ibid). It was the culmination of a research and development project from mid-1997 until mid-1998 in the company Melbourne IT Pty Ltd, then a wholly-owned subsidiary of the University of Melbourne. Note: The company was *floated* – the *IPO* initial public offering - on the ASX (Australian Stock Exchange) in the year 1999, raising some $90 million for the university.

Creator was an integrated system that provided an end-to-end solution to authoring, management and presentation of web-based online learning materials, in the genre of what now is the LMS. It had three primary functions:

- Content Authoring
- Content Storage and Management
- Content Presentation and Delivery

The central concept introduced in Creator was the *learning object*, of which there are two categories: *simple* and *complex* (composite in nature). Creator also defined a number of *views* of the overall system, as seen by users with distinctly different *roles,* to help users navigate what had become a large and sophisticated system.

Simple Learning Objects

Simple learning objects can be one of the following: Plain Text (paragraphs); Tables (HTML <table>); Images; Audio; Video; Interactive Animation (e.g. Flash, Shockwave); Programmed Component (Javabeans, Java Applet, Microsoft COM objects); Question (Simple True/False; Multiple Choice; Mutually-exclusive Choices; Matching (2D matrix of choices); or, Free text entry).

Composite Learning Objects

Composite (also called complex) learning objects can be one of the following:

- **Page:** A HTML page that may contain numerous and any combination of the simple learning objects above.
- **Reference Work:** A hierarchy of sequentially linked *Pages*.
- **Learning Activity:** A complex web of *Pages* linked in a non-linear sequence (a network graph), with conditional paths based on student choices and progress.

- **Document:** An externally authored document in one of various formats including MS/WORD, Adobe Acrobat (PDF), and RTF.

Figure 1 is a conceptual data model of the learning objects, and how they are inter-related within the unifying model. This logical model can be easily detailed further into the physical model of the server-side database, which stores the current state of a Creator-hosted online learning system in a Relational DBMS server, a type of system that later became known as a Web 2.0 approach (2005).

Note 1: Each of the main entities shaded in yellow in Figure 1 (REFERENCE_WORK, PAGE, LEARNING_ACTIVITY, QUESTION_OBJECT, KEYWORK/KEYWORK_LIST and RESOURCE_PALETTE) had a dedicated authoring tool written in the Java language. Figure 4 is an example of the interface of one of the authoring tools: the *Learning Activity Tool.*

Note 2: The entities shaded in grey are associative entities (which represent many-to-many relationships); those in light-blue are less-significant objects, such as icons and images, which do not need custom authoring tools; while those in white are simply less significant entities in the model, included for completeness.

Figure 1. Part 1 of the Conceptual Data Model that stores the Learning Objects in Creator

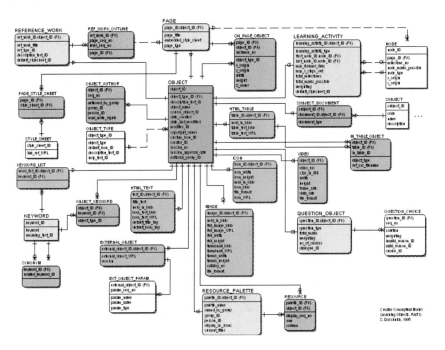

415

The Page as Fundamental Unit in Course Delivery

Early in the life of the project, a one-week discussion between many stakeholders took place, regarding the prominent place of *objects* in the design *versus* the prominent place of *pages* in the design – with effectively two sides of roughly equal numbers of stakeholders, leaning each way. (In a sense, it was parallel to the self-dialogue in Downes (2005), where he effectively dismisses the 'atoms' that are learning-objects in an LMS, structured together into activities, subjects and courses; but then he outlines his alternative vision of the web-page (in blogs, etc), similarly aggregated together into a loose structure, of more personally suited content via RSS aggregation). The resulting conceptual schema in Creator places both *Pages* and *Objects* in the design, with each holding a significant foundational position in the underlying structure: the OBJECT entity is a so-called *super-type* to the simple learning objects, such as IMAGE, VIDEO, HTML_TXT, HTML_TABLE, and others (shaded in aqua in Figure 1); while PAGE can appear in both REFERENCE_WORKs and LEARNING_ACTIVITYs.

Figure 2 is a sub-section of the model in Figure 1, showing the central structure and the relationships between OBJECTs and PAGEs. All of the large variation of types of learning-objects listed above have the common visual quality (apart from *Audio*) that they may each be represented on a user's screen in a rectangular sub-area of a larger section of screen - the PAGE. This is a more obvious choice in the age of the iPad, than it was in 1997/98 as HTML V4 was just becoming available.

Figure 2. Detail from Figure 1 showing the relationship between Objects, Pages and Reference_Works

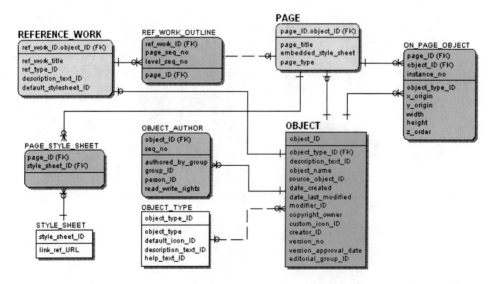

While a PAGE is itself one of the OBJECT_TYPEs, the structure named ON_PAGE_OBJECT (rhs in Figure 2) represents the flexible relationship between a given PAGE and a number of OBJECTs that appear on that PAGE. It allows a given OBJECT to appear on any number of authored PAGEs in the system, and ultimately allows for *personalised pages* in a *learning trajectory*. In data modelling terminology it is of type *associative entity* (these are generally shaded in light-grey in Figures 1,2 and 3). The data attributes within it named: *x_origin,y_origin, width, height* – hold the few necessary values that the CSS code needs to place an object on the page, just so, as the PAGE author intended it (WYSIWYG – what-you-see-is-what-you-get). This placing of objects on a page by absolute positioning (allowed by CSS) ran contrary to the flowing nature of HTML mark-up, which in turn tended to upset many page designers using HTML. That dichotomy appears again in the two types of ebooks allowed in Apple's iBookstore today: the flowing text format, and the fixed-page format - added in a subsequent version.

Note 1: The OBJECT attributes *version_no, version_approval_date* and *editorial_group_id* – which allowed for a formal process regarding the creation and subsequent evolution of all types of learning-objects in the system. While *copyright_owner* allowed for attributions right down at the individual learning object level.

Note 2: The OBJECT_AUTHOR entity allowed for the authorship of learning objects to be either by an individual or a group of authors.

Figure 2 also shows the arrangement of a set of PAGEs into REFERENCE_WORKs. Clearly from its name, a Reference Work can be seen as an online ebook with interactivity, but what is less obvious is that the Reference Work may actually be customised down to the Page level, for individual learners, as we will see further down. That is, the PAGE was designed as the fundamental unit of course/subject delivery in the Creator system. The entity REF_WORK_OUTLINE is the structure that holds the data to build the Contents of a Reference Work. The authorship of the Page (and the complex learning objects) is not restricted to teachers and tutors – it is entirely in the hands of the administration rights in the Creator system (which are non-hierarchical), such that a PLE of a sort is possible with little change to the tools.

The Learning Activity Learning Object

The most complex learning-object in Creator is the *Learning Activity*. It also interacts with the *Question Object* – which appears on the Page as a question that a student answers. A Learning Activity here is a pre-designed series of PAGEs that a learner encounters, the order of which is dynamic and generally non-linear, depending on the learner's interaction with it; as opposed to the sequential movement through a Reference_Work.

Figure 3. Part 2 of the Conceptual Data Model that stores the Learning Objects in Creator, but also student responses as they move through a Learning Activity

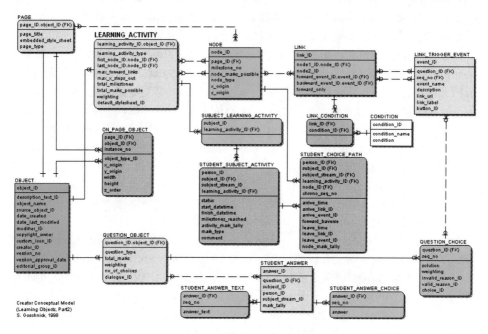

As with a REFERENCE_WORK the PAGE is the fundamental unit of delivery for a LEARNING_ACTIVITY. The overall structure of a Learning Activity is that of a *network graph* (see Figure 4 for an example of a network graph of Pages within the authoring tool), as opposed to the hierarchical structure of a Reference Work or an ebook. The entities directly involved in a Learning Activity are portrayed in Figure 3. A *NODE* represents a Page in the network graph which includes a *milestone* manually set by the author of a particular Learning Activity.

The *LINK* entity represents the *arc* between two NODEs, the IDs of which are stored in attributes *node1_ID* and *node2_ID*. LINKs can be either one or two-way, at the authors discretion. The learner can back-step if it is designated a two-way link. The transition of the learner from one NODE/PAGE to the next, depends on an *event* stored in the *LINK_TRIGGER_EVENT* entity. One such triggering event is a particular *QUESTION_CHOICE* that a learner has selected within a multiple-choice Question, as they negotiate the Learning Activity. This allows for a dynamic *path* through the network of PAGEs, based on the learning outcomes of an individual learner. E.g. if they pick the right answer it goes in one direction, if not, then it goes a different way, possibly a remedial learning path to make sure they achieve a particular learning milestone. Another trigger event type is the simple pressing of a particular button with *button_ID*. In addition to the trigger event, a number of filtering *Conditions* can be placed on the *Link*, for example, that a particular video was watched in-full by the learner.

An individual student's *personal learning trajectory* is recorded in the entity *STUDENT_CHOICE_PATH*. We take a deeper look at it in Section 4 where we press the concept and technique into finer-grained *personalised learning trajectories*, taking the student's current context into consideration with respect to the types of events that can trigger a particular path through a Learning Activity.

What is not immediately clear in Figure 3 is that the concatenated primary-keys (the attributes above the dividing-line in an entity box) in the two entities STUDENT_SUBJECT_ACTIVITY and subsequently, STUDENT_CHOICE_PATH, include several foreign-keys (FK) from entities that don't appear in Figure 3, namely, *person_ID, subject_ID* and *subject_stream_ID*. Those identifiers come from entities left out of Figure 3 for clarity sake. We will revisit them down in Section 4. Enough to say here that there is a whole other Creator sub-model that deals with the *administration* of *subjects, students* and *subject-streams,* some of which necessarily appear down in Figure 9 (the white entities).

Figure 4. The interface of (one of) the actual authoring tool for creating Learning Activities - clearly showing the network graph structure of such an activity

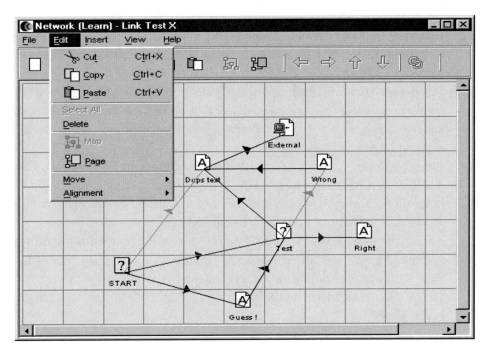

What can be gleaned from the details in Figure 3 is that the entity STUDENT_ SUBJECT_ACTIVITY records an individual student's progress within a particular Learning Activity, via their enrolment in a particular SUBJECT_STREAM, storing the state of that progress in the appropriate data attributes: *start_datetime, finish_ datetime, milestone_reached, activity_mark_tally* and *comment*.

Finer-grained detail of a student's navigation through a Learning Activity, node-by-node, is recorded in the STUDENT_CHOICE_PATH entity, in the data attributes: *arrive_time, arrive_event, arrive_link_ID, arrive_event, leave_time, leave_link_ID, leave_event_ID,* and *node_mark_tally.* Such data could be data-mined to identify general problems in a given Learning Activity.

User Views and Roles, and the Tools That Service Them

User Views and User Roles

There are five *User Views* that facilitate the chunking of functionality in the Creator system, with respect to locating and using the right tool for the right task. Very briefly, these views are as follows:

1. **Authoring (Roles: Teacher/Author/Senior Tutor):** This view brings together the Authoring Tools, the Search Tools and Version Controls Services to facilitate the creation of subject and course content, down to the page level.

2. **Learning (Roles: Student/ Tutor):** This view brings together the Session Control interface, the Search Tools and the Communication Tools (see immediately below).

3. **Discussion (Roles: Teacher/Author/Tutor):** The Communication Tools represent the totality of this view. Note: Melbourne IT Creator used off-the-shelf tools for *email, newsgroups* and *conferencing* – namely Microsoft NetMeeting and Exchange Server, for expediency.

4. **Library (Roles: Content Administrator/IP Manager):** This view included the Reference Works accumulated in the system, external documents included in various Learning Activities, the Search Tools, the Keyword Manager tool, and Version Control and IP Management services.

5. **Administration (Roles: Course Administrator/ System Administrator):** bCourse, Subject and Student administration tools formed one side of this view, with System Administration and Database Administration from the OS vendor (Windows Server and Microsoft SQL Server) forming the other part of this view.

As can be glimpsed from these five user views the breadth of application of Melbourne IT Creator was designed to facilitate up to the level of the content creation and teaching for a whole online University or School, and hence is a full-blown LMS. However, the granularity of detail goes right down to individual paragraphs and questions in the content, and down to an individual student's progress through Learning Activities, including their responses to questions, and page-by-page trajectories taken through such an activity – suggesting the applicability of those aspects to a personalised learning system (a PLE). Furthermore, the authoring tools were highly usable, and available to anyone given the appropriate rights to do so (*rights* were not hierarchical in their application, but were set on a 128-bit access key) – meaning students could themselves be given access to these tools, on any desktop computer that runs the Java language.

Authoring Tools

There were five distinct Java-language based authoring applications, that made up the one integrated software tool, which were:

1. **Page Designer:** An innovative (for the time) WYSIWYG editor for creating pages in HTML with absolute positioning of learning-objects, using the CSS standard. A Page thus created, could be used in either: a Reference Work, and/ or a Learning Activity.
2. **Page Linker:** Used to create the innovative Learning Activities as seen in Figure 4 and described above in Section 2.4.
3. **Resource Palette:** Used to amass a collection of learning-objects, both simple and complex, that may then be easily accessed and drag-and-dropped onto a Page within the Page Designer.
4. **The Outliner:** Used to create a Reference Work from pre-authored Pages.
5. **Keyword Manager:** Used to populate the keyword-related entities in Figure 1, namely: KEYWORD, SYNONYM, OBJECT_KEYWORD and KEYWORD_ LIST – in turn used in keyword searches across the *internal* store of learning-objects. I.e. Within the other authoring tools, keyword searches can be done by an author to locate appropriate objects in the overall Creator system, during an authoring session.

Search and the FAME Agent

While the Keyword Manager built indexes against the learning-objects held *within* a Creator system, there was a need for external Internet-wide search, particularly with regard to research-paper citations, often needed by the authors of subject-based learning materials. To cater for this gap in Creator a research project was undertaken by researchers from the Intelligent Agent Lab within the Department of Computer Science & Software Engineering at the University of Melbourne, who had expertise in precisely this area (Cassin & Sterling, 1997; Loke, Davison, & Sterling, 1996; Goschnick & Cassin, 1997).

The intelligent software agent was thereafter known as the Finder and Minder Agent Engine (FAME Agents). The snippets of information from content authors lead to URLs that were then used to *seed* deep web-crawling searches of the site and its links on a regular basis. I won't expand any further in this chapter on the FAME Agent. However, the current field of *recommendation systems* use either software agents or other AI techniques in a similar way to FAME usage in Creator, suggesting many potential applications within PLEs with regard to the personalisation of learning content, and the alignment of collaborative tasks across individual learners.

CONCEPTUAL MODELS FROM A SOCIAL NETWORKING PLATFORM (FACEBOOK)

While Downes (2010), Mott (2010) and others saw benefits of social networking software within PLEs, they mainly saw them as linked informally by the student themselves in their daily learning, in the form of light-weight mashups. Functionally, that could be as simple as a learner having multiple windows from multiple apps on the one screen, or using an RSS aggregator to pull information in from such sites on the web. In more recent times there has been a growing body of research that directly investigates the use of social software (the terms used vary but have similar or overlapping meanings: social media, social semantic web, social networks, social software) with respect to learning, particularly personalised learning: Halimi et al (2014) investigate personalised *recommendations* based on similarity using the social semantic web; Leung (2015) investigates the use of social media against academic performance and perceived social support; Dabbagh & Kitsantas (2012) investigate the combination of social media and self-regulated learning with personalised learning environments (PLEs); while Archee (2012) suggests that the lure of Facebook as an external tool being embraced by educational institutions is 'mistaken' and that the proponents thereof (those that '*regard Facebook as a pedagogical model*' at least) are '*technological determinists*'. None of those studies looks at a specific social network platform from an *information system design* point-of-view, to investigate either: *how* the key features that attract people to social networking platforms such as *Facebook, LinkedIn, Twitter* and *Google+*, might be put into a PLE technology; or alternatively, how easily the vendor of such a platform could focus it into a PLE, should the vendor decide to point their respective considerable commercial focus toward the PLE marketplace.

We investigate these two scenarios in the next Section, but before doing so we need to outline the *why* and the *what* of social network platforms, that are of such interest and potential in the creation of PLEs.

The Why of Social Software in a PLE

Looking at the functionality of current-day social networking platforms, they generally eclipse the earlier use of email and newsgroups in the Creator LMS, regarding social functionality. Beyond communication and collaboration possibilities, the sheer ease that some simple content can be created and the speed that it can be uploaded and shared in the social media platforms, has set the precedence regarding usability and immediacy for a generation or two of what learners now expect in any current or forthcoming PLE.

The What of Social Software in an Advanced Smart PLE

While Facebook has a programming API available to third-party developers, they do not publish a formal or even a conceptual *data model* overview of what is clearly a structured data system behind the scenes. Recently, the author inferred a complete conceptual model of the Facebook platform (Goschnick, 2014), one that fits the data textual descriptions in the publicly available Facebook Graph API V2.0 (Facebook, 2017). The inferred conceptual model has 85 entities – a mid-range information system, in terms of conceptual scope.

The first point of note about the Facebook model is the number of entities – the Facebook platform is far from the light-weight service that the earlier cited PLE enthusiasts (e.g. Mott, 2010; Attwell, 2007) were considering for inclusion in their mashups. Despite its relatively easy to use desktop interface - and discarding the sheer scale and logistics of its physical model and infrastructure to cope with upwards of 2 billion users - underlying the Facebook platform is a sophisticated and extensive *conceptual data model*. As pointed out in (Goschnick, 2014), Facebook has gone to considerable lengths to deny an underlying logical structure, instead saying it is simply a realtime Graph, they call the '*People Graph*, akin to Google's *Search Graph*'. And yet they gather information that fits strict, limited pigeon holes that they themselves define and provide to users, unlike Google's search engine which must deal effectively with the unstructured or widely different structured data from hundreds of millions of independent content creators. That is, the Facebook platform has a definite structure, albeit an extensive one of enterprise system proportions.

However, Facebook has shown considerable innovation in making their enterprise-scale data model highly usable on smartphones and tablets, demonstrated with their more recently released apps: *Facebook Groups* (November, 2014) and *Messenger* (August, 2011 on Android; July, 2014 on iPad). Each app provides limited but focused slices of functionality from the enterprise-scale model, in a highly user-friendly manner on every-day devices. This is a usability strategy that many more enterprise-scale platforms could learn from.

In this chapter, in the next 5 sub-sections we will look in detail at five of the sub-models from the overall Facebook model - those we perceive as having some value to our cross PLE/Social network software comparison, in our goal for an improved smart PLE. They are: the part of the model that deals with *Posts* (which can give *context* to and about the learner's situation); the part that deals with *Groups* (which can replicate the sorts of groups represented in learning environments but also the wider social groups that a learner is a part of – even extending to a global community of traditional and other sub-groups, according to Zuckerberg (2017) more recently); the part that deals with *Events* (which can chart future events such as lectures, project meetings, reading group meetings, etc. - and facilitate all sorts of contextual dialog around them); and the part that deals with *Pages* - given the central place that *Pages* has in both LMS and envisaged PLEs, as discussed above; and *Apps* the part that can bring in unprecedented levels of personalisation through both self-written apps by a new code-savvy generation, and/or via an app store dedicated to learning.

The Facebook Posts Sub-Model

Goschnick (2014) begins with a general description of social networks, with particular reference to Facebook, saying that they "are about connecting people and collecting data; they are communication services upon which further services can be added and customised. The 'people' part leads to *groups* (of friends, family and associates), *sub-groups* and *events*. The 'communication' part leads to *posts, messages, comments* and *questions*. The 'collecting data' part leads to *links, photos, albums, videos, photo-tags, video-tags* and *check-ins* to particular *places* (including *locations* in the real world)".

A *User* has a set of *Friends* who each receives the user's *Posts* and vice-versa. The *Posts* may be a simple text message (status update), but it may be accompanied with a *Photo*, a *Video* or a *Link* (to some web page – often taking a graphic and a headline from that www page). Posts appear in a user's *Newsfeed* – which is effectively a *default home page*, of chronologically listed posts for one's social network (depending on various privacy settings). The Newsfeed is increasingly being peppered with news from outside one's personal social group. This is for both commercial reasons and also now claimed by Zuckerberg (2017) to help counter the problems associated with a 'filter bubble' and 'fake news'. There is a *timeline* version of the newsfeed, which is generally just the full list of a User's own Posts, each entry timestamped.

This simple mechanism can be supported by the *conceptual data model* in Figure 5. Note: the entities *Link, Video*, and *Photo* are sub-types of *Post* - itself a so-called super-type in ER modelling terminology. The *Profile* entity is a generalised way of representing a profile in Facebook of more than just people, which is discussed in the next section. The *With_Tags* entity (an associative entity) is a simple mechanism to store the presence of various friends or peers, with the user when they posted a Post – this is separate from the people 'tagged' in an actual photo which are stored down the bottom in the *Photo_Tags* entity. The *Media* and *Interest* entities are a simple method of storing the various books, music, movies, bands and other things from popular culture, that a user has flagged as of particular interest to them (Note: there is a more extensive way of flagging interests via *Pages*, covered further down). Facebook stores a variety of resolutions of a single image in the *Image* entity to

Figure 5. Users, Friends and their Posts, taken from (Goschnick, 2014 – Figure 3.1)

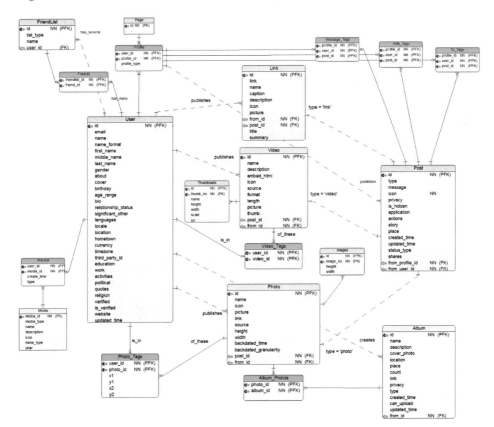

deliver a version that is most appropriate (efficiency-wise) to the current device of the post-receiving user.

The *Users, Friends* and *Posts* are foundational to Facebook and go back to its early history. *FriendList* allows some basic grouping of one's Friends. The free-flowing newsfeed of content (which is conceptually and procedurally similar to a dynamically updated *report* coming from a database system of underlying data), by way of text, photos, video and links, provides a simple and quick content publishing system using a basic stylesheet, broadcast to one's social network. People in that social network may show their support via a *Like* (a one-button click/touch response), and/or a *Comment*, which can expand into an ongoing conversation, involving anyone who has access to that item in the newsfeed.

This simple, authoring and communication mechanism, with the immediacy of affirmation and feedback from friends and peers, is now the norm of a generation or two. The smartphone has placed access to it wherever the mobile user currently is. Images from the smartphone can be posted to one's social networks almost instantly and via a user-interface with indiscernible friction. (Note: the *Instagram* app is also now owned by Facebook).

Video requires somewhat more bandwidth, but the evolving telecommunication infrastructure and data plans, means that uploading video will soon be nearly as painless as uploading images for a large percentage of users.

That usability and the responsiveness of the communication is now what a PLE needs to use or to replicate, to meet learner expectations with regard to personalised authoring of content, broadcasting it, and communicating around it with peers, friends and others. Simple in its use, complex but efficient in its delivery infrastructure, and powerful regarding the consequences upon the emotional aspects of learning.

The Facebook Groups Sub-Model

Groups in Facebook are like a series of generalised *FriendLists* (see entity top-left in Figure 5), with extra capabilities and features. For example the *link* attribute in the *Group* entity in Figure 6, holds a *url* to the external Home Page website of the group, who may be a more traditional community. The members of a particular Group are all represented in the associative entity *Member*. A user may join an existing group or start a new one. The Group has a record in the *Profile* entity (together with the user_id of the *User* who first set-up or 'owns' the *Group*). This is a clever mechanism which allows a Group to have a newsfeed of *Posts* by members, just like an individual User has a newsfeed of Posts. All posts emanating from the group via its members, are referenced by records in the associative entity *Group_Feed*. The users get *alerts* when new *Posts* emanate from another group member.

Figure 6. Facebook Groups reproduced here from (Goschnick, 2014; Figure 4.1)

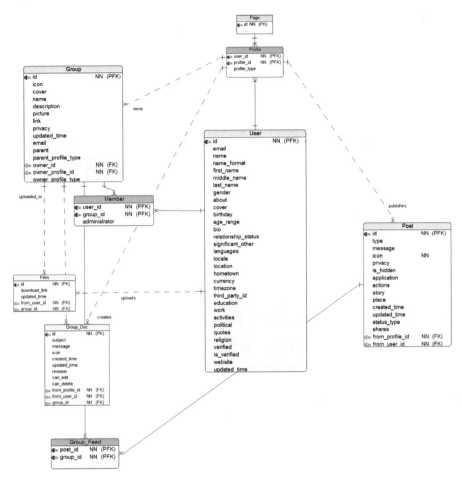

External files created by all sorts of external applications can be uploaded to the Group, as recorded in the *Files* entity. In addition to those, internal *Group_Doc* documents can be created within Facebook (using HTML formatting), and these can be jointly edited by the members of the group.

The attribute in the *Group* entity named *parent* represents the *id* of its parent (if it has one), while *parent_profile_type* can be either: a *Page*, an *App* or another *Group*. I.e. Groups can recursively own other Groups, creating a hierarchical structure of groups that is entirely similar to the *newsgroups* from earlier Internet times, and to *forums* in various wikis and most traditional LMS.

The Groups feature was only added to Facebook in 2010 and when it was introduced, it quickly became their most popular feature (Goschnick, 2014). A free smartphone app (named: *Facebook Groups*) dedicated to just those features in

Groups was released by Facebook in 2014 - currently available from both: the Apple App Store for iOS devices, and the Google Play Store for Android OS devices. The features available through this app replicate most of those available through the web browser interface for Groups.

The Facebook Events Sub-Model

Events in either the virtual or real world can be organised, tracked and recorded in Facebook. The *What? When? Where? Who's invited? Who is coming? And who can't make it?* - are all captured and broadcast via the features of the Event part of the Facebook platform.

Figure 7. Conceptual model of Facebook Events taken from (Goschnick, 2014; Figure 8.1)

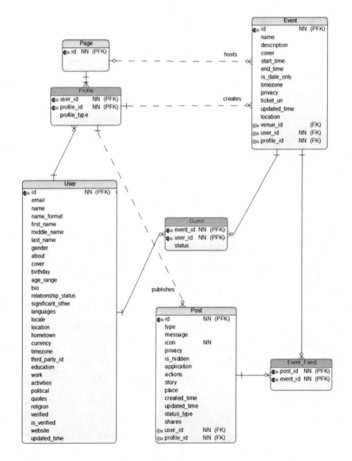

Furthermore, as with Groups (via the same *Profile* mechanism), *Events* have their own *newsfeed* of *Posts* coming from those users *posting* to the event. The *Event* entity has a *privacy* attribute (see Figure 7) which can be set to either: *Invite-Only*, *Public*, or *Friend-of-Guests* – which are self-descriptive in terms of who can see and join an *Event*. As noted earlier, a timetabled lecture, a project meeting, or a tutorial are each *events* forward in time - all ideal candidates for Facebook *Events*.

Another attribute of the *Event* entity of interest here is *venue_id*, which is the id of a *Page* (described in the next section), of either the: *place*, *location*, *organisation* or some other entity hosting the *event*.

The Facebook Pages Sub-Model

The Page, the fundamental unit of the www was introduced into Facebook as an entity separate from a User, in April 2010. It became the way that Facebook allowed corporate and other identities (e.g. celebrities by stage-name), into what had previously been a people-identity-only system – where everybody was supposedly going by their real names and identities. (Note: that has been a point of contention over the years, where a number of effectively anonymous trolls have seemed to continue on in Facebook with impunity).

Figure 8. Pages, Places and Locations, from (Goschnick, 2014; Figure 9.1)

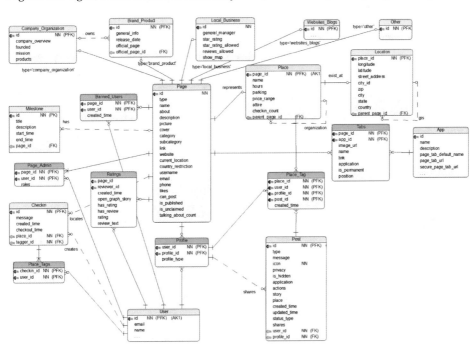

The *Page* entity in the conceptual model is a super-type (see Figure 8) with numerous specialised sub-types across the top of the Figure: *Company_Organization, Brand_Product, Local_Business, Websites_Blogs, Other*. Each of the sub-types have a few extra attributes beyond what they have in common in the *Page* entity. They also each have a distinct stylesheet, evident when the different types are displayed in the browser. Facebook has scores of categories and sub-categories of the Page types, with little or no current variation across many of them with-respect-to the attributes available in the Graph API, so only five sub-types are currently necessary in the conceptual model. This aspect of Facebook renders it much like a content management system (CMS), where the default presentation of a *page* is provided by carefully designed stylesheets. That also means that authoring such pages is inflexible, compared to an LMS or a CMS with WYSIWYG editing tools available to the content creator, such as Creator covered above.

In 2010 Facebook also added *Places* (see the *Place* and *Location* entities in Figure 8) to their platform, which have a one-to-one relationship with *Page*, but only with pages that represent *a place in the real world* – such as a store/shop, the head office of an organisation, or a park, and so on. This was Facebook's foray into location-based services (e.g. attributes in the *Place* entity include *parking* and the opening *hours*), whereby Facebook users can check-in and check-out of actual places in the real world (see the *Checkin* entity between Page and User), either by themselves or via their friends. Note that *Location* has a self-relationship such that hierarchies of locations (e.g. a store in a street, in a suburb, in a city, in a state, in a country) can be represented, in a GIS-fashion (Geographical Information System). That is, the Page and Place entities can be used to tie in location-based educational or other facilities related to one's learning activities.

A second location-services inspired feature was added to the Facebook platform in the recent rendition of the Graph API in April 2014: it is represented in Figure 8 by the three-way *Place_Tag* associative entity between *Place, Profile* and *Post*. It allows for people other than the user sending the *post*, to also be tagged at a *Place*, at the time the user posted the *Post*. I.e. Though currently enacted by people, it technically allows for automatic recorded check-ins by GPS, or via other sensors as the Internet of Things (IoT) progresses, of people from a user's friendlist, placing them at the scene, at the time of the post. The privacy issues associated with such an automation are substantial.

Other entities from this model of specific interest to us here, include:

- **Ratings:** Ratings and user-stories about a Page can be accumulated via this associative entity. E.g. a Subject can have a Page, as can a finer-grained Learning Activity.

- **Banded_Users:** People who have offended the owner of a page in some non-resolved way, can be banned from viewing and interacting with a given page, by the page owner.
- **Milestone:** Milestones there-in are a special type of post that appears in the timeline of a Page, so that it is visibly flagged in the chronological history of the Page.

All these features and others could be put to very good use within an advanced PLE.

The Facebook Apps Sub-Model

On July 10, 2008 Apple released the App Store in the then new second version of iOS. It allowed third party app developers to write and sell apps for Apple smartphones for the first time. Google followed suit between 2009-2011, initially only allowing third party developers from the US and the UK for the first year. With the Apple App Store, Steve Jobs created another revolution in the software world: "Apps are the software artifacts that allowed the previously inert mobile/cell phone to take over the computing world, no less" Goschnick (2014). Facebook had long had apps (games mainly) that could run within a page on Facebook, including their own *Notes* app for writing longer stories with some basic HTML formatting. With the release of their Graph API V2, Facebook introduced functionality that allowed third party app developers who publish in the Apple, Google, web and Windows app stores, to integrate with Facebook at some level, rather than attempt to woo them into Facebook's own App Center (which then, as now, is nearly all *games*). In particular, by placing an advertisement for an app within a Facebook user's newsfeed, courtesy of Facebook's business model, when/if the user clicked on it, they could be taken to the app publishers web page, or to the link in the App Store or the Play Store for app installation.

Facebook correctly identified a marketing problem for indie app developers, centred on *app discoverability* as there was soon millions of apps to choose from in each of the two main stores. Instead of competing with Apple's App Store and Google's Play Store via their own App Center which houses Facebook games, they decided instead to leverage the marketing power of the social groupings within Facebook, as a solution to that discoverability of apps in the major app stores, and tap into a significant revenue stream coming from app advertising. While this chapter has no interest in the advertising side of Facebook, the structures related to apps within the Facebook Graph API V2, are of interest with a view to the potential of educational apps within possible future PLEs.

Figure 9. Apps and Related Entities, from (Goschnick, 2014; Figure 10.1)

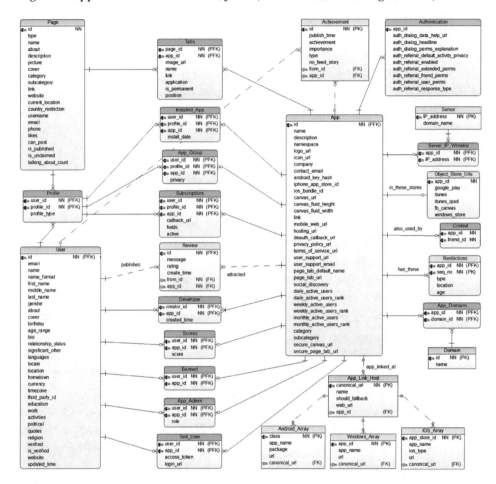

Of the 27 entities in Figure 9 the ones of most interest here, are within the column of entities second from the left, as it represents the relationships between the User and an App, or else between a particular Facebook Page and an App.

Of those entities the ones of specific interest here, include:

- **Tabs:** Is an associative entity between Page and Apps, such that user-selected Facebook apps can be installed-on/accessible-from a specific page (via a tab), making them directly clickable from that Page. Note: this is a bit analogous to the complex Learning Objects that can be placed on a Page in Creator – though less flexible in its placement on the page, it is potentially more powerful regarding a broad selection of third-party apps that might be installed on a Page (although most/all apps currently in the Facebook App Center are games, of which there is no educational-games category).

- **Installed_App:** This simply records which apps a given user has. As an associative entity it can be used to list all users of a particular app, or alternatively, all apps that a particular user has installed.
- **App_Group:** This entity associates an app with a Group. The link here includes the profile of the user who is the administrator of that particular Group.
- **Subscriptions:** Used to enact subscriptions to an app, which may expire after a period of time. Used to post updates or to flag the need for a user to renew their subscription.
- **Review:** An associative entity such that a user can post reviews of many apps, and a app can receive many reviews.
- **Scores**: A simple score that a user has attained in an app.
- **Achievement:** For apps such as game that have leader boards, but within the Facebook environment if the inclusive attribute no_feed_story is set 'false' than the particular achievement a user reached will be broadcast to the newsfeeds of the users 'friends'.
- **Domain:** Represents a web site domain out on the greater Internet that has become known within the Graph API, for the purposes of Facebook Insights (a marketing dashboard). A third party developer/publisher can 'claim' a domain as their own, such that forward of the claim, traffic related to Facebook users to their web site will appear in their Insights statistics, which can be drilled down on various user demographics to aid their future marketing campaigns.

Each of these features could be put to some good use within an advanced PLE that allowed app plugins as such. Apps can bring in unprecedented levels of personalisation in learning.

A MERGING OF MODELS

There is some recent research regarding how students use existing social networking platforms with respect to their working patterns within current study routines, alongside the traditional learning technologies (Arndt & Guercio, 2012), but none we could find regarding how the social networking platforms could be enhanced to incorporate such working routines; or conversely, how an LMS or PLE platform could be modified to bring in the best features of the social network platforms. There is a paper outlining a planned set of features researchers would like in a conventional

LMS, mirroring something of the features in social networking platforms, but when it comes to the specifics, there are vague ideas about how such features could be used to make learning more personalised and adaptive. For example, in Tsolis et al (2011), in which they propose modifying the Moodle LMS given its adaptability, they outline a brief plan to: expand the user profile page allowing the user to add tags (keywords) indicating their interests; have shared bookmarks; have shared galleries of digital content (this last proposal is like the shared *Resource Palette* in Creator covered earlier, though they make no mention of learning-objects).

In the section on the Conceptual Data Models from the Facebook platform, we investigated numerous aspects of them, with an open mind regarding two possible future directions that PLEs and social networking platforms might advance, regarding personalised learning, namely: what can be gained from such a case study with respect to folding similar social functionality into a PLE; and conversely, to gauge how accommodating is the current Facebook structural design, should that vendor choose to move their market focus in the personalised education direction. Interestingly, we can examine both those scenarios in the one design exercise: by folding appropriately selected aspects of the two models (those from Creator and those from Facebook) into the one model.

While the concept of *posts* to one's *friendlist* was a central early strength of social networking software, when looking across the models in Figures 6, 7, 8 and 9 five *generic* concepts stand out: *Groups*; *Events*; *Pages*; *Places* and *Apps* – all of which were added much later to the Facebook platform (mainly in 2010). The generic nature of the four makes them highly adaptable to other software application areas; not just applications in the small-feature *app* sense, but applications *at the platform level*, such as a personalised PLE, or an adaptive LMS.

Looking at Figure 8, the way that a number of Page *sub-entities* are *derived* from the generic *Page* super-type, is indicative of what can also be done by sub-typing GROUP in service of our aim, e.g.: *Class, Tutorial-Group, Study Group, Year-level, Reading Group, Project Team, Lab Group*, and so on for the more traditional groupings in an educational setting. Similarly, sub-types of EVENT could include: *Lecture, Lab Session, Workshop, Demonstration, Tutorial, Seminar, Research Seminar*, and so on. In other words, the *current* Facebook platform is already well endowed with generic structures and capabilities that could be specialised into an LMS of some capability, by the vendor should they choose such a path (note: not an infeasible decision given the Facebook company founder's large donations to public education in the US: $100M in New York in 2010, and $150M in the San Francisco Bay area public school system in 2014).

Furthermore, if we take a finer-grained view of learning down at a single *Learning Activity* level as demonstrated in Creator (i.e. where a *Learning Activity* which in that system may be as small as a single page with learning-objects on that

Figure 10. Merging models from Figures 3, 6 and 7

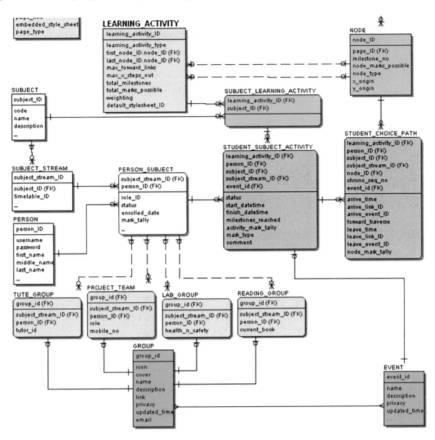

page, that in turn may or may not also be a sub-section of a more traditional *Lab Session*, a *Workshop*, a *Tutorial* and so on), it can be very personalised in a PLE that incorporates social networking capabilities. As a *small* illustration, Figure 10 combines the *Learning Activity* concepts represented in Figure 3, with the generic entities from the Facebook Platform model in Figures 6 (*Groups*) and 7 (*Events*) – the rest of Figures 6 and 7 are assumed to be part of the merged model, without the need to re-present them and clutter-up the figure. Alternatively, *Groups* and *Events* are also generic entities (they may have different names) in many LMS and indeed other systems too, such as multi-agent systems, e.g. the ShaMAN multi-agent meta-model has them as *SocialWorlds* and *Events* (Goschnick, Sonenberg & Balbo, 2008).

Events are fine-grained via a possible relationship between *Event* and *Student_ Subject_Activity*. We have also introduced four sub-entities of *Group*, namely - *Tute_Group, Project_Team, Lab_Group, Reading_Group* – each of which may have extra specific attributes. E.g. *tutor_id, mobile_no, health_n_safety,* and *current_book* respectively as simple examples. Furthermore, *Events* and *Groups* are related via a many-to-many relationship, as one is often related to the other.

The combined structure would enable new features such as:

- An automatic *posting* of the achievement of reaching a *milestone* in a single learning activity, to one's friends and family (those that have the right *privacy* setting);
- The many-to-many relationship means that some events can involve many groups, and some groups will be involved in many events – and which-are-which can easily be set and/or discovered;
- Those people reading the same *current_book* within and across different *reading groups* can be alerted to the possibility of fruitful discussions, if so sort out;
- Those learners that are up to the same *milestone* can be alerted to their common situation;
- A course administrator can quickly see if there are any lab groups that have no one that has yet completed the pre-requisite health-and-safety course – and post them on their mobiles about the observation (A 'smart' Lab, could check that all by itself – see next paragraph);
- And more;

To be implemented with straight-forward/light-weight procedural coding. And furthermore, if entities like many of those in Figures 8 and 9 were also merged in the combined structure:

- A location-based service across a university campus could likewise be interfaced model-wise, at the *Location* entity in Figure 8.
- An *app* from a library of subscribed-to or purchased educational apps, could be placed by the author (may be a student) at the individual *Page* level in the PLE, via the *Tab* entity in Figure 9.
- Both students and teachers could provide significant feedback at the individual Page level via the *Review* entity in Figure 8, *any time* rather than just at Quality-of-Teaching/Student-Experience survey time; and so on.
- The *Tabs* on a Facebook page is simply a parallel with Learning Objects in Creator – i.e. educational apps can be thought of as smart learning objects that could be plugins to a page in the PLE, down at the granularity of the individual learner for a highly customized personal learning experience.

- The *App_Group* structure in Facebook demonstrates how to make an app available to a specific group of learner in the PLE. To a: tutorial, lab, workshop, or other cohort of learners.
- App *Subscriptions* clearly would allow for a pay-as-you-go series of learning apps, where that is desired feature.
- The *Installed_App* would be useful to know who has got what installed from an administration point of view, down to the user level of granularity.
- While the app *Achievement* entity would allow for gamification in apps *within* learning activities, similar to the milestone feature *at* the learning activity level already mentioned.

CONCLUSION

The Merging of Models section above highlighted some of the key features evident in a social network platform like Facebook, that could be included in the blueprint of an advanced PLE platform. Also sketched out were *just a few* of the new features that could be built upon such a merged model.

Furthermore, in demonstrating aspects of that merged model, we have also shown how 'education-ready' the current Facebook platform is, given the number of generic structures such as *Groups* and *Events,* that have been folded into the Facebook platform in recent times. With relatively superficial technical modifications at the level of the foundational structures, and a changed or additional direction in the marketing focus of that company, Facebook Inc. could enter an emerging PLE marketplace, for better or for worse. Given Zuckerberg's (2017) more recent grander plan for "building a global society" which aims to also motivate the self-inclusion of "tradition groups" into Facebook in greater numbers, the personalized learning goals made possible in a PLE, is possibly subsumed in that grand Facebook plan.

Either way, an advanced PLE by whom ever, based on such a merged conceptual model would be capable of a significant degree of personalisation, adaptability and socialisation.

Another aspect of the Facebook platform touched upon, is their strategic slicing up of functionality into discrete apps (each simpler than their desktop/web interface), as a way to keep the usability high and the individual user focused on specific sub-sections or *views* (i.e. the *Facebook Groups* and *Messenger* apps) of their system. This works, despite the enterprise-system scale of their overall platform. Both LMSs and future PLEs could also benefit from such an approach, particularly the LMS given the typical enterprise nature of them.

FUTURE DIRECTIONS

We have touched on how the *Apps* part of the Facebook conceptual data model, when merged into a PLE, would afford certain features; however, our future research will focus more on how *educational apps* are brought into Personalised Learning Environments. I believe that apps can bring unprecedented levels of personalisation into learning through both an app store dedicated to learning accessible within the PLE; and, by allowing the incorporation of self-written apps by a new code-savvy generation in block-based and text-based programming languages. In a sense, the Scratch environment is a very rudimentary forerunner to the PLE proper – one simply dedicated to lessons on coding and story telling – that shows something of the personalised planned and unplanned collaborations that take place. It gives us a glimpse of the learner taking control of what they learn and how they learn. Similarly, the near universal ownership of a smartphone by students down to a certain age level (and the age is getting lower all the time), gives each student a remarkable sensing and recording device that can be folded into the PLE, through an array of innovative apps. Again, the potential for personalized learning with respect to smartphone apps and the sensors in the phone (and in the environment itself) offers unprecedented opportunities to empower learners and teachers, and the impact and outer usefulness of their mutual learning (See iNaturalist.org for an example use of the humble smartphone coupled with an entusiastic individual).

The future of learning environments lies with the merging of the better aspects of flexible Learning Management Systems with features popularised in Social Networking platforms, supplemented with the smartphone, to personalise and energise the individual learning experience in Personal Learning Environments. I believe we have underlined such a possibility in this paper by demonstrating how that can be done at the conceptual schema level.

REFERENCES

Arndt, T., & Guercio, A. (2012). Social Networking and E-Learning: Towards a More Effective Online Learning Experience. *GSTF Journal on Computing*, 2(2), 89–94. doi:10.5176/2010-2283_2.2.173

Attwell, G. (2007). The Personal Learning Environments – the future of eLearning? *eLearning Papers*, 2(1).

Berners-Lee, T., Hendler, J. & Lassila, O. (2001). The Semantic Web. *Scientific America*, 284(5), 34-43.

Cassin, A., & Goschnick, S. B. (1998). *FAME Agent System Design and Specifications. Internal Document, Melbourne IT Pty Ltd*. University of Melbourne.

Cassin, A., & Sterling, L. (1997). IndiansWatcher: Single Purpose Software Agent. *Proceedings of the Second International Conference on the Practical Application of Intelligent Agents and Multi-Agent Technology (PAAM 97)*, 529-538.

Chatti, M. A., Jarke, M., & Frosch-Wilke, D. (2007). The future of e-learning: A shift to knowledge networking and social software. *International Journal of Knowledge and Learning*, *3*(4/5), 404–420. doi:10.1504/IJKL.2007.016702

Dabbagh, N., & Kitsantas, A. (2012). Personal Learning Environments, social media, and self-regulated learning: A natural formula for connecting formal and informal learning. *Internet and Higher Education*, *15*(1), 3–8. doi:10.1016/j. iheduc.2011.06.002

Downes, S. (2005). E-learning 2.0. *eLearning Mag*. Retrieved from http://elearnmag. acm.org/featured.cfm?aid=1104968

Downes, S. (2010). *Elements of a Personal Learning Environment*. ITK Conference, Keynote address, Hameenlinna, Finland. Accessed here: http://www.downes.ca/ files/Personal%20Learning%20Environments.pdf

Facebook. (2017). *Facebook's Graph API 2.0*. Accessed Nov 30, 2017 at: https:// developers.facebook.com/docs/graph-api

Felder, R.M., & Silverman, I.K. (1988). Learning and teaching styles in engineering education. *Engineering Education*, *78*(7).

Goschnick, S. (1998). Design and Development of Melbourne IT Creator – a System for Authoring and Management of Online Education. Academic Press.

Goschnick, S. (2014). *Facebook from Five Thousand Feet: A Visual Mapping from Conceptual Model to Ground-level Graph API Data*. EbookDynasty.net.

Goschnick, S., Balbo, S., & Sonenberg, L. (2008). From Task Models to Agent-Oriented Meta-models, and Back Again. *Proceedings, TAMODIA-2008 the 7th Workshop on Task Models and Diagrams*. 10.1007/978-3-540-85992-5_4

Goschnick, S. B., & Cassin, A. (1997). *Requirements Document – Agents-in-cMILE V1.0. Internal Document, Melbourne IT Pty Ltd*. University of Melbourne.

Halimi, K., Seridi-Bouchelaghem, H., & Faron-Zucker, C. (2014). An enhanced personal learning environment using social semantic web technologies. *Interactive Learning Environments*, *22*(2), 165–187. doi:10.1080/10494820.2013.788032

Leung, L. (2015). A Panel Study on the Effects of Social Media Use and Internet Connectedness on Academic Performance and Social Support. *International Journal of Cyber Behavior, Psychology and Learning, 5*(1), 1-16. doi:10.4018/ijcbpl.2015010101

Limongelli, C., Sciarrone, F., Temperini, M., & Vaste, G. (2011). The Lecomps5 framework for personaliszed web-based learning: A teacher's satisfaction perspective. *Computers in Human Behavior, 27*(4), 1301–1320. doi:10.1016/j.chb.2010.07.026

Loke, S. W. D., & Sterling, L. (1996). *CiFi: An Intelligent Agent for Citation Finding on the World-Wide Web.* Technical Report 96/4. Department of Computer Science, the University of Melbourne.

Luckin, R. (2008). The Learner Centric Ecology of Resources: A Framework for using Technology to Scaffold Learning. *Computers & Education, 50*(2), 449–462. doi:10.1016/j.compedu.2007.09.018

Mayer, C., Linongelli, C., Orlandini, A., & Poggioni, V. (2007). Linear temporal logic as an executable semantics for planning languages. *Journal of Logic Language and Information, 1*(16).

Mott, J. (2010). Envisioning the Post-LMS Era: The Open Learning Network. *Educause Review Online.* Accessed: http://www.educause.edu/ero/article/envisioning-post-lms-era-open-learning-network

Tsolis, D., Christia, P., Kampana, S., & Tsakalidis, A. (2011). OWLearn: An Open Source e-Learning Platform Supporting Adaptability, Personalization and Mobile Learning. *Proceedings of the International Conference on Information Technologies (InfoTech-2011)*, 383-392.

Valtonen, T., Hacklin, S., Dillon, S., Vesisenaho, M., Kukkonen, J., & Hietanen, A. (2012). Perspectives on personal learning environments held by vocational students. *Computer Education, 58*(2), 732–739. doi:10.1016/j.compedu.2011.09.025

W3C. (2014). *The web standards model – HTML CSS and JavaScript.* Accessed: http://www.w3.org/wiki/The_web_standards_model_-_HTML_CSS_and_JavaScript

Zuckerberg, M. (2017). *Building Global Community.* Retrieved on Nov 30, 2017 from https://www.facebook.com/notes/mark-zuckerberg/building-global-community/10154544292806634/

Compilation of References

Abelson, H. (2009, July 31). App inventor for android. *Google Research Blog.*

Abraham, R., & Erwig, M. (2008). Test-driven goal-directed debugging in spreadsheets. *2008 IEEE Symposium on Visual Languages and Human-Centric Computing*, 131–138. 10.1109/VLHCC.2008.4639073

Adams, J. (2014). *Alice 3 in Action: Computing Through Animation.* Cengage Learning.

ADL. (2012). *Sharable Content Object Reference Model (SCORM).* Retrieved from http://www.adlnet.org

Al Muhaideb, S., Hammami, S., & Mathkour, H. (2010). Towards a Distributed Architecture for Adaptive E-Learning System. *Int. Conf. On Advanced Learning Technologies*, 632-636. 10.1109/ICALT.2010.180

Alario-Hoyos, C., Bote-Lorenzo, M. L., Gómez-Sánchez, M. L., Asensio-Pérez, J. I., Vega-Gorgojo, G., & Ruiz-Calleja, A. (2013). GLUE! An architecture for the integration of external tools in Virtual Learning Environments. *Computer Education, 60*(1), 122–137. doi:10.1016/j.compedu.2012.08.010

Allcott, H., & Gentzkow, M. (2017). Social Media and Fake News in the 2016 Election. *The Journal of Economic Perspectives, 31*(2), 211–236. doi:10.1257/jep.31.2.211

Allen, E., Cartwright, R., & Stoler, B. (2002). DrJava: A lightweight pedagogic environment for Java. *Proceedings of the 33rd SIGCSE Technical Symposium on Computer Science Education, 34*(1), 137-141. 10.1145/563340.563395

Amershi, S., Cakmak, M., Knox, W. B., & Kulesza, T. (2014). Power to the people: The role of humans in interactive machine learning. *AI Magazine, 35*(4), 105–120. doi:10.1609/aimag.v35i4.2513

Anderson, B. (2006). *Imagined Communities: Reflections on the Origin and Spread of Nationalism.* London: Verso. (Original work published 1983)

Anderson, J. (2005). IT, E-Learning and Teacher Development. *International Education Journal, 5*(5), 1–14.

Andrade, J., Ares, J., Garcia, R., Pazos, J., Rodriguez, S., & Silva, A. (2004). A methodological framework for viewpoint-oriented conceptual modeling. *Software Engineering. IEEE Transactions on, 30*(5), 282–294.

Android com.google.android.gms.vision.face APIs. (2015). Retrieved from https://developers.google.com/android/reference/com/google/android/gms/vision/face/package-summary

Annet, J. (2004). Hierarchical Task Analysis. In D. Diaper & N. Stanton (Eds.), *The Handbook of Task Analysis for Human-Computer Interaction* (pp. 67–82). Lawrence Erlbaum Associates.

Aoki, P. M., & Woodruff, A. (2005). Making space for stories: ambiguity in the design of personal communication systems. In *Proceedings of ACM Conference on Human Factors in Computing Systems, CHI '05* (pp. 181-190). New York: ACM Press.

Apple Inc. (2013). *Designed by Apple in California.* Retrieved June 30, 2013, from http://www.apple.com/designed-by-apple

Aqda, M. F., Hamidi, F., & Ghorbandordinejad, G. (2011). The impact of constructivist and cognitive distance instructional design on the learner's creativity. *Procedia Computer Science, 3*, 260–265. doi:10.1016/j.procs.2010.12.044

Armoni, M., Meerbaum-Salant, O., & Ben-Ari, M. (2015). From scratch to "real" programming. *ACM Transactions on Computing Education, 14*(4), 25. doi:10.1145/2677087

Arndt, T., & Guercio, A. (2012). Social Networking and E-Learning: Towards a More Effective Online Learning Experience. *GSTF Journal on Computing, 2*(2), 89–94. doi:10.5176/2010-2283_2.2.173

Arnold, M. (2004). The Connected Home: Probing the Effects and Affects of Domesticated ICTs. In *Proceedings of PDC '04* (pp. 1-6). ACM Press.

Assareh, A., & Hosseini Bidokht, M. (2011). Barriers to e-teaching and e-learning. *Procedia Computer Science, 3*, 791–795. doi:10.1016/j.procs.2010.12.129

Astrachan, O., Bruce, K., Koffman, E., Kölling, M., & Reges, S. (2005). Resolved: Objects early has failed. *ACM SIGCSE Bulletin, 37*(1), 451–452. doi:10.1145/1047124.1047359

Attwell, G. (2007). The Personal Learning Environments – the future of eLearning? *eLearning Papers, 2*(1).

Auinger, A., & Stary, C. (2005). Didaktikgeleiteter Wissenstransfer - Interaktive Informationsräume für Lern-Gemeinschaften im Web Deutscher Universitäts-Verlag. GWV Fachverlage GmbH.

Avison, D. E., & Fitzgerald, G. (2003). Where Now For Development Methodologies. *Communications of the ACM, 46*(1), 79–82. doi:10.1145/602421.602423

Badaracco, M., & Martínez, L. (2013). A fuzzy linguistic algorithm for adaptive test in Intelligent Tutoring System based on competences. *Expert Systems with Applications, 40*(8), 3073–3086. doi:10.1016/j.eswa.2012.12.023

Balbo, S., Ozkan, N., & Paris, C. (2004). Choosing the Right Task-modelling Notation: A Taxonomy. In D. Diaper & N. Stanton (Eds.), *The Handbook of Task Analysis for Human-Computer Interaction* (pp. 445–465). Lawrence Erlbaum Associates.

Bandura, A. (1976). *Social Learning Theory*. Englewood Cliffs, NJ: Prentice Hall.

Banks Gatenby, A. (2017). Developing Critical Understanding of Computing With the Raspberry Pi. *International Journal of People-Oriented Programming*, *6*(2), 1–19.

Bardram, J., & Bossen, C. (2005). Mobility Work: The spatial dimension of collaboration at a hospital. *Computer Supported Cooperative Work*, *14*(2), 131–160. doi:10.100710606-005-0989-y

Barnes, D., & Kölling, M. (2002). *Objects First with Java - A Practical Introduction using BlueJ*. Prentice-Hall.

Bau, D. (2015). Droplet, a blocks-based editor for text code. *Journal of Computing Sciences in Colleges*, *30*(6), 138–144.

Bau, D., Bau, D. A., Dawson, M., & Pickens, C. (2015). Pencil Code: Block code for a text world. In *Proceedings of the 14th International Conference on Interaction Design and Children* (pp. 445-448). ACM. 10.1145/2771839.2771875

Baxter, G., & Sommerville, I. (2011). Socio-technical systems: From design methods to systems engineering. *Interacting with Computers*, *23*(1), 4–17. doi:10.1016/j.intcom.2010.07.003

Beeri, C. (1980). On the membership problem for functional and multivalued dependencies in relational databases. *ACM Transactions on Database Systems*, *5*(3), 241–259. doi:10.1145/320613.320614

Beeri, C., & Bernstein, P. A. (1979). Computation problems related to the design of normal relational schemata. *Communications of the ACM*, *4*(1), 30–59.

Beetham, H. (2005). e-Learning research: Emerging issues? *Research in Learning Technology*, *13*(1). doi:10.3402/rlt.v13i1.10976

Begel, A., & Klopfer, E. (2007). StarLogo TNG: An introduction to game development. *Journal of E-Learning*.

Bell, G., & Gemmell, J. (2009). *Total recall: How the e-memory revolution will change everything*. New York: Dutton.

Bentley, T., Johnston, L., & Von Baggo, K. (2002) Putting some emotion into requirements engineering. *Proc. of the 7th Australian Workshop on Requirements Engineering*, 227-244.

Bergin, J., Pattis, R., Stehlik, M., & Roberts, J. (1997). *Karel*. Wiley.

Bergin, J., Stehlik, M., Roberts, J., & Pattis, R. (2005). *Karel J Robot: A gentle introduction to the art of object-oriented programming in Java*. Dream Songs Press.

Berners-Lee, T., Hendler, J. & Lassila, O. (2001). The Semantic Web. *Scientific America*, *284*(5), 34-43.

Bernstein, P. A. (1976). Synthesizing third-normal-form relations from functional dependencies. *ACM Transactions on Software Engineering and Methodology*, *1*(4), 277–298.

Berry, D. M., Kamsties, E., & Krieger, M. M. (2003). *From Contract Drafting to Software Specification: Linguistic Sources of Ambiguity - A Handbook Version 1.0*. Retrieved from http://se.uwaterloo.ca/~dberry/handbook/ambiguityHandbook.pdf

Berry, D. M. (2008). Ambiguity in Natural Language Requirements Documents. In B. Paech & C. Martell (Eds.), *Innovations for Requirement Analysis: From Stakeholders' Needs to Formal Designs* (pp. 1–7). Berlin: Springer. doi:10.1007/978-3-540-89778-1_1

Beyer, H., & Holzblatt, K. (1998). *Contextual Design: Defining Customer-Centered Systems*. San Francisco: Morgan Kaufmann.

Biermann, A. W. (1983). Natural language programming. In *Computer Program Synthesis Methodologies* (pp. 335–368). Springer. doi:10.1007/978-94-009-7019-9_10

Biermann, A. W., Ballard, B. W., & Sigmon, A. H. (1983). An experimental study of natural language programming. *International Journal of Man-Machine Studies*, *18*(1), 71–87. doi:10.1016/S0020-7373(83)80005-4

Black, A. P., Bruce, K. B., Homer, M., Noble, J., Ruskin, A., & Yannow, R. (2013). Seeking Grace: a new object-oriented language for novices. *Proceeding of the 44th ACM technical symposium on Computer science education*, 129-134. 10.1145/2445196.2445240

Blackwell, A. F., Whitley, K. N., Good, J., & Petre, M. (2001). Cognitive factors in programming with diagrams. *Artificial Intelligence Review*, *15*(1), 95–114.

Blaha, K., Monge, A., Sanders, D., Simon, B., & VanDeGrift, T. (2005). Do students recognize ambiguity in software design? A multi-national, multi-institutional report. In *Proceedings of the 27th international conference on Software engineering, ICSE '05* (pp. 615-616). ACM Press.

Bleiberg, J., & West, D. M. (2015). *Political Polarization on Facebook*. Retrieved Nov 30, 2017 from https://www.brookings.edu/blog/techtank/2015/05/13/political-polarization-on-facebook

Boehner, K., Vertesi, J., Sengers, P., & Dourish, P. (2007). How HCI interprets the Probes. In *Proceedings of the 2007 SIGCHI Conference on Human Factors in Computing Systems* (pp. 1077-1086). New York, NY: ACM. 10.1145/1240624.1240789

Bonar, J., & Soloway, E. (1985). Preprogramming knowledge: A major source of misconceptions in novice programmers. *Human-Computer Interaction*, *1*(2), 133–161. doi:10.120715327051hci0102_3

Boshernitsan, M., & Downes, M. (2004). *Visual Programming Languages: A Survey*. Technical report No. UCB/CSD-04-1368, December 2004, Computer Science Division (EECS) University of California Berkeley.

Compilation of References

Bouzeghoub, M., Gardarin, G., & Metais, E. (1985). Database design tools: An expert system approach. In *Proceedings of 11th International Conference on Very Large Data Bases* (pp. 82-95). Academic Press.

Bowers, J. M. (1991). The Janus face of design: some critical questions for CSCW. In J. M. Bowers & S. D. Benford (Eds.), *Studies in Computer Supported Cooperative Work* (pp. 333–350). Amsterdam: Elsevier Science Publishers.

Boyd, D. (2011). *Faceted Id/entity: Managing representations in a digital world* (Master's Thesis). MIT Media Lab's Sociable Media Group. Retrieved on July 17, 2011 from http://smg.media.mit.edu/people/danah/thesis/thesis/

Bozdag, E., & Timmerman, J. (2011). Values in the filter bubble Ethics of Personalization Algorithms in Cloud Computing. In *Proceedings, 1st International Workshop on Values in Design – Building Bridges between RE, HCI and Ethics* (pp. 7-15). Lisbon, Portugal: Academic Press.

Bresciani, P., Perini, A., Giorgini, P., Giunchiglia, F., & Mylopoulos, J. (2004). Tropos: An Agent-Oriented Software Development Methodology. *Autonomous Agents and Multi-Agent Systems*, *8*(3), 203–236. doi:10.1023/B:AGNT.0000018806.20944.ef

Brown, B. A. T., Sellen, A. J., & O'Hara, K. P. (2000). A diary study of information capture in working life. In *Proceedings of the 2009 International Conference on Human Factors in Computing Systems* (pp. 438-45). New York, NY: ACM Press. 10.1145/332040.332472

Brown, N. C. C., Kölling, M., Crick, T., Peyton Jones, S., Humphreys, S., & Sentance, S. (2013). Bringing computer science back into schools: lessons from the UK. *Proceeding of the 44th ACM technical symposium on Computer science education*, 269-274. 10.1145/2445196.2445277

Brown, N., Altadmri, A., & Kölling, M. (2016). Frame-Based Editing: Combining the Best of Blocks and Text Programming. *Proceedings of the Fourth International Conference on Learning and Teaching in Computing and Engineering*. 10.1109/LaTiCE.2016.16

Brown, N., & Kölling, M. (2013). A Tale of Three Sites: Resource and Knowledge Sharing Amongst Computer Science Educators. *Ninth Annual International Computing Education Research Conference (ICER)*, 27-34. 10.1145/2493394.2493398

Buckeridge, A. M., & Sutcliffe, R. F. E. (2002). Using Latent Semantic Indexing as a Measure of Conceptual Association for Noun Compound Disambiguation. *Proceedings of AICS*, *02*, 12–19.

Burnett, M., Cook, C., Pendse, O., Rothermel, G., Summet, J., & Wallace, C. (2003). End-user software engineering with assertions in the spreadsheet paradigm. *Proceedings of the 25th International Conference on Software Engineering*, 93–103. 10.1109/ICSE.2003.1201191

Burns, L., Gassert, A., & Cipriano, P. (2008). Smart technology, enduring solutions. *Journal of Healthcare Information Management*, *22*(4), 24–30. PMID:19267016

Burrows, A., Gooberman-Hill, R., & Coyle, D. (2015). Empirically derived user attributes for the design of home healthcare technologies. *Personal and Ubiquitous Computing*, *19*(8), 1233–1245. doi:10.100700779-015-0889-1

Button, G., & Sharrock, W. (1994). Occasioned practices in the work of software engineers. In M. Jirotka & J. A. Goguen (Eds.), *Requirements Engineering: Social and technical issues* (pp. 217–240). Academic Press.

Butz, B. P., Duarte, M., & Miller, S. M. (2006). An Intelligent Tutoring System for Circuit Analysis. *IEEE Transactions on Education*, *49*(2), 216–223. doi:10.1109/TE.2006.872407

Candy, F. J. (2003). The fabric of society: a proposal to investigate the emotional and sensory experience of wearing denim clothing. In *Proceedings of the 2003 International Conference on Designing Pleasurable Products and Interfaces* (pp. 28-33). New York, NY: ACM. 10.1145/782896.782904

Carroll, J. M. (1997). Scenario-based design. In M. Helander & T. K. Landauer (Eds.), *Handbook of human-computer interaction* (2nd ed.; pp. 383–406). Amsterdam: North-Holland. doi:10.1016/B978-044481862-1.50083-2

Carroll, J. M. (2000). *Making use: scenario-based design of human-computer interactions*. MIT press. doi:10.1145/347642.347652

Carroll, J. M., & Kellogg, W. A. (1989). Artifact as Theory-Nexus: Hermeneutics Meets Theory based Design. In *Proceedings of the Conference on Human Factors in Computing Systems* (pp. 7–14). ACM Press. 10.1145/67449.67452

Casanova, D., Moreira, A., & Costa, N. (2011). Technology Enhanced Learning in Higher Education: Results from the design of a quality evaluation framework. *Procedia: Social and Behavioral Sciences*, *29*, 893–902. doi:10.1016/j.sbspro.2011.11.319

Caspersen, M. E., & Christensen, H. B. (2000). Here, there and everywhere–on the recurring use of turtle graphics in CS1. *Proceedings of the Fourth Australasian Computing Education Conference* (ACE 2000), 34-40. 10.1145/359369.359375

Cassin, A., & Goschnick, S. B. (1998). *FAME Agent System Design and Specifications. Internal Document, Melbourne IT Pty Ltd*. University of Melbourne.

Cassin, A., & Sterling, L. (1997). IndiansWatcher: Single Purpose Software Agent. *Proceedings of the Second International Conference on the Practical Application of Intelligent Agents and Multi-Agent Technology (PAAM 97)*, 529-538.

Castro, J., Kolp, M., & Mylopoulos, J. (2001). A Requirements-Driven Development Methodology. *Proceedings of CaiSE*, *01*, 108–123.

Cellan-Jones, R. (2017). *Raspberry Pi scores UK's top engineering award*. BBC. Retrieved from http://www.bbc.com/news/technology-40444356

Ceri, S., & Gottlob, G. (1986). Normalization of Relations and Prolog. *Communications of the ACM*, *29*(6), 524–544. doi:10.1145/5948.5952

Cernosek, G. (2004). *The Value of Modeling*. IBM.

Chai, D. (2010). *New Groups: Stay Closer to Groups of People in Your Life.* The Facebook Blog. Retrieved April 2, 2013 from http://blog.facebook.com/blog.php?post=434700832130

Chaiyasut, P., & Shanks, G. (1994). *Conceptual data modelling process: a study of novice and expert data modellers.* Dept. of Information Systems, Monash University.

Chang, K. S.-P., & Myers, B. A. (2014). Creating interactive web data applications with spreadsheets. *Proceedings of the 27th Annual ACM Symposium on User Interface Software and Technology*, 87–96. 10.1145/2642918.2647371

Chatti, M. A., Jarke, M., & Frosch-Wilke, D. (2007). The future of e-learning: A shift to knowledge networking and social software. *International Journal of Knowledge and Learning*, *3*(4/5), 404–420. doi:10.1504/IJKL.2007.016702

Cheverst, K., Clarke, K., Dewsbury, G., Hemmings, T., Hughes, J., & Rouncefield, M. (2003). Design with Care: Technology, Disability and the Home. In R. Harper (Ed.), *Inside the Smart Home* (pp. 163–180). London: Springer. doi:10.1007/1-85233-854-7_9

Cheverst, K., Dix, A., Fitton, D., Rouncefield, M., & Graham, C. (2007). Exploring awareness related messaging through two situated-display-based systems. *Human-Computer Interaction*, *22*(1), 173–220.

Cheverst, K., Fitton, D., Rouncefield, M., & Graham, C. (2004). 'Smart Mobs' and Technology Probes: Evaluating Texting at Work. In *Proceedings of the 2004 European Conference on Information Technology Evaluation* (pp. 73-80). Royal Netherlands Academy of Arts and Sciences.

Chung-Chih, L., Ming-Jang, C., Chun-Chieh, H., Ren-Guey, L., & Yuh-Show, T. (2006). Wireless Health Care Service System for Elderly With Dementia. *Information Technology in Biomedicine. IEEE Transactions on*, *10*(4), 696–704.

Chung, L. K., Nixon, B. A., Yu, E., & Mylopoulos, J. (2000). *Non-Functional Requirements in Software Engineering.* Kluwer Publishing. doi:10.1007/978-1-4615-5269-7

Churchill, E. (2017). The Ethnographic Lens: Perspectives and Opportunities for New Data Dialects. *EPIC2017*. Retrieved from https://www.epicpeople.org/ethnographic-lens/

CoA. (2011). *Don't fall for it. Falls can be prevented!* Canberra: Commonwealth of Australia.

COBALT. (2013). *Older people have a thirst for technology.* The University of Sheffield. Retrieved 20 November, 2013, from http://www.shef.ac.uk/news/nr/older-people-and-technology-1.275964

Codd, E. F. (1970). A relational model of data for large shared data banks. *Communications of the ACM*, *13*(6), 377–387. doi:10.1145/362384.362685

Codd, E. F. (1971). *Further normalization of the database relational model. Courant Computer Science Symposia 6: Data Base Systems.* Englewood Cliffs, NJ: Prentice-Hall.

Colmerauer, A., & Roussel, P. (1993). The birth of Prolog. In *Proceedings of HOPL-II The second ACM SIGPLAN conference on history of programming languages*. New York, NY: ACM. 10.1145/154766.155362

Constine, J. (2017). *Facebook now has 2 billion monthly users... and responsibility*. Retrieved on 30 Nov 2017, from https://techcrunch.com/2017/06/27/facebook-2-billion-users/

Cooper, S., Dann, W., & Pausch, R. (2003). Teaching objects-first in introductory computer science. *Proceedings of the 34th SIGCSE Technical Symposium on Computer Science Education* (pp. 191-195). New York: ACM Press. 10.1145/611892.611966

Coyne, R. (2011). *Profile yourself (Narcissus on line)*. Retrieved February 20, 2013, from http://richardcoyne.com/2011/02/12/narcissus-on-line/

Crabtree, A., French, A., Greenhalgh, C., Benford, S., Cheverst, K., Fitton, D., ... Graham, C. (2006). Developing digital records: Early experiences of Record and Replay. *Computer Supported Cooperative Work*, *15*(4), 281–319. doi:10.100710606-006-9026-z

Crabtree, A., Hemmings, T., Rodden, T., Cheverst, K., Clarke, K., Dewsbury, G., ... Rouncefield, M. (2003). Designing with care: Adapting Cultural Probes to inform design in sensitive settings. In *Proceedings of the 2003 Australasian Conference on Computer-Human Interaction* (pp. 4-13). Brisbane, Australia: Ergonomics Society of Australia.

Crabtree, A., Rodden, T., Tolmie, P., & Button, G. (2009). Ethnography considered harmful. In *Proceedings of the 2009 International Conference on Human Factors in Computing Systems* (pp. 879-88). New York: ACM.

Cross, N. (2011). *Design Thinking*. London: Bloomsbury Publishing. doi:10.5040/9781474293884

Culter, K.-M. (2010). Why Mark Zuckerberg needs to come clean about his views on privacy. *SocialBeat*. Retrieved on July 15, 2011 from http://social.venturebeat.com/2010/05/13/zuckerberg-privacy/

Dabbagh, N., & Kitsantas, A. (2012). Personal Learning Environments, social media, and self-regulated learning: A natural formula for connecting formal and informal learning. *Internet and Higher Education*, *15*(1), 3–8. doi:10.1016/j.iheduc.2011.06.002

Dahl, O. J., Myhrhaug, B., & Nygaard, K. (1967). *Simula 67 common base language*. Academic Press.

Dalmau, M. (2003). *Ambiguity as a Conceptual Framework for Design*. Technical Report: Contemporary Issues and Concepts in HCI, 7 November 2003. Retrieved from http://mcs.open.ac.uk/yr258/amb_frame/

Daniel, M. B., & Brown, D. M. (2007). Communicating design: developing web site documentation for design and planning. Berkeley, CA: Peachpit Press.

Dann, W. P., Cooper, S., & Pausch, R. (2011). *Learning to Program with Alice*. Prentice Hall Press.

Darke, P., & Shanks, G. (1996). Stakeholder viewpoints in requirements definition: A framework for understanding viewpoint development approaches. *Requirements Engineering, 1*(2), 88–105. doi:10.1007/BF01235904

Davies, J. N., Comerford, P., Grout, V., Rvachova, N., & Korkh, O. (2012). An investigation into the effect of rule complexity in access control list. *Радіоелектронні I Комп'ютерні Системи*, (5), 33–38.

Davis, H., Skov, M., Stougaard, M., & Vetere, F. (2007) Virtual Box: Supporting Mediated Family Intimacy through Virtual and Physical Play. In *Proceedings of the 19th Australasian Conference on Computer-Human Interaction, OZCHI '07* (pp. 151-159). CHISIG Australia. 10.1145/1324892.1324920

De Botton, A. (2014). *The News, A User's Manual*. Penguin.

De San Miguel, K., & Lewin, G. (2008). Brief Report: Personal emergency alarms: What impact do they have on older people's lives? *Australasian Journal on Ageing, 27*(2), 103–105. doi:10.1111/j.1741-6612.2008.00286.x PMID:18713202

Demirbilek, O., & Sener, B. (2003). Product design, semantics and emotional response. *Ergonomics, 46*(13-14), 1346–1360. doi:10.1080/00140130310001610874 PMID:14612324

Demiris, G., Rantz, M. J., Aud, M. A., Marek, K. D., Tyrer, H. W., Skubic, M., & Hussam, A. A. (2004). Older adults' attitudes towards and perceptions of 'smart home' technologies: A pilot study. *Informatics for Health & Social Care, 29*(2), 87–94. PMID:15370989

Demoly, F., Monticolo, D., Eynard, B., Rivest, L., & Gomes, S. (2010). Multiple viewpoint modelling framework enabling integrated product–process design. *International Journal on Interactive Design and Manufacturing, 4*(4), 269–280. doi:10.100712008-010-0107-3

Dennett, D. (1976). Conditions of Personhood. In A. O. Rorty (Ed.), *Identities of Persons* (pp. 175–196). Berkeley, CA: University of California Press.

Department for Education. (2013). *The National Curriculum in England: Computing programmes of study*. Available from: https://www.gov.uk/government/publications/national-curriculum-in-england-computing-programmes-of-study

Desmet, P. (2005). Measuring Emotion: Development and Application of an Instrument to Measure Emotional Responses to Products. In M. Blythe, K. Overbeeke, A. Monk, & P. Wright (Eds.), *Funology* (Vol. 3, pp. 111–123). Springer Netherlands. doi:10.1007/1-4020-2967-5_12

Desmet, P. M. A., & Hekkert, P. (2009). Special issue editorial: Design & Emotion. *International Journal of Design, 3*(2), 1–6.

Dewey, J. (1938). Experience and Education. *Touchstone (Nashville, Tenn.)*.

Dey, A. K., & De Guzman, E. (2006). From awareness to connectedness: the design and deployment of presence displays. In *Proceedings of the SIGCHI Conference on Human Factors in Computing Systems, CHI '06* (pp. 899-908). ACM Press. 10.1145/1124772.1124905

Dorling, M., & White, D. (2015). Scratch: A way to logo and python. *Proceedings of the 46th ACM Technical Symposium on Computer Science Education*, 191-196. 10.1145/2676723.2677256

Dourish, P. (2001b). *Where the Action Is: The Foundation of Embodied Interaction*. Cambridge, MA: MIT Press.

Dourish, P., Graham, C., Randall, D., & Rouncefield, M. (2010). Social Interaction and Mundane Technologies. *Theme Issue of Personal and Ubiquitous Computing*, *14*(3), 171–180. doi:10.100700779-010-0281-0

Downes, S. (2005). E-learning 2.0. *eLearning Mag*. Retrieved from http://elearnmag.acm.org/featured.cfm?aid=1104968

Downes, S. (2010). *Elements of a Personal Learning Environment*. ITK Conference, Keynote address, Hameenlinna, Finland. Accessed here: http://www.downes.ca/files/Personal%20Learning%20Environments.pdf

Durrant, A., Kirk, D., Pisanty, D. T., Moncur, W., Orzech, K., Schofield, T., ... Monk, A. (2017). Transitions in Digital Personhood: Online Activity in Early Retirement. In *Proceedings of the 2017 CHI Conference on Human Factors in Computing Systems (CHI '17)* (pp. 6398-6411). New York: ACM. 10.1145/3025453.3025913

Easterbrook, S., & Chechik, M. (2001). A framework for multi-valued reasoning over inconsistent viewpoints. *Software Engineering, 2001. ICSE 2001. Proceedings of the 23rd International Conference on*.

Edwards, K., & Grinter, R. (2001). At home with ubiquitous computing: Seven Challenges. In G.D. Abowd, B. Brumitt, & S.A. Shafer (Eds.), Lecture Notes In Computer Science: Vol. 2201. *Proceedings of the 3rd international Conference on Ubiquitous Computing* (pp. 256-272). London: Springer-Verlag. 10.1007/3-540-45427-6_22

Eichelberger, H., & Laner, C. (2010). *Unterrichtsentwicklung via eLearning*. München: Oldenbourg. doi:10.1524/9783486704754

Eichelberger, H., Laner, C., Kohlberg, W. D., Stary, E., & Stary, C. (2008). *Reformpädagogik goes E-Learning – neue Wege zur Selbstbestimmung von virtuellem Wissenstransfer und individualisiertem Wissenserwerb*. Oldebourg.

Enders, B. E., Heverhagen, T., Goedicke, M., Tröpfner, P., & Tracht, R. (2002). Towards an integration of different specification methods by using the Viewpoint Framework. *Journal of Integrated Design & Process Science*, *6*(2), 1–23.

Fabrini, F., Fusani, M., Gnesi, S., & Lami, G. (2001). An Automatic Quality Evaluation for Natural Language Requirements. In *Proceedings of the Seventh International Workshop on Requirements Engineering: Foundations for Software Quality, REFSQ '01, Lecture Notes in Computer Science*. Springer-Verlag.

Facebook. (2017). *Facebook's Graph API 2.0*. Accessed Nov 30, 2017 at: https://developers.facebook.com/docs/graph-api

Facebook. (2017). *Open Graph Reference Document*. Retrieved from https://developers.facebook.com/docs/reference/opengraph

Fagin, R. (1977). Functional dependencies in a relational database and propositional logic. *IBM Journal of Research and Development*, *21*(6), 534–544. doi:10.1147/rd.216.0534

Feiler, J. (2008). *How to do everything with Web 2.0 mashups*. New York, NY: McGraw-Hill.

Felder, R.M., & Silverman, I.K. (1988). Learning and teaching styles in engineering education. *Engineering Education*, *78*(7).

Feurzeig, W., & Papert, S. (1967). LOGO. *ODP-Open Directory Project*.

Fielding, N. (1994). Ethnography. In N. Gilbert (Ed.), *Research in Social Life*. London: Sage.

Fincher, S. (2015). What are we doing when we teach computing in schools? *Communications of the ACM*, *58*(5), 24–26. doi:10.1145/2742693

Fincher, S., Kölling, M., Utting, I., Brown, N. C. C., & Stevens, P. (2010). Repositories of Teaching Material and Communities of Use: Nifty Assignments and the Greenroom. *Proceedings of the Sixth international workshop on Computing education research*, 182-196. 10.1145/1839594.1839613

Finkelstein, A., Kramer, J., Nuseibeh, B., Finkelstein, L., & Goedicke, M. (1992). Viewpoints: A framework for integrating multiple perspectives in system development. *International Journal of Software Engineering and Knowledge Engineering*, *2*(01), 31–57. doi:10.1142/S0218194092000038

Fisher, P. T., & Murphy, B. D. (2010). *Spring Persistence with Hibernate*. Apress. doi:10.1007/978-1-4302-2633-8

Fletcher, G., & Lu, J. (2009). Human computing skills: Rethinking the K-12 experience. *Communications of the ACM*, *52*(2), 23–25. doi:10.1145/1461928.1461938

Forbes Inc. (2017). *Fortune 500*. Retrieved October 14, 2017 from http://fortune.com/fortune500/apple/

Fowler, M. (2009). *Refactoring: improving the design of existing code*. Pearson Education India.

Fox, J. (2011). *Five million Facebook users are 10 or younger*. ConsumerReports.org. Retrieved on July 15, 2011 from http://news.consumerreports.org/electronics/2011/05/five-million-facebook-users-are-10-or-younger.html

Fraser, N. (2013). Blockly: A visual programming editor. *Google developers*. Retrieved Feb 14, 2016 from: https://developers.google.com/blockly/

Friedman, R. S., & Deek, F. P. (2003). Innovation and Education in the Digital Age: Reconciling the Roles of Pedagogy, Technology, and the Business of Learning. *IEEE Transactions on Engineering Management*, *50*(4), 403–412. doi:10.1109/TEM.2003.819650

Garfinkel, H. (1996). Ethnomethodology's Program. *Social Psychology Quarterly, 59*(1), 5–21. doi:10.2307/2787116

Gause, D. C., & Weinberg, G. M. (1989). *Exploring Requirements: Quality Before Design*. New York: Dorset House.

Gaver, W. (2001). *Designing for Ludic Aspects of Everyday Life*. ERCIM News. No.47, October 2001. Retrieved at http://www.ercim.org/publication/Ercim_News/enw47/gaver.html

Gaver, B., Dunne, T., & Pacenti, E. (1999b). Cultural probes. *Interactions: New Visions of Human-Computer Interaction, 6*(1), 21–29. doi:10.1145/291224.291235

Gaver, W. H., Hooker, B., & Dunne, A. (1999a). *The Presence Project*. London: Department of Interaction Design.

Gaver, W., Beaver, J., & Benford, S. (2003). Ambiguity as a Resource for Design. In *Proceedings of CHI '03* (pp. 233-240). ACM Press. 10.1145/642611.642653

Gaver, W., Boucher, A., Pennington, S., & Walker, B. (2004). Cultural probes and the value of uncertainty. *Interactions: New Visions of Human-Computer Interaction, 11*(5), 53–56. doi:10.1145/1015530.1015555

Gaver, W., & Dunne, A. (1999). Projected Realities: Conceptual Design for Cultural Effect. *Proceedings of the 2003 SIGCHI Conference on Human Factors in Computing Systems* (pp. 600-7). New York, NY: ACM. 10.1145/302979.303168

Geertz, C. (2000). *Available Light*. Princeton, NJ: Princeton University Press.

Geron, T. (2011). *Facebook Moves Beyond 'Like'--To Listen, Watch, Eat, Run*. Retrieved on March 20, 2012, from http://www.forbes.com/sites/tomiogeron/2011/09/22/facebook-moves-beyond-like-to-listen-watch-eat-run/

Gilbert, N., & Terna, P. (2000). How to build and use agent-based models in social science. *Mind & Society, 1*(1), 57–72. doi:10.1007/BF02512229

Goguen, J., & Linde, C. (1993). Techniques for Requirements Elicitation. *Proceedings of RE, 93*, 152–164.

Goldberg, A., & Robson, D. (1983). *Smalltalk-80: the language and its implementation*. Addison-Wesley Longman Publishing Co., Inc.

Gonzalez-Sanchez, J., Chavez-Echeagaray, M. E., Vanlehn, K., & Burleson, W. (2011). From behavioral description to a pattern-based model for intelligent tutoring systems. In *Proceedings of the 18th Conference on Pattern Languages of Programs* (paper 26). ACM. 10.1145/2578903.2579164

Good, J. & de Boulay. (2014). Guest Editorial Preface. *Special Issue on Personalised Learning. International Journal of People-Oriented Programming, 3*(2).

Good, J. (2011). Learners at the Wheel: Novice Programming Environments Come of Age. *International Journal of People-Oriented Programming, 1*(1), 1–24. doi:10.4018/ijpop.2011010101

Good, J. (2018). Novice Programming Environments: Lowering the Barriers, Supporting the Progression. In S. Goschnick (Ed.), *Innovative Methods, User-Friendly Tools, Coding, and Design Approaches in People-Oriented Programming*. Hershey, PA: Information Science Publishing.

Good, J., & Howland, K. (2017). Programming language, natural language? Supporting the diverse computational activities of novice programmers. *Journal of Visual Languages and Computing*, *39*, 78–92. doi:10.1016/j.jvlc.2016.10.008

Good, J., Howland, K., & Nicholson, K. (2010). Young people's descriptions of computational rules in role-playing games: An empirical study. In *2010 IEEE Symposium on Visual Languages and Human-Centric Computing (VL/HCC)* (pp. 67-74). IEEE. 10.1109/VLHCC.2010.18

Good, J., & Robertson, J. (2006). CARSS: A framework for learner-centred design with children. *International Journal of Artificial Intelligence in Education*, *16*(4), 381–413.

Google. (2011). *Google Terms of Services*. Retrieved from http://www.google.com/accounts/TOS

Goschnick, S. (1998). Design and Development of Melbourne IT Creator – a System for Authoring and Management of Online Education. Academic Press.

Goschnick, S. (2005). *The FUN File Manager*. Accessed Nov 30, 2017 from http://digitalfriend.org/knowledge-tree/know.html

Goschnick, S. (2006). *The DigitalFriend: The First End-User Oriented Multi-Agent System*. OSDC 2006, the third Open Source Developers Conference, Melbourne, Australia.

Goschnick, S. (2009). People-Oriented Programming: from Agent-Oriented Analysis to the design of interactive systems. In J.A. Jacko (Ed.), Lecture Notes In Computer Science: Vol. 5610. *Human-Computer Interaction: New Trends. Proceedings of the 13th International Conference of HCI International* (pp. 836-845). Berlin: Springer-Verlag. 10.1007/978-3-642-02574-7_93

Goschnick, S. (2014). Facebook From Five Thousand Feet: a visual mapping from conceptual model down to ground level graph api data. eBookDynasty.net.

Goschnick, S. B. (2001). *Shadowboard: An agent architecture for enacting a sophisticated Digital Self* (Thesis). Dept. of Computer Science and Software Engineering, University of Melbourne, Melbourne, Australia.

Goschnick, S. B., Balbo, S., Sterling, L., & Sun, C. (2006). TANDEM - a design method for integrating Web services into multi-agent dystems. In *Proceedings, Fifth Joint Conference on Autonomous Agents and Multi-Agent Systems (AAMAS-06)* (pp.939-941). Academic Press. 10.1145/1160633.1160799

Goschnick, S., & Balbo, S. (2005). Game-first programming for information systems students. *Proceedings of the second Australasian conference on Interactive entertainment*. Creativity & Cognition Studios Press.

Goschnick, S., & Graham, C. (2006). Augmenting Interaction and Cognition using Agent Architectures and Technology Inspired by Psychology and Social Worlds. Universal Access in the Information Society, 4(3), 204-222.

Goschnick, S., Sterling, L., & Sonenberg, L. (2015). Modelling Human Activity in People-Oriented Programming with Metamodels. International Journal of People-Oriented Programming, 4(2), 1-24. doi:10.4018/IJPOP.2015070101

Goschnick, S. (2006) The DigitalFriend: the First End-User Oriented Multi-Agent System. *Proceedings of the 3rd Open Source Developers Conference (OSDC-2006).*

Goschnick, S. (2014). *Facebook from Five Thousand Feet: A Visual Mapping from Conceptual Model to Ground-level Graph API Data.* EbookDynasty.net.

Goschnick, S. (2015). App Review: ScratchJr (Scratch Junior). *International Journal of People-Oriented Programming, 4*(1), 50–55. doi:10.4018/IJPOP.2015010104

Goschnick, S. B., & Cassin, A. (1997). *Requirements Document – Agents-in-cMILE V1.0. Internal Document, Melbourne IT Pty Ltd.* University of Melbourne.

Goschnick, S., & Balbo, S. (2005). Game-first programming for information systems students. In *Proceedings of the Second Australasian Conference on Interactive Entertainment* (pp. 71-74). Creativity & Cognition Studios Press.

Goschnick, S., Balbo, S., & Sonenberg, L. (2008). From Task Models to Agent-Oriented Meta-models, and Back Again. *Proceedings, TAMODIA-2008 the 7th Workshop on Task Models and Diagrams.* 10.1007/978-3-540-85992-5_4

Goschnick, S., & Graham, C. (2006). Augmenting Interaction and Cognition using Agent Architectures and Technology Inspired by Psychology and Social Worlds. *Universal Access in the Information Society, 4*(3), 204–222. doi:10.100710209-005-0012-x

Goschnick, S., & Sterling, L. (2003). Enacting and Interacting with an Agent-based Digital Self in a 24x7 Web Services World. In *Proceedings, IEEE Joint Conference on Web Intelligence and Intelligent Agent Technology (WI/IAT).* Halifax, Canada: IEEE.

Gosling, J. (2000). *The Java language specification.* Addison-Wesley Professional.

Graham, C., Cheverst, K., & Rouncefield, M. (2006). Technology For The Humdrum: Trajectories, Interactional Needs and a Care Setting. *AJIS. Australasian Journal of Information Systems, 13*(2). doi:10.3127/ajis.v13i2.43

Graham, C., & Rouncefield, M. (2008). Probes and Participation. In *Proceedings of the Tenth Anniversary Conference on Participatory Design 2008 (PDC '08)* (pp. 194-197). Indianapolis, IN: Indiana University.

Graham, C., Rouncefield, M., Gibbs, M., Vetere, F., & Cheverst, K. (2007). How probes work. In *Proceedings of the 19th Australasian Conference on Computer-Human interaction, OZCHI '07* (pp. 29-37). ACM Press.

Graham, C., Rouncefield, M., Gibbs, M., Vetere, F., & Cheverst, K. (2007). How probes work. In *Proceedings of the 2007 Australasian Conference on Computer-Human Interaction: Entertaining User Interfaces* (pp. 29-37). New York, NY: ACM.

Graham, C., Rouncefield, M., & Satchell, C. (2009). Blogging as 'therapy'? Exploring personal technologies for smoking cessation. *Health Informatics Journal*, *15*(4), 1–15. doi:10.1177/1460458209345897 PMID:20007652

Gray, J. A. (1985). The whole and its parts: Behaviour, the brain, cognition and emotion. *Bulletin of the British Psychological Society*, *38*, 99–112.

Green, T. R. G., & Petre, M. (1996). Usability analysis of visual programming environments: A cognitive dimensions framework. *Journal of Visual Languages and Computing*, *7*(2), 131–174. doi:10.1006/jvlc.1996.0009

Grinter, R. E., & Eldridge, M. (2003). Wan2tlk?: Everyday text messaging. In *Proceedings of the 2003 SIGCHI Conference on Human Factors in Computing Systems* (pp. 441-448). New York, NY: ACM.

Gross, H. (2005). *Component-based Software Testing with UML*. Springer.

Gross, P. A., Herstand, M. S., Hodges, J. W., & Kelleher, C. L. (2010). A code reuse interface for non-programmer middle school students. *Proceedings of the 14th International Conference on Intelligent User Interfaces* (pp. 219-228). New York: ACM Press. 10.1145/1719970.1720001

Gross, S., Mokbel, B., Hammer, B., & Pinkwart, N. (2013). Towards a domain-independent its middleware architecture. In *13th International Conference on Advanced Learning Technologies (ICALT)*. IEEE.

Grover, S., Cooper, S., & Pea, R. (2014). Assessing computational learning in K-12. In *Proceedings of the 2014 Conference on Innovation & Technology in Computer Science Education* (pp. 57-62). ACM.

Grudin, J. (1990). The Computer Reaches Out: The Historical Continuity of Interface Design. In J. C. Chew, & J. Whiteside (Eds), *Proceedings of the 1990 SIGCHI Conference on Human Factors in Computing Systems: Empowering People* (pp. 261-268). New York, NY: ACM. 10.1145/97243.97284

Guédria, W., & Naudet, Y. (2014). Extending the ontology of enterprise interoperability (ooei) using enterprise-as-system concepts. In *Enterprise Interoperability VI. Proceedings of the I-ESA Conferences* (*vol. 7*, pp. 393–403). Springer International Publishing Switzerland. 10.1007/978-3-319-04948-9_33

Guédria, W., Gaaloul, K., Naudet, Y., & Proper, H. (2013). A Modelling Approach to Support Enterprise Architecture Interoperability. In Y. T. Demey & H. Panetto (Eds.), *OTM 2013 Workshops, LNCS 8186* (pp. 189–198). Heidelberg, Germany: Springer Berlin. doi:10.1007/978-3-642-41033-8_27

Guizzardi, R., & Perini, A. (2005). Analyzing requirements of knowledge management systems with the support of agent organizations. *Journal of the Brazilian Computer Society, 11*(1), 51–62.

Gulwani, S., & Marron, M. (2014). NLyze: Interactive programming by natural language for spreadsheet data analysis and manipulation. *Proceedings of the 2014 ACM SIGMOD International Conference on Management of Data*, 803–814. 10.1145/2588555.2612177

Guzdial, M. (2004). Programming environments for novices. In S. Fincher & M. Petre (Eds.), *Computer Science Education Research* (pp. 127–154). London: Taylor & Francis.

Guzdial, M. (2008). Paving the way for computational thinking. *Communications of the ACM, 51*(8), 25–27. doi:10.1145/1378704.1378713

Hadjerrouit, S. (2005). Learner-Centered Web-based Instruction in Software Engineering. *IEEE Transactions on Education, 48*(1), 99–104. doi:10.1109/TE.2004.832871

Halimi, K., Seridi-Bouchelaghem, H., & Faron-Zucker, C. (2014). An enhanced personal learning environment using social semantic web technologies. *Interactive Learning Environments, 22*(2), 165–187. doi:10.1080/10494820.2013.788032

Hammami, S., Mathkour, H., & Al-Mosallam, E. A. (2009). A multi-agent architecture for adaptive E-learning systems using a blackboard agent. *Int. Conf. On Computer Science and Information Technology*, 184-188 10.1109/ICCSIT.2009.5234741

Hanson, E., & Magnusson, L. (2011). The role of ICT support services to promote ageing in place: The ACTION service. *Eurohealth (London), 17*(2-3), 24–26.

Harms, K. J., Rowlett, N., & Kelleher, C. (2015). Enabling independent learning of programming concepts through programming completion puzzles. In *Proceedings of the 2015 IEEE Symposium on Visual Languages and Human-Centric Computing (VL/HCC)* (pp. 271-279). IEEE. doi:10.1145/2485760.2485764

Harms, K. J., Cosgrove, D., Gray, S., & Kelleher, C. (2013). Automatically generating tutorials to enable middle school children to learn programming independently. In *Proceedings of the 12th International Conference on Interaction Design and Children* (pp. 11-19). ACM.

Hart, J. (2015). *2014 Top 100 Tools for Learning*. Available at http://c4lpt.co.uk/top100tools/

Harvey, B., & Mönig, J. (2010). Bringing "no ceiling" to Scratch: Can one language serve kids and computer scientists. *Proc. Constructionism*, 1-10.

Harvey, B., & Mönig, J. (2015). Lambda in blocks languages: Lessons learned. *IEEE Blocks and Beyond Workshop (Blocks and Beyond)*, 35-38. 10.1109/BLOCKS.2015.7368997

Hassling, L., Nordfeldt, S., Eriksson, H., & Timpka, T. (2005). Use of cultural probes for representation of chronic disease experience: Exploration of an innovative method for design of supportive technologies. *Technology and Health Care, 13*(2), 87–95. PMID:15912006

Hemmings, T., Clarke, K., Crabtree, A., Rodden, T., & Rouncefield, M. (2002). Probing the Probes. In *Proceedings of PDC '02* (pp. 42-50). ACM Press.

Henriksen, P., & Kölling, M. (2004). Greenfoot: combining object visualisation with interaction. *Companion to the 19th annual ACM SIGPLAN conference on Object-oriented programming systems, languages, and applications,* 73-82.

Heo, J., Kim, J., & Won, Y.-S. (2011). Exploring the Relationship Between Internet Use and Leisure Satisfaction Among Older Adults. *Activities, Adaptation and Aging, 35*(1), 43–54. doi: 10.1080/01924788.2010.545975

Hoffer, J. A., Prescott, M. B., & McFadden, F. R. (2007). *Modern Database Management* (8th ed.). New Jersey: Pearson Prentice Hall.

Homer, M., & Noble, J. (2014). Combining tiled and textual views of code. In *2014 Second IEEE Working Conference on Software Visualisation (VISSOFT)* (pp. 1-10). IEEE. 10.1109/VISSOFT.2014.11

Homer, M., & Noble, J. (2014). Combining tiled and textual views of code. *Software Visualization (VISSOFT), 2014 Second IEEE Working Conference on Software Visualization,* 1-10.

How to pick the best temperature sensor for your Arduino project. (2015, February 16). Retrieved from http://www.intorobotics.com/pick-best-temperature-sensor-arduino-project/

Howland, K., Good, J., & Robertson, J. (2006). Script Cards: A visual programming language for games authoring by young people. In *Proceedings of the 2006 IEEE Symposium on Visual Languages and Human-Centric Computing (VL/HCC)* (pp. 181-184). IEEE.

Howland, K., & Good, J. (2015). Learning to communicate computationally with Flip: A bi-modal programming language for game creation. *Computers & Education, 80,* 224–240. doi:10.1016/j.compedu.2014.08.014

Howland, K., Good, J., & du Boulay, B. (2008). A game creation tool which supports the development of writing skills: Interface design considerations. In *Proceedings of Narrative and Interactive Learning Environments (NILE 08),* 23-29.

Howland, K., Good, J., & du Boulay, B. (2013). Narrative Threads: A tool to support young people in creating their own narrative-based computer games. In *Transactions on Edutainment X* (pp. 122–145). Berlin: Springer. doi:10.1007/978-3-642-37919-2_7

Howland, K., Good, J., & Nicholson, K. (2009). Language-based support for computational thinking. In *Proceedings of the 2009 IEEE Symposium on Visual Languages and Human-Centric Computing (VL/HCC),* (pp. 147-150). IEEE. 10.1109/VLHCC.2009.5295278

Hughes, J. A., Randall, D., & Shapiro, D. (1993). From Ethnographic Record to System Design: Some Experiences from the Field. *Computer Supported Cooperative Work, 1*(3), 123–141. doi:10.1007/BF00752435

Hughes, J., O'Brien, J., Rodden, T., Rouncefield, M., & Sommerville, I. (1995). Presenting Ethnography in the Requirements Process. *Proceedings of RE, 95*, 27–34.

Hulkko, S., Mattelmäki, T., Virtanen, K., & Keinonen, T. (2004). Mobile probes. In *Proceedings of the Third Nordic Conference on Human-Computer Interaction* (pp. 43-451). New York, NY: ACM. 10.1145/1028014.1028020

Hundhausen, C. D., Farley, S. F., & Brown, J. L. (2009). Can direct manipulation lower the barriers to computer programming and promote transfer of training?: An experimental study. *ACM Transactions on Computer-Human Interaction, 16*(3), 13. doi:10.1145/1592440.1592442

Hung, J. (2012). Trends of e-learning research from 2000 to 2008: Use of text mining and bibliometrics. *British Journal of Educational Technology, 43*(1), 5–16. doi:10.1111/j.1467-8535.2010.01144.x

Hussain, N., & Kahn, M. K. (2005). Service-Oriented E-Learning Architecture Using Web Service-Based Intelligent Agents. *Int. Conf. On Information and Communication Technologies*, 137-143. 10.1109/ICICT.2005.1598570

Hutchinson, H., Mackay, W., Westerlund, B., Bederson, B.B, Druin, A., Plaisant, C., ... Eiderbäck, B. (2003). Technology probes: Inspiring Design for and with Families. In *Proceedings of the 2003 SIGCHI Conference on Human Factors in Computing Systems* (pp. 17-24). New York, NY: ACM.

Iacob, M., Jonkers, H., Lankhorst, M., Proper, H., & Quartel, D. (2012). *ArchiMate 2.0 Specification*. The Open Group.

Iacucci, G., & Kuutti, K. (2002). Everyday life as a stage in creating and performing scenarios for wireless devices. *Personal and Ubiquitous Computing, 6*(4), 299–306. doi:10.1007007790200031

Ingalls, D., Kaehler, T., Maloney, J., Wallace, S., & Kay, A. (1997). Back to the future: The story of Squeak, a practical Smalltalk written in itself. *ACM SIGPLAN Notices, 32*(10), 318–326. doi:10.1145/263700.263754

Intille, S., Kukla, C., & Ma, X. (2002). Eliciting User Preferences Using Image-based Experience Sampling and Reflection. In *CHI '02 Extended Abstracts on Human Factors in Computing Systems* (pp. 738–739). New York, NY: ACM. doi:10.1145/506443.506573

Isikdag, U. (2015). Internet of Things: Single-Board Computers. In Enhanced Building Information Models (pp. 43-53). Springer International Publishing.

Iversen, O. S., & Nielsen, C. 2003. Using digital cultural probes in design with children. In S. S. MacFarlane, T. Nicol, J. Read, & L. Snape (Eds.), *Proceedings of the 2003 Conference on Interaction Design and Children* (pp.154-154). New York, NY: ACM. 10.1145/953536.953564

JACK, Autonomous Decision Making Software. (2015). Retrieved at http://aosgrp.com/products/jack

Jonkers, H., & Proper, H. A. (2009). *TOGAF and ArchiMate: A Future Together*. White Paper W192. The Open Group.

Jordan, M. I., & Mitchell, T. M. (2015). Machine learning: Trends, perspectives, and prospects. *Science, 349*(6245), 255–260. doi:10.1126cience.aaa8415 PMID:26185243

Juan, T., Pearce, A., & Sterling, L. (2002). *ROADMAP: Extending the Gaia Methodology for Complex Open Systems*. Paper presented at the First International Joint Conference on Autonomous Agents and Multiagent Systems, AAMAS 2002, Bologna, Italy. 10.1145/544741.544744

Jureta, I. J., & Faulkner, S. (2007) Clarifying goal models. *Proc. ER 2007*, 139-144.

Jureta, I. J., & Faulkner, S. (2007). Clarifying Goal Models: Conceptual Modeling. In *Proceedings of 26th International Conference on Conceptual Modeling, ER 2007*(pp. 139-144). Australian Computer Society.

Jureta, I. J., Faulkner, S., & Schobbens, P. Y. (2006). A More Expressive Softgoal Conceptualization for Quality Requirements Analysis Conceptual Modeling. In *Proceedings of 25th International Conference on Conceptual Modeling, ER '06* (pp. 281-295). Springer.

Jureta, I. J., Mylopoulos, J., & Faulkner, S. (2008). Revisiting the Core Ontology and Problem in Requirements Engineering. In *Proceedings of 16th IEEE International Conference on Requirements Engineering, RE '08* (pp. 71-80). Springer. 10.1109/RE.2008.13

Kamsties, E., Berry, D. M., & Paech, B. (2001). Detecting Ambiguities in Requirements Documents Using Inspections. In *Proceedings of the First Workshop on Inspection in Software Engineering, WISE '01* (pp. 68-80). IEEE Computer Society.

Kay, A. (2005). *Squeak Etoys Authoring & Media*. Viewpoints Research Institute.

Kelleher, C. (2008). Using storytelling to introduce girls to computer programming. *Beyond Barbie & Mortal Kombat: New Perspectives on Gender and Gaming*, 247–264.

Kelleher, C., Cosgrove, D., Culyba, D., Forlines, C., Pratt, J., & Pausch, R. (2002). Alice 2: Programming without syntax errors. In *Proceedings of the 2002 Conference on User Interface Software and Technology*. Available from: https://uist.acm.org/archive/adjunct/2002/pdf/demos/p35-kelleher.pdf

Kelleher, C., & Pausch, R. (2005). Lowering the barriers to programming. *ACM Computing Surveys, 37*(2), 83–137. doi:10.1145/1089733.1089734

Kelleher, C., & Pausch, R. (2007). Using storytelling to motivate programming. *Communications of the ACM, 50*(7), 58–64. doi:10.1145/1272516.1272540

Kelleher, C., Pausch, R., & Kiesler, S. (2007). Storytelling Alice motivates middle school girls to learn computer programming. In *Proceedings of the SIGCHI Conference on Human Factors in Computing Systems* (pp. 1455 - 1464). New York: ACM Press. 10.1145/1240624.1240844

Kent, W. A. (1983). A simple guide to five normal forms in relational database theory. *Communications of the ACM, 26*(2), 120–125. doi:10.1145/358024.358054

Kerrigan, F., & Hart, A. (2016). Theorising Digital Personhood: A Dramaturgical Approach. *Journal of Marketing Management, 32*(17-18), 1701–1721. doi:10.1080/0267257X.2016.1260630

Kerschberg, L. (1984). Expert database systems. *Proceedings, The 1st International Conference on Expert Database Systems.*

Khalid, S. U., Basharat, A., Shahid, A. A., & Hassan, S. (2009). An adaptive E-learning Framework to supporting new ways of teaching and learning. *Int. Conf. On Information and Communication Technologies*, 300-306. 10.1109/ICICT.2009.5267175

Kiersch, J. (2007). *Die Waldorfpädagogik.* Verlag Freies Geistesleben.

Kim, K. O. (2012). *The emotional responses of older adults to new technology (Ph.D.).* University of Illinois at Urbana-Champaign.

Kirikova, M., Grundspenkis, J., Wojtkowski, W., Zupancic, J., & Wrycza, S. (2002). *Information Systems Development: Advances in Methodologies, Components, and Management.* Springer. doi:10.1007/978-1-4615-0167-1

Kirkpatrick, D. (2010). *The Facebook Effect: The Inside Story of the Company that is Connecting the World.* Simon & Schuster.

Kissoon-Curumsing, M., Pedell, S., & Vasa, R. (2014). Designing an Evaluation Tool to Measure Emotional Goals. International Journal of People-Oriented Programming, 3(1), 22-43.

Kitchen, R. (2014, April). Big Data, New Epistemologies and Paradigm Shifts. *Big Data & Society*, 1–12.

Kjeldskov, J. (2014). *Mobile Interactions in Context: A Designerly Way Toward Digital Ecology. Synthesis Lectures on Human-Centered Informatics.* Morgan & Claypool Publishers.

Kjeldskov, J., Gibbs, M., Vetere, F., Howard, S., Pedell, S., Mecoles, K., & Bunyan, M. (2005). Using Cultural Probes To Explore Mediated Intimacy. *AJIS. Australian Journal of Information Systems, 1*(12), 102–115.

Kleppe, A. G., Warmer, J. B., & Bast, W. (2003). *MDA explained: the model driven architecture: practice and promise.* Addison-Wesley Professional.

Ko, A. J., Myers, B. A., & Chau, D. H. (2006). A linguistic analysis of how people describe software problems. In Visual Languages and Human-Centric Computing (VL/HCC'06) (pp. 127–134). Academic Press. doi:10.1109/VLHCC.2006.3

Kölling, M. (1999a). *The Design of an Object-Oriented Environment and Language for Teaching* (Ph.D. thesis). Basser Department of Computer Science, University of Sydney.

Kölling, M. (2010). The Greenfoot programming environment. ACM Transactions of Computing Education, 10(4), Article 14.

Kölling, M. (2010). The Greenfoot Programming Environment. *ACM Transactions on Computing Education, 10*(4), 182-196.

Kölling, M., Brown, N., & Altadmri, A. (2017). Frame-Based Editing. *Journal of Visual Languages and Sentient Systems, 3*.

Kölling, M. (1999b). The Problem of Teaching Object-Oriented Programming, Part 1: Languages. *Journal of Object-Oriented Programming, 11*(8), 8–15.

Kölling, M. (1999c). The Problem of Teaching Object-Oriented Programming, Part 2: Environments. *Journal of Object-Oriented Programming, 11*(9), 6–12.

Kölling, M. (2015). Lessons from the Design of three educational programming environments: Blue, BlueJ and Greenfoot. *International Journal of People-Oriented Programming, 4*(1), 5–32. doi:10.4018/IJPOP.2015010102

Kölling, M. (2016). *Introduction to Programming with Greenfoot: Object-Oriented Programming in Java with Games and Simulations* (2nd ed.). Pearson.

Kölling, M. (2018). Blue, BlueJ, Greenfoot: Designing Educational Programming Environments. In S. Goschnick (Ed.), *Innovative Methods, User-Friendly Tools, Coding, and Design Approaches in People-Oriented Programming*. Hershey, PA: Information Science Publishing.

Kölling, M., Brown, N., & Altadmri, A. (2015). Frame-Based Editing: Easing the Transition from Blocks to Text-Based Programming. *Proceedings of the 10th Workshop in Primary and Secondary Computing Education*, 29-38. 10.1145/2818314.2818331

Kölling, M., & Henriksen, P. (2005). Game programming in introductory courses with direct state manipulation. In *Proceedings of the 10th ACM–SIGCSE Annual Conference on Innovation and Technology in Computer Science Education* (pp. 59-63). New York: ACM Press. 10.1145/1067445.1067465

Kölling, M., Koch, B., & Rosenberg, J. (1995). Requirements for a First Year Object-Oriented Teaching Language. *Proceedings of the 26th SIGCSE Technical Symposium on Computer Science Education*, 173-177. 10.1145/199688.199770

Kölling, M., Quig, B., Patterson, A., & Rosenberg, J. (2003). The BlueJ system and its pedagogy. *Computer Science Education, 13*, 249–268. doi:10.1076/csed.13.4.249.17496

Kölling, M., & Rosenberg, J. (1996). An object-oriented program development environment for the first programming course. *ACM SIGCSE Bulletin, 28*(1), 83–87. doi:10.1145/236462.236514

Kölling, M., & Rosenberg, J. (2000). Objects first with Java and BlueJ (seminar session). *ACM SIGCSE Bulletin, 32*(1), 429. doi:10.1145/331795.331912

Kortuem, G., Kawsar, F., Fitton, D., & Sundramoorthy, V. (2010). Smart objects as building blocks for the internet of things. *IEEE Internet Computing, 14*(1), 44–51. doi:10.1109/MIC.2009.143

Kotonya, G., & Sommerville, I. (1996). Requirements Engineering With Viewpoints. *Software Engineering Journal, 11*(1), 5–18. doi:10.1049ej.1996.0002

Kowalski, R. A. (1988). The early years of logic programming. *Communications of the ACM*, *31*(1), 38–43. doi:10.1145/35043.35046

Latham, A., Crockett, K., McLean, D., & Edmonds, B. (2012). A conversational intelligent tutoring system to automatically predict learning styles. *Computers & Education*, *59*(1), 95–109. doi:10.1016/j.compedu.2011.11.001

Law, J. (2004). *After Method: Mess in Social Science Research*. Oxon, UK: Routledge.

Lee, K. D. (2011). Event-Driven Programming. In Python Programming Fundamentals (pp. 149-165). Springer London. doi:10.1007/978-1-84996-537-8_6

Lee, R. M. (1985). Database inferencing for decision support. *Decision Support Systems*, *1*(1), 57–68. doi:10.1016/0167-9236(85)90197-6

Leonard, A. (2010). *JSF 2.0 Cookbook: Over 100 simple but incredibly effective recipes for taking control of your JSF applications*. Packt Publishing Ltd.

Leung, L. (2015). A Panel Study on the Effects of Social Media Use and Internet Connectedness on Academic Performance and Social Support. *International Journal of Cyber Behavior, Psychology and Learning*, *5*(1), 1-16. doi:10.4018/ijcbpl.2015010101

Lieberman, H., & Ahmad, M. (2010). *Knowing what you're talking about: Natural language programming of a multi-player online game. In No Code Required: Giving Users Tools to Transform the Web*. Morgan Kaufmann.

Lillard, A. S. (2007). *Montessori – The Science behind the Genius*. Oxford Press.

Limongelli, C., Sciarrone, F., Temperini, M., & Vaste, G. (2011). The Lecomps5 framework for personaliszed web-based learning: A teacher's satisfaction perspective. *Computers in Human Behavior*, *27*(4), 1301–1320. doi:10.1016/j.chb.2010.07.026

Lindley, J., & Coulton, P. (2015). Back to the Future: Ten Years of Design Fiction. In *Proceedings of the 2015 British HCI Conference* (pp. 210-211). New York, NY: ACM. 10.1145/2783446.2783592

Liu, X., Holden, B., & Wu, D. (2017). Automated Synthesis of Access Control Lists. In *Software Security and Assurance (ICSSA), 2017 International Conference on*. IEEE.

Liu, X., Jiang, Y., Wu, L., & Wu, D. (2016). Natural Shell: An Assistant for End-User Scripting. *International Journal of People-Oriented Programming*, *5*(1), 1–18. doi:10.4018/IJPOP.2016010101

Liu, X., & Wu, D. (2014). PiE: Programming in Eliza. In *Proceedings of the 29th ACM/IEEE International Conference on Automated Software Engineering* (pp. 695–700). ACM.

LiuX.WuD. (2016). *PiE-LOGO*. Available: http://bambool.github.io/pie-logo/index.htm

Li, Y., Chen, Z., Huang, R., & Cheng, X. (2009). New e-Learning system architecture based on knowledge engineering technology. *IEEE Int. Conf. On Systems, Man and Cybernetics*, 5140-5144. 10.1109/ICSMC.2009.5346013

Loizou, G., & Thanish, P. (1983). Testing a dependency-preserving decomposition for losslessness. *Information Systems*, *8*(1), 25–28. doi:10.1016/0306-4379(83)90026-1

Loke, S. W. D., & Sterling, L. (1996). *CiFi: An Intelligent Agent for Citation Finding on the World-Wide Web*. Technical Report 96/4. Department of Computer Science, the University of Melbourne.

Lopez-Lorca, A., Miller, T., Pedell, S., Mendoza, A., Keirnan, A., & Sterling, L. (2014). One size doesn't fit all: diversifying "the user" using personas and emotional scenarios. In *Proceedings of the 6th International Workshop on Social Software Engineering* (pp. 25-32). New York: ACM Press. 10.1145/2661685.2661691

Lorence, D., & Park, H. (2006). New technology and old habits: The role of age as a technology chasm. *Technology and Health Care*, *14*(2), 91–96. PMID:16720952

Lucchesi, C. L., & Osborn, S. L. (1978). Candidate keys for relations. *Journal of Computer and System Sciences*, *17*(2), 270–280. doi:10.1016/0022-0000(78)90009-0

Luckin, R. (2008). The Learner Centric Ecology of Resources: A Framework for using Technology to Scaffold Learning. *Computers & Education*, *50*(2), 449–462. doi:10.1016/j.compedu.2007.09.018

Macgregor, P. (1995). Chinese? Australian? the limits of geography and ethnicity as determinants of cultural identity. In J. Ryan (Ed.), *Chinese in Australia and New Zealand: a multidisciplinary approach* (pp. 5–20). New Delhi: New Age International.

MacLaurin, M. (2009). Kodu: End-user programming and design for games. *Proceedings of the 4th International Conference on Foundations of Digital Games*, 2. 10.1145/1536513.1536516

MacLean, A., Bellotti, V., & Young, R. (1990). What rationale is there in design? In *Proceedings of the IFIP TC13 Third International Conference on Human-Computer Interaction* (pp. 207-212). Amsterdam: North-Holland Publishing Co.

Maloney, J., Resnick, M., Rusk, N., Silverman, B., & Eastmond, E. (2010). The Scratch programming language and environment. *ACM Transactions on Computing Education, 10*(4), 16:2-16:15.

Maloney, J., Peppler, K., Kafai, Y. B., Resnick, M., & Rusk, N. (2008). Programming by choice: Urban youth learning programming with Scratch. In *Proceedings of the 39th SIGCSE Technical Symposium on Computer Science Education* (pp. 367-371). New York: ACM Press. 10.1145/1352135.1352260

Maloney, J., Resnick, M., Rusk, N., Silverman, B., & Eastmond, E. (2010). The Scratch programming language and environment. *ACM Transactions on Computing Education*, *10*(4), 16. doi:10.1145/1868358.1868363

Mamykina, L., & Mynatt, E. D. (2007). Investigating and supporting health management practices of individuals with diabetes. In *Proceedings of the 1st ACM SIGMOBILE International Workshop on Systems and Networking Support For Healthcare and Assisted Living Environments* (pp. 49-54). New York, NY: ACM. 10.1145/1248054.1248068

Mamykina, L., Mynatt, E. D., & Kaufman, D. R. (2006). Investigating health management practices of individuals with diabetes. In *Proceedings of the 2006 SIGCHI Conference on Human Factors in Computing Systems* (pp. 927-36). New York, NY: ACM. 10.1145/1124772.1124910

Marca, D. A., & McGowan, C. L. (1988). *SADT: Structured analysis and design technique.* New York, NY.

Marriott, K., & Stuckey, P. J. (1998). *Programming with Constraints: An Introduction.* Cambridge, MA: The MIT Press.

Marshall, J. (2018). Agent-Based Modelling of Emotional Goals in Digital Media Design Projects. In S. Goschnick (Ed.), *Innovative Methods, User-Friendly Tools, Coding, and Design Approaches in People-Oriented Programming.* Hershey, PA: Information Science Publishing. doi:10.4018/978-1-5225-3822-6.ch034

Mattelmäki, T. (2005). Applying Probes – From Inspirational Notes to Collaborative Insights. *CoDesign*, *1*(2), 83–102. doi:10.1080/15719880500135821

Mattelmäki, T., & Battarbee, K. (2002) Empathy Probes. In *Proceedings of the 2002 Participatory Design Conference* (pp. 266-271). Palo Alto, CA: CPSR.

Matthews, L. (2011). Google CEO confirms Google+ has more than 10 million users. *International Business Times*. Retrieved from http://www.ibtimes.com/articles/180869/20110715/google-google-google-circles-google-1.htm

Mayasari, A., Pedell, S., & Barnes, C. (2016). "Out of sight, out of mind", investigating affective intergenerational communication over distance. In *Proceedings of the 28th Australian Conference on Computer-Human Interaction, OzCHI '16 1* (pp. 282-291). New York: ACM Press.

Mayer, C., Linongelli, C., Orlandini, A., & Poggioni, V. (2007). Linear temporal logic as an executable semantics for planning languages. *Journal of Logic Language and Information*, *1*(16).

McAfee, A., Brynjolfsson, E., Davenport, T. H., Patil, D. J., & Barton, D. (2012). Big Data. The Management Revolution. *Harvard Business Review*, *90*(10), 61–67. PMID:23074865

McCarthy, J., & Wright, P. (2004). *Technology as Experience.* MIT Press.

Meerbaum-Salant, O., Armoni, M., & Ben-Ari, M. (2013). Learning computer science concepts with scratch. *Computer Science Education*, *23*(3), 239–264. doi:10.1080/08993408.2013.832022

Meese, J., Nansen, B., Kohn, T., Arnold, M., & Gibbs, M. (2015). Posthumous Personhood and the Affordances of Digital Media. Mortality. *Promoting the Interdisciplinary Study of Death and Dying*, *20*(4), 408–420.

Meyer, B. (1988). Eiffel: A language and environment for software engineering. *Journal of Systems and Software*, *8*(3), 199–246. doi:10.1016/0164-1212(88)90022-2

Michael, M. (2003). Between the mundane and the exotic: Time for a different sociotechnical stuff. *Time & Society*, *12*(1), 127–143. doi:10.1177/0961463X03012001372

Microsoft. (2016, February 14). *Visual Studio Express*. Retrieved from https://www.visualstudio.com/en-us/products/visual-studio-express-vs.aspx

Mihalcea, R., Liu, H., & Lieberman, H. (2006). NLP (natural language processing) for NLP (natural language programming). In *International Conference on Intelligent Text Processing and Computational Linguistics* (pp. 319–330). Academic Press. 10.1007/11671299_34

Mikroyannidis, A., Lefrere, P., & Scott, P. (2010). An Architecture for Layering and Integration of Learning Ontologies, Applied to Personal Learning Environments and Cloud Learning Environments. *Int. Conf. on Advanced Learning Technologies*, 92-93. 10.1109/ICALT.2010.33

Miller, T., Pedell, S., Mendoza, A., Keirnan, A., Sterling, L., & Lopez-Lorca, A. A. (2014). *Emotionally-driven models for people-oriented requirements engineering: the case study of emergency systems*. Academic Press.

Miller, G. A. (1995). WordNet: A lexical database for English. *Communications of the ACM*, *38*(11), 39–41. doi:10.1145/219717.219748

Miller, T., Pedell, S., Sterling, L., Vetere, F., & Howard, S. (2012). Understanding socially oriented roles and goals through motivational modelling. *Journal of Systems and Software*, *85*(9), 2160–2170. doi:10.1016/j.jss.2012.04.049

Mirsky, Y. (2011). Identity =? *Jewish Ideas Daily*. Retrieved on March 17, 2013 from http://www.jewishideasdaily.com/839/features/identity/

Mobile Vision – Google Developers. (2015). Retrieved from https://developers.google.com/vision/

Mönig, J., Ohshima, Y., & Maloney, J. (2015). Blocks at your fingertips: Blurring the line between blocks and text in GP. *Blocks and Beyond Workshop (Blocks and Beyond)*, 51-53. 10.1109/BLOCKS.2015.7369001

Montefoschi, F. (2015, March 06). fmntf/appinventor-sources: MIT App Inventor Public Open Source. *GitHub*. Retrieved from https://github.com/fmntf/appinventor-sources

Montessori, M. (1917). The advanced Montessori method - The Montessori Elementary Material. Frederick A. Stokes Company.

Moody, D. L., & Shanks, G. (2003). Improving the quality of data models: Empirical validation of a quality management framework. *Information Systems*, *28*(6), 619–650. doi:10.1016/S0306-4379(02)00043-1

Moody, D. L., Shanks, G., & Darke, P. (1998). *Improving the quality of entity relationship models: experience in research and practice. In Conceptual Modeling-ER'98* (pp. 255–276). Berlin: Springer.

Morris, M., Ozanne, E., Miller, K., Santamaria, N., Pearce, A., Said, C., & Adair, B. (2012). *Smart Technologies for older people*. Retrieved 20 February, 2014, from http://broadband.unimelb.edu.au/resources/Smart-technologies-for-older-people.pdf

Mott, J. (2010). Envisioning the Post-LMS Era: The Open Learning Network. *Educause Review Online*. Accessed: http://www.educause.edu/ero/article/envisioning-post-lms-era-open-learning-network

Mullery, G. P. (1979). CORE - a method for controlled requirement specification. *Proceedings of the 4th international conference on Software engineering*.

Munroe, S., Miller, T., Belecheanu, R. A., Pechoucek, M., McBurney, P., & Luck, M. (2006). Crossing the agent technology chasm: Lessons, experiences and challenges in commercial applications of agents. *The Knowledge Engineering Review*, *21*(04), 345–392. doi:10.1017/S0269888906001020

Murdoch, S. (2015). Exploring Primary and Emotional Goals within an Agent-Oriented, Animation Production Process. *ASPERA Annual Conference 2015: "What's This Space? Screen Practice, Audiences and Education for the Future Decade"*.

Myers, B. A., Pane, J. F., & Ko, A. (2004). Natural programming languages and environments. *Communications of the ACM*, *47*(9), 47–52. doi:10.1145/1015864.1015888

Mynatt, E. D., Rowan, J., Craighill, S., & Jacobs, A. (2001). Digital family portraits: supporting peace of mind for extended family members. *Proceedings of the SIGCHI Conference on Human Factors in Computing Systems*. 10.1145/365024.365126

Nagasaki, H., & Nagasaki, M. (2007). A system architecture model for web-based adaptive e-learning systems. *Proceedings of the 14th European conference on Cognitive ergonomics: Invent! Explore!* 129-132. 10.1145/1362550.1362576

Nardi, B., Whittaker, S., & Bradner, E. (2000). Interaction and Outeraction: Instant Messaging in Action. In *Proceedings of the 2000 ACM Conference on Computer Supported Cooperative Work* (pp. 79-88). New York, NY: ACM.

Naudet, Y., Latour, T., Guédria, W., & Chen, D. (2010). Towards a systemic formalisation of interoperability. *Computers in Industry*, *61*(2), 176–185. doi:10.1016/j.compind.2009.10.014

Nelson, G. (2006). *Natural Language, Semantics Analysis and Interactive Fiction*. Available from: http://inform7.com/learn/documents/WhitePaper.pdf

Norman, D. (1998). *The invisible computer: Why good products can fail, the personal computer is so complex and information appliances are the solution*. Cambridge, MA: MIT Press.

Novak, J. D., & Cañas, A. J. (2008). *The Theory Underlying Concept Maps and How to Construct and Use Them*. Retrieved from http://cmap.ihmc.us/Publications/ResearchPapers/TheoryUnderlyingConceptMaps.pdf

Oluyomi, A., Karunasekera, S., & Sterling, L. S. (2007). A comprehensive view of agent-oriented patterns. *Autonomous Agents and Multi-Agent Systems*, *15*(3), 337–377. doi:10.100710458-007-9014-9

Orbitco. (2015). *What is ACLs Error? Solutions to ACLs errors Examples*. Retrieved from http://www.orbit-computer-solutions.com/network-troubleshooting-access-control-lists-errors/

Orchard, L. M. (2005). *Hacking RSS and Atom*. Indianapolis, IN: Wiley Publishing.

Oulhaci, M. H. A., Tranvouez, E., Espinasse, B., & Fournier, S. (2013). Intelligent Tutoring Systems and Serious Game for Crisis Management: A Multi-agents Integration Architecture. In *22nd International Workshop on Enabling Technologies: Infrastructure for Collaborative Enterprises (WETICE)*. IEEE. 10.1109/WETICE.2013.78

Overmars, M. (2004). Learning object-oriented design by creating games. *Potentials, IEEE, 23*(5), 11–13. doi:10.1109/MP.2005.1368910

Paay, J. (2008). From Ethnography to Interface Design. In J. Lumsden (Ed.), *Handbook of Research on User Interface Design and Evaluation for Mobile Technology*. Idea Group, Inc. doi:10.4018/978-1-59904-871-0.ch001

Paay, J., Pedell, S., Sterling, L., Vetere, F., & Howard, S. (2010). The Benefit of Ambiguity in Understanding Goals in Requirements Modelling. *International Journal of People-Oriented Programming, 1*(2), 24–49. doi:10.4018/ijpop.2011070102

Paay, J., Sterling, L., Vetere, F., Howard, S., & Boettcher, A. (2009). Engineering the Social: The Role of Shared Artifacts. *IJHCS, 67*(5), 437–454.

Paay, J., Sterling, L., Vetere, F., Howard, S., & Boettcher, A. (2009). Engineering the Social: The Role of Shared Artifacts. *International Journal of Human-Computer Studies, 67*(5), 437–454. doi:10.1016/j.ijhcs.2008.12.002

Pacey, A. (1999). *Meaning in Technology*. MIT Press.

Pädagogisches Institut f. d. deutsche Sprachgruppe. (2015). Retrieved from http://blikk.it

Padgham, L., & Winikoff, M. (2003). Prometheus: A Methodology for Developing Intelligent Agents. In F. Giunchiglia, J. Odell, & G. Weiß (Eds.), *Agent-Oriented Software Engineering III* (Vol. 2585, pp. 174–185). Springer Berlin Heidelberg. doi:10.1007/3-540-36540-0_14

Padgham, L., & Winikoff, M. (2004). *Developing Intelligent Agent Systems: a practical guide*. Chichester, UK: John Wiley & Sons. doi:10.1002/0470861223

Palazzetti, E. (2015). *Getting Started with UDOO*. Packt Publishing Ltd.

Palen, L., & Salzman, M. (2002). Voice-mail diary studies for naturalistic data capture under mobile conditions. In *Proceedings of the 2002 ACM Conference on Computer Supported Cooperative Work* (pp. 97-95). New York, NY: ACM. 10.1145/587078.587092

Pan, N., Lau, H., & Lai, W. (2010). Sharing e-Learning Innovation across Disciplines: An Encounter between Engineering and Teacher Education. *Electronic Journal of e-Learning, 8*(1), 31-40.

Pandit, S., Acharya, H., Sanvedi, A., Nahar, P., Soni, S. K., Saxena, P., & Ramani, A. K. (2010). An architecture solution for E-Learning System ESSA. *Int. Conf. On Technology for Education*, 56-62.

Pane, J. F., Myers, B. A., & Miller, L. B. (2002). Using HCI techniques to design a more usable programming system. In Human Centric Computing Languages and Environments, 2002. Proceedings. IEEE 2002 Symposia on (pp. 198–206). IEEE. doi:10.1109/HCC.2002.1046372

Pane, J. F., Ratanamahatana, C. A., & Myers, B. A. (2001). Studying the language and structure in non-programmers' solutions to programming problems. *International Journal of Human-Computer Studies*, *54*(2), 237–264. doi:10.1006/ijhc.2000.0410

Panetto, H. (2007). Towards a classification framework for interoperability of enterprise applications. *International Journal of Computer Integrated Manufacturing*, *20*(8), 727–740.

Papert, S., & Harel, I. (1991). Situating constructionism. In S. Papert & I. Harel (Eds.), *Constructionism*. Norwood, NJ: Ablex Publishing Corporation. Available from: http://www. papert.org/articles/SituatingConstructionism.html

Papert, S. (1980). *Mindstorms: Children, Computers, and Powerful Ideas*. New York, NY: Basic Books, Inc.

Papert, S. (1980). *Mindstorms: Children, computers, and powerful ideas*. New York: Basic Books.

Parkhurst, H. (2010). *Education On The Dalton Plan*. Nabu Press. (original publication 1923)

Patterson, A., Kölling, M., & Rosenberg, J. (2003). Introducing Unit Testing With BlueJ. *Proceedings of the 8th conference on Information Technology in Computer Science Education (ITiCSE 2003)*, 11-15.

Pattis, R. E. (1981). *Karel the Robot: A gentle introduction to the art of programming*. New York: John Wiley & Sons, Inc.

Paulos, E., & Jenkins, T. (2005). Urban probes: encountering our emerging urban atmospheres. In *Proceedings of the 2005 SIGCHI Conference on Human Factors in Computing Systems* (pp. 341-50). New York, NY: ACM. 10.1145/1054972.1055020

Pavon, J., Arroyo, M., Hassan, S., & Sansores, C. (2008). Agent-based modelling and simulation for the analysis of social patterns. *Pattern Recognition Letters*, *29*(8), 1039–1048. doi:10.1016/j.patrec.2007.06.021

Pedell, S., Lopez-Lorca, A., Miller, T., & Sterling, L. (2014). Don't Leave me Untouched: Considering Emotions in Personal Alarm Use and Development. In Healthcare Informatics and Analytics: Emerging Issues and Trends. IGI Global.

Pedell, S., Vetere, F., Miller, T., Howard, S., & Sterling L. (2014). *Tools for Participation: Intergenerational Technology Design for the Home*. Academic Press.

Pedell, S., Lopez-Lorca, A. A., Miller, T., & Sterling, L. (2015). Don't Leave Me Untouched: Considering Emotions in Personal Alarm Use and Development. In M. Tavana, A. Ghapanchi, & A. Talaei-Khoei (Eds.), *Healthcare Informatics and Analytics: Emerging Issues and Trends* (pp. 96–127). Hershey, PA: IGI Global. doi:10.4018/978-1-4666-6316-9.ch006

Pedell, S., Sterling, L., Keirnan, A., & Dobson, G. (2013). *Emotions around emergency alarm use: A field study with older adults: Report for smart services crc*. Swinburne University of Technology.

Peeters, P. H. F. (2000). Design criteria for an automatic safety-alarm system for elderly. *Technology and Health Care*, *8*(2), 81–91. PMID:10955763

Pencil Code. (2016, February 14). Retrieved from https://pencilcode.net

Perera, C., Aghaee, S., & Blackwell, A. (2015). Natural Notation for the Domestic Internet of Things. In *International Symposium on End User Development* (pp. 25–41). Academic Press. 10.1007/978-3-319-18425-8_3

Perry, M., O'Hara, K., Sellen, A., Brown, B., & Harper, R. (2001). Dealing with mobility: Understanding access anytime, anywhere. *ACM Transactions on Computer-Human Interaction*, *8*(4), 323–347. doi:10.1145/504704.504707

Petrelli, D., van den Hoven, E., & Whittaker, S. (2009). Making history: intentional capture of future memories. In *Proceedings of the SIGCHI Conference on Human Factors in Computing Systems, CHI '09* (pp. 1723-1732). New York: ACM Press. 10.1145/1518701.1518966

Petre, M., & Blackwell, A. F. (2007). Children as unwitting end-user programmers. In *Proceedings of the 2007 IEEE Symposium on Visual Languages and Human-Centric Computing* (pp. 239 – 242). IEEE.

Philip, G. C. (1998). Software design guidelines for event-driven programming. *Journal of Systems and Software*, *41*(2), 79–91. doi:10.1016/S0164-1212(97)10009-7

Plowman, L., Rogers, Y., & Ramage, M. (1995). What are Workplace Studies For? In *Proceedings of the Fourth European Conference on Computer-Supported Cooperative Work ECSCW '95* (pp. 309-324). Dordrecht: Kluwer Academic Publishers, Springer.

Pollock, L., Vijay-Shanker, K., Hill, E., Sridhara, G., & Shepherd, D. (2013). Natural language-based software analyses and tools for software maintenance. In *Software Engineering* (pp. 94–125). Springer. doi:10.1007/978-3-642-36054-1_4

Potter, W. D. (1984). Design-Pro: A multi-model schema design tool in Prolog. In *Proceedings, The 1st International Conference on Expert Database Systems* (pp. 747-759). Academic Press.

Powers, K., Ecott, S., & Hirshfield, L. M. (2007). Through the looking glass: Teaching CS0 with Alice. *ACM SIGCSE Bulletin*, *39*(1), 213–217. doi:10.1145/1227504.1227386

Preece, J. (2017, March-April). How two billion smartphone users can save species! *Interaction*, *24*(2), 26–33. doi:10.1145/3043702

Prensky, M. (2001). Digital Natives, Digital Immigrants. *On the Horizon*, *9*(5), 1–6. doi:10.1108/10748120110424816

Price, D., Rilofff, E., Zachary, J., & Harvey, B. (2000). NaturalJava: a natural language interface for programming in Java. In *Proceedings of the 5th International Conference on Intelligent User Interfaces* (pp. 207–211). Academic Press. 10.1145/325737.325845

Price, T. W., & Barnes, T. (2015). Comparing Textual and Block Interfaces in a Novice Programming Environment. *Proceedings of the eleventh annual International Conference on International Computing Education Research*, 91-99. 10.1145/2787622.2787712

Procter, R., Greenhalgh, T., Wherton, J., Sugarhood, P., Rouncefield, M., & Hinder, S. (2014). The day-to-day co-production of ageing in place. *Computer Supported Cooperative Work*, *23*(3), 245–267. doi:10.100710606-014-9202-5 PMID:26321795

Python Software Foundation. (2012). *Python standard library: Turtle graphics for tk*. Retrieved May 08, 2015 from http://docs.python.org/library/turtle.html

Ramakrishnan, R., & Gehrke, J. (2003). *Database Management Systems* (3rd ed.). New York, NY: McGraw-Hill.

Ramos, I., Berry, D. M., & Carvalho, Á. (2005). Requirements engineering for organizational transformation. *Information and Software Technology*, *47*(5), 479–495. doi:10.1016/j.infsof.2004.09.014

Randall, D., Hughes, J., & Shapiro, D. (1994). Steps toward a partnership: ethnography and system design. In M. Jirotka & J. A. Goguen (Eds.), Requirements Engineering: Social and technical issues (pp. 241-254). Academic Press.

Randall, D., Harper, R., & Rouncefield, M. (2004). *Fieldwork for design: Theory and practice*. Amsterdam: Kluwer Academic Press.

Reas, C., & Fry, B. (2003). Processing: A learning environment for creating interactive Web graphics. *ACM SIGGRAPH 2003 Web Graphics*, 1-1.

Reekie, H. J., & McAdam, R. J. (2006). *A Software Architecture Primer: A Primer*. Angophora Press.

Resnick, M. (2014). Give P's a chance: Projects, peers, passion, play. In *Constructionism and Creativity: Proceedings of the Third International Constructionism Conference*. Austrian Computer Society.

Resnick, M. (2017). *Lifelong Kindergarten: Cultivating Creativity through Projects, Passion, Peers, and Play*. Cambridge, MA: MIT Press.

Resnick, M. (2017). *Lifelong Kindergarten: Cultivating Creativity Through Projects, Passion, Peers, and Play*. MIT Press.

Resnick, M., Maloney, J., Monroy-Hernández, A., Rusk, N., Eastmond, E., Brennan, K., ... Kafai, Y. (2009). Scratch: Programming for all. *Communications of the ACM, 52*(11), 60–67. doi:10.1145/1592761.1592779

Rheingold, H. (2003). *Smart Mobs: The Next Social Revolution Transforming Cultures and Communities in the Age of Instant Access*. New York, NY: Basic Books.

Rizvi, M., Humphries, T., Major, D., Jones, M., & Lauzun, H. (2011). A CS0 course using scratch. *Journal of Computing Sciences in Colleges, 26*(3), 19–27.

Rizzo, A, Montefoschi, F., Caporali, M. & Burresi. (2018). UAPPI: A platform for extending App Inventor towards the worlds of IoT and Machine Learning. In S. Goschnick (Ed.), *Innovative Methods, User-Friendly Tools, Coding, and Design Approaches in People-Oriented Programming*. Hershey, PA: Information Science Publishing.

Rizzo, A., Marti, P., Decortis, F., Rutgers, J., & Thursfield, P. (2005). Building narrative experiences for children through real time media manipulation: POGO World. In Funology (pp. 189-199). Springer Netherlands.

Robertson, J., & Good, J. (2006). Supporting the development of interactive storytelling skills in teenagers. In Z. Pan, R. Aylett, H. Diener, X. Jin, S. Göbel, & L. Li (Eds.), Technologies for E-Learning and Digital Entertainment. Edutainment 2006 (pp. 348–357). Lecture Notes in Computer Science Springer; doi:10.1007/11736639_46.

Robertson, J., & Good, J. (2005). Story creation in virtual game worlds. *Communications of the ACM, 48*(1), 61–65. doi:10.1145/1039539.1039571

Robertson, J., & Nicholson, K. (2007). Adventure Author: A learning environment to support creative design. In *Proceedings of the 6th International Conference on Interaction Design and Children* (pp. 37 - 44). New York: ACM Press. 10.1145/1297277.1297285

Rodden, T., & Benford, S. (2003). The evolution of buildings and implications for the design of ubiquitous domestic environments. In *Proceedings of the SIGCHI Conference on Human Factors in Computing Systems, CHI '03* (pp. 9-16). ACM Press. 10.1145/642611.642615

Rode, J., & Rosson, M. B. (2003). Programming at runtime: requirements and paradigms for nonprogrammer web application development. In *Human Centric Computing Languages and Environments, 2003 IEEE Symposium on* (pp. 23–30). IEEE.

Roque, R. V. (2007). *OpenBlocks: An extendable framework for graphical block programming systems* (Doctoral dissertation). Massachusetts Institute of Technology.

Rouncefield, M., Crabtree, A., Hemmings, T., Rodden, T., Cheverst, K., Clarke, K., ... Hughes, J. (2003). Adapting Cultural Probes to Inform Design in Sensitive Settings. In *Proceedings of OZCHI '03*. Ergonomics Society of Australia.

Roussos, G., Peterson, D., & Patel, U. (2003). Mobile Identity Management: An Enacted View. *International Journal of E-Commerce, 8*(1), 81–100.

Russell, H. (2011). Later life ICT learners ageing well. *International Journal of Ageing & Later Life, 6*(2), 103–127. doi:10.3384/ijal.1652-8670.1162103

Samson, T. (2011). *Will Linkedin Suffer Facebook's privacy problems?* Retrieved on Nov 30, 2017, from http://www.infoworld.com/t/internet-privacy/will-linkedin-suffer-facebooks-privacy-problems-677

Sanders, D., & Dorn, B. (2003). Jeroo: A tool for introducing object-oriented programming. *Proceedings of the 34th SIGCSE Technical Symposium on Computer Science Education*, 201-204. 10.1145/611892.611968

Sarkar, A., Blackwell, A. F., Jamnik, M., & Spott, M. (2014). Teach and try: A simple interaction technique for exploratory data modelling by end users. In *2014 IEEE Symposium on Visual Languages and Human-Centric Computing (VL/HCC)* (pp. 53–56). IEEE. 10.1109/VLHCC.2014.6883022

Satchell, C., Shanks, G., Howard, S., & Murphy, J. (2006). Knowing me, knowing you: end user perceptions of identity management systems. *Proceedings of the 14th European Conference on Information System (ECIS 2006)*, 795-806.

Sawyer, P., Rayson, P., & Cosh, K. (2005). Shallow Knowledge as an Aid to Deep Understanding in Early Phase Requirements Engineering. *IEEE Transactions on Software Engineering, 31*(11), 969–981. doi:10.1109/TSE.2005.129

Schiller, J., Turbak, F., Abelson, H., Dominguez, J., McKinney, A., Okerlund, J., & Friedman, M. (2014, October). Live programming of mobile apps in App Inventor. In *Proceedings of the 2nd Workshop on Programming for Mobile & Touch* (pp. 1-8). ACM. 10.1145/2688471.2688482

Schorch, M., Wan, L., Randall, D. W., & Wulf, V. (2016). Designing for Those who are Overlooked: Insider Perspectives on Care Practices and Cooperative Work of Elderly Informal Caregivers. In *Proceedings of the 19th ACM Conference on Computer-Supported Cooperative Work & Social Computing, CSCW'16* (pp. 787-799). New York: ACM Press. 10.1145/2818048.2819999

Seaton, D. T., Reich, J., Nesterko, S. O., Mullaney, T., Waldo, J., Ho, A. D., & Chuang, I. (2014). *6.00 x Introduction to Computer Science and Programming MITx on edX Course Report*. Academic Press.

Selwyn, N. (2004). The information aged: A qualitative study of older adults' use of information and communications technology. *Journal of Aging Studies, 18*(4), 369–384. doi:10.1016/j.jaging.2004.06.008

Selwyn, N., Gorard, S., Furlong, J., & Madden, L. (2003). Older adults' use of information and communications technology in everyday life. *Ageing and Society, 23*(05), 561–582. doi:10.1017/S0144686X03001302

Sengers, P., & Gaver, B. (2006). Staying open to interpretation: engaging multiple meanings in design and evaluation. In *Proceedings of the 6th Conference on Designing Interactive Systems, DIS '06* (pp. 99-108). New York: ACM Press. 10.1145/1142405.1142422

Sheller, M., & Urry, J. (2006). Introduction: mobile cities, urban mobilities. In M. Sheller & J. Urry (Eds.), *Mobile Technologies and the City* (pp. 1–17). London: Routledge.

Silverstone, R., Hirsch, E., & Morley, D. (1992). Information and communication technologies and the moral economy of the household. In R. Silverstone & E. Hirsch (Eds.), *Consuming Technologies: Media and Information in Domestic Spaces* (pp. 13–58). London: Routledge. doi:10.4324/9780203401491_chapter_1

Simsion, G. C. (2006). *Data Modeling: Description or Design* (Doctoral thesis). University of Melbourne.

Simuth, J., & Sarmany-Schuller, I. (2012). Principles for e-pedagogy. *Procedia: Social and Behavioral Sciences*, *46*, 4454–4456. doi:10.1016/j.sbspro.2012.06.274

Skiera, E. (2003). Reformpädagogik in Geschichte und Gegenwart: Eine kritische Einführung, R. *Oldenburg Verlag*, *2003*, 514.

Slack, J. M. (1990). *Turbo Pascal with turtle graphics*. St. Paul, MN: West Publishing Co.

Soloway, E. (1993). Should we teach students to program? *Communications of the ACM*, *36*(10), 21–24. doi:10.1145/163430.164061

Sommerville, I. (2015). Software Engineering. Pearson Higher Ed.

Sommerville, I. (2007). *Software Engineering* (8th ed.). Harlow, UK: Addison Wesley.

Sommerville, I., Sawyer, P., & Viller, S. (1998). Viewpoints for Requirements Elicitation: A Practical Approach. *Proceedings of the 3rd International Conference on Requirements Engineering: Putting Requirements Engineering to Practice*. 10.1109/ICRE.1998.667811

Soro, A., Brereton, M., Lawrence Taylor, J., & Hong, L. A. & Roe, P. (2016). Cross-Cultural Dialogical Probes. In *Proceedings of the First African Conference on Human Computer Interaction, AfriCHI'16* (pp. 114-12), New York: ACM Press. 10.1145/2998581.2998591

Stary, C. (2009). The Design of e-Learning Contracts: Intelligibility Catchers in praxis. *IEEE/WIC/ACM International Joint Conferences on Web Intelligence and Intelligent Agent Technologies, WI-IAT '09*, *3*, 203-206. 10.1109/WI-IAT.2009.263

Stary, C., & Weichhart, G. (2012). An e-Learning Approach To Informed Problem Solving. *Knowledge Management & E-Learning International Journal (Toronto, Ont.)*, *4*, 195–216.

Stead, A. G. (2016). *Using multiple representations to develop notational expertise in programming*. University of Cambridge, Computer Laboratory, Technical Report, (UCAM-CL-TR-890).

Stead, A., & Blackwell, A. F. (2014). Learning syntax as notational expertise when using DrawBridge. In *Proceedings of the Psychology of Programming Interest Group Annual Conference (PPIG 2014)* (pp. 41-52). Academic Press.

Sterling, L. (2002). Patterns for Prolog Programming. Computational Logic: Logic Programming and Beyond, 374-401. doi:10.1007/3-540-45628-7_15

Sterling, L., Lopez-Lorca, A., Pedell, S., & Goschnick, S. (2017). Developing Emotionally Supportive Technology for Monitoring Sleep Disorders. In Proc. Design4Health Conference. Swinburne University.

Sterling, L., Lopez-Lorca, A., Pedell, S., & Goschnick, S. (2017, December). *Developing Emotionally Supportive Technology for Monitoring Sleep Disorders.* Paper presented at Design4Health Conference, Hallam, UK.

Sterling, L. S., & Taveter, K. (2009). *The art of agent-oriented modeling.* Massachusetts Institute of Technology.

Sterling, L., & Shapiro, E. (1994). *The Art of Prolog.* Cambridge, MA: The MIT Press.

Sterling, L., & Taveter, K. (2009). *The Art of Agent-oriented Modeling.* The MIT Press.

Sterling, L., & Taveter, K. (2009). *The Art of Agent-Oriented Modelling.* Cambridge, MA: MIT Press.

Storey, M. A., Damian, D., Michaud, J., Myers, D., Mindel, M., German, D., ... Hargreaves, E. (2003). Improving the usability of Eclipse for novice programmers. *Proceedings of the 2003 OOPSLA workshop on eclipse technology eXchange*, 35-39. 10.1145/965660.965668

Strauss, A. (1978). A Social World Perspective. *Studies in Symbolic Interaction, 1*, 119–128.

Strauss, A., Fagerhaugh, S., Suczek, B., & Weiner, C. (1985). *Social Organisation of Medical Work.* Chicago: University of Chicago Press.

Stroustrup, B. (1986). *The C++ programming language.* Pearson Education India.

Sun, C. Y. (2012). Something Old, Something New, Something Borrowed, Something Blue: The Construction of online Identity and Its Consequences. *International Journal of People-Oriented Programming, 2*(1), 53–73. doi:10.4018/ijpop.2012010103

Sutcliffe, A. G., Maiden, N., Minocha, S., & Manuel, D. (1998). Supporting scenario-based requirements engineering. *IEEE Transactions on Software Engineering, 24*(12), 1072–1088. doi:10.1109/32.738340

Sutherland, I. B. (1963). Sutherland, I. B. SKETCHPAD, a man-machine graphical communication system. *Proceedings of the Spring Joint Computer Conference*, 329–346.

Tanimoto, S. L. (2013, May). A perspective on the evolution of live programming. In *Proceedings of the 2013 1st International Workshop on Live Programming (LIVE)* (pp. 31-34). IEEE. 10.1109/LIVE.2013.6617346

Taveter, K. (2005). Towards Radical Agent-Oriented Software Engineering Processes Based on AOR Modeling. In H.-S. Brian & G. Paolo (Eds.), *Agent-Oriented Methodologies* (pp. 277–316). Hershey, PA: IGI Global. doi:10.4018/978-1-59140-581-8.ch010

Taylor, A. S., & Harper, R. (2002). Age-old practices in the 'New World': A study of gift-giving between teenage mobile phone users. In *Proceedings of the 2002 ACM Conference on Computer-Supported Cooperative Work* (pp. 439-446). New York, NY: ACM. 10.1145/503376.503455

Taylor, N., & Cheverst, K. (2009). Social interaction around a rural community photo display. *International Journal of Human-Computer Studies*, *67*(12), 1037–1047. doi:10.1016/j.ijhcs.2009.07.006

Taylor, N., Cheverst, K., Fitton, D., Race, N. J., Rouncefield, M., & Graham, C. 2007. Probing communities: study of a village photo display. *Proceedings of the 2003 Australasian Conference on Computer-Human Interaction* (pp. 17-24). New York, NY: ACM. 10.1145/1324892.1324896

Tehranian, J. (2011). Parchment, Pixels & Personhood: User Rights and the IP (Identity Politics) of IP (Intellectual Property). *University of Colorado Law Review*, *82*(1), 1–84.

Thew, S., & Sutcliffe, A. (2008). *Investigating the Role of 'Soft Issues' in the RE Process*. Academic Press.

Thomas, N., Farhall, J., Foley, F., Leitan, N., Villagonzalo, K., Ladd, E., ... Kyrios, M. (2016). Promoting personal recovery in people with persisting psychotic disorders: Development and pilot study of a novel digital intervention. *Frontiers in Psychiatry*, *7*, 196. doi:10.3389/fpsyt.2016.00196 PMID:28066271

Tibbets, L. (2010). *IFTTT the beginning*. Available: https://ifttt.com/blog/2010/12/ifttt-the-beginning

TimeLine Past'n Future Exhibition. (2015, October 27). Retrieved from http://hub.garden/timeline

Tjong, S. F., Hartley, M., & Berry, D. M. (2007). Disambiguation Rules for Requirements Specifications. In *Proceedings of Workshop in Requirements Engineering* (pp. 97-106). Springer.

Tolmie, P., Crabtree, A., Egglestone, S., Humble, J., Greenhalgh, C., & Rodden, T. (2010). Digital plumbing: The mundane work of deploying UbiComp in the home. *Personal and Ubiquitous Computing*, *14*(3), 181–196. doi:10.100700779-009-0260-5

Tsolis, D., Christia, P., Kampana, S., & Tsakalidis, A. (2011). OWLearn: An Open Source e-Learning Platform Supporting Adaptability, Personalization and Mobile Learning. *Proceedings of the International Conference on Information Technologies (InfoTech-2011)*, 383-392.

Tsou, T. M., & Fischer, P. C. (1982). Decomposition of a relation scheme into Boyce-Codd normal form. *ACM-SIGART*, *14*(3), 23–29.

Turbak, F., Sherman, M., Martin, F., Wolber, D., & Crawford Pokress, S. (2014, June). Events-first programming in APP inventor. *Journal of Computing Sciences in Colleges*, *29*(6), 81–89.

UDOO - Developing an App for IoT with App Inventor and UDOO. (2015, October 16). Retrieved from http://www.makerfairerome.eu/en/events/?ids=544

Urry, J. (2003). Social Networks, Travel and Talk. *The British Journal of Sociology*, *54*(2), 155–175. doi:10.1080/0007131032000080186 PMID:12945865

Urry, J. (2004). Connections. *Environment and Planning. D, Society & Space*, *22*(1), 27–37. doi:10.1068/d322t

Valtonen, T., Hacklin, S., Dillon, S., Vesisenaho, M., Kukkonen, J., & Hietanen, A. (2012). Perspectives on personal learning environments held by vocational students. *Computer Education*, *58*(2), 732–739. doi:10.1016/j.compedu.2011.09.025

van Lamsweerde, A., & Letier, E. (2003). From Object Orientation to Goal Orientation: A Paradigm Shift for Requirements Engineering. In Radical Innovations of Software and Systems Engineering in the Future, Revised Papers from RISSEF '02 (pp. 325-340). Springer.

Van Lamsweerde, A., Darimont, R., & Letier, E. (1998). Managing conflicts in goal-driven requirements engineering. *Software Engineering. IEEE Transactions on*, *24*(11), 908–926.

van Lamsweerde, A., & Letier, E. (2004). From Object Orientation to Goal Orientation: A Paradigm Shift for Requirements Engineering. In M. Wirsing, A. Knapp, & S. Balsamo (Eds.), *Radical Innovations of Software and Systems Engineering in the Future, Revised Papers from RISSEF '02, LNCS 2941* (pp. 325–340). Springer. doi:10.1007/978-3-540-24626-8_23

Vetere, F., Martin, R., Kjeldskov, J., Howard, S., Mueller, F., Pedell, S., Mecoles, K., & Bunyan, M. (2005) Mediating intimacy: designing technologies to support strong tie relationships. In *Proceedings of the 2005 SIGCHI Conference on Human Factors in Computing Systems* (471-80). New York, NY: ACM. 10.1145/1054972.1055038

Vetting Wolf, T., Rode, J. A., Sussman, J., & Kellogg, W. A. (2006). Dispelling Design as the 'Black Art'. In *Proceedings of the 2006 SIGCHI Conference on Human Factors in Computing Systems* (pp. 521-30). New York, NY: ACM.

Viller, S., & Sommerville, I. (2000). Ethnographically Informed Analysis for Software Engineers. *International Journal of Human-Computer Studies*, *53*(1), 169–196. doi:10.1006/ijhc.2000.0370

Voida, A., & Mynatt, E. D. (2005). Conveying user values between families and designers. In *CHI '05 Extended Abstracts on Human Factors in Computing Systems* (pp. 2013–2016). New York, NY: ACM. doi:10.1145/1056808.1057080

von Glasersfeld, E. (1989). Constructivism in Education. In T. Husen & T. N. Postlethwaite (Eds.), *The International Encyclopedia of Education* (Vol. 1, pp. 162–163). Oxford, UK: Pergamon Press.

Von Koch, H. (1993). On a continuous curve without tangents constructible from elementary geometry. In *Classics on Fractals*. Westview Press.

Vygotsky, L. S. (1978). *Mind and society: The development of higher psychological processes*. Cambridge, MA: Harvard University Press.

W3C. (2014). *The web standards model – HTML CSS and JavaScript*. Accessed: http://www.w3.org/wiki/The_web_standards_model_-_HTML_CSS_and_JavaScript

Wagner, A., Gray, J., Corley, J., & Wolber, D. (2013, March). Using app inventor in a K-12 summer camp. In *Proceeding of the 44th ACM technical symposium on Computer science education* (pp. 621-626). ACM. 10.1145/2445196.2445377

Walls, C. (2008). *Spring im Einsatz*. Hanser.

Wang, Y., Berant, J., & Liang, P. (2015). Building a semantic parser overnight. Association for Computational Linguistic (ACL). doi:10.3115/v1/P15-1129

Weichhart, G. (2013). The Learning Environment as a Chaotic and Complex Adaptive System. *Systems, 1*(1), 36-53. Available at: http://www.systems-journal.eu/article/view/130/138

Weichhart, G. (2012). *S-BPM Education on the Dalton Plan: An E-Learning Approach*. S-BPM ONE – Education and Industrial Development.

Weichhart, G. (2014a). *Der Dalton Plan im E-Learning: Transformation einer Reformpädagogik ins Web*. Trauner Verlag.

Weichhart, G. (2014b). Learning for Sustainable Organisational Interoperability. *Proceedings of the 19th IFAC World Congress, International Federation of Automation and Control (IFAC)*.

Weiner, J., & Battelle, J. (2010). A Conversation with Jeff Weiner. *Web 2.0 Summit 2010*. Retrieved from http://www.youtube.com/watch?v=R1yNDDLiHyY&feature=player_embedded

Weining, K., Junzhou, L., & Tiantian, Z. (2005). A workflow based e-learning architecture in service environment. *Int. Conf. On Computer and Information Technology*, 1026-1032. 10.1109/CIT.2005.56

Weintrop, D., & Wilensky, U. (2015a). To block or not to block, that is the question: students' perceptions of blocks-based programming. *Proceedings of the 14th International Conference on Interaction Design and Children*, 199-208. 10.1145/2771839.2771860

Weintrop, D., & Wilensky, U. (2015b). Using commutative assessments to compare conceptual understanding in blocks-based and text-based programs. *Proceedings of the Eleventh Annual International Conference on International Computing Education Research, ICER 15*, 101-110. 10.1145/2787622.2787721

Wei, X., & Yan, J. (2009). An E-learning System Architecture Based on Web Services and Intelligent Agents. *Int. Conf. On Hybrid Intelligent Systems*, 173-177. 10.1109/HIS.2009.147

Weizenbaum, J. (1966). ELIZA. *Communications of the ACM, 9*(1), 36–45. doi:10.1145/365153.365168

Wenger, E. (1988). *Communities of Practice: Learning, Meaning and Identity*. Cambridge, UK: Cambridge University Press.

Wenger, E. (1999). *Communities of practice. Learning, meaning and identity*. Cambridge, UK: Cambridge University Press.

Wenger, E. (2014). *Artificial intelligence and tutoring systems: computational and cognitive approaches to the communication of knowledge*. San Francisco: Morgan Kaufmann.

Wherton, J., Sugarhood, P., Procter, R., Rouncefield, M., Dewsbury, G., Hinder, S., & Greenhalgh, T. (2012). Designing Assisted Living Technologies 'In the Wild': Preliminary Experiences with Cultural Probe Methodology. *BMC Medical Research Methodology, 12*(1), 188. doi:10.1186/1471-2288-12-188 PMID:23256612

Whittaker, S., Frohlich, D., & Daly-Jones, O. (1994). Informal Workplace Communication: What Is It Like and How Might We Support It? In *Proceedings of the 1994 ACM Conference on Computer Supported Cooperative Work* (pp. 131-7). New York, NY: ACM.

Wikipedia. (2016). *IBM Watson*. Author.

Wikipedia. (2017). *Criticism of Facebook*. Retrieved on Nov 30, 2017 from http://en.wikipedia.org/wiki/Criticism_of_Facebook

Wing, J. (2006). Viewpoint-Computational Thinking. *Communications of the ACM, 49*(3), 33–35. doi:10.1145/1118178.1118215

Wiszniewski, D., & Coyne, R. (2002). Mask and Identity: The Hermeneutics of Self-Construction in the Information Age. In Building Virtual Communities: Learning and Change in Cyberspace (pp. 191-214). Cambridge University Press.

Wolber, D. (2011, March). App inventor and real-world motivation. In *Proceedings of the 42nd ACM technical symposium on Computer science education* (pp. 601-606). ACM. doi:10.1145/1953163.1953329

Wolber, D., Abelson, H., & Friedman, M. (2015). Democratizing computing with app inventor. GetMobile. *Mobile Computing and Communications, 18*(4), 53–58. doi:10.1145/2721914.2721935

Wolber, D., Abelson, H., Spertus, E., & Looney, L. (2011). *App Inventor*. O'Reilly Media, Inc.

Wooldridge, M. (2009). *An introduction to MultiAgent Systems* (2nd ed.). John Wiley & Sons.

Wooldridge, M., & Ciancarini, P. (2000). Agent-Oriented Software Engineering: The State of the Art. In P. Ciancarini & M. Wooldridge (Eds.), *Agent Oriented Software Engineering* (pp. 1–24). Springer.

Wooldridge, M., Jennings, N., & Kinny, D. (2000). The Gaia Methodology For Agent-Oriented Analysis And Design. *Journal of Autonomous Agents and Multi-Agent Systems, 3*(3), 285–312. doi:10.1023/A:1010071910869

Yau, J., Lam, J., & Cheung, K. S. (2009). A review of e-Learning Platforms in the Age of e-Learning 2.0. *Hybrid Learning and Education, Lectur Notes in Computer Science, 5685*, 208–217. doi:10.1007/978-3-642-03697-2_20

Yu, E. (1995). *Modelling Strategic Relationships for Process Reengineering* (PhD thesis). Department of Computer Science, University of Toronto, Canada.

Yu, E. (1997). Towards modelling and reasoning support for early-phase requirements engineering. *Paper presented at the Requirements Engineering, 1997, Proceedings of the Third IEEE International Symposium on.*

Yu, E. (2002). Agent-Oriented Modelling: Software versus the World. In M. Wooldridge, G. Weiß, & P. Ciancarini (Eds.), *Agent-Oriented Software Engineering II* (Vol. 2222, pp. 206–225). Springer Berlin Heidelberg. doi:10.1007/3-540-70657-7_14

Zahn, Q., & Chengyang, C. (2008). A Study of E-Learning Architecture Based on Knowledge Innovation. *Int. Conf. On Computer Science and Software Engineering*, 781-784.

Zambonelli, F., Jennings, N., & Wooldridge, M. (2003). Developing Multiagent Systems: The Gaia Methodology. *Transactions on Software Engineering and Methodology*, *12*(3), 317–370. doi:10.1145/958961.958963

Zarandi, M. H. F., Khademian, M., Minaei-Bidgoli, B., & Türkşen, I. B. (2012). A Fuzzy Expert System Architecture for Intelligent Tutoring Systems: A Cognitive Mapping Approach. *Journal of Intelligent Learning Systems and Applications*, *4*(1), 29–40. doi:10.4236/jilsa.2012.41003

Zardas, G. (2008). The Importance of integrating Learning Theories and Pedagogical Principles in AHES (Adaptive Hypermedia Educational Systems). *Int. Conf. On Advanced Learning Technologies.* 10.1109/ICALT.2008.204

Zerubavel, E. (1985). *Hidden Rhythms: Schedules and Calendars in Social Life.* California: University of California Press.

Zimmerman, J., & Forlizzi, J. (2014). Research through design in HCI. In *Ways of Knowing in HCI* (pp. 167–189). Springer New York; doi:10.1007/978-1-4939-0378-8_8

Zimmerman, J., Forlizzi, J., & Evenson, S. (2007, April). Research through design as a method for interac- tion design research in HCI. In *Proceedings of the SIGCHI conference on Human factors in computing systems* (pp. 493-502). ACM. 10.1145/1240624.1240704

Zimmer, Z., & Chappell, N. L. (1999). Receptivity to new technology among older adults. *Disability and Rehabilitation*, *21*(5/6), 222–230. PMID:10381234

Zuckerberg, M. (2017). *Building Global Community.* Retrieved on Nov 30, 2017 from https://www.facebook.com/notes/mark-zuckerberg/building-global-community/10154544292806634/

About the Contributors

Steve Goschnick is an Adjunct Professor at Swinburne University of Technology. He was previously a Senior Research Fellow at the University of Melbourne between 2000 and 2012, developing and teaching undergraduate and masters level subjects in Computing & Information Systems. He was the Research & Business Manager of the Interaction Design Lab (IDEA Lab) at the same university for 4 years within that time interval. He came to academia in 1998 with 20 years experience in various professional ICT roles.

* * *

Giovanni Burresi graduated in Computer Science at University of Siena (2011). He worked on machine learning, parallel programming, financial simulation and distributed computing. He has a PhD in Computer Science from the University of Florence in Telematics and Information Society focused in Physical Computing and Internet of Things. Now he is a Postdoctoral researcher in Electrical and Computer Engineering at Carnegie Mellon University (Pittsburgh, PA). He is focusing on Internet of Things applications and Smart Environments Services design.

Maurizio Caporali is the CEO and co-founder of AIDILAB s.r.l. (www.aidilab.com) and the co-founder and Product Manager of UDOO (www.udoo.org). He is Adjunct Professor at the University of Siena IDA Interaction Design Laboratory (www.discom.unisi.it/ida/) where he teaches Physical Computing. He has a Master's Degree in Mathematics, with specialization in Computer Science, and a PhD in Information and Communication Technologies from the Electronic Engineering Department of the University of Florence, Italy. Currently Maurizio is mainly involved in the UDOO lifecycle management and he is working on different projects regarding the design of new technological products for the home automation, wearable, and cyber-physical system market, and acts as WP Leader for the EU project AXIOM (www.axiom-project.eu/).

Maheswaree Kissoon Curumsing is the Hub Manager for the ARC Industry Transformation Research Hub for Digital Enhanced Living at Deakin University. She holds a Bachelor degree in Information Systems and a Master's degree in Software Engineering. Her PhD is in the area of Software Engineering, more specifically, emotion-oriented requirements engineering. Maheswaree has 12+ years of experience in software engineering industry, research and academia. Since she started her PhD in 2013, she has been engaged in large industry and government funded projects, including smart home technologies for the elderly. Maheswaree's main research focus is on capturing users' emotional expectations and incorporating those expectations within the software development life cycle.

Judith Good is Professor of Interaction Design and Inclusion in the School of Engineering and Informatics at the University of Sussex. She has a PhD in Artificial Intelligence from the University of Edinburgh. Her research interests include supporting the development of children's computational skills, the design of novice programming environments, participatory design methodologies for children (both with and without disabilities), and the design of technologies to enable individuals with disabilities, particularly autism. Her funded research grants have included Flip, described in this paper; ECHOEs, an environment designed to support the development of social and communication skills in typically developing children and children with autism spectrum conditions; Shyness, looking at how technology can mediate social interaction, and the Green Revolution Game, an online simulation designed to highlight the influence of policy decisions on small scale farmers in Africa.

Connor Graham is a senior lecturer at Tembusu College and a research fellow at the Asia Research Institute at the National University of Singapore. His research centers on living and dying in the time of the Internet, with a particular focus on the use and design of everyday, 'social' technologies in people's lives. His work explores different approaches to and uses for ethnography e.g. for design. Recently he has been situating his research in Asia.

Steve Howard was the Director of the Melbourne School of Information, at The University of Melbourne. Over a 26-year career he worked in many areas of HCI, including usability engineering, use-centered innovation, and 'post-usability' interpretations of user experience. Steve worked at the intersection between the computational and social sciences, trying to understand IT in its social context. Specifically, thinking about applications of pervasive and ubiquitous computing to problems of real societal concern (e.g. health, sustainability, ageing, distributed families, community engagement). His research approach was inspired by design ethnography, interleaving qualitative field work and use-centered innovation. He had a positive impact on the lives of all those he taught, all he collaborated with, and on many people beyond.

Michael Kölling is a Professor at the Department of Informatics at King's College London, UK. He holds a PhD in computer science from Sydney University, and has worked in Australia, Denmark and the UK. Michael's research interests are in the areas of object-oriented systems, programming languages, software tools, computing education and HCI. He has published numerous papers on object-orientation and computing education topics and is the author and co-author of two Java textbooks. Michael is the lead developer of BlueJ and Greenfoot, two educational programming environments. He is a UK National Teaching Fellow, Fellow of the UK Higher Education Academy, Oracle Java Champion, and a Distinguished Educator of the ACM. In 2013, he received the ACM SIGCSE Award for Outstanding Contribution to Computer Science Education. Michael is a founding member of 'Computing At School', a UK organisation furthering computing teaching at school level.

Xiao Liu is a Ph.D. student at the College of Information Sciences and Technology at Pennsylvania State University, USA. Her research interests mainly focus on software engineering, program analysis and software security. She is also interested in building applied tools for end-user programming, testing and debugging.

Antonio Lopez-Lorca is a level A academic at the School of Computing and Information Systems at The University of Melbourne, Australia. He holds a PhD in Information Technology from the University of Wollongong, Australia. He first studied ways of applying semantic web techniques to agent-oriented models to validate them prior to software development. His research then shifted to looking at ways of introducing design processes into software engineering by considering the emotional needs of users throughout the complete lifecycle of the system. In his teaching philosophy, he believes in bringing together university and industry needs. He teaches agile processes and other current industry practices in the fields of HCI or UX design. He also coordinates capstone project units and he is very active networking with industry to source the projects for these subjects. He also supervises teams of up to 10 students working on these real-world projects, to ensure good interactions with all stakeholders and good agile practices.

James Marshall is a Senior Lecturer and the Major Discipline Coordinator of Digital Media Design at Swinburne University of Technology in Melbourne, Australia (www.swinburne.edu.au/design). James received a Bachelor of Technology, Industrial Design from Monash University, and a Masters in Multimedia from Swinburne University. James's primary research interests are in agent-oriented modelling and game design.

Francesco Montefoschi obtained the Bachelor's degree in Computer Science Engineering at University of Siena in 2015. He worked as software developer in the passenger transportation domain at Allbus srl. He is currently holding a research position at University of Siena on the H2020 AXIOM Project, about FPGA accelerated Machine Learning. He is also part of the UDOO Team, maintaining the operating systems for the boards, Ubuntu and Android. His interests include embedded boards and systems, Deep Learning, hardware hacking, do-it-yourself, open source software and web application development.

Jeni Paay has a cross disciplinary PhD in HCI and Architectural Design. She is currently Associate Professor in Interaction Design at Swinburne University of Technology, Melbourne, where she is program leader in both the Smart Cities Research Institute, and the Centre for Design Innovation. She has recently returned to Australia after working at Aalborg University in Denmark for the past 7 years, as an Associate Professor in HCI. Prior to this she was Lead Interaction Designer on the "Blended Interaction Spaces" project with CSIRO Australia. Jeni has a cross-disciplinary background spanning architecture, computer science, and interaction design, and has published widely within the area of Human-Computer Interaction. She has worked within the overall research themes of human computer interaction, design methods and interaction design for urban and domestic computing for over twenty years.

Sonja Pedell is Director of Swinburne's Future Self and Design Living Lab. The FSD Living Lab has core development capabilities in the area of innovative socio-technical systems and design solutions for health and wellbeing with a focus on the ageing population. Alongside this role, Dr Pedell is also Department Research Director for Swinburne's Department of Communication and Digital Media Design. She contributes knowledge of human-computer interaction (HCI) and co-design methods to the teaching of digital media and communication design. Prior to taking up these roles at Swinburne University, Dr Pedell completed a Masters of Psychology from the Technical University of Berlin and was employed as an Interaction Designer, Usability Consultant and Product Manager in industry for several years.

Antonio Rizzo is Full Professor of Cognitive Science and Technology at the University of Siena (2002-Present). Co-founder of UDOO (www.udoo.org, 2013-Present). Director of the Academy of Digital Arts and Science – ArsNova Siena (2004 – 2010). Chair of the European Association of Cognitive Ergonomics (2000 – 2006). Member of the Scientific Committee of the Programme Incitatif de Recherche sur l'Education et la Formation (PIREF) of the French Government (2002-2003). Member of the WG30 NATO Human Factors and Human Reliability

Group (1999 – 2002). Head of the Human Factor Group of the Italian National Railways (1996 – 1999). University Liaison for Apple Inc, for the Apple Design Project (1996-1997). Web site: http://Bit.ly/AntonioRizzo.

Mark Rouncefield is a Senior Research Fellow within the School of Computing and Communications at Lancaster University in the United Kingdom. He is co-editor of the book Ethnomethodology at Work.

Christian Stary is Head of the Department of Business Informatics / Communications Engineering, Johannes Kepler University Linz, Austria.

Leon Sterling received a BSc(Hons) from the University of Melbourne and a PhD in Pure Mathematics from the Australian National University. He has worked at universities in the United Kingdom, Israel, the United States and Australia. His teaching and research specialties are software engineering, artificial intelligence, and logic programming. He is currently Professor Emeritus in the Centre for Design Innovation, Swinburne University of Technology. From 2010–13, he was Dean of the Faculty of ICT at Swinburne University of Technology, and Pro Vice-Chancellor (Digital Frontiers) from 2014–15. He is past president of the Australian Council of Deans of ICT and a fellow of Engineers Australia and the Australian Computer Society.

Christine Yunn-Yu Sun is a bilingual writer, translator, reader, reviewer and independent scholar. She is currently the manager of eBookDynasty, an Australian publisher of Chinese digital and print books. She has a PhD in Languages, Cultures and Linguistics from Monash University.

Frank Vetere is Professor of Human-Computer Interaction at the University of Melbourne. He leads the Interaction Design Laboratory and is director of the research centre for Social Natural User Interfaces, a collaborative initiative with Microsoft Research. His research interests are in human-centred innovation, design thinking and technologies for ageing-well. His research aims to generate knowledge about the use and design of information and communication technologies for human wellbeing and social benefit.

Georg Weichhart is a lecturer in the Department of Business Informatics at Johannes Kepler University Linz (JKU), Austria. He has a PhD in Business Informatics from JKU. He is also a Senior Scientist and Head of Flexible Production Systems at Profactor GmbH.

Dinghao Wu is an Associate Professor with the College of Information Sciences and Technology at Pennsylvania State University, USA. He currently holds the PNC Technologies Career Development Professorship. He does research on cyber security and software systems. He received his Ph.D. degree in Computer Science from Princeton University in 2005 and was a research engineer at Microsoft from 2005-2009. He received the NSF CAREER Award, George J. McMurtry Junior Faculty Excellence in Teaching and Learning Award, and College Junior Faculty Excellence in Research Award.

Index

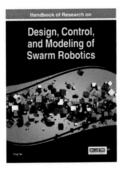

Stay Current on the Latest Emerging Research Developments

Become an IGI Global Reviewer for Authored Book Projects

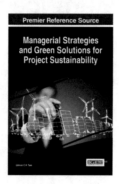

The overall success of an authored book project is dependent on quality and timely reviews.

In this competitive age of scholarly publishing, constructive and timely feedback significantly decreases the turnaround time of manuscripts from submission to acceptance, allowing the publication and discovery of progressive research at a much more expeditious rate. Several IGI Global authored book projects are currently seeking highly qualified experts in the field to fill vacancies on their respective editorial review boards:

Applications may be sent to:
development@igi-global.com

Applicants must have a doctorate (or an equivalent degree) as well as publishing and reviewing experience. Reviewers are asked to write reviews in a timely, collegial, and constructive manner. All reviewers will begin their role on an ad-hoc basis for a period of one year, and upon successful completion of this term can be considered for full editorial review board status, with the potential for a subsequent promotion to Associate Editor.

If you have a colleague that may be interested in this opportunity, we encourage you to share this information with them.

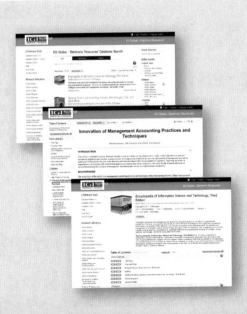

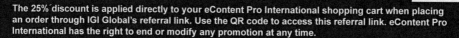
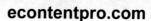

Information Resources Management Association

Advancing the Concepts & Practices of Information Resources Management in Modern Organizations

Become an IRMA Member

Members of the **Information Resources Management Association (IRMA)** understand the importance of community within their field of study. The Information Resources Management Association is an ideal venue through which professionals, students, and academicians can convene and share the latest industry innovations and scholarly research that is changing the field of information science and technology. Become a member today and enjoy the benefits of membership as well as the opportunity to collaborate and network with fellow experts in the field.

IRMA Membership Benefits:

- **One FREE Journal Subscription**
- **30% Off Additional Journal Subscriptions**
- **20% Off Book Purchases**
- Updates on the latest events and research on Information Resources Management through the IRMA-L listserv.
- Updates on new open access and downloadable content added to Research IRM.
- A copy of the Information Technology Management Newsletter twice a year.
- A certificate of membership.

IRMA Membership $195

Scan code or visit **irma-international.org** and begin by selecting your free journal subscription.

Membership is good for one full year.

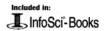